# A History of Singapore
## 1819–1975

# A HISTORY OF
# SINGAPORE
## 1819–1975

## C.M. TURNBULL

KUALA LUMPUR
OXFORD UNIVERSITY PRESS
LONDON   NEW YORK   MELBOURNE
1977

*Oxford University Press*
OXFORD LONDON GLASGOW
NEW YORK TORONTO MELBOURNE WELLINGTON
IBADAN NAIROBI DAR ES SALAAM LUSAKA CAPE TOWN
KUALA LUMPUR SINGAPORE JAKARTA HONG KONG TOKYO
DELHI BOMBAY CALCUTTA MADRAS KARACHI
© *Oxford University Press 1977*

ISBN 0 19 580354 x

*Filmset by T.P. Graphic Arts Services, Hong Kong
Printed by Hing Yip Printing Co.
Published by Oxford University Press*

*For Leonard*

# Acknowledgements

THE Lee Foundation generously financed a Visiting Fellowship at the Institute of Southeast Asian Studies in Singapore in July/August 1972 and a further research trip to Singapore in the summer vacation of 1973 to enable me to carry out research for this book.

I wish to record my gratitude for the constant helpfulness shown to me over many years by Miss M. Namazie of the University of Singapore Library, and by Professor Kernial Singh Sandhu, Director, and Datin Patricia Lim Pui Huen, Librarian of the Institute of Southeast Asian Studies, Singapore. I am also indebted to the staff of the National Library and National Archives in Singapore, the Public Record Office, India Office Library and Royal Commonwealth Society Library in London, Rhodes House Library in Oxford, and the University of Hong Kong Library.

For helpful criticism and comments I owe much to my former colleagues in the Department of History in the University of Singapore, and to the late Professor Maurice Freedman of All Souls' College, Oxford, who read the manuscript and offered a number of suggestions.

I am grateful for information and advice to the Earl of Selkirk and to innumerable Singaporeans, whom it would be invidious to thank individually, since in many cases their opinion was given in confidence.

His Highness, the Sultan of Johor, graciously arranged for a copy to be made of the photograph from his family collection of his great-grand-father, Temenggong Ibrahim. Mr. Eric Jennings has given me valuable advice on illustrations and generously allowed me to use photographs from his collection. My thanks are due to Mr. Lee Seng Gee for the photograph of his grandfather, Mr. Tan Kah Kee, and to Mr. David Marshall and Mr. Lee Kuan Yew for their photographs.

Miss Adelina Tang Mee Fu and Miss Rosie Khoo Suat Lian have shown patience and forbearance in cheerfully typing a number of drafts, while Mr. Martin Chiu carefully re-drew the map of contemporary Singapore from the author's composite draft.

Above all my thanks go to my husband, Leonard Rayner, for his unstinting encouragement and wise counsel.

University of Hong Kong                                     C. MARY TURNBULL
September 1975

# Contents

| | | |
|---|---|---|
| *Acknowledgements* | | vii |
| *Illustrations* | | x |
| *Maps* | | x |
| *Abbreviations* | | xi |
| *Introduction* | | xiii |
| I | THE FOUNDATION OF THE SETTLEMENT, 1819–1826 | 1 |
| II | 'THIS SPIRITED AND SPLENDID LITTLE COLONY', 1826–1867 | 34 |
| III | HIGH NOON OF EMPIRE, 1867–1914 | 78 |
| IV | 'THE CLAPHAM JUNCTION OF THE EASTERN SEAS', 1914–1941 | 128 |
| V | WAR IN THE EAST, 1941–1942 | 162 |
| VI | SYONAN: LIGHT OF THE SOUTH, 1942–1945 | 190 |
| VII | THE AFTERMATH OF WAR, 1945–1955 | 220 |
| VIII | THE ROAD TO MERDEKA, 1955–1965 | 257 |
| IX | INDEPENDENCE: THE FIRST DECADE, 1965–1975 | 297 |
| | *Bibliography* | 335 |
| | *Index* | 364 |

# Illustrations

*facing*

1. Sir Thomas Stamford Raffles. Portrait by G.F. Joseph, A.R.A., 1817. (By permission of the Trustees of the National Portrait Gallery, London.)    12

2. Colonel William Farquhar. (By permission of the National Archives, Singapore.)    13

3. Daeng Ibrahim, Temenggong of Johor. (By permission of H.H. the Sultan of Johor.)    51

4. Dr. Lim Boon Keng. (By permission of the National Archives, Singapore.)    104

5. Dr. and Mrs. Song Ong Siang. (By permission of Mr. Eric Jennings.)    105

6. Tan Jiak Kim. (By permission of Mr. Eric Jennings.)    113

7. Tan Kah Kee. (By permission of Mr. Lee Seng Gee.)    136

8. Sir Cecil Clementi. (By permission of the National Archives, Singapore.)    137

9. Lt. General Tomoyuki Yamashita. (By permission of Kyodo Photo Service.)    171

10. David Marshall after his election triumph April 1955. (*Straits Times.*)    252

11. Lee Kuan Yew. (By permission of the Prime Minister's Office, Singapore.)    253

# Maps

1. Plan of the Town of Singapore by Lieutenant Jackson, from John Crawfurd, *Journal of an Embassy to the Courts of Siam and Cochin-China* (London, 1828)    xvi

2. Singapore in 1975    296

# Abbreviations

| | |
|---|---|
| ANZUK | Australia, New Zealand, United Kingdom |
| ASEAN | Association of South-East Asian Nations |
| BMA | British Military Administration |
| CAB | Cabinet Papers |
| CO | Colonial Office |
| COD | Colonial Office Despatches |
| GD | Governor's Despatches |
| JIA | *Journal of the Indian Archipelago* |
| JMBRAS | *Journal of the Malaysian Branch, Royal Asiatic Society* |
| JSBRAS | *Journal of the Straits Branch, Royal Asiatic Society* |
| JSEAH | *Journal of Southeast Asian History* |
| JSEAS | *Journal of Southeast Asian Studies* |
| JSSS | *Journal of the South Seas Society* |
| MCA | Malayan Chinese Association (subsequently Malaysian Chinese Association) |
| PAP | People's Action Party |
| PRO | Public Record Office |
| PUTERA | Pusat Tengga Ra'ayat |
| SEP | *Singapore Free Press* |
| SSR | Straits Settlements Records |
| ST | *Straits Times* |
| UMNO | United Malays National Organization |
| WO | War Office |

# Introduction

---

MODERN Singapore is unique in that she was founded in 1819 on the initiative of one individual, Sir Stamford Raffles, despite almost universal opposition. An unwanted child, foisted upon the English East India Company, Singapore managed to survive and flourish, but her story was not one of steady development and unchecked progress. Her prosperity and sometimes even her existence were threatened many times.

In 1824 the East India Company purchased control of the whole island and Britain's legal sovereignty over Singapore was acknowledged. Two years later she became part, and subsequently the capital, of the Company's Straits Settlements, which were converted into a British crown colony in 1867. Throughout these years Singapore's position remained precarious, but the opening of the Suez Canal in 1869 and the extension of British political influence over the rich hinterland of the Malay states in the last quarter of the century assured her permanent status as one of the world's wealthiest and busiest ports. She became a separate crown colony in 1946 and acquired internal self-governing status in 1959. In 1963 she achieved independence as part of the new Federation of Malaysia but was expelled after two troubled years to become a fully independent nation.

Interest in the history of Singapore as a separate entity is a comparatively new phenomenon, and until recently her story has been treated as part of Malayan history. Early attempts at writing a history of Singapore made little progress. Raffles's own manuscripts and papers, from which he intended to compose an account of the station's origins and early administration, perished in a shipwreck in 1824. Thomas Braddell, later Singapore's first Attorney-General, planned a history of the settlement but published only a collection of official documents as 'Notices of Singapore' in the *Journal of the Indian Archipelago* in the 1850s.

Britain's political intervention in the Malay states from 1874 onwards and the development of peninsular tin and rubber production diverted the attention of officials, developers and writers away from the Straits Settlements. An enterprising new generation of colonial officials became absorbed in the Malay states. Singapore acquired her own civil service only in 1954, eight years after she became a separate crown colony, and up to that time service in Singapore constituted only an interlude from which most adventurous officials were glad to escape to more challenging and exotic postings up-country. Furthermore, specialization in Chinese affairs, which was most appropriate to work in Singapore, generally blocked the path of officials to the highest appointments, so that most ambitious civil servants chose to study Malay, and those with an academic bent concentrated their research into the history, customs and literature of the Malay states.

Sir Richard Winstedt, the leading British colonial historian of Malaya, dismissed Singapore's history before 1941 as 'a scene of peaceful commercial development, disturbed only for a few years by pirates who molested its sea traffic and by pitched battles among Chinese secret societies'.[1] This is too simple a view. There have been many paradoxes and vicissitudes in Singapore's history, and much that has defied the laws of probability. Modern Singapore's birth was an exciting individual triumph, while her post-war history has been full of colour and incident, the clash of personalities and ideologies. The long intermediate years of adolescence have usually been dismissed as being dull as ditchwater, but of course ditchwater is never dull. The apparently placid surface of Singapore life covered a ferment of mixing and change, which produced a unique society, so that Singapore, one of the world's smallest nations, now commands a commercial and political influence out of proportion to her physical size.

In recent years various factors have inhibited the attempt to write a history of Singapore. With nationhood unexpectedly thrust upon her in 1965, her attention has focused upon creating national consciousness and working for future prosperity. In building up loyalties to the new state, Singaporeans concentrated on the present and future, neglecting their history, which originated under European colonial rule, with many of its Asian traditions and values also stemming from alien cultures. But ultimately nation-building implies a need to establish an identity based upon the consciousness of the development of a country, as distinct from the interests of the individuals collected together in it.

This present account traces the story of Singapore from 1819, when the modern settlement was founded, up to 1975, which completed the first decade of independence. In most newly independent countries there is a time lag of several years between acquiring political independence and loosening colonial economic and security ties or shedding colonial-based attitudes. The last formal links with Malaysia were cut in 1973 with the separation of the currency, the stock exchange and the rubber market. The same year witnessed Britain's entry into the European Economic Community, the winding up of the British Malaysia Association, the virtual folding up of the Commonwealth security umbrella. The Sino-American *détente* beginning in 1972, the oil crisis of 1973–4, the Paris Peace Agreements on Indo-China of 1973, the triumph of communism and humiliating defeat of United States policy in Cambodia and South Vietnam two years later, all combined to force Singapore to seek a new identity in a changed world. She had to forge links with her regional neighbours, to come to terms with hostile ideologies in the Far East and to face a new economic situation in which the terms of trade suddenly swung away from the advanced industrial nations, whose ranks she had aspired to join.

It is difficult to see that any 'standard' history of Singapore can be written for some time to come, since the diversity of cultural background and experience is so great that no foreigner or Singaporean of any one community can speak for the society as a whole. The author offers this book as a sympathetic personal interpretation by one who lived and worked in Singapore and Malaysia for nearly twenty years. It is presented in the hope that its limitations, omissions and faults may spur historians, sociologists, political scientists, anthropologists and others to fill in the gaps and correct misconceptions, in order that we may ultimately come to a greater understanding of the background of this young nation.

1. R.O. Winstedt, *Malaya and its History* (London, 1948), p. 61.

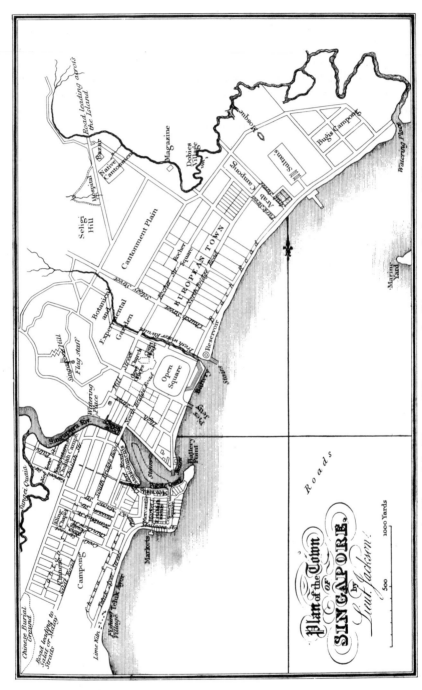

1. Plan of the Town of Singapore by Lieutenant Jackson, 1828

# I

# The Foundation of the Settlement
# 1819–1826

MODERN Singapore dates from 30 January 1819, when the local chieftain, the Temenggong of Johor, signed a preliminary treaty with Sir Stamford Raffles, agent of the East India Company, providing for the foundation of a British trading post. On the following day, camped on the banks of the Singapore river, with the Union Jack flying within the crumbling ramparts of old Singapura, Raffles wrote contentedly to his friend, the distinguished orientalist, William Marsden, 'in the enjoyment of all the pleasure which a footing on such classic ground must inspire'.

Sentiment and romantic yearnings after vanished glories played a large part in bringing Raffles to this particular spot, whose fascination was all the more tantalizing because the past was so obscure. The very name Singapura was a paradox, for no lion had ever set foot in this Lion City. In 1819 little of the old settlement remained. An earth wall, some 16 feet broad at the base and 8 to 9 feet high, stretched from the sea about a mile inland along the Bras Basah stream to Fort Canning Hill, which was then known as Bukit Larangan, or Forbidden Hill, because it was the reputed burial place of Singapura's kings. Only one grave remained in 1819, but an outline of terraces, some sandstone foundation blocks and old fruit trees indicated former occupation, and a century later, in 1928, some jewellery of Javanese Majapahit origin was unearthed nearby. The only other relic, a huge stone about 10 feet high and 9 to 10 feet long, inscribed supposedly in Majapahit characters, was found at the river's mouth. Badly worn by the tides, it defied all attempts to decipher its message and was blown up in 1843 by the government engineer to make way for new construction, leaving only fragments which can be seen in Singapore and Calcutta museums.

Written records relating to Singapore in ancient times are fragmentary. It may have been the second-century Sabara of Ptolemy's Golden Khersonese.[1] It could probably be P'u Luo Chung, a Chinese rendering of the Malay Pulau Ujong, or 'island at the end of the peninsula', mentioned briefly by a Chinese envoy, K'ang T'ai, in the third century. According to this hearsay account the inhabitants were reputed to be primitive cannibals with tails 5 or 6 inches long.[2] Singapore might be the island of Ma'it, recorded by Arab sailors in the ninth century.[3] The late thirteenth century Venetian traveller, Marco Polo, refers at second hand to Chiamassie, which could be Temasek, 'a very large and noble' city on the island of Malayur 'with a king and language of their own'.[4]

The first indisputable evidence of a settlement at Singapore dates from the fourteenth century. The earliest indigenous South-East Asian reference is in the Javanese *Nagarakretagama* of 1365, which named a settlement called Temasek on Singapore island.

The first eye-witness description was given by a Chinese trader, Wang Ta-yüan, who travelled extensively in the southern seas over a period of twenty years in the first half of the fourteenth century.[5] According to Wang Ta-yüan, Temasek had some Chinese inhabitants who lived and dressed in native style. He portrayed it as a place of dread for traders, infertile and unproductive, and 'everything the inhabitants possess is a product of their plundering of Chinese junks'. Arab writers in the thirteenth century had spoken of the neighbouring islands 'from which armed black pirates with poisoned arrows emerge, possessing armed warships'.[6] Wang Ta-yüan told how west-bound ships were allowed to pass without hindrance, but on the homeward run junks put up padded screens as protection and prayed for fair winds to carry them safely past the savage Tan-ma-hsi, or Temasek, pirates, who lurked in wait with as many as two or three hundred boats.

The most exciting and bloodstained chapter of Temasek's history came in the last years of the fourteenth century, but accounts are confusing. At that time the first Ming emperor forbade his subjects trading privately to the Nanyang, so that there were no Chinese travellers to record events, and the Chinese had to rely on information from South-East Asian tributary missions. Sixteenth-century Portuguese historians wrote extensively about the area but pieced their stories together more than a century after Temasek ceased to be important. Moreover Chinese and Portuguese evidence conflicts with the seventeenth-century *Sejarah Melayu,* or *Malay Annals,* the earliest, most colourful and vivid of Malay histories, and the only one which purports to give a full account of Temasek/Singapura's past.

According to the *Malay Annals,* Raja Chulan, mighty warrior king of India and descendant of Alexander the Great, encamped at Temasek on his way to conquer China. The Emperor of China tricked him by sending to Temasek a boat carrying a cargo of rusty needles and trees in full fruit, manned by a crew of senile, toothless men, who pretended that they had aged from lusty youths, the needles had rusted from iron bars and the trees matured from seeds on the long voyage. So Raja Chulan, deceived into thinking China was far away, gave up his enterprise and married the daughter of the god of the sea.

According to the *Annals,* a son of this marriage, Sang Utama, 'the Highest', became ruler of Palembang, heart of the great Malay maritime empire of Srivijaya, and took the title of Sri Tri Buana. While touring the nearby islands, Sri Tri Buana saw the gleaming white shore of Temasek and determined to explore it, but a great storm blew up, threatening to wreck his ship and forcing him to jettison everything, including his crown. Landing at Kuala Temasek, estuary of the present Singapore river, Sri Tri Buana encountered a strange beast with a red body, a black head and a white breast, whom he took to be a lion. This good omen induced the prince to found a settlement at Kuala Temasek, which he called Singapura or lion city.

The *Annals* go on to tell how, under the wise government of Sri Tri Buana and four successors. Singapura blossomed into a trading city, 'to which foreigners resorted in great numbers so that the fame of the city and its greatness spread throughout the world'. Singapura's wealth attracted the envy of the Javanese empire of Majapahit. The city succeeded in repelling a first Javanese raid, but during a subsequent attack a treacherous minister opened the gates to the Javanese. Blood flowed 'like a river in spate' and dyed the soil of the Singapore plain red for ever. The ruler, fleeing into the jungle with his faithful followers, escaped by the Seletar river to the mainland, and, after wandering for several years, eventually founded a new and more fortunate settlement at Malacca.

The *Malay Annals* aimed to establish the claim of the Malacca rulers to trace their descent from Alexander the Great and the ancient ruling house of Srivijaya Palembang. Despite this, the stories are not mere contrived romantic fancy but grew round a kernel of solid historical truth. A small Malay trading dependency of the far-flung Srivijaya empire existed for centuries at the southern end of the peninsula, probably at Temasek. With the fragmentation of the Srivijaya empire and the loosening of its hold over the seas and local chieftains, the island peoples living to the south of the Malay peninsula degenerated into piracy, and Temasek was laid open to attack from the rival expanding empires of Majapahit and Thailand. Temasek survived at least one long Thai siege and repelled initial Javanese attacks in the mid-fourteenth century, but by 1365 Majapahit claimed the island as a vassal state.

About the year 1390 an ambitious and aggressive young Palembang ruler, who was known as Iskander in Malay histories and Parameswara by the Portuguese, decided to cast off allegiance to Majapahit. Mounting a lion throne, he staged a religious ceremony of consecration as a god-king, symbolizing the revival of Palembang's former claims over the Srivijaya empire. In anger the Javanese drove Iskander out of Palembang. He fled first to Bintang, where he mustered the support of neighbouring island chiefs. After being granted asylum in Temasek, according to Portuguese accounts he murdered his host and assumed command himself.[7] The usurper's triumph was short-lived, and Iskander was driven from Singapura, possibly by Majapahit but more probably by the rising Thai state of Ayuthia or one of its Malayan dependencies.

The parallel between the activities of Sri Tri Buana and Iskander/ Parameswara is so close that it has been suggested that the genealogist who composed the opening chapters of the *Malay Annals* attributed to the mythical Sri Tri Buana the career of the factual Iskander and invented the tale of Singapura's five kings in order to gloss over three centuries of inglorious Palembang history. The period when any ruler of note held sway in Temasek appears to have been very short, probably from the early 1390s when Iskander seized control to 1398 when the Thais attacked the settlement.

The name Singapura came into use about the end of the fourteenth century. Chinese and Javanese in the fourteenth century used the term Temasek, but fifteenth-century seamen referred to Singapura. The origin of the name remains a mystery. Possibly Iskander named his settlement Lion City to signify that he was re-establishing there the lion throne which he had set up in Palembang, symbolizing his claims to independence. This is a more convincing explanation than attempts to link the name with Singosari in Java or with a religious sect, adherents of early Majapahit Bhairava Buddhism, who were known as lions because of their wild orgies. Certainly it is less fanciful than the Sri Tri Buana legend or the common suggestion that the island was over-run with tigers which early settlers mistook for lions.

The great trading city of the *Malay Annals* was probably a myth. There is no corroboration for this role of Temasek/Singapura. Wang Ta-yüan mentions Chinese inhabitants in the early fourteenth century, but there is no indication that they were drawn there by legitimate trade. The Portuguese writer, Tomé Pires, speaks of the Parameswara living on plunder during his few years on the island. Certainly the settlement's story in the fourteenth century was one of violence, bloodshed and war. The unique geographical situation of Singapore island at the southern-most tip of the Asian mainland, which has been a cause of Singapore's commercial success in modern times, was not of comparable importance in ancient days, when the routes dependent on the trade winds centred on south-east Sumatra and the crossing to China was made by west Borneo. Lying off the main commercial route with no natural resources to attract traders, Temasek was at most a small outpost of Srivijaya, its people harnessed to the seapower of the empire or in more troubled times exploiting their position to prey on others' trade.

Singapore was not completely deserted after Iskander's flight. In the early fifteenth century it was a Thai vassal state, but the Malacca sultanate, which Iskander founded, quickly extended its authority over the island. It became the dwelling place of a senior vassal of Malacca and provided the Sultan with fighting ships. After the Portuguese seized Malacca in 1511, the Malay *laksamana*, or admiral, fled to Singapura, and when the Sultan established his new capital at Johor Lama he kept a *shahbandar*, or port officer, in Singapura. The Portuguese destroyed Johor Lama in 1587, and the end of Singapura probably dates from 1613 when the Portuguese reported burning down a Malay outpost at the mouth of the river.

The Keppel Strait remained a major highway between the Straits of Malacca and the China Sea until the end of the sixteenth century, when the Portuguese discovered what was to become the main Singapore Strait to the south of Sentosa island.[8] The Dutch considered setting up a station on Pulau Brani in the early seventeenth century but abandoned the idea. By the second half of the eighteenth century western seamen had forgotten the very existence of the Keppel passage, and the area was left to *orang laut,* or sea nomads, who were known as the Celates, *orang selat,* or 'straits people'. They led a nomadic existence in the waters round Singapore, sometimes trading with passing ships in fish and fruit, or lying in wait to plunder craft which got into difficulties in the nearby treacherous shoals and shallows.

The headquarters of the Johor empire was re-established in the Riau-Lingga archipelago. Johor itself, together with Singapore, neighbouring islands and parts of eastern Sumatra, were in the fief of the Temenggong, one of the Sultan's two senior ministers. In the first decade of the nineteenth century, the Temenggong Abdu'r Rahman, with a small band of Malays, set up a village on the site of the old town of Singapura, where he gathered about him the *Orang Gelam* tribe who probably came over from Bulan island.

The *orang laut* of the Riau-Lingga archipelago were organized into tribes or *suku.* In return for protection and trade they had duties to Malay overlords according to their status. High ranking *suku,* such as the fierce *Orang Gallang* from the south of the archipelago, were organized into pirate armadas, led by Malay war-boats, and were feared throughout the archipelago. The humbler *Orang Gelam* were obliged to act as boatmen to the Temenggong and supply him with fish.[9] Their piratical activities were restricted to pillaging helpless craft and slaughtering their crews, which gave Singapore a bad reputation.

Other more primitive people lived on the island: the *Orang Seletar,* who roamed the northern creeks along the present Johor Strait, and the *Biduanda Orang Kallang,* who were the indigenous inhabitants of Singapore and had lived in the swamps at the mouth of the Kallang river as far back as their traditions went. These river peoples were boat dwellers but avoided the open sea. Shy, timid, shunning contact with other people, they had no agriculture but lived on fish and produce gathered from the jungle.[10]

A few Chinese settlers lived near the Temenggong's village under the charge of their own headman or Kapitan China, while others grew gambier on the nearby hills.[11]

Altogether in January 1819 Singapore had perhaps a thousand inhabitants, consisting of some 500 *Orang Kallang,* 200 *Orang Seletar,* 150 *Orang Gelam* in the Singapore river, other *orang laut* in the Keppel Harbour area, twenty to thirty Malays in the Temenggong's entourage and a similar number of Chinese.

At that time the settlement on the Singapore river was a typical Malay-ruled, *orang laut* village, consisting of the Temenggong's substantial wooden house, surrounded by a few huts, with large numbers of boats clustered in the river nearby. The inhabitants grew fruit but no rice and depended for their livelihood on collecting jungle produce, fishing, small-scale trading and piracy. In 1818 the Singapore Strait was reputed to be one of the regular rendezvous spots for the main Gallang pirate fleet, which consisted of about fifty ships crewed by twelve hundred men and made regular annual raiding expeditions round the island of Java and in the waters off south-east Sumatra. Captured boats were sometimes brought to the Singapore river, where in 1810 a British man-of-war retook a pirated European ship.[12] But Lingga was the fleet's main mart for selling plunder, and the Singapore village played only a modest role as a collecting centre. She did not attract the enterprising American arms dealers and the large numbers of Chinese, Bugis and others who flocked to more flourishing centres to trade in slaves, arms and loot.

The Temenggong Abdu'r Rahman, however, may well have had a major interest in the Gallang pirate fleet. Energetic, resourceful and shrewd, he was quick to recognize opportunities for acquiring wealth and influence and to appreciate the new horizons of ambition and power opened up by the unexpected arrival in Singapore of Sir Stamford Raffles.

Raffles was an official of the English East India Company, which had settlements at Bencoolen in West Sumatra and at Penang. During the wars with France which lasted till 1815, the East India Company took temporary possession of Dutch colonies in the East Indies, including Malacca and Java. Penang was elevated in 1805 to the status of fourth presidency of India, but at the end of the war both the British government and the East India Company wished to reduce their commitments in South-East Asia, and to reach an accommodation with the Dutch to secure peace and fair trading conditions in the region. Britain restored Java and Malacca to the Dutch, and opened negotiations to hand over Bencoolen and possibly Penang to the Netherlands in exchange for the remaining Dutch territories in India.

This withdrawal from South-East Asia was resisted by private British merchants, who had expanded their trading activities during the wartime disruption of Dutch rule, and by the East India Company's officials on the spot, of whom Raffles was the most inveterate opponent of the revival and extension of Dutch power. Born in 1781, Raffles joined the East India Company in London as a clerk and in 1805 was promoted as Assistant Secretary to the newly-formed Penang presidency. He served as Lieutenant-Governor of Java from 1811 to 1816, and was appointed Lieutenant-Governor of Bencoolen in 1818.

Despite the wealth of literature about Raffles, he remains an enigma, a man of fascinating contradictions. A frail diffident youth, 'meek as a maiden' in his own description, he nursed vast ambitions for himself and his country. His lack of formal education gave him an insatiable appetite for learning. Coming from a background of genteel poverty, he revelled in the company of the rich, the powerful and the aristocratic. A man of deep friendships, magnanimous and generous, with a passion for liberty and truth, he could be capable of petty meanness and deceit in his dealings with subordinates and colleagues and of gullible favouritism in advancing the fortunes of relatives and friends. Above all he was a man for whom

life was a perpetual challenge and who acted with courage and resilience
in face of the many disappointments and disasters which overtook him.

Raffles's personal ambitions and concern to boost British trade were
backed by a sense of messianic mission. He did not seek territorial
aggrandizement for Britain but rather a blend of commercial and moral
pre-eminence. Fascinated by the romance of faded civilizations and fired
with confidence in British liberal politics and commercial freedom, he
saw his country's role in South-East Asia almost as a crusade, to free the
peoples of the eastern archipelago from civil war, piracy, slavery and
oppression, to restore and revive their old cultures and independence
under the influence of European enlightenment, liberal education,
progressive economic prosperity and sound law.

Like many men of dreams and imagination who look beyond their
own age, Raffles was an impractical administrator. He had overturned
the traditions of Java's complicated society, involved the Company in
heavy financial loss and was recalled in disgrace. With good reason the
Company subsequently condemned his administration of Bencoolen as
extravagant, wasteful and over-ambitious. A source of embarrassment to
his employers and to the British government, his name was anathema to
the Dutch, whose system of government and commercial monopoly he
openly regarded as 'contrary to all principles of natural justice and un-
worthy of any enlightened and civilized nation'. The return of Java,
the Moluccas and Malacca to the Dutch and his own ignominious recall
to England in 1816 shattered Raffles's dream for using Java as a base
for extending British influence throughout the Indies. In London Raffles
urged the East India Company's Board of Control to establish a chain
of British stations in Acheh, west Sumatra, the Sunda Straits, the Riau
archipelago and west Borneo, which would protect the Company's
China trade, develop British commerce with the archipelago and compel
the Dutch to liberalize their economic policy. The Board of Control
showed no interest.

On his arrival in Bencoolen in 1818, Raffles was appalled at the expansion of Dutch control in Sumatra and warned the Company's Directors, 'The Dutch possess the only passes through which ships must sail
into the Archipelago, the Straits of Sunda and Malacca; and the British
have now not an inch of ground to stand upon between the Cape of
Good Hope and China, nor a single friendly port at which they can water
and obtain refreshment.'

The East India Company repudiated Raffles's attempts to thwart
Dutch expansion in south Sumatra but Lord Hastings, the Governor-
General of India, permitted him to visit Calcutta in 1818 and outline
his ideas. Raffles failed to win Hastings over to his ambitious plans for
diffusing British influence throughout Sumatra, but he succeeded in
obtaining permission to undertake a more limited project for protecting
Britain's trade route through the Straits of Malacca. Hastings authorized
him to secure an agreement with Acheh at the northern end and establish
a post at Riau, Johor or some other southern point, provided he did

not bring the Company into conflict with the Dutch.

For this purpose Raffles was permitted to enlist the services of an old friend, Colonel William Farquhar, who was then in Penang preparing to return to Britain on retirement. Farquhar, who joined the Madras Engineers in 1790 at the age of twenty, had served in wartime occupied Malacca for twenty-three years, acting as Resident from 1803 until the Dutch returned in 1818. Farquhar enjoyed Raffles's complete trust. He had long Malayan experience, an intimate knowledge of Riau-Lingga politics, and he shared Raffles's antipathy towards the Dutch. Farquhar had negotiated a treaty with Riau in 1818 on behalf of the Governor of Penang to safeguard British trade against the revival of Dutch privileges and had himself urged the Company to acquire a base there.

Raffles reached Penang in December 1818 to learn that the Dutch had forestalled him in Riau, annulled Farquhar's treaty, established their own Resident and garrison and claimed authority over all Riau's dependent territories, including Johor and neighbouring islands. Despite this, Raffles was even more eager to press on with his plans and dispatched the like-minded Farquhar to choose and establish a base in the south while he himself finalized arrangements at Acheh. Colonel Bannerman, Governor of Penang, jealous of Raffles's ambitions and irritated by the intervention of an outsider in what the Governor considered to be Penang's sphere of influence, insisted that Raffles defer his Acheh expedition pending further reference to Calcutta. Raffles agreed but, to Bannerman's annoyance, seized this opportunity to slip out of Penang secretly by night and chase after Farquhar.

But for Bannerman's intervention, Raffles would not have taken part in the expedition which resulted in founding modern Singapore, and the British settlement might have been established on the Carimon islands, which Farquhar favoured. But Singapore island already exerted a sentimental attraction for Raffles. On the voyage from Calcutta to Penang, even before he heard of the closure of Riau, Raffles wrote to William Marsden, 'You must not be surprised if my next letter to you is dated from the site of the ancient city of Singapura.' When the expedition found the Carimons to be rocky, inhospitable and unsuitable for a commercial station, the quest for an alternative site brought Raffles on 28 January 1819 to anchor his little fleet of eight ships off St. John's island, close to the mouth of the Singapore river. *Orang laut,* coming from the village to investigate, told him that the Temenggong of Johor was living in Singapore, and also brought the welcome news that there were no Dutchmen on the island.

The following morning Raffles and Farquhar disembarked and met the Temenggong.

The astute Temenggong Abdu'r-Rahman, who knew and trusted Farquhar, readily appreciated the material advantages which he would gain from permitting the British to found a settlement on Singapore island, but he needed to safeguard his position in the Malay hierarchy.

By that time little remained of the once powerful Malay empire. From his capital in the Riau-Lingga archipelago, the Sultan claimed suzerainty over Johor, Pahang and some of the East Sumatran states. In practice the authority of the throne was undermined by disputes and intrigues between Bugis and Malay factions at court. The two most senior vassals, the Bendahara who lived in Pahang, and the Temenggong, whose fief was Johor, Singapore and neighbouring islands, enjoyed an increasing measure of independence.

The succession to the throne had been in dispute since 1812 when the previous Sultan had died, leaving no heirs by his royal marriages but two sons by commoner wives. Hussein, the elder, seemed to be marked for succession by his father. Marriages were arranged for him with relatives of the Bendahara and Temenggong, and he was attending his wedding in Pahang when his father died. In his absence, the Bugis faction acclaimed the younger son Abdu'r-Rahman as Sultan. Abdu'r-Rahman held court at Lingga while Hussein returned to live in obscurity in Riau, but no formal coronation ceremony could take place because the late Sultan's royal widow, who favoured Hussein, refused to give up the regalia. Abdu'r-Rahman's succession was acknowledged neither by the Temenggong nor the Bendahara, but the Dutch recognized him, and Farquhar in his treaty with Riau in 1818 had also by implication acknowledged Abdu'r-Rahman as the rightful ruler. It was legally desirable to obtain his consent to the proposed British settlement at Singapore but unlikely that the Dutch would permit this. Raffles, perhaps urged by Farquhar, who was familiar with the background to the disputed succession, and by the Temenggong, who was Hussein's father-in-law, decided that, in order to establish legality for the British station at Singapore, it would probably be necessary to recognize the elder claimant. Farquhar was dispatched immediately in style with a party of forty European soldiers and sailors to seek Abdu'r-Rahman's consent to the Singapore settlement, but at the same time the Temenggong secretly sent messengers to bring Hussein to Singapore.13

Meanwhile the Temenggong and Raffles made a provisional agreement for the East India Company to set up a trading post. Raffles raised the British flag and began landing troops, clearing the ground, erecting tents, and surveying the harbour and possible defence positions. The site seemed ideal. While the south-west bank of the river was swampy, the ground on the north-east was level and firm. There was an abundance of drinking water, and the river mouth formed a natural sheltered harbour. Singapore commanded the southern entrance to the Straits of Malacca and was conveniently placed as a centre for trade with China and the eastern archipelago.

Farquhar met with the expected rebuff from Abdu'r-Rahman, but Hussein came to Singapore, rather frightened and suspicious at this turn in his fortunes. Raffles acknowledged him as Sultan, and on 6 February signed a formal treaty with the Temenggong and 'His Highness the Sultan Hussein Mahomed Shah Sultan of Johor', confirming the right given by the Temenggong to the East India Company to establish a post, subject to the payment of $5,000 a year to Sultan Hussein and $3,000 to the Temenggong. The formalities were carried out with as fine a ceremony as circumstances permitted. The day was auspiciously clear and sunny, and the Chinese planters arrived from the country to join the throng of Malay and *orang laut* spectators. Malay dignitaries came in their finery, British officials and soldiers were smartly turned out, the ships were dressed overall for the occasion, speeches were read, the treaty was formally signed and sealed, guns fired salutes, and presents were exchanged.

Raffles left Singapore the following day, making Farquhar Resident, with responsibility to himself as Lieutenant-Governor of Bencoolen.

Raffles was delighted with the foundation of Singapore. 'It breaks the spell,' he wrote from Penang on 19 February 1819, 'and they (the Dutch) are no longer the exclusive sovereigns of the eastern seas.' He thought this was the last opportunity to establish an effective counterweight to Dutch commercial dominance. 'This will probably be my last attempt,' he wrote to Marsden from Singapore the day after his landing. 'If I am deserted now, I must fain return to Bencoolen and become philosopher.' As he feared, Dutch opposition and bitter hostility from the Company's administration in Penang combined to threaten Singapore's very existence. The infant settlement's survival was little short of a miracle, the result of courage and grit on the spot, the slowness of communications, and a large measure of luck.

The Temenggong and Sultan Hussein fully anticipated Dutch reaction. After shocking Raffles by suggesting the British should consolidate the bargain by murdering the Dutch in Riau, Hussein set out to safeguard his position by disclaiming responsibility. The new Sultan wrote to his brother, Sultan Abdu'r-Rahman, and to the Raja Muda or under-king at Riau, while the Temenggong also wrote to the Riau authorities and to Dutch friends in Malacca, claiming that Raffles had intimidated them into making the agreement. The Dutch were furious. They regarded Singapore as part of Riau and thus under their own control, and they feared economic competition from Britain as the stronger commercial power. The Dutch Governor of Malacca protested to Penang and contemplated driving the British out of Singapore. Prompt military action would have easily ousted Farquhar's party, which comprised only thirty European military officers and civilians, with a hundred discontented Indian sepoys. Raffles had left Farquhar one barely seaworthy gunboat, and, in face of rumours of an impending attack from Malacca, Farquhar appealed urgently to Penang for reinforcements.

Governor Bannerman refused and urged Farquhar to evacuate Singapore to avoid any embarrassing clash with the Dutch. Bannerman assured the Dutch Governor of Malacca that Raffles had acted on his own initiative at Singapore, and he appealed to Calcutta. He criticized Raffles's impetuous behaviour and his apparent irresponsibility in leaving his new settlement almost defenceless, acting 'like a man who sets a house on fire and then runs away'.

The Dutch had good reason to believe that the British would repudiate Raffles's venture. In January 1819, on the day before Raffles dropped anchor off Singapore, the Board of Control in London dispatched instructions to Calcutta forbidding Raffles's mission to the east, and at the same time the British Foreign Office assured the Dutch that Raffles was only the Company's commercial representative with no authority to make any political arrangements.

The instructions were issued too late to stop Raffles, but van der Capellen, Governor-General of the Netherlands Indies, expected that Calcutta would immediately disavow Raffles's action without reference to London. Armed with Bannerman's assurances and with the claims from Hussein and the Temenggong that they had acted under duress, van der Capellen protested to Calcutta in moderate terms.

By that time, however, Raffles's action had caused a stir in Calcutta. In March 1819 the *Calcutta Journal* welcomed the establishment at Singapore 'as a fulcrum for the support of our commercial views and speculations'. Bannerman unwittingly helped to ensure the survival of Singapore not only by lulling Dutch suspicions but also by aggravating the Governor-General of India into giving Raffles his support. While Hastings was irritated when Raffles went ahead at Singapore despite finding the Dutch had occupied Riau, he was even more angry at Bannerman's imputation against his own authority and wished to justify his position in face of any reprimands from London. The Governor-General assured Raffles, 'The selection of Singapore for a post is considered as to locality to have been highly judicious,' and he agreed provisionally to the arrangement pending London's approval. Meanwhile Hastings reproached Bannerman and ordered him to give every assistance to Singapore. Grudgingly, Bannerman sent two hundred troops and some money to Farquhar, who had also succeeded in intercepting and diverting to Singapore five hundred Indian troops returning from Bencoolen to India.

Farquhar's courage brought Singapore through her first crisis, and the Dutch lost the opportunity to destroy the vulnerable settlement, whose future would now be determined not by military force but by the outcome of a paper war between London and The Hague.

The news of Raffles's action in Singapore, which reached London in August 1819, came as an unpleasant shock to the East India Company, who feared this move threatened the success of the entire Anglo-Dutch negotiations in Europe. 'If the Dutch should forcibly expel our garrison at Singapore we must either submit in silence or demand reparation at hazard of war which may involve all Europe.' Despite this, Lord Castlereagh, the British Foreign Minister, saw the commercial and strategic danger of leaving the Dutch 'all the military and naval keys of the Straits of Malacca' and recognized that a British station to the south of Malacca was desirable. While the British government would have preferred a less controversial post, free from embarrassing association with Raffles's name, no other site offered the same advantages. The British legal claim to Singapore was weak, but the island's potential attractions induced the British government to play for time by adding the question to the subjects already under negotiation with The Hague.

Raffles was placid about the delay: the longer the negotiations dragged on, the stronger would be the case for Singapore's retention.

Raffles left Farquhar with instructions to clear the ground, put up simple defence works, post a responsible European on St. John's island to inform passing ships about the new settlement, and encourage trade by imposing no duties for the time being.

Farquhar sent messages to Malacca seeking settlers and supplies. Despite a Dutch ban, many Malacca traders were attracted by the considerable profits to be made from selling foodstuffs and other necessities at inflated prices. Farquhar's reputation as wartime Resident did much to attract settlers from Malacca. Popularly known as 'Rajah of Malacca', he had married a Malacca girl and spoke fluent Malay. A tall soldierly figure, Farquhar commanded respect and was always accessible to hear complaints and judge disputes, fair to rich and poor alike.

Farquhar quickly set about clearing the plain on the north-east bank of the river, which soon boasted a flourishing bazaar and a cantonment of temporary huts. Regular supplies and food from Malacca, though expensive, saved Singapore from the customary privations and malnutrition suffered by pioneer settlements. Within six weeks more than a hundred small Indonesian craft were anchored in the harbour, in addition to two European merchant ships and a Siamese junk.

When Raffles returned at the end of May 1819, bringing immigrants from Penang and welcome supplies of timber, tiles and implements, he was thrilled with the settlement's progress. 'My new Colony thrives most rapidly,' he wrote to the Duchess of Somerset, adding with pardonable exaggeration, 'We have not been established four months and it has received an accession of population exceeding five thousand, principally Chinese, and their number is daily increasing.' To another correspondent he wrote enthusiastically that Singapore 'bids fair to be the next port to Calcutta; ... this is by far the most important station in the East; and, as far as naval superiority and commercial interests are concerned, of much higher value than whole continents of territory'.

Raffles spent four weeks in Singapore on this second visit. He made a further agreement with Sultan Hussein and the Temenggong in June 1819, defining the boundaries of the British settlement, which was to stretch from Tanjong Malang on the west to Tanjong Katong on the east and inland as far as the range of a cannon shot. He established a plan for the town, which was designed partly for aesthetic effect, but primarily for order and control by grouping the different communities in specified areas under their own headmen.

Apart from the Temenggong's village, the left bank of the river and

1. Sir Thomas Stamford Raffles. A portrait by George Francis Joseph
(By permission of the Trustees of the National Portrait Gallery, London)

2. Colonel William Farquhar, Resident of Singapore, 1819–1823
(By permission of the National Archives, Singapore)

the plain were to be reserved for the cantonment and official quarter, together with the land on the opposite bank at the river mouth. The European town was to be laid out east of the cantonment, and all Chinese were to settle on the right bank of the river. Farquhar was ordered to build a bridge to link the Chinese town with the Malay village and the cantonment.

No duties were to be imposed or agreements made without the concurrence of the Resident and the two Malay chiefs, who had authority over their own followers. Other Asians were put under the jurisdiction of their own *kapitans,* who would keep the peace and settle disputes among their own community. In conjunction with the Sultan and Temenggong, Farquhar was to hold court once a week, when the *kapitans* would present grievances and reports, and their people could appeal against their judgments. The Resident was to make final decisions according to his own common sense.

Raffles left Singapore in June 1819 and did not return for more than three years. Farquhar was responsible to Bencoolen, but communications were so poor that Singapore developed on her own. In March 1820 Farquhar wrote to Raffles telling him that he had heard nothing from Calcutta for nearly seven weeks and nothing from Bencoolen for three months.

Singapore's trade expanded rapidly. Raffles wrote to his cousin in July 1820, 'My settlement continues to thrive most wonderfully; it is all and everything I could wish and if no untimely fate awaits it, promises to become the emporium and the pride of the East.' To strengthen the case for Singapore's retention, he painted its successes in glowing colours to correspondents in England, but there was no need to exaggerate its achievements.

Her convenient location, free trade policy and comparative orderliness were responsible for much of Singapore's early success. But the main reason for her spectacular growth was not that she was a new phenomenon but rather that she offered unique attractions to an already highly-developed regional trade, conducted by prosperous Asian and European traders, who appreciated the opportunities offered by this new outlet. Singapore quickly captured the bulk of the flourishing trade of Riau, hitherto the headquarters for south Sumatra and Bugis trade and a prosperous centre of Chinese gambier production. She soon took over a large part of Penang's commerce, and from her early months attracted junks from Siam, Cambodia and Cochin China and western shipping from India. The first Amoy junk arrived in February 1821, the first European China trade vessel five months later, and in the first two and a half years nearly three thousand vessels came to Singapore. In that time the import and export trade totalled $8 million, of which $5 million was carried in Asian craft and $3 million in European. Private merchants had demonstrated their faith in Singapore at a time when her future was still doubtful to the British government.

Singapore soon became a cosmopolitan town. Farquhar encouraged all comers to settle and by 1821 there were about five thousand inhabitants, of whom nearly three thousand were Malays, more than one thousand Chinese, and five or six hundred Bugis, together with Indians, Arabs, Armenians, Europeans, Eurasians and other minority groups.

The new-found fortunes of the Temenggong and Sultan Hussein attracted a throng of followers, who settled in the Temenggong's village on the Singapore river or round the Sultan at Kampong Glam to the east of the town. Hussein built himself a palace or *istana* there soon after the founding of the settlement and brought his whole family and entourage over from Riau in hundreds of boats. Other Malays came in a steady influx from Malacca, the Riau islands and Sumatra, including Bencoolen men, who built Kampong Bencoolen on the Bras Basah river.

Singapore was particularly attractive to the Nanyang Chinese, who for many years had settled throughout the region as traders, farmers and miners and operated a network of commerce in Riau, Malacca, Penang, Bangkok, Manila, Batavia and other Javanese ports. Since they had no support from their own government, which officially prohibited emigration or private overseas trading, the Nanyang Chinese congregated where conditions were favourable. None of the centres in the Nanyang was ideal. Penang was geographically inconvenient, and elsewhere alien traders were subject to heavy duties, erratic laws, irksome restrictions and extortion. The attractions of Singapore as the natural centre for South-East Asian trade were immediately obvious to established Chinese, who moved in from other ports in the Nanyang. The first Chinese immigrants came from Riau and Malacca, many of them from long-settled families, who had intermarried with Malay women to form a distinct Baba Chinese community.

The most important of Singapore's Chinese pioneers was Tan Che Sang, who left his native Canton in 1778 at the age of fifteen, and after making his fortune in Riau, Penang and Malacca, came to Singapore in 1819, where he built the first warehouse and was agent for the early Chinese junks. Known to Farquhar from his Malacca days, Tan Che Sang promoted Chinese immigration by standing surety for newcomers who wanted to obtain goods on credit. When he died in Singapore in 1836 a huge crowd, said to be between ten and fifteen thousand, attended his funeral. But he had no social contact with the ruling community and was a strange withdrawn man, an inveterate gambler, obsessed with making money and reputed to sleep with his money chests in his bedroom.

In contrast the Hokkien Chua Chong Long, born in 1788, son of the *Kapitan China* of Dutch Malacca and the only Chinese who could rival Tan Che Sang's wealth in the early days of Singapore, was an open-handed extrovert. He entertained Europeans to lavish entertainments and was the government's most trusted go-between with the Chinese community until he left Singapore for China in 1836.

Most of the influential early settlers were already prosperous when they arrived and did not fit the popular 'rags to riches' success stories of penniless youths rising by hard work and acumen to wealth and eminence. The Hokkien Tan Tock Seng was an exception. Born in Malacca, he came to Singapore as a vegetable hawker in 1819 at the age of twenty-one and rose to be one of the richest merchants.

For many years Bugis traders, who dominated the commerce of the eastern islands of the archipelago, had flocked to Riau, where their countrymen were strongly entrenched politically. The imposition of Dutch control in Riau threatened their position and led to armed clashes, as a result of which in February 1820 five hundred Bugis fled from Riau to Singapore under their chieftain Arong Bilawa. The initial appearance of the fierce, warlike Bugis fleet terrified the inhabitants of Singapore, but Farquhar was relieved to find they came as settlers, bringing their women and children. They constituted the largest single body of immigrants, and the Resident was delighted to welcome a balanced community of families, who would act as a magnet to attract the prized Bugis trade. He refused to hand Arong Bilawa over to a Dutch envoy, who demanded his extradition, and instead granted him asylum in Singapore, where the Bugis built their *kampong* on the Rochore river. The Dutch later permitted Arong Bilawa to return to Riau, but many Bugis remained in Singapore, which soon became the headquarters of Bugis trade in the western archipelago.

Most Indians in early Singapore were soldiers or camp followers. But there were a few merchants, drawn mainly from Penang's large Indian mercantile community. The most notable was Naraina Pillai, who accompanied Raffles on his second visit to Singapore in May 1819. Naraina Pillai started a brick kiln, became Singapore's first building contractor and also opened a shop for cotton piece goods. He went bankrupt when the shop burned down in 1822, but Raffles helped him restore his fortunes and soon Naraina Pillai became rich once more.

Armenians were well established in trade in Brunei and the Philippines, and an Armenian merchant, Aristarchus Moses, settled in Singapore in 1820, the first of a small but wealthy minority.

Raffles hoped Singapore would attract a large community of Arabs, who had played a dominating role in South-East Asian trade for more than a thousand years and by the eighteenth century had begun to settle in various parts of Sumatra and Borneo.[14] The first to arrive in Singapore in 1819 were two wealthy Palembang merchants, Syed Mohammed bin Harun Al-Junied and his nephew, Syed Omar bin Ali Al-Junied. They settled at Kampong Glam, where Syed Mohammed died a very rich man in 1824, and Omar lived on till 1852 as leader of the Arab community.

Apart from the East India Company's officials, few Europeans came to settle in Singapore during the earliest years. They were not deterred by the East India Company's ruling that private European residents needed licences to settle in its territories, because in practice Calcutta turned a blind eye to this regulation in the Straits. Their reluctance to settle stemmed rather from uncertainty about whether Singapore would be retained as a permanent British possession and the consequent difficulties about buying land.

Most of the earliest Europeans were former merchant navy men or agents of Calcutta firms. The doyen of the mercantile community was a Scotsman, Alexander Laurie Johnston, a former ship's owner/captain, who settled in July 1820, founded the firm of A.L. Johnston & Company and remained the leader of the European merchants until his retirement from Singapore in 1841. Another Scot, Alexander Guthrie, founder of Singapore's oldest surviving firm, arrived from the Cape of Good Hope in January 1821. That same year James Pearl, who was captain of the *Indiana* which first brought Raffles to Singapore and had afterwards made a fair fortune trading in and out of the port, decided to settle in Singapore. He bought up Chinese gambier plantations and built a fine country house on the hill which still bears his name. In 1822 John Purvis, a former partner of John Matheson in Canton, left China to found a firm in Singapore.

Raffles ordered Farquhar to hold expenses to a minimum, since London would baulk at keeping Singapore if it became an expensive burden like Penang or Bencoolen. Farquhar had to administer the rapidly expanding settlement on a shoestring budget and spent less on salaries in a year than Bencoolen did in a month. At first an Assistant Resident handled civil affairs, but in 1820 Calcutta cut the Resident's establishment to one clerk, and by 1822 Farquhar was forced to employ two extra clerks at his own expense. Farquhar had few means of raising revenue, since he was forbidden to impose trade dues and could not sell permanent land titles. In May 1820 he imposed small port clearance charges to cover the cost of the master attendant's establishment. Four months later, defying Raffles's instructions, he introduced a tax farming system, auctioning monopoly rights to sell opium and arrack, or Asian spirits, and to run gambling dens.

With this revenue Farquhar embarked on a public works programme, which was ambitious in view of Singapore's precarious legal position but helped to boost confidence in her future. In January 1820 Calcutta had warned Farquhar not to encourage Asian immigration, since Singapore was still a temporary military post. Rumours that the Company might abandon the settlement led the Sultan, the Temenggong and the *kapitans* to call on Farquhar to confirm that the British intended to stay and would defend them. Reassured by the subsequent flurry of public building, Chinese and European merchants began to seek land for godowns.

This development posed new problems for Farquhar. Raffles had left no instructions about land grants, and Farquhar felt no permanent allocation could be made until the British title was settled. Moreover he held the view that the East India Company was a mere tenant in Singapore and could not alienate the Malay chiefs' land by granting permanent titles to settlers.

To complicate matters, East Beach, which Raffles had set aside as the European commercial quarter, was unsuited to the purpose, since shallow water and sandbanks made it impossible to land goods. European merchants complained it was not worth the expense of developing sites there, and Alexander Guthrie threatened to quit Singapore unless he was given more suitable land.

Farquhar referred the matter to Bencoolen in April 1821 but received no reply until eleven months later, when Raffles prohibited the erection of substantial buildings. When merchants insisted on putting up brick warehouses to protect their goods against fire, Farquhar gave Guthrie and others provisional grants of land on the firm north bank of the river but warned them that they went there at their own risk and might have to move later.

In addition to a temporary ban on customs duties, Raffles sought to attract trade by keeping port charges to a minimum. The Sultan and Temenggong at first put pressure on *nakodahs*, (or ships' captains), to present them with 'gifts', but in April 1820 the master attendant was instructed to impress on shipmasters that any gifts made to the Sultan and Temenggong were voluntary.

In June 1820 Farquhar referred to Raffles a request by the Sultan and Temenggong for permission to levy a fee on property accumulated by Chinese passengers returning to China. No reply had been received when eight months later Sultan Hussein arrested the *nakodah* of the first Amoy junk to arrive in Singapore and put him in the stocks, allegedly for not giving a sufficiently expensive present. Farquhar ordered the *nakodah's* release but was angry when a group of leading European merchants presented a letter of protest to Hussein, demanding an apology and a promise not to repeat such demands. Farquhar considered this protest 'an improper, premature and very unnecessary interference'. The merchants argued that the line of demarcation between courtesy presents and trade dues was so thin that news of such demands and the ill treatment of *nakodahs* might frighten away the Chinese junk trade. Once more Farquhar appealed in vain to Raffles for a definite ruling on presents and on fees levied on Chinese returning home.

The question of trade dues highlighted the ambiguity of the Malay chiefs' position. The Temenggong, in making the initial bargain with Raffles, was not only attracted by the immediate offer of money but envisaged a settlement like former trade centres in the region, where a Malay hierarchy would preside over a cosmopolitan trading community, leasing land, judging law suits and exacting dues.

With his long experience of the region, Farquhar was prepared to accept this situation. He insisted the Malay chiefs should be accorded respect and recognized as lords of the soil. Farquhar also admitted the judicial authority of the Temenggong and Sultan, and in place of the trade levies, which were the customary due of chiefs, be paid them an allowance out of the taxes from May 1820 to cover their assistance in police and judicial duties.

A pioneer town of rootless immigrants, early Singapore was notoriously lawless, and there was little money to provide a police force. In May

1820 Farquhar established the first regular force, headed by his son-in-law, Francis Bernard, as superintendent, with one constable, one jailer, one writer, one tindal and eight peons, at a total monthly cost of three hundred dollars. In 1821 the leading European and Asian merchants agreed to contribute fifty-four dollars a month as a night-watch fund to provide for an extra constable and nine peons.

The Malacca immigrants, both Chinese and Malay, were a peaceable community, who did not carry arms, and the main trouble-makers were the followers of the Temenggong and the Sultan, who quarrelled constantly with the Malacca Malays 'like tigers towards goats'.[15] Stabbings and robberies took place frequently in broad daylight and many people were murdered on the path to Kampong Glam.

For more than three years Singapore developed on its own under Farquhar's guidance. While Raffles welcomed the reports of Singapore's rapid expansion, at that time she played only a minor role in his ambitions.

Raffles aspired to gather under his control all the Company's possessions in South-East Asia: Penang, Province Wellesley, Singapore and Bencoolen, and ultimately to become Governor-General of India and a peer of the realm. Bannerman's sudden death in 1819 sent Raffles hurrying to Calcutta to push his claims, but without success. While Hastings agreed in principle that it would be beneficial to put all the Company's eastern possessions under one authority, he deferred any such decision pending the settlement of the protracted Anglo-Dutch negotiations in London.

Returning to Sumatra depressed and empty-handed, Raffles soon threw off his dejection and tried to make Bencoolen a model colony and the centre of new ambitions. Excited by travels in the remote interior, he dreamed of reviving the ancient glories of the Menangkabau empire and simultaneously extending British influence throughout Sumatra. This was probably the most contented period of his life, years of domestic happiness, when, delighting in the company of an adoring wife and talented children, he could indulge his fascination in natural history and the romantic past.

The idyll was shattered by a series of cruel disasters. In six months, between July 1821 and January 1822, three of his four children, several relatives and close friends, all died in Bencoolen, while Raffles and his wife fell seriously ill. Crushed, dispirited and numbed, his personal happiness destroyed, his career an apparent futile waste, Raffles abandoned his dreams for the resurrection of Sumatra. Prematurely aged, 'a little old man, all yellow and shrivelled', as he described himself, he decided to jettison his ambitions and turn his back on the accursed Bencoolen and the East.

Before his retirement he arranged to pay a last visit to settle the administration of Singapore, but immediately he landed in October 1822 the sight of the settlement with its activity, bustle, cheerfulness and sense of purpose jolted Raffles out of his depression and gloom. Perhaps the greatest of Raffles's qualities was his resilience to misfortune and defeat, his ability to create new ideas out of shattered dreams, to snatch triumph out of apparent failure. Now he narrowed his horizons from planning the revival of the ancient glories of Sumatra and Java to achieving perfection in this one small place. 'It is here that I think I may have done some little good, and instead of frittering away the stock of zeal and means that may yet be left me in objects for which I may not be fitted, I am anxious to do all the good I can here, where experience has proved to me that my labours will not be thrown away.'

As his wife commented, 'Sir Stamford's heart again expanded with the hope of happiness and rejoiced in the consciousness of possessing the power of diffusing civilization and blessings around him.' Despite bouts of sickness and blinding headaches which left him prostrate for weeks on end, it was the sense of mission and the imaginative and enlightened measures taken by Raffles during the last eight months he spent in Singapore which largely determined the future character of the settlement.

In June 1819 Raffles had written of Singapore, 'It...is a child of my own and I have made it what it is.' Now this feeling of proud paternalism surged up again even more strongly. 'I feel a new life and vigour' [in seeing] 'this my almost only child,' he confided to a friend in England on the day after he returned to Singapore, and he wrote to the Duchess of Somerset enthusiastically the following month, 'Here all is life and activity; and it would be difficult to name a place on the face of the globe with brighter prospects or more present satisfaction.'

Despite his delight with Singapore's progress, Raffles disapproved of many of Farquhar's pragmatic measures and was angry that some of his own instructions had not been carried out to the letter. He objected to Farquhar's allocation of land, although his own orders for land distribution were impractical. He considered Farquhar had paid too much deference to the Sultan and Temenggong and was shocked by Farquhar's support of legalized gambling and his lax attitude towards slavery. Raffles ignored the difficulties under which Farquhar had laboured, the shortage of staff and revenue, the difficulty of communications, and Raffles's own insistence that all matters, however trivial, should be channelled through Bencoolen, although he himself often failed to answer letters. Raffles set aside the considerable achievements of Farquhar, and their former friendship soured into mounting irritation which culminated in Raffles ousting Farquhar from office.

The two men quarrelled over policies and personalities. Farquhar had already angered Raffles by clinging to the post of Resident. Originally he intended to retire once the settlement was firmly established and he sent his resignation to Bencoolen in October 1820. Raffles dispatched Captain Thomas Travers to succeed him, but Farquhar changed his mind, and, after waiting several months for Farquhar to hand over to him, Travers had finally quarrelled with the Resident and sailed for England.[16]

Even more galling was Farquhar's feud with Captain William Flint, Raffles's brother-in-law. Flint arrived in Singapore in April 1820, when Raffles appointed him master attendant in place of Farquhar's son-in-law, Francis Bernard. Farquhar had reason to be irritated by Flint, who was arrogant, overbearing, greedy, extravagant, and prepared to push his relationship with the Lieutenant-Governor to the limit. In contrast to Farquhar's staff of one clerk, Flint enjoyed an establishment of one European assistant, two clerks and several peons. Flint monopolized the hire of lighters to government and private individuals and pocketed the profits for himself. Raffles insisted that Flint send his statistics direct to Bencoolen, not through Farquhar, and when the Lieutenant-Governor returned to Singapore in 1822 he stayed for the first few months with Flint and took his part against Farquhar. He gave Flint more powers, including authority as magistrate over seamen and the right to collect anchorage and port clearance fees.

Raffles humiliated Farquhar by handing some of his duties over to junior officials. He put the sale of land and collection of licence revenue in the hands of a twenty-year-old writer, George Bonham. In January 1823 Raffles wrote to Calcutta declaring Farquhar to be incompetent, and in March 1823 Calcutta accepted the resignation which Farquhar had sent in 1820 but subsequently withdrawn. The following month Raffles took over the responsibilities of Resident himself, putting executive control in Bonham's hands, and in May 1823 Raffles stripped Farquhar of his powers as Commandant.

Farquhar remained in Singapore for a few months as a private resident and left for Scotland at the end of 1823. The Europeans contributed three thousand rupees to buy him a present of silver plate, and the Chinese gave him a gold cup. Farquhar's final send-off has probably not been surpassed in warmth and spontaneous enthusiasm in the history of the island. There was such a crush of people on the waterfront that it took him two hours to say his farewells, and hundreds of small *prahus* followed him out to his ship in the roads, their occupants singing and firing crackers. The Governor-General of India later reinstated Farquhar's reputation, reproving Raffles for his harsh treatment of the Resident.

Farquhar's understandable bitterness against Raffles led him in later years to claim that he, not Raffles, was responsible for the choice of Singapore as a base. This brought Farquhar little credit. Certainly he had long argued in favour of securing a base to command the southern end of the Malacca Straits, and his acquaintance with the Malay chiefs and background knowledge of the Johor succession dispute, of which Raffles was ignorant, were invaluable in the initial negotiations. The Malay authorities believed that the British search for a foothold was taken on Farquhar's initiative. But Farquhar had advocated the Carimons. On the other hand Raffles's claims that he alone knew of the existence of Singapore through his study of Malay literature were exaggerated. Singapore island may have been known to few in Calcutta or London, but it was familiar enough to sailors, traders and officials in South-East

Asia. The story of the British Captain Alexander Hamilton, who claimed that the Sultan of Johor offered him Singapore island in 1703, appeared in William Milburn's *Oriental Commerce,* which was published in London in 1813.[17] Abraham Couperus, who surrendered wartime Malacca to the British, suggested in 1808 that Singapore would be a superior site to Malacca as a future Dutch settlement. Despite this, it is true that by visiting Calcutta, winning over the Governor-General and being prepared to exceed his orders, Raffles made it possible for the base to be secured. He alone appreciated the historical associations of Singapore, 'once the great emporium of these seas, whose history is lost in the mists of antiquity'.

Raffles's treatment of Farquhar was perhaps the shabbiest episode in his career, the unfair repudiation of a friend, who had withstood all the difficulties and dangers in the first precarious years and nursed the settlement into the life and vigour which so inspired Raffles on his return in 1822. At the same time Farquhar's old-fashioned ideas stood in the way of Raffles's far-seeing vision for Singapore. At the very time when Raffles was stooping to his lowest in ousting and humiliating the unfortunate Farquhar, he reached the highest point in his career in drawing up his plans for the future of Singapore.

From the beginning Raffles had regarded Singapore as a commercial centre. He had written in June 1819, 'Our object is not territory but trade; a great commercial emporium and a fulcrum whence we may extend our influence politically as circumstances may hereafter require.' He aimed to blend commercial interest and moral influence, and he now set out to ensure Singapore's prosperity as a great port, to abolish slavery and injustice, to devise a way of government giving 'the utmost possible freedom of trade and equal rights to all, with protection of property and person', and to make Singapore a beautiful and orderly city, the intellectual and educational centre of South-East Asia.

Within a week of his return, Raffles set out to revise the layout of the town. The major modification was in providing for the commercial quarter. While Raffles was angry with Farquhar for allowing merchants to encroach on the government area, he had to admit that East Beach was unsuitable for commerce. He decided to move the business sector to the opposite bank of the Singapore river, a swampy area where many Chinese had built their houses. In addition to moving these settlers further inland, the new location of the business area involved levelling a hill to form Commercial Square, the present Raffles Place, and using the earth to fill in the swamp on the south-west river bank, to form the present Boat Quay. This area became the commercial heart of the city. The project was galling for Farquhar. It justified his arguments against the East Beach development, but Raffles financed his expensive reclamation scheme by spending all the money saved through Farquhar's frugal administration.

The other major change was to move the Temenggong's sprawling village, which by then comprised more than six hundred people, to a two-hundred-acre land reserve three miles to the west of the town, along the coast between Tanjong Pagar and Telok Blangah. This cleared the river for trade and removed the Temenggong and his lawless followers from their dominating position in the heart of the town.

An area of about three miles along the coast and half a mile to a mile inland was reserved for the official and commercial quarter, with the government retaining the east bank and Forbidden Hill, and keeping the south-west tip at the river's mouth for a defence point.

The Rochore plain east of the government quarter was reserved as a residential area for affluent Europeans and Asians. The Arabs were given land to the east of this zone, adjoining the fifty-acre site at Kampong Glam allotted to Sultan Hussein, and the Bugis were moved further east beyond Kampong Glam.

Since the Chinese were expected to form the bulk of future town dwellers, Raffles allocated to Chinatown the whole area west of the river adjoining the commercial quarter, to be divided among the various dialect groups. The lower classes of Indians were allotted land further up-river.

In the town area houses had to be built in orderly straight roads of specified width, meeting at right angles. All commercial buildings were to be constructed of masonry with tiled roofs. *Kapitans* were allocated larger plots of land than their countrymen, and well-to-do merchants were not compelled to live in the areas assigned to their community. Similarly in the commercial sector, big Asian and European shops, offices and godowns adjoined one another. Naraina Pillai and Tan Che Sang were two of the first to move their premises to Commercial Square. Prosperous Asians and Europeans were encouraged to live and trade side by side, thus founding the basis of Singapore's multiracial society, where from the start the colour of men's money counted for more than the colour of their skins.

Raffles built himself a wooden bungalow on the Forbidden Hill, later renamed Government Hill, partly to escape in his sickness from the oppressive heat of the plain below, partly in a death wish to be buried among the Malay rulers of old Singapura. In 1819 he had dispatched a European gardener from Bencoolen to plant clove and nutmeg trees at the foot of the hill. These flourished, and Raffles now allocated 48 acres of adjoining land as a Botanic Garden. Working in collaboration with Dr. Wallich of the Calcutta Botanic Garden, who paid periodic visits to Singapore, Raffles hoped his experimental garden would provide the foundation for Singapore's agricultural prosperity.

The revised town plan involved a large-scale resettlement of the existing population, and to help him Raffles appointed a committee in November 1822 consisting of one European merchant and two officials, who were to consult representatives of the Malay, Chinese, Bugis, Javanese, and Arab communities.

Financial compensation and free land were offered to people who were forced to move from their houses and the old bazaar, but the upheaval caused considerable trouble and inconvenience, and the police had to be called in to evict residents and pull down buildings. The days of haphazard building were at an end. Singapore from these early times was a planned town, and the pattern of Raffles's Singapore still remains in the heart of the city.[18]

Raffles then set about drawing up a composite series of administrative regulations, which would preclude the Sultan or the Temenggong from putting any brake on the development of his settlement.

In the agreements made in 1819 the Malay chiefs had merely permitted the setting up of a British post and Farquhar, following Malay custom, believed that this did not confer ownership of land or rights to make laws. This interpretation did not suit Raffles, whose professed admiration for the Malay people tended to pale when he was faced by actual flesh and blood individuals with their ambitions and foibles. He despised Hussein and distrusted the Temenggong. Raffles was prepared to pay lip service to the chiefs' dignity but to tolerate no obstruction of his plans. He attempted to reform their ways and bring them up to date by offering to arrange shipments of goods from Calcutta for them to sell on commission, but they scorned the role of trader as beneath the dignity of Malay princes. They also rejected Raffles's offer to send their sons to be educated in India at the Company's expense. After that Raffles gave up any attempt to turn the chiefs and their successors into enlightened partners in government. He paid their allowances promptly, and apart from disarming their followers, which drew angry protests from the chiefs, he left them undisturbed in their own private enclaves but gradually eased them out of public life. In December 1822 he commuted to a fixed monthly payment all their claims to a share in the revenue, and on the eve of his final departure in June 1823 he made an agreement to buy out their judicial powers and rights to land, except the areas specially reserved for them.

The first of a series of administrative regulations which Raffles passed in 1823 dealt with the registry of land, which was to be sold on permanent lease by public auction.

A second regulation concerned the port. Originally Raffles saw free trade as a bait to attract shipping to the new mart until commerce became worth taxing, although even in the early days the Company doubted the wisdom of foregoing trade dues in order to attract Asian immigration. Raffles was so delighted with the success of early Singapore, which he attributed to 'the simple but almost magic result of that perfect freedom of trade, which it has been my good fortune to establish', that he decided to preserve absolute freedom of trade as a permanent principle. When he finally left Singapore in June 1823 he assured the merchants 'that no sinister, no sordid view, no considerations either of political importance or pecuniary advantage, should interfere with the broad and liberal principles on which the British interests have been established. Monopoly and exclusive privileges, against which public opinion has long raised its voice, are here unknown...that Singapore will long and always remain a free port and that no taxes on trade or industry will be established to check its future rise and prosperity, I can have no doubt.' This became the central tenet of the Singapore merchants' creed, to be defended with almost religious fervour for more than a hundred years.

A third regulation provided for the administration of justice. Raffles decided that indigenous Muslim laws were to be applied in dealing with religious practice, marriage and inheritance among the Malay population, 'where they shall not be contrary to reason, justice or humanity'. But the general law of Singapore should be English law, modified 'with due consideration to the usage and habits of the people', applied with mildness and common sense 'and a patriarchal kindness and indulgent consideration for the prejudices of each tribe'. Murder was the only capital offence, and the principle of paying compensation to the injured was as important as punishment for the offender.

Raffles aimed to give an active role in government and legislation to the non-official European community and a measure of participation to Asians. He had put this into practice by choosing the committee of European members and Asian representatives to help in laying out the town. Under the new judicial regulation twelve responsible Europeans were chosen to serve as magistrates for a year. They were to assist the Resident in his court and hold their own magistrates' court, which dealt with petty crimes and minor civil cases. The Resident was to seek their advice in drawing up laws and was obliged to refer to Calcutta any proposed regulations to which the magistrates objected. By giving the magistrates a share in government, Raffles hoped to avoid the friction between government and private European residents, which was so common in small colonies without representative institutions.

Considering it was the government's duty to prevent crime and to reform rather than punish criminals, Raffles extended to Singapore the training schemes to turn convicts into useful settlers, which he had adopted in Bencoolen. He set out to discourage violence by banning the carrying of weapons and to curb vices which bred crime, notably gambling and cock fighting, which he considered 'disgraceful and repugnant to the British character and government'. Angry to find that Farquhar had licensed gambling in Singapore, in May 1823 he closed all gambling dens and cockpits. He aimed to use heavy taxation to discourage other vices, such as drunkenness and opium smoking, and while he appreciated that in a predominantly male immigrant society it would be unrealistic to attempt to ban prostitution, his laws forbade men living off the earnings of prostitutes.

Raffles shared the aversion of humanitarian and radical men of his generation to the practice of slavery, which he had abolished in Bencoolen, but Farquhar had condoned slave dealing in Singapore as a local custom. Bugis traders, who were the main slave dealers of the region, brought in large numbers of slaves, whom they frequently herded round the town on display. Other slaves were imported in Malay boats from Sumatra, and there was a particularly brisk trade in young girls. Raffles was scandalized within days of his returning to Singapore in October 1822, when Bugis traders sold fifty slaves near the Resident's house and offered a few as presents to Raffles and Farquhar.

He resolved to put an end to this traffic in human flesh and in May 1823 issued a regulation prohibiting the slave trade in Singapore and declaring that no-one who had come since 29 January 1819 could be regarded as a slave. Slave debtors, who were numerous among the Malay population, were to work off their debts in a maximum period of five years. Raffles also attempted to control the semi-slavery of penniless Chinese immigrants, who pledged their labour to employers in return for payment of their passage money. He laid down that *nakodahs* could demand no more than twenty dollars for passage money, which had to be worked off in a maximum of two years, and such contracts had to be registered in the presence of a magistrate.

Outright slavery was abolished, but it was more difficult to wipe out debt bondage, and the hidden slavery of immigrant labour persisted for decades since the registration of contracts remained a dead letter. The interpretation of slavery was open to ambiguity, particularly in Malay society where everyone had obligations for service, although they might not be bought and sold for money. The Bugis continued to import slaves, ostensibly as debtors, selling them to Chinese middlemen, who paid off the debt and then consigned most of them to neighbouring territories.[19] As late as 1873 it was alleged in the legislative council that nearly all Arab households employed slaves, and at that time many Javanese and Boyanese gardeners and syces in Singapore were virtual slaves, taking employment in exchange for payment of their debts to pilgrim shipmasters. The regulations about Chinese immigrant labour could not be enforced until the Chinese Protectorate was established in the 1870s. But blatant slave dealing was checked from these early years and the principle of personal liberty established.

While in many ways Raffles was enlightened and ahead of his time, his puritanical moral zeal fathered harsh measures designed to root out corrupting vices. He ordered that buildings used for gaming were to be confiscated and gaming-house keepers and gamblers should be flogged. Despite his claim to an insight and understanding of the Malay character, he was on occasion remarkably insensitive to deep-seated feelings. He was savage in his reaction when an Arab, Sayid Yasin, escaped from prison in March 1823 and ran *amok,* killing a police *peon* and wounding Farquhar. Farquhar's son killed the attacker on the spot, but there was pandemonium among the panic-stricken Europeans, who at first suspected the Temenggong's men had perpetrated the outrage. Raffles refused the Sultan's request for the body, and had the corpse carried round the town in a bullock cart and then hung up on display for a fortnight in an iron cage at Telok Ayer. The Malay community watched in sullen fury at this desecration of a Muslim body, and subsequently Sayid Yasin's grave at Tanjong Pagar became a holy shrine. The incident hung like a menacing shadow over Singapore for a long time, both

European and Chinese merchants fearing Malay retribution and conscious that the tiny garrison could give them little protection.

Perhaps most dear to Raffles's heart was his project for higher education, since he believed that 'education must keep pace with commerce in order that its benefits may be ensured and its evils avoided'. 'Let us not be remembered as the tempest whose course was desolation, but as the gale of spring.' It had long been his dream to revive the cultural heritage of the region, which he considered had been degraded by Chinese, Arab and Dutch exploitation and by the influence of the Muslim 'robber religion'. He wished to ally the reborn indigenous culture with the best in modern western scholarship for the intellectual enrichment of Asians and Europeans alike. In 1819 he tried to interest William Wilberforce in the creation of a college in the Malay archipelago to be attached to Wilberforce's African Institution. Singapore's geographic position, historical associations and commercial prosperity marked her out as the ideal centre 'for the cultivation of Chinese and Malayan literature and for the moral and intellectual improvement of the Archipelago and the surrounding countries'.

As his stay in Singapore drew to a close, Raffles determined to found his Singapore Institution as 'my last public act', and he told his friend Wallich, 'I trust in God this Institution may be the means of civilizing and bettering the condition of millions...our field is India beyond the Ganges, including the Malayan Archipelago, Australia, China, Japan and the islands of the Pacific ocean.' Raffles saw his projected institution as a means of instructing the Company's officials about the background in which they worked, educating the sons of neighbouring rulers and chiefs, and creating a class of Asian teachers and government servants. He anticipated a great rush for education from all over South-East Asia, particularly from the local aristocracy.

Without waiting to obtain approval from Calcutta, Raffles laid the foundation stone of the Singapore Institution three days before he left Singapore. Immediate provisions were made to appoint three Siamese, one Chinese and several Malay masters, and also Javanese and Buginese masters, when such could be found.

Raffles led the way by contributing $2,000 himself to the school, committing the East India Company to a contribution of $4,000, and using his powers of charmed persuasion to press the Sultan, Temenggong and Farquhar into parting with $1,000 each. Other officials and private residents followed suit and soon subscriptions totalled more than $17,000. The East India Company considered the scheme premature but grudgingly allotted a maintenance grant of $300 a month.

A few days before Raffles's final departure the European and Asian merchants of Singapore presented him with an address praising his 'comprehensive view...and principles the operation of which has converted, in a period short beyond all example, a haunt of pirates into the abode of enterprise, security and opulence'. Raffles himself was pleased with his work. Writing to Wallich in July 1823, he claimed, 'The constitution which I have given to Singapore is certainly the purest and most liberal in India.' And to another correspondent he explained, 'I have had everything to new-mould from first to last—to introduce a system of energy, purity and encouragement. . .to look for a century or two beforehand and provide for what Singapore may one day become.'

It was characteristic of Raffles that he should plunge into the task of creating a society, looking ahead for a hundred years, in a settlement whose very existence was still under dispute and in which he had no legitimate authority to frame laws. But Raffles was sure that Singapore was already too flourishing to be given up by Britain.

In view of Raffles's impending retirement, the Company decided to separate Singapore from Bencoolen and make it a direct dependency of Calcutta. On his final departure Raffles handed over the Singapore Residency to Dr. John Crawfurd, a Scotsman who had served under him in Java. Crawfurd had joined the East India Company's medical service in 1803 at the age of twenty and was posted to Penang in 1808, but his interests lay in languages, history and political administration rather than in medicine. After the war he returned from Java to Britain, where he published, in 1820, *A History of the Indian Archipelago,* which established him as an authority on the East. Shortly afterwards he was sent on a diplomatic mission to Siam and Cochin China, in the course of which he visited Singapore for the first time in January 1822 and was greatly impressed with its development.

Raffles had confidence in Crawfurd, whom he considered to be 'bold and fearless', 'devoting his mind exclusively to objects in which my heart and soul are deeply interested'. He wrote to Wallich in November 1823, 'Crawfurd has promised most solemnly to adhere to and uphold all my arrangements,' but in this Raffles was to be disappointed.

Crawfurd was an austere and forbidding character. Hard, cold, intolerant of criticism, 'bent down by a love of the goods of this world', as Munshi Abdullah described him, he inspired little affection. His brusque impatience offended the Asian community and Europeans considered him tight-fisted. But he was conscientious, painstaking and canny. He was familiar with Raffles's ways, which he regarded with a mixture of admiration and scepticism. In Java Crawfurd had on several occasions acted on his own initiative against Raffles's wishes, and Raffles once admitted 'Two of a trade can never agree; and Crawfurd and I are perhaps running too much on the same parallel not now and then to be jostling each other.' Crawfurd regarded Raffles's provisions for representative government, higher education and moral upliftment as visionary, utopian and premature. He jettisoned them in order to promote what he held to be Raffles's most sensible ideas, notably his commercial policy.

The first casualty was Raffles's illegal judicial system and attempt to associate non-officials in government, which collapsed almost immediately. When the honorary magistrates used the wide powers authorized by Raffles to flog and banish gamblers and confiscate their property, Crawfurd annulled the proceedings. To Raffles's consternation, and over-riding the magistrates' protests, in August 1823 Crawfurd licensed ten gaming houses in town and a cockpit in Kampong Bugis. He argued that gambling was endemic among Chinese, Malays and Bugis, and since it could not be eradicated, the state should profit by it.

Crawfurd replaced the magistrates by a court of requests under an Assistant Resident, which dealt with petty civil cases, and tried all other cases himself. He had no legal powers over Europeans, as the merchants well knew. Serious cases involving Britons could be referred to Calcutta, and in 1824 Crawfurd sent one merchant, John Morgan, to Calcutta on charges of insubordination. This could be dangerous, as Farquhar had found to his cost when he sent to Calcutta a Captain Gillon accused of raping one of his passengers. Gillon was acquitted and successfully sued Farquhar for compensation. In practice the Resident's only legal remedy was to banish troublesome Britons, since the settlement was the Company's private preserve, but fortunately the early British community were a law-abiding group, unlike their countrymen in other pioneer settlements. Crawfurd appealed for a charter of justice to be granted to Singapore to put the administration of law on a proper footing.

Crawfurd was justifiably sceptical about Raffles's idealistic ambitions of cultural revival and the grandiose education programme which Raffles instructed him to carry out. In 1826 Crawfurd urged Calcutta to concentrate on primary education and reported to the Directors, 'The native inhabitants of Singapore have not yet attained that state of civilization and knowledge which would qualify them to derive advantage from the enlarged system of education held by the Singapore Institution.' Calcutta gladly accepted Crawfurd's view about dispensing with higher education but unfortunately did not follow up his proposals to encourage primary schooling, with the result that education schemes at both levels lapsed and Raffles's cherished ideal withered.

Raffles's other wishes Crawfurd carried out with enthusiasm. He continued his measures to suppress slavery, obeyed the instructions on town planning, and continued the campaign to whittle down the Malay chiefs' influence. Above all he pursued Raffles's commercial policy with ardent devotion.

Raffles instructed Crawfurd before he left to practise economy and keep the cost of administration down, 'avoiding unnecessary expense rather than seeking revenue to cover it'. Crawfurd found these orders congenial, promoting free trade and restraining government expenditure with more zeal than Raffles himself. Whereas Raffles was a late convert to the principle of free trade, Crawfurd had for a long time been its staunch devotee. By pruning administrative expenses and removing the impositions of Captain Flint, the master attendant, he was able to abolish anchorage and other fees, making Singapore unique as a port which was free not only from tariffs but also from port charges.

Crawfurd eased out Raffles's and Farquhar's relatives. The Resident deprived Flint of his office of magistrate and threw open to competition the master attendant's monopoly rights of wooding, watering and ballasting ships. He commandeered as an official Residency the house on the hill, which Raffles had built and subsequently given to Flint. Flint continued as master attendant until his death in 1828 but his powers were gradually stripped away and he died in debt.

The period of Crawfurd's administration, which lasted from June 1823 to August 1826, was a time of vigorous upsurge in population, trade and revenue. According to the first official census taken in January 1824 Singapore had nearly eleven thousand inhabitants, of whom the Malays still formed the largest community, with the Chinese in second place. Third were the Bugis, and there were 756 Indians, 74 Europeans, 16 Armenians and 15 Arabs. By that time there were twelve European firms, most of them agents for London or Calcutta houses. There was a steady trickle of European immigration, mostly young commercial assistants in their late teens, but also a few slightly older men with wives and children. Nearly all were British, but December 1825 saw the arrival of a former Portuguese naval surgeon, Dr. Jozé d'Almeida, who came from Macao to set up a dispensary and subsequently became one of Singapore's leading merchants.

With the rise in population and trade, Crawfurd succeeded in extracting more revenue from the opium and arrack farms and sold licences for pawnbrokers and for the manufacture and sale of gunpowder. But his major innovation was to revive the gambling farm, which became the most profitable source of revenue. The revenue from tax farms rose from less than $26,000 in 1823 to more than $75,000 in 1825, of which nearly half came from gambling. By 1826 Singapore's revenue outstripped that of Penang.

Raffles's new town took shape under Crawfurd's direction. He enforced the standards laid down by Raffles for 'beauty, regularity and cleanliness'. Commercial Square was cleared and laid out, and a sound bridge was constructed across the river. The town streets were widened, levelled and given English street signs, and street lighting by means of coconut oil first appeared in 1824. Land was allotted for religious buildings. The troops were moved from the town centre to a new cantonment on the north-west outskirts at Sepoy Lines at the end of 1823.

In 1824 Singapore was acknowledged as a permanent British possession as a result of two treaties: the Anglo-Dutch Treaty of London signed in March 1824, which was the outcome of negotiations in Europe in which the Singapore authorities had no part; and a Treaty of Friendship and Alliance between the East India Company, Sultan Hussein and the Temenggong in August 1824, which was negotiated by Crawfurd.

The Treaty of London marked the end of the 'paper war' over Singapore. Among its territorial stipulations, the Dutch ceded Malacca to Britain, withdrew objections to the British occupation of Singapore and undertook not to make any establishment in the Malay peninsula, while the British agreed not to interfere in the islands south of the Singapore Strait. This treaty put an end to territorial friction between the Dutch and British in the Malay peninsula and the Riau archipelago.

A Dutch visitor, Colonel Nahuijs, who visited Singapore soon after, in June 1824, was grudgingly impressed but still rather bitter that the British had seized what he regarded as Dutch territory. But he concluded that Singapore was not likely to become the great port Raffles had visualized or the Dutch had feared, and considered that the existing twelve European firms were as much as Singapore could support. He thought Raffles had made a fatal mistake in negotiating with the Malay chiefs, and in particular the Temenggong and his piratical 'sea scum', instead of rooting them out.[20]

The Anglo-Dutch treaty gave the British a freer hand in dealing with the local chiefs. Despite the agreement made by Raffles in June 1823, the relationship remained ambiguous, and Crawfurd feared the Company might be drawn into the political disputes of the Johor-Lingga empire. He clashed with the chiefs on the interpretation of slavery and quarrelled over money. The Temenggong demanded compensation in addition to the $3,000 which he had already been paid to move to Telok Blangah, and Sultan Hussein was deep in debt to the Company and to private individuals. Crawfurd regarded both the chiefs as 'utterly unfit for any useful employment', and in January 1824 he advised the East India Company to secure the outright cession of Singapore, in order to cut the Company free from Malay politics.

Calcutta authorized him to negotiate a new agreement. The chiefs were reluctant but Crawfurd put pressure on them by holding back payment of their allowances for three months. Eventually in August 1824, in exchange for cash payments and increased pensions, they signed a Treaty of Friendship and Alliance, whereby they ceded to the East India Company and its heirs perpetual title to Singapore and all islands within ten miles of her shores. They were permitted to live on the land reserved for them in Singapore but were not to have any dealings abroad without the Company's consent. If they decided to withdraw from Singapore, the Sultan would receive $20,000 compensation and the Temenggong $15,000.

The treaty did not go as far as Crawfurd wished. He would have liked to oust the chiefs from Singapore and hoped the promised compensation would be sufficient bait to induce them to leave. He tried to make their life uncomfortable and prodded them as far as he could. In September 1824 he freed twenty-seven female slaves who escaped from the Sultan's palace complaining of ill-treatment, and a month later he drove a road to Kampong Bugis through Hussein's compound, smashing down his wall. While these measures failed to dislodge the chiefs and their continued residence in Singapore brought embarrassment to the British administration, the treaty effectively removed them from any control over Singapore's future.

Crawfurd sailed round Singapore island in August 1824 to take formal possession. Outside of the town area there was no sign of habitation except a few wood-cutters' huts on Pulau Ubin in the Johor Strait. Most of the island was still uninhabited and unexplored jungle, and in 1825 the *Singapore Chronicle* declared it would be easier to go to Calcutta than cover the difficult terrain to Bukit Timah hill, the centre of Singapore island and its highest point.

Of the party who landed with Raffles in January 1819, only Francis Bernard remained to see the signing of the August 1824 treaty. The settlement had experienced many changes in those five years and by 1824 was a well-established thriving port, with an orderly administration, a healthy trade and a population of nearly 11,000.

Singapore was fortunate in her three early pioneer administrators: Raffles, a man of extraordinary vision, but for whom Singapore would never have existed; Farquhar, who by his energy, good sense, and courage, nursed the infant settlement through its first dangerous years; and Crawfurd, shrewd and sensible, with his feet firmly on the ground, who converted into reality Raffles's most practical dreams. These diverse characters combined to set the pattern of administration which was maintained throughout the nineteenth century.

Farquhar played no further role in Singapore after he departed in 1823, and Raffles died in July 1826. Crawfurd left in August 1826 and, after undertaking a diplomatic mission to Burma, returned to England in 1830. He never revisited the East but maintained his contacts with Singapore. For some years he tried unsuccessfully to enter parliament and spent the rest of his life on the fringe of politics, battling against the East India Company, first of all as agent for the Calcutta merchants and later on behalf of the Singapore trading community. From 1853 he devoted most of his energies to advancing the cause of the Straits merchants in London, composing petitions and memoranda for parliament and organizing deputations. In 1868, in the last year of his life, when he was eighty-five years old, Crawfurd was made the first President of the Straits Settlements Association, which was formed to protect the new colony's interests. It was a fitting end to his career.

Despite this long association, Crawfurd's name, like Farquhar's, has faded almost into obscurity, and of Singapore's pioneers only Raffles's fame and reputation have grown over the years. In some ways history has been unfair to Farquhar and Crawfurd, who gave early Singapore the efficient administration which Raffles could not supply. Despite his great imagination and vision, Singapore was Raffles's only successful project, and this was largely because he had little hand in the actual running of the settlement. Singapore was fortunate in that, after the bold stroke of its founding, Raffles remained almost out of touch with the settlement during the first three formative years, when the port grew and prospered under Farquhar's careful administration. She was fortunate again in that after the whirlwind activity of Raffles's last stay, the actual implementation of his policy should have been left to the hard-headed Crawfurd. Raffles drew broad sweeping outlines, and it was left to other less imaginative but more practical and realistic men to fill in the details.

In the process it was inevitable that they should shed some of Raffles's altruistic idealism. Singapore quickly achieved a commercial success beyond Raffles's hopes, but his moral and educational policy soon crumbled, and Singapore developed into a highly materialistic society. While the Singapore merchants revered Raffles's memory and invoked his name as the high priest of free trade, many of the features of mid-nineteenth century Singapore would have saddened and disappointed its founder.

Despite this, Raffles's idealism later became an inspiration to intelligent and enterprising men, and he was a more influential force on later generations of empire builders than any other Briton connected with Singapore. Despite his lack of schooling and his long years of comparative isolation in the East as an employee of an old-fashioned monopolistic company, Raffles reflected to a remarkable degree the most advanced radical, intellectual, and humanitarian thinking of his day. The type of society he tried to establish in Singapore was ahead of that in contemporary England or India. His horror of slavery and vision of the moral influence of government were in tune with Wilberforce and the Evangelicals. His enlightened penal system and concern for law were in line with Jeremy Bentham and the Utilitarians. And in his final conversion to the cause of free trade he established in Singapore a free port following the principles of Adam Smith and *laissez faire* at a time when Britain herself was still a protectionist country.

1. P. Wheatley, *The Golden Khersonese* (Kuala Lumpur, 1961), p. 152.
2. Hsü Yün-ts'iao, 'Notes on Malay Peninsula in Ancient Voyages', *JSSS*, V, 2 (1948), pp. 1–16; Hsü Yün-ts'iao, 'The Historical Position of Singapore', *Papers on Malayan History*, ed. K.G. Tregonning (Singapore, 1962); Hsü Yün-ts'iao, 'Singapore in the Remote Past', *JMBRAS*, XLV, 1 (1973), pp. 6–9. Of K'ang T'ai's *The Book of the Native Customs of Funan*, describing his embassy to that country about 231 A.D., only fragments survive in Sung texts.
3. G.R. Tibbetts, 'The Malay Peninsula as known to the Arab Geographers', *Malayan Journal of Tropical Geography*, IX (Singapore, 1956), pp. 40–2; B.F. Colless, 'The Ancient History of Singapore', *JSEAH*, X, 1 (1969), pp. 5–7.
4. Hsü Yün-ts'iao, 'The Historical Position of Singapore', *Papers on Malayan History*, ed. K.G. Tregonning (Singapore, 1962), pp. 232–3.
5. W.W. Rockhill, 'Notes on the Relations and Trade of China with the Eastern Archipelago and the Coast of the Indian Ocean during the Fourteenth Century, part II', *T'oung Pao*, XVI (Leiden, 1915), pp. 61–159, gives translated excerpts from Wang Ta-yüan, *Tao-i Chih-lioh (Description of the Barbarians of the Isles)* (1349).
6. Ibn Said, quoted in O.W. Wolters, *The Fall of Srivijaya in Malay History* (Ithaca, 1970), p. 11.
7. A. Cortesão, (ed. and trans.), *The Suma Oriental of Tomé Pires*, 2 vols. (London, 1944), II, pp. 231–2.
8. For disputes concerning early sea-routes and the possible identification of the Lung-ya-men, or Dragon's Teeth Gate, with the modern Keppel Harbour, see J.V. Mills, 'Arab and Chinese Navigators in Malaysian Waters in about A.D. 1500', *JMBRAS*, XLVII, 2 (1974), pp. 1–82; C.A. Gibson-Hill, 'Singapore Old Strait and New Harbour, 1300–1870', *Memoirs of the Raffles Museum*, No. 3 (Singapore, 1956), pp. 11–115;

C.A. Gibson-Hill, 'Singapore: notes on the history of the Old Strait, 1580–1850', *JMBRAS*, XXVII, 1 (1954), pp. 163–214; R. Braddell, 'Lung-ya-men and Tan-ma-hsi', *JMBRAS*, XXIII, 1 (1950), pp. 37–51; reprinted in *JMBRAS*, XLII, 1 (1969), pp. 10–24.

9. D.E. Sopher, 'The Sea Nomads', *Memoirs of the National Museum*, No. 5 (Singapore, 1965), p. 105.

10. J.R. Logan, 'The Orang Biduanda Kallang of the River Pulai in Johore', *JIA*, I (1847), pp. 299–302; J.R. Logan, 'The Orang Sletar of the Rivers and Creeks of the Old Strait and Estuary of the Johore', *JIA*, I (1847), p. 302; J.T. Thomson, 'Remarks on the Seletar and Sabimba Tribes', *JIA*, I (1847), pp. 342[+]–4[+]; W.W. Skeat and H.N. Ridley, 'The Orang Laut of Singapore', *JSBRAS*, XXXIII (1900), pp. 247–50; reprinted *JMBRAS*, XLII, 1 (1969), pp. 114–16.

11. W. Bartley, 'Population of Singapore in 1819', *JMBRAS*, XI, 2 (1933), p. 177, reprinted *JMBRAS*, XLII, no. 1, (1969), pp. 112–13.

12. J.R. Logan, 'The Piracy and Slave Trade of the Indian Archipelago', *JIA*, III (1849), p. 632.

13. R.O. Winstedt, 'Abdul-Jalil, Sultan of Johor (1699–1719),' Abdu'l Jamal, Temenggong (c.) 1750, and Raffles' Founding of Singapore', *JMBRAS*, XI, 2 (1933), p. 165. Based on a nineteenth century Pahang MS.

14. J.A.E. Morley, 'The Arabs and the Eastern Trade', *JMBRAS*, XXII, 1 (1949), p. 155.

15. A.H. Hill, (ed. and trans.), 'Hikayat Abdullah', *JMBRAS*, XXVIII, 3 (1955), p. 142; reprinted Kuala Lumpur, 1970.

16. J. Bastin (ed.), 'The Journal of Thomas Otho Travers, 1813–1820', *Memoirs of the Raffles Museum*, No. 4 (Singapore, 1957), pp. 142–56.

17. W. Milburn, *Oriental Commerce*, 2 vols. (London, 1813), I, p. 320.

18. The reconstruction and lay-out are described and illustrated in H.F. Pearson, 'Singapore from the sea, June 1823', *JMBRAS*, XXVI, 1 (1953), pp. 43–55; reprinted *JMBRAS*, XLII, 1 (1969), pp. 133–44; and 'Lt. Jackson's plan of Singapore', *JMBRAS*, XXVI, 1 (1953), pp. 200–4; reprinted *JMBRAS*, XLII, 1 (1969), pp. 161–5.

19. *Singapore Chronicle*, 8 April 1830.

20. H.E. Miller (trans.), 'Extracts from the Letters of Col. Nahuijs', *JMBRAS*, XIX, 2 (1941), p. 195.

# II

# 'This Spirited and Splendid Little Colony', 1826–1867

IN 1826 the East India Company united Singapore with Penang and Malacca to form the Presidency of the Straits Settlements, with Penang as the capital and Penang's Governor, Robert Fullerton, as first Governor of the Straits Settlements. The merger put an end to Singapore's pioneering days: she came under Penang's executive and judicial control, and regular civil servants of the East India Company from Penang and Bencoolen brought her administration into line with the Company's practice. The Singapore establishment was enlarged. It was headed by a Resident Councillor with three Assistant Residents, but in the first four years Resident Councillors followed each other in rapid succession and none left a distinctive mark.[1]

The royal charter of justice, which Crawfurd had requested, was granted to the Straits Settlements in 1826, giving Singapore her first judicial system and providing for citizens of standing to be appointed as justices of the peace or grand jurymen. But at first the charter brought little improvement. The Recorder was supposed to travel on circuit from his Penang base and preside over a court in conjunction with the Governor and senior councillor in each settlement in turn. But this machinery could not be put into operation because the Recorder, Sir John Claridge, refused to leave Penang following disputes about travelling arrangements and expenses. Fullerton was compelled to hold the first Singapore assizes himself in 1828, while Claridge was recalled to England the following year and dismissed.

The Straits Settlements Presidency was overshadowed from the beginning by the menacing clouds of financial storm and doomed to an early death. Saddled with a big civil establishment and an elaborate judicial system, the government could not extract enough revenue to administer the scattered settlements. Fullerton's plans to raise a land revenue failed, and London vetoed his proposals to tax trade. While the deficit in the Straits Settlements swelled, the Company faced an acute financial crisis in India, and in 1830 it swept away the expensive superstructure in the Straits Settlements. The Presidency, the Governor, and his Council were abolished, and the Settlements were reduced to the status of a Residency dependent on the Presidency of Bengal.

The constitutional change generated an immediate judicial crisis. No

Recorder had arrived to replace Claridge, and with the disappearance of the offices and titles of Governor and Resident Councillors, Fullerton ruled that no-one was entitled to administer justice under the terms of the existing charter. When he departed for England in 1830 he closed the courts and dismissed the judicial establishment. The Assistant Resident of Singapore opened a temporary court but soon closed it again when he was warned that he possessed no legal authority. Merchants in Singapore and Penang appealed to the British parliament, but by then the Company had decided that Fullerton's interpretation was incorrect. The courts reopened in 1832, and a new Recorder arrived the following year.

To support judicial authority the titles of Governor and Resident Councillor were revived, but without their former powers or status. Governors were in practice mere Residents, and were either civil servants who had spent most of their career in the eastern settlements, such as George Bonham, Governor from 1836 to 1843, and Edmund Blundell, Governor from 1855 to 1859, or they were former Indian Army colonels, such as William John Butterworth, who ruled the Straits from 1843 to 1855, and Orfeur Cavenagh, who was Governor from 1859 until the end of Indian rule in 1867.

In 1833 Singapore faced another crisis when the East India Company lost its monopoly of the China trade, which the Straits Settlements had been acquired to protect and supply. While the Company could not jettison the useless burden, after 1834 she pursued a negative policy in the Straits, trying to avoid financial deficit and to insulate the settlements from problems in the Malay states by a rigid policy of non-intervention.

The civil service was drastically reduced in 1830. Senior posts in the Straits were cut from nineteen to eight, only two of these tenable in Singapore. Many officials were dismissed and the survivors suffered big salary cuts. This skeleton civil service survived almost unchanged until the end of Indian rule, despite the fact that between 1830 and 1867 Singapore's population quadrupled and her trade increased more than three-fold. Consequently officials could not cope with the growing complexity of administration.

At that period the Company's senior officials were usually respectable, intelligent men who carried out policy in an orthodox way. None stamped his personality so strongly on Singapore as the pioneers, Raffles, Farquhar and Crawfurd. There was no room in mid-nineteenth century Singapore for the flair and genius of a Raffles, but it was inevitable, and in many ways desirable, that informal personal rule, often accompanied by irresponsible nepotism, should give way to a more orderly if less colourful bureaucracy.

The officials of this period were a frustrated class. With few exceptions official salaries remained static between 1830 and 1867, although the cost of living rose steeply. Calcutta's obsession with the collection of reports and statistics put a heavy burden on bureaucrats in Singapore, where there was no literate clerical class. Officials had to correlate reports from the three settlements, compiling narratives and statistics, and converting local figures into Indian weights and currencies. Frustration and futility, compounded by long service in an enervating climate, sapped efficiency and sense of purpose. The Governor-General of India, Lord Canning, acknowledged in 1859 that the shortcomings of the bureaucracy were 'the greatest evil' in the Straits. Officials had little time to become acquainted with local languages and customs. Schemes introduced by Fullerton to pay tuition fees and bonuses to officials who attained proficiency in Malay, Siamese or Chinese were abolished in 1830. In the mid-nineteenth century many officials were barely fluent in Malay, and none could speak Chinese. Chinese translations of new laws had to be made in Hong Kong, and the *Singapore Free Press* commented in 1857, 'There is probably no other government in the world so incapable of addressing the people as that of the Straits.'

The judicial establishment was also inadequate. The Recorder paid periodic visits to Singapore but left the bulk of judicial work to the Governor and Resident Councillor. Cases remained unheard for months and the jails were packed with men awaiting trial. Eventually in 1855, after long years of agitation, a new charter of justice was granted, which provided for two Recorders, one to administer Singapore and Malacca, and the second, Penang. For the first time Singapore had her own judicial establishment, but the Governor and Resident Councillor still retained their anomalous position alongside the professional judge.

Singapore was the most flourishing of the Straits Settlements but Penang remained the seat of government for several years and the judicial headquarters until 1856. In practice George Bonham, who acted as Governor from 1833 to 1835 and became substantive Governor in 1836, spent most of his time in Singapore, but it was his successor, Governor Butterworth, who formally established Singapore as the permanent capital.

The contrast between drab official frustration and private commercial success was dramatic. Singapore's population expanded rapidly. In 1827 it stood at less than 16,000, by 1836 had nearly doubled to more than 30,000 and in 1860 numbered 81,000.

By 1827 the Chinese were the largest single community and in 1867 constituted 65 per cent of the population, numbering 55,000. Nearly all Chinese immigrants came from the provinces of Kwangtung and Fukien in south-east China, and comprised four major dialect groups: Hokkien, Teochew, Cantonese and Hakka. Most numerous were the Hokkiens who dominated Singapore's commercial life from the beginning. Their main business rivals were the Teochews, who were the second largest community. Cantonese generally came as agricultural labourers, tin miners or artisans and included most of Singapore's carpenters, tailors, goldsmiths and masons. Most Hakka immigrants passed through the port to the tin mines of the interior but some settled in Singapore, mainly as labourers. There was some affinity among Hokkiens and Teochews in speech and customs but a great gulf in dialect and character between the Cantonese and Hakkas.

Straits-born and many successful China-born immigrants settled down to permanent family life in Singapore, and several leading merchants became British subjects under a naturalization law passed in 1852. These were a minority, and most immigrants hoped to make enough money to return permanently to China after a few years. To this end they were prepared to work hard and live frugally, sending regular remittances of their savings to their families in China.

The Malay community continued to expand but soon lost its position of predominance. Immigrants from Malacca, Sumatra, and the Riau archipelago mingled easily and unobtrusively with the existing Malay population and with Javanese, Boyanese and others from the eastern islands.

The *orang laut* disappeared as a separate community. Soon after the British arrival, the Temenggong moved the *Orang Kallang* to the Pulai river in Johor, where most of them died in a small-pox epidemic.[2] The *Orang Seletar* continued their wandering existence undisturbed until the 1850s when the Johor Strait became more frequented. Some then drifted off to more peaceful creeks on the mainland, while the remainder became absorbed in the shore population. Some *Orang Gelam* settled on islands in Keppel Harbour, others in Malay villages ashore, but a large collection of *Orang Gelam* boats remained in the Singapore river, attracting a shifting population of *orang laut* from the Riau-Lingga archipelago.[3] In the late 1840s the government dispersed this floating village because it obstructed port traffic and was rumoured to harbour pirates, and from the middle of the century the *orang laut* and their descendants merged into the Malay population, generally as boatmen and fishermen.

By the 1860s the Malays had fallen to third place in Singapore's population. Most were peaceful industrious immigrants, employed in humble occupations as boatmen, fishermen, wood cutters or carpenters. Their one day of glory was the New Year's sports when the Malays and *orang laut* in boats of their own design invariably triumphed over Europeans, Chinese, Bugis and all other competitors.

Indians comprised less than 10 per cent of Singapore's inhabitants in 1845 but by 1860 had become Singapore's second largest community, totalling 13,000. Most came as traders or labourers, some as garrison troops or camp followers and others as convicts. The majority were south Indians, but there were also Sikhs, Punjabis, Gujaratis, Bengalis and a few rich Parsis.

Most Indian immigrants were young men, who skimped and saved to accumulate enough money to return home to settle. Very few Indian women came to Singapore until the 1860s, but Indian Muslims sometimes married Malay girls and settled down, producing a mixed class of descendants commonly known as Jawi-Peranakan.

The Bugis were the only community which declined in actual numbers. From a peak of 2,000 in the 1830s, when Bugis traders almost monopolized Singapore's trade with the eastern islands of the archipelago, their numbers sank to 900 by 1860. The opening of Macassar as a free port in 1847, the lifting of trading restrictions in the Dutch Indies, and the growing dominance of big western sailing ships and steamers in the archipelago trade loosened the Bugis' hold. The number of Bugis craft coming to Singapore dropped steadily, but the arrival of their annual fleet was still a picturesque and exotic sight in the early years of the twentieth century.

Of the smaller minority groups, the Arabs began to bring their womenfolk to settle in the 1830s. Many were affluent before they arrived and the major families accumulated enormous wealth, but Arabs only began to arrive in substantial numbers in the latter decades of the century. The first Jew from Baghdad came to settle in 1836, but the big influx of Middle East Jews came in the 1870s. Like the Arabs, the Jews often became extremely wealthy men.

The European population expanded steadily but remained a tiny minority. In 1827 they numbered ninety-four and in 1860 there were still fewer than 500 Europeans, only 271 of whom were adult British men. Their influence was disproportionate to their numbers. Britons filled all upper- and middle-grade official posts and provided most of the trading capital. Crawfurd had described the European minority in 1824 as 'the life and spirit of the Settlement', without whom there would be 'neither capital, enterprise, activity, confidence or order'.[4]

By the end of Indian rule Singapore was a predominantly Chinese town, with an upper crust composed of the European minority with a handful of wealthy Chinese, Arabs, Parsis, Indians, Armenians, and Jews.

The majority of immigrants were attracted to Singapore as a trading centre. In addition to British and Indian commerce, which was controlled almost exclusively by European merchants, Singapore quickly became an important focus for Asian-dominated Indonesian, Siamese, Chinese, and Malayan trade. Her harbour presented a picturesque spectacle of exotic Asian craft, often hundreds at one time: Malay *prahus,* Chinese junks, Bugis and Arab vessels.

In the days of sail the trade winds determined the pattern of Singapore's life, which centred round two main trading periods: the junk and the Bugis seasons. Junks from China, Cochin-China and Siam came with the north-east monsoon which blows from November to March, and left with the south-west monsoon which sets in during April. Most Chinese junks arrived in January and February, which was a time of great bustle and excitement. Swarms of boats went out to escort in the first junk of the season. The town was crowded with employers coming to hire new immigrants and shopkeepers competing with each other to buy the wares, which were spread out on the decks for their inspection.

Even during the East India Company's monopoly of the China trade, private merchants in Singapore conducted a flourishing trans-shipment trade by means of Chinese junks, and Singapore aspired to take over Canton's role as the focal point for western trade with China. She enjoyed a short-lived boom when Canton was closed during the first Opium War, but the founding of Hong Kong in 1841, followed by the opening of five China treaty ports, dashed Singapore's hopes of cornering the China trade.

The main Bugis fleet, coming from Celebes, Bali, southern Borneo and other ports south of the equator, usually reached Singapore in September or October, leaving for home in November with the onset of the north-west monsoon in the southern tropics. The strange-looking Bugis *prahus* anchored as floating shops along the shore at Kampong Glam. In the 1830s about two hundred Bugis craft came to Singapore every season, each manned by about thirty men. The arrival of six thousand such daring and quick-tempered men threatened the peace, and although the Bugis were forbidden to bring arms ashore, they were often involved in violent brawls, particularly with Chinese middlemen.

Singapore has always depended heavily upon Indonesian trade, for which she provides essential services. At the same time her position as an entrepot created an undercurrent of envy and resentment in Indonesia which goes back to Dutch colonial times. In the 1820s and 1830s Batavia imposed restrictions, surcharges and heavy duties on goods trans-shipped at Singapore and excluded her from direct access to Dutch outports in Sumatra, Borneo, Celebes and Timor. But Malay and Bugis *prahus* continued to smuggle goods between Singapore and these ports. After the heaviest Dutch restrictions were lifted in 1841, Singapore's Indonesian trade expanded steadily.

By 1826 Singapore had supplanted Batavia as the entrepôt for Siamese trade with the archipelago, but this trade was dominated by Siamese and Chinese junk-masters living in Bangkok. Attempts by European and Asian merchants of Singapore to invade this monopoly were frustrated until the Anglo-Siamese Bowring Treaty of 1855 opened Siam to British traders.

Chinese traders dominated Singapore's commerce with the east-coast Malay peninsular ports, selling opium and other supplies to colonies of Chinese miners and traders in exchange for gold, tin and rattans. Until the last quarter of the century there was little trade along the west coast of the peninsula, which, apart from the towns of Malacca and Penang, was almost uninhabited.

American ships were at first formally excluded from Singapore. Under an Anglo-American convention of 1815 Americans were permitted to trade with Indian presidency ports, including Penang, but no provision was made to extend this right to Singapore. Raffles detested Americans as 'commercial interlopers' and gun runners, but a few American ships came to Singapore until 1825, when one was seized and taken to Calcutta for trial on the grounds of illegal trading. After that American ships anchored at Riau, or at Battam some 14 miles away, to conduct their trade with Singapore, until eventually in 1840 American trade was formally admitted.[5]

Of 43 merchant houses in 1846, 20 were British, 6 Jewish, 5 Chinese, 5 Arab, 2 Armenian, 2 German, 1 Portuguese, 1 American and 1 Parsi. Singapore's commercial system rested mainly on an interrelation of European capital and Chinese enterprise. Most Europeans received goods on consignment which they sold on commission. To support this trade they relied on Chinese middlemen, who handled dealings with their own countrymen, and with Bugis, Siamese, Malays and other Asian traders. Some early Europeans put down roots of companies, such as Guthries and Bousteads which survive to this day, and Singapore's Europeans always formed an affluent class. Few were poor, but no individual European at that time appears to have made a fortune to match the most successful Chinese. Singapore's spectacular success as a port brought great profits for manufacturers in Britain, but for the individual European merchant the fluctuating entrepôt trade in the mid-nineteenth century provided at best 'a long drudgery which men enter upon in their youth and leave in their old age'.[6]

Some Chinese were adept at property dealing and short term speculation, which offered great prizes in early Singapore. Many had no capital but obtained goods from Europeans in exchange for promissory notes, which encouraged recklessness and wild speculation. Some successful ventures enriched both parties. Some Chinese failed and could not repay their debts, while others absconded to China with their gains. Many European fingers were burned, and on several occasions from the 1830s onwards European merchants agreed among themselves to restrict credit. But all such schemes broke down, because westerners found the Chinese middlemen indispensable, and in general this form of joint enterprise was mutually profitable.

Regular steamship services to India, Britain and China were introduced in the 1840s, but most cargoes continued to be carried in sailing ships for another thirty years. However the pattern of trade changed in other ways at this time. Western square-rigged sailing ships invaded the archipelago trade, displacing Malay and Bugis craft, and by 1854 more than three-quarters of Singapore's trade was carried in square-rigged vessels.[7]

Private commercial facilities and institutions came in the wake of trade expansion. The Oriental Bank was established in 1846, followed in 1855 by the Mercantile Bank and in 1859 by the Chartered Bank of India, Australia and China. The first telegraph was laid between Singapore and Batavia in 1859. The first dry-dock was opened in 1859, and in 1864 the Tanjong Pagar Dock Company was formed.

Lack of revenue and interest on the part of the East India Company meant that public facilities and commercial legislation lagged behind the private sector.

One major difficulty was the currency. The East India Company's rupee was the official currency but appeared only in paper transactions, and the common currency of South-East Asian trade was the Spanish silver dollar. This was supplemented by Dutch copper coins and copper tokens manufactured in England and imported into Singapore as a commercial venture by European merchants. While the Company disliked the circulation of a fluctuating foreign currency over which it had no control, Calcutta did not propose to abolish the dollar. But it wished to tidy up the currency system by also providing for a copper currency based on fractions of the rupee. The Singapore merchants wrongly assumed that an Act to this effect passed by the Indian legislative council in 1855 was the first stage in trying to oust the dollar. As a result of their protests the unpopular Act was withdrawn in 1857, but the currency question was not settled until colonial rule was established in 1867, when dollars and cents became the official currency.[8]

Piracy menaced Singapore's trade throughout the period of Indian rule. The most dangerous and highly organized were those from the Sulu archipelago and the Illanun from Mindanao, whose fleets of large, heavily-armed boats made annual voyages to ravage the waters of the eastern archipelago and the Malay peninsula. Dyaks and Brunei Malays preyed on trade with the west coast of Borneo, while Malays and *orang laut* from the Riau-Lingga archipelago often attacked sailing boats as they lay helplessly becalmed in the Malacca Straits, and easily escaped into the labyrinth of shallow mangrove creeks which line the shore of the southern part of the Malay peninsula.[9]

In the early years pirates battened on the swarms of small Asian craft coming to the new port, and it was an open secret that the pirates were receiving help from Temenggong Abdu'r-Rahman. Piracy brought legitimate trade almost to a standstill along the east coast of the Malay peninsula in the early 1830s. Singapore merchants were increasingly reluctant to entrust goods on credit for fear they would be lost to pirates, and in 1831 Bugis *nakodahs* complained that unless the east coast pirates were suppressed, they would abandon trading from Singapore.[10]

In the port itself vessels were attacked within view of the seafront by pirates, who traded openly in arms and loot in the town and waylaid passengers travelling out on sampans to ships in the roads. In 1832 and again in 1833 a group of Chinese merchants fitted out armed boats to patrol the waters just outside the harbour.

Since she had no Admiralty jurisdiction, Singapore had to send captured pirates to Calcutta for trial, and it was common practice among ships' captains to inflict irregular but effective justice by throwing captured pirates overboard. Admiralty jurisdiction was eventually granted in 1837 but was limited to piracy committed within Straits Settlements' territorial waters.

In 1835 Bonham complained to Calcutta that piracy was threatening the Asian trade with 'total annihilation', and in answer to a petition from the European merchants of Singapore a royal naval sloop H.M.S. *Wolf* was dispatched to the Straits to co-operate with the Company's steamer *Diana* against pirates. The *Wolf* and the *Diana* brought terror to the pirates, who had never encountered steamers before, and alarmed the late Temenggong's young heir, Ibrahim, into abandoning piracy.

For a few years the waters round Singapore were safe but in the early 1850s a new and more virulent menace surged up in the form of large-scale Chinese piracy, which the weak Manchu government could not curb. Chinese pirates attacked large junks as well as smaller craft and killed Singapore's trade with Formosa and Cochin China. The pirates were openly using Singapore to provision and arm their boats and sell loot.

Pirate attacks became so frequent that in 1854 it was alleged only half the Asian craft from the archipelago succeeded in reaching Singapore.[11] As the junk season began, empty but heavily-armed junks carrying large crews left Singapore every day. It was obvious they were bent on piracy but there was no legal authority to intercept them. Nor could the government take action against pirates with its 'lilliputian fleet' of three gunboats, which were supposed to provide both protection and official transport for all three Settlements.

In 1855 the Singapore merchants sent fruitless petitions to the Governor-General of India, the Royal Navy and both Houses of Parliament, pleading for naval protection and for legislation to permit the arrest of suspected pirates. The Singapore newspapers reported cases of piracy in nearly every issue, and in 1866 the *Singapore Free Press* complained about Chinese pirates plundering ships 'within the sound of our guns'.[12]

But by that time the heyday of piracy in South-East Asian waters was coming to an end. Treaties signed between the western powers and China in 1860 provided for co-operation to wipe out piracy, and the increasing importance of the China trade led to greater activity by the British navy in the Far East, with the suppression of piracy in the China Sea and the Straits of Malacca as one of its main functions. The extension of Dutch power in Sumatra from 1858 onwards, and the spread of British protection over the west Malay states after 1874 contributed to the rapid decline of large-scale piracy.

Almost entirely dependent on a fickle entrepôt trade, Singapore's position in the mid-nineteenth century was delicate, and her trade was subject to violent fluctuations and to years of uncertainty and depression. Singapore's progress came in fits and starts. Merchants regarded booms as times of freak prosperity and slumps as the herald of permanent ruin. They were constantly haunted by the fear that prosperity might wither as quickly as it had grown, if rival free ports appeared or if the Indian government undermined Singapore's free-port status.

Before 1841 Singapore traders resented Dutch restrictions on Indonesian trade as a threat to their enterprise, but from the 1840s they began to complain instead about the steady liberalizing of Dutch trade policy, because they feared the opening of free ports in the Indies would entice trade away from Singapore. When Macassar was opened as a free port in 1847 many merchants predicted that Singapore's Bugis trade was doomed. The founding of Hong Kong and the opening of the China treaty ports to foreign trade plunged Singapore merchants in gloom. 'I think the trade of Singapore has reached its maximum; and that the town has attained to its highest point of importance and prosperity,' a merchant, G.F. Davidson, wrote in 1846.[13] The majority of his contemporaries agreed with this gloomy prediction, fearing the settlement faced economic depression and possibly extinction.

Commerce revived in the early 1850s. A record number of vessels came to Singapore during the official year 1851/2, and the trade figures induced the Calcutta newspaper, *The Friend of India,* to hail Singapore as 'this spirited and splendid little colony, the most important of the outlying marts of Great Britain'.[14]

Forebodings about competition from Macassar, Hong Kong and the China treaty ports melted away since the expansion of commerce with China and the Indies in fact boosted Singapore's trade. After the Bowring treaty of 1855 Singapore quickly became an important centre for the Bangkok trade. By 1857 the value of Singapore's trade had nearly doubled over the figures of fifteen years before.

The boom burst in the early 1860s, when Singapore's trade was hit by the extension of Dutch control in Celebes, which deflected more of the Bugis trade, by the American civil war, and by the opening of further Chinese ports to direct western trade at the end of the second Opium War. In 1862 Cavenagh reported, 'Singapore has ceased to be the great port of transhipment, either for native produce or European goods; vessels from England now pass through without breaking bulk whilst the native trade is naturally attracted to the nearest marts.'

These were no idle fears because 1864, the worst year of the slump, brought disaster to many firms, big and small, Asian and European. The most sensational was the bankruptcy of D'Almeida & Sons, one of the oldest and most respected of Singapore business houses.

Despite this, the setback to Singapore's expansion was only temporary and Cavenagh's fears about her permanent eclipse as a great international trading centre proved unfounded. When she was handed over to the Colonial Office in 1867, Singapore was one of the most flourishing ports in the British Empire.

In contrast to Singapore's commercial success, her industrial progress was disappointing and the story of agriculture was one of almost unrelieved gloom.

Part of the problem was shortage of labour, which afflicted Singapore throughout the nineteenth century. The Malays concentrated on fishing, wood-cutting and small-scale subsistence farming, and rarely went into trading or became hired labourers. The Bugis did not adapt to organized labour, while Indian labourers emigrated to Penang rather than Singapore.

Chinese labourers were highly prized but preferred to work on their own account or for their own countrymen. Most European estates relied on Javanese, or Boyanese from the island of Bawean off Java. In 1860 there were three thousand such immigrants in Singapore, but it was difficult to import Javanese and Boyanese labour on a regular basis. Many were pilgrims returning from Mecca, who pledged their labour to Singapore plantation owners in return for payment of their debts to the ship's master.

Singapore's only industry of any note was sago manufacture. The technique of pearling sago was imported from Malacca or Siak into early Singapore, which quickly became the centre for producing high-quality sago for export to India and Europe. By 1849 there were fifteen Chinese and two European sago factories in Singapore, but Europeans found it impossible to compete with Chinese proprietors, who lived and worked in their factories alongside their workmen.[15]

The lushness of her tropical jungle deceived early settlers into believing the island to be very fertile, and in 1836 a group of enthusiasts, mainly Europeans, formed the Singapore Agricultural and Horticultural Society to experiment with crops. Nutmegs were the most popular and in the middle of the century nutmeg-growing was described as 'a sort of mania in Singapore',[16] but disease struck the plantations and by the mid-1860s only one blight-stricken nutmeg plantation remained under cultivation. The town was surrounded by sinister acres of dying nutmeg trees.

Coconuts were the second favoured crop but grew only in the sandy coastal Katong area of south-east Singapore and brought only a modest return on capital. Sugar-planting proved disastrous and in 1848 bankrupted the American consul, Joseph Balestier, who was the most ambitious sugar-planter. Coffee, cotton, cinnamon, cloves, and indigo, which were planted on a more cautious experimental scale, all ended in failure, and by the 1860s European estate-type agriculture had been defeated by soil deficiencies, plant diseases, pests, and the absence of seasonal change.[17]

Only the Chinese gambier and pepper plantations flourished. These crops complemented each other, since gambier waste provided an essential fertilizer for pepper, which was more profitable but quickly exhausted the soil. Gambier leaves required boiling soon after picking, and the virgin forests of Singapore island furnished plenty of wood for the burners.

There were about twenty gambier plantations in 1819 when the British arrived, some worked by Chinese and others by Malays, and the product was exported to China. In the 1830s British dyeing and tanning industries became the chief market for Singapore's gambier. Rising prices encouraged the opening of new plantations and Chinese pushed into the interior of the island, particularly to the north and west.[18]

Gambier production reached its peak in the late 1840s, by which time there were 600 gambier and pepper plantations under cultivation, employing about 6,000 Chinese labourers. But it was an uncertain form of agriculture because prices fluctuated widely. By the middle of the century many plantations had exhausted their soil, and farmers began to move to Johor. Nearly all planters borrowed their initial capital at stiff interest rates from town shopkeepers, in return for which they were obliged to buy food and supplies from their creditors and to sell them their gambier and pepper. This system tied farmers to creditors for years, and the established Singapore dealers continued to control the new enterprises in Johor.[19]

In addition to declining productivity, gambier planters were scared off by the growing tiger menace. Tigers were first reported in 1831, when two Chinese were killed not far from town. As more plantations encroached on the virgin jungle, the danger became so acute that by the middle of the century Singapore was famous for its tigers, which were rumoured to be carrying off on average one victim a day. A tiger was even found in Orchard Road in 1846.

At first estate owners tried to suppress stories of ravages by tigers for fear of deterring labour, but by the mid-1840s they gave up trying to disguise the truth. Creditors dared not visit their estates, and in 1859 one village near Bukit Timah was abandoned after tigers killed many of its inhabitants.

Tiger-hunting became a favourite sport. The government offered rewards for killing tigers, and their flesh and skins commanded sufficiently high prices to induce two Eurasians to make tiger-hunting a full-time living. In 1860 Governor Cavenagh sent parties of convicts to hunt tigers in the jungles. Gradually the menace faded as the island was more thoroughly opened up and developed, but a man was killed by a tiger at the seventh milestone Thomson Road in 1890, two tigers were shot on the Bukit Timah Road in 1896, and the last tiger was shot at Goodwood House in 1904.[20]

'Slash and burn' gambier and pepper cultivation was disastrous for Singapore. In his efforts to get rich quickly, the immigrant Chinese peasant, forsaking the intensive care, the cherishing and replenishing of the soil to which he was accustomed in his homeland, raped the earth and deserted it. The soil was exhausted, the forest destroyed and the ground left open to the encroachment of coarse lalang grass. The gambier and pepper planter moved on 'as the locust leaving a tract of desolation behind him'. By 1867 much of the interior of Singapore island was laid waste and abandoned.

Only the superstitious believed Singapore's agriculture was doomed by the curse of Temasek's bloodstained history, but none could deny the stark curse put on her land by gambier and pepper planters five centuries later.

By the early 1830s Singapore was known as 'the Queen of the Further East'.[21] Her regal qualities lay in her great economic bustle, the natural beauty of her setting, and the fine houses and godowns of her prosperous merchants. The government had no money to build public buildings to match. Merchants' stores were used as government offices, and a private

European house was rented as the court house. The Resident lived in the flimsy attap-roofed wooden bungalow which Raffles had built, a structure so frail that people looked up after a stormy night to see if it was still there. The botanical garden at the foot of Government Hill was overgrown by weeds, and the Singapore Institution on the beach was a half-finished shell, the first sight which greeted travellers on entering the harbour. This imposing ruin gave the settlement an antique appearance belying its recent origin. Visitors were puzzled, but first impressions were correct: a contrast between the penury of government and the ruin of intellectual ambitions on the east bank, compared with the lusty pursuit of wealth across the river.

The Singapore river was the heart of the town, and up to the 1840s all shipping congregated at its mouth and along the crescent of Boat Quay. Merchants had their offices and *godowns,* or warehouses, either on Boat Quay or Commercial Square, which then backed on to the sea. In the early days many Europeans lived above their offices, but by 1830 most had moved across to the east bank fronting the Esplanade and along the beach. Here in the 'Mayfair of Singapore' they built themselves elegant houses in spacious compounds.

In the early 1830s much of the town area was still swamp, the main roads mere causeways over the marsh, and whole districts were subject to frequent floods. Fire was a major hazard in the Asian quarters and in the main business area. In 1830 a fire raged for three days in the centre of the town, burning down Philip Street and part of Market Street. There was no fire-fighting service and the police acquired fire-engines only in 1846. Even these were not effective in combating a fire which destroyed a large part of Kampong Glam the following year.[22]

The town improved with the appointment in 1833 of George Drumgold Coleman, a talented Irish architect, as superintendent of public works. Coleman began the practice of making extensive use of convict labour in Singapore. The first Indian convicts were transferred from Bencoolen in 1825, and Singapore quickly became the major convict centre in the Straits, 'the Sydney convict settlements of India'. In view of the chronic shortage of labour in Singapore, convicts carried out entire projects from quarrying stone, felling timber and making bricks, to actual construction of lighthouses, churches, government offices and other public buildings.[23]

Coleman reclaimed land along the sea front towards Kampong Glam, drained marshes, constructed roads, and built many elegant private houses in a gracious Palladian style, which set the fashion for Singapore's delicate, graceful colonial architecture. When he died in 1844 he left behind many impressive buildings, of which only a few survive today. Most notable are the Armenian Church, a private house which forms the nucleus of the present Parliament Building, and the Registrar's house, which now forms part of the Convent of the Holy Infant Jesus. Coleman's own magnificent house, built in 1829 in the street bearing his name, was leased to a Frenchman, who opened the London Hotel there in 1831.

The mansion housed a succession of hotels and boarding houses but by the 1930s degenerated into a tenement slum, which was finally pulled down in 1969.

In the 1830s solid religious buildings began to replace the flimsy make-shift original structures. Coleman completed the Armenian Church in 1835 and the first St. Andrew's Church in 1836. The first Roman Catholic church was built in 1833 and a second church, which was later consecrated as the Cathedral of the Good Shepherd, was completed in 1846. The main Chinese temple was the Thian Hok Keong in Telok Ayer Street, then fronting the sea. Finished about 1842, it is still one of the sights of Singapore. Most of the materials, including the granite pillars, ornamental stone work and a statue of the sea goddess Ma-Cho-Po, were imported from China at the expense of wealthy Hokkien junk owners. The first mosque was built in Kampong Glam in 1824, but the oldest surviving and most attractive mosque was erected, also in Kampong Glam, in 1846 by a prosperous Malacca lady, mother-in-law of an Arab merchant Syed Ahmed Alsagoff. The reconstruction of Indian temples reflected the burgeoning prosperity of the Indian community. The Siva temple in Orchard Road was rebuilt as a solid structure in the early 1850s, the wood and attap Sri Mariamman temple was replaced by a brick building in 1862, and rich *chettiars* built the imposing Subramaniam temple in Tank Road in 1859.[24] The first Jewish synagogue opened in Synagogue Street in 1845.

By the middle of the century there were three reputable hotels. The most fashionable was the London Hotel, which in 1845 took over another splendid house originally built by Coleman for a leading merchant, Edward Boustead. It occupied an imposing position on the Esplanade, the site of the present Supreme Court. In 1865 the hotel was renamed the Hotel de l'Europe, predecessor of the present Cockpit and Singapore's oldest surviving hotel.

Most of the urban population were Chinese, but nearly all the Europeans and Indians and a large number of Malays lived in the town. The eastern rural district of Kampong Glam and its environs supported a mixed population, mainly Malay, Bugis, Arab, and Javanese, but with a sizeable community of Chinese. The western country districts were more sparsely peopled. More than half of the inhabitants there were Chinese. The remainder were mainly Malays, centring on the Temenggong's settlement at Telok Blangah, and *orang laut* in the New Harbour area. This pattern of racial settlement persisted in Singapore up to the mid-twentieth century.[25]

The town area was still very small and surrounded by swamps. Chinese market gardeners grew fruit and vegetables behind the town along Orchard Road, which was a country lane lined with bamboo hedges and shrubbery, with trees meeting overhead for its whole length. In the late 1830s some wealthy Chinese and European merchants began to move to country houses, often surrounded by nutmeg plantations, on the town fringes. Some settled to the west along the coast adjoining Telok Blangah, notably William Wemys Kerr at Bukit Chermin, James Guthrie at St. James and Joaquim d'Almeida at Raeburn. Others moved eastward, such as Joseph Balestier, who planted sugar on the plain bearing his name, Thomas Dunman who grew coconuts at Katong, and Hoo Ah Kay (nicknamed Whampoa) who built himself a mansion with a magnificent ornamental garden on Serangoon Road. Most preferred to move north towards Tanglin, where the roads were better and the approach to town was prettier. Dr. Thomas Oxley, the government surgeon and an ardent nutmeg planter, moved to Killiney in 1837, and was followed by Charles Carnie at Carnie's Hill (Cairnhill), Thomas Hewetson at Mount Elizabeth, and Dr. Martin at River Valley.

The interior of the island beyond these suburbs was still a mystery to Europeans despite the fact that Singapore was such a small flat island. They were put off by the swampy coasts, the thick jungle terrain, the complex drainage system of many small rivers, and apparently by sheer lack of curiosity. Expansion to the interior was left to Asian settlers, primarily the Chinese, and Europeans rarely ventured far beyond the town limits. But by 1840 roads extended to Bukit Timah and Serangoon, each about seven miles long. In 1843 a road was constructed to the top of Bukit Timah hill, and the idea of building a miniature hill station was mooted but abandoned because of the fear of tigers. In 1845 the Bukit Timah road was extended through to the Johor Strait, giving access to the hitherto isolated plantations in the north of the island.

The Singapore river remained the heart of the business sector but became increasingly congested. Businessmen and military engineers complained that Raffles had made a mistake in siting the town on the river, where commerce was cramped and defence impossible. Keppel Harbour, then known as New Harbour, a fine large deep harbour, which was sheltered and easy to defend, had been brought to Farquhar's notice in July 1819, but Raffles vetoed Farquhar's suggestions to develop it. Established firms were reluctant to move from Boat Quay until forced by the advent of steamers, which needed deep water and coal supplies. The P. & O. Company was the first to establish itself at New Harbour in 1852, and was quickly followed by Jardines, the Borneo Company and other big firms. Despite this, three-quarters of all shipping business in the 1860s was still done at Boat Quay in the heart of the town.[26]

Despite its lovely setting and orderly planning, many parts of Singapore in the mid-nineteenth century were still unsightly. The main streets frequently flooded at high tide and were lit by feeble coconut-oil lamps. The town was plagued by stray dogs, and dead ponies were left to rot on the beach. The city's refuse was thrown into the swamps, the roads were littered with garbage, and the Singapore grand jury complained at almost every sessions about pollution and stench. The problem was money. Residents demanded more amenities but refused to pay higher property assessment, while Calcutta did not consider that lightly-taxed Singapore deserved further government subsidies. They refused to build a new bridge near the river mouth or to mend the two existing bridges, which could not cope with traffic and were in a dangerous state of repair. Traffic jams and reckless driving led to many accidents, which were aggravated because the authorities could not enforce any rule about keeping to one side of the road.

Despite the phenomenal growth of population and trade, throughout the period of Indian rule Singapore's merchants lived on their nerves, vulnerable to every slump in international commerce, and frequently at loggerheads with the government of India and Straits officials. Haunted by a basic insecurity, which drove them to an obstinate and sometimes hysterical defence of their privileges, they opposed all proposals to impose new taxes which would have provided better port facilities, security or social amenities. For its part the East India Company, which already subsidized Singapore's general revenue, refused to incur a greater deficit and was forced into a neglectful parsimony.

The drastic economies of 1830 failed to make the Straits Settlements solvent, and the Singapore government could benefit only indirectly from increased prosperity and expanding population in the form of excise revenue, licences and property taxes. Until the last few years of the Indian regime these were insufficient to cover costs and the loss had to be made good by Calcutta.

The right to collect excise taxes was auctioned to private Chinese bidders, except in the case of the Indian-held toddy farm. This gave the government a comparatively secure income without any administrative cost. Direct excise collection seemed impracticable. As Crawfurd said, 'The government would be brought into a frequent and odious collision with the natives, and compelled to employ a vile, expensive and corrupt crew of native excise officers.'[27] A few officials and private residents argued that taxing vices encouraged moral corruption, but the majority of the ruling class had no compunction and agreed with Fullerton that 'the vicious propensities of mankind are the fittest subjects of taxation'.[28]

The major battle centred on gambling. The gambling farm, started by Farquhar, banned by Raffles and restored by Crawfurd in 1823, was the most lucrative of all the Singapore revenue farms. But the temptation offered to immigrants to get rich quickly led to such misery, destitution and crime, that the grand jury demanded the prohibition of gambling. In 1829 it was declared illegal and the gambling farm was never restored, despite many suggestions in later years that it would be a palatable means of balancing the revenue.

From time to time other minor taxes were imposed on pork, toddy and betel nuts, while pawnbrokers and market stall holders paid licence fees, but the opium and arrack farms remained the main sources of revenue throughout the nineteenth century. As the secretary of state for India commented in 1859, the revenue was 'derived more from the vices than from the industry of the people'. This fitted the self-righteous philosophy of Singapore's European ruling class. The predominantly Scottish merchant group tended to be puritanical, stressing the spartan qualities of thrift and hard work. Many were kind, charitable, generous men, contributing handsomely to relieve individual distress or support worthy causes, but collectively their harsh *laissez faire* cult and emphasis on the virtues of self-help and industry gave moral backing to callous practices.

In seeking to balance the budget, officials in Singapore and India made periodic proposals to tax trade, which the European mercantile community resisted indignantly. They argued that, apart from her geographical position, Singapore was blessed with few natural advantages, and her prosperity depended upon her liberal policy. Raffles had converted a temporary expedient to attract trade into a promise of permanent freedom from custom duties, which Crawfurd extended to include port charges. The principle of free trade was accepted by the East India Company's Board of Control in London in 1826 and thereafter preserved zealously by the Singapore merchants. Free trade became a sacred cardinal principle and any threatened infringement was opposed vehemently as commercial heresy.

The merchants defeated suggestions made by Fullerton in 1829 to impose export duties and stamp dues and to tax aliens' exported capital. In 1836 they succeeded in obtaining a veto from the Company in London on port dues proposed by Calcutta to finance anti-piracy measures in Singapore. In this way Singapore was guaranteed freedom not only from trade tariffs but also from tonnage and port dues, wharfage and anchorage dues, port clearance fees and stamp duties, and the government was deprived of the chance to share in commercial prosperity.

Hampered by lack of money and shortage of officials, administration was light and lax, providing a semblance of law and order but scarcely touching the lives of the inhabitants. This *laissez faire* policy and the absence of taxes and restrictions benefited trade but led to deficiencies of government, particularly in the provision of security and social services. It also meant that the different communities retained and developed their own organizations, virtually outside the pale of official administration.

After the *kapitan* system was supplanted by the charter of justice in 1826, the government's control over the Asian population was tenuous. It enlisted the co-operation of influential members of different communities but gave them no formal functions. The result was an unsatisfactory compromise, with the authorities expecting community leaders to keep their own people in order but giving them no definite authority.

Most Indonesian and Arab immigrants settled with men of their own community in parts of the town still bearing their names, such as Kampong Jawa, Kampong Sumbawa, Bugis Street and Arab Street. They adapted peaceably to their new environment without coming into much contact with the government.

The Malays lacked leadership and organization. Sultan Hussein did not possess the ability to profit from the sudden upward turn in his

3. Daeng Ibrahim, Temenggong of Johor, 1841–1862
From a photograph in Istana Bukit Serene, Johor Bahru
(By permission of His Highness, the Sultan of Johor)

fortunes. The Company recognized him as Sultan to give a cloak of legality to the founding of their Singapore factory, but he commanded no respect or firm following among the Malays. By the early 1830s, exhibiting a Pickwickian syndrome, Hussein had become 'so enormously stout that he appears to be continually on the point of suffocation... and exists only in a torpid state'.[29] Family scandals and mounting debts compelled him to move to Malacca, where he died in 1835. His fifteen-year-old son Ali returned to Singapore in 1840 and took possession of his father's property in Kampong Glam, but for many years the Straits government refused to acknowledge his claim to be Sultan.

Temenggong Abdu'r-Rahman died in 1825, by which time Raffles and Crawfurd had thwarted any ambitions which he may have harboured of turning Singapore into another Malacca, with a foreign trading community subservient to the Malay authorities. No successor was appointed to the office of Temenggong for nearly twenty years. But during the 1830s the late Temenggong's intelligent and enterprising younger son, Daing Ibrahim, who had been brought to Singapore in 1819 when he was eight years old, grew up to lead the Telok Blangah community. At first he emulated his father in exacting tribute from the swarms of small Asian craft which frequented Singapore, and the *Singapore Free Press* accused Ibrahim of being in command of all the pirates in the neighbourhood. But outwardly Ibrahim cultivated the British Governor's favour and, profiting from Hussein's disgrace and Ali's youth, he increased his prestige among neighbouring Malay chiefs.

The vigorous campaign undertaken by the Straits authorities to suppress piracy induced the prudent Ibrahim to turn pirate hunter himself. This change of policy paid dividends. In 1841 the Bendahara of Pahang formally installed him as Temenggong at Telok Blangah in the presence of Governor Bonham, and at a glittering ceremony five years later Governor Butterworth presented a sword to the Temenggong in token of his vigilance in suppressing pirates. Many of the European merchants considered the occasion a mockery, but Ibrahim's decision to abandon piracy made the seas immediately round Singapore safe for small ships. It also changed the role of his followers, whom the authorities had up till then regarded as idle good-for-nothing mischief-makers.

From the mid-1840s the Temenggong turned his attention to establishing a profitable monopoly over the gutta percha trade of southern Malaya and east Sumatra, with Singapore as its centre, and the development of New Harbour in the early 1850s made Ibrahim's property along the Telok Blangah waterfront very valuable.

While the Temenggong grew rich, the would-be Sultan, Ali, was in a desperate financial plight, facing the threat of being thrown into a debtor's prison. Constantly bemoaning the insufficiency of his allowance but refusing to soil his hands with trade, Ali was unable to pay his diminishing band of followers, and his government pension was pledged to an Indian money-lender to pay the interest on his debts.

The Singapore authorities welcomed Ibrahim's conversion from pirate to businessman, and with their blessing he became influential in Singapore's commercial life. He struck up friendships with European merchants, particularly with his neighbour at Bukit Chermin, William Kerr, who became his business associate. After Kerr returned to England, his partners, William Paterson and Henry Simons, continued to act as the Temenggong's agents, and the firm of Paterson & Simons was the first European company in Singapore to extend its operations to Johor and taste the tempting fruits of the peninsular trade.

While merchants such as Kerr, Paterson, and Simons hitched their fortunes to the Temenggong's rising star, others, and notably William Henry Read of A.L. Johnston & Co, tried to manipulate Ali's weakness to their own advantage. Alarmed by the intrigues among the European commercial community, Governor Butterworth attempted to stop this meddling in Johor politics. In 1855 he negotiated a treaty between Ali and Ibrahim, whereby Ali acknowledged Ibrahim as actual ruler of Johor but received a fixed allowance from the state's revenue and acquired the long-coveted title of Sultan. It was an empty and meaningless honour. Ali's son lost the title, and the family declined into obscure poverty in Kampong Glam.

The Johor treaty failed to settle the unrest. Commercial intrigue continued, particularly between Johnstons and Paterson & Simons. The Temenggong quarrelled with the Singapore authorities over leasing his land in New Harbour to private companies and over the alleged mistreatment of Chinese British subjects in Johor.

Governor Cavenagh succeeded in settling the difficult problem of Johor politics. He managed to establish a cordial working relationship with Ibrahim's intelligent son, Abu Bakar, who became Temenggong in 1862. Abu Bakar transferred his headquarters to Johor Bahru where he removed sources of friction by bringing his administration and legal system into line with the Governor's wishes. In 1885 the British recognized Abu Bakar as Sultan of Johor.

Singapore continued to control Johor's foreign policy and dominate her economy, and the Malay chiefs' political influence in Singapore disappeared. The new Johor royal family kept residences in Singapore and remained prominent in the city's sporting and social life but associated with Europeans and Chinese more often than Malays. With the diversion of Telok Blangah's interest to the mainland and the decline of the Kampong Glam aristocracy into penury, no other Malay leaders emerged to take their place.

Despite their numbers and their concentration in the urban area, the Indian community made comparatively little impact. The vast majority were labourers, ferrymen, or petty tradesmen. They had no leadership and were divided in background, language and religion. In the mid-nineteenth century there were seventeen Parsi, Tamil and north Indian businessmen of standing in Singapore, but they were notable as individuals rather than community leaders. Indeed the rich Parsis stood aloof from the Indian community and the ruling class did not regard them as Indians.

The Chinese facility to organize themselves and run their affairs independently produced a blend of admiration and dread among the ruling community. Officials respected the Chinese as hard-working and self-reliant settlers but feared the clan feuds and secret societies which they brought with them.

The vast majority of Chinese immigrants came from the coastal strip of east Kwangtung and south Fukien, where conditions bred hardy, resourceful pioneers. In these hilly provinces, cut off from central China by mountain ranges, a considerable part of the population was engaged in fishing, junk building and trade rather than agriculture, and ambitious young men were accustomed to emigrate in search of a living. The inhabitants of these regions were used to working long hours of gruelling labour, to living frugally and also to gambling in overseas junk ventures. Young emigrants coming from such a background were ideal pioneers in facing the hardships, dangers and deprivations of a new life in the Nanyang.[30]

Most Chinese immigrants to Singapore were illiterate youths who had never been outside their home village, and when they moved to the bewildering new world of Singapore they sought out familiar organizations among their own people. Having no guidance from the Straits government and no contact with their own, they joined earlier settlers with the same family surname, coming from the same neighbourhood in China, speaking the same dialect, and they adopted similar occupations. They formed *pangs* or guilds, which went beyond the normal western trade guilds in that they covered social and economic as well as purely occupational activities.[31]

This family and regional loyalty and the constructive ability to form associations helped Chinese immigrants to fit into the new society, but at the same time Fukien and Kwangtung were notorious for their bitter clan feuds. These provinces were also the major source of strength for the Triad or Heaven and Earth Society, a political secret society dedicated to the overthrow of Manchu imperial rule in China. Triad branches were set up in the early days of Singapore and in 1824 several people were killed in secret society clashes. By 1840 the Triad Society was said to have some five to six thousand members in Singapore, and rival societies sprang up in the middle years of the century. They were behind much of the violence and crime which plagued Singapore.

The Straits authorities did not outlaw the Chinese secret societies, or *hoeys,* until 1889, because their political subversion remained directed only against the Manchus, and they performed many useful social functions. They protected young immigrants, arranged their employment and admitted them to a brotherhood which provided a sense of belonging in a strange foreign land. They settled disputes among their own people who found the official judicial system remote, complicated and difficult to understand. But the secret societies' insistence on complete obedience and defence of their fellow brethren to the point of perjury impeded the British judicial system. Officials believed that the remedy lay in undermining the authority of the *hoey* tribunals and attracting the Chinese into the British courts by opening up more magistrates' courts to deal speedily and effectively with petty crimes, by punishing firmly any obvious perjury and by applying the law impartially to rich and poor. This was a slow process.

The Singapore authorities were loathe to apply force against the societies. Governor Butterworth refused to support pleas by the Singapore grand jury for the *hoeys* to be suppressed and assured Calcutta in 1848, 'I am of the opinion that the Chinese are the best and most peaceable colonists in the world.'[32] Grand juries continued to plead for suppression and wanted to ban Chinese from jury service, for fear they might be secret society members themselves.

The secret societies sought to enrol all Chinese immigrants to their ranks and bitterly opposed the conversion of Chinese to Christianity, which constituted a threat to their own authority. In 1851 the *hoeys* sent out gangs to wipe out Christian converts on the plantations in the interior. It was rumoured that 500 Christians were slaughtered and nearly thirty agricultural settlements destroyed.

By the middle 1850s Chinese immigration reached a new peak. Chinese youths in their thousands defied the Manchu empire's prohibition on emigration in order to escape land hunger and civil war. In the official year 1853/4 more than thirteen thousand Chinese immigrants arrived, many of them dangerous men, rebels and refugees from the civil war raging in southern China. Singapore Hokkiens supplied much of the money and leadership for the Short Daggers Rebellion, in which rebels seized temporary control of Amoy city in 1853. Most of these rebels subsequently fled to Singapore where their arrival upset the balance of the existing societies. After weeks of tension, fighting broke out in 1854 which led to great bloodshed. There were reports of terrible atrocities, impaling and mutilation of men, women and children, of whole villages being wiped out, and rumours that hundreds of Chinese were massing on the outskirts to attack the town. Possibly about four hundred Chinese were killed and many Chinese shops looted, and after the fighting died down in the town, strife continued in the country areas for a week. But the disturbance was a domestic dispute among the Chinese themselves and not directed against the government nor the non-Chinese communities.

The secret societies battened on the coolie trade and prostitution, which offered great scope for exploiting a floating population of young unattached men. Demands for labour led to gross abuses in the coolie traffic. Many youths were drugged, kidnapped or tricked by recruiting agents in China, and for most of them the voyage to Singapore was a nightmare. Confined to sweltering holds, hundreds died on the journey, and dead bodies were often found thrown overboard in Singapore harbour. On one junk which arrived from Macao in 1863 only one hundred and twenty of its three hundred passengers were still alive.[33]

Immigrants were kept imprisoned in the hold until prospective employers paid off the passage money to the junkmasters. Sick men, whom no-one would hire, often died, but the able-bodied were quickly snapped up by employers. The immigrant worker, or *sinkheh,* was obliged to serve his employer for one year, during which he was housed, fed, clothed and given a small allowance. He was then free to find his own employment.

The British authorities used prominent Chinese merchants as go-betweens with the different dialect groups. Experience of European ways and an ability to speak Malay and sometimes a little English gave an initial advantage to the Baba Chinese, such as Chua Chong Long, Tan Che Sang, Tan Tock Seng, and Tan Kim Seng. Tan Tock Seng was Singapore's first Asian justice of the peace. Tan Kim Seng, a third-generation Baba, born in Malacca in 1805, accumulated great wealth in property and trade in Singapore and at the time of his death in 1864 was reputed to be worth $2 million.

China-born immigrants, who had a reputation for greater energy and acumen, soon began to challenge this Baba supremacy. Seah Eu Chin and Hoo Ah Kay were the two most prominent China-born immigrants in the nineteenth century. Seah Eu Chin, a well-educated Teochew and son of a minor mandarin, settled in Singapore in 1830. He became a ship's chandler and invested in land, particularly in gambier and pepper planting. An early member of the Singapore chamber of commerce, a justice of the peace and one of the first Chinese to become a naturalized British subject, Seah was the Singapore government's trusted go-between with the Teochew community. He retired in Singapore in 1864, devoting the remaining nineteen years of his life to the study of Chinese literature.

The Cantonese Hoo Ah Kay, nicknamed Whampoa after his birth-place, also came to Singapore in 1830, at the age of fifteen, and built up a flourishing ship's chandling business. He diversified his interests, opening a department store, a bakery, and an icehouse, and speculating profitably in land. Remaining in Singapore until his death in 1880, Whampoa was probably the wealthiest Chinese and certainly the best-known and most popular in European circles.[34] He rose to higher political office than any other Singapore Chinese in the nineteenth century, becoming the first Asian member of the legislative council and subsequently an extraordinary member of the executive council.

The traditional pattern of leadership in mainland China, based on respect for scholarship and the dominance of the mandarin class, was broken by immigration to Singapore. Wealth and material success, rather than learning, commanded respect, and rich Chinese acquired prestige in building hospitals, schools, poor-houses and markets, and sponsoring entertainments.

Outwardly the wealthy Chinese merchants were co-operative with the Singapore authorities. Whampoa in particular cultivated the friendship of the British and was said to be 'almost as much an Englishman as he is a Chinaman'.[35] To some extent the Chinese merchants leagued them-

selves with the ruling class against the rank and file of their own countrymen. Men like Tan Kim Seng and Chua Chong Long were lavish in
entertaining Europeans to dinners and balls, while Whampoa, who
spoke excellent English, frequently invited European friends to his own
house. But however hospitable and cordial their behaviour towards the
ruling community, even the most westernized clung to their Chinese
customs, traditions and sense of values. They continued to wear Chinese
dress, to shave their heads and wear pigtails. The private life of the well-
to-do Chinese was a mystery to their closest European associates, who
did not know whether they had any connexions with Singapore's underworld. No respectable Chinese merchant would admit to membership
of a secret society, but it was rumoured that Whampoa and others were
*hoey* leaders.

Despite its weakness, the government was not unduly alarmed, since
it faced no serious challenge to its authority. The natural divisions in
Singapore's mixed population were so deep that the authorities had no
need to employ any conscious 'divide and rule' policy. Except at the
highest level, Chinese, Malays and Indians were separated in language,
religion, customs, social organization and economic activity. The divisions among the Chinese dialect groups were wide. While they brought
their local and regional quarrels to Singapore, the Chinese showed no
hostility to the local government, even when Britain was at war with
China. In 1857 Lord Elgin, the British High Commissioner and Pleni-
potentiary, passing through Singapore with troops to fight in China,
was astonished to receive an address from the leading Chinese merchants,
expressing loyalty and appreciation of the advantages the Straits Chinese
enjoyed under British rule.[36] The Chinese were a potential danger 'not
from their sympathy with the country from which they sprang but from
their want of sympathy with the country in which they have taken up
their abode'.[37] There were times of rumour and panic but no revolts
and on the whole Singapore was a little haven of order and calm in a
stormy South-East Asia.

Many merchants did not share the government's optimism. Europeans
were apprehensive at being a tiny minority among thousands of Asians,
and well-to-do merchants of all races looked with misgiving at the mass
of poor, illiterate, half-starving youths who came to make their fortune.
They also began to appreciate that cheap convict labour was being
recruited at the cost of flooding Singapore with dangerous criminals.
In 1851 the *Free Press* lamented that the Straits Settlements were 'the
common sewer...for all the scum and refuse of the populations of
nearly the whole British possessions in the East',[38] and three years later
declared, 'We have in this small island the very dregs of the population
of south eastern Asia.'[39]

In the early years Indian convicts supplied Singapore with a steady
supply of cheap labour for public works. Since there was insufficient
revenue to provide guards for the large convict body, prisoners were

allowed a great deal of freedom. This situation bred an enlightened system, in which they were supervised almost entirely by senior convict petty officers, promoted for good behaviour, and trained in useful trades.

After a probationary period working in gangs on heavy manual labour, convicts were taught a skill to enable them to be useful during their confinement and to earn an honest living after their release. They learned brick making, weaving, tailoring, rope making, printing. carpentry and even photography.

Forced into being by financial necessity, this convict administration became a matter of pride. Observers came from the Dutch East Indies, Siam and Japan to study its applicability to their own society, and the prison was a tourist attraction in the 1860s. The accent was on training, reformation and useful employment rather than punishment. In convict administration mid-nineteenth century Singapore came nearer to advanced Benthamite thinking than anywhere else in the world.

Most convicts were Indians. Small numbers of Chinese convicts were transported from Hong Kong but with the help of the secret societies they easily escaped to merge into the general population, and, after many years of agitation, transportation of Chinese convicts was stopped in 1856.

The mass of the population were afraid of the Indian convicts. During the worst scare in 1853 when the first St. Andrew's Church was struck by lightning, rumours spread that the Governor had sent out Indian convicts to collect human heads to pacify the spirits who were harming the church. Official proclamations failed to allay the panic and leading Chinese merchants had to be called upon to restore calm among their people.

At first the European merchants welcomed convicts as an essential source of cheap labour, but by the middle of the century they worried about the violent undercurrents in Singapore society and were alarmed at the large numbers of dangerous criminals coming from Calcutta, who included dacoits and thugs.

As a labour force the convicts contributed much to Singapore, but their long-term effect upon the character of the population is difficult to gauge. There was no provision before 1859 for repatriating convicts at the end of their sentence, and even after that date many released convicts remained as permanent settlers. Female convicts were in great demand as brides for Indian bachelors, and the government was so eager to rehabilitate them that even a murderess rarely had to spend more than two or three years in jail.[40] Only a few former convicts were charged with subsequent crimes, but ex-convicts figured prominently among the turbulent Indo-Malay Jawi-Peranakan class, and the Hindu Dusserah and Muslim Muharram festivals, when convicts were given leave to stage street processions, were invariably times of unrest and violence.

The much-prized freedom of immigration contributed to Singapore's growth and success but it brought a transitory, unbalanced population, consisting in the main of poverty-stricken young men, which made it difficult to maintain law and order. For many decades Singapore retained the qualities of a pioneering town: virile, bustling, active, lawless and disorderly.

The ratio between the sexes was balanced among the Malays, Bugis and Eurasians but in the Chinese, European and Indian communities men outnumbered women by a large majority. This problem was particularly serious among the Chinese, who regarded the emigration of women from their homeland not only as illegal but socially unacceptable. Wives and families sought refuge with their husbands in Singapore in times of exceptional upheaval, such as the Amoy rebellion in 1853, but only temporarily. Even after China relaxed her emigration laws in 1859, it was many years before respectable Chinese women came to Singapore in any numbers. The only 'Chinese' women were of mixed blood or young prostitutes imported by the secret societies.

The disparity between numbers of Chinese men and women was a major social problem. The ruling class wanted to promote Chinese female immigration in order to encourage permanent settlement, to divert shifting, rootless youths from crime, to curb the secret societies' hold over prostitution and to stem the drain to China of family remittances which could have been used to develop Singapore.

In 1856 a group of European merchants offered to pay a bonus to Chinese who brought their wives to Singapore. Five years later Governor Cavenagh, in considering a scheme to legalize gambling, suggested using part of the gaming licence money to subsidize Chinese female immigration, in order to wean men from the gaming table to 'the comforts of a home' and to build up a permanent resident labour force. None of these ideas bore fruit and in the mid-1860s there was still only one 'Chinese' woman to fifteen men.

Weak government, lack of finance, secret-society power and a transitory population combined to make early Singapore a violent place. The main danger came from gang robberies, which were reputed to be the work of Chinese secret societies. Gangs of up to two hundred Chinese with blackened faces raided parts of the town almost every night. Their chief targets were the Malay districts, but they sometimes attacked Indians and Europeans too, breaking into buildings, ransacking and murdering. The whole town lived in fear, and the tiny police force prudently kept out of the way until the gangsters had gone.

The hundreds of Chinese who lived on the isolated pepper and gambier farms in the interior were beyond the writ of government, and the authorities did not pretend to exert any control in the country districts.

In 1843 violent crime reached such a pitch that the English-speaking merchants held a protest meeting and persuaded the government to appoint Thomas Dunman, a young commercial assistant, as first superintendent of police. A vigorous and sensible man, respected by European officials and merchants, Dunman also had useful contacts with the Chinese community. His initial difficulties were immense. The Netherlands Indies authorities frequently shipped trouble-makers to Singapore, and three thousand Chinese immigrants arriving from Riau in 1846 included a number of deported secret-society leaders, who instigated a wave of crime. This reached a climax with the ransacking of Hewetson's plantation bungalow at Mount Elizabeth by a large gang of thieves, and led nervous householders in the Claymore and Tanglin districts to appeal for protection.

Dunman battled hard to produce an efficient force, but his material was unpromising. Police work was so arduous, dangerous and badly paid that the only recruits were unemployed men in desperate financial straits, many of them stranded sailors who became policemen as a temporary stopgap occupation. An underpaid, overworked force had no inducement to court danger with possible injury or death. It was more profitable for policemen to accept bribes from gambling-house keepers and more prudent to keep away from violence. Dunman struggled to improve the calibre of his policemen, fighting for better conditions and higher wages. He reduced their hours of work and taught them to read and write.

Within a few years he managed to check gang robberies. He was promoted to be Singapore's first full-time commissioner of police in 1857 and within the limitations of his position achieved a striking improvement in the police in the last years of Indian rule. The force was still small, but its calibre and morale were greatly improved. The police were beginning to become more effective in the country districts, and police posts were established along the coasts. The lack of money hampered police work but brought compensating advantages. Authority could not rest on brute force but on persuasion and co-operation, and by the time he retired in 1871 Dunman had laid the foundations for an efficient and humane force.

The police force and the government continued to fight an uphill battle in face of the great influx of immigrants. By the middle of the century Singapore was the focal point of Chinese immigration for the entire region. The 1854 riots alarmed the European community. They led to further demands for strengthening the police force, and to the European and Eurasian inhabitants forming a Singapore Volunteer Rifle Corps in July 1854, the first such body in Britain's possessions in the East.

On occasions the authorities proposed checks on immigration to prevent the influx of criminals or sick paupers, to stem the evils of the coolie trade and the traffic in prostitutes. But the merchant community would tolerate no restrictions on immigrant labour. Free immigration was a cardinal principle, second only to the preservation of free trade.

The attitude towards external defence was initially very different. In the first half of the nineteenth century Singapore had no fears of being engulfed in an international war, and neither officials nor merchants showed much interest in providing for her defence. The Singapore merchants begrudged even the small amount spent on the modest Indian garrison.

Military and naval officers appreciated Singapore's defence needs. In

1827 Captain Edward Lake of the Bengal Engineers was sent to advise on fortifications. Realizing the potential strategic and commercial value of New Harbour, Lake incorporated it into his scheme of defence and also recommended constructing a line of batteries to protect the town from a sea attack. Nothing was done, except to begin erecting a battery at the entrance to the Singapore river, which fell victim to the 1830 economy campaign and was left half finished. In 1843 Captain Best of the Madras Engineers drew up an ambitious scheme to protect New Harbour and to construct a chain of batteries along the coast with forts to accommodate 3,000 troops. These expensive suggestions were also ignored. Captain (later Admiral Sir Henry) Keppel surveyed New Harbour and reported its advantages to the Admiralty in 1848, but the British government eventually chose Hong Kong instead of Singapore as its Far East naval headquarters.

The Singapore merchants were rudely jolted out of their complacency by the outbreak of the Crimean War in 1854. Singapore's defenceless prosperity could make her an attractive target and throughout the war the British community feared that a surprise naval attack or an isolated Russian warship might blast the heart out of the town. Tension persisted even when peace was signed because of the possibility of revolt on the part of her own lawless people.

After decades of inactivity, Calcutta suddenly launched into constructing elaborate fortifications in Singapore. In 1858 Captain Collyer of the Madras Engineers was sent, in response to an appeal made by Governor Blundell for the construction of simple defence works and a place of refuge for the European population in the event of a local rebellion. Carried away by enthusiasm, Collyer planned a line of shore batteries and recommended constructing extensive fortifications on Government Hill overlooking the town and harbour, with an arsenal, workshops, commissariat, powder house and barracks. These, together with smaller forts on neighbouring hills and a refuge area to enclose the government buildings, court house, church and town hall, would turn the whole into a quasi-military cantonment. Collyer also advised building forts on the islands commanding New Harbour and cutting a canal through to the Singapore river.[41]

These proposals appalled Blundell, who warned Calcutta that converting Singapore into 'a great military fortress' might kill her trade. Collyer was ordered to modify his schemes, but he had already pulled down the old Government House and levelled the top of the hill to make way for Fort Canning, which was completed in 1860 and named after the Governor-General of India. A useless fortification, it might perhaps more appropriately be named Collyer's Folly. It could not provide refuge for the European population during internal riots, because it had no independent water supply. Its guns could not protect the town against external attack because they were out of range of enemy ships and would merely destroy the town and shipping in the harbour. Indeed one puzzled Dutch observer concluded erroneously that the guns were purposely fixed to destroy Chinatown in time of local trouble.

Lack of revenue and the transient unbalanced nature of the population made it difficult to develop an education policy or provide social services.

Raffles's dreams of Singapore as an educational centre soon faded and she did not prove a magnet for learning in the way that she attracted trade. The East India Company showed no enthusiasm in educating its officials in the languages and customs of the region and withdrew its meagre education maintenance grant in the 1830 retrenchment.

Raffles's educational schemes were defeated not only by the Company's parsimony and indifference but also by the nature of Singapore society. Until late in the nineteenth century there was no public demand for education. Immigrants came to make money, not to settle and raise families, and neighbouring rulers ignored invitations to educate their sons in Singapore.

The Christian missions showed only passing interest in early Singapore, where they were more influential in promoting printing than religion or education.[42] Protestant missionaries, who had their eyes on the forbidden land of China, established temporary headquarters in Singapore. The London Missionary Society opened its first school there in 1822 with twelve pupils learning Malay and English, and by 1829 the Society had four schools. In 1834 the American Board of Commissioners of Foreign Missions made Singapore its base for China, and within three years the Board had nineteen missionaries in Singapore and more than three hundred Chinese pupils.

When China was opened to Christian missionaries after the First Opium War, the American and British Protestant missionary societies pulled up their Singapore roots, the Americans in 1842 and the London Missionary Society five years later. They closed all their schools, except the Anglican St. Margaret's, Singapore's oldest surviving girls' school. The Roman Catholic community was torn by the rival claims of the Goa-based Portuguese mission and the Siam-based French mission, whose conflict was not settled until 1886. Meanwhile the task of building up education was left to private philanthropists and individual missionaries.

In 1835 a group of European merchants raised funds to complete the Singapore Institution, which was renamed Raffles Institution in 1868. It comprised an upper English-medium school and a lower school, teaching partly in English and partly in vernacular languages, including Malay, Tamil, Bugis, Siamese and various Chinese dialects. The school committee was particularly keen to promote Malay education, and employed five Malay teachers in 1838-9.

The upper school attracted resident European children, some Portuguese from Macao and the sons of affluent Chinese merchants. But the standard was low, and most Asian children were withdrawn once they had learned enough English to find a job or carry on commercial dealings with European customers. The lower school was a failure. Teachers were paid according to the number of pupils they could recruit, and despite vigorous touting for students, Tamil, Bugis, Siamese. Malay, and most Chinese classes had to be closed down. By 1843 only one Hokkien group of twenty-five pupils remained.

The Singapore Institution and its sister school for girls continued as indifferent primary schools. Fees and subscriptions barely covered the costs, and the government would provide no money for repairs to the building, which by 1851 was in a dangerous state of dilapidation.

Roman Catholic effort in the education field was left to an individual French priest, Father Beurel, who opened St. Joseph's Institution in 1852 and a sister school, the Convent of the Holy Infant Jesus, two years later. Beurel financed the schools from private subscriptions and his own personal fortune.

The most promising educational experiment resulted from the labours of a lone Protestant missionary, Benjamin Peach Keasberry, who remained behind when the London Missionary Society moved to China and founded a school for Malay boys which he financed largely by a printing press. The Temenggong Ibrahim subsidized the school generously, and enrolled his own and his retainers' children as pupils.

In the middle years of the century education in Singapore was in a parlous state, despite the East India Company's renewed interest in promoting education in its territories. A law passed in Calcutta in 1854, 'the intellectual charter of India', sought to establish throughout the Company's domains a properly graded vernacular education from the primary stage to university. Singapore did not profit from this reform, which indeed proved a setback. Since the Company agreed only to equal public contributions and fees, it matched the Temenggong's donations to Keasberry's school but reduced the official grant to the Singapore Institution and withdrew subsidies altogether from charity non-fee-paying schools such as Father Beurel's.

The East India Company disapproved of the preoccupation of Singapore pupils with acquiring basic English in order to secure jobs. They preferred that children should become literate first in their own language, and successive Governors tried to boost vernacular education in Singapore by providing free primary schooling in the Malay medium. This provoked conflict with European merchants, who complained that it was unfair to enforce Indian educational policy on Singapore. Malay was the indigenous vernacular, but it was the language only of a minority. The Chinese at that stage showed no interest in having Chinese-medium schools. Consequently the European merchants, backed by the English-language press, argued, but without success, that English should be promoted as the *lingua franca*.

For the remaining years of Indian rule education remained in the doldrums. Basic English education reached only a tiny minority. There were no Chinese schools and no opportunities to study Chinese apart from sporadic attempts to set up classes within the Singapore Institution. Despite the emphasis on providing free Malay education, the results were disappointing. The Koran schools were of low standard and did not help Malay pupils to enter the mainstream of Singapore's life. Even in Keasberry's school, which was generously subsidized by the Temenggong and the government, there were only fifty-two boys on the roll in 1863 and half were usually absent.[43] In 1872 it was proposed to convert Keasberry's school into a Malay teachers' training college, but Keasberry died suddenly in 1875 and his school closed down. He was influential in training the first generation of Johor state officials but failed to lay the sound basis for westernized modern Malay-medium education in Singapore.

The struggling educational establishments of the mid-nineteenth century survived to rank today among Singapore's finest schools: Raffles Institution, St. Joseph's, St. Margaret's, Raffles Girls' School, and the Convent of the Holy Infant Jesus.

In social welfare and education Singapore fell below even the rudimentary standards expected of mid-nineteenth century governments, but it was impossible to counteract poverty, destitution or disease, or to provide the background for improved living or working conditions, without putting some check on immigration.

There were no hospitals and, apart from one or two government doctors and a few private practitioners, there were virtually no medical services prior to the 1840s. An apprentice scheme to produce locally-trained Eurasian subordinate medical staff was started in 1823 but failed to attract many recruits because of the small salaries and lack of prospects. Only two Singapore boys graduated under this scheme in the 1830s.[44]

Fortunately Singapore's climate proved to be exceptionally healthy, despite the constant damp heat, marsh and swamp, rotting vegetation, filth and stench. Malaria and leprosy were uncommon, while cholera and smallpox were normally confined to the overcrowded slums. Cholera in particular was a social rather than a medical problem, arising from water pollution caused by the filth and bad drainage, which the government had no money to remedy. Like most health hazards in Singapore, it was largely man-made.

The well-to-do, who included the Europeans, Jews, Armenians, Eurasians, Parsis, and rich Chinese, suffered mainly from over-indulgence in food and alcohol. Most European men counteracted this by dressing informally and taking vigorous physical exercise. It was customary to rise at dawn, take long early morning walks, and to ride or sail in the evening. The younger men played fives or cricket. Mercantile life was leisurely, except on mail days, and work rarely interfered with regular sport, since office hours normally ended by four o'clock. 'We are the healthiest community in the East,' the *Straits Times* claimed in 1861, 'and attribute no small share of it to our activity and love of outdoor sports.'[45] Singapore's early Christian burial grounds are perhaps the dullest in Asia, because nearly all prominent Europeans lived to retire to Britain. Most of those buried in Singapore were visiting sailors, young women and children.

Among the mass of the population poverty, malnutrition, over-crowding and excessive opium-smoking took the heaviest toll. The annual influx of penniless Chinese and the fluctuations of demand for labour threw many immigrants on to the streets, and the number of destitute was swelled by European seamen, who were often stranded in Singapore for months looking for work.

Initially, with the consent of the leading Chinese, the government levied a tax on the sale of pork to finance the erection and maintenance of an attap shed to house sick paupers. But in 1837 Calcutta prohibited this tax on the grounds that it was immoral to tax an essential foodstuff. After that only chronic cases were admitted to the pauper shed.

Both Chinese and European merchants began to feel ashamed that social services were so poor, and in 1844 Tan Tock Seng chaired a public meeting which appealed to the government to build a pauper hospital. The merchants objected to Governor Butterworth's proposals to prohibit the landing of diseased immigrants and to finance the hospital out of the property assessment. A compromise was reached whereby the bulk of the money came from private charity, supplemented by a small property assessment, and the government supplied medical assistance, medicines and a financial grant.

Tan Tock Seng presented $7,000 to build the pauper hospital and the foundation stones for this and a European seamen's hospital were laid on adjoining sites at Pearl's Hill in 1844. While Tan Tock Seng's hospital was under construction the position became desperate. In 1845 at least seventy Chinese beggars died from starvation, and four years later the Recorder, commenting on inquests where verdicts of death through starvation had been returned, said such deaths were 'a disgrace to a Christian community like Singapore'.[46]

When the hospital opened in 1849 it only touched the surface of the problem. The hospital was a grim place, fronting a swamp which was used as the town's main rubbish dump. Paupers were brought in with ulcers, sores and dropsy, many of them with limbs dropping off with gangrene. Not surprisingly the mortality rate was high. In the official year 1852/3 one third of the patients died, and in 1857 the hospital committee admitted, 'No-one will enter who can crawl and beg, unless compelled by the police.'[47]

Much of this misery stemmed from the deadly habit of opium-smoking which was the centre of controversy. Most Europeans regarded it merely as a bad habit, soothing and soporific, evil only if taken to excess. A private practitioner, Dr. Robert Little, and a few other Europeans campaigned to open the eyes of the government and the community at large to the medical and social evils of opium-smoking.[48] Little estimated in 1848 that 20 per cent of the entire population and more than half the Chinese adults were opium addicts. Rich Chinese, who smoked high-quality opium, were not seriously harmed, but the poor smoked the refuse. Addicts were reduced to begging and living on rotten fish and decaying vegetables round the market, ending up in prison or the pauper hospital, or driven to suicide. Little tried in vain to persuade leading Chinese merchants to form a society to suppress opium addiction. The well-to-do Chinese found the opium farm lucrative, other Asians made no protest, while European merchants were content to see the bulk of the revenue levied on opium rather than on commerce, property or salaries. and they dismissed Little as a crank. The opium farm continued to be the mainstay of the revenue up to the twentieth century.[49]

The ruling class was embarrassed by the problem of destitute European sailors, but the extension to Singapore of Indian legislation designed to protect seamen and their conditions of service, to supervise taverns and control prostitution, was delayed for many years because of financial deadlock. The plight of able-bodied unemployed sailors was acute, and there were so many destitute Australians, who arrived in charge of shipments of horses, that in 1863 Australian state governments warned men not to come to Singapore unless they had a definite promise of work.[50] The situation attracted many shady characters to Singapore to set up brothels and taverns where sailors were often given drugged liquor, robbed and beaten up. In the early 1860s there were more than two hundred disreputable taverns and so many foreign prostitutes that the *Straits Times* complained there were almost as many whores as respectable women among the European female population.[51] The situation improved somewhat after 1863, when Calcutta gave the Singapore authorities the legal right to close objectionable taverns, and many seedy underworld characters drifted away to happier hunting grounds.

Singapore's social life underwent great changes during this period. Among the upper class respect for material success blurred racial divisions. In the early days the small European society of Singapore was a friendly hospitable community, where differences of wealth, colour, race or age counted for little. They mixed freely with their Asian counterparts and were delighted to welcome strangers and visitors with first-hand knowledge of Europe.

They were a self-contained group, cut off from Britain. Sailing ships took four months to reach Singapore from England, and even mail coming by the expensive, uncertain 'overland' service, trans-shipped in Egypt and transported by camel across the Suez Isthmus, seldom arrived in less than two months. Britons could not afford the time or money to visit Europe and expected to spend their whole working lives in the East.

The affluent enjoyed a constant round of dances, suppers and sporting entertainments. A billiards club was formed in 1829, the first regatta was held in 1834, St. Andrew's night was first celebrated in 1835, a fives club was set up in 1836, and the first cricket match was held in 1837. Snipe shooting in the marshes skirting the town became a favourite sport in the 1830s. In 1840 the first tiger hunt was staged, and two years later the Singapore Sporting Club was founded to promote horse racing.

Changes came over Singapore in the mid-1840s, in her appearance, in commerce, and in the attitudes of the upper class. Visitors were amazed at the physical improvements but complained that much of her exotic charm and her friendliness had gone.[52] This reflected changes in her pattern of life.

Steamships, which were rarely seen in Singapore during the first twenty years, began to frequent the port in the 1840s. In 1845 the Peninsular and Oriental Steamship Company began monthly sailings to the Far East, and the following year a regular steamship service was inaugurated between Singapore and Calcutta. In 1855 the P. & O. Company expanded its schedule to provide a fortnightly service from Europe. The Suez railway, opened in 1858, provided greater comfort and safety to passengers and security for mail, and it was so reliable that by the mid-1860s people complained if English mail took more than five weeks to reach Singapore.

The steamship did not revolutionize trade overnight, but speeded up commercial activity and produced marked social changes in the British community. Some Britons could now afford to visit England periodically, and all of them could keep their links with 'home' through up-to-date newspapers, regular letters and new books. The old free and easy, uniquely Singaporean, way of life changed to a more formal, consciously British middle-class society, staid, honest, respectable, unadventurous, narrow-minded, reflecting the values of mid-Victorian Britain.

The European community drew apart from Asians, while at the same time they did not open their doors so whole-heartedly to visitors from Europe, who were no longer such a rare reminder of a far distant homeland. The advent of steam also brought greater pressure of office work, with merchants rushing to prepare documents for the mail, so that visitors complained their compatriots were too busy making money to welcome strangers.

British Governors, Asian and European merchants continued to hold multiracial dinners, balls and celebrations. But much of this conviviality was superficial, and people tended increasingly to find relaxation among their own community. By the 1860s the Europeans sought entertainment of a western type in amateur theatricals and formed their own clubs, such as the Cricket Club in 1852, the German Teutonia Club in 1856, the British Tanglin Club in 1865 and the Swimming Club in 1866. Social life among Europeans became more sophisticated, snobbish and exclusively western. This alienation was apparent to some extent too in commercial life, and in 1860 the Chinese withdrew from the chamber of commerce, leaving it predominantly a European institution.

At the mass level there was little mingling among the different communities, who were kept apart by deep differences in language, religion and custom. Even the New Year sports, in which all communities competed and which were for many years considered the best means to promote racial harmony, were described in 1865 as 'a mercenary affair on the part of the natives and a somewhat absurd and tiresome spectacle to the European'.[53]

There was a great gulf between the way of life of prosperous Asians and the mass of the population, but there was plenty of entertainment to temper the hardships of life. Troupes of strolling players performed frequent *wayangs*, or theatrical entertainments, in the streets. Most of the numerous religious festivals were celebrated with processions and public festivities. At Chinese New Year Whampoa opened his gardens to the public and the place became a fairground, with throngs of merry-makers and hawkers. The gambling laws were lifted for a fortnight at Chinese New Year, and indeed gambling and cock fighting were carried on widely all year round with the connivance of the police.

Singapore still had the air of a pioneer town, a man's world, with a predominantly young adult male population. Despite the spectacular growth in numbers, the population still consisted primarily of shifting transients who did not regard Singapore as home.

Despite the shortcomings of government, there were few complaints or signs of unrest among either the Asian or European inhabitants before the middle of the century. There was general contentment with the administration of Governor George Bonham, who came to Singapore in September 1819 as a writer, rose to be Assistant Resident, Resident Councillor, Acting Governor, and finally Governor in 1836. He provided a continuity of experience and influence dating from the early months of Singapore and was an approachable, gregarious and cheerful bachelor, an excellent social mixer. There was no demand for formal organization when municipal affairs could be settled at the Governor's dinner table.

This cordial atmosphere changed with the arrival of Colonel William John Butterworth of the Madras army, who succeeded Bonham in 1843 and remained Governor of the Straits for twelve years. A newcomer to Singapore, the stiff and pompous Butterworth was nicknamed 'Butterpot the Great'. His arrival put an end to the friendly informality which characterized Bonham's administration, and two years later the European merchants made their first demands for representation in municipal affairs and for more control over the police and property assessment. This led to bitter wrangles, to stormy scenes between the Governor and the grand jury and to angry correspondence in the press.

In 1847, with Butterworth's approval, Calcutta rescinded the rights of the justices of the peace to appoint and control the police force. All the non-official J.P.s resigned in protest and for the next fifteen years men of standing refused to accept the office. In 1848 Bengal created a committee of officials and non-officials to administer the assessment in Singapore, but this first milestone in the development of municipal government aroused no public enthusiasm. Non-official members were appointed by the Governor, and the Singapore press dismissed the municipal committee as 'a mere government bureau...serving as a breakwater to protect the executive government from shocks'.

Butterworth's early years as Governor coincided with the commercial depression of the 1840s, when the atmosphere of worry and frustration led some of the European merchants to question whether Singapore would fare better as a crown colony rather than an appendage of the

East India Company. By that time commercial bonds with Calcutta were weakening, and the growth of European trade and steamship communications made Singapore merchants look increasingly to London as their economic and political centre. By the middle of the century most British firms in Singapore were agency houses for London companies.

The proposal to convert Singapore into a crown colony had been talked about in Singapore for several years, but was now taken up as a practical issue by the young merchant, William Henry Read. Tiny in stature but dynamic and aggressive in manner, Read was born in Scotland in February 1819, within a few days of Singapore's foundation, and his fortunes were closely linked with the island throughout his long life. Arriving in 1841 to join the leading firm of A.L. Johnston & Company, he quickly became involved in public affairs and took part in the agitation for municipal representation. He returned to England in 1848 at the height of Singapore's commercial worries and of Butterworth's unpopularity. There he had lengthy discussions with John Crawfurd, who was fighting the cause of the Bengal merchants against the East India Company in England. By the time Read returned to Singapore in 1851, he and Crawfurd had decided to agitate for a complete break with India and the transfer of the Straits Settlements to the Colonial Office.

In England Crawfurd devoted his efforts to Singapore's interests, but Read, on his return to Singapore, found the situation unpromising for political agitation. Learning from his mistakes, Butterworth had set out with remarkable success to conciliate the merchant community, while Singapore was riding high on a new wave of prosperity.

A visit by Lord Dalhousie, the Governor-General of India, in 1850, had left the Singapore merchants expecting a dramatic improvement in administration. Calling briefly at Singapore in the course of a convalescent voyage to China, Dalhousie was feted with enthusiasm. Europeans and Chinese alike vied for invitations to meet him, and 'the whole settlement was drunk with loyalty'.[54] Promising to give the Straits Settlements his personal attention, Dalhousie separated them from the Bengal Presidency in 1851 and put them under the direct charge of the Governor-General.

For the moment Singapore's merchants basked in the sunshine of commercial prosperity but this euphoria could not last for ever. Singapore was a thriving port, a triumph for the most advanced theories of free trade and *laissez-faire*, but ultimately she needed more modern and sophisticated administration, and prosperous European merchants became increasingly frustrated by the autocratic nature of the Company's Governors and its inefficient bureaucracy. Businessmen resented exclusion from public affairs which was out of keeping with their growing economic power.

The merchants also complained that the East India Company neglected to provide public works and commercial amenities in keeping with Singapore's position as a thriving international port. During the 1850s Calcutta brought in many measures in India to improve ports and shipping facilities, to establish shipping offices and curb abuses in passenger traffic, to provide lights and pilots, to register seamen and check desertion. Merchants complained loudly whenever Calcutta hesitated on financial grounds to extend the benefits of new legislation to Singapore but were adamant in refusing to pay charges to cover the costs of reforms. In 1852 battle was joined between the Singapore merchants and the Company over a levy made on all ships calling at Singapore to pay for part of the construction and maintenance of Horsburgh lighthouse, but eventually the European merchants agreed to pay lighthouse fees provided Asian shipping was exempt.

Set against the rising discontents and frustrations of the mid-1850s, the Singapore merchants were disillusioned with constitutional reforms from which they had expected so much. Dalhousie's move to take the Straits Settlements under his own wing produced no tangible change, and the sole result of his visit was the Dalhousie monument, erected by the Singapore merchants in his honour, which stands today in front of the central government offices, a suitably graceful and useless reminder of this pleasant but unproductive interlude.

The East India Company's charter was renewed in 1853 and a new legislative council with enlarged powers was set up in Calcutta the following year. While Singapore had no representative on this council, her merchants hoped it would be more energetic and enlightened in introducing reforms. In fact Singapore was to suffer more than any other Indian-administered territory from the council's policy of enforcing uniformity, and the vigorous centralization campaign waged by this legislative council eventually goaded the Singapore merchants to demand a break with India.

The storm could not be foreseen at the time of Butterworth's departure in 1855. His early quarrels with the mercantile community were long forgotten, and Butterworth retired in an aura of affection and respect. His successor, Edmund Blundell, was welcomed as a man with long experience of the East, where he had served for more than thirty years as Commissioner of Tenasserim, Resident Councillor of Malacca, and subsequently Resident Councillor of Penang.

Blundell was worthy and conscientious, an excellent paternal administrator in pioneer conditions, but he was obstinate and autocratic. The office of Governor in the 1850s required particular intelligence and tact, since he had no legislative council to strengthen his hand in dealing with Calcutta or to protect him against irresponsible opposition from the merchant community. Blundell did not possess these qualities. As Governor in the crucial years from 1855 to 1859, when the Indian legislative council was most energetic, he acted in defiance of popular opinion and encouraged Calcutta to pass unpopular legislation.

Blundell soon came into collision with the small active group of European constitutional reformers. They objected most fiercely to his proposal that Calcutta should finance port improvements by levying modest port dues and charging fees for clearance documents. The Singapore merchants countered by suggesting that the Company should raise the money by halving the Governor's salary, but in any event Calcutta withdrew the controversial port dues proposal.

The vocal minority of European merchants set out to rally public opinion against the Company's policy and against the Governor, using the press, the grand jury, and public meetings. Despite the absence of representative institutions, the European mercantile community had plenty of opportunities for making their views known, since throughout the period of Indian rule Singapore enjoyed free speech and assembly, and press censorship was abolished in 1835.[55]

In the absence of a legislative council Singapore's newspapers played a significant political role and provided an outlet for European public opinion. There was no vernacular press, but the first English-language newspaper, the *Singapore Chronicle*, was founded in 1824. A second newspaper, the *Singapore Free Press*, appeared in 1835 and a rival weekly, the *Straits Times*, in 1845.

Senior merchants could exert influence as justices of the peace or grand jurymen. At the close of each court sessions the grand jury presented a statement of comments and grievances, including matters which would normally have been the responsibility of a legislative council or elected municipal authority. Before Blundell's day merchants regarded jury service as a tiresome duty, because it disrupted their business. In 1854 the European merchants petitioned for the grand jury to be abolished, but they changed their tune after 1855 when the grand jury became a rallying point for growing opposition to the government.[56]

In the hands of a vocal opposition group, the public meeting developed into a regular means of agitating against official policy. In the mid-1850s the Indian legislative council's activities provoked the calling of many public meetings in Singapore at which petitions were drawn up to complain about alleged grievances, such as the failure to give adequate protection against piracy, the transportation of European convicts from India to Singapore, delays in passing judicial reforms, threats to the dollar, and proposals to impose port dues.

In 1855 the *Straits Times* urged the formation of a Reform League to agitate for radical changes in administration.[57] A motion seeking to throw off Indian rule was rejected at a public meeting but a small group remained dedicated to freedom from India. They were dominated by Read, Abraham Logan, editor of the *Singapore Free Press*, Robin Woods, editor of the *Strait Times*, and Joaquim d'Almeida, prominent merchant and son of Sir Jozé d'Almeida.

Mounting discontent reached its peak in the crisis year of 1857. This began innocently with the implementation of tighter police regulations and municipal reforms, which for the first time gave ratepayers the right to elect the majority on a reconstituted municipal committee with enlarged powers. But the clumsy enforcement of this new legislation provoked a strike among the Chinese and riots among the Indians. In February 1857 a Chinese rebellion in Kuching, resulting in the murder of several of Rajah Brooke's men, came at a time when the British were fighting in China and was misinterpreted by the nervous European merchants as part of a widespread anti-British conspiracy which would engulf Singapore. Further fuel was added to this argument in March when disturbances broke out among the Penang Chinese over the new municipal laws. Blundell's low-key handling of these crises brought hostile criticism from European and Asian merchants, and in May the Singapore grand jury complained 'at no period in the history of the settlement have the representations and remonstrances of the European community received so little attention at the hands of the local authorities'.[58]

The first reports of the Indian Mutiny, reaching Singapore late in May 1857, brought the mood of nervous tension to the pitch of dismay. There was in fact little reason to fear that the Indian violence would extend to the Straits, as the predominantly South Indian population showed no signs of sympathy with the mutineers. But Singapore was soon affected by indirect repercussions of the Mutiny when Calcutta imposed a twelve-month press censorship throughout all Indian territories. Blundell took no steps to enforce this 'Gagging Act' on the Singapore newspapers, which he held in contempt, but the press attacked the measure as further proof of Calcutta's refusal to recognize the special position of the Straits.[59]

In August 1857 rumours swept through Singapore of a planned rising among the Indian convicts, who then numbered nearly three thousand, and it was learned that Calcutta intended to send dacoits and dangerous prisoners to Singapore to make room for mutineer prisoners in Calcutta's jails. The general panic sent some families fleeing aboard ships in the harbour for safety and brought resentment against the Company's rule to a head. The European merchants called a public meeting, which resolved to support a petition sent to the British parliament by the European merchants of Calcutta demanding the abolition of the East India Company. The Singapore merchants asked further that the Straits Settlements be separated from India and ruled directly from London.[60]

The object was to secure a local legislative council and participation in government. The petition claimed that Calcutta had treated the Settlements as a part of continental India and persistently disregarded the wishes of the Straits communities. It complained that the Indian legislative council gave no representation to the Straits, while the Governor ruled as a despot with no council to advise or control him. To prove their general complaints the petitioners recited specific grievances, such as alleged attempts to impose duties and tonnage dues and to standardize the rupee as the legal currency. They criticized the Company's reluctance to provide an adequate judicial establishment, its failure to wipe out piracy or build up British influence in the peninsula and the archipelago. They argued that Calcutta's policy towards the Chinese was weak and concluded by dealing at length with the problem then uppermost in their minds: the danger and humiliation of using Singapore as a dumping ground for convicts.[61] While the petition was being prepared mutineers and other dangerous prisoners arrived from Calcutta's maximum-security prisons. Singapore's open prison system was ill-designed to cope with such an influx, and worried European merchants pleaded for transportation to Singapore to be discontinued altogether.

Singapore's petition began a process which, after ten years of confused negotiations, led to the transfer of the Straits Settlements to the Colonial Office in 1867. The petition came from Singapore alone. At a public meeting in Penang only three people backed a motion to support Singapore's demands, and the overwhelming majority voted against adding to the Company's tribulations in its hour of danger.[62]

The House of Commons received the Singapore petition favourably and success seemed assured. The Singapore merchants had many contacts in England who were eager to support their cause. They had built up links with members of parliament interested in the East, with chambers of commerce and other commercial bodies. The more prosperous Singapore merchants visited England from time to time and there was an influential group of former Straits officials and merchants, who had returned to head their London offices.

India was glad to give up the Settlements but unwilling to spend time unravelling the Straits' complicated accounts to the British Treasury's satisfaction. The Colonial Office complained in 1860, 'The India Office seem in the same breath to admit a deficit and claim a surplus.'[63] The enthusiasm of those who clamoured for the change also harmed the cause of transfer since Read, Crawfurd, other former Straits residents in London, and the Singapore chamber of commerce, all produced optimistic but conflicting financial estimates, which only served to increase suspicion in the Treasury and the Colonial Office.

The British government was particularly worried about the potential expense of defending Singapore. Collyer's complicated and expensive fortifications which would require substantial and costly garrisons were particularly unwelcome in Britain, since she was embarking on a policy of withdrawing troops and military aid from her colonies. In 1862 the secretary of state for the colonies promised a select parliamentary com-committee that the British government would only acquire dependencies in future if they were no burden on the Exchequer.[64]

Consequently the British Treasury broke off the negotiations. It was obvious that Singapore would be granted crown colony status only if her revenue could be increased to cover all her civil and military expenses, or if she could establish a claim to be of vital strategic and commercial importance to the British Empire.

Meanwhile the extinction of the East India Company in 1858 and the transfer of India to the direct rule of the British crown made little impact in the Straits Settlements, which continued to be administered by Calcutta. In 1859 the unpopular Blundell was succeeded by Colonel Orfeur Cavenagh, the last and best-liked of all the Indian Governors. A warm-hearted, honest and practical leader, firm but fair, Cavenagh consulted public opinion, paid heed to the press, the chamber of commerce, the grand jury and the municipal committee, winning not only respect but affection. He removed much of the friction between merchants and government, securing wise legislation and, within the severe limitations of finance and manpower, promoting considerable improvements in administration, in public works, in police and prisons and in the judicial field.

Cavenagh opened law courts in the country districts and backed Dunman in strengthening the police force. He made maximum use of convict labour to improve amenities. In 1860 Calcutta decided to stop transportation to the Straits, but the last Indian convicts were not withdrawn until 1873, six years after Singapore became a crown colony, and in the last years before the convicts were finally taken away the Straits authorities rushed through an ambitious programme of public works, many of which survive in Singapore today. Convict labour was used to build Fort Canning in 1860 and the present St. Andrew's Cathedral, which was completed in 1862. Convicts constructed roads and official buildings, including a town hall, a court house, which forms the nucleus of the Empress Place government offices, a general hospital, lunatic asylum, new pauper hospital, and Government House, the present Istana. Gas lighting replaced the feeble coconut-oil street-lamps in 1864. The old wooden bridge linking North and South Bridge Roads was replaced by an iron bridge in 1862 and renamed Elgin Bridge. Land to the seaward of Commercial Square, now known as Collyer Quay, was reclaimed between 1861 and 1864 and protected by a sea wall. By 1866 it carried a complete line of buildings, 'one of the sights of the Far East', many of which could still be seen a century later.

The town was beginning to look impressive. The prosperous commercial sector on the west bank faced the official quarter across the river, with the government offices, the Town Hall, the Singapore Institution, now extended and completed, and St. Andrew's Cathedral, all set in well-kept green lawns. Fort Canning dominated the town, flanked by hills crowned with fine houses. The town was still small, extending scarcely anywhere more than a mile from the centre. But the rest of the island was now accessible, with a network of roads, many villages, police stations along the coasts, and government rest-houses at outlying Seletar and Changi. Singapore was one of the beauty spots of the East. 'For forty-five years have the hands of man been busy accumulating wealth on its bosom and yet scarce a scar is visible.'[65]

Cavenagh's popularity was strong enough to weather the storms of economic depression, which had battered his predecessors, and the problem of the Straits deficit was solved during his regime. The merchants fought hard to avert the extension to Singapore of an Indian Stamp Act, but this eventually was forced through in 1863, and after a painful initial teething period it settled once and for all the apparently insoluble problem of how to balance revenue and expenditure.

Singapore was fortunate in escaping various other unpopular taxes, which Calcutta proposed to impose during the financial crisis which followed the Indian Mutiny. The merchants successfully warded off an attempt to levy port dues in 1862, and Calcutta withdrew a proposal to extend income tax to the Straits. In doing so it stifled an interesting experiment at birth. Lacking officials to collect such a tax, Cavenagh proposed to grade the population in fifty-two classes according to their financial standing and levy a flat tax at each level. Since Singaporeans identified status with wealth, he envisaged leading citizens would vie for position in the social scale and probably claim membership of a higher class carrying a heavier rate of tax than their actual income demanded. When Calcutta decided after all not to tax incomes in the Straits Settlements, Singapore lost the opportunity to put this novel pyschological theory to the test and to determine whether the social-climbing ambitions of a *nouveau riche* society could be adapted to the painless extraction of revenue. When income tax was eventually introduced in 1947 it came in the conventional form of a secret and confidential tussle between reluctant citizens and a complicated bureaucratic machine.

During his beneficent régime Cavenagh enjoyed the support of the local press, the grand juries, the municipal committee, the chamber of commerce and the leading Chinese. He received unquestioning loyalty from his officials and warm respect from the general public. Grand juries gave up making presentments of grievances, municipal politics quietened down into a concern with workaday improvements and attempting to make ends meet. Cavenagh made the Indian régime more popular than it had ever been, and stilled the aspirations for constitutional change.

Only a radical minority, comprising Read, Logan, Woods and a few like-minded enthusiasts, kept the transfer issue alive and, with the help of their London friends, they persuaded the British government to revive the negotiations.

The Colonial Office would not accept their claim that Singapore was of vital strategic importance to the Empire, 'at once the Gibraltar and the Constantinople of the East'. The British government could be convinced only by a proof of financial solvency, and this became possible after the new Stamp Act made the Straits Settlements self-supporting. At the end of 1863 the British government deputed Sir Hercules Robinson, Governor of Hong Kong, to report on the state of Singapore. His recommendations favoured a transfer to colonial rule, but negotiations dragged on, mainly over arguments about responsibility for military expenditure.

London refused to take on any financial commitment to defend the Straits Settlements, but in 1866 the War Office suddenly took an interest in Singapore as an alternative base for part of the British forces stationed in Hong Kong, where the mortality rate among troops and families threatened to become a public scandal.

A bill was rushed through and final arrangements for the take-over by the Colonial Office were made in such haste that the senior Indian officials found themselves compulsorily retired, since India refused to take them and the Colonial Office wanted to put in their own men. Nor was Cavenagh officially informed that a Colonial Office appointee had been chosen to succeed him. Learning by chance from a private resident in Singapore that a new Governor was already on his way from England, Cavenagh departed from Singapore in high dudgeon. On 1 April 1867 the Indian administration came to an end and the Straits Settlements became a Crown colony.

1. J. Kathirithamby-Wells, 'Early Singapore and the inception of a British administrative tradition in the Straits Settlements (1819–1832)', *JMBRAS*, XLII, 2 (1969), pp. 48–73, deals with early administration in Singapore.

2. J.R. Logan, 'The Orang Binua of Johore', *JIA*, I (1847), p. 300.

3. C.A. Gibson-Hill, 'The Orang Laut of the Singapore River and the Sampan Panjang', *JMBRAS*, XXV, 1 (1952), pp. 161–74; reprinted *JMBRAS*, XLII, 1 (1969), pp. 118–32.

4. J. Crawfurd, *Journal of an Embassy from the Governor General of India to the Courts of Siam and Cochin China*, 2 vols. (London, 1828; reprinted Kuala Lumpur, 1967), II, p. 383.

5. Sharom Ahmat, 'American Trade with Singapore, 1819–65', *JMBRAS*, XXXVIII, 2 (1965), pp. 241–57; Sharom Ahmat, 'Joseph Balestier: the First American Consul in Singapore, 1833–52', *JMBRAS*, XXXIX, 2 (1966), pp. 108–22.

6. *ST*, 10 January 1865.

7. *SFP*, 6 January 1854.

8. F. Pridmore, 'Coins and Coinages of the Straits Settlements and British Malaya, 1786 to 1951', *Memoirs of the Raffles Museum*, No. 2 (Singapore, 1955), pp. 28–40; C.H. Dakers, 'Some Copper Tokens in the Raffles Museum, Singapore', *JMBRAS*, XV, 2 (1937), pp. 127–9; E. Wodak, 'Some Coins and Tokens of Malaya', *JMBRAS*, XXIII, 3 (1950), pp. 143–7.

9. 'Oriental pirates', *United Service Journal*, III (1835), pp. 31–42; 'The Malay pirates', *United Service Journal*, I (1837), pp. 450–65; E.G. Festing (ed.), *Life of Commander Henry James, R.N.* (London, 1899), p. 262.

10. J.R. Logan, 'The Piracy and Slave Trade of the Indian Archipelago', *JIA*, IV (1850), p. 145.

11. *SFP*, 17 March 1854.

12. *SFP*, 18 January 1866. H. Miller, *Pirates of the Far East* (London, 1970) gives a readable general account of piracy in the region.

13. G.F. Davidson, *Trade and Travel in the Far East* (London, 1846), p. 69.

14. Quoted in *SFP*, 6 August 1852.

15. J.R. Logan, 'Sago', *JIA*, III (1849), pp. 288–313.

16. J. Cameron, *Our Tropical Possessions in Malayan India* (London, 1865; reprinted Kuala Lumpur, 1965), p. 168.

17. J.T. Thomson, 'General Report on the Residency of Singapore Drawn up Principally with a View of Illustrating its Agricultural Statistics', *JIA*, III (1849), pp. 618–28, 744–55, IV (1850), pp. 27–41, 102–6, 134–43, 206–19; J. Balestier, 'View of the State of Agriculture in the British Possessions in the Straits of Malacca', *JIA*, II (1848), pp. 139–50; T. Oxley, 'Some Account of the Nutmeg and its Cultivation', *JIA*, II (1848), pp. 641–60; J. Crawfurd, 'Agriculture of Singapore', *JIA*, III (1849), pp. 508–11: reprinted from *Singapore Chronicle*, 1824.

18. J.C. Jackson, *Planters and Speculators: Chinese and European Agricultural Enterprise in Malaya, 1786–1921* (Kuala Lumpur, 1968), pp. 7–30; J.C. Jackson, 'Chinese Agricultural Pioneering in Singapore and Johore', *JMBRAS*, XXXVIII, 1 (1965), pp. 77–105; P. Wheatley, 'Land Use in the Vicinity of Singapore in the 1830s', *Malayan Journal of Tropical Geography*, II (Singapore, 1954), pp. 63–6.

19. C.M. Turnbull, 'The Johore Gambier and Pepper Trade in the mid-Nineteenth Century', *JSSS*, XV, 1 (1959), pp. 43–55.

20. E.A. Brown, *Indiscreet Memories* (London, 1935), pp. 257–8.

21. G.W. Earl, *The Eastern Seas* (London, 1837; reprinted Kuala Lumpur, 1971), p. 145.

22. Munshi Abdullah bin Abdul Kadir gave an eye-witness description of the 1830 fire in *Shaer Singapura Terbakar* and of the 1847 fire in 'Shaer Kampong Gelam Terbakar oleh Abdullah B. Abdul-Kadir', romanized version, edited with notes by C. Skinner, *JMBRAS*, XLV, 1 (1972) pp. 21–56.

23. K.S. Sandhu, 'Tamil and Other Indian Convicts in the Straits Settlements, A.D. 1790–1873', *Proceedings of the First International Conference Seminar of Tamil Studies, Kuala Lumpur, Malaysia, 1966* (Kuala Lumpur, 1968), I, pp. 197–208; C.M. Turnbull, 'Convicts in the Straits Settlements, 1826–1867', *JMBRAS*, XLIII, 1 (1970), pp. 87–103; for the construction of Horsburgh Lighthouse see J.T. Thomson, 'Account of the Horsburgh Lighthouse', *JIA*, VI (1852), pp. 376–498, and J.A.L. Pavitt, *First Pharos of the Eastern Seas: Horsburgh Lighthouse* (Singapore, 1966).

24. J.P. Mialaret, *Hinduism in Singapore* (Singapore, 1969) describes the Hindu temples of Singapore and their past history.

25. B.W. Hodder, 'Racial Groupings in Singapore', *Malayan Journal of Tropical Geography*, I (Singapore, 1953), pp. 25–36.

26. C.A. Gibson-Hill, 'Singapore Old Strait and New Harbour, 1300–1870', *Memoirs of the Raffles Museum*, No. 3 (Singapore, 1956), p. 11–115; C.A. Gibson-Hill, 'Singapore: Notes on the History of the Old Strait, 1580–1850', *JMBRAS*, XXVII, 1 (1954), pp. 163–214; and C.D. Cowan, 'New Harbour, Singapore and the Cruise of H.M.S. "Maeander", 1848–49', *JMBRAS*, XXXVIII, 2 (1965), pp. 229–40, discuss the development of New Harbour.

27. J. Crawfurd, 'Remarks on the revenue', 21 October 1825, *JIA*, VIII (1854), p. 414.

28. SSR, H 13, 24 December 1824.

29. Earl, *Eastern Seas*, p. 383.

30. M. Freedman, *Lineage Organisation in Southeastern China* (London, 1958), and M. Freedman, *Chinese Lineage and Society: Fukien and Kwangtung* (London, 1966) provide valuable background studies.

31. T. Suyama, 'Pang Societies: the Economy of Chinese Immigrants', in K.G. Tregonning (ed.), *Papers on Malayan History* (Singapore, 1962), p. 198.

32. SSR, R17, pp. 65–6.

33. SSR, V37, p. 155.

34. See vivid descriptions in J.T. Thomson, *Some Glimpses into Life in the Far East* (London, 1864), pp. 307–11; H. Keppel, *A Sailor's Life under Four Sovereigns*, 3 vols. (London, 1899), III, p. 13.

35. *ST*, 21 December 1869.

36. L. Oliphant, *Narrative of the Earl of Elgin's Mission to China and Japan*, 2 vols. (Edinburgh and London, 1859; reprinted Kuala Lumpur, 1970) has some interesting comments on the Singapore Chinese.

37. *SFP*, 29 December 1859.

38. *SFP*, 25 July 1851.

39. *SFP*, 21 July 1854.

40. R.C. Penang to Governor, 26 June 1861, SSR, DD 34, Item 86.

41. SSR, W27, Item 231A.

42. C.K. Byrd, *Early Printing in the Straits Settlements, 1806–58* (Singapore, 1971), pp. 13–17.

43. *Annual Report on the Administration of the Straits Settlements for 1862–63*.

44. Y.K. Lee, 'Medical education in the Straits, 1786–1871', *JMBRAS*, XLVI, 1 (1973), pp. 101–22.

45. *ST*, 17 August 1861.

46. *SFP*, 29 March 1849.

47. SSR, S25, Item 152.

48. R. Little, 'On the Habitual Use of Opium in Singapore', *JIA*, II (1848), pp. 1–79; T. Braddell, 'Gambling and Opium Smoking in the Straits of Malacca', *JIA*, New Series, I (1857), pp. 66–83.

49. Cheng U Wen, 'Opium in the Straits Settlements', *JSEAH*, II (1961).

50. SSR, V 37, p. 52; SSR, W 46, Item 247.

51. *ST*, 18 June 1864.

52. F.S. Marryat, *Borneo and the Indian Archipelago* (London, 1848), p. 213. E. Belcher, *Narrative of the Voyage of H.M.S. 'Samarang' during the Years 1843–6*, 2 vols. (London, 1848), II, pp. 179–80; J.D. Ross, *Sixty Years: Life and Adventure in the Far East*, 2 vols. (London, 1911; reprinted London, 1968), I, pp. 58–9.

53. *ST*, 14 January 1865.

54. Correspondent 'ZZ' to *SFP*, November 1850.

55. C.A. Gibson-Hill, 'The Singapore Chronicle, 1824–37', *JMBRAS*, XXVI, 1 (1953), pp. 175–99.

56. Y.K. Lee, 'The Grand Jury in Early Singapore, 1819–1873', *JMBRAS*, XLVI, 2 (1973), pp. 55–150.

57. *ST*, 3 July, 7 August 1855.

58. *SFP*, 14 May 1857; C.M. Turnbull, 'Communal Disturbances in the Straits Settlements in 1857', *JMBRAS*, XXXI, 1 (1958), pp. 96–146.

59. SSR, W 25, Item 339; *ST*, 7 July 1857; *SFP*, 23 July 1857.

60. *SFP*, 17 September 1857; *ST*, 22 September 1857.

61. *PP*, 1862, xl (H. of C.), 259, pp. 585–8.

62. *PG*, 19, 26 September, 10 October, in *SFP*, 1, 8, 22 October 1857.

63. C.O. correspondence and minutes, 7–10 July 1860, CO 144/18.

64. *PP*, 1861, XIII, no. 423, pp. 69–373.

65. Cameron, p. 48.

# III

# High Noon of Empire, 1867–1914

THOMAS Carlyle's 'Happy the people whose annals are blank in history books,' could well be applied to Singapore during the decades which followed the transfer to colonial rule. For almost three-quarters of a century she enjoyed unbroken peace with orderly administration, and her steady expansion and prosperity were checked only temporarily by periodic international economic depressions.

Despite this outward calm, the character of Singapore society during these decades changed fundamentally. The conversion of the Straits Settlements into a crown colony was followed by three developments which did not revolutionize Singapore's role overnight but combined to accelerate and consolidate her growth in the last quarter of the nineteenth century: the opening of the Suez Canal in 1869, the extension of British protection to the Malay states, which began in 1874, and the steady conversion of cargo shipping to steam from the mid-1860s.

Singapore ceased to be an isolated settlement, divorced from the hinterland, looking out to sea, living on her nerves and her wits in the uncertainties of international trade. She acquired permanent status as a major entrepôt on the leading east-west Malacca Straits trade route, the focus for the trading wealth of the Malay peninsula and the East Indies, and one of the most vital commercial keypoints of the British Empire.

When the India Office gave up Singapore in 1867, its government scarcely impinged on the life of the Asian population. An official commission reported in 1875, 'We believe that the vast majority of Chinamen who come to work in these Settlements return to their country not knowing clearly whether there is a government in them or not.' By 1941, while the inhabitants had not yet been assimilated into a specifically Singaporean society, the government had succeeded in bringing the whole community into its executive and judicial system, developing specialized departments of administration and making provisions for education, health and social welfare, which formed the foundations for the modern state. Many changes in the fabric of society were produced not in the legislative chamber but quietly and unobtrusively in government offices, the law courts, the schools, the professional offices and business houses.

The first colonial Governor, Sir Harry St. George Ord, formerly Governor of Bermuda, applied for the more challenging post in Singapore to act as a 'new broom' in sweeping away the supposed inefficiency of Indian rule.[1] 'Essentially a man of progress', the *London and China Telegraph* described him in January 1867,[2] and as a military officer experienced in colonial administration Ord seemed admirably fitted to govern the new colony.

He expected to find eager support for the new régime and for his spring-cleaning campaign. The deputations, letters, memorials and petitions, with which the minority of enthusiasts had bombarded the British government for the past ten years, deceived both Ord and the Colonial Office into believing that Singaporeans were unanimous in seeking change. The *Straits Times* hailed the transfer as 'the greatest political event which has occurred since the foundation of the settlement',[3] and the European mercantile community welcomed the new constitutional arrangements, providing for formal consultation which had been the major object in seeking colonial status. Yet there was a strong under-current of anxiety. Asian merchants had shown no interest in the political change. Few Europeans raised their voices in protest while the transfer remained a remote possibility, but once it became a certainty many began to have doubts, fearing it might bring increased expense and higher taxation. Many of the grievances which led the merchants to petition for separation from India in 1857 had since disappeared. The problems of piracy, commercial taxation, currency, and convicts had all been settled. Cavenagh's popular term of office had produced a golden sunset for the Indian régime, and the merchants were sorry to lose him.

In accordance with normal British crown colony practice, the Governor was to rule with the help of executive and legislative councils. In 1867 the executive council consisted of the Governor, the Officer commanding the troops in the Straits and six senior officials. The legislative council comprised members of the executive council, together with the Chief Justice and four non-officials nominated by the Governor.

The principle of the Governor's executive supremacy, subject to the Colonial Office's ultimate control, remained intact up to the Second World War. The executive council met in private and constituted a type of cabinet, but it was not responsible to the legislative council. Its advice was not binding on the Governor, who initiated most legislation and had the power of assent or veto on all bills. Official members were obliged to support him, but non-officials were free to speak and vote as they pleased. The Governor was instructed to pay deference to their views, particularly on questions of taxation and expenditure, and to report and explain any occasion when he over-rode their unanimous opinion. Legislative council debates were held in public and reported in the local press. The success of the British colonial constitutional system depended upon the willing co-operation of the Governor and his council, and in practice a Governor's full powers were rarely invoked.

Some modifications were made over the years to broaden the basis of consultation. The numbers of non-officials and Asians were increased, the first Asian non-official, Whampoa, being appointed in 1869. By 1924 the legislative council comprised equal numbers of officials and non-officials, but the Governor had the casting vote, so that final authority still rested with him and the Colonial Office.

The colony of the Straits Settlements comprised Singapore, Penang, and Malacca, with additional entities attached from time to time for administrative convenience: the Dindings area of Perak was part of the colony from 1874 to 1934, Labuan from 1906 to 1946, the Cocos Keeling islands from 1886 to 1955, and Christmas Island from 1900 to 1958.

Singapore was the centre of government, commerce, and policy making. Each of the three Straits Settlements was supposed to have at least one non-official legislative councillor, but it was difficult in Penang and impossible in Malacca to find suitable people who could spare time to serve. Of the four non-officials appointed in 1867, three came from Singapore. The government was so Singapore-dominated that Penang, which had not supported the movement for colonial rule in the first place, became increasingly resentful at the alleged neglect of its interests. In 1872 the Penang chamber of commerce demanded separation from Singapore or the creation of a separate Penang legislative council. Tension eased in the later years of the century when Penang prospered with the development of Perak and trade with Thailand, but there were perennial rumblings about the proportion of the colony's revenue spent on Singapore.

The adjustment to colonial rule was painful.[4] After long years of opposition without responsibility, the vocal minority was disappointed to find how little political power they were allowed, while the majority, who had not actively sought the transfer, looked back nostalgically to the old days whenever difficulties arose.

The transfer petition was granted as a concession by the British government, with no thought of strategic military or naval advantage and with no intention of introducing any radical change. Ord was merely instructed to rule efficiently and keep within his budget, but was given no authority to initiate any new policies in dealing with the Malay states or the Chinese secret societies. Those who had fought for the transfer were angry to find that the Colonial Office had no intention of taking a more active line than Calcutta on these two problems, and Ord found himself in a frustrating position.

The new Governor was temperamentally unsuited for the delicate task of moulding Singapore into the colonial pattern. The situation called for patience and tact rather than energy and reforming zeal, but Ord's abrasive personality and autocratic disposition aggravated the irritations of the early colonial years.

Within three months of his arrival the Governor warned the Colonial Office that critics of the new régime claimed the term 'crown colony'

was not suitable for the Straits Settlements,[5] to which the Colonial
Office replied that 'There is scarcely any colony under the English
dominion in which the authority of the Crown and control of the home
government is so indispensable as in the Straits Settlements.'[6]

Ord provoked considerable ill-feeling in reorganizing the administration, in clearing up carelessness and corruption and demanding higher
standards of efficiency.[7] His attack upon nepotism and abuses of patronage, which had been accepted as normal practice before 1867, roused
a fury of resentment. In his attempt to make the judiciary conform to
normal colonial practice, Ord found himself in head-on collision with
the Chief Justice, Sir Benson Maxwell, who as Recorder of Singapore
had enjoyed personal independence and considerable rights of patronage
under the Indian régime. Maxwell marshalled the non-official members
of the legislative council to support him in open conflict with the Governor,
but the Colonial Office insisted on bringing the Straits judiciary into
line with all other crown colonies, by making the Chief Justice responsible
to the Governor in Council. A Supreme Court Bill was passed to this
effect in 1868.

Ord brought down upon himself accusations of personal extravagance
when he ordered a new government steamer and built a palatial Government House, which still stands as the President's palace in independent
Singapore. The existing steamer was not seaworthy, and the Governor
of a thriving colony could not continue living in a rented house, as his
predecessors had done for the past ten years, since the original Governor's
bungalow was demolished to make way for Fort Canning. Both items
of expenditure were justified but unfortunately they were associated with
the new Governor's personal comfort.

His worst blunder was to question the revenue system, which he
felt bore too heavily on the poor, letting affluent merchants escape
lightly. The government was in a healthy financial state but Ord incautious-
ly told the legislative council at the end of 1867 that if further revenue
were ever required, he proposed to raise it by direct taxation, adding
that it would be undesirable to tax trade 'except under the pressure of
necessity which could hardly arise'.[8] This intended reassurance had the
opposite effect, and the idea that the sacred creed of free trade might
be violated in any circumstances whatsoever unleashed the resentment
which had been building up for months. The *Straits Times* declared the
Governor had 'thrown down the gauntlet to public opinion on a point
that has never yet been questioned by any one at all conversant, even
rudimentally, with the history of the Settlement and the circumstances
of its commerce'.

The former opposition group banded together once more. In January
1868 the ex-Straits residents who had fought for the transfer in England
met in Bousteads' London office and formed the Straits Settlements
Association, 'to guard against any legislation that might prejudicially
affect the interests of the Straits Settlements, and in particular that might
be calculated to check or interfere with their commercial prosperity as

free ports of trade'.[9] John Crawfurd was elected president, and local branches of the Association were formed in Singapore and Penang.

The Straits Settlements Association in London sent a memorandum to the Colonial Office in April 1869 claiming that the first two years of colonial administration had been 'most disastrous to the colony'. They objected that the legislative council was 'a mere mockery, representing as it does, the will of the Governor alone; and that such a system is wrong in principle, demoralising and altogether objectionable'.[10] This led to angry exchanges with the Governor, and to the organizing of public protest meetings in Singapore under the chairmanship of Read, the senior non-official in the legislative council.

The Colonial Office was at first unaware of the immense Chinese problem which it had inherited, since the Indian régime had taken no steps to tackle the inter-related problems of secret societies, immigration, labour, coolie traffic, poverty and prostitution. A commission of enquiry was appointed following secret-society riots in Penang in 1867, and as a result of its findings a Dangerous Societies Suppression Ordinance was passed in 1869. Despite its name, this measure did not aim to suppress but merely to register associations. Societies were obliged to admit magistrates or police officers to meetings, and it became illegal to administer oaths or to recruit members by force.

The ordinance was ineffective, and the secret societies thrived on the growing coolie traffic as Chinese immigrants flooded into Singapore, attracted by the opportunities for work in the British Protected Malay States and the Dutch Indies. By the mid-1870s the November-February junk season brought 30,000 Chinese to Singapore each year. The immigrants included numbers of *samsengs* or professional thugs, attracted by the demand for fighting men in the Perak tin mines and other troubled areas. In 1872 it was said that the Singapore Ghee Hok society alone had four thousand *samsengs* at its command.

Many *sinkhehs* were kept under guard on the coolie ships or locked up in filthy conditions in secret-society depots ashore and then forcibly re-shipped to Sumatra and other places in South-East Asia, where conditions were too deplorable to attract free labour. This practice of kidnapping was highly organized in the 1870s, sometimes entrapping even free immigrants who had paid their own passage.[11] On one occasion *samsengs* marched a band of more than eighty *sinkhehs* openly through the Singapore streets for shipment to Siak.

Rioting among the Chinese in Singapore in 1872 led to the appointment of a further official commission, which recommended the controversial steps of reviving the former *kapitan* system and curbing Chinese immigration. Leading Chinese, including Whampoa and Seah Eu Chin, petitioned the government to superintend coolie immigration and to prevent the forcible diversion of *sinkhehs* away from Singapore, where 'they know that in this fine country they will find a peaceful home, where the whole population are so prosperous that they sing for joy'.

With this backing, Ord tried to make the first onslaught on the abuses of the coolie trade by means of a Chinese Coolie Immigration Bill, which he introduced in 1873. This modest bill proposed merely to register immigrants, not to enforce contracts nor provide reception depots, but it provoked a fury of opposition from European merchants, legislative councillors and the English-language press, in defence of the treasured principle of free immigration, which was held to be the life blood of the Straits economy. The bill became law but was never implemented.

Perhaps the most frustrating aspect of all Ord's work related to the Malay states, since he was secretly in sympathy with those who favoured positive action. Despite the official policy of non-interference, which the Colonial Office took over from India, in practice the Straits government had become increasingly involved in the affairs of the interior.

The rising demand for tin in world markets stimulated the search for tin in Malaya from the middle of the century, and Chinese labourers poured into Perak, Sungei Ujong and Selangor. Mining operations were organized by Chinese entrepreneurs, often with backing from European merchants, who occasionally financed such enterprises directly. These men began to clamour for more protection for their capital and for the lives of the Chinese pioneers who braved the dangers and hardships of the interior.

In Johor, Abu Bakar's government produced safe and stable conditions in which Singapore merchants could operate. Elsewhere the Singapore authorities had failed to establish the indirect hold over Malay rulers through education and influence, which had been Raffles's ideal, and enterprise fell prey to growing anarchy. The rapid expansion of the tin trade and the influx of Chinese miners hastened the disintegration of traditional authority in Perak, Selangor, and Negri Sembilan. Civil war in Pahang, which lasted from 1857 to 1864, closed the Kuantan tin mines and cut off the valuable gold trade of the interior in which Singapore merchants were deeply involved.

The merchants' petition for transfer to colonial rule in 1857 was based mainly on domestic and constitutional issues, and policy in the Malay states was a minor grievance. By the end of Indian rule ten years later, the situation in the Malay states had become a crucial concern. These years had brought disaster to thousands of Chinese miners and severe setbacks to European and Chinese speculators. By 1867 the merchants had discovered to their cost that without official backing there could be no security. Conflicts between immigrants and Malay authorities and among rival Chinese societies themselves brought bitter commercial rivalry to Singapore and the threat of bloodshed in Penang. Sooner or later political intervention was inevitable.

The Singapore merchants were disappointed to find that the Colonial Office did not intend to make Singapore the focus for extending British territorial power. In 1868 the Secretary of State instructed Ord that 'The policy of Her Majesty's government in the Malayan peninsula is not one of intervention in native affairs,' and 'If merchants or others penetrate disturbed and semi-barbarous independent states...they must not anticipate that the British government will intervene to enforce their contracts.'[12] While Ord was in England on leave in 1871/2 he had long personal discussions with the Secretary of State, in which he pressed for a more active policy on the grounds that it was unrealistic for the British authorities to stand aloof and watch the rich trade of the hinterland disintegrate in the turmoil of Malay politics and secret-society fighting. But the Colonial Office refused his request and Ord's hands were tied.

In July 1873, with civil war raging in Perak and Selangor, the leading Chinese merchants of Singapore presented a formal petition seeking British intervention. Ord backed the appeal, and by that time the Colonial Office was beginning to feel that it might be necessary to strengthen British influence in the Malay states for fear other foreign powers might intervene. But Ord's activities over the past seven years convinced them he was not the man to enforce such a policy. They had no confidence in his tact or judgement. Not realizing the strength of opposition which had already grown up before 1867 and refusing to admit Ord's argument that the majority did not want the transfer, they saw all the troubles of his régime as his own making.

Shortly before his final departure from Singapore in 1873, Ord introduced a Criminal Procedure Bill, with a controversial clause abolishing the grand jury. Twenty years earlier the merchants themselves had agitated to get rid of the jury, but Ord's proposals provoked a violent outcry from the non-official legislative councillors and from a public meeting, where Read alleged that the abolition of the grand jury would remove 'the last check between arbitrary government and justice to the people'.[13] The European merchants sent a telegram of protest to the Colonial Office and, with the exception of Whampoa, all the non-officials resigned. This important bill, which reconstituted the Supreme Court, provided for four puisne judges, and created a court of appeal, was passed in their absence and approved by the Colonial Office. The Secretary of State rejected a plea from European and Chinese merchants that the non-officials be reinstated and that future ordinances should not be put into force until approve: by London, since he objected to the principle that the non-official minority should exert even a temporary veto on legislation.

The conflict highlighted the inherent problems of legislative councils and colonial constitutions. The Directors of the East India Company had opposed granting colonial-type institutions in India on the grounds that this would put power in the hands of expatriate non-officials, probably to the detriment of the indigenous population. This happened in Singapore and other crown colonies, where both European and Asian non-official legislative councillors tended to represent hard commercial interests. Ord wrote scathingly to the Colonial Office in one of his last dispatches, 'The mercantile community which constitutes the society of the place takes hardly any interest in anything beyond their own immediate business.

Many of them openly avow that they come here solely to make money.'

Despite Ord's personal unpopularity he reorganized the administration efficiently and his régime was a time of great material progress. Singapore's trade figures jumped from just over £58 million in 1868 to nearly £90 million in 1873, and Ord retired from Singapore in the autumn of 1873 at a time of unprecedented prosperity. His successor, Sir Andrew Clarke, found the teething troubles of the new régime were over. Both the British government and the Singapore merchants looked to Clarke to smooth away friction and the Colonial Office instructed him to investigate and report on the state of affairs in the west-coast states of Malaya.

The new Governor was more in tune with the Singapore business community, more willing to 'dance to the bagpipes of Singapore'. Despite misgivings in the Colonial Office, Clarke immediately reinstated the non-official legislative councillors. He also readily adopted the leading merchants' views favouring a more vigorous policy in the Malay states.

Clarke visited Perak where, exceeding the instructions given him in London, he made the Pangkor Engagement in January 1874. This provided for a British Resident to advise the Sultan, paved the way for similar arrangements in Selangor and Sungei Ujong and began the process leading to British domination in these states. In view of the changed feeling then prevailing in London, Clarke's actions were not repudiated, and the way was open for the development of the resources of the Protected Malay States, for which Singapore became the main port.

Clarke also succeeded in 1874 in winning the support of Chinese and European merchants to an ordinance to regulate passenger ships, which put the first modest check on some of the abuses of coolie travel.

It has been said that 'the course of running a Crown colony, like love, rarely runs smoothly',[14] but for the moment administration ran more smoothly in Singapore than in most crown colonies. In January 1874 the *Straits Times* admitted, 'It is very hard to be without a grievance, and we confess we are somewhat in this condition here at the present time.'[15] The colony was set on a course of constitutional and political calm which lasted almost without interruption for nearly seventy years.

One of the main benefits of colonial rule was the development of a separate Straits Civil Service. After 1867 young men were recruited in England specifically for service in the Straits, at first by Colonial Office nomination. From 1869 nominees had to sit for an examination and in 1882 the Straits Civil Service was thrown open to public competition.

Young cadets were trained in Malay on arrival in the colony, and from the 1880s those who were required to specialize in Chinese affairs were sent to learn Chinese dialects in Amoy, Swatow or Canton. Normally they served their whole career in the Straits, so that many officials exerted a stronger influence on government policy through their long connexion with Singapore than Governors who came for a relatively short span of time.

Little happened on the surface of politics. Periodic trade fluctuations frayed political tempers, but not to the same extent as in the precarious pre-Suez days. The feeling of greater security induced more responsible, if still rather selfish, politics. The colony's military contribution was the most common source of discord, particularly when demands came at times of commercial depression.

In 1867 the British government did not admit that Singapore had any imperial strategic importance and insisted that defence costs were her own responsibility, apart from the support of the contingent of imperial troops transferred from Hong Kong on health grounds. The colony's contribution was fixed at £59,300 out of a total defence expenditure of £66,000, which was a heavier proportion than in most other colonies.

There was not much to be seen for this expenditure. In 1869 Sir William Drummond Jervois, then Deputy Inspector-General of Fortifications and subsequently Governor of the Straits Settlements, reported that the existing fortifications in Singapore were useless, except possibly against a civil revolt. Four years later the general commanding the China station reported to the War Office that the forts at Singapore were 'totally incapable of effective defence'.[16]

With the opening of the Suez Canal and the use of the Malacca Straits as the main route to the Far East, Singapore became an essential link in the chain of British ports and coaling stations, which stretched from Gibraltar, through Malta, Suez, Aden, Trincomalee and on to Hong Kong or Australia. Consequently in 1871 the British government agreed to assume part responsibility for Singapore's defence, to station a full-strength European regiment there and to pay 45 per cent of garrison costs. At the same time the War Office proposed to fortify Singapore against naval attack and offered to pay for the guns and armament but expected the colony to meet the construction costs. The Governor supported his legislative council's objections to this demand, but the secretary of state refused to accept the principle that Singapore's defence was an imperial obligation and that the home government should bear the entire cost of erecting permanent defence works.

Since there was no prospective enemy in sight and the Singapore merchants protested so hotly, the matter was left in abeyance.

The Colonial Office began to prod the Straits authorities into taking more positive action to stem the scandalous labour abuses in Singapore. A commission appointed by Jervois, who became Governor of the Straits Settlements in 1875, reported the following year that 'The government knows little or nothing of the Chinese, who are the industrial backbone of these Settlements; and the immense majority of them know still less of government.' It recommended firmer control with more official protection for new immigrants, and its findings led in 1877 to the establishment of a Chinese Protectorate, with William Pickering as first Protector of Chinese.

Housed modestly in a Chinese shophouse in North Canal Road, the

Protectorate marked a reversal of *laissez faire* policy in favour of paternal, personal direct contact. The foundation of the Protectorate was timely since Chinese immigration was rising to new peaks in response to demand for labour in the tin mines of the Protected Malay States. Numbers of Chinese immigrants increased from 34,000 in 1878 to 103,000 in 1888, and the Chinese population of Singapore rose threefold in the last thirty years of the century.

Pickering had worked in China for eight years before being appointed interpreter in Singapore in 1872. The first European official who could speak and read Chinese, he was appalled at the corruption of the court interpreters, and at the language used to describe the administration. Chinese translations of official government proclamations styled Europeans as 'red-haired barbarians', judges as 'devils', and police as 'big dogs'.

The Protector's first task was to tackle the abuses of the coolie trade. A Chinese Immigrants Ordinance and a Crimping Ordinance, which were passed in 1877, authorized him to license recruiting agents and board incoming ships. He was to discharge passengers who had already paid their passages and send others to government depots, where employment contracts would be officially registered. Little opposition was offered to these sweeping new laws, since the revelations of cruelty and oppression practised on immigrants had touched the public conscience in the four years since Ord attempted to tackle the problem.

In the early days *hoey* agents often attempted to get coolies off incoming ships and clashed with the Protector and his staff, but gradually these disorderly scenes petered out. A Labour Commission in 1890 confirmed that there were still considerable abuses in hiring coolie labour but by the end of the century immigration supervision became an administrative routine, handled by cadets and subordinate officials.

The Protectorate made a great impact from the beginning, and with his strong personality, unique knowledge, and flair for practical administration Pickering rapidly extended his authority from the protection of immigrants to general supervision of the Chinese community.

As a result of shocking disclosures about brutality and degradation in Singapore brothels, in the 1880s the Protectorate extended its activities to supervision of Chinese women and girls.[17] The authorities did not seek to ban prostitution, nor to discourage the immigration of willing professional female prostitutes. Such a prohibition would have been unrealistic in Singapore, which in 1884 had 60,000 Chinese men, compared with 6,600 Chinese women, of whom Pickering estimated that at least two thousand were prostitutes. A ban would also have encouraged homosexual prostitution which was fostered for many years by the importation of Hainanese boys. The Protectorate merely aimed to stop forced prostitution, since it was believed that 80 per cent of the young Chinese girls who came to Singapore in the late 1870s were sold to brothels.

In 1881 the Protectorate took over the administration of a Contagious

Diseases Ordinance, which had been passed in 1870 to provide for the registration of brothels. It also registered prostitutes and founded the Po Leung Kuk, or 'Office to protect virtue', which was administered with the advice of a committee of prominent Chinese and offered protection to girls who had been sold or unwillingly lured into prostitution. It did not seek to inhibit the activities of voluntary prostitutes, but at first roused great opposition from brothel keepers, and there were angry scenes at the Protectorate, with the brothel madams 'throwing back their licence boards, dancing on the floors with wooden clogs and howling furiously'. The Protectorate rescued many women from prostitution but Pickering found European juries reluctant to convict in cases of alleged abduction, and complained:

> If in these trials they do as the Judge charges them to do—use the same common sense and judgement which they use in their ordinary business concerns—then it is no wonder the Chinese in the Straits are buying up all the land, building splendid houses and have the best carriages and horses, while the Europeans and Eurasians toil year after year in order to get a mere competency.[18]

The Protectorate also acquired the task of coping with the secret societies. In 1876 the Chinese leaders showed their power to organize their community in opposition to government measures during the 'post office riots'. This protest was instigated by Teochew merchants who had monopolized remittances to China when a special post office was opened to handle such payments. They put up proclamations offering a reward for the heads of the new post-office managers, and in ensuing riots the sub-office was sacked. The police acted firmly, the riot was quelled, the merchants involved arrested and the ringleader banished to China, after which the sub-post office was reopened.

In 1877 Pickering was appointed joint Registrar of Societies with Major S. Dunlop, the Inspector-General of Police. Pickering was confident that he could gradually bring the Chinese under government control by working through the *hoeys,* converting the headmen into government agents and undermining their judicial power by providing in the Protectorate a more attractive arbitration centre. Gradually the Protectorate supplanted the societies in settling financial and domestic disputes.

As the societies lost their grip over immigration, labour and prostitution, they switched their interest to gambling. In 1886 an official commision of enquiry revealed widespread gambling abuses. It was common practice to rig gambling sessions at which coolies on the point of returning to China were cheated of their lifetime savings. Gambling was highly organized, the laws prohibiting it blatantly flouted, and regular subscriptions were levied from gaming houses to buy police connivance.

The commission considered it was impossible to suppress gambling but thought it immoral to resurrect the gaming farm. Pickering again urged strict measures, and this may have been the cause for a savage attack upon him by a Teochew carpenter, who wounded him seriously with an axe in the Protectorate Office in 1887.

By that time the Straits Settlements were unique in recognizing secret societies, which were banned in Hong Kong, the Protected Malay States and the Dutch colonies. Both Pickering and Dunlop agreed that it was time to begin a gradual elimination of the secret societies, but they were not prepared to accept the immediate abolition proposed by the Governor, Sir Cecil Clementi Smith.

An accomplished Chinese scholar, Clementi Smith had spent his career in the East. He joined the colonial service as a cadet in Hong Kong in 1864, and with the exception of two years in Ceylon, he served from 1878 to 1893 in Singapore as Colonial Secretary, Acting Governor and finally as Governor. A forceful and efficient administrator, he resolved on taking strong action to get rid of the secret societies as 'a standing menace to all good government and a great scandal to British administration'. 'The government must be the paramount power, and it is not so in the eyes of many thousands of the Chinese in the Straits Settlements.'

Pickering, Dunlop and the non-official legislative councillors argued that total suppression would be precipitate, driving the societies underground, breaking the government's contact with society leaders and registered members without substituting any alternative control machinery.

With Colonial Office backing, Clementi Smith persisted with his policy, gradually winning public support. Dunlop and Pickering, who never fully recovered from his wounds, both retired in 1888, and the last opposition evaporated the following year when Clementi Smith created a Chinese Advisory Board to provide a formal link between the government and the Chinese community. A law to suppress dangerous societies and register harmless benevolent associations was passed in 1889 and brought into force in 1890 without any riots or disturbances. Six years later the Protector commented, 'There exists at present no society which is in any way dangerous to the peace of the Colony.'[19]

The Societies Ordinance did not succeed in eliminating secret societies altogether, but it broke the big *hoeys* up into small bands of thugs, who continued to extort 'protection money' from shops, gambling dens, opium dens, brothels, hawkers, and fought among themselves for control of areas. In times of economic depression or political weakness the criminal activities of these secret societies became widespread and at certain periods they used political developments to resume an air of pseudo-respectability. But they were never able to reconstruct the large organizations or recover the widespread power which they wielded before 1890. Gang fights remained frequent but the days of large-scale secret society riots which paralysed Singapore were over. The power of banishment was a particularly effective deterrent, because the Chinese government often arrested deportees on their return to China and sometimes executed them.

The Societies Ordinance was an important landmark in the development of Singapore. It was rare for a Governor to carry through legislation in the face of initial opposition from leading officials and unanimous objections from non-officials in the legislative council, but Clementi Smith's authority, tact, and long experience of the East enabled him to win over public opinion. He left Singapore in 1893 in an aura of great prestige, widely admired among all communities, including the Chinese, who petitioned for the extension of his period of office.

With Pickering's departure the Protectorate entered a more prosaic phase, but he had created, shaped it and given it the traditions which were maintained up to the Second World War. Long after his death the Chinese Protectorate Office continued to be known among the Singapore Chinese as the Pi-ki-ling.

The establishment of the Chinese Protectorate and the ban on secret societies brought more law and order into Singapore society. This was helped too by police reforms carried out in the 1880s following a commission of enquiry into the alleged inefficiency of the force. At that time most policemen were south Indians, with a few Boyanese and Malays, since Whampoa, Seah Eu Chin and other leading Chinese had consistently resisted suggestions to recruit Chinese policemen for fear that secret society men might infiltrate into the police. As a compromise, from 1881 some Sikhs and a few European ex-army officers, inspectors and constables, were added to the force, a police training school was opened in 1881 and a separate detective force established three years later. In 1904 a cadet system was started to recruit young Englishmen as police officers and give them specialist training.

The last quarter of the nineteenth century saw a dramatic rise in Singapore's trade. The Suez Canal established the supremacy of her geographical position, because it meant that the Malacca Straits supplanted the Sunda Straits as the major waterway from Europe to the Far East. While the Canal experienced many troubles in its early years and did not lead to an immediate switching of trade routes, its opening was a significant milestone in Singapore's development. It hastened the decline of sailing ships, because the clippers could not use the Canal, and enhanced Singapore's role as a coaling station for steamers.

Singapore profited from the increase in European trade in Siam following the accession of King Chulalongkorn in 1868, and from the expansion of trade which came in the wake of colonization by other European powers in South-East Asia in the last decades of the century. The French occupation of Indo-China, the extension of Spanish rule in the Philippines, and in particular the liberalization of Dutch commercial policy made Singapore the focal point for trade in the Far East.

In Malaya itself British influence spread quickly. After the first Resident of Perak was murdered in 1875, the British tightened their control and strengthened the Residents' authority in the Protected States. In 1888 a British Resident was established in Pahang and in the same year Sarawak, North Borneo and Brunei became British protectorates. In 1896 the protected states of Selangor, Perak, Pahang, and Negri Sembilan were formed into a Federation, which encouraged investment in the Malay states, most of which came through Singapore.

The opening of the Suez Canal and the extension of European colonial rule in South-East Asia coincided with a rapid expansion of the steamship in merchant shipping. This not only stimulated east-west trade and entrepôt commerce, but gave an impetus to local commercial development throughout the region. Britain, as undisputed mistress of the seas, held the key ports and controlled international shipping lanes, with Singapore as one of the most vital links in the chain.

Singapore's trade expanded eight-fold in the period from 1873 to 1913 and shifted from the rather exotic wares of the early nineteenth century to the bulk movement of primary products, chiefly rubber and tin, but also copra and sugar. Singapore's activities also expanded from mere trans-shipment to include preliminary processing, such as tin smelting, rubber processing and pineapple canning.

The Malayan tin industry expanded rapidly with the extension of peace and order in the interior and in response to growing demands from the new American canning industry.[20] Smelting was Singapore's first modern industry. In 1890 the Straits Trading Company, backed mainly by local European capital, built a tin smelter on Pulau Brani. Ore was brought from the Malay states, later from Bangka and Billiton in the Dutch East Indies, and by the early years of the twentieth century from Siam, Australia, Alaska and South Africa.[21]

In 1877 the first Brazilian rubber seeds were sent from England to the Botanic Garden at Tanglin, which was developed in the 1860s as a public park and experimental station for new crops. Singaporeans were still disillusioned by the agricultural failures of the 1840s and 1850s, and the potential of rubber as an agricultural crop was ignored until the arrival of Henry Ridley as Director of the Botanic Gardens in 1888. By 1897 he devised a method of tapping the tree without damaging the bark and for years 'Mad' Ridley pressed Malayan coffee planters to grow rubber. Rubber only came into its own in the early years of the twentieth century as a substitute crop when Brazilian competition ruined the Malayan coffee plantations.[22] The first rubber grown commercially in Singapore was on the Trafalgar Coconut Plantation at Ponggol, whose owner began growing rubber alongside his coconuts about 1907.

The rise of the new motor-car industry, which created a demand for rubber tyres, soon brought a rubber boom. Malayan rubber exports rose from 104 tons in 1905 to 196,000 tons in 1914, which represented more than half the total world supply, most of it exported through Singapore.

At first rubber from the big European estates was sent to London for sale, but in 1908 British firms in Singapore began to sell rubber locally, despite vociferous objections from London. In 1911 the Singapore chamber of commerce established a Rubber Association which organized sales in Singapore and made her an important international rubber market.

Oil became the third important commodity in Singapore's trade. At the end of the nineteenth century Syme and Company constructed a tank depot on the offshore island of Pulau Bukum, since they were forbidden to store bulk oil in town. A few years later Dutch and British oil interests in the archipelago merged to form the Asiatic Petroleum Company, which later became the Shell Company, and by 1902 Bukum was the oil supply centre for the Far East.

Singapore now had a natural and secure place in the pattern of world trade as the entrepôt for South-East Asian raw materials and western manufactured goods, and she was building up the infrastructure of commercial institutions and expertise to support this economy.

At the beginning of the century most banking business was in the hands of three British banks: the Chartered Bank of India, Australia and China, the Hongkong and Shanghai Banking Corporation, and the Mercantile Bank of India. The first American bank opened an office in Singapore in 1902, the first Chinese bank, the Kwong Yik Bank, in 1903, and the first French bank in 1905.

The currency was stabilized for the first time. Hitherto the dollar had fluctuated, ranging in value from 4 shillings and 6 pence in 1874 to 1 shilling and $8\frac{1}{2}$ pence in 1902. This caused commercial confusion, individual hardship and perennial uncertainty in planning the government's budget. A new Straits dollar was introduced in 1903, the rate of exchange was fixed at 2 shillings and 4 pence in 1906 and remained at that level up to 1967.[23]

Communications were improving. The European telegraph was extended from India to Singapore in 1870, and during the 1880s telegraph communication built up with the Protected States. Singapore's first private telephone service was opened in 1879, and in 1882 it was taken over by the Oriental Telephone and Electric Company, which extended the service to Johor.

These economic changes brought to an end the fears and uncertainties of the precarious and vulnerable position which Singapore held during her first half century. Recessions were only temporary setbacks. Singapore's superb geographical position, Britain's unchallenged naval supremacy and the general growth of world trade guaranteed her increasing prosperity. Singapore merchants ceased to live on their nerves, although increased business brought new strains, or, as the *Straits Times* complained in May 1872, 'everlasting hurry and brain labour'.[24]

By 1867 there were sixty European companies in Singapore, and in the last decades of the century European commercial houses expanded, some as general import and export businesses, others with special interests in rubber, tin or shipping. Many long-established firms acquired a new prosperity, although the oldest, A.L. Johnston & Co., which continued under Read's personal management up to the 1880s, went out of business in 1892. Most of the others were more fortunate, such as Syme & Company founded in 1823, or Boustead & Company and Maclaine, Fraser & Company both formed in 1827, the German Behn Meyer & Company founded in 1840, the Borneo Company, which established itself in

Singapore in 1851, McAlister & Company founded in 1857, or Paterson, Simons & Company, which began trading under that name in 1859 but grew from a firm first formed in 1828.

Most successful of all was the firm of Guthries, today Singapore's oldest surviving company.[25] Founded in 1821 by Alexander Guthrie, a nephew, James Guthrie, took over the management from 1846 to 1876 and subsequently handed over to Thomas Scott, who was a partner for forty-five years. Guthries steadily extended their trading, banking and insurance interests in Singapore, while the retired partners, Alexander and James, looked after the company's interests in London. Guthries first branched into the mainland in 1896, buying coffee estates, later turning to rubber, and they were one of the few firms in a position to profit from the early rubber boom. After the death of James Guthrie in 1900, followed by Thomas Scott two years later, the firm blossomed under the command of John Anderson. The son of a sea captain who had settled in Singapore, Anderson was educated at Raffles Institution and joined Guthries as a boy in 1876. By the early twentieth century he was undisputed leader of the Singapore business community and of the rubber industry. Anderson headed the Opium Commission in 1907, he was knighted in 1912, and he kept control of Guthries until he retired in 1923 at the age of 71.

Many new firms sprang up, such as Adamson & Gilfillan, which was established in 1867, and Straits Trading Company, which was formed to smelt tin ore in 1887. The versatile Fraser and Neave partnership was formed by a banker, John Fraser, and David Neave, who bought up Keasberry's mission press, renaming it Fraser and Neave. In 1883 Fraser and Neave started an Aerated Water Company, and John Fraser became involved in so many different enterprises that by the time he retired from Singapore in 1896 he was called the 'Jolly Old Octopus'. Fraser & Neave became a limited company in 1898 and later opened branches up-country, becoming one of the wealthiest organizations.

Steamship companies also began to flourish, although the Singapore business community was slow to realize the potential of steam. The established companies, such as the P. & O. Company, which was founded in 1837 and extended its services to Singapore in 1845,[26] and the Ben Line, founded in 1825 in the days of sail,[27] stepped up their operations in the Far East. They were joined by a new competitor, the Ocean Steamship Company (the Blue Funnel Line), founded by Alfred and Philip Holt of Liverpool in 1865. Three years later Holts gave the then unwanted Singapore agency to a struggling ship-chandling business, Mansfield & Company, which was headed by the far-seeing Walter Mansfield.[28] Thus began a flourishing partnership, which helped to make Singapore a centre of steamship communications, 'the second doorway of the wide world's trade'.[29] By the 1880s the German Norddeutscher Lloyd Company was strongly entrenched in Singapore, and French, Dutch, Italian and Scandinavian shipping lines established offices there. From the 1860s increasing numbers of Continental merchants and shippers settled in

Singapore; and the Germans in particular were vigorous competitors with the British firms, although British capital was still predominant.

Substantial though the European sector's prosperity might be, it was strikingly obvious to the most casual observer that the greatest individual wealth lay in the hands of the Chinese. 'England is by the uninformed supposed to own the island,' Rudyard Kipling commented on first visiting Singapore.[30] Chinese business developed rapidly.[31] Most early immigrants sent their savings back to China, but by the middle of the century some Chinese merchants began investing their accumulated capital in land and trade in the Straits Settlements. Unlike the Europeans, the Chinese set up small family firms, and proprietors worked alongside their employees. From the beginning many Chinese family businesses in Singapore had close personal links with Malacca, but from the 1860s enterprising Chinese began extending their family and regional connexions outside of the Straits Settlements. Tan Beng Swee opened a branch of Kim Seng & Company in Shanghai, and Tan Kim Ching set up rice mills in Siam and Saigon. These were the forerunners of the big individually-dominated Nanyang commercial empires of the twentieth century, often centred in Singapore and holding sway over interests throughout the East.

In the 1880s European business activities were still largely confined to Singapore and Penang, while enterprise in the peninsular states was a Chinese preserve. In the last decade of the century European firms extended traditional friendly contacts into more formal links with the Chinese in order to break in to the peninsular economy.

The first such joint enterprise was the Straits Steamship Company, registered in Singapore in 1890 and founded by directors of Mansfields, together with three Chinese, Tan Jiak Kim, Tan Keong Saik and Lee Cheng Yam. All three were members of former Malacca Baba families with interests in shipping and long connexions with European companies. Tan Jiak Kim, grandson of Tan Kim Seng, took over Kim Seng & Company in 1884, Tan Keong Saik inherited the family business on the death of his uncle Tan Choon Bock in 1880. Lee Cheng Yam had founded his firm, Chin Joo & Company, as a youth in 1858. The Straits Steamship Company dominated the Malayan coastal trade, and from the 1890s European firms began to branch out into the Malay states and acquire a tightening grip upon the economy. Companies such as Guthries led the rush into rubber in the mid-1890s. European capital flooded into the tin mining and smelting industry. In 1912 the first tin dredge was brought into operation and by the 1930s the tin industry was western dominated.[32]

Singapore's port facilities expanded less rapidly than her trade. During the 1870s the volume of cargo handled and ships berthed in the port increased considerably, but the rough dirt track across the marshes was still the only link between New Harbour and the town. In the 1880s the government levelled the coastal hills to reclaim land from Telok Ayer Bay and form the present day Robinson Road/Anson Road area. The marshes were drained and the former nutmeg plantations which lay between the harbour and the town began to give way to building.

In 1861 the Patent Slip and Dock Company was formed and later became the New Harbour Dock Company, largely controlled by Paterson & Simons. Under the leadership of Guthries and Tan Kim Ching, a rival Tanjong Pagar Dock Company was set up in 1864. Both companies faced several lean years in the trade doldrums of the 1860s when there was insufficient work to warrant even one dock company, but business improved with the opening of the Suez Canal and the revival of world trade. The Tanjong Pagar Dock Company paid its first dividend in 1872. It built the Victoria Dock in 1878 and the Albert Dock in 1879, by which time it employed about 2,500 men.

By the end of the century, with the exception of the P. & O. Company which had its own wharf, the Tanjong Pagar Dock Company had swallowed up all rivals: the Borneo Company's wharf, Jardine's wharf, and finally in 1899 the New Harbour Dock Company.

By 1903 Singapore was the world's seventh largest port in tonnage of shipping, but the facilities offered were grossly inadequate, cramped and congested. Her services were expensive and subject to long delays. The quay, built at different times in sections, had an irregular face line which was difficult for large ships, and the wooden wharves were worm-eaten and dangerous. Her four graving docks could only service small ships, which had to queue for repairs. She lacked modern equipment. There was no railway to service the docks, since railway schemes mooted thirty years earlier had fallen victim to the clash of vested interests between Singapore companies and the government. The result was that in the early years of the twentieth century ox-carts still transported all goods to and from the docks.

Large-scale modernization of Singapore's port facilities was needed to cope with the existing volume of traffic and to counter competition from Hong Kong and potential rivalry from Saigon and Javanese ports. But in its anxiety to maintain dividends, the London board rejected schemes of improvement put forward in 1904 by the local management of the Tanjong Pagar Dock Company, which would have cost the company $12 million. The government was forced to step in. In 1905 the Tanjong Pagar Dock Company was expropriated and transformed into a public-owned Tanjong Pagar Dock Board. During the next few years the port was modernized. All the old wharves were replaced, new roads and godowns were built, modern machinery was installed, the recently reclaimed Telok Ayer Basin was developed, a wet-dock was constructed, and electric power introduced. In 1913 the Board was transformed into the Singapore Harbour Board, and by that time improvements were almost complete. The graving dock, the second largest in the world, was opened later in 1913, and the giant Empire Dock was finished in 1917.

The Singapore Harbour Board was a corporate statutory body, for many years the most important public utility in Singapore, with responsibility for its own public health, public works and fire brigade. Motor lorries replaced the ox-carts to transport goods between the docks and the town. In 1909 the peninsular railway was completed, linking Johor and Prai, and the Singapore railway was extended from the harbour to Kranji, opposite Johor Bahru.

The modernization of the port came just in time to cope with the rapid opening up of the interior and spiralling world demand for rubber and tin. By that time investment in the tin and rubber industries had become a flood, but the economic expansion highlighted political complications. British influence in Malaya had grown in a haphazard fashion, producing an untidy pattern of administration. The Straits Settlements colony itself was a motley collection, with Penang and Malacca limping rather reluctantly in the wake of the more powerful Singapore. In the Malay states Singapore's political influence did not match her economic hold.

Early British Residents were responsible to the Governor of the Straits Settlements but in practice pursued their activities in the Protected States for twenty years with little control from Singapore. The federation of the Protected States in 1896 brought them more firmly into Singapore's orbit, although a proposal to include the Straits Settlements in the Federation was rejected.[33] The Governor of the Straits Settlements also became High Commissioner of the Federation, and the civil services of the Straits Settlements and the former Protected States joined to form a united Malayan Civil Service. In practice the Federation's chief executive, the Resident-General, enjoyed considerable autonomy, and officials were rarely transferred between Singapore and the Malay states until the second decade of the twentieth century.

Federation satisfied neither the Sultans, who saw their powers whittled away, nor the Governor who regarded the Resident-General in Kuala Lumpur as a rival rather than a subordinate. In 1909 the picture was complicated by the extension of British protection to the former Siamese states of Kelantan, Trengganu, Kedah, and Perlis, whose rulers retained more powers than their counterparts in the Federation, and in 1914 the British presence was completed when a British Adviser was posted to Johor. This confused political situation was compounded by commercial strains and competition, since Kuala Lumpur merchants continually resisted Singapore's domination of the Federation's economy.

The Singapore authorities wished to streamline the complicated structure, and from time to time, particularly in periods of economic depression, they produced schemes of simplification.

The first such attempt arose as a result of an international trade slump in 1908, at that time described as 'the most serious financial and commercial depression in (the Colony's) history'.[34] It hit Singapore at a time when the government had acquired big debts in taking over the Tanjong Pagar Dock Company and developing port facilities. In 1909 the Colony's expenditure exceeded revenue, but the Federation's revenue was expanding with the rising demand for tin and the rapid expansion of rubber. Many in Singapore wanted to amalgamate with the Federated Malay

States, on the grounds that Singapore deserved to share in the Federation's prosperity since she provided its defence and port facilities.

The Governor at that time was Sir John Anderson, not to be confused with his namesake and contemporary, the head of Guthries. Anderson, who held office from 1904 to 1911, had previously served in the Colonial Office in London for twenty-five years and had the complete confidence of the British government, but at first he was considered an outsider in Singapore. A lawyer by training, formal and serious, he seemed rather daunting, but he was an energetic and shrewd man, 'an actor and not a talker',[35] and he came to be respected as one of the ablest of Malayan Governors.

Anderson wanted to draw the Malay states and Singapore closer but considered it was too early to unite Malaya. To annex the Federated states would mean breaking faith with the Sultans and alarming the rulers of the northern states and of independent Johor. In 1909 Anderson created a Federal Council and the following year changed the Resident-General's title to Chief Secretary as a first step to reducing his status. Federation businessmen opposed the measure as the 'thin end of the wedge by which the Colony will gradually get control of the revenues of these states'. Bowing to their protests, Anderson agreed to leave financial control in the hands of the Federal Council, and the Chief Secretary retained powers as great as the former Resident-General. In this way Anderson's intentions were defeated and his reforms made little difference.

Trade revived in 1911 and the years immediately leading up to World War I were a time of unprecedented prosperity in Singapore. Commercial contentment and the outbreak of the war stilled discussions about political reorganization and produced a decade of constitutional calm.

Singapore's rapidly expanding economy attracted ever-increasing numbers of immigrants in the last quarter of the nineteenth century. The population increased by over 40 per cent in the decade 1871–81, and in 1911 Singapore had more than 185,000 inhabitants. By the end of the nineteenth century she was the most cosmopolitan city in Asia: nearly three-quarters of the population were Chinese, but there were sizeable minorities of peninsular Malays, Sumatrans, Javanese, Bugis, Boyanese, Indians, Ceylonese, Arabs, Jews, Eurasians and Europeans. The population was still predominantly male, and in 1911 men out-numbered women by eight to one.

The largest number of immigrants were Chinese, of whom 50,000 landed in 1880, 200,000 in 1900 and 250,000 in 1912. Most passed through to the Malay states or the Dutch Indies, but Singapore's Chinese community rose from 55,000 in 1871 to 87,000 in 1881 and nearly doubled in the next twenty years to 164,000.

The Malay population, coming from Sumatra and the peninsular states, also increased dramatically from less than 12,000 in 1860 to more than 22,000 in 1881, while the combined Javanese, Boyanese and Bugis population more than doubled in the same period, rising from little over 4,000 to nearly 11,000.

The Indian community was the only one to decline, falling from nearly 13,000 in 1860, when Indians comprised the second largest group, to little over 12,000 twenty years later.

The European population increased but still numbered fewer than 3,000 in 1881. There were about 1,000 Arabs in the later years of the century and some 4,000 Jews.

The Eurasian population expanded steadily and settled mainly in the Katong area. They were a very mixed community, comprising people of Portuguese or Dutch extraction from Malacca and growing numbers of Anglo-Indians and Anglo-Chinese. Most of them spoke English as their mother tongue and found employment as clerks and subordinates in commercial or government offices.

A big influx of Middle Eastern Jews began in the 1870s, and by the turn of the century the Singapore Jewish community formed a prosperous and prominent group. The best known Jewish resident was Manasseh Meyer, who was born in India in 1846 and finished his education at St. Joseph's in Singapore. After some years in the family business in Calcutta and Rangoon, in 1873 he came back to found a branch in Singapore. This prospered greatly as the biggest import and export firm in the Indian trade. In the 1880s Manasseh Meyer bought land on a big scale, and in 1905 at his own expense he built the impressive synagogue which is still in use today. Manasseh Meyer served as a municipal councillor from 1893 to 1900 and was knighted in 1906.

Most Indian labourers sought work in the Malay states rather than in Singapore. Until 1903 Penang was the sole port of entry for assisted Indian immigrants into Malaya, and even after that Singapore took third place to Penang and Port Swettenham for Indian immigration. But in the last years of the nineteenth century an increasing number of Indian commercial immigrants came to Singapore as traders, shop assistants and clerks. Some of these white-collared workers settled permanently in Singapore, but most Indians planned to return home and the Indian community was perhaps even more transitory than the Chinese.

Indians tended to concentrate in five districts. The oldest, dating from the 1820s, was the west fringe of the business area around Chulia and Market Streets, where south Indian chettiars, money changers, small shopkeepers, boatmen, and quayside workers congregated. The second group, living in the High Street area, were mainly Sindhi, Gujarati and Sikh cloth merchants. Other Gujarati and Muslim Indian textile and jewellery merchants congregated in the Arab Street neighbourhood and a group of Tamil shopkeepers on the Serangoon Road, while Tamil, Telugu, and Malayali labourers lived near the docks and railways.

Although Indian immigrants grouped together, they did not develop any strong local organizations or leadership. There was a rift between north and south Indians. Most Tamils were labourers and small shopkeepers, whereas the north Indians were usually more affluent. Muslims, Sikhs and Hindus all had their own mosques and temples, while the small Indian Christian group belonged to the poorer section of the south Indian community.

In addition to their role as shopkeepers and clerks, Indians figured prominently in transport. Until the 1860s they held a virtual monopoly as river boatmen, dock coolies and ox-cart drivers, and although others began to encroach on these activities in the later years of the century, Indians still predominated in transport, harbour and communications up to the Second World War.

In the last quarter of the nineteenth century Singapore was the economic and cultural centre of the Malayo-Muslim world in South-East Asia, a focus for Indonesian immigration and for the peninsular and archipelago trade. She was a publication centre for Muslim religious writings, and Malay was one of the leading languages of the Islamic world.

Singapore became a staging post for Indonesian as well as Chinese labourers in the last decades of the century. Javanese, recruited by agents or *orang tebunan*, pledged their labour against recovery of passage money in the same way as the Chinese. Between 1886 and 1889, 21,000 Javanese labourers signed contracts with the Chinese Protectorate in Singapore,[36] and with the expansion of rubber planting from the last years of the century the numbers of immigrant Javanese agricultural labourers swelled.

With the advent of steamers, Singapore also became the centre for the Mecca pilgrim trade. By the end of the century most of the 7,000 Indonesians who made the pilgrimage each year left from Singapore, where shipping was geared to the pilgrim trade and there were fewer restrictions on travel than in the Dutch Indies. Many would-be pilgrims spent months, sometimes years, in Singapore accumulating money for their journey. Some never saved sufficient to make the journey and stayed in Singapore permanently. Others stopped off to work there on their return in order to pay off debts incurred on the pilgrimage.

By 1901 the Malayo-Muslim population stood at more than 36,000, comprising some 23,000 peninsular Malays, over 12,000 from Riau, Sumatra, Java, Bawean, Celebes and other islands, about 1,000 Arabs and 600 Jawi-Peranakan.

The Arabs and Jawi-Peranakan, most Indonesian immigrants and many Malays lived within the town limits, congregating in the areas set aside for their communities in Raffles's day: Kampong Glam and its environs, Telok Blangah, Kampong Malacca and Kampong Bencoolen.

Malay and Indonesian immigrants assimilated quietly and unobtrusively. They quickly adopted the Sumatran Malay *lingua franca,* adhered to the same religion and customs, and married freely with the established Malay population. Of all the immigrant peoples, Indonesians kept the fewest links with their original homeland. Only a minority returned and few sent family remittances.

Some Indonesian and Malay immigrants became prosperous. The Buginese family, of which Haji Embok Suloh was in later years the most outstanding figure, owned much property in Singapore, had pepper and gambier plantations in Borneo and Sumatra and conducted trade in their own ships. The Sumatran Menangkabaus were particularly successful as shopkeepers. Other immigrants became mosque officials, religious teachers and petty traders. But the bulk of Malays, whether local-born, peninsular or Indonesian immigrants, drifted into humble employment as watchmen, drivers, gardeners, domestic servants or policemen.

By the end of the nineteenth century steeply-rising land values drove new Malay immigrants to seek cheaper land further out from the city. Urban Malays found themselves submerged in a European-ruled Chinese city and their commercial life wilted in face of Chinese competition. There was little opportunity for them to rise in society. Most were illiterate or educated only in the Malay vernacular schools which were so elementary that up to 1894 they had not produced one clerk, interpreter or translator for government service.[37] Religion, language and ethnic affinity took on a new meaning in binding the Malay community together in face of western and Chinese pressures and the increasing complexity of urban life.

In the late nineteenth century Singapore was the centre of considerable political intrigue, with many peninsular chiefs coming to deal with officials, lawyers and businessmen. It also provided a refuge for chiefs who were dislodged by British intervention in the Malay states. Ex-Sultan Abdullah of Perak lived in Singapore from the time of his return from exile in the Seychelles in 1894 until his death in 1922. The Mantri of Larut, the Dato' Bandar of Sungei Ujong, Rajah Mahdi and Rajah Mahmud of Selangor all retreated to live in retirement in Singapore. The descendants of Sultan Ali of Singapore still lived in Kampong Glam, and the new Sultans of Johor, Abu Bakar and his son Ibrahim, figured largely in Singapore social life. Abu Bakar gave up his Telok Blangah house and built a new European-style residence at Tyersall in fashionable Tanglin, where he associated mainly with Europeans and wealthy Chinese, 'a man much petted and decorated by the British government for unswerving fidelity to British interests'.[38]

These colourful individuals were not the dominating influence in the Malayo-Muslim world of Singapore at the turn of the century. Leadership passed to new classes, notably to the largely English-educated Jawi-Peranakan, who were most au fait with the colonial administration, and to wealthy Arabs who could compete with Chinese and Europeans in the economy.

For centuries Arabs had played a significant part in the archipelago as traders, teachers and missionaries, but it was not until the last quarter of the century that their numbers increased and they came to fill the vacuum in Muslim leadership in Singapore.

Some Arab families, such as the Aljunieds, had been established in South-East Asia long before the founding of Singapore, and since female

emigration from the Hadramaut was forbidden. Arab immigrants intermarried with local Muslim women. However mixed their blood, the
Singapore Arabs kept close contacts with Arabia, often sending their
sons to school there, observing Muslim custom strictly, seeking sons-in-
law of pure Arab blood, using the Arabic language, wearing Arab dress
and adopting Arab titles, such as Sayyid or Shaykh. At the turn of the
century, when the Singapore Arabs reached the height of their influence
among the Malayo-Muslim community, few of them knew any English.
This was true even of the wealthy philanthropist, Syed Shaik Alkaff,
who in 1909 built the Arcade, which still survives and was then the most
outstanding commercial building in Singapore.

The Arab community was replenished in the late nineteenth century
with fresh immigrants from the Hadramaut, who were often cultivated
men, devout and learned. Prominent Arabs were acknowledged in the
last years of the century as respected leaders. The main families were
very wealthy, controlling the Mecca pilgrim traffic and much of the
inter-archipelago sailing-ship trade. Many owned tea, pepper and
gambier estates in nearby regions of the archipelago and in the later
years of the century acquired large landed properties in Singapore,
particularly in the Geylang and Serangoon areas. The three wealthiest
families were the Alkaffs, the Alsagoffs, and the Aljunieds, who were all
active in charity work, endowing hospitals and schools, building mosques
and financing religious feasts and festivals.

At the turn of the century the ability of the small Jawi-Peranakan
community to speak Malay and English gave them an entrée into Singapore's commercial world. Some flourished as shopkeepers, many were
employed as clerks, interpreters, school teachers, and a few, following
Keasberry's tradition, took to journalism and printing. The *Jawi Peranakan,* which was the first Malay-language newspaper in Malaya or Indonesia, was published in 1876[39] and from that time until World War I
Singapore was the centre for Malay journalism. In the first twenty years
of the twentieth century she became the focal point of reformist Muslim
thought and literature in South-East Asia. The Middle East Pan-Islamic
reform movement, with its accent on modernism, appealed to Singapore's
urban commercial Muslim community, and Singapore reformers challenged the traditional Islam practised by the aristocratic élite and the
conservative *ulama* of the Malay states.

Arabs and Jawi-Peranakan began to adopt the European and Chinese
practice of forming clubs and associations, notably the Persekutuan
Islam Singapura, or Muslim Association of Singapore, which was founded
about 1900 and is still in existence. Most of these clubs were cultural,
largely concerned with education, language and Malay custom. They
were patronized by the small middle class and the well-to-do Arabs,
Jawi-Peranakan and educated Malays, who tended to look down upon
the sports clubs favoured by the uneducated mass of Malays and Indonesians as a symbol of Malay backwardness.

The Chinese population expanded rapidly in this period. By the outbreak of World War I they constituted a little over three-quarters of Singapore's population and have maintained that proportion ever since. The majority at that period were China-born, and at the 1881 census the Straits-born took fourth place after the immigrant Hokkien, Teochew and Cantonese communities. But the handful of Baba Chinese leaders commanded disproportionate influence through their contacts with the European official and commercial class.

In the 1860s a new generation of Singapore-born leaders emerged. Most were Hokkiens, such as Tan Tock Seng's son, Tan Kim Ching (1829-92); Cheang Hong Lim (1825-93), shipowner, opium and spirit tax farmer, and property magnate; Tan Kim Seng's son, Tan Beng Swee (1828-84), and Beng Swee's own son. Tan Jiak Kim (1857-1917); Malacca-born Gan Eng Seng (1844-1899), compradore, labour contractor and landed proprietor; Tan Choon Bock (1824-1880) and his nephew, Tan Keong Saik, importers and shipowners. Traditionally to the fore in trade and shipping, the Hokkiens strengthened their hold in banking, industry and sugar production in the late nineteenth century, and they became the largest and dominating element in the Chinese chamber of commerce, which was founded in 1906.

The Teochews remained the second most influential community, notably Perak-born Tan Seng Poh (1830-79), opium and spirit tax farmer and gunpowder magazine proprietor, and Seah Eu Chin's son, Seah Liang Seah (1850-1925). Already dominant in gambier and pepper production, the Teochews led the way in promoting new forms of export agriculture, in rubber production and pineapple canning, saw milling, rice milling and fish distribution.

The majority of Cantonese in Singapore were artisans and labourers, but the prosperous minority tended to make their money in tin. The Hakkas were a smaller and poorer community, and were overtaken in numbers in the early twentieth century by the Hainanese, or Hailams, who were at the bottom of the social and economic scale. Most Hainanese were sailors, domestic servants, or unskilled labourers, and they formed a particularly unsettled group because up to 1918 Hainanese women were forbidden to emigrate and Hainanese rarely married outside of their own community.

Tan Kim Ching, Tan Beng Swee, Tan Jiak Kim, Cheang Hong Lim and Seah Liang Seah all inherited considerable fortunes, but Gan Eng Seng rose from poverty on his own merit, starting as a clerk in Guthries' warehouse.

The colonial government continued to seek the co-operation of the Straits Chinese leaders by appointing them to positions of authority. Chinese frequently became justices of the peace. After 1869 there was always a Chinese representative on the legislative council, and the first Chinese municipal commissioner, Tan Seng Poh, was appointed in 1870. To be effective in public life required an adequate command of English. Tan Beng Swee refused a seat on the legislative council in 1882 because of his indifferent knowledge of the language, but his English-educated son, Tan Jiak Kim, was appointed to the legislative council in 1889 and in 1912 was awarded a C.M.G.

The Chinese Advisory Board gave proportional representation to the various Chinese dialect groups. As its name implied, it had the right to advise and provided an airing ground for grievances but had no executive authority.

Clementi Smith toyed with the idea of making membership of the Board elective, but the small group of influential Straits Chinese who were near to the British authorities consistently resisted the principle of election, not only for the Chinese Advisory Board, but also for the legislative council and the municipal commission. Their influence derived not from authority within the Chinese community but rather from their close relationship with the colonial power, and men like Tan Jiak Kim, who was a nominated legislative councillor from 1889 to 1892 and again from 1902 to 1915, displayed a co-operation with the colonial authorities amounting almost to servility.

As in former days, the Singapore Chinese leaders aimed to increase their prestige through charitable works. They constructed hospitals, roads, temples, gardens, markets, and above all schools. They wielded great influence through the numerous regional associations which sprang up in the third quarter of the nineteenth century, notably the Hokkien Huay Association, formed in 1860; the Cantonese Ku Seng Wui Kun Association, founded in 1873; and the Teochew Ngee Ann Kongsi. These were economic and benevolent social associations, which dealt with such matters as cemeteries, hospitals, schools, religious festivals and social insurance.

Wealth remained the sole key to social standing among the Singapore Chinese until the emergence of a university-trained professional class at the end of the century. The first of this new breed, Lim Boon Keng (1869–1957), a medical doctor, and Song Ong Siang (1871–1941), a lawyer, were both Singapore-born Hokkiens. They were the recipients of Queen's scholarships, established by Clementi Smith in 1889 to enable outstanding students to proceed to British universities.

Over the years the proportion of Chinese born in the Straits increased. In 1901 they constituted only 10 per cent of the total population, but ten years later 25 per cent of Singapore's Chinese were Straits-born.[40] This resulted largely from the steady increase in the number of Chinese women immigrants from the 1880s.

By the turn of the century there was a warm and genuine feeling of mutual respect and co-operation between the Baba leaders and the British colonial authorities. It rested upon confidence in the security and seemingly permanent strength of the British Empire, the rising prosperity of Singapore and the spread of western education and professional activities among the Straits Chinese. In 1900 Tan Jiak Kim, Seah Liang Seah, Lim Boon Keng and Song Ong Siang formed the Straits Chinese British Association, designed to promote interest in the British Empire and loyalty to the Queen, to advance the welfare of Chinese British subjects in the colony and to encourage higher education. Starting with 800 members, the Association included most Chinese professional leaders, legislative and municipal councillors up to the Second World War.

The Straits Chinese began to value British citizenship not merely for the protection it offered in visiting China or travelling abroad but for its association with the British Empire. There were frequent displays of loyalty. Queen Victoria's golden jubilee was celebrated in 1887 with much warmth, and the Baba community presented a statue of the queen, which was unveiled in the dining room of Government House.

British royal visitors, such as the Duke of Clarence who came in 1882, the Duke and Duchess of York in 1901, and the Duke of Connaught in 1905, were welcomed with enthusiasm in their drives round Chinatown, which was always a part of every visiting dignitary's itinerary. In 1901, as a result of an appeal by Song Ong Siang and Tan Jiak Kim, a Chinese company was created to serve alongside Europeans in the Volunteer Corps. Song Ong Siang and Lim Boon Keng went as members of the Volunteers to Edward VII's coronation, and Tan Jiak Kim represented the colony at the coronation of George V.

British victories, such as the capture of Pretoria in 1900 and the end of the Boer War, were celebrated by mammoth Chinese processions. British crises, such as the First World War, roused the generosity of the Straits Chinese, who contributed large sums of money to the British war effort.[41]

Increasing numbers of Straits Chinese adopted western customs, took to European sports and pastimes and became Christians. In 1885 a Straits Chinese Recreation Club was founded, which offered facilities for tennis and billiards, and later on for cricket and hockey, and in 1911 the Straits Chinese Football Association was formed. Christianity became a fashionable religion, and missionaries, who had previously found it hard to make headway among the Chinese community, became very successful in the later years of the century, particularly in converting Baba women. The Presbyterians, who established themselves in Singapore in 1856, and the Methodists, who set up their mission in 1885, were more successful than the Anglicans or Roman Catholics, since they had more women missionaries.[42]

Europeans came to think of the Straits Chinese as a prosperous, English-educated, westernized community, but in reality these were the characteristics only of the upper crust. The vast majority of the Straits Chinese were no better educated, affluent or oriented towards Britain than their immigrant China-born contemporaries.

The last years of the nineteenth century and first decade of the twentieth century were a time of confused loyalties among the Singapore Chinese, since they coincided with the upheaval of reform, reaction and revolution in China. The Baba Chinese respected British power upon which their own prosperity was based, and sought westernized education in Singapore

4. Dr. Lim Boon Keng
(By permission of the National Archives, Singapore)

5. Dr. and Mrs. Song Ong Siang
(By permission of Mr. Eric Jennings)

English-medium schools or sent their sons to universities in Britain as the key to a successful career in business or the professions. Yet those who had been most thoroughly educated in the western tradition were most concerned to preserve the roots of their Chinese culture and to see China modernize. The founders of the Straits British Chinese Association were the keenest supporters in Singapore of China's Hundred Days' Reform Movement.

Lim Boon Keng, who studied medicine in Edinburgh, and Song Ong Siang, who read law in London, both returned to Singapore in 1893. They formed the spearhead of the new group of Chinese professional men who came to challenge the apathy towards education which prevailed among the Singapore Chinese and to attempt to extend mainland reforms to Chinese schools in Singapore.

Up to that time even the most westernized Singapore Chinese had clung to traditional Chinese ways. Whampoa, probably the first to send his son to school in England, was horrified when the boy returned in 1847, shorn of his pigtail and professing to be a Presbyterian, and he sent him back to Canton to mend his ways. An English visitor to Singapore, meeting the legislative councillor Seah Liang Seah in 1889, was impressed by the fact that although he spoke perfect English, knew Europe well and had never visited China, yet in habits and dress he was thoroughly Chinese.[43] As the century progressed, despite the increasing westernization of the Straits Chinese and their willing co-operation with the British colonial authorities, they also strengthened their ties with their Chinese background. The relaxation of China's emigration laws, combined with the protection of British citizenship and the co-operation by treaty between Britain and China, gave greater legal security to successful Singapore Chinese in visiting China. The journey by steamship was quicker, safer and more comfortable than by the sailing junks of the past. Even long-established Singapore Chinese revived family links, visited China frequently, sent their sons to school in China and sometimes retired there in old age. While the early Chinese settlers had often married local women, by the second half of the nineteenth century Baba Chinese preferred their daughters to marry pure-blooded immigrants and often sent their sons to seek wives in China. Those Chinese who were most exposed to contact with the European official and commercial community in Singapore put an increasing value on Chinese culture and customs. At the same time the Straits Chinese spoke Malay, or at least a Baba Malay patois. Lim Boon Keng and Tan Jiak Kim both spoke Malay at the inaugural meeting of the Straits Chinese British Association in 1900, and Song Ong Siang produced the first romanized Malay newspaper, the *Bintang Timor*, for the benefit of the Straits Chinese.

This counter pull of three different cultural loyalties threatened a 'crisis of identity' among the rising younger generation of Singapore Chinese in the last years of the century, which was typified by Lim Boon Keng. A third-generation Baba born in Singapore in 1869, Lim Boon Keng was educated at Raffles Institution, became the first Chinese

Queen's scholar, a legislative councillor from 1895 to 1902, founder member of the Straits Chinese British Association, member of the Chinese Advisory Board, and the first to enrol in Britain's support in the Chinese Volunteer Company in 1901. Lim had a triple loyalty to Britain, China and Singapore and set out to resolve the problem of confused cultural identity by modernizing Chinese traditions along western lines, discarding what he considered to be old-fashioned superstitions and practices but reviving and strengthening Confucian morality and confidence in Chinese culture. In 1897 he founded the Philomathic Society and that same year, with Song Ong Siang, published the first issue of the *Straits Chinese Magazine.* Lim Boon Keng took up in Singapore the movement begun in China in 1898 to discard the pigtail and helped launch the first serious campaign against opium smoking.

Lim Boon Keng's main concern was education. He deplored the superficial schooling of most Straits Chinese and preached the need for a sounder foundation. Straits Chinese sent their boys to English-medium schools, neglecting their Chinese education, and Chinese classes run in English-medium schools were so poorly attended that the last to survive, which was held in Raffles Institution, closed down in 1894.

There were more than fifty Chinese 'schools' in Singapore,[44] mostly small private classes but a few endowed by wealthy Chinese merchants, such as the Chiu Eng Si, or Chinese Free School, opened by Tan Kim Seng in 1854, and the Cheang Wan Seng School founded by Cheang Hong Lim in 1875. The Chinese schools taught in dialect, most of them in Hokkien and along traditional Confucian lines, but the standard was so poor that in 1889 the editor of the *Lat Pau* suggested there was no point in keeping them open. They were designed to satisfy the philanthropic spirit of the wealthy merchants rather than to provide an up-to-date education.

Well-to-do Chinese merchants preferred to send their sons to China or to the local English-medium schools, and it was growing concern that Chinese children in Singapore were losing their cultural background which in 1893 led Gan Eng Seng to open an Anglo-Chinese Free School, later renamed the Gan Eng Seng Free School. Its aim was to provide bi-lingual education, but it eventually became an English-medium school.

Lim Boon Keng condemned 'the absolute staleness of our education', the narrow concentration upon English as a means to secure a job, breeding 'neither patriotism nor piety, nor virtue nor wisdom'. He deplored the divorce of the Singapore Chinese from their background, since 'a people, like a tree severed from its roots, must wither away and degenerate'. He urged Singapore Chinese to educate their children first in the Chinese tradition, which was designed 'to ennoble man's mind and purify his character'. But he wanted a more modern scientific curriculum, not merely the classics. The Baba reformers favoured Mandarin as a medium of instruction. Lim Boon Keng began teaching Mandarin to students in 1899, and classes were subsequently started at the Chinese consulate and the Straits Chinese Recreation Club.

The Baba reform group also opened educational opportunities to Straits Chinese women, who by tradition were secluded and guarded from the age of puberty, prepared only for serving their husband and mother-in-law in a marriage arranged by their parents. Most were illiterate or could at best read romanized Malay. They knew no English or Chinese, spoke Baba Malay, and took no part in activities outside their own household. As the Director of Public Instruction declared in 1906, 'There is no more absolutely ignorant, prejudiced and superstitious class of people in the world than the Straits-born Chinese woman.'[45]

Lim Boon Keng started the first English-medium school for Chinese girls in 1899, with a curriculum which included Malay, music, sewing, cookery and later Chinese. The first Chinese-medium girls' school, the Chung Hua Girls' School, was opened in 1911. Straits Chinese women began to emerge from the isolation to which they had hitherto been condemned, and in 1913 a Chinese girl student enrolled in the Medical School.

In the early years of the twentieth century the Manchu government began belatedly to encourage education among the overseas Chinese in order to win their loyalty. In 1907 a special school for overseas Chinese was opened in Nanking, which attracted many Singapore students. In addition the Manchu government sent officials to raise money to found Chinese schools in the Nanyang, and the Chinese consul-general helped to collect these funds and supervised education.

The reform movement in China itself had a strong impact upon Singapore youths sent to school in China, notably upon Khoo Seok Wan, son of a wealthy Singapore businessman. Khoo returned to Singapore in 1895 disgusted with the old-fashioned imperial Chinese government. With Lim Boon Keng he encouraged the setting up of modern-type Chinese-medium schools in Singapore in the early years of the twentieth century.

As the main spokesman of the Baba reform group, Lim Boon Keng, whose command of English was better than his predecessors on the legislative council, argued more outspokenly but with little success against certain government measures. The Baba reformers encountered resistance not only from the colonial authorities but also from Christian missionaries and from the more conservative elements in their own community. While they agreed with Christian missionaries in attacking practices such as opium smoking or foot-binding in women, the reformers' concern to strengthen Confucian morality brought them to clash with some Christian teaching in the mission schools.

Conventional Babas, such as Tan Jiak Kim, frowned upon the movement to discard the pigtail, and while modern-minded Singapore Chinese began cutting off their queues from the early years of the century, the practice was not generally adopted in Singapore until after the 1911 revolution. The campaign against opium smoking received little support either from the government or initially from the Chinese chamber of commerce, some of whose leading members had a vested interest in the opium tax farm.

Despite these difficulties, the Baba reformers did succeed in gradually changing the attitudes of their community. Pigtails became a rarity after the second decade of the century, opium smoking came to be regarded as a disreputable habit, the status of Chinese women and the standard of Chinese education improved.

The character of the China-born and the Chinese-educated changed even more markedly than the Baba Chinese in this period. Chinese immigrants arrived in large numbers in the early years of the century, their numbers fluctuating according to the state of prosperity in Malaya and harvest conditions in China. In 1907, 227,000 Chinese immigrants landed in Singapore, in 1909 only 152,000, but a record figure of 270,000 arrived in 1911, which was a year of flood and famine in southern China. These immigrants, and the Chinese-educated in Singapore, were more interested in the changing scene in their homeland than in their new surroundings.

Before the Chinese imperial government legalized emigration, Peking did not recognize the overseas Chinese or seek to establish contact with them. Her attitude changed in the 1870s, when she decided to set up consulates in the Nanyang, not to protect the overseas Chinese but to harness their loyalty to China by promoting interest in Chinese culture and education and by seeking their financial support. The first Chinese consulate was established in Singapore in 1877, with Whampoa as consul, and the British authorities welcomed this appointment of a trusted Singapore Chinese.[46]

After Whampoa's death in 1880, Tso Ping-lung (Tzu-hsing), an able young career diplomat with experience in Europe, was appointed Chinese consul and held the post for ten years. Tso was active in extending his influence with the Chinese community and strengthening their cultural links with China, but the consulate's relationship with the Straits authorities remained amicable. Tso co-operated with the Straits authorities in supplying information on secret societies and promoting the protection of women and girls. The consul was said to be behind the launching in 1881 of the *Lat Pau,* Singapore's first Chinese newspaper. He started the Hui-hsien Cultural Club for the Chinese speaking and in 1882 founded the Celestial Reasoning Society, which held debates in English and attracted many Straits Chinese members. He also encouraged wealthy Chinese to found Chinese-medium schools and in 1884 started a medical dispensary for the poor.

A major function of the Singapore consulate was to raise money from the overseas Chinese in Malaya and the Dutch Indies, and prominent Babas, such as Tan Beng Swee, frequently served on fund-raising committees. The Straits authorities took no exception if the funds were for charitable purposes, such as the relief of flood and famine victims in China. They were less happy about some of the consulate's other activities, notably when it published an appeal from Peking to the Nanyang Chinese during the Sino-French conflict in 1884 to poison all Frenchmen and scuttle French ships.

In the main the consulate's activities were neither political nor anti-British but they changed the attitude of the Singapore Chinese towards Peking. In 1889 the Singapore Chinese officially celebrated the accession and marriage of Emperor Kuang-hsu and the following year welcomed the Chinese navy on a visit to Singapore. These were the first public expressions of loyalty to the Manchus, towards whom the Singapore Chinese had traditionally been hostile.

In the last decade of the century the Manchu empire adopted a radically different stance towards the overseas Chinese, demanding their loyalty and trying to secure their wealth and talents to serve China. Peking started a process, which was continued by Chinese royalist reformers, revolutionaries and the Kuomintang for more than half a century. In Malaya it was to cause strains within the Chinese community, to create communal distrust and to embitter the relationship between the government and the Chinese.

In 1891 the Chinese consulate's status was raised to a consulate-general, and two years later the prohibition on emigration from China, which had been a dead letter in practice since 1860, was formally repealed. Peking actively encouraged emigration to ease the pressure of over-population and to raise financial help from overseas Chinese for the mother country.

The first consul-general, an energetic Hakka named Huang Tsun-hsien, who had served for fourteen years as a diplomat in Tokyo, Washington and London, made Singapore the major centre for collecting funds from the Nanyang. The Straits authorities became alarmed about the extent of the consulate's influence. They resented Huang's campaign to extend fund-raising on a large scale into the Protected Malay States, and the British Foreign Office was contemplating means of having him removed, when Huang was recalled to China in 1894.

Huang brought the consulate-general to the peak of its influence and prestige, but its position weakened as a result of China's shock defeat by Japan and the first stirrings of national discontent in China. The dismay of the Singapore Chinese was heightened by the fact that in March 1894 they had feted the imperial navy which surrendered to the Japanese eleven months later.

The humiliating peace dictated by Japan in 1895 was followed by the scramble for concessions by the western powers and threats to the very existence of China. During the last years of the nineteenth century the Singapore consulate put aside cultural activities and gave priority to raising money for investment in railways and other enterprises in China which would keep foreign capital out. One method was by the sale of imperial titles and honours. A price list for such honours was published in 1889 and titles were sold in large numbers to Singapore Chinese up to the end of the Manchu dynasty.[47]

The new consul-general, Chang Chen-hsun (sometimes known as

Thio Tiauw Siat), was not a professional diplomat but a wealthy Nanyang Chinese businessman. Born into a poor Hakka family, Chang emigrated from China to Batavia at the age of seventeen. He moved to Penang in 1876, acquired control of the excise tax farms in Penang and Singapore, and through his trading and shipping interests provided a link between the overseas Chinese of Malaya and the Dutch Indies. Chang set out to extract the maximum from the Nanyang Chinese. He sold Chinese titles and honours on such a scale that the Straits authorities persuaded London to offer British honours in competition. In 1898 Chang returned to China, where he became a prominent industrialist, but he continued his interest in the Straits and was one of the leaders behind the formation of the Singapore Chinese commercial association a few years later.

Peking sought talent as well as money from the overseas Chinese and wooed qualified men to return home to serve China in her 'hour of need'. A Malacca-born lawyer, Ng Ah Choy, became Chinese minister to Washington in 1896, and Penang-born Dr. Wu Lien-teh, the 'plague fighter', went as a doctor to China in 1907.[48]

While the consulate-general concentrated on economic and financial projects, its cultural activities were taken over by a group of Chinese, who had studied abroad, either in China or in Britain. Most notable were Khoo Seok Wan, Song Ong Siang, Lim Boon Keng, and Lim's father-in-law, Huang Nai-seng, a wealthy newspaper editor.

The Hundred Days' Reform Movement launched in China in 1898, with its emphasis on educational modernization, met with enthusiastic response from the interested minority of reformers in Singapore. After the Empress-Dowager crushed the short-lived movement in China, Singapore became a fertile field for exiled royalist reformers and later for more violent revolutionaries who wished to destroy the Chinese empire. Khoo Seok Wan started a progressive newspaper, the *T'ien Nan Shin Pao,* in 1898 in support of the Chinese reform movement, and in 1900, at his own expense, Khoo invited K'ang Yu-wei, one of the exiled reform leaders, to come to Singapore. K'ang roused considerable support both among the well-educated China-born or China-educated and among English-educated Babas.

The new Chinese consul-general, Lo Tsung-yao, asked the Governor, Sir Frank Swettenham, to banish K'ang Yu-wei. Swettenham refused, although he would have been delighted to see K'ang leave and was worried by rumours that the Empress-Dowager was sending assassins to kill the former Chinese leader.[49]

The revolutionary Dr. Sun Yat-sen came to Singapore in 1900 to try to make a bargain with K'ang Yu-wei, but the latter refused to have anything to do with him. The reform and revolutionary movements took different paths, and Singapore Chinese were forced to take sides, as the Manchu government, royalist reformers and revolutionaries competed for their support and money. As part of its policy, Peking promoted the setting up of commercial organizations among the overseas Chinese, and in 1906 the consul-general and Shih Chu Ching, a Ch'ing official, founded the Singapore Chinese commercial association, which was renamed the Singapore Chinese chamber of commerce in 1917. In 1909 Peking asserted the principle of *jus sanguinis,* claiming as Chinese nationals all people of Chinese blood through the male line, regardless of where they were born or how long their ancestors had lived outside of China.

K'ang Yu-wei founded the Protect Emperor Party in Singapore early in 1900 but he moved to Penang shortly afterwards, by which time Khoo Seok Wan and other supporters had become disillusioned with the former Chinese minister and the political side of the reform movement flagged. In 1907 some wealthy Singapore Cantonese brought an able editor, Hsu Ch'ing, from China to edit the reformist *Union Times* (the *Nanyang Chung Hwei Pao*), but the most permanent influence of the reform movement was in education.

Singapore professional and businessmen favoured reform rather than revolution, since the revolutionaries' sole interest in the Nanyang was to raise money to stage uprisings in China. Rich Singapore *towkays* contributed handsomely to support local educational institutions but were wary about financing revolutionary movements. While not wishing to alienate the potential future rulers of China, Singapore businessmen needed persuading of the likelihood of success before they parted with their money.

Sun Yat-sen visited Singapore eight times in the first decade of the century but only came to appreciate her potential as a support centre for the revolutionary cause in 1906.[50] One of his early followers, Yiu Lieh (or Yiu Lit), who came to Singapore in 1901, started workers' clubs, set up a clinic in Chinatown and roused a following among the poor. These included secret-society members, who saw in the political revolutionary movement a chance to restore their *hoeys* to a pseudo-respectable footing. Yiu also won the support of a few wealthy business-men, including Chen Tsu-nan, Teo Eng Hock and his nephew, Lim Nee Soon, who, in 1904, contributed $50,000 to found the first revolutionary Nanyang Chinese newspaper in Singapore, the *T'oo Nan Daily News.*

At that time Sun Yat-sen was concentrating his political activities in Japan where he founded the Tung-ming Hui or Chinese Revolutionary League, fore-runner of the Kuomintang, in 1905. Too impatient and impetuous to devote himself to the careful building up of an organizational framework among the overseas Chinese, Sun Yat-sen was impressed by Yiu Lieh's efforts when he visited Singapore once more in 1906.[51] He decided to found a Singapore branch of the Tung-ming Hui, which began with fifteen members and became the base for his movement in the Nanyang. Sun Yat-sen's revolutionaries worked through the new modern Chinese schools and other ostensibly innocent institutions, such as Chinese Young Men's Christian Associations or literary societies. The first was the YMCA of the Chinese Presbyterian Church, which stocked revolutionary literature and held lectures for young people, many of whom joined the Tung-ming League.

Singapore was the planning centre for several Chinese risings in 1907 and 1908 but the failure of these risings, which coincided with the commercial depression in 1907–8, hit the Tung-ming League in Singapore very hard. Ex-rebels, who flooded into Singapore after the risings failed, clashed with the reformists, became involved in crime and discredited the revolutionary movement. The slump ruined Chen Tsu-nan and Teo Eng Hock. Lim Nee Soon survived to make a fortune in rubber but was reluctant to invest further in revolution. The *T'oo Nan Daily News*, with a circulation of only thirty, was forced to close, and its equipment was bought by the reformist *Union Times*.

Sun Yat-sen visited Singapore regularly in these years and continued to inspire loyalty among humbler supporters but found it increasingly difficult to raise money from the rich. In 1909 he moved his Nanyang headquarters to Penang, whence he was deported the following year. Yiu Lieh was arrested in 1909 and left Malaya on his release, after which his organization degenerated into gangsterism and was suppressed. The Singapore Chinese turned their backs on the revolutionary cause.

The atmosphere changed dramatically after the successful Wu-ch'ang rising in 1911. The Singapore Chinese went wild with excitement and joy and gave a tumultuous welcome to Sun Yat-sen when he passed through as a conquering hero en route to China. Hokkien and Cantonese leaders co-operated to collect funds for China, and young Singapore Chinese flocked to join the rebel army's ranks. Singapore money played an important role in the final revolution which brought Sun Yat-sen to power. Even the poorest contributed to the rebels' fund, and the culminating victory produced a wave of warm patriotism towards China. Young men enthusiastically cut off their queues and sometimes forcibly chopped off those of their more conservative countrymen, while the British, perturbed at the sudden upsurge of national pride, bemoaned 'the mutinous tone of the lowest classes'.[52]

Singapore Chinese basked in the praise bestowed by Sun Yat-sen on the Nanyang as 'mother of the revolution' but few had contributed until the final stage. Sun Yat-sen seemed to look kindly upon Singapore in the hope of favours to come rather than gratitude for favours received. He had been bitterly disappointed at the lack of support in his early struggling days.

The growing pressure exerted by China upon the overseas Chinese, enthusiasm for Chinese nationalism and the spread of modern Chinese education brought great changes to the Singapore Chinese community. In some ways they accentuated the differences between the leading Straits-born and immigrant Chinese.[53] The English-educated Straits-born minority looked to the Straits Chinese British Association as their mouthpiece. Their leaders were merchants or successful professional men, lawyers, doctors and teachers. The Straits Chinese dominated the professions, were favoured for public office and worked closely with the colonial authorities, concentrating on social and educational matters rather than politics. The China-oriented leaders, banded together in the

6. Tan Jiak Kim
(By permission of Mr. Eric Jennings)

Singapore Chinese chamber of commerce, wielded great power in the Chinese community. Drawn exclusively from the rich merchants, some were exceedingly wealthy, presiding over commercial empires which spread throughout the Nanyang, but usually they had little formal education and their English was poor. They neither sought, nor were sought after, for public office in the colony, and their interests lay in Chinese politics, Chinese schools and philanthropic works.

Most outstanding of the China-born was Tan Kah Kee, who was born near Amoy in 1873 and came to Singapore as a penniless immigrant at the age of seventeen to work in a rice shop. He then set up his own rice shop and a pineapple factory in 1904, extended his activities to rubber, rice milling and shipping, and by the time World War I broke out Tan Kah Kee & Company was Singapore's premier Chinese firm, with interests in Malaya, Siam, and China.[54] In the midst of riches Tan Kah Kee remained unpretentious, considering wealth an evil if not put to good use. He ploughed much of his early profit into founding primary schools and supplied the major part of the finances for Amoy University, which he established in 1924.

The interests and energies of the Straits-oriented and China-oriented diverged but did not necessarily clash at this time. The Straits Chinese British Association and the Singapore Chinese chamber of commerce were markedly different institutions but not exclusive in composition. Tan Kah Kee was a member of the Straits Chinese British Association, while Lim Boon Keng was a pioneer in Chinese education in Singapore and a founder member of the Singapore branch of the Kuomintang.

Prosperity transformed the physical appearance of the town in the last quarter of the century. Cavenagh Bridge, opened in 1869 to link Commercial Square and the government quarter near the river mouth, was the final major work carried out by Indian convicts, and after 1873 official building became the responsibility of a Public Works Department. A general hospital was built on its present site in 1882, the Central Police Station in 1882, Coleman Bridge in 1886, and Raffles Museum and Library in 1887. The Esplanade was widened by reclaiming land from the sea to form the present Connaught Drive.

Successful Chinese businessmen built mansions in traditional mainland style. The first such house, erected by Tan Seng Poh in Hill Street in 1869, later became the Chinese consulate. The only one to survive was put up by a wealthy Teochew, Tan Yeok Nee, about 1885 and is now the Salvation Army headquarters in Clemenceau Avenue. Affluent Chinese businessmen continued to provide amenities as a form of philanthropy, such as Cheang Hong Lim, who in 1876 presented $3,000 to plant the green which still bears his name in crowded Chinatown where open spaces were urgently needed.

The centre of the town was very congested, although it retained some of the characteristics of more leisurely days, and horse sales continued to be held in Commercial Square until 1886. Business houses congregated in the Commercial Square/Collyer Quay area, and most big firms had offices along Collyer Quay where they could observe the coming and going of shipping through their telescopes. It was not until the early years of the twentieth century that such observation became obsolete and the telephone enabled firms to spread out from the traditional business centre.

In the later years of the nineteenth century the narrow roads in the heart of the town were crowded with a motley assortment of bullock-carts, private carriages, pony-carts, public hack-gharries, jinrikishas, introduced in 1880 from Shanghai, joined in 1882 by the first 'noiseless but deadly' bicycles. Battery Road was jammed with traffic all day long, there were no parking restrictions and no regulations to force vehicles to use one side of the road. Rickshaws caused most accidents. Rickshaw pullers had to be licensed, but the vehicle owners by-passed the regulations, exploited the pullers, working them long hours, transferring licence badges indiscriminately, and often hiring, as the cheapest form of labour, inexperienced immigrants newly arrived from villages in China who had never seen heavy traffic before. As late as 1901 Singapore was paralysed by a rickshaw strike when the police attempted to enforce traffic rules to cut the accident rate, and the Governor had to summon the leading Chinese *towkays* to Government House and enlist their efforts to put an end to the strike.

Changes in municipal administration were needed to cope with the rapid expansion of the town. In the interests of efficiency Ord had proposed to abolish the municipal committee and absorb its work into the general government, but the legislative council opposed this as yet one more example of the Governor's authoritarianism, and the elective committee of voluntary amateurs was retained.

The need for change became more urgent with the expansion of municipal expenditure, which rose from less than $63,000 in 1857 to more than $500,000 in 1886. Accordingly a Municipal Ordinance was passed in 1887. The town area was separated from the rural districts, which were put under direct government control. A full-time paid municipal president was to be appointed by the Governor. The municipality's finances were separated from general revenue so that it could no longer treat the government as 'a municipal milch cow',[55] but expenditure in excess of $10,000 could only be incurred with government approval.

This measure went only a small way towards modernization, but in the circumstances the new municipal commission achieved a great deal. It drew up many schemes of improvement in the 1880s, including the provision of a professional fire-brigade in 1888. It took over the existing waterworks, made a reservoir at Thomson Road and constructed the first filter-beds in 1889. Most of this was the work of James MacRitchie, who held the post of municipal engineer for twelve years.

In the next decade municipal schemes underwent a severe setback, falling victim to a world slump which triggered off a disastrous fall in the sterling value of the Straits dollar in 1893. This led to a sharp rise in the cost of imported raw materials and to a rigorous official economy campaign. Discontented municipal officials lost 20 per cent of the real value of their salaries through the depreciation of the dollar. Many resigned, and MacRitchie's death in 1895 robbed the municipality of one of its most far-seeing officers.

As the economy picked up in the late 1890s, the municipality revived its schemes. It enlarged the Thomson Road reservoir in 1904, completed the Pearl's Hill reservoir in 1907 and the Kallang Extension River Scheme (now named the Peirce reservoir) in 1911. The Town Hall was renovated and reopened as the Victoria Memorial Hall in 1905, and the Victoria Theatre was finished in 1909. In 1900 the municipality took over the inefficient Gas Company. In 1906 it provided electric street lighting in the central area and arranged for electricity to be supplied to private consumers by the private Singapore Tramway Company.

The Singapore Tramway Company, started in 1882, ran trams from New Harbour to Collyer Quay and east to Rochore. For the first twenty years they operated on steam but switched to electricity early in the twentieth century. The Tramway Company found difficulty in competing with rickshaws, despite the fact that rickshaws were very uncomfortable and only adopted rubber tyres in 1904.

Many people objected to the tramway, including one unofficial legislative councillor, who called trams the 'modern car of Juggernaut' which would fill the hospitals with casualties. But the fast-spreading town needed efficient public transport.

At the turn of the century, Singapore was a cosmopolitan city but largely an Anglo-Chinese preserve. The British rulers held a monopoly of official political power, provided protection, justice and administration. To the visitor from Britain Singapore was very English in appearance, 'so flourishing and enlightened, so advanced and well-governed'.[56] The heterogeneous society existed 'in order and sanitation, living and thriving and trading, simply because of the presence of English law and under the protection of the British flag. Remove that piece of bunting from Government House, and all that it signified, and the whole community would go to pieces like a child's sandcastle when the tide rises. Its three supports are free trade, fair taxation and even handed justice'.[57]

The mystique of British imperialism was at its height, and the death of Queen Victoria in 1901 plunged Singapore into silence 'like a city struck with plague'.[58] Britain's commercial and naval power seemed permanent and unshakeable, and Singapore's economy was largely dominated by western firms, mostly based in Britain. But superficial impressions were in some ways deceptive. Most Europeans lived in comfort and style as the agents and employees of Europe-based managements. The greatest individual wealth lay with a handful of Asians: Chinese, Jews, Indians and Arabs, who made personal fortunes out of trade and property.

For the affluent life was becoming more pleasant. More people could afford their own carriages, and improvements in roads enabled them to live in spacious comfort in the suburbs. The first motor-car was imported in 1896, but motor traffic remained a novelty for many years, and in 1908 only 214 people had driving licences. The first decade of the twentieth century saw the peak of horse-drawn vehicles, and this mobility encouraged more entertaining in private houses and parties which went on to a later hour.

Raffles Hotel opened in 1899 and social clubs provided a wide choice of entertainment for Europeans. The Yacht Club was formed in 1881, the Golf Club opened at the old race course in 1891, the new Swimming Club in 1894 and the Polo Club in 1899. Liveliest of all was the German Teutonia Club, the centre of European social life and of musical activity, which had a strong following among the western community at the turn of the century. In 1900 the Teutonia built a luxurious new clubhouse, with a first-class restaurant, concert room and sports facilities, later forming the nucleus of the present Goodwood Park Hotel.

There were plenty of opportunities for sport. Tennis became fashionable in the 1870s, association football came into vogue in 1889, and horse-riding parties on Sundays and early mornings were very popular. The first movie, depicting Queen Victoria's funeral, was shown in the Town Hall in July 1901.

The discomforts of life in the tropics lessened. The first consignment of frozen meat, fresh butter and fruit from Australia was imported by the Singapore Cold Storage Company in 1905.[59] Electric fans were installed in Government House in 1904, and after 1906 electric lighting and fans came to replace oil lamps and punkahs in private houses.

But for the poor life grew worse. In 1896 a commission of enquiry headed by Dr. Lim Boon Keng produced a grim picture of mass living conditions. Singapore's mortality rate was higher than in Hong Kong, Ceylon or India, ranging between 44 and 51 per thousand in the first years of the twentieth century. The senior army medical officer had warned in 1872 that 'the town is a nursery for disease'. Spectacular epidemics were surprisingly rare, but their absence cloaked the seriousness of endemic killing diseases, such as beri-beri, tuberculosis, malaria, enteric fever and dysentery, which were caused by poverty, overcrowding, malnutrition and dirt. There was no adequate water supply nor any sewerage scheme, since night-soil was collected for market gardens on a private basis. Tan Kim Seng had presented $13,000 in 1857 to provide a water supply, but this represented only a fraction of the sum needed for this costly amenity. Acrimonious discussions about how to raise the balance dragged on for years, until in the end the works were completed in 1879 out of public funds and most of Tan Kim Seng's gift was spent on an ornamental fountain, which stands today on the Esplanade. By the end of the century the supply was again inadequate.

Government hospitals were substandard and official health services few. The mass of the population had no medical facilities or relied on a few charitable institutions founded by Chinese philanthropists. Most notable was the Thong Chai Medical Institution, set up in Chinatown in 1867, which still survives. Generously financed by Chinese merchants, notably by Gan Eng Seng, the dispensary was given free land by the government in 1892. It examined *sinsehs,* who trained in China on traditional lines, and provided free treatment to poor people of all races.

In 1905 a cholera epidemic carried off 759 victims, and the legislative council became alarmed at the general high mortality rate. Malaria was the main killer, accounting for 1,410 out of 9,440 deaths in 1909. But much of the high mortality and ill health was attributed to vice, notably to opium addiction, and at the beginning of the twentieth century the opium farm still provided half of the colony's revenue.

Lim Boon Keng and his partner, Dr. Yin Suat Chuan, launched a campaign to discourage opium smoking which attracted support from European missionaries and a few Chinese, mainly young men who had been educated abroad and a handful of Baba merchants. Peking wanted to see the Nanyang Chinese conserve their savings for the benefit of China rather than squander their money on opium, and in 1906 the Chinese consul-general founded a Singapore Anti-Opium Society with Tan Boon Liat as president. He also established an experimental rehabilitation centre in the consulate, which was run by Yin Suat Chuan and Lim Boon Keng and financed by a group of Baba merchants.

The consumption of opium and the revenue it generated began to decline, but the anti-opium movement encountered opposition from the tax farmers, from most Chinese and European merchants, and from the English-language press. The government was torn between financial and moral considerations, but at Colonial Office insistence it appointed a commission in 1907 to investigate the opium question. The commission advised that opium smoking was a fairly harmless, fashionable vice among the rich but the effects were more pernicious among the poor, who could only afford to smoke the dregs of used opium. It concluded that addiction was not widespread, except among Singapore's rickshaw pullers, who rarely lived to be more than 35 or 40 years old. The Governor, Sir John Anderson, was prepared to prohibit the vice and to tax income as an alternative but had to withdraw this proposal in face of bitter opposition from non-official legislative councillors, European and Asian businessmen, who not only objected to the proposed income tax but feared a prohibition on opium smoking might deter immigration.[60]

As a compromise, in 1910 the government took over the manufacture and sale of opium. A government factory at Pasir Panjang monopolized the production of good-quality opium and the authorities bought up and burned all opium refuse. This stemmed the worst abuses, but the sale of opium still contributed nearly half of Singapore's revenue up to the mid-1920s, and the government continued to manufacture opium until the Second World War. By that time opium could only be purchased under licence, and the policy was gradually to eliminate the vice. By 1934 opium excise accounted for only one-quarter of the revenue and had been overtaken by duties on tobacco, petrol, and alcohol.

An official commission of enquiry in 1909/10 into the high mortality rate and chronic slum conditions led to the municipality being reorganized. Municipal elections had roused little interest for years and few voters turned out to cast their ballot. Governor Anderson wanted the government to take over full control of policy and finance, employing professional, technical executive officers and using the municipal board as a mere advisory body, but this suggestion roused protest from both European non-officials and the Chinese commercial association. A Municipal Ordinance of 1913 retained the municipal commission but abolished elections and put control of the municipal budget into the hands of the Governor, who was to nominate commissioners. Two European non-official legislative councillors protested at dropping the elective principle, but Tan Jiak Kim, legislative councillor and a powerful voice in the Chinese commercial association, declared the Chinese community did not oppose the nomination of municipal councillors.

The 1913 ordinance remained in force, with minor amendments, up to the Second World War.

Education did not keep pace with economic development. In 1870 the Woolley Committee reported to the legislative council that 'the state of education in the Colony has been and is in a backward state'. The committee suggested reorganizing all the existing schools under a Director of Education, encouraging secular education, extending vernacular instruction, both in Malay and Chinese, and improving the education of girls. These recommendations went further than the authorities were prepared to go at that time. In 1872 they appointed an Inspector of Schools, A.M. Skinner, but ignored the other proposals.

Like its Indian predecessor, the colonial administration acknowledged a special responsibility for providing free vernacular primary education in Malay. There was no public demand nor was it feasible for the government to provide education in the diverse Indian languages and Chinese dialects spoken by the immigrant majority.

Malay education did not flourish despite the efforts of Christian missionaries and of Skinner, who held the post of Inspector of Schools in the Straits Settlements for thirty years. In 1876, the Temenggong converted his Telok Blangah residence into a Malay college, with an ambitious programme to provide secondary education in Malay and English and to train Malay teachers. The project did not succeed, secondary education in Malay did not take root, and teacher training was transferred to peninsular colleges.

Raffles Institution resumed Malay classes in 1885 but these had to be abandoned eight years later for lack of support. A Methodist missionary, Dr. W.G. Shellabear, tried to promote Christian education among the Malay community in the early 1890s but he found that attitudes had hardened since Keasberry's day and Muslims showed a growing resistance to Christian teaching. Education among Malay boys reached a low ebb and attempts to provide schooling for Malay girls were a total failure. After a select committee reported in 1893 on the inefficiency of Malay education in Singapore many small schools were closed, but this led to no improvement in the quality of the remainder, which offered very elementary Malay instruction with no opportunity to learn English as a second language.

Chinese-medium education was left to the Chinese community. The government set up two Anglo-Tamil schools in 1873 and 1876, but these were converted into English schools because of lack of demand for schooling from the Tamil community. A similar fate overtook the Methodist Girls' School, which was created to cater for Tamil girls but soon became an English-medium school. By the end of the nineteenth century no government-aided school offered any Tamil classes.

Throughout the nineteenth century the Singapore authorities accepted no responsibility to provide English education but subsidized private English-medium schools, most of which were run by Christian missions. Despite the lack of official encouragement, the vocational benefit of English gave a boost to primary English-medium education in the later years of the nineteenth century. The existing mission schools raised their standards and the secular Raffles Institution blossomed under the headship of R.W. Hullett, who was principal from 1871 to 1906 and later became Inspector of Schools and Director of Public Instruction for the Straits Settlements.[61] New mission schools were opened: St. Andrew's in 1871, St. Anthony's in 1879. The American Methodist Mission set up its base in Singapore in 1885, founding the Anglo-Chinese Boys' School in 1886 and the Methodist Girls' School in 1887. By 1915 it had seven schools in Singapore.

The only school which provided secondary education was Raffles Institution, which began post-primary classes in 1884. As Colonial Secretary and later as Governor in the 1880s, Clementi Smith tried to promote tertiary education but with little success. Only a minority of prosperous Chinese and Eurasians were interested, and Clementi Smith was ahead of his time in his schemes for technical training, a survey school and a college for general education. A medical school for training apothecaries opened in 1889 but only two students enrolled and the school closed the following year. Clementi Smith's one success was to found two Queen's scholarships in 1889, and in 1891 to introduce the Senior Cambridge examination which was the basis for awarding these scholarships and has since remained the criterion for university selection in Singapore.

Clementi Smith's educational proposals were criticized at the time by the European community, and particularly by the *Singapore Free Press,* for concentrating resources at the top and ignoring the broader base of primary education. But the Queen's scholarship scheme justified the thesis that the quickest and most effective way to raise general educational standards is to start at the top. Over the years Queen's scholars returned to Singapore as doctors, lawyers, and teachers. There was no outlet for their talents in government administration since the senior ranks of the civil service were reserved for Britons of pure European descent, but they became leaders in the professions and took their place alongside the wealthy merchants as legislative councillors, municipal councillors and justices of the peace. The English-educated professional Asian élite provided a new type of leadership and began a subtle westernizing and modernizing of Singapore society, inculcating a respect for western education and professional success, opening the way for the Asian community to assimilate and accept western medicine, the British judicial system and European educational methods. It also became fashionable for prosperous Singapore parents to send to England at their own expense children who were not scholastically brilliant enough to win Queen's scholarships. This practice persisted even after independence and was partially checked only in 1971 when the government imposed penalties on sending boys overseas to school. The influence of the minority educated in England and of the growing numbers of children educated in the English medium in Singapore produced a gradual but significant revolution in the attitudes and character of Singaporeans.

By the beginning of the twentieth century, in addition to providing free Malay primary schooling, the Straits authorities were prepared to take more responsibility for English-medium education but continued to leave Chinese and Tamil education to private charity.

An Education Code laid down in 1902 formed the basis for official education policy for the next twenty years. For the first time the government provided English-medium primary schools. In 1903 it took over Raffles Institution, making it an exclusively secondary school, and in 1909 it founded an Education Board. Between 1904 and 1911 the number of places in English-medium schools doubled, and English education progressed steadily for the first two decades of the twentieth century.

Under pressure from the Straits Chinese, led by Tan Jiak Kim, the Singapore authorities agreed to establish and maintain a medical school, provided the petitioners could raise $71,000 towards the initial cost. To the surprise of officials, there was such public enthusiasm for this project that a sum of $87,000 was raised almost overnight. The first class of twenty-three students was opened in 1905 and the school was named the Edward VII Medical School in 1912. At first the school was staffed by part-time lecturers from government service and private practice, but in 1920 it was upgraded to become the King Edward Medical College and acquired a full-time teaching staff. The College was built in the grounds of the new Outram General Hospital, and formed the first constituent part of the future University of Singapore.

The effect of this impetus in English education, coinciding with the rapid expansion of modern Chinese schools inspired by the reforming movement in China, produced a great change in Singapore society. It led to the emergence of an upper professional class and a literate middle class, it put a new value on education as giving status in the community, and it began the slow process of emancipating women.

English education was a link between the upper classes, since those children of the well-to-do of all races who remained in Singapore for their education invariably attended English-medium schools. For the clever, English education provided a path to professional eminence, and for many others it opened the way to clerical or commercial employment.

But the overall effect was socially divisive, separating the English- and vernacular-educated, widening the gap between the different communities except at the highest level, accentuating racial, cultural and linguistic differences and stressing the rift between rich and poor. Malay- and Tamil-medium education was of a very elementary standard. For all but the few exceptionally talented Malay students who were promoted to English-medium secondary schools, Malay and Tamil education was a dead end, offering no prospect for advancement in the framework of Singapore society. Chinese schools provided a full education but directed outlook towards China and confined pupils to the Chinese sector of Singapore's economy and society. Particularly among the Chinese community the division between Chinese-educated and English-educated became the major classification, blurring former dialect divisions.

The process of westernization, the expansion of English and Chinese education, the spread of the Reform Islam movement from the Middle East, the increase in international commerce and the growing awareness of events in China, the Middle East and elsewhere, stimulated the growth of the English press and gave birth to the first vernacular newspapers in the last quarter of the nineteenth century.

The *Singapore Free Press* was wound up in 1869, leaving the *Straits Times* as the only newspaper in Singapore. A disastrous fire almost put an end to its existence, its assets were sold for $40 at public auction, and John Cameron, the proprietor-editor, went bankrupt. He managed to revive the newspaper but it continued to suffer financial difficulties. Cameron died in 1881, and in 1887 his widow appointed as editor a young Scottish professional journalist, Arnold Reid, who held the post for twelve years and succeeded for the first time in raising circulation above the two hundred mark. After his retirement a talented English journalist, Alexander William Still, was editor for eighteen years and made the *Straits Times* a great commercial success.

The *Singapore Free Press* re-emerged under the able leadership of W.G. St. Clair, who edited the newspaper from 1887 to 1916. The *Free Press* was a morning paper whereas the *Straits Times* remained an afternoon newspaper up to the time of the Japanese occupation. Under Still and St. Clair the rival newspapers attracted growing numbers of readers from the expanding English-educated community.

In contrast to the fortunes of the English press, most early vernacular newspapers had a difficult time. The *Jawi Peranakan*, established in 1876, survived for nearly twenty years. Owned by Jawi-Peranakan, the newspaper was edited until 1888 by Mohammed Said bin Dada Mohyiddin, Penang-born of Malay and Indian Muslim stock and a teacher at Raffles

Institution. The *Jawi Peranakan* devoted much of its space to commercial information and was not critical of government policy. Its news was taken largely from the local English newspapers and also from the Egyptian and Arabic press. But its correspondence columns were lively, it was concerned about the general backwardness of the Malay community and anxious to foster vernacular education and promote the Malay language.

Other Malay-language journals were short-lived. These included the *Bintang Timor*, the only journal then printed in romanized Malay script, which was brought out by Song Ong Siang for the Baba Chinese in 1894 but survived less than a year, and the religiously oriented *Al-Imam*, which ceased publication after two years. As Singapore's first reformist journal, *Al-Imam*, or *The Leader*, was launched in 1906, with the financial backing of Indonesian and Arab merchants, and its main sponsors had extensive contacts with the Middle East modernist movement. *Al-Imam* was apolitical but aimed to raise the moral and material well-being of the Muslim population through reviving the purity and strength of Islam and modernizing Muslim education. *Al-Imam* survived only until 1908 and probably had more readers in Sumatra than Singapore, but it set the tone for other pan-Islamic Malay journals, which supported religious and moral reform and appealed to religious teachers and the educated Muslim mercantile classes.

The Malay press came into its own and flourished for a quarter of a century under the inspiration of Mohammed Eunos bin Abdullah, 'the father of Malay journalism'. Born in Sumatra in 1876, the son of a wealthy Menangkabau merchant, Mohammed Eunos grew up in Kampong Glam and was educated at Raffles Institution. In 1907 the proprietor of the *Singapore Free Press* invited him to edit the *Utusan Melayu* as a Malay edition of the newspaper.

The *Utusan Melayu* was the first major national Malay newspaper and circulated throughout the Straits Settlements and the Malay states. Secular in outlook, it emphasized issues of interest to urban Malay readers. At first it was published three times a week, partly in Jawi and partly in romanized script for Baba Chinese readers. It became a daily newspaper in 1915, but the *Free Press* sold it in 1918 to a group of Indian businessmen and it was forced to close down in 1922 after being crippled financially by damages awarded against it in a libel case.

Meanwhile in 1914 Mohammed Eunos Abdullah became editor of the *Lembaga Melayu*, the Malay version of a new English-language paper, the *Malaya Tribune*. Like the *Utusan Melayu*, the *Lembaga Melayu* was moderate and progressive in character, appealing to urban middle-class Malays, generally supporting the colonial regime but sometimes mildly critical of official policy towards the Malays.[62]

A *Singapore Eurasian Advocate*, started in 1888, lasted only three years, and a second English-language Eurasian newspaper appeared only briefly in 1900. A Tamil newspaper *Singai Nesan* was published in 1888 but had a small circulation.

The first Chinese newspaper, the *Lat Pau,* was founded in 1881 by See Ewe Lay, a fifth-generation Baba, whose grandfather came from Malacca to Singapore in the 1820s. See Ewe Lay was *compradore* of the Hongkong Shanghai Bank and prominent in European commercial circles. He also had close connexions with China and, like many of his generation, sought to strengthen the cultural bonds between the Singapore Chinese and China. In 1900 the *Lat Pau's* circulation still stood at under 500 and ran at a loss until the second decade of the twentieth century,[63] when the Chinese-reading public expanded with the development of Chinese education.

The *Lat Pau* was not concerned with Singapore's affairs, apart from its commerce, and offered no criticism of the colonial regime. It was a conservative newspaper, supporting the Manchus and opposing infringement of Chinese traditions, such as the queue-cutting campaign which divided the Singapore Chinese in the late 1890s. This gained it the support of many of the well-to-do among the Chinese community, but its position was challenged by the reformist *Union Times,* launched in 1907.

In 1909 See Ewe Lay's nephew, See Tiong Wah, took the newspaper over. Like his uncle, See Tiong Wah was a Hongkong Shanghai Bank *compradore* and a prominent public figure, a justice of the peace, municipal councillor, president of the Chinese commercial association and head of the Hokkien Huay-kuay. He lifted the newspaper out of debt, but it went into a decline after the chief writer's death in 1921 and was wound up in 1932.

By the 1880s growing international commercial competition and possible threats to the Pax Britannica led official and mercantile interests in London and Singapore to renew the debate about the colony's defences. The immediate worry was Russia's re-emergence as a naval power. In 1885, amid mounting fears of an Anglo-Russian war over Afghanistan, the Straits Settlements Association of London petitioned the Colonial Office to provide for the defence of the Straits of Malacca and recommended that the colony should foot the bill for constructing defence works in Singapore if the War Office supplied the guns and equipment.

The British government was prepared to defend the port area but the Singapore merchants sought protection also for the town, and in 1886 there was an outcry in the legislative council when Britain began erecting fortifications only for New Harbour and Blakang Mati island (the modern Sentosa). The Colonial Office insisted that Britain did not intend to create 'a naval fortress' in Singapore, but merely to protect the port area from casual small-scale attack and to leave Singapore's main protection to the Royal Navy.

In 1890 London demanded £60,000 towards the cost of barracks and other new military buildings and proposed to double the Straits Settlements' annual military contribution to £100,000. The legislative council agreed to the barracks, but the non-officials unanimously protested against the revised contribution, and the English-language press denounced Colonial Office demands as 'imperial robbery'. Public meetings were called and a petition to parliament drawn up, arguing that Singapore was now an essential imperial station.[64] The Governor, Clementi Smith, supported the petition, warning the Colonial Office that the soured relationship 'has tended to imperil good government', but London persisted in demanding full payment.

The trade depression which set in during 1891 and the fall in the value of silver forced the colony to draw on its reserves to meet the military contribution. This caused retrenchment in government departments, delays in executing public works and cheese-paring in education. In 1895, after bitter and long drawn-out arguments about military expenditure, the unofficial legislative councillors resigned, followed by the justices of the peace and the Chinese Advisory Board. The legislative council had to go into recess for some months. Eventually London agreed to a slightly reduced figure which would also include defence works, and this remained the basis of contribution until the 1920s, when London tried to increase the payment as a contribution towards the new naval base. Singapore resisted stoutly. The arguments raged throughout the 1920s and the forty-year battle was finally brought to an end in 1933 when the colony reluctantly agreed to pay $4 million a year, or 20 per cent of its revenue.

Singapore's case was weakened by the circumstances of the constitutional transfer in 1867, when she became a crown colony at her own request and on condition that she financed her own military expenditure. The Governors consistently fought on the colony's behalf against London on this issue, but were forced to use the official majority to outvote non-officials, which was almost the only occasion on which this had to be done.

Britain's naval supremacy was threatened not only by Russia but also by France, who had united Indo-China under her control and in 1887 was discussing cutting a canal across the Kra isthmus. Even Japan was a potential rival. In February 1886 the Governor, Sir Frederick Weld, wrote privately to a friend, 'We have two Japanese ironclads of a very superior type built at Newcastle stopping here. Nothing in these parts could look at them. One of our naval men who went over them said either was worth all our fleet in these seas—which is made up of the greatest rubbish—put together, if it came to a fight.'[65]

The troubled uncertainty of international relations, combined with the development of steamships and ironclads, led the Admiralty in 1885 to investigate various ports with a view to creating a naval dockyard in the east. At one time Singapore was favoured, but negotiations over choosing a site and acquiring land dragged on until 1889, by which time the immediate crisis was over and the Admiralty lost interest.

The proposal was revived in 1896 in face of deepening British anxiety over the implications of the new Franco-Russian alliance and fears of German economic rivalry and colonial ambitions. During the 1890s the theory of 'the new navalism', which held that national strength depended upon sea power and the key to naval power lay in heavy battleships, became an internationally-accepted fashionable cult. Many nations, notably Germany, rushed to build up their navies.

The naval race and growing competition in her hitherto unchallenged international trade revived the British government's interest in creating a naval base at Singapore, but the very intensity of the new international rivalry eventually killed this scheme. It induced Britain to concentrate her fleet in home waters in face of the German naval threat and to seek protection for her overseas empire through alliances with other powers. In 1902 Britain made a defensive pact with Japan, whose victory over Russia in the Russo-Japanese war three years later destroyed the long-standing Russian threat to British sea power in the East. The Anglo-French Entente of 1904 removed the dangers of French rivalry and gave Britain an ally to guard the Mediterranean sea lane. Admiral Sir John Fisher, who became First Sea Lord in 1904, concentrated British naval strength in the North Sea, withdrew battleships from the East and Mediterranean, closed down existing naval dockyards abroad and abandoned the Singapore scheme.

Britain's ability to mass her naval strength in home waters was of vital importance in her struggle with Germany in World War I. But the long-term implications were not generally appreciated. Contemporary Englishmen might claim with pride that 'the port, phenomenal as its past progress has been, is only on the threshold of its career'.[66] 'All live at peace and prosper abundantly under the Union Jack, and the statue of Raffles looks down benignantly on a scene so much in harmony with the aspirations and policy of the original founder of the city.'[67]

Behind this complacency lay the ominous truth that Britain needed French and Japanese friendship to guard her trade and in the event of international war she had already abdicated defence of her eastern empire to Japan.

---

1. Ord to Parker (CO), 6 July 1866, Carnarvon Papers, PRO 30/6.
2. *London and China Telegraph,* 26 January 1867.
3. *ST,* 21 March 1867.
4. For a satirical sketch of these early years see G. Dana, *Letters of 'Extinguisher' and Chronicles of St. George* (Singapore, 1870).
5. Ord to C.O., 15 July 1867, GD 1, No. 61.
6. COD 2, No. 71.
7. For early colonial impressions about the inefficiency of the Indian administrative system, see A. Anson, *About Others and Myself* (London, 1920).
8. Straits Settlements Legislative Council minutes, 18 December 1867, 1 E 1, p. 41.
9. Minutes of meeting to form the Straits Settlements Association in Napier to Buckingham, 7 February 1868, in Buckingham to Ord, 17 February 1868, COD 3, No. 27.
10. Straits Settlements Association, *Memorandum regarding the government of the Straits Settlements,* 26 April 1869, in S. of S. to Ord, 1 June 1869, COD 7, No. 95.

11. P.C. Campbell, *Chinese Coolie Emigration to Countries Within the British Empire* (London, 1923, reprinted London, 1971), pp. 6–7.

12. S. of S. to Ord, 1868, COD 4, Nos. 77, 99, 119 and 166.

13. *ST*, 15 September 1873; CO 273/70, Nos. 290 and 291.

14. *SFP*, 24 April 1936.

15. *ST*, 12 January 1874.

16. Extract of report of 1 January 1873, in C.O. to Ord, 11 June 1873, COD/C 5.

17. See Lim Joo Hock, 'Chinese Female Immigration into the Straits Settlements, 1860–1901', *JSSS*, XXII, 2 (1967), pp. 58–110.

18. R.N. Jackson, *Pickering: Protector of Chinese* (Kuala Lumpur, 1965), p. 97.

19. Quoted in Ng Siew Yoong, 'The Chinese Protectorate in Singapore, 1877–1900', *JSEAH*, II, 1 (1961), p. 95.

20. Wong Lin Ken, *The Malayan Tin Industry to 1914* (Arizona, 1965) is a well-researched study of the early tin industry.

21. K.G. Tregonning, *Straits Tin: a Brief Account of the First Seventy-Five Years of the Straits Trading Company Ltd., 1887–1962* (Singapore, 1962).

22. See J.H. Drabble, *Rubber in Malaya, 1876–1922* (Kuala Lumpur, 1973) for the early rubber industry.

23. Chiang Hai Ding, 'The Origin of the Malayan Currency System', *JMBRAS*, XXXIX, No. 1 (1966), pp. 1–18; W.A. Shaw and Mohammed Kassim Haji Ali, *Paper Currency of Malaysia, Singapore and Brunei, 1849–1970* (Kuala Lumpur, 1971); and F. Pridmore, 'Coins and Coinages of the Straits Settlements and British Malaya, 1786 to 1951', *Memoirs of the Raffles Museum*, No. 2 (Singapore, 1955) deal with various aspects of the currency question.

24. *ST*, 16 May 1872.

25. The history of the firm of Guthries is told in S. Cunyngham-Brown, *The Traders* (London, 1970).

26. B. Cable, *A Hundred-Year History of the P. & O. (Peninsular and Oriental Steam Navigation Company), 1837–1937* (London, 1937).

27. G. Blake, *The Ben Line, 1825–1955* (London, 1956).

28. E. Jennings, *Mansfields: Transport and Distribution in Southeast Asia* (Singapore, 1973). The early struggles of the firm are poignantly described in the 'Diary of George John Mansfield, 1863–1866', MSS Ind. Ocn. r 11 (Rhodes House, Oxford).

29. Rudyard Kipling, 'The Song of the Cities' in *The Seven Seas* (London, 1896).

30. Quoted in J. Morris, *Pax Britannica* (London, 1968), p. 148, which gives a vivid portrait of the imperial background in the 1890s.

31. Discussed in T. Suyama, 'Pang Societies: the Economy of Chinese Immigrants' in K.G. Tregonning (ed.), *Papers on Malayan History* (Singapore, 1962), pp. 193–213.

32. See Yip Yat Hoong, *The Development of the Tin Mining Industry of Malaya* (Kuala Lumpur, 1969).

33. Philip Loh Fook Seng, *The Malay States: Political Change and Social Policy, 1877–1895* (Kuala Lumpur, 1969), pp. 104–5.

34. *PG*, 20 August 1908.

35. *PG*, 7 June 1906.

36. W.R. Roff, *The Origins of Malay Nationalism* (New Haven and Kuala Lumpur, 1967), p. 37.

37. Roff, *Malay Nationalism*, p. 35.

38. I.L. Bird, *The Golden Chersonese and the Way Thither* (New York, 1883, reprinted Kuala Lumpur, 1967), p. 119.

39. See E.W. Birch, 'The Vernacular Press in the Straits', *JSBRAS*, IV (1879), pp. 51–5, reprinted in *JMBRAS*, XLII, 1 (1969), pp. 192–5.

40. For the characteristics and subdivisions within this group, see Png Poh Seng, 'The Straits Chinese in Singapore: a case of local identity and socio-cultural accommodation', *JSEAH*, X, 1 (1969), pp. 95–114.

41. Tan Jiak Kim, Lim Boon Keng and Song Ong Siang (eds.), *Duty to the British Empire during the Great War* (Singapore, 1915).

42. C.E. Ferguson-Davie (ed.), *In Rubber Lands* (London, 1921).

43. F. Caddy, *To Siam and Malaya in the Duke of Sutherland's Yacht 'Sans eur'* (London, 1889), p. 84.

44. Lee Ah Chai (Ting Hui), 'Policies and Politics in Chinese Schools in the Straits Settlements and the Federated Malay States, 1786–1941', M.A. thesis, University of Malaya (Singapore), 1957, p. 1.

45. J.B. Elcum, Director of Public Instruction, in *Straits Settlements Annual Report for 1906*.

46. Wen Chung-chi, 'The Nineteenth Century Imperial Chinese Consulate in the Straits Settlements: origins and development', unpublished M.A. thesis, University of Singapore, 1964, is an absorbing study of the consulate's early years.

47. Yen Ching-Hwang, 'Ch'ing's Sale of Honours and the Chinese Leadership in Singapore and Malaya, 1877–1912', *JSEAS*, I, 2 (1970), pp. 20–32; M.R. Godley, 'The Late Ch'ing Courtship of the Chinese in Southeast Asia', *JAS*, XXIV, 2 (1975), pp. 361–5.

48. Wu Lien-teh, *Plague Fighter: the Autobiography of a Modern Chinese Physician* (Cambridge, 1959).

49. Wang Gungwu, 'Chinese Reformists and Revolutionaries in the Straits Settlements, 1900–11', unpublished B.A. academic exercise, University of Malaya (Singapore 1953), p. 14.

50. Wang Gungwu, 'Sun Yat-sen and Singapore', *JSSS*, XV, 2 (1959), pp. 55–68.

51. H.Z. Schiffrin, *Sun Yat-sen and the Origins of the Chinese Revolution* (California, 1968). The early revolutionary movement in Singapore is discussed in Png Poh Seng, 'The KMT in Malaya', *JSEAH*, II, 1 (1961), pp. 1–32, and in K.G. Tregonning (ed.), *Papers on Malayan History* (Singapore, 1962), pp. 214–25.

52. *ST*, 25 January 1912.

53. Discussed in Yong Chin Fatt, 'A Preliminary Study of Chinese Leadership in Singapore, 1900–41', *JSEAH*, IX, 2 (1968), pp. 258–85.

54. W. Feldwick (ed.), *Present Day Impressions of the Far East and Prominent and Progressive Chinese at Home and Abroad* (London, 1917), pp. 836–7.

55. Gov. to S. of S., 19 September 1887, GD 25.

56. Caddy, p. 227.

57. H. Norman, *The People and Politics of the Far East* (London, 1895).

58. E.A. Brown, *Indiscreet Memories* (London, 1935), p. 17.

59. K.G. Tregonning, *The Singapore Cold Storage, 1903–1966* (Singapore, 1966).

60. For a discussion of the opium question, see Cheng U Wen, 'Opium in the Straits Settlements, 1867–1910', *JSEAH*, II, 2 (1961), pp. 52–75.

61. E. Wijeysingha, *A History of Raffles Institution, 1823–1963* (Singapore, 1963), pp. 83–107.

62. Zainal Abidin bin Ahmad (Za'ba), 'Malay Journalism in Malaya', *JMBRAS*, XIX, 2 (1941), pp. 244–50: W.R. Roff, *Bibliography of Malay and Arabic Periodicals in the Straits Settlements and Peninsular Malay States, 1876–1941* (London, 1972).

63. Cheng Mong Hock, *The Early Chinese Newspapers of Singapore, 1881–1912* (Singapore, 1967), p. 52.

64. *Straits Settlements Legislative Council Proceedings*, 13 February 1890, GD No. 28, 19 February 1890.

65. Quoted in A. Lovat, *The Life of Sir Frederick Weld* (London, 1914), p. 383.

66. A. Wright and H.A. Cartwright, *Twentieth Century Impressions of British Malaya* (London, 1908), p. 49.

67. A. Wright and T.H. Reid, *The Malay Peninsula: a Record of Progress in the Middle East* (London, 1912), p. 236.

# IV

# 'The Clapham Junction of the Eastern Seas'[1]
# 1914–1941

SINGAPORE stood on the sidelines while World War I and the Chinese Revolution were played out, but these two events combined to change the course of her history. The inter-war years at the time seemed to be a period of undiminished imperial authority, with Singapore the pillar of the eastern empire and scarcely a ripple of political or nationalist dissent to ruffle her serenity. Looking back, this era of deceptive calm can be seen as merely a prelude to the cataclysm of 1942, which set in chain the political storms of the following years. It was a period when Singapore's future was determined largely by external events, by developments in China and Japan, by decisions in Tokyo, Washington, and London.

When World War I broke out in August 1914, German residents in Singapore were interned, German ships were seized and German property taken over. British residents had mixed feelings about this. British merchants had viewed with some distaste and resentment the invasion in the early years of the century of a new breed of aggressive young German businessmen, very different from their suave countrymen of earlier days. German goods flooded the Singapore market, the German community expanded rapidly, and the opulent Teutonia Club overshadowed the nearby British Tanglin Club, which was almost deserted and its building in a dangerous state of disrepair. But the Germans were a hospitable and gregarious group, the life and soul of the western community's social life. Consequently at the outbreak of war they were comfortably installed with their servants in the Teutonia Club, and Diehn, the senior German merchant and head of Behn Meyer & Company, was allowed into town to look after the firm's affairs.

In the early months of the war Singapore feared an attack by the German East Asiatic squadron and particularly the cruiser *Emden,* which raided Penang in October 1914. But the *Emden* sailed past Singapore, making no attempt to attack the now fortified harbour. The *Emden's* destruction off the Cocos islands in November 1914 put an end to any threat of German naval action.

The turmoil and bloodshed of the European war seemed comfortably far away. To free men for active service, the Singapore garrison was reduced to one Indian regiment, the 5th Light Infantry, with a few

British Artillery and Royal Engineers. The Singapore Volunteer Rifles had been wound up in 1904 after languishing for some years, but a new Singapore Volunteer Artillery, 450 strong, was formed in 1914.[2] In addition a party of Sikh Malay States Guides was posted from Perak to bolster Singapore's defence.

After the German naval threat had evaporated, the 5th Light Infantry were ordered to Hong Kong in February 1915 but the regiment mutinied on the eve of their departure. This rising came as a shock to the placid calm of Singapore, which had always assumed that any danger would come from the sea and that a small garrison could cope with internal unrest. No provision had been made to defend Singapore against its own garrison.

Trouble had in fact been brewing for some time. Slack discipline and poor leadership undermined the morale of the 5th, which unlike most Indian regiments was a one-class regiment, consisting solely of Punjabi Muslims. Bitter that the British were fighting against Muslim Turkey, they came under the influence of Kassim Mansoor, a Gujarati Muslim coffee-shop owner, who lived near the Alexandra barracks and who wrote a letter in December 1914 to the Turkish consul in Rangoon, petitioning the Turks to send a warship to Singapore to collect pro-Turkish Indian Muslim troops.

Kassim Mansoor's attempts to sow disaffection among Malay policemen, who constituted the bulk of the police force, were unsuccessful, but Jagat Singh, a Sikh resident of Singapore, incited the Sikh Malay States Guides into refusing to embark for active service in December 1914, after which most of them were sent back to Taiping.

The Indian troops were put to guard the German military prisoners at Tanglin barracks, who included some of the *Emden's* crew. The senior officer was the enterprising Oberleutnant Julius Lauterbach, the *Emden's* navigation officer. A fat, jovial ex-merchant navy skipper and old China hand, Lauterbach knew Singapore well and had been accorded almost a hero's welcome by his British captors when he returned as a prisoner. The Germans struck up a cordial relationship with their Indian guards and Lauterbach in particular fanned resentment against their British masters.

As their departure for Hong Kong approached, bitterness and suspicion spread among the Indian troops, with rumours that they were being taken not to Hong Kong but to fight in France or Turkey, or even that their ship was to be deliberately sunk. When they asked Lauterbach's guidance, he advised them to resist, and on 15 February Indian soldiers murdered their officers, seized Alexandra barracks, released the German prisoners and then roamed the town in small groups murdering any Europeans they encountered.

With competent leadership, the Indian regiment, over eight hundred strong, could have had the town at their mercy, since they had caught the authorities unawares in the middle of the Chinese New Year holiday. But after the initial success, their leaders did not know what to do.

They appealed in vain to the Germans to lead them. Lauterbach, Diehn, and a few others took the opportunity to slip away by night and eventually got back to Germany, but most of the German prisoners were less enterprising and remained in their camp.

Once alerted, the government shepherded European women and children from the suburbs to safety in town hotels or on ships in the harbour. The officer in charge of the troops marshalled a motley collection of supporters: police, the Singapore Volunteer Artillery, British sappers, gunners and sailors, together with troops brought from Johor by the Sultan in person. Altogether there were about 500 men, only half of whom had military training. Nearly four hundred civilian special constables were also recruited, together with the crews of Allied French, Japanese and Russian ships which rushed to Singapore to help.

Mopping-up operations took ten days. The mutineers dispersed to the west and north of the island, some fleeing to Johor where they were rounded up and sent back by the Sultan. After trials which lasted from February to May 1915, Kassim Mansoor was hanged and 36 mutineers, including 2 Indian officers, were shot, 77 transported and 12 imprisoned. The executions of the soldiers were carried out in public at Outram Prison. At the time there was no dissent to these public shootings, which were attended by thousands from all communities, including a number of European women.

The commanding officer of the 5th Light Infantry was dismissed and the regiment was sent on active service. The Singapore police were reorganized, European men were obliged to undergo military training, and for the remainder of the war Singapore was garrisoned by a small detachment of British troops supported by the Volunteers.

All Indian residents in Singapore were compelled to register, which caused considerable ill-feeling among a basically loyal section of the community. Other Singaporeans dismissed the mutiny as a ten-day wonder. In itself it achieved nothing. It revealed no concerted plot, leadership or plan. It failed to rouse any support among the general population. The eastern part of the island was unaffected by the trouble and in Chinatown the New Year celebrations continued uninterrupted. But the incident contained a warning. Peace had been restored only with the help of Allied ships, and two of the four warships which came to British aid were Japanese cruisers. Almost half of the civilian special constables were Japanese. In time of international crisis Singapore's security rested on the Anglo-Japanese alliance, and the full implication of the lesson was to be driven home in Singapore on Chinese New Year's Day twenty-seven years later.

Singapore's centenary was not marked by any event as striking as the opening of the Suez Canal, which had coincided with her fiftieth birthday, but it was a time of general rejoicing. The war was over, the world was returning to normal, and for the moment trade was booming. Wartime shortages stimulated a healthy demand for imported goods, particularly motor-cars, which augured well for the rubber industry.

The post-war boom gave way to a recession in 1920. Rubber, which fetched $1.15 a lb in February 1920, slumped to 30 cents by December. Tin, which was $212 a picul in February, fell to $90 in December. But by 1922 Malaya was pulling out of the slump. The Stevenson rubber restriction scheme, imposed in 1922, laid down export quotas which helped maintain rubber prices. Firms such as Guthries, which bought up rubber land cheaply during the depression, started new planting schemes and diversified into oil palm. By 1923 the black times were over and demand for tin, rubber and petroleum was rising. The Johor Causeway linking Singapore with the mainland by road and rail was opened in 1923, giving a new boost to Singapore's trade. Tin prices rose to a peak in 1926 and 1927. Immigration soared, and in 1927 Chinese immigration figures achieved an all-time record of nearly 360,000.

Enormous fortunes were amassed almost overnight. Tan Kah Kee claimed to have made $8 million in a single year in 1925, and there were other multi-millionaires: Lee Kong Chian, born in Fukien in 1894, who began his career in Singapore as a school teacher, turned to business, married Tan Kah Kee's daughter, and formed his own Lee Rubber Company; Tay Koh Yat, born in Fukien in 1880, who came to Singapore at the age of twenty-two and became the leading bus-company magnate; Tan Lark Sye, born in 1896, who came to Singapore as a youth and became a wealthy rubber merchant and industrialist; Aw Boon Haw, one of Singapore's few prominent Hakka businessmen, who was born in Rangoon in 1893 and made his fortune in patent medicine, earning the soubriquet of 'Tiger Balm King'.

In these boom years government spending increased rapidly, particularly in the hitherto neglected fields of police, education, and medical services. The municipal commission, whose works had been interrupted during the war, was enlarged and launched big improvement schemes to cope with Singapore's rising population and to repair past deficiencies.

In the years immediately preceding the outbreak of war the municipality had begun the attack on malaria-breeding mosquitoes and from 1911 deaths from the disease fell steadily. In 1913 the first sewage pipes were laid and the government began taking over night-soil collection. Infant mortality, which stood at 345 per thousand in 1910, began to decline after 1912 with the provision of home visiting by nurses.

The Middleton Isolation Hospital had been opened in 1913, and in the 1920s the government embarked on an ambitious programme of building hospitals, staffed largely by the graduates of the King Edward College of Medicine. The new Outram General Hospital and the Trafalgar Home for lepers were both opened in 1926, the Woodbridge Mental Hospital in 1927 and the Kandang Kerbau Maternity Hospital in 1928.

By the end of World War I the growing popularity of motorized transport presented both opportunities and problems. The change from horse-drawn to motorized fire-engines in 1912 resulted in a dramatic improvement in tackling fires. Motor transport enabled people to move away from the crowded town centre, but private motor-cars increased from 842 in 1915 to 3,506 in 1920 and caused acute congestion on the inadequate roads. Public transport facilities were poor, depending largely on trams and rickshaws, but Chinese-operated seven-seater 'mosquito' buses came into vogue soon after the war. Following the failure of the Electric Tramways Company, the Singapore Traction Company, the first public motor-transport firm, was set up in 1925 to operate trolley buses and omnibuses, while the small Chinese bus owners amalgamated to form two bus companies in 1935. The municipality resurfaced roads to cope with the heavier traffic, and rail travel improved with the opening of a modern station, the present terminus, at Tanjong Pagar in 1932.

Electric lighting was a rarity outside the town centre in the early 1920s, but the first municipal power-station was opened at St. James in 1927. The Pulai reservoir in Johor was brought into use to supply Singapore with water in 1929, and the Seletar reservoir was completed in 1940.

A first attempt was made on slum clearance with the creation in 1927 of the Singapore Improvement Trust, a government-financed statutory body which worked in liaison with the municipality.

Many new public buildings were constructed, notably Fullerton Building, which included the General Post Office, in 1928, and the new Municipal Building (later City Hall) in 1929 on part of the site of the Hotel de l'Europe.

An American visitor, returning to Singapore in 1929 after an eight-year absence, commented, 'It is marvellous how you have progressed. Why, I hardly know the place.'[3]

The attitudes of the Singapore Chinese to the colonial authorities changed radically in the inter-war years. Affection for their motherland and active sympathy for budding Chinese nationalism had not conflicted with passive loyalty to the colonial régime in the early years of the century, and the initial exhilaration in Singapore when the Chinese Republic was founded gave way to disillusionment during the new régime's troubled early years.

During World War I the Straits Chinese leaders pledged their support for Britain and marshalled the resources of their community. They called on Straits-born Chinese youths to volunteer for military service, campaigned to raise funds for the National War Loan, gave generous donations for the purchase of aeroplanes and other equipment, and supported a War Tax Bill to levy income tax, which the legislative council passed in 1917.

The British put great store by these demonstrations of support but they affected only a minority even of the Straits Chinese. The basic feeling of the mass of the Singapore Chinese lay towards China, and the Chinese Republic's claims to command the loyalty of the Nanyang Chinese created mounting trouble for the Singapore authorities.

Sun Yat-sen's revolutionary Tung-ming Hui was reorganized as the

Kuomintang after the revolution and formed a branch in Singapore in 1912, with Lim Boon Keng and Lim Nee Soon among the first office-bearers. The Kuomintang aimed to enlist the financial support of the Nanyang Chinese in rebuilding China's economy, but the movement soon ran into trouble. President Yuan Shi-k'ai outlawed the parent Kuomintang in China when he seized power in 1913. Wilting under the strain of internal dissensions and colonial government suspicion, the Singapore branch of the Kuomintang formally dissolved the following year.

The Chinese business community in Singapore had shown its sympathy with China's cause on a number of occasions. In 1905 they boycotted American trade in protest against the United States Exclusion Act against Chinese immigration. Three years later they boycotted Japanese goods in support of the Manchus' quarrel with Japan over the seizure of a ship, and in 1915 they again boycotted Japanese goods on account of Japan's Twenty-One Demands against China. These were peaceful protests, confined to the merchant group, but after 1919 the masses became caught up in China's politics, changing the whole character of overseas Chinese involvement and their relationship with the Singapore authorities.

Young Hokkiens who had been prominent in the 4 May 1919 movement in China came to Singapore to rally support, provoking a mass demonstration which led to violence, with the looting of Japanese shops, factories, workshops and houses. The colonial authorities acted firmly to repress the outburst and looked with disapproval at the peaceful boycotts organized by the Singapore Chinese chamber of commerce and the Chinese consul-general in 1923 and 1928 in protest against Japanese encroachments on Chinese territory.[4]

The Kuomintang's fortunes revived in the early 1920s when Sun Yat-sen tried to put new life into the movement. The Kuomintang worked to bring Chinese schools in the Nanyang under its direction, sending teachers and textbooks from China, and in 1924 Sun Yat-sen established an Overseas Affairs Bureau to keep in close touch with the Nanyang.

Sun Yat-sen found a ready response among the Singapore Chinese, who contributed handsomely to establishing schools both in Singapore and China and invested large sums in industries in China. Tan Kah Kee in particular founded a number of schools in Fukien and contributed more than $4 million to build and maintain Amoy university, which was founded in 1921 with Lim Boon Keng as its first president.

Interest in China's politics encouraged the growth of political clubs in Singapore and gave new zest to the Chinese press. The 1920s witnessed a new type of financially profitable newspaper backed by China oriented businessmen, notably Tan Kah Kee's *Nanyang Siang Pau*, started in 1923, and the *Sin Chew Jit Poh,* founded in 1929 by Aw Boon Haw.

The Chinese chamber of commerce also fostered the sense of Chinese nationalism. Up to the Second World War nearly all of the chamber's leaders were China-born. Chinese-educated multi-millionaires, such as

Tan Kah Kee, Aw Boon Haw and Lee Kong Chian, who had little pull with the colonial authorities, were very influential among the immigrant Chinese.

The main nursery for Chinese nationalism in Singapore was the Chinese-medium schools. Patriotic Singapore Chinese often sent their children to China for secondary education, particularly to the Chi Nan school in Nanking, but in 1919 Tan Kah Kee raised money to open the first Singapore middle school, the Nanyang Hua Chiao Middle School or Hua Chung, which taught boys up to pre-university level. The new schools taught in Mandarin or Kuo-yu, which was not the dialect of any Singapore group but supported by Manchus, royalists, revolutionaries and Kuomintang alike as a unifying factor.

The Singapore authorities continued their traditional aloof policy towards Chinese-medium schools until the active participation of Chinese students and teachers in the violent anti-Japanese demonstration in 1919 made the Straits government realize the danger of political subversion in Chinese schools. In 1920 an Education Ordinance was passed which required the registration of all schools, teachers and managers, and gave the government powers to make regulations concerning the conduct of schools.

The Chinese schools objected strongly to this measure, organizing petitions and protest meetings. When government grants were offered to them for the first time in 1923, few applied for assistance, which entailed increased government supervision and an undertaking to teach in local Chinese dialects instead of Kuo-yu.

The authorities became more worried in the mid-1920s because of the growth of radical left-wing politics among the Chinese, which for the first time expressed anti-British and anti-colonial sentiments. During the period from 1924 to 1927 when the Kuomintang and the communists leagued together to unify China, the communists came to dominate the left wing of the Kuomintang in Singapore. Fu Ta Ching, a Chinese Communist Party agent, arrived from Shanghai in 1925 to build up the movement in Singapore, which was used as a base in plotting communist insurrection for Indonesia. Communist teachers and professional cadres were most successful among young Hainanese pupils in Kuo-yu medium night-schools, many of which had sprung up in the early 1920s, and in 1926 the communists formed the South Seas General Labour Union.

The secret societies had recruited many Hainanese *sinkhehs* to their ranks during the 1920–2 slump and battened on the left-wing political movement, which gave them a new lease of life. To counter this the government passed a Societies Ordinance in 1924 stiffening the penalties against secret-society gangsters, and it pressed more harshly on the Kuomintang as communist and *hoey* influence spread within it. Kuomintang branches were officially banned throughout Malaya in 1925, although a secret branch, dominated by the left wing, operated in Singapore. The authorities closed twelve troublesome Singapore schools in 1926, banished several teachers and students, and passed tougher legislation to tighten registration requirements.

At that time Singapore was known as the 'Chicago of the East', the haven of gunmen and street gangs, who carried out a reign of terror in Chinatown and the rural districts. A record number of murders was reported in 1927 and secret-society fights were an everyday occurrence. The Singapore police force was ill-prepared to cope with violence and subversion on such a scale, despite recent reforms. A Special Branch was created in 1919 to deal specifically with political subversion, and a police depot was established in 1924 to step up recruitment and raise educational and physical standards. But the force was under strength and riddled with corruption. There were very few British police officers working in the field and they were required to learn Malay rather than Chinese, although 90 per cent of criminal activity involved Chinese people. The growing tendency of the ruling class to hold itself apart from Asians meant that the police leadership was remote from the realities of Singapore's underworld.

The Kuomintang's left-wing extremism began to alienate the Straits Chinese and many of the China-born. Violence erupted in March 1927 at a mass meeting held to commemorate the death of Sun Yat-sen. About 2,000 Hainanese demonstrators, many of them schoolchildren, protested when the organizers launched into anti-communist speeches. The Hainanese then set out to march to Kreta Ayer and refused to disperse when ordered by the police, who panicked and opened fire. Seven people were killed and the ill-managed Kreta Ayer incident caused great bitterness among the Chinese. The official enquiry which followed opened the authorities' eyes to the extent of communist influence, particularly in schools. The government closed more night-schools, banned textbooks and from that time exerted constant vigilance to suppress communism.

The movement received a setback throughout South-East Asia in 1927 when the Dutch put down a communist rising in Java and the Kuomintang Nationalists broke away from the communists in China. After the failure of the Java revolt Tan Malaka, chief Comintern agent for South-East Asia, decided that future hope for communism lay with the urban Chinese and tried to reorganize the Nanyang communist movement in Singapore.

In 1928 the Comintern set up a Nanyang Communist Party, comprising mainly Hainanese members. The party infiltrated schools and organized strikes but these were broken by the police, the South Seas General Labour Union was banned and leading communists put in prison. In the late 1920s the fortunes of the Nanyang Communist Party were at a low ebb. Outlawed and harried by the Singapore police and the Chinese Protectorate, ordered by the Comintern to pursue a strict line of promoting proletarian revolution and to avoid collaboration with liberal or nationalist elements, the party was spurned by all but the poorest of Singapore Chinese.

In 1930 the communists attempted to remodel their organization in the Nanyang and held a secret meeting in Singapore, which was attended by Ho Chi-minh representing the communist Third International. A Malayan Communist Party was established, centred on Singapore and responsible to the Far Eastern Bureau of the Comintern in Shanghai. The communists set out to infiltrate schools and created two front organizations, the Singapore Chinese Middle School Teachers' Federation and the Singapore Students' Federation, which staged student strikes in the Chinese High School and Tiong Wah Girls' School in 1931.

The party's success was short-lived. In April 1931 a French communist leader, Joseph Ducroux, calling himself Serge Lefranc, came to Singapore to supervise the reorganization of the communist movement in Malaya. He was arrested two months later, and his address book revealed the ramifications of the communist movement in the Far East. These disclosures led to further arrests and to the complete disruption of the Malayan Communist Party, which was almost wiped out by the early months of 1932.

Initially the Kuomintang profited from the communists' disarray. At the time of the split in 1927 most Singapore Chinese sided with the Kuomintang and were impressed with its northern expedition and re-unification campaign in China. Once it had consolidated its position at home, the Kuomintang attempted to assert a more positive control over the Nanyang Chinese. The Chinese Republic continued to uphold the *jus sanguinis* principle established in the last years of the Manchu empire, and restated this in a Nationality Law of 1929, which claimed as Chinese nationals all persons of Chinese descent on the paternal side. Demanding loyalty from all Nanyang Chinese associations, Peking issued new laws in 1929 covering the activities of chambers of commerce and set up an Overseas Party Affairs Department three years later.

Education again became a prime concern and one of the Kuomintang's slogans was 'Without Chinese education there can be no overseas Chinese'. In 1927 the Kuomintang established a bureau of education and drew up regulations to register overseas Chinese schools, to supervise their curriculum and to encourage Nanyang Chinese to go to China for higher education. In 1929 the Chinese Ministry of Education launched a five-year plan for overseas education, and a year later drew up a twenty-year plan to finance overseas education through local levies from wealthy individuals and organizations. Kuo-yu was to be the medium of instruction and was universally adopted in all Singapore Chinese schools by 1935.

During the late 1920s the Kuomintang's policy of demanding loyalty from the overseas Chinese evoked a positive and enthusiastic response in the Nanyang, and the party's overseas membership expanded rapidly. In Singapore it attracted the support of many prominent Chinese and the Straits authorities took a lenient view of the Kuomintang and its anti-communist activities.

This situation changed at the end of 1929, with the appointment of Sir Cecil Clementi as Governor. Proficient in Cantonese and Mandarin, Clementi arrived with a reputation for sympathy and tact in dealing

7. Tan Kah Kee
(By permission of Mr. Lee Seng Gee)

8. Sir Cecil Clementi, Governor of Singapore, 1929–1934

with Chinese problems. He had begun his colonial service as a cadet in Hong Kong, rose to be Colonial Secretary, and after serving in British Guiana and Ceylon he returned to Hong Kong as Governor in 1925. He came to Singapore at a critical time when Malaya was facing the first brunt of the great international slump and a sudden change from prosperity to depression. But the strong measures which Clementi took to counteract subversion and deal with economic distress were racially divisive and roused widespread opposition.

In an attempt to suppress anti-colonial propaganda, which was mainly Chinese and communist in origin, he censored the vernacular press, enforced the ban on the Kuomintang in Singapore, and prohibited fund-raising for the party in China. The renewed ban came as a shock to many eminent Malayan Chinese supporters and roused a chorus of protest. As a compromise the British government permitted Singapore Chinese to be members of the Chinese Kuomintang but refused to permit branches to be established in Malaya.

While many of the leading Baba Chinese were not sorry to see re-strictions put on the Kuomintang, they were incensed at Clementi's other measures regarding education and immigration, which they took to be racially discriminatory and anti-Chinese. As an economy, in 1932 Clementi withdrew grants-in-aid from Chinese and Tamil vernacular schools, which meant that only Malay education was provided free and primary education in English was subsidized.

Immigration restrictions roused greater fears. An Immigration Restriction Ordinance had been drafted before the onset of the slump to improve labour standards and balance the sex ratio of immigrant communities by restricting the immigration of unskilled male labourers. The bill encountered such opposition from employers and the Singapore chamber of commerce that it was held in abeyance but was brought into force in 1930, in the teeth of European commercial opposition, in order to cope with rising unemployment.[5] Chinese immigrants could only come by recognized ships, which were allotted quotas, and these quotas were reduced in 1931 and further in 1932. The effect was dramatic. Chinese immigrants dropped from 242,000 in 1930 to less than 28,000 in 1933, and the fall was most marked among adult males, against whom the legislation was primarily aimed. From 158,000 in 1930, their numbers fell to less than 14,000 in 1933.

The Secretary for Chinese Affairs admitted in the legislative council that immigration restrictions were designed partly to ban those 'suspected of being likely to promote sedition or to cause a disturbance of public tranquillity'. It was almost exclusively the Chinese whom the government regarded as trouble-makers. In 1933 the Immigration Restriction Ordinance was replaced by an Aliens Ordinance, imposing quota restrictions and charging landing fees on aliens. In practice aliens meant Chinese, since the law did not affect Britons, nor Indians who were British subjects. Straits-born and immigrant Chinese united in opposing the social, racial and political implications of the Aliens Bill. They accused the colonial government of abandoning its neutral policy in favour of active discrimination against the Chinese. The Chinese chamber of commerce protested, and the attack was led in the legislative council by Tan Cheng Lock, himself a scion of a Hokkien Malacca Baba family which had settled in Malaya in the seventeenth century, who complained that this was a poor reward for the services which the Chinese had contributed to Malaya over many centuries.

Tan Cheng Lock stated bitterly in the legislative council in October 1932, 'The government has no fixed and constructive policy to win over the Straits and other Malayan-born Chinese, who are subjects of the country, and foster and strengthen their spirit of patriotism and natural love for the country of their birth and adoption.... One is driven to the conclusion that the Bill is part and parcel of an anti-Chinese policy, probably with a political objective, based on distrust and fear, which the Chinese on the whole as a community have done nothing and have given absolutely no cause to merit.'

For the first time government policy created racial tensions, and the legislation of the depression caused the Straits Chinese to question their future in Malaya.

In addition to imposing immigration restrictions, the government repatriated large numbers of Chinese and Indians at public expense during the slump years. 1931 was the first year in Singapore's history in which emigrants outnumbered immigrants, and the trend continued for the next two years. There was, however, some migration from the peninsula, particularly of unemployed Indian rubber plantation workers who drifted to Singapore.

The depression hit Singapore particularly hard, since she was so dependent upon international trade and notably upon the export of Malayan tin and rubber to the American market. Even before the slump, producers of these vulnerable commodities faced problems of over-production. The Stevenson restriction scheme was only partly successful in limiting rubber production and was abandoned in 1928 because the Dutch Indies refused to co-operate. Soaring tin prices in 1926 and 1927 bred over-confidence and over-production. The world economic crash converted these problems into a major crisis. The price of rubber fell from an average of 34 cents in 1929 to an all-time low of 4.95 cents in June 1932. Tin dropped to an average of $60 per picul in 1931. Singapore's revenue plummeted, while public expenditure reached a record high in 1931, partly because the authorities initially embarked on public works to stem unemployment. The following year the government slashed salaries, dismissed many officials, cut back on public works and health services, and at the same time increased taxation. It was a time of great hardship, and the island was a depressing place for all communities, for unemployed rubber planters and tin miners, who came down from the peninsula seeking work, for businessmen, shopkeepers, retrenched civil servants, commercial employees and labourers.

With the gradual revival of world confidence, Singapore recovered from the slump, helped by higher taxation rates and more effective output restriction schemes. In 1933 the budget balanced again. The first international tin-control scheme was introduced in 1931, and slowly the price of tin began to rise. Rubber restriction was more difficult to negotiate, but in 1934 an international agreement was eventually signed, regulating rubber exports and restricting new planting, which remained in force until the outbreak of World War II.

Measures to protect imperial trade provoked more controversy. There were fierce objections in 1932 when the Colonial Office instructed colonies and protectorates to introduce imperial preference tariffs, and the Singapore chamber of commerce and legislative council stoutly resisted British demands for quotas to be imposed on foreign textiles. The measure, which was aimed primarily at cheap Japanese textiles, had to be forced through the legislative council in 1934 using the official majority. Thus the twin principles of free trade and free immigration both fell casualty to the depression.

The slump also led to significant changes in Chinese business methods. Hitherto the Singapore Chinese had been slow to develop modern capitalist organization or banking, preferring to rely on regional associations and family links in a more personal form of trading. When European capital started to flood into the Malayan tin and rubber industries at the end of the nineteenth century the Singapore Chinese adapted themselves to the new western capitalism by the *compradore* system. The *compradore* was a go-between commission merchant, who provided financial guarantees to western organizations and personal credit to Chinese traders, receiving a salary from the European firm who employed him and a commission from both sides. This worked smoothly and oiled the wheels of economic development and investment, but it made the Chinese subordinate to western capital. The world slump taught the dangers of relying on European capital, particularly in primary production, and from that time enterprising Chinese turned to direct capital investment in secondary industries and to modern banking.[6]

Singapore did not regain the high pitch of prosperity which she had enjoyed in the late 1920s and faced many economic problems up to the outbreak of World War II. Her entrepôt trade suffered through imperial preference schemes and also from Dutch policy to develop rubber milling and grading in the Indies. Singapore's trade was badly affected, but enterprising Singapore Chinese set up their own rubber factories in Sumatra and Dutch Borneo.

The end of the slump and the return to normal conditions coincided with the arrival in 1934 of Sir Shenton Thomas as Governor. Clementi's departure was greeted with relief both by the Chinese, who had been alienated by his immigration and education policies, and by the Europeans, both officials and non-officials, who found him an uncomfortable man to deal with. His Inspector-General of Police admitted. Clementi was 'far too clever for his advisers',[7] and in the words of a prominent Malayan Ceylonese journalist he was 'too much an intellectual for the average "hail fellow, well met" and club back-slapping Malayans of those days'.[8]

The *Straits Times* stated in July 1934, 'What is needed is a man of pronounced administrative ability and a large measure of tact, who will... soothe feelings which have been sadly ruffled during the past three years.'[9] Shenton Thomas was ideal for this role. Approachable and sympathetic, he soon struck up an easy relationship with the European community. He diverted funds to relieve unemployment, revived schemes for public works, and in 1935 restored government grants to Chinese and Tamil vernacular schools.

On the surface life had never been so pleasant for the prosperous and the well-to-do, particularly for the European community. It was an era of gracious living in beautiful houses surrounded by green lawns and tended by plenty of servants. Singapore was an exceptionally clean city by Asian standards, and the city centre and fashionable residential areas were meticulously kept.

Everyday living was easier and healthier than ever before, to a large extent due to the Singapore Cold Storage Company, which pioneered the processing and distribution of hygienic food supplies in Malaya. In 1923 the company manufactured the first ice cream in Singapore, in 1926 it ousted its competitors to become the sole ice manufacturer, in the same year it set up a pig farm in Singapore and in 1929 established a dairy farm at Bukit Timah. In 1930 it began producing bread and three years later set up a groceries department. It brought in vegetables from the Cameron Highlands, meat from New Zealand, fruit from South Africa and the United States, and groceries from Europe. In addition to fresh milk, fruit, vegetables and tinned groceries, Singaporeans could also enjoy local-made beer. Malayan Breweries opened in 1932 and a German brewery was set up the following year.

Club life provided swimming, tennis, bridge, golf and flying, and the wireless and cinema were added attractions. The first commercial wireless station was established in 1915, but wireless sets did not come into common use until the British Malayan Broadcasting Corporation was set up in Singapore in 1936.

The increasingly popular motor-car permitted the affluent to travel further afield for their pleasures and encouraged a different life style. The golf club moved to a new and magnificent site at Bukit Timah in 1924, a second Island Club for golf opened nearby in 1927, the Singapore Flying Club was founded the same year, and in 1937 horse-racing was transferred to the new Turf Club at Bukit Timah, the most beautiful race-course in Asia. With the Hotel de l'Europe temporarily closed to make way for new public buildings, in the 1930s Raffles Hotel was the social centre for the European community, while the Seaview Hotel, which opened in the mid-1930s, became their favourite Sunday meeting place. The Swimming Club was lively, and there was one open air night-club, the Coconut Grove at Pasir Panjang. Cocktail parties and elaborate dinners became the fashion. Entertainment was pleasant but restrained, and all hotels, restaurants and clubs closed at midnight.

The wireless and the aeroplane, speeding up contact with the outside world, had a social impact on Singapore's European society comparable to the early steamships nearly a century earlier. The first aeroplane was flown by a Frenchman in Farrer Park in 1911, and in 1919 Captain Ross Smith landed there on his epic solo flight to win the first England to Australia air race. Singapore was a regular transit stop for many pioneer fliers, but its own aviation developed slowly. In 1923 the British government decided to construct a seaplane base at Sembawang, near the proposed naval base, and a Royal Air Force base at Seletar. The Seletar aerodrome was completed in the late 1920s and at first served civil aircraft as well as the Royal Air Force, but regular air communications did not come until the 1930s.

Clementi told the legislative council in 1931 that Singapore would become 'one of the largest and most important airports in the world'. The first airmail was delivered from London that year, and in 1934 Imperial Airways and Qantas began weekly flights. A civil airport with a grass runway was opened at Kallang in 1937, and by the late 1930s there were daily flights from Singapore to Kuala Lumpur, Ipoh, and Penang. Commercial flying was still a hazardous and novel form of passenger transport, but speedy postal and newspaper services brought Singapore into closer contact with world affairs.

Despite this, the western community was still parochial in its attitudes. The atmosphere of spaciousness, serenity and ease represented gracious living at its most superficial, and Singapore was a place of 'high living and low thinking'.[10] The love of music and the excellent concerts which the city enjoyed at the turn of the century had gone, and in the inter-war years Singapore lacked cultural depth, as occasional visiting performers of the arts found to their cost. When the world's premier ballerina, the exquisite Anna Pavlova, gave a charity performance in 1922, she was excluded from the Town Hall by the Amateur Dramatic Society's rendering of Gilbert and Sullivan and forced to dance on the small stage of the Teutonia Club. After an over-enthusiatic Chinese stage hand emptied the contents of several waste paper baskets over her during her snow dance, the enraged ballerina refused to dance a second performance.

The development of more complex administration, the expansion of schools and technical services, the growth of commerce and the new military bases brought in greater numbers of Europeans. The post-war practice of recruiting young university graduates and upper middle-class ex-public school boys for commercial posts, and the short-tour postings of army, navy and air force·officers, meant that former rather rigid hierarchical distinctions became blurred and the European community mingled more easily on terms of equality. Paradoxically, as elsewhere in colonial South-East Asia, the closer involvement of the government in everyday life, which brought in greater numbers of Europeans, inhibited social contact between rulers and ruled. It led to a widening chasm between Asians and the European minority, who developed a swollen-headed 'Singaporitis'. The ruling class encouraged this aloofness in order to preserve the last vestiges of the mystique of superiority, which had largely been stripped away by exposure through the cinema, western education, and the popular press.

Even the Christian religion did not draw Asians and Europeans together. While Europeans attended services at St. Andrew's Cathedral or the Roman Catholic Cathedral of the Good Shepherd, Chinese Roman Catholics went to the St. Peter and Paul Church, and Indians to the Church of Our Lady of Lourdes. The only social meeting places of Asians and Europeans were the three slightly disreputable entertainment parks or 'worlds'.

The mass of the population still lived in squalor. Rickets and malnutrition were common and the child mortality rate from beri-beri was high. But in the 1930s most Europeans could lead a life oblivious to the poverty, slums and crime of the more crowded sectors of the city. Singapore was a comfortable place also for the affluent Asian, and some of the benefits of the new amenities filtered through to the mass of the population, in the form of improved health facilities, cheap entertainment, better law and order.

Gang fights were still common, but by the 1930s the police force was much more efficient. Telephones, motor vehicles and radio communications made police work easier, and by that time senior posts were filled by officers who had gone through the police cadet system. A large proportion of public funds was devoted to police training in the 1930s and, apart from the Supreme Court, which was completed in 1939, the most impressive public works put up in Singapore in that decade were police buildings. The police were vigilant in keeping secret-society activity and subversion in check. The force was expanded to about 2,000 strong and powers to banish troublemakers were used frequently, so that Singapore in the 1930s became a more peaceful and safe place for the bulk of the population.

There was little blatant vice, and in the 1930s tourists in search of the lurid and picturesque were disappointed to find Singapore an outwardly staid and strait-laced port, which no longer lived up to its name of 'Sin-galore'. Opium dens were fast disappearing with the controls and restrictions on opium smoking, and brothels were illegal.

Until the 1920s the notorious Malay Street red-light district was the haunt of prostitutes, many of them women of East European origin, whose career brought them eastwards over the years with Singapore as the lowest point of degradation. In 1914 the sale of girls for prostitution was forbidden and restrictions on brothel-keepers were tightened during the 1920s. In 1927 the importation of girls for prostitution was stopped, and three years later brothels were closed after much argument, although prostitution remained legal. The law was only partially successful and tended to drive brothels underground, putting their inmates at the mercy of secret-society gangsters. By the 1930s Malay Street had lost its custom to the more discreet Lavender Street, to the popular Japanese 'hostesses' of Middle Road and the Japanese restaurant at Changi, or to the girls who waited in the 'rickshaw parade' at Dhoby Ghaut to ply their trade.

Other attempts were made to improve the status of women. The government tried, but with little success, to reform the *mui tsai* practice, whereby rich families 'adopted' girls from poor homes. The buying and selling of children was common in Singapore in the 1930s. Such adoption could be beneficial but was open to abuse and *mui tsai* were often exploited as unpaid domestic servants and prostitutes. Laws passed in 1926 and 1933 to prohibit the purchase of *mui tsai* and the employment of servants under the age of ten were ineffective since it was almost impossible to prove the age or the circumstances of acquiring *mui tsai*. The Colonial Office then appointed a commission to investigate the *mui tsai* question in Malaya and Hong Kong. The commission's majority report was optimistic about the position in Singapore where the shortage of women gave *mui tsai* a good chance to marry, but the government accepted the minority report, which claimed that the *mui tsai* system exploited young women. Legislation to abolish the system and protect young girls was passed in 1939 but not enforced because of the outbreak of war.[11]

A number of Straits Chinese leaders advocated marriage reform on western lines but most of the China-born wanted to retain traditional practice. The Singapore government was wary of interfering in Chinese marriage customs, beyond making legal provision for concubines and their children on the father's death. A Chinese Marriage Committee, appointed by the colonial authorities in 1926, made no progress in face of divided opinion within the Chinese community itself. In 1940 a Civil Marriage Ordinance provided for the voluntary registration of mono-gamous marriages, but Chinese traditional marriages also continued to be recognized.

The authorities made some attempt to improve working conditions. Chinese indentured labour was abolished in 1914, and a series of labour ordinances passed in 1920, 1923 and 1930 provided more protection for workers. Chinese labourers were able to bring wage disputes to the Protectorate for settlement free of charge in the 1930s. But the colonial government did not favour the formation of western-type trade unions, which failed to take root in Singapore before World War II. Nor did the nature of Singapore society lend itself to the growth of organized labour. Few Malays were engaged in enterprises involving large numbers of workers, although a Malay Seamen's Association was formed in 1916. Indians showed no interest in forming labour organizations before the abolition of their indentured labour system in 1938. The Chinese already had trade guilds and were the first to move towards modern labour organizations, but the identification of these early labour associations with Kuomintang and communist politics laid them open to government repression and inhibited the emergence of a genuine labour movement.

The Kuomintang encouraged the growth of trade unions in the Nanyang as a means to rally Chinese backing and tap workers' money, and the communists vied for Chinese working-class support. The South Seas General Labour Union was renamed the Malayan General Union in 1930, after the Malayan Communist Party was formed, and was affiliated to the Pan-Pacific Trade Union Secretariat, a branch of the Comintern. It attracted mainly unskilled workers, particularly Hainanese.

The Kuomintang/communist split, followed by the economic slump and the destruction of the Malayan Communist Party in 1931–2, hit the infant trade union movement hard. In the mid-1930s employers held the whip hand, so that wages and working conditions did not improve in step with the revival of the economy. Singapore experienced her first real labour trouble in 1936 when the communists tried to exploit this resentment. Singapore seamen made a bid to break the hold of licensed lodging-houses over recruitment of sailors, and there were strikes among municipal and transport workers, pineapple-factory employees, building and construction workers.

The strikes were broken and throughout the 1930s the colonial authorities were intent on keeping communist influence out of trade unions. The Special Branch of the police was often overzealous in viewing genuine grievances as subversion and employers took advantage of this situation. The Chinese Protectorate succeeded to some extent in tempering police repression and employers' exploitation, but its own popularity declined in the inter-war years because it was so much involved in enforcing restrictions, censoring the press and investigating political subversion.[12]

Shortly before the outbreak of war in Europe, Britain set out to extend the British type of labour legislation to her colonies. An Industrial Courts Bill and Trade Union Bill were passed in Singapore in 1940 and a Trade Disputes Ordinance in 1941. Neither employers nor workers showed enthusiasm for the measures, which were based on British conditions, and no trade union was registered in Malaya under the 1940 Ordinance up to the outbreak of the Pacific War. In August 1941 the government outlawed strikes in essential industries and in public transport, and the Japanese invasion put an end to labour disputes.

The expansion of the economy and growth of employment opportunities led to an increasing demand for education. Government expenditure on education nearly doubled in the period from 1924 to 1932, although it still accounted for less than 6 per cent of the revenue. Most of the finance went into English-medium education, although this did not keep pace with demand, particularly from the Straits Chinese.

In 1917 the Straits Chinese British Association appealed for tertiary and technical education. It was decided to establish a college of Arts and Sciences to mark Singapore's centenary, and Raffles College was opened in 1928. The college awarded diplomas, and most of its graduates went into secondary school teaching or into subordinate official posts. Singapore's second government English-medium secondary school, the Victoria School, was opened in 1931.

English-educated Singaporeans had no difficulty in finding jobs before the great slump, but the sudden shock of unemployment led them for the first time to criticize English education for being too bookish. More emphasis was put in the 1930s on practical and vocational training and on suiting the content of teaching to local needs. The first government trade school had been set up in 1929, and in 1938 an official commission recommended an expansion of vocational and scientific education.

This commission, led by Sir William McLean, was appointed to investigate the state of higher education in Malaya. Many Straits Chinese and Indians wanted a university, but the Straits government and the British community in general thought the time was not ripe for such an institution. The McLean Commission concurred with this view.[13] The Medical College, to which a dental school had been added in 1937, enjoyed a high reputation in the East, but the commission considered Raffles College was not up to international university standard, nor was it geared to meet local conditions. The commission recommended that the College should establish departments of Chinese and Malay, with a view to expanding vernacular teaching in the schools, and it also proposed that a technical college be built adjoining Raffles College. These recommendations were not carried out and the whole question of higher education was left in abeyance.

The Methodist Mission contemplated setting up an Anglo-Chinese College of tertiary education and formed a council which included Tan Kah Kee and Tan Cheng Lock, but the scheme was shelved and the funds were eventually transferred to the Anglo-Chinese School.

By 1939 there were 72,000 children at school in Singapore, of whom 38,000 studied in Chinese-medium schools, 27,000 in English schools, nearly 6,000 in Malay schools and 1,000 in Tamil schools.[14] Large numbers of children, particularly girls, did not attend school at all, since all institutions other than the government Malay schools charged fees. Even Malay parents showed little interest in educating their daughters, and as late as 1916 there were barely one hundred Malay girls in school in Singapore.

The Straits authorities provided four years of free primary vernacular schooling for Malay children, gave substantial subsidies to government and aided English-medium schools, and small financial grants to certain Chinese and Tamil schools. Secondary education was supposed to be self-supporting. Scholarships at Raffles Institution and Victoria School were confined to very gifted pupils, to avoid creating a frustrated educated class. The scholarship scheme produced some prominent men, who invariably came from middle-class and well-to-do families, but it provided few opportunities for the mass of school children.

Malay education received a boost with the appointment of Richard Winstedt as Director of Education for the Colony and the Federated

Malay States in 1916. From 1919 provision was made for bright Malay children to transfer to and receive free tuition in English-medium schools, and in 1924 special remove classes gave intensive English instruction to such children. But it required considerable ability, effort and parental backing to pass from the Malay primary to English secondary schools.

Education for the vast majority of Malay children in Singapore was hampered by being tied to the policy followed in the Malay states. Here the aim was to avoid social dislocation and keep Malays contented in their traditional way of life by educating them to be better farmers and fishermen, with an emphasis on practical arts, crafts and gardening. Malay schools were no gateway to the commercial life of Singapore, and rudimentary vernacular education held most Malay children back from the mainstream of Singapore's development.

Tamil schooling in Singapore offered no outlets for pupils except to become unskilled labourers. When schools were first registered in 1920 there was only one Tamil vernacular school, which was run by the American Methodist Mission. A few others sprang up after 1923 when government grants were offered, and by 1941 there were eighteen Tamil schools registered in Singapore, run either by Tamil Associations or Christian missions.

Chinese schools continued to stand aloof from the government as far as they could. Few accepted grants with the controls which these entailed. Despite attempts at government supervision, closure of schools and banishment of teachers, the Chinese schools still brought in their teachers and textbooks from China and oriented children towards their mother-land. Wealthy Singapore Chinese businessmen contributed generously to Chinese schools, and despite friction with the government and rivalry between the Kuomintang and the communists, many Chinese schools made good progress in the 1930s. But they provided no avenue to government service nor to the commercial world outside the Chinese sector. The vast majority of Chinese-educated children received only primary schooling and went into manual jobs.

Repeated, if not very vigorous, attempts by the authorities to base education on vernacular teaching in the nineteenth century had all failed, and, apart from the Chinese schools, vernacular education did not extend beyond the primary stage because it had no commercial value. In the first decades of the twentieth century the government followed the public demand in expanding English secondary education, which created a common bond between the talented and ambitious élite of different racial groups. Such unity was achieved at the expense of cutting them off from their cultural roots and separating them from the mass of their own community.

This danger was beginning to be appreciated in the 1930s even among the non-Chinese English-educated, and the McLean Commission tried to produce a better balance by encouraging the teaching of vernaculars as second languages in English-medium schools. Nothing came of this before World War II and the education system was racially and socially divisive. It offered a promising career for the English-educated minority but condemned the mass of the vernacular-educated to unskilled work with no opportunity to rise in the government or international commercial fields.

While English-medium education was valued mainly as a means to a career, it inevitably imparted some western ideas, attitudes, and ways of life. English and American films and sports, such as cricket and tennis, enjoyed great vogue. Among Singapore men traditional dress gave way to European attire. Many younger Asian women also adopted western fashions, and sleeveless frocks, high heels and cigarette cases became the mark of sophistication among Straits Chinese girls in the 1930s.

The growth of an educated Asian middle class gave an impetus to newspapers, both vernacular and English. The Penang *Straits Echo*, started in 1911, was the first English-language newspaper to cater for the Straits Chinese, but much more influential was the *Malaya Tribune*, which began publication in 1914, with the support of Lim Boon Keng and a group of Eurasians, 'to express the views and aspirations of the domiciled communities'.

Whereas the two existing English-language newspapers were both European in outlook, the *Tribune* appealed to the English-speaking of all races. It filled a need and prospered, despite opposition from St. Clair of the *Free Press* and Still of the *Straits Times*. In the 1930s the *Tribune* claimed a circulation of 18,000 to 20,000, rising to a peak of 24,900 copies on weekdays and 31,500 on Sundays in 1941. In face of this competition the *Straits Times* struggled to expand its circulation, which fell to 6,000 during the depression. By the late 1930s it rose to 15,000 after a determined sales effort, including a price reduction to 5 cents a copy, and on the eve of World War II the newspaper claimed more Asian than European readers.

The expansion of Chinese education and increasing interest in affairs in China boosted the sale of Chinese newspapers. By 1935 Aw Boon Haw's *Sin Chew Jit Poh* had a readership of 30,000 in Malaya and Singapore, and Tan Kah Kee's *Nanyang Siang Pau* nearly 10,000.

The character of the Malay press changed. Up to that time the leading Malay newspapers had been linked to the English-language press, but the *Lembaga Melayu* closed down in 1931 and during the 1930s Singapore's Malay-language press was controlled by the Arab community. The Alsagoff family launched the *Warta Melayu*, which was published daily from 1930 to 1941. Onn bin Jaafar, who edited the *Warta Melayu* for its first three years, then founded and edited a *Lembaga Malaya*, which was Arab financed and was published in Singapore from 1934 to 1937, after which it moved to Johor Bahru.

In an attempt to shake free from Arab control, Malay journalists founded a new *Utusan Melayu*, which was issued daily in Singapore from 1939 until the fall of Singapore to the Japanese. The first Malay-controlled newspaper, the *Utusan Melayu* was financed by widespread subscriptions raised from Malay peasants, taxi drivers and other ordinary people, and edited by the distinguished Abdul Rahim Kajai.

The Malay press matured during the 1930s and a generation of professional Malay journalists came to the fore, but Malay newspapers devoted their interest to peninsular affairs and the centre of Malay political and cultural life swung away from Singapore to Penang and the Malay states.

The steep rise in land values in the inter-war years bore perhaps most heavily upon the Malays, who wished to preserve a semi-rural way of life. They found themselves a neglected minority in an Anglo-Chinese city, but their immediate resentment was often directed towards wealthy Arab families who had bought up enormous tracts of land.

The Arab community reached the height of its prosperity in these years. Wealthy Arabs continued to finance charitable works and public amenities, such as the Japanese-style public gardens opened by the Alkaff family in 1929, but the new generation of Arabs lived in European style and drew away from the mass of the Muslim community. Many of them, such as Syed Mohammed bin Omar Alsagoff, the leader of the Arab community in the 1920s, were educated in England, and some married Europeans.

The leadership of the Arabs and the Jawi-Peranakan, who had dominated the Malayo-Muslim community for fifty years, now came to be challenged by enterprising young Malays, many of them English-educated and influenced by western secular ideas. Mohammed Eunos Abdullah was the most outstanding of this group. He was prominent in Malay social welfare organizations and a member of the Muslim Advisory Board set up by the government during World War I. Mohammed Eunos was appointed a justice of the peace and in 1922 became the first Malay municipal commissioner. He gathered about him a group of modern-minded educated Malays, notably Dr. Abdul Samad, the first Malay doctor, and Tengku Kadir, who belonged to the Kampong Glam royal family. They objected to the Persekutuan Islam Singapura (the Muslim Association of Singapore) as a rich man's club and founded a rival Muslim Institute to care for the needs of ordinary Malays.

Rivalry between these two associations came to a head when the colonial authorities decided to appoint a further Asian representative to the legislative council in 1924. The Persekutuan wanted a Muslim nominee but the Muslim Institute wanted a Malay. The British preferred to choose on a racial rather than religious basis, and appointed Eunos Abdullah as the first Malay legislative councillor.

In order to give Eunos Abdullah support as the mouthpiece for the Malay community, in 1926 the Kesatuan Melayu Singapura or Singapore Malay Union was formed, with Eunos Abdullah as its first president.[15] It appealed specifically to Malays, and membership was confined to Malay people, indigenous to the peninsula and the archipelago, thus excluding Arabs and Indian Muslims.

One of the Kesatuan's first acts was to back Eunos Abdullah's appeal in the legislative council in 1927 for land to be set aside for Malay settlement, which led to over 600 acres of land on the eastern outskirts of the city being designated to form Kampong Melayu.

Kesatuan Melayu Singapura leaders were mainly English-educated Malay journalists, government officials and middle-class merchants, who differed greatly from the aristocratic Malay élite of the peninsular states. They pressed the Singapore authorities to improve the condition of the Malays, particularly in education opportunities, and Mohammed Eunos Abdullah's campaign in the legislative council led to the opening of a trades school for Malays in 1929. When Eunos Abdullah died in 1934 Embok Suloh took his place on the legislative council and as president of the Kesatuan Melayu Singapura. Under his leadership the party continued throughout the 1930s to co-operate with government, offering only mild criticism of official policies concerning the Malays and steering clear of more extreme Indonesian radicals.

The Kesatuan Melayu Singapura was the first political Malay association but could hardly be described as a nationalist party. It did not oppose British rule but was concerned to safeguard Malay interests in face of the rising political ambitions of the Straits Chinese. Kesatuan leaders were instrumental in establishing the new *Utusan Melayu,* which was not anti-British but often anti-Chinese and sometimes criticized the non-Malay Muslim community. Its chief concern was with Malay problems, particularly relating to education.

Politically the Kesatuan Melayu Singapura was important mainly as the fore-runner of the post-war United Malays National Organization. The Kesatuan Melayu Singapura stimulated the founding of similar Malay associations in the Malay states in the late 1930s, and at the second conference of the Malay associations in Singapore in 1940 Onn bin Ja'afar expressed the conviction that the Malay associations would enable Malays to 'regain the political and civil rights which have slipped from them'. When Dato Onn succeeded in rousing Malay political feeling six years later, this centred in peninsular Malaya, not Singapore.

Even if their work took them to the city as civil servants, clerks, drivers or labourers, urban Malays could preserve some of their traditional way of life in Singapore in the 1930s, living in peaceful surroundings in kampong-style houses in almost exclusively Malay districts such as Kampong Melayu and Geylang Serai. Some small Malay communities were able to resist modernization almost entirely. A large enclave of Malays moved along the coast at Pasir Panjang as shipping and business interests took over Telok Blangah. They lived by fishing, making charcoal and driving bullock carts in the harbour area. Another settlement grew up about a mile further west along the coast beyond Pasir Panjang in the 1930s, when the construction of Kallang airport displaced them from their former homes. In their new settlement they resumed a livelihood of fishing and growing fruit.

In the southern islands and at points along the north and east coasts of the island, Malay villages remained almost untouched by modern progress. When the development of the naval base, military installations and airfields forced villagers to move, they settled at other points on the coast to carry on their traditional occupations.

Official educational policy encouraged Malays to cling to their accustomed way of life. With the growth of urban opportunities the city's pull became stronger, but it was not yet irresistible.

The English-educated Asian middle class grew rapidly in the inter-war years, and the proportion of Straits-born Singaporeans increased. In 1921 only a quarter of the Singapore Chinese were Straits-born. Ten years later the proportion had risen to 36 per cent, and the change in immigration policy in the 1930s reduced the inflow of the China-born. In 1933 adult male immigration was restricted to a quota of one thousand a month, and Chinese immigrants tended to remain in the Straits for fear that if they revisited China they might be unable to return to Singapore. Since no restriction was put on women immigrants until 1938, Chinese men had more opportunity to marry in Singapore than in previous times, and the birth rate among Straits Chinese in the mid-1930s was higher than among any other racial group.[16]

Despite this, up to the Second World War immigrant Chinese continued to outnumber the Straits-born in Singapore, and the vast majority even of the Straits-born attended Chinese schools, if they received any education at all.

The growth of Chinese nationalism and of Kyo-yu education fostered a distinction between the Chinese and English-educated, which was accentuated by the growing fashion among well-to-do Singapore Chinese to send their sons either to universities in Britain or to the Sun Yat-sen, Peking or Amoy universities in China. The development also weakened but did not destroy traditional groupings along lines of dialect or regional loyalty.

The political interests of the Chinese-educated were absorbed with the problems of China and the Japanese threat. Anti-Japanese feeling had been growing in Singapore for many years. Chinese in Singapore boycotted Japanese goods when the Kuomintang clashed with the Japanese in Shantung in 1928 and when the Japanese invaded Manchuria in 1931.

At that time Kuomintang fortunes in Singapore were at a low ebb, but revived rapidly in the face of Japan's invasion of Manchuria, followed in 1937 by the outbreak of the Sino-Japanese War. The Kuomintang's call for the Nanyang Chinese to raise money and send young volunteer helpers to the mother country found a ready response from many influential Chinese in Singapore, particularly from Tan Kah Kee. Having spent a large part of his fortune on educational projects after the First World War, Tan Kah Kee went bankrupt during the great depression in 1933. After that time he left his son-in-law, Lee Kong Chian, to rebuild the family fortunes in the rubber and pineapple industries and in banking. Meanwhile Tan Kah Kee devoted his energies to serving the cause of China and became the leading figure in the Nanyang Chinese National Salvation Movement.

In August 1937, one month after the outbreak of war in China, the dominant Hokkien group in the Chinese chamber of commerce formed the Singapore Chinese General Association for the Relief of Refugees in China, with Tan Kah Kee as president. In October 1937 he became head of the Malayan fund-raising movement, with Singapore as his base, and the Kuomintang sent a former consul-general, Tiao Tso-chi'en, to organize the sale of Chinese government subscription bonds among the Malayan Chinese.

Tan Kah Kee was on friendly terms with the Chinese consul-general, Kao Ling-pai, and with Chiang Kai-shek and other Kuomintang leaders. The Chinese government sent agents to organize boycotts of Japanese goods with the help of local associations, such as the Chinese chamber of commerce, and also enrolled secret societies in the patriotic cause.

The Singapore government became alarmed as anti-Japanese feeling grew. Chinese gave up patronizing Japanese shops, dentists, doctors and barbers. The boycott led to a dramatic fall in Japanese trade with Malaya, which showed a drop in 1938 of nearly 70 per cent from the previous year. Chinese property-owners evicted Japanese tenants, Chinese schools taught anti-Japanese propaganda, Chinese students stoned Japanese school-children, Chinese picketed not only Chinese shops but also Indian and Malay shops selling Japanese goods. Bands of youths, notably the Red Blood Brigade, intimidated Chinese traders who broke the boycott, damaging their shops, cutting off their ears and sometimes murdering them. The Japanese consul-general, Gunji Kiichi, protested, and the colonial authorities forbade anti-Japanese demonstrations, banned the import of anti-Japanese textbooks from China, and forbade the teaching of inflammatory propaganda and anti-Japanese songs in Chinese schools. They also prohibited the collection of funds for the war in China and were sceptical of Tan Kah Kee's assurances that the subscriptions were to help refugees and the bereaved.

The British were particularly worried because of increasing communist infiltration in the National Salvation Movement. The communists had been thrown into disarray following the arrest of Serge Lefranc in 1931, and the constant vigilance of the police and the Chinese Protectorate, 'the uncrowned kings of Malaya', prevented the remnants of the Malayan Communist Party exploiting the hardships of the depression years.

But the communists made a new start in 1934 with the arrival of an Annamese Comintern agent, Wong Kim Geok, alias Lai Teck, who became secretary-general of the Malayan Communist Party. The Comintern Far East Bureau ordered the party to concentrate first on gaining control over labour, and communists played a big role in the strikes and labour disputes which broke out in 1936. In 1935 the Comintern adopted a radical change in policy, abandoning its insistence on direct proletariat revolution in favour of allying with anti-imperial national struggles.

The Malayan Communist Party could now exploit patriotic Chinese resistance to Japanese aggression. After the Chinese Communist Party formed a united front with the Kuomintang against Japan in December 1936, communists quickly infiltrated the Nanyang Chinese National Salvation Movement and changed the names of their organizations to give them a patriotic ring, so that the General Labour Union, for instance, became the Labouring Classes' Anti-Enemy-Backing-Up Society.

The outbreak of the Sino-Japanese War in 1937 gave the Malayan Communist Party the chance to widen its support. Although the party was illegal, it posed in the guise of the All-Malayan National Liberation movement. Between 1937 and 1941 the communists used anti-Japanese activities to extend their influence from young impressionable students and disgruntled labourers to more prominent community leaders. The Malayan Communist Party formed a series of committees, some secret bodies of hard core members and other open organizations such as the Chinese National Liberation Vanguard Corps, to which they attracted Tan Kah Kee and other patriot leaders.

Anti-Japanese feeling intensified in Singapore as the Japanese swept into south-east China, seizing Amoy in May 1938 and bombing Canton, Swatow and Hainan. Demonstrations and protest meetings were broken up by the police. Parades and street meetings were banned, and the police raided a number of underground associations. Arrests and banishments in turn provoked more disturbances and unrest. The British authorities were now deeply alarmed at the evidence of communist influence and of connexions with the secret societies.

Supported by the Chinese consul-general and by Lee Kong Chian, who was then chairman of the Chinese chamber of commerce, Tan Kah Kee stepped up contributions for China and put the collection on a systematic basis, making each dialect group responsible for raising funds from its own community. The object was to extract payment from all Singapore Chinese, including the Straits-born, ranging from a contribution of 1 per cent of a labourer's wages to large donations from the rich. This was supplemented by fund-raising drama shows and flag days. At first the response from the immigrant Chinese was enthusiastic, but the demands came at a difficult time when rubber and tin prices were low. The Kuomintang put pressure on Tan Kah Kee to step up donations and Chinese newspapers published the names of donors and of people who refused to contribute.

In October 1938 delegates from all the Nanyang countries attended a conference in Singapore, at which it was decided to create a Nanyang Chinese Relief General Association, to co-ordinate patriotic efforts. Tan Kah Kee was elected chairman, his *Nanyang Siang Pau* was the mouthpiece of the Association, and the committee was dominated by Chinese from Malaya and Singapore. The Nanyang Chinese Relief General Association had thirty sub-committees in the Nanyang and an active membership of over 20,000. It raised money, encouraged the purchase of Chinese government bonds, stimulated investment in industries in China and recruited youths to work on the Burma Road, China's vital life-line to the west.

The Association was the nearest to a united overseas Chinese movement, but its strength was undermined by clannishness and personal rivalries. Tan Kah Kee was the most prominent leader but Tan Ean Kiam, a Hokkien financier and managing director of the Oversea Chinese Bank, and Aw Boon Haw, who commanded support from the Cantonese as well as the Hakka *pangs,* also vied for power.

The predominantly Hokkien committee was at loggerheads with the Cantonese, and there was no Hakka representation. Aw Boon Haw organized fund-raising independently through his *Sin Chew Jit Poh* and the Hakka Association. No prominent Baba served on the committee, and the Straits Chinese as a community showed reluctance to contribute funds to the movement.

The Nanyang Chinese National Salvation Movement attained the height of its effectiveness in 1939, when the Nanyang Chinese closed ranks against Wang Ching-wei, who deserted Chiang Kai-shek in December 1938, came to terms with the Japanese, set up a puppet government in Nanking and tried to win the Nanyang Chinese over to his policy. Wang Ching-wei had long-established links with Malaya going back to the early years of the century before the Chinese Revolution, but Tan Kah Kee refused to support him and urged Chiang Kai-shek to continue fighting. The Singapore Chinese backed Tan Kah Kee's stand, and the *Nanyang Siang Pau,* the *Sin Chew Jit Poh* and the other Chinese newspapers in Singapore condemned Wang Ching-wei as a traitor.

At that point the prestige of Chiang Kai-shek and the Kuomintang stood at its highest point with the Singapore Chinese, who appeared to have been brought together in united opposition to the Japanese, but, under the banner of a united front, the Kuomintang and the communists were in reality competing for power, and these divisions eventually undermined the Nanyang Chinese Relief General Association.

In April 1939 the Malayan Communist Party called for an 'All Races United Front to strive for a democratic system and oppose the Jap-Axis bloc'. The party gained great prestige because of its vociferous opposition to the Japanese and by May 1940 claimed a membership of between 50,000 and 60,000.[17] It competed with the Kuomintang for the support of men such as Tan Kah Kee, who had no bent towards socialism but were Chinese patriots.

The Kuomintang tried to strengthen its hold over the overseas Chinese. In 1939 Chungking opened an Overseas Chinese Investment Information Office, and early the following year sent General Wu T'ieh-ch'eng, Minister of Overseas Party Affairs, to try to step up investment by the Malayan Chinese in China's new industries. Following Wu's visit an anti-Japanese youth organization, the San-Min-Chu-I Youth Corps, was established, and Chungking followed this up with further attempts to establish a tighter control over the Chinese National Salvation Movement in Malaya.

With the boom in the Malayan economy following the outbreak of the war in Europe, the Singapore Chinese increased their investment in Chinese industries, but there was growing criticism of the Kuomintang. Tan Kah Kee was irritated by Chungking's interference in the Singapore movement and worried by reports of conditions in China. He decided to accept an invitation extended by Wu T'ieh-ch'eng to visit China and left Singapore for Chungking in March 1940. For the next nine months Tan travelled widely in the country and was distressed at the conditions under which Nanyang volunteers were working on the Burma Road, shocked at the corruption of many of Chiang Kai-shek's supporters and impressed by the spartan sense of discipline shown by Mao Tse-tung and his communist followers in Yenan.

By the time he returned to Singapore Tan Kah Kee was openly critical of the Kuomintang and at the second congress of the Nanyang Chinese Relief General Association in Singapore in March 1941 he clashed with the consul-general, Kao Ling-pai, in bitter invective against the government's activities in China. Tan was re-elected chairman of the Association, but the Kuomintang worked to discredit him and this rift threatened to wreck the whole Nanyang Chinese National Salvation movement.

The small minority of pro-British Baba 'King's Chinese', who prided themselves on being British subjects, were not deeply involved in Chinese politics or committed to the Kuomintang's activities. They aspired rather to secure a larger share in Singapore's public life, and through the Straits Chinese British Association and their representatives on the legislative council they agitated for better education opportunities and more political powers.

The Baba leaders consistently pressed for English-medium education. Their community had been largely instrumental in financing the Medical School in 1905 and Raffles College in 1928. In the 1930s they appealed for free primary English-medium education and more scholarships in English secondary schools. Some wanted to see English as the *lingua franca* and campaigned to found a university.

With the steady expansion of English education many Straits Chinese, Indians and Eurasians became highly anglicized professional or business men, the most prominent admitted to the executive, legislative and municipal councils and the recipients of British honours. Yet the very prevalence of this westernization led to a hardening of aloof attitudes among Europeans and to social barriers. The Governor held multi-racial receptions, but there was little mixing in private homes. Inter-racial marriage was frowned upon, and Asians were rigidly barred from senior posts in the Malayan Civil Service and from membership of European social clubs.

This led to frustration but not to smouldering discontent, and as yet the vague resentments of the Straits Chinese were not channelled into any organized opposition. The colonial regime was snobbish, condescending, somewhat contemptuous but benign. While talented English-educated Asians had little prospect of a political or bureaucratic career, there were considerable material rewards to be gained in professional life and in business.

On the eve of the Second World War the Singapore government remained in many ways remote from the ordinary lives of the mass of the population. Top-level administration was in the hands of a small group of officials of the Malayan Civil Service, which was confined to 'natural-born British subjects of pure European descent on both sides', although British subjects of all races could apply for middle-ranking executive and technical posts. The Straits Medical Service was opened to Asians in 1932, but few Asian doctors rose above the bottom rungs of the service. A Straits Civil Service was created in 1934 and a Straits Legal Service in 1937, to which Asians who had graduated from British universities could apply, but few were admitted each year and there was no provision for transfer to the Malayan Civil Service. The expansion of opportunities for Singaporeans was held back by political considerations in the rest of Malaya, where the Malay rulers opposed the entry of non-Malay Asians to the civil service.

Under the constitution,[18] which had not changed in principle since 1867, the Governor worked in consultation with the upper strata of European non-officials and with a tiny section of the wealthy and professional English-speaking Asian community.

The most popular, and often the most successful, Governors were those who did not seek to rock the boat. In the words of Sir Laurence Guillemard, who was Governor from 1919 to 1927, 'The main duty of the Governor must be to keep the colony in peace, prosperity and security.'[19] Innovative and enterprising Governors, such as Guillemard himself or Clementi, stirred up opposition and difficulty, whereas less gifted but genial Governors, such as Arthur Young during the First World War or Shenton Thomas in the 1930s, often presided over periods of quiet construction.

The inefficient structure of British administration in Malaya came into question again during the inter-war years, and attempts to reform the constitution and make administration more effective were initiated by the two outstanding Governors of the period, Sir Laurence Guillemard and Sir Cecil Clementi.

Guillemard, who came with a brilliant record from the British Treasury, re-examined Anderson's proposals for strengthening the High Commissioner's authority over Kuala Lumpur and making administration more uniform between Singapore and the Malay states. In 1925 he proposed to abolish the post of Chief Secretary, to transfer some of Kuala Lumpur's powers to the separate state governments and to bring the states into more direct contact with the High Commissioner. Guillemard promised this would not mean any new centralization in Singapore, 'no dark schemes of annexation or fusion with the Colony', but the proposals met with strong resistance from commercial interests in the Federation and were set aside in the prosperous years which followed.

In 1931, at a critical time in the slump, Clementi announced plans to decentralize federal powers to the state governments. Clementi saw this as a prelude to uniting the whole peninsula into a Malayan League, which would lead 'to the emergence of the brotherhood of Malay nations, each proudly guarding its historical individuality and autonomy but joining hands with the rest in enterprise that may be for the good of the Malays of this peninsula as a whole and of the immigrants of other races who have made this country their home'.

On paper Clementi's scheme seemed sensible and tidy. The Malay sultans welcomed the prospect of greater local authority, and there was some support for the idea of creating a Malayan nation. In 1926 Tan Cheng Lock had declared in the legislative council that 'the ultimate goal should be a united self-governing British Malaya with a Federal government and Parliament for the whole of it' and had called for the creation of a 'Malayan spirit and consciousness amongst its people to the complete elimination of racial or communal feeling'.

But this was a minority view, and the majority looked with suspicion upon a Malayan League. The Unfederated States feared they would lose their individuality in a closer association. Federation businessmen once more baulked at being subjected to Singapore, while their Singapore counterparts dreaded the prospect of a Malayan common market with external tariffs, which would damage Singapore's treasured free trade entrepôt status. In 1931 Clementi appointed a committee, largely composed of Singapore businessmen, to investigate the possibilities of a Malayan customs union, but the committee reported unequivocally that such a union was 'essentially opposed to the interests of the colony and undesirable in any circumstances that can be foreseen'. It claimed that 'the interests of Singapore and Penang are largely extra-Malayan'.

The Chinese in the Federation were afraid that as a minority their interests would be threatened in a united Malaya. The new constitutional proposals, coinciding with immigration restrictions, vernacular press censorship, the ban on the Kuomintang, cuts in government grants to Chinese schools, and compounded by the hardships of the depression, evoked unprecedented racial bitterness throughout Malaya and Singapore.

The British government sent Sir Samuel Wilson, permanent under secretary of state for the colonies, to investigate the position. In his report, published in 1933, Wilson advised that, while the unification of the country under one central government would be economically sound, the British were commited to preserving the individual states. 'The maintenance of the position, authority and prestige of the Malay rulers must always be a cardinal point in British policy: and the encouragement of indirect rule will probably prove the greatest safeguard against the political submersion of the Malays which would result from the development of popular government on western lines.'[21]

Wilson found that officials and commercial leaders in the Federation regarded the Chief Secretary as one who could 'fight the battles of the Federated Malay States against the High Commissioner and the colonial authorities in Singapore'. Wilson recommended reducing the Chief Secretary's status and gradually devolving to the separate states the work of technical departments, such as agriculture, education, medical services and public works.

The Colonial Office adopted Wilson's proposals, which were welcomed generally in Malaya as a fair compromise, and the implementation proceeded smoothly in the hands of the conciliatory new Governor, Sir Shenton Thomas.

In 1935 the Chief Secretary was replaced by a Federal Secretary of somewhat lower status. Many functions devolved upon the individual states, while at the same time pan-Malayan departments were created, and other departmental directors stationed in Singapore acted as advisers for the Malay states. This gave Singapore more control over policy and encouraged more uniform administration, but the ambitious proposals for a political and economic union faded away. In later years many came to admit that Clementi was far-seeing in his vision of a united Malaya, but at the time neither the Federation, the Unfederated States, nor Singapore was ready to make the necessary sacrifices. The result was to assuage regional and sectional fears and jealousies at the expense of leaving Malaya divided and disorganized.

Guillemard was able to make more headway in constitutional reform in the colony itself. In Singapore there was no demand for change before the 1920s, and the system of nomination and official majority rule was generally accepted. Indeed commentators before the First World War had deemed it 'a commendable feature of a place like Singapore that there is comparatively little self seeking in municipal and colonial politics'.[21] Such matters were left to the heads of firms and if they showed no interest it was not deemed fitting for juniors to meddle.

In an attempt to increase public participation, in 1921 Guillemard introduced the practice of allowing certain organizations to nominate municipal commissioners. The Singapore branch of the Straits Settlements Association nominated three, the Singapore and Chinese chambers of commerce two each, the Straits Chinese British Association, the Eurasian Association, the Muhammedan Advisory Board and the Hindu Advisory Board one each.

In 1920 a select committee which Guillemard appointed to consider reforming the legislative council recommended creating an unofficial majority, comprising seven Europeans and eight Asians, as compared with twelve officials, but empowering the Governor to suspend proceedings. The Straits Settlements (Singapore) Association welcomed this suggestion, but the Colonial Office refused to admit 'a departure from the principle that responsibility and control must be in the same hands'.[22] Guillemard introduced some modifications in 1924. Two unofficial members of the legislative council were to be nominated by the Governor to sit on the executive council. The legislative council was enlarged to comprise twenty-six members, with equal numbers of unofficials and officials, the Governor having the casting vote. The Penang and Singapore European chambers of commerce were each permitted to nominate one non-official and the remainder were nominated by the Governor on a racial basis: five Europeans, including one from Penang and one from Malacca, three Chinese British subjects, one Malay, one Indian and one Eurasian.

In 1930 the Straits Settlements (Singapore) Association proposed a similar equality of officials and non-officials in the executive council, and recommended that non-official legislative councillors should be elected by a panel of British subjects of all races. There was little support for this suggestion, which the Straits Times labelled 'a ludicrous scheme' and 'crass folly'.[23] In a community so divided by race, religion and language, with a large number of aliens, transients and illiterates, it was argued that a Governor was better able to reconcile justice for society than a 'popularly' elected government, which would in practice mean the representatives of the prosperous commercial class.

Initially only the western community showed any interest in constitutional reform, the only vocal bodies being the Straits Settlements (Singapore) Association and the Association of British Malaya, which were both predominantly European in membership.

The Association of British Malaya was formed in London in 1920 as a successor to the parent Straits Settlements Association, in order to extend activities to cover planting, mining and commercial interests in the Malay states as well as the Colony. Initially the Association invited the Singapore branch of the Straits Settlements Association to dissolve itself and transfer its members to the new organization, but the Singapore branch refused, insisting that it could look after Straits Settlements interests satisfactorily itself.

The rivals quickly sank their differences in opposition to a Straits Settlements Income Tax Ordinance, which Guillemard introduced in 1921, and which C.W. Darbishire, president of the Association of British Malaya, said was 'enough to make Sir Stamford Raffles turn in his grave'.[24] He went on to attack Guillemard's alleged 'squandermania' and extravagance on an official yacht and Government House servants, issues reminiscent of the opposition to Ord which gave birth to the original Straits Settlements Association.

The unpopular income tax proposal was withdrawn, but the issue served to draw the two bodies together and co-operation was maintained from that point. By 1927 the Straits Settlements (Singapore) Association had more than 700 members and was described as 'rapidly becoming the most important unofficial body in the Straits Settlements'.[25]

By that time, however, the Straits Chinese British Association was beginning to assume the lead in political agitation, mild though this was. The most vocal spokesman was Tan Cheng Lock, who was born into a wealthy Baba family in Malacca in 1883, worked as a schoolmaster for six years and then went into the rubber industry, where he became director of several companies.[26] Tan Cheng Lock served as a municipal commissioner in Malacca from 1912 to 1922, as a legislative councillor from 1923 to 1934 and an executive councillor from 1933 to 1935. He represented the Colony at King George V's coronation in 1937. In 1928 Tan Cheng Lock called in vain for an unofficial majority and direct popular representation in both legislative and executive councils by all who had made their home in the Straits.[27] The Straits Chinese British Association pressed Clementi for increased Chinese representation on the legislative and executive councils but without success. Tan Cheng Lock continued the agitation throughout the 1930s, speaking forcefully in the legislative council against Clementi's discriminatory anti-Chinese legislation and addressing a memorial to Sir Samuel Wilson in 1932 entitled *Why the Chinese are Perturbed.*[28] While in London in June 1939 Tan Cheng Lock established contact with Arthur Creech-Jones, then a socialist backbencher, who had queried in parliament the means used to suppress sedition in the Straits. Through Creech-Jones Tan tried to arrange for regular communication with members of parliament sympathetic to colonial reform, but the outbreak of the European war a few weeks after Tan's return to Malaya put an end to this dialogue.[29]

Tan Cheng Lock represented only a minority view. Most Asians seemed content with opportunities to participate in Singapore's public life, which had improved by the 1930s. All born in Singapore were automatically British subjects and eligible for appointment to the executive, legislative or municipal councils, or for admission to the Straits Settlements Civil Service. They could serve on administrative boards, such as the Education Board, the Singapore Harbour Board, the Licensing Board and Hospital Management Committees. They could share in the work of racial and religious advisory boards, which were consulted by the government, or on the committees of the chambers of commerce. In practice the numbers of Asians in public life were very few. Chambers of commerce were dominated by a small clique of wealthy businessmen, and only a minority of the English-educated took any interest in official and quasi-official activities.

Local apathy and the absorption of politically-active Chinese with affairs in China minimized racial friction in Singapore in the immediate pre-war years of relative peace and prosperity, which were not conducive to the growth of political movements. Of the three semi-political parties, the Kesatuan Melayu Singapura had no specific political programme, and the mildly liberal Straits Chinese British Association and Straits Settlements (Singapore) Association numbered only a few hundred members.

The constitution satisfied the limited objective of colonial rule. The wealthy and well-educated had a voice in government which was usually heeded, although they had no ultimate control or power. The mass of the population was indifferent to government but not actively hostile. Singapore remained a collection of immigrant communities, with their culture, interests and loyalties rooted in foreign countries, their ultimate ambition often to return to the land of their origin, whether it was Britain, India or China. Singaporeans were content to leave government in the hands of the colonial authorities, and on the whole this produced tolerably efficient administration. One European non-official in the legislative council in 1932 pictured 'some future historian referring to the present era of the Straits Settlements as its "golden age", when the art of governing was left to trained experts and the ordinary people were allowed to pursue their ordinary avocations unhampered by the virus of politics'.

While the official majority was rarely used to over-rule non-officials, the legislative council did not pretend to be democratic but was designed as an advisory body to air the views of various communities, to give the government a public platform and to test popular reaction to new legislation.

The official and nominated character of the council made it appear more an organ of government than a guardian of public interest. The official majority crushed the council's vitality, meetings were poorly attended, proceedings were for the most part 'formal, dull and brief',[30] where 'a mumbled rigmarole is being carried on with very little relation to the realities of the life of the Straits'.[31]

The late 1930s were a time of peace, increasing comfort and leisure for the upper and middle strata of Singapore society. Some of the benefits from improved public works and amenities permeated through to the mass of the population. But, as an acute young American observed in 1937, 'The government of the colony is run by a small group of insiders living a life the comforts and luxuries of which are rarely impaired by too close contact with the sordid poverty which has set its stamp on the great bulk of the population'...and 'it is still no exaggeration to say that it is a government run by and for those who have won through to power and wealth, and devil take the hindermost'.[32]

British colonial rule had lost the zest and vitality that characterized the early years of the century. It had become jaded, smug, complacent, but it seemed as firmly rooted in Singapore as ever. 'Imperialism appears always to be committed to perpetuating its own rule unless it is challenged by a force which makes it necessary or expedient for it to withdraw.'[33]

1. F. Swettenham, *British Malaya* (London, 1948; reprinted London, 1955), p. 342.
2. See T.M. Winsley, *A History of the Singapore Volunteer Corps* (Singapore, 1937).
3. Quoted in F.M. Luscombe, *Singapore, 1819–1930* (Singapore, 1930), p. 66.
4. Discussed in Y. Akashi, 'The Nanyang Chinese Anti-Japanese and Boycott Movement, 1908–1928', *JSSS*, XXIII, 2 (1968), pp. 89–96.
5. J.N. Parmer, *Colonial Labor Policy and Administration: a History of Labor in the Rubber Plantation Industry in Malaya, 1910–1941* (New York, 1960), p. 93.
6. Naosaku Uchida, *The Overseas Chinese* (Stanford, 1959), p. 48; Tan Ee Leong, 'The Chinese Banks Incorporated in Singapore & the Federation of Malaya', *JMBRAS*, XXVI, 1 (1953), pp. 113–39, reprinted in *JMBRAS*, XLII, 1 (1969), pp. 256–81; Dick

Wilson (assisted by S.Y. Lee and others), *Solid as a Rock: the first Forty Years of the Oversea Chinese Banking Corporation* (Singapore, 1972).

7. R.H. de S. Onraet, *Singapore: a Police Background* (London, 1947), p. 33.

8. Manicasothy Saravanamutu, *The Sara Saga* (Penang, 1970), p. 48.

9. *ST*, 16 July 1934.

10. Saravanamutu, p. 54.

11. M. Freedman, 'Colonial Law and Chinese Society', *Journal of the Royal Anthropological Institute*, LXXX (1950), pp. 114–15; W. Woods and C.A. Wills, *Report of the Commission on Mui Tsai in Hong Kong and Malaya* (London, 1937); E. Picton-Turbervill, *Report of the Commission on Mui Tsai in Hong Kong and Malaya* (minority report), (London, 1937).

12. Chu Tee Seng, 'The Singapore Chinese Protectorate, 1900–1941', *JSSS*, XXVI, 1 (1971), pp. 5–45.

13. Colonial Office, *Higher Education in Malaya: Report of the Commission appointed by the Secretary of State for the Colonies, June 1939* (London, 1939), (the McLean Report).

14. T.R. Doraisamy (ed.), *150 Years of Education in Singapore* (Singapore, 1969), p. 38.

15. See Radin Soenarno, 'Malay Nationalism, 1900–45', *JSEAH,*' I, 1 (1960), pp. 9–11.

16. Chen Ta, *Immigrant Communities in South China: a study of Overseas Migration and its Influence on Standards of Living and Social Change* (Shanghai, 1939, and New York, 1940), p. 118.

17. Y. Akashi, *The Nanyang Chinese Anti-Japanese National Salvation Movement, 1937–41* (Kansas, 1970), p. 74.

18. Described in R.O. Winstedt, *The Constitution of the Colony of the Straits Settlements and of the Federated and Unfederated Malay States* (Royal Institute of International Affairs, London, 1931), and War Office, *Malaya and its Civil Administration prior to the Japanese Occupation* (London, 1944).

19. L. Guillemard, *Trivial Fond Records* (London, 1937), p. 99.

20. *Report of Brigadier General Sir Samuel Wilson, G.C.M.G., K.C.B., K.B.E., Permanent Under-secretary of State for the Colonies on his Visit to Malaya 1932* (London, 1933).

21. A. Wright and T.H. Reid, *The Malay Peninsula: a Record of Progress in the Middle East* (London, 1912), p. 232.

22. W. Churchill to Guillemard, 24 June 1922, CO 273/510, quoted in Yeo Kim Wah, *Political Development in Singapore, 1945–1955* (Singapore, 1973).

23. *ST*, 14 November 1930.

24. President's speech, annual general meeting, Association of British Malaya Minute Books, Vol. I, 26 July 1922.

25. Annual report for 1926–7, Association of British Malaya Minute Books, Vol. II.

26. Tan Cheng Lock's career is discussed in Soh Eng Lim, 'Tan Cheng Lock', *JSEAH*, I, 1 (1960), pp. 29–55.

27. *Proceedings of the Straits Settlements Legislative Council, 1928*, pp. 147–8.

28. Printed also in *ST*, 23 December 1932.

29. Creech-Jones Papers, MSS Brit. Emp. (Rhodes House, Oxford), Box 26, File 11.

30. *Malaya Tribune*, 20 December 1930.

31. R. Emerson, *Malaysia: a Study in Direct and Indirect Rule* (New York, 1937; reprinted Kuala Lumpur, 1964), p. 287.

32. Ibid., p. 306.

33. Ibid., p. 519.

# V

# War in the East
# 1941–1942

IN the early hours of the morning of 8 December 1941 Japanese aircraft raided Singapore. Their main targets were the Seletar and Tengah airfields, but they also bombed Raffles Place in the heart of the town. The unsuspecting city was at rest, the streets and the ships in the harbour ablaze with light, the headquarters of the civil air raid precautions organization unmanned. For the civilian population these bombs, and the newspaper headlines which greeted them next morning, were the first indications of war, beginning a train of disaster, which within seventy days forced the British to surrender Singapore to the Japanese army.

The origins of the debacle went back to the beginning of the century when, in her preoccupation with meeting the German naval threat in Europe, Britain had relied on her alliance with Japan to safeguard her interests in the East and had left the Japanese navy in undisputed mastery of the China Seas. The extent of this dependence on the Japanese was highlighted by the sepoy mutiny in 1915, which threw the first doubts on Britain's ability to defend her eastern empire.

After World War I the British government re-examined its naval policy. In Europe the German naval threat had been destroyed, but in the East the balance of power was changing, since the extension of Japan's control over parts of China and former German Pacific islands transformed her into a rival and potential enemy.

To deal with this changed situation, in 1919 Lord Jellicoe, the British First Sea Lord, proposed the creation of a powerful eastern imperial fleet, comprising British, Australian, and New Zealand ships. The suggestion found little favour in Britain, which had fought a 'war to end all wars' and placed her trust for the future in disarmament and international co-operation, rather than in military might and alliances. In deference to the United States Britain allowed the Japanese alliance to lapse when it came up for renewal in 1921. In its place a Naval Limitation Treaty was signed in Washington in 1922 whereby Britain, the United States, Japan and France agreed to restrict the size of their navies and not to erect military or naval bases in the Pacific. In effect Britain exchanged the definite commitment of an alliance with a country whose interests in the Pacific had been complementary to her own for a shadowy alignment with the United States.

Precluded under the terms of the Washington Agreement from building up a Far East fleet, Britain intended to send contingents of her home-based navy to meet any emergency in the East, but she needed a local base to offer repair and docking facilities to the new breed of large battle-ships. In 1923 the British government voted £11 million to begin con-structing a naval base at Singapore, supplemented by contributions from the Malay states, Australia, New Zealand and Hong Kong.

The choice of Singapore, which lay outside of the area prohibited under the Washington Agreement, had been made before the Naval Limitation Treaty was signed. It was too far away to pose any threat to Japan and the Singapore base was a purely defensive move, designed to protect Britain's eastern trade and empire, and to give confidence to Australia and New Zealand.

Any danger of war in the East seemed so unlikely in the 1920s that the progress of the naval base was dictated not by strategic but by domestic British political considerations. The base was the Conservative party's project, while the Labour party opposed from the beginning what its leader, Ramsey MacDonald, dubbed 'the wild and wanton escapade of Singapore', as a threat to international goodwill and a waste of precious resources.

Rather than develop the crowded and vulnerable Keppel Harbour area, it was decided to site the naval base on the Johor Straits, with an airfield and sea-plane base at nearby Seletar. Drainage schemes, which were needed to prepare the swampy mangrove area, were con-tinued as a general health measure under MacDonald's short-lived Labour government, which came to power in Britain in 1924, and by the time the preliminary clearing and draining work was finished the Conservatives were back in office. Construction proceeded slowly until 1929, when a new Labour government suspended all further work on the Singapore base in a bid towards international disarmament.

Japan's growing aggressiveness put an end to these vacillations of British policy. In 1931 Japan occupied Manchuria and the following year resigned from the League of Nations. Work on the Singapore base was resumed and speeded up as the danger from Japan increased. In 1935 Japan withdrew from the London disarmament conference, in 1936 she terminated the Washington Agreement and made an Anti-Comintern Pact with Germany, and in 1937 she invaded China. Construction went ahead full speed in Singapore. In 1938 the King George VI dry dock was opened, which was capable of taking the largest vessels afloat, and the base was hailed by the *Sydney Morning Herald* as 'The Gibraltar of the East...the gateway to the Orient...the bastion of British might'.[1] New airfields were constructed at Tengah and Sembawang, while virgin jungle was cleared and mangrove swamps were drained at Changi to provide heavy artillery and anti-aircraft defences covering the eastern approaches to the naval base. In 1938 barracks were completed at nearby Selarang to house a full battalion of infantry, so that by 1941 the naval base and its protective 'Changi fortress' were complete. It inspired journalistic hyperbole, 'a new, bigger and better Gibraltar, one of the most formidable concatenations of naval, military and strategic power ever put together anywhere'.[2]

The fortifications themselves were impressive, but their effectiveness depended on the strength and quality of military, naval, and air force manpower and equipment. During the initial stages a British general had expressed concern lest 'we ourselves put a half way house and then— garrisoning it, as is our wont—make a present of it to the wrong people'.[3] A strong but inadequately manned base conjured up in larger and more dangerous form the spectre which had made the Colonial Office so wary about accepting Singapore as a crown colony in 1867.

Singapore came second only to the United Kingdom as the keystone to defence of the British Commonwealth, but London did not propose to station a peace-time fleet in the East. It was estimated that a relief naval force could reach Singapore in seventy days, and Singapore's defence was geared to providing military and air cover to protect the naval base until the British navy could come to the rescue. With the Japanese navy 1,700 miles away and no Japanese air bases within striking distance of Singapore, a small garrison and strong seaward defences were deemed sufficient to repel any initial attack.

In 1937 the British service commanders on the spot made an appreciation that defence of the Singapore naval base was bound up with the defence of the whole Malay peninsula. The General Officer Commanding Malaya, Major-General William Dobbie, and his senior staff officer, Lt.-Colonel Arthur Percival, visualized a wartime situation in which the British navy would not be able to reach Singapore in time and the Japanese might attack down the Malay peninsula. Percival drew up a plan from the Japanese view-point which bore an uncanny resemblance to the actual Japanese attack made four years later. His assessment was based upon landings on the north-east of the peninsula, probably at Singgora, with subsidiary landings at Patani and Kota Bharu, and showed that these would not only be feasible during the December/March north-east monsoon but might profit from the bad visibility common at that time. From this Dobbie argued that defending the naval base involved holding the whole peninsula and urged the construction of defence works for north Malaya and Johor. These plans were rejected by the War Office. Airfields were constructed at Kota Bharu, Kuantan and in east Johor but were not provided with adequate military protection.

As early as 1926 Australia had queried whether the British were correct in assuming they would have sufficient ships to send to the East in time of war. The Chiefs of Staff warned the Imperial Conference in 1937 that the Singapore base in itself, without a fleet, was an inadequate deterrent, and Australia and New Zealand appealed for a peace-time fleet to be stationed in the Far East. Britain reiterated her policy of concentrating her naval strength in Europe and dispatching a fleet only if war broke out in the East.

The Japanese occupied Canton in October 1938 and seized Hainan island early in 1939. Britain and the United States grew closer in response to Japanese expansion but still aimed to maintain friendly relations with Japan. In Malaya itself there was general apathy and complacency among officials, British civilians and the Asian population. There was little co-operation between the services and civilian authorities, nor between the arms of the services themselves.

When war broke out in Europe in September 1939 the time estimate for sending naval reinforcements to deal with any crisis in Singapore was extended from seventy to 180 days. But Winston Churchill, then First Lord of the Admiralty, promised that the defence of Singapore, Australia, and New Zealand would take precedence over the Mediterranean if the eastern empire were menaced.

In the early months of the European war the spread of the conflict to the Far East seemed unlikely, and London allocated Malaya the comfortable role of 'a dollar arsenal', concentrating on production rather than defence. In 1939 Malaya produced nearly 40 per cent of the world's rubber and nearly 60 per cent of its tin, most of it for the American market. She came second only to Canada as the Commonwealth's biggest dollar earner.

For civilians the European war transformed Singapore into a centre of purposeful energy. The depressing restrictions on tin and rubber production of the 1930s were replaced by a drive for maximum output. Profit and patriotism lay in the same direction to produce a sense of virtuous activity. The only source of distress among Singapore's mercantile community was income tax, which the Governor forced through the legislative council in February 1941, using the official majority.

The European war stimulated an appetite for news and boosted circulation of Singapore's English-language newspapers. Of these the largest, the *Malaya Tribune,* edited by E.M. Glover, maintained its original policy of catering for local Asian interests. Its rival, the *Straits Times,* edited by Seabridge, bought up the *Singapore Free Press* and represented the local European commercial community, often in opposition to official policy. Both newspapers were hostile to the Japanese-owned English-language *Singapore Herald,* which started in April 1939. Under its lively and energetic managing editor, Tatsuki Fujii, the *Herald* set out to put the Japanese in the best light and to counter the pro-Chungking stand taken by the *Malaya Tribune.*

In view of the non-aggression pact signed between Germany and Russia in August 1939, the Comintern instructed the Malayan Communist Party to step up its attempts to foment labour trouble in order to impede the British war effort. In the early months of the European war the Malayan General Labour Union organized a number of strikes in Singapore and staged an illegal mass rally on May Day 1940. Communist influence in the labour movement was strong but its main support came from unskilled workers in Chinese firms, and it failed to capture the key sectors, namely the railways and bus companies, the harbour board, the municipality, and the naval base. The Singapore authorities acted swiftly to arrest and banish agitators and dissolve unions which engaged in subversive activities. But they were fully aware, probably through information supplied by Lai Teck, of the limitations to communist strength and shifts in policy. The party's pro-Russian, anti-British stand was self-defeating, since it weakened the party's hold over anti-Japanese Chinese patriots. In September 1940 the Chinese Communist Party instructed the party in Malaya to stop all anti-British movements and consolidate the anti-Japanese front.[4] From that time strikes in Singapore petered out.

The collapse of France and Holland and Italy's entry into the war as an ally of Germany forced Britain to reappraise her defence position in June 1940. Threatened with invasion, heavily engaged in the Middle East and battling to preserve her Atlantic lifeline, Britain realized that she was in no position to increase Far Eastern commitments and she relied on the American fleet based at Pearl Harbor to deter Japan.

In July 1940 the United States imposed the first economic sanctions to stem the flow to Japan of arms, iron, oil and other vital raw materials. This began a process which eventually forced Japan to choose between calling off her China campaign or seizing for herself the main sources of war materials she needed. In face of hardening American opinion, Japan occupied northern Indo-China in September, signed a ten-year pact with Germany and Italy and sent missions to the Axis powers to gain military information and discuss policy.

Public feeling was tense and Singaporeans suspected all Japanese residents of being spies. Tokyo had already ordered the return of the once flourishing group of Japanese prostitutes as degrading to their country's reputation, but about four thousand Japanese remained: 1,500 were fishermen and the rest businessmen, journalists, dentists, photographers and barbers. The Special Branch of the police kept them under scrutiny, and several were arrested on charges of espionage in the first year of the European war, including Mamoru Shinozaki, press attaché to the Japanese consulate-general.

A retired sixty-two-year-old Air Chief Marshal, Sir Robert Brooke-Popham, arrived in Singapore in November 1940 as Commander-in-Chief of land and air forces in the Far East, but without powers over the navy, civil defence or any aspect of civil administration. Reinforcements of Indian and British infantry began arriving in the last weeks of the year, in February 1941 the first troops of a newly-raised Australian 8th Division landed, followed in March/April by a second Indian division. The number of Commonwealth troops stationed in Malaya trebled between June 1940 and April 1941, but they lacked supporting artillery and tanks. Brooke-Popham appealed for more aircraft, but there was no chance of supplying anything approaching the desired number, and in view of British losses at Dunkirk and new demands in the Middle East, Malaya's equipment needs could not be met.

The uneasiness of the summer months of 1940 gave way to renewed complacency in Singapore, as army reinforcements continued to arrive, while the Anglo-American relationship grew warmer and the Japanese were bogged down in China. Social life among expatriate civilians and servicemen alike was relaxed and carefree. Far from the spartan privations and the tense life-and-death struggles in Europe and the Middle East, Singapore was 'a little spot of paradise',[5] where there was peace and plenty, no food rationing, no sense of urgency or danger. The local government, following Whitehall's instructions, continued to give priority to rubber and tin production over the training of military volunteers or the construction of defence works. The Volunteer force expanded but its equipment was basically World War I material, and service was of necessity a part-time activity.

The immigration restrictions enforced since the great depression meant that the labour force was inadequate by the time war broke out. Labour for defence works could not be attracted freely since the War Office fixed wage rates unrealistically low, at less than half the market rate, and there was no question of conscripting labour away from tin and rubber production.

'The majority of well-informed people do not believe that the Japanese in their present difficulties will branch out on fresh ventures,' the *Singapore Free Press* declared in January 1941,[6] and most military men were confident that Japan's growing difficulties in China and her fear of a Russian attack in her rear would dissuade her from ventures in South-East Asia. Britain and the United States held secret talks in Washington in the early months of 1941 to discuss co-operation in the East. Britain favoured having American ships stationed at Singapore, but the United States preferred to keep her Pacific fleet intact at Pearl Harbour. Both powers agreed that Europe was the area of first priority.

The German invasion of Russia in June 1941 put an end to Japan's fears of attack from the rear and gave her more freedom of action. Germany urged her ally to attack Russia, and Churchill believed that Japan would agree, rather than launch into a new type of warfare in tropical South-East Asia, which would bring her into conflict not only with Britain and the Netherlands but also with the United States.

The immediate impact of the outbreak of war between Germany and Russia was to put an end to the last vestiges of communist-inspired labour unrest in Singapore and to bring communist and Kuomintang supporters together again. The Malayan Communist Party was illegal still but very strong. With a central committee in Singapore and state committees on the mainland, it claimed some five thousand members and 100,000 sympathizers.[7] It dominated the Overseas Chinese Anti-Japanese Mobilization Committee and set up a secret Special Operations Executive in Singapore to train guerrillas in sabotage. But the colonial authorities, anxious not to provoke Japan, continued to make frequent arrests of Chinese communist sympathizers and to discourage anti-Japanese activities generally. They were particularly worried about the San-Min-Chu-I Youth Corps and the propaganda taught in Chinese schools. The Nanyang Chinese National Salvation Movement continued to be an embarrassment to the authorities up to the outbreak of the Pacific war.

The atmosphere of ease and plenty in Singapore seemed unreal and almost indecent to new arrivals, such as Percival, by now Vice-Chief of Imperial General Staff in London, who returned as General Officer Commanding Malaya in May 1941, or Brigadier Ivan Simson, who was appointed Chief Engineer Malaya Command three months later. Fresh from organizing defences in beleaguered Britain, Simson in particular was appalled at the soft living among troops in Singapore and the lack of attempts to organize the local population for their own defence.

Most European civilians were very busy, working hard and devoting much of their leisure time to civil defence duties, and Singapore had less of a brittle escapist pleasure-seeking atmosphere than wartime London's West End, but the realities of war seemed remote. 'There'll Always Be An England' was Singapore's theme song in 1941 and expressed the general feeling that Britain was battling for survival, with Singapore as a sympathetic and helpful but faraway onlooker. The ruling class had no wish to involve the Asian population in defence, doubting both their capabilities and their loyalties. There were few openings for Asians in the Volunteers and none in the British armed services, although the *Malaya Tribune* had called for conscription in May 1939.[8] It was assumed that the local population would panic at any hint of trouble, that they would not be willing to suffer and die for an alien regime. In particular the Singapore authorities clung to their pre-war suspicion about Kuomintang activities, despite a personal secret telegram to Shenton Thomas in February 1941 from the secretary of state for the colonies, urging that, since Japan was now openly committed to the Axis, increased British support for Chiang Kai-shek should be reflected in Singapore's attitude to 'Free China' though not 'unnecessarily provocative to Japan'.[9]

Japan's major concern was to finish the war in China and to secure the raw materials she needed for this purpose from South-East Asia. Japanese talks with Dutch authorities in Batavia about oil supplies broke down in June 1941, and the next month the United States, followed by Britain and the Netherlands Indies, froze Japanese assets, strangling her foreign trade and cutting off crucial oil supplies. Up to that point the Malayan authorities had applied trade restrictions sparingly in an attempt to appease Japan, but now Japan was suddenly deprived of her iron, bauxite and shipping interests in the peninsula.[10]

The Japanese cabinet decided to continue the China campaign, even at the risk of war with the United States and Britain. Tokyo forced Vichy France to provide her with bases in southern Indo-China, which gave Japan a naval base 750 miles from Singapore and airfields only 300 miles from northern Malaya. Percival appealed for reinforcements, but Churchill and the British service chiefs were not prepared to rush forces from the active Middle East sector to meet what was still only a potential threat.

For the moment Singapore and Malaya were dangerously vulnerable to attack. They had few planes and no battleships, no aircraft carriers, no heavy cruisers, no submarines. Defence depended on preserving peace with Japan, or at least in postponing war until the spring of 1942, by which time it was envisaged that military reinforcements and a fleet could be sent to the East. There was still little sense of urgency in Singapore. Brooke-Popham continued to feed the British cabinet with optimistic information. On 1 October 1941 he reported to London that 'the last thing Japan wants at this juncture is a campaign to the South'.

Despite the growing informal co-operation with the Americans and the Dutch, no unified command was agreed, nor was any attempt made to streamline administration and consolidate British military command in Malaya. In September 1941 a British cabinet minister, Duff Cooper, was sent to Singapore with vague terms of reference to enquire into the various forms of civil administration in the Allied countries of South-East Asia and Australasia. To co-ordinate the complicated structure he recommended the appointment of a commissioner-general for the Far East, but this proposal was still under consideration in London when the Pacific war broke out.

The authorities remained reluctant to divert manpower to defence works or to take any action which might shake civilian morale and public confidence. Suggestions made by Simson in October 1941 to construct defences along the northern shores of Singapore island with an outer defence round Johor Bahru were set aside. Proposals to dig air-raid shelters were rejected on the grounds that the water table was too high.

In October 1941 Percival called on Asians to come forward for military service with the Volunteers but gave no hint of urgency. That same month Brooke-Popham declared publicly that Britain did not need American naval support, and assured a press conference early in December that the Japanese were too afraid of British power to attack Malaya.[11]

The Singapore authorities were still trying to preserve friendly relations with Japan. Representatives of the Japanese-owned *Singapore Herald* were admitted to press conferences and military demonstrations as late as September 1941. Japanese businessmen remained in large numbers until their business dried up as a result of the embargo, and an official evacuation ship repatriated about 600 of them early in October. The Japanese consul-general, Tsurumi Ken, was recalled later that month, but most of the Japanese photographers, barbers, and dentists remained, while the *Singapore Herald* and the Japanese-language *Singapore Nippo* continued to operate until the day war broke out.

The *Singapore Herald* declared as late as 6 December that 'Peace can still be saved', a message which was welcomed by the British authorities as good for morale. Foreign correspondents and local journalists seethed at the official policy of suppressing any potentially disturbing information or opinions. 'Malaya is in the drowsy languid interval between sleep and awakening,' declared the *Malaya Tribune* in October 1941.

'We in Malaya are metaphorically still in bed.'

In the confused uncertainty of the summer and autumn of 1941, political considerations outweighed strategy in British defence decisions, in an effort to balance Russian appeals for help against Australia's demands for a build-up of military strength in Malaya and Singapore. The Australians, the military men on the spot in Singapore, and the service chiefs in London all realized that air power was the vital key to cripple any invading force before it established a foothold. The British service chiefs recommended sending aircraft and a fleet of four veteran battleships to the East, to be supplemented by two more ships in early 1942. Churchill, however, decided instead to send spare tanks and fighter planes to Russia, and to dispatch *Prince of Wales,* accompanied by the veteran cruiser *Repulse* and an aircraft carrier, to Singapore. The Prime Minister was convinced that this fast and most modern of battleships, nicknamed H.M.S. *Unsinkable* and pride of the British navy, would deter the Japanese into keeping the peace and that it would 'exercise a vague general fear and menace all points at once'.

Churchill took the decisions to send aircraft and tanks to Russia and *Prince of Wales* to Singapore against the advice of all professional experts, including the First Sea Lord and Admiral Sir Tom Phillips, who was to be commander-in-chief of the Eastern fleet. The decisions had no strategic justification. The manoeuvrable modern Hurricane fighters, which would have been invaluable in Singapore, were of little use in the Russian campaign. *Prince of Wales* had no deterrent impact on the Japanese, who had already decided that time had run out on their diplomatic wrangles and were preparing for war.

Early in 1941 Colonel Masanobu Tsuji, a veteran of the China campaign, was allocated a shoe-string budget and put in charge of a small Southern Military Studies research group in Taiwan to investigate problems of jungle warfare. Tsuji was given a report drawn up by two senior Japanese army officers, who had visited Malaya during the critical time in September 1940. They advised that any attack on Singapore would have to come from the north and reported that the British air force in Malaya was understrength and its planes obsolete.[12] Tsuji appreciated, as Percival and Dobbie had pointed out, that a frontal attack on Singapore was scarcely feasible but her back door stood open, and he realized that British propaganda was deluding only her own people.

Tsuji embarked on his task with enthusiasm and verve. The challenge was enormous, for the Japanese army had no experience of fighting jungle warfare. Soldiers accustomed to cold weather fighting had to be trained to face tropical conditions, and cavalry, which was used in China, had to be abandoned in favour of bicycles. The Japanese set up an espionage centre in Bangkok under Major Iwaichi Fujiwara, and in the three months before the outbreak of war spies speaking fluent Malay, English, Cantonese or Hokkien were sent to Singapore and Malaya, to gather information and to stir up dissension and unrest among

9. Lt. General Tomoyuki Yamashita, Commander of the Japanese 25th Army
(By permission of Kyodo Photo Service)

Indian troops in north Malaya.

Japan's major long-term war plan was geared to an attack on Russia, and it was only in September 1941 that the Japanese cabinet decided to concentrate on a southward thrust, if negotiations to persuade the United States to lift economic sanctions were unsuccessful. In October 1941 the moderates in the Japanese cabinet resigned and the aggressive General Hideki Tojo became prime minister. In November the Japanese decision to attack was confirmed. Japan did not aspire to total victory but aimed to force a compromise peace on the United States and Britain in order to guarantee the resources needed to complete her war in China.[13]

The 25th Japanese Army, which was hurriedly assembled for the invasion of Malaya, was put under the command of Lt.-General Tomoyuki Yamashita, probably Japan's most able general. The son of a humble village doctor, Yamashita was then fifty-six years old and was Tojo's contemporary and rival. He had headed the Japanese military mission to Germany and Italy in 1940 and served in Korea and North China until in November 1941 he was summoned from Manchuria to command the attack on Singapore.

Yamashita was offered five divisions but decided to employ only three, knowing that this was the maximum force which could be fed and maintained as his supply lines became extended south. The 25th Army comprised the Imperial Guards, the seasoned 18th Division and the highly experienced crack 5th Division, which was one of the best in the Japanese army. The able Lt.-General Sosaku Suzuki was Yamashita's chief of staff, while Tsuji became head of operations staff. With the exception of Takuma Nishimura, commander of the Imperial Guards, the leaders quickly responded to the impressive personality of Yamashita, who inspired respect among his officers and hero worship among the rank and file. Even Tsuji, who was Tojo's protégé and in a sense belonging to a rival faction, acknowledged Yamashita as a man 'who enforced upon all under his orders a military and moral discipline as rigorous as the autumn frost'.

Meanwhile, Duff Cooper, Brooke-Popham, and other British leaders were still convinced that Japan would attack Russia and would certainly not invade Malaya during the north-east monsoon. They were sure the Japanese were weary after long years of fighting in China, that their soldiers were inferior and their aircraft obsolete.

Singaporeans were reassured by the sight of *Prince of Wales* and *Repulse* as they sailed proudly up the Johor Strait to the naval base on 2 December 1941. The Governor, Brooke-Popham, Percival, Duff Cooper, the air force and naval commanders, and many other dignitaries were there to greet them and the base was 'like Portsmouth in Navy Week'.[14] In the words of Duff Cooper, the ships 'conferred a sense of complete security'.[15] But they had been forced to sail without their accompanying aircraft carrier, which had run aground, and their only support was four small destroyers, two of them in poor shape. As a senior Australian officer commented, the fleet 'went quickly from cream to skimmed milk'.[16]

Without protective air cover, the ships were too vulnerable in Singapore, and Phillips proposed to remove them to Manila.

By the end of the first week of December the air was alive with expectancy in Singapore. Servicemen were recalled on duty, sailors summoned back to their ships and the naval base blacked out. No similar precautions were taken in the town, and neither civil nor military authorities were prepared for the speed and intensity of Japan's onslaught, the quality of her aircraft or the fighting mettle of her soldiers.

The Japanese appreciated that success depended on surprise, to deal an immediate crippling blow against the United States Pacific fleet and to establish a firm foothold on the Malay peninsula. Within a few hours on the night of 7–8 December the Japanese destroyed the American fleet in Pearl Harbor, invaded Hong Kong and the Philippines, landed troops in southern Thailand at Singgora with ancillary landings at Patani and Kota Bharu, and dropped the first bombs on Singapore.

From the start the British lost the initiative. Prevarications in Whitehall made it impossible to launch a proposed 'Matador' plan to enter southern Thailand and pre-empt any Japanese attack before it reached Malaya. The Thais put up virtually no resistance to the landing of Yamashita's main force, and within a few hours 27,000 Japanese troops were established ashore at Singgora, Patani, and Kota Bharu.

The British defence plan depended upon preventing the Japanese effecting a large-scale landing, and Admiral Phillips, faced with the necessity of removing his fleet from its exposed position in Singapore, decided to dash north to intercept any further Japanese invading force. Without a supporting aircraft carrier this was at best a highly risky undertaking, but it was not until the fleet was well under way that Phillips learned that the Kota Bharu airfield was already in Japanese hands and there would be no air support at all. Sighted by the Japanese, Phillips turned back but was too late to escape the Japanese air force and by the afternoon of 10 December the two great ships were sunk, the commander-in-chief of the British eastern fleet was dead, and the Japanese had control of the sea. No single incident did more to wound the defenders' morale and to exhilarate the Japanese.

Japanese air superiority was crucial. Within twenty-four hours they had mastery of the air, they had knocked out more than half the British aircraft operational in north Malaya and seized the inadequately-protected British airfields in the north, which were invaluable to them in the ensuing campaign.

British defence plans had depended upon control of the air to repel attacks until the arrival of the fleet, with the army playing an ancillary role to hold the beaches, protect the airfields, and concentrate on the naval base and Singapore island. In the first two days of the Malayan campaign the basis of this defence was destroyed. Air control was lost. The naval base was nearly empty. The army thenceforth had to bear the brunt of the campaign and to fight the whole length of the peninsula.

On the outbreak of war Duff Cooper was made Resident Minister for Far Eastern Affairs, with cabinet rank, and formed a Far East war council which met daily and comprised the Governor, Percival, the naval and air force commanders, and an Australian representative. Japanese newspapers were closed down, all Japanese residents were arrested and subsequently sent to internment camps in India. As Commander-in-Chief Far East, Brooke-Popham issued an order of the day, declaring that Malaya was prepared and ready 'to cripple the power of the enemy to endanger our ideals, our possessions and our peace', and to destroy the force of 'a Japan drained for years by the exhausting claims of her wanton onslaught on China'.

The battle for Singapore became a question of time, depending on whether Japanese troops could be held back in the peninsula until reinforcements reached Singapore. At the outbreak of war Malaya had three full infantry divisions, one Australian and two Indian, but a large proportion of the troops were poorly trained and badly equipped. They had no tanks, few armoured cars, few anti-tank or mobile anti-aircraft weapons. The chiefs of staff in London decided to divert to Singapore the 18th British Division, together with some anti-tank and anti-aircraft regiments then en route to the Middle East, but a Far East fleet could not be reassembled for several months and there was little prospect of supplying much air support.

The Japanese swept down the Malay peninsula, carried forward by audacious planning, good fortune and the exhilaration bred by success. The main body of the force were disciplined, hardy and vigorous soldiers, who had fought together in the China campaign. Yamashita used his mastery of the air and the coastal waters to conduct a dynamic technique of infiltration, enveloping and outflanking which bewildered the defenders and compelled them to withdraw to avoid being cut off from the rear. Confined by the communications system of one trunk road and railway line, the British defence lacked mobility and the Japanese could defeat them in detail. Without tanks and anti-tank guns or prepared lines of defences, the Commonwealth retreat was inevitable, and the Japanese drove relentlessly south.

The Commonwealth commanders were at loggerheads. In particular Major-General Gordon Bennett, the fearless but irascible commander of the Australian Division, was critical of the retreat tactics employed by Major-General Lewis Heath, commander of the Indian troops in north Malaya, and also disputed the disposition of Australian and Indian troops made by Percival in Johor.

Refugees streamed south into Singapore but, in an effort to maintain morale, a strict censorship was put on all news of military disasters. Newspapers were forbidden to report the fall of Penang on 18 December but it was soon common knowledge. Singaporeans were horrified to learn that Europeans had been evacuated from the island, leaving the local people to their fate, and at a tense press conference community leaders demanded assurance from Brooke-Popham that there would be no such racial discrimination in Singapore.

On Christmas Day the Japanese began broadcasting propaganda from the Penang wireless station and three days later dropped their first leaflets on Singapore. They urged Asians to rise against their European masters and to light up their homes in order to protect themselves from Japanese bombers. This made the authorities even more vigilant in stiffening morale, and 'the mutiny of 1915 lay like a shadow over the conversation'.[17]

The Governor refused to demand or encourage the evacuation of foreign women and children, in order to avoid discrimination charges. Apart from the American community, only a trickle of people departed, and ships left Singapore throughout December 1941 half empty. The same routine prevailed in administration, the same concern for official memos, files and procedure, the same bickering between officials, the same meticulous regard for petty legalities, the same air of suspicion between officials and non-official legislative councillors, the same official unwillingness to trust either European or Asian civilians.

In the confusion there was widespread criticism of the top leadership, its unwillingness to divulge accurate information and its inability to harness the community to the war effort. The ageing Brooke-Popham was a hesitant speaker, lacking incisiveness, and he inspired no public confidence. Before the Pacific war broke out it had been arranged that General Sir Henry Pownall should take over from Brooke-Popham, and Pownall's arrival on 23 December 1941 was hailed with enthusiasm and high expectations.

The strongest criticisms were levelled at the civil administrators, and in particular at the Governor, Sir Shenton Thomas, whom an American journalist described as 'an uninformed individual...a slave to Civil Service clichés, bromides and banalities...he lives in a dream world'.[18] Kindly and conscientious, Thomas had been chosen as Governor eight years before to soothe ruffled feelings created by his predecessor and guide Malaya prudently out of the economic depression. In this task he had succeeded admirably, and his relationship with his officials and with European and Asian civilians was cordial. But he was not a man to lead or inspire the colony in his charge for all-out war. The qualities of compromise and conciliation, the willingness to consult and if need be defer to the opinions of his officials, which had made him an effective and popular peace-time Governor, left him a weak, vacillating, and indecisive leader in a crisis. Thomas loved to broadcast but his aimless, rambling discourses failed to create confidence and trust.

Criticism of the Governor extended to the Malayan Civil Service, described as 'a nineteenth century organization run by privileged mediocrities, trying to cope with a twentieth century crisis'.[19] The Australian representative on the Far East war council complained to his government that 'in the Malayan civil service there seems to be too much of the old bureaucratic doctrine that action means to risk making blunders and inaction means safety'.[20] The *Straits Times,* under its outspoken editor, Seabridge, thundered at the civil service throughout the Malayan campaign, and was largely instrumental in effecting the replacement of the much criticized Colonial Secretary in late January.

The press and vocal elements of the public pinned their main hopes on Duff Cooper, who was decisive, energetic and an impressive broadcaster, clear, straightforward and not given to clichés. The *Straits Times* backed Cooper, calling on him to devise machinery to assume control in Singapore,[21] but his powers as chairman of the Far East war council were ill-defined. He proposed to appoint Brigadier Simson as Director-General of Civil Defence with plenary powers in Singapore and Johor, but in practice Simson's scope was limited by the Governor. Thomas was reluctant to accede to Cooper's proposals to proclaim martial law. Eventually, at the end of December, a modified form of martial law and a curfew were imposed, but the military authorities had limited powers and Singapore never came under full martial rule even at the end.

Despite disillusionment with some of the military and civilian leaders, there was still in Singapore an air of unreal calm. The use of the word 'fortress' convinced Singaporeans that their island was in fact defended on all sides, although their eyes could tell them it was not. After the first night of the war there were few air raids on Singapore throughout the rest of December, and on New Year's Day the *Strait Times* commented, 'Terrible changes have taken place with a rapidity that still leaves us a little bewildered,' but 'We are not overwhelmed: we shall not be over-whelmed...we shall be rejoicing before 1943 comes round.'

In a last minute attempt to provide overall military leadership, Field-Marshal Wavell was appointed Supreme Commander in the Far East, over British, American, Australian and Dutch forces. Wavell arrived in Singapore on 7 January 1942 but established his headquarters in Java, taking Pownall with him as chief of staff. The first result of Wavell's appointment was the recall to London of Duff Cooper, whose post lapsed with the creation of a generalissimo. Cooper's transfer led to a public outcry. He had accomplished very little but seemed like a breath of fresh air, and the *Straits Times* appealed in vain for his retention as 'the last bulwark against that minute paper mentality to which many of our present anxieties must be attributed'.[22]

With Cooper's departure the *Straits Times* called for the appointment of a military governor for Singapore to give overall direction and cut through red tape, but Wavell made no move to create such an office. Shenton Thomas instructed the Malayan Civil Service, 'The day of minute papers has gone...the day of letters and reports is over... the essential thing is speed in action,' but, as the *Straits Times* commented, 'The announcement is about two and a half years too late.'

By the time of Wavell's appointment the Malayan campaign had reached a critical stage. On the day of his arrival in Singapore the Japanese routed the 11th Indian Division and the Argyll and Sutherland Highlanders at Slim River. On 11 January they occupied Kuala Lumpur and five days later broke the Australian defences at the Muar River. This was the last defensive position on the peninsula, and Percival had warned General Gordon Bennett, the Australian commander, that 'if this position is lost, the battle of Singapore is lost'.

On 19 January Wavell cabled Churchill to warn him that Singapore could probably not hold out once Johor was lost. Churchill was aghast. He had presumed the Japanese advance would be checked while they waited for the arrival of artillery to attack Singapore's fortifications and that this would give time for British reinforcements to take up their positions. For the first time he now realized that the northern shores of Singapore were not fortified. 'Seaward batteries and naval base do not contitute a fortress, which is a *completely encircled* strong place,' he protested.

Up to that time political leaders in Britain, ignorant of conditions in Singapore, were blinded by their own terminology, and the use of terms 'fortress' and 'Gibraltar of the East' deceived them as well as Singaporeans. The legend of Singapore's invincibility had spread so wide that everyone except the Japanese planners and some of the British military commanders were lulled into a sense of superficial security. As Churchill later commented, 'The possibility of Singapore having no landward defences no more entered into my mind than that of a battleship being launched without a bottom.'[23]

Churchill ordered that the 'entire male population' be conscripted for defence works. 'The most rigorous compulsion is to be used.' 'The whole island must be fought for until every single unit and every single strongpoint has been separately destroyed: finally, the city of Singapore must be converted into a citadel and defended to the death. No surrender can be contemplated.' 'I want to make it absolutely clear that I expect every inch of ground to be defended, every scrap of material or defences to be blown to pieces to prevent capture by the enemy, and no question of surrender to be entertained until after protracted fighting among the ruins of Singapore city.'

But Churchill now feared that at best Commonwealth forces could only turn the inevitable Japanese capture of Singapore into a Pyrrhic victory, and he asked his chiefs of staff whether it would be better to cut losses and divert fresh reinforcements to defend Burma. The ultimate decision to prolong the fight was made on political rather than military grounds, and dictated partly by mingled feelings of responsibility to Singapore and Malaya, of matching the ferocious defence of their homeland put up by Britain's Russian allies, and the stout American resistance in the Philippines. But Britain's prime consideration was her obligation to Australia, who considered Singapore the keystone of her own defence. On Christmas Day Churchill had promised the Australian prime minister, John Curtin, that Singapore would be held 'with the utmost tenacity'. Reports that the British government was discussing abandoning Singapore provoked the Australian war cabinet into holding an emergency meeting on 23 January, when Curtin cabled Churchill that any such withdrawal would be 'an inexcusable betrayal' of his country, and complained, 'We have acted and carried out our part of the bargain. We expect you not to frustrate the whole purpose by evacuation.' There were bitter recriminations in the Singapore war council when the Australian representative accused the British of regarding Singapore as having 'nothing more than sentimental value' and deplored the prospect of the Australian 8th Division being cooped up and sacrificed in Singapore, while British reinforcements were diverted to Burma.

Fresh Commonwealth forces poured into Singapore. The 45th Indian Brigade landed at the beginning of January, 7,000 Indians of the 44th Brigade on 22 January, 3,000 Australians two days later, the main body of the British 18th Division on the 29th and its remaining battalions on 5 February. The Indians were semi-trained, the Australians raw recruits, many of them posted within a fortnight of enlisting, and the British who were diverted en route for the Middle East desert war, were fresh, fit but inexperienced, fed on a diet of contempt for their Japanese adversary on the ship, and, in the words of one of them, 'so much greener than the lushest grass around'.[24]

Belated attempts were made to rally the local population to their own defence. About 8,000 civilians were already enrolled for voluntary service, nearly 2,000 of them forming the Singapore battalion of the Straits Settlements Volunteer Corps. Five thousand others were attached to auxiliary medical, fire and air-raid precaution organizations and a further 1,000 in the volunteer police reserve and local defence.

The Japanese invasion drew the Singapore Chinese together in united opposition. Tan Kah Kee and the Kuomintang sank their differences and a deputation of Chinese leaders called on the Governor to offer their help. Shenton Thomas accepted without reservation. 'Post-war repercussions do not concern us in this emergency,' he informed the secretary of state.[25] Kuomintang officials called on Tan Kah Kee to form a committee and on the last day of December 1941 the Chung Kuo council for general mobilization came into being. Members of the still technically illegal Malayan Communist Party were welcomed as 'loyal supporters of the British cause'. Communist manifestoes urging all-out war were printed in the three English-language newspapers, and political prisoners were released from jail.

Thousands of Chinese flocked to help from all sectors of society, old and young, rich and poor, students, rickshaw pullers, young girls and elderly men. Tan Kah Kee urged the government to arm a Chinese force, and thousands of demonstrators paraded the streets singing Chinese war songs and carrying placards saying 'Give us guns and we will fight'. With some misgivings the government agreed to form a Singapore Chinese Anti-Japanese Volunteer Battalion, known as Dalforce, under the command of Lt.-Colonel John Dalley of the Federated Malay States police force. Dalley set up his headquarters in a Chinese school, equipped the volunteers with uniforms and elementary weapons, mostly shotguns, parangs and hand grenades, and put them through ten days' crash training.

The mobilization council met daily at the Chinese Protectorate and harnessed labour for manning essential services and constructing defences, under the leadership of Lim Bo Seng, a prominent Hokkien businessman. A former student of Raffles Institution and Hong Kong University, Lim Bo Seng had taken such an active part in anti-Japanese activities before the war that the British had considered banishing him. At the Governor's request he now formed a Chinese liaison committee for civil defence, with the help of the Malayan Communist Party, which claimed to control about seventy labour unions including construction workers and dockers. Belatedly, on 29 January, the legislative council rushed through a measure to legalize conscription of labour, and two days later the British government agreed to pay higher wages and compensation rates. By that time it was too late either to attract or to impress labour, because constant air raids made work so dangerous in vital areas, and Lim Bo Seng's committee was the only organization which could marshall workers.

Even in this hour of peril old enmities still threatened the new-found unity of the Singapore Chinese. Chungking appealed to the British government to remove Tan Kah Kee as head of the mobilization committee, but the Governor insisted that Tan was not a communist and his retention was essential.[26]

It was not until the second half of January that air raids on Singapore became intense. While the main targets were the airfields, which were Singapore's only hope of counter attack, many bombs fell in the town, causing terrible casualties in the crowded streets. Often there would be three air raids in one night and three more by day.

Despite the carnage, there was no panic among the local population, and the expatriate community, not crediting that danger was so near, tried to maintain a 'normal' life. Evacuees only began to leave in large numbers in late January, priority being given to mothers and children. The elderly and childless had to wait, and exit permits were refused for European and Asian men of military age, who were all required to register for service. Banks were so crowded that clients could hardly get in the doors, and transport became difficult after cars and bicycles were requisitioned in the last week of January. Hotels, boarding houses and private homes were crowded with refugees from up-country, and many restaurants and night clubs closed down, but Raffles Hotel continued to hold its nightly dances, while the cinemas and the New World cabaret remained open up to the final days before the surrender.

On 27 January Wavell gave Percival permission to withdraw to the island when necessary but told him that Singapore itself must be held at all cost. On the last day of the month the remaining 30,000 Commonwealth troops withdrew without casualty across the Causeway, marching in good order, with the ninety surviving Argyll and Sutherlanders and the bagpipes of the Gordon Highlanders bringing up the rear. With the help of Lim Bo Seng's Quarry Workers' Union, a sixty-yard gap was then blown in the Causeway. It was a tense day, with the remnants of the Navy standing by to ferry survivors if need be across to the island, but no Japanese planes came to molest the retreat.

It was twenty-four hours before the bewildered people of Singapore realized their island was beleaguered, but the censor still refused to allow correspondents to use the word 'siege' and most civilians failed to appreciate the danger.

The troops who arrived back after seven weeks of continuous retreat and disaster, weary, hungry, dirty and decimated, were appalled. All remaining bombers and most fighters had been withdrawn to Sumatra, since Tengah, Seletar and Sembawang airfields were under constant artillery fire from the mainland. The one fighter squadron of eight Hurricanes and six slow Brewster Buffaloes remaining at Kallang found it difficult to operate from the bomb-pitted runway. No defences had been prepared for the north coast of the island, and the exhausted soldiers retreating from the peninsular campaign had to set to work to construct the last-ditch defences themselves.

Singapore's peacetime population of 550,000 had nearly doubled as refugees poured over from the mainland. Military leaders deplored this influx, which complicated defence and put great strain on supplies of food and water, but the civilian authorities refused to risk racial disharmony by barring entry to Asians while admitting the European minority.

Throughout eight days of brilliant weather the two armies faced each other across the Johor Strait, divided by less than a thousand yards of water, the Japanese massing for their final onslaught, the Commonwealth forces hurriedly preparing their defences. Yamashita installed his headquarters in the Sultan's palace at Johor Bahru, from the heights of which he could survey Singapore island, the naval base and Tengah airfield.

Since Japanese reconnaissance aircraft could fly without hindrance over Singapore, it was difficult to construct defensive positions. Singapore's guns remained almost silent, partly to conserve ammunition and partly in an attempt even at this late stage to allay civilian alarm. No move was made to mine the Johor Strait, presumably in order not to harm soldiers escaping from the mainland or to impede Australian patrols which crossed the Strait at night to reconnoitre.

The major object of Singapore's defence plan, the protection of the naval base, was now shattered. With the opposite shore in enemy hands, the naval base was useless and the remaining ships had gone. On the day on which the troops withdrew to the island most European naval and civilian dockyard staff quit Singapore for Ceylon, leaving to the bewildered and battle-worn soldiers the disheartening task of destroying the base which it had been their prime duty to protect.

Now the object was to hold Singapore island as long as possible and inflict maximum damage on the Japanese, a contingency for which the defence plans had never provided. The permanent defences of Singapore were designed to protect the base and harbour from sea attack. There were fixed coastal defences at the Changi entrance to the naval base and the approaches to Keppel Harbour. For twenty miles from Changi along the south coast the beaches were strongly defended, with pill boxes, anti-tank obstacles, barbed wire and land mines, well supported by anti-naval artillery. The whole northern shore lay naked and vulnerable to attack, and although the guns could be adapted to fire landwards, they were of little use, since they had only armour-piercing and no anti-personnel shells.

Government offices, shops and commercial houses continued to operate, but the city was 'a ship without a rudder'.[27] The defence of Singapore in this unexpected crisis depended upon dynamic leadership and adaptability, but neither the Governor nor the military commander were men to inspire a sense of urgency and strength in such an emergency.

Shenton Thomas's prestige had already sunk very low. His main concern was to prevent panic, and he was probably the only individual in authority who genuinely believed that Singapore could hold out after Johor had been abandoned. Thomas appealed to Singaporeans to stand as one people and he ordered expatriate and local officials alike to stay at their posts, forbidding any repetition of the demoralizing and unauthorized evacuation of Europeans which had taken place in Penang. He opposed any rigid scorched earth policy, and as a colonial Governor he saw his first duty to the colony under his charge, not to imperial interests.

Arthur Percival, who assumed direct command of the Allied forces once they withdrew to the island, was also a man wholly unsuited for the role fate had suddenly thrust on him. A courageous, humane and intelligent soldier of great integrity, he was 'a brilliant blue-print general'[28] but not a born leader and field commander in the mould of Slim or Montgomery. While he impressed many people who knew him well, Percival lacked public presence. Slight in build, he appeared shy and over-sensitive, while in a crisis his unruffled calm could easily be mistaken for apathy and weakness.

Tired and exhausted after seven weeks of travelling to the front by day and working most of the night, Percival planned for a three-month siege but was convinced the battle was already lost. Seeing the Japanese attack sweeping down the Malay peninsula almost exactly with the same strength and in the same way he had predicted four years before, Percival seemed to be going through a nightmare already worked out to its conclusion and was mesmerized into accepting defeat. He saw all the locust years of wasted opportunities and unheeded warnings, when the War Office had neglected the advice of experts on the spot, including himself, and the Singapore legislative council had refused money for defences. He saw clearly the divisions of command, the futility of a naval base without ships and airfields with virtually no aircraft or ground forces to protect them, the hollowness of a defence plan in which the army, which was supposed only to play a role auxiliary to the navy and air force, had been forced to take the whole brunt of the attack. And it was clear to him that in the last resort Britain could not fight on western and eastern fronts at the same time. In a global struggle the defence of the eastern empire depended on bluff and when Japan called Britain's bluff, the East had to be sacrificed.

Percival was all too conscious of the contradictions in his orders to fight to the finish while carrying out a scorched earth policy and systematic demolition. Late in January when the War Office wanted assurances that everything of value would be destroyed, Percival protested, 'You cannot fight and destroy simultaneously with 100 per cent efficiency in both.'[29] Nor was it possible to evacuate useless mouths in preparation for a grim last battle, when only limited numbers could be taken to safety and no discrimination could be made between European and Asian without destroying morale.

It was said of Percival at the time that 'he had a mind that saw the difficulties to any scheme before it saw the possibilities'.[30] Possibilities there were. Singapore had adequate supplies of oil and ammunition, enough food to last six months, and, with rigid economies, the island could manage indefinitely on its water supplies. The defenders had a numerical advantage, since Yamashita had only 30,000 troops left to launch against Singapore, whereas Percival had 85,000, of whom 70,000 were operational. A large proportion of the Commonwealth forces were worn out and shaken in morale after weeks of retreat, but they had a short spell to reorganize and recoup their energies before the battle started afresh. There were also the Singapore Volunteers, the Malay Regiment, which had just been expanded to two battalions on the eve of war, and Dalforce, whose members had everything to lose in the case of failure and were prepared for all-out resistance. Wavell asked for Singapore to hold out one month until reinforcements came to save the day. An armoured brigade was due to arrive early in March, more ships were on their way, and fifty-one Hurricanes had been landed in crates, ready to be assembled.

If the former complacency had not given way to almost paralysing shock and defeatism, the defenders could have exploited many potential weaknesses among the Japanese. In this first encounter with a bewildering Japanese enemy the initial misplaced contempt for the Japanese changed to a feeling of awe and to over-rating their capabilities. While the Japanese were excellent field soldiers, they were not strong in staff work and supply. Divisions of command, obsession with seniority and personal honour encouraged inter-service jealousies, and a rigid devotion to timetables led to recriminations and sometimes to near panic in face of unexpected setbacks.

The success of the Malayan campaign had produced a sense of euphoria and a harmony which was unusual among the Japanese. The speed of the advance had enabled the leaders to push ahead without much interference from Tokyo or from the Southern Army headquarters in Saigon. Indeed Tsuji referred to an 'unparalleled co-operation between Army, Navy and Air Force',[31] free from the wranglings and jealousies which invariably plagued Japanese commands elsewhere. But from the early days of the campaign Yamashita was worried by the insubordination of Nishimura, the headstrong and temperamental commander of the Imperial Guards. Unlike the other contingents of the 25th Army, the Guards, though an élite force, had seen no action since the Russo-Japanese war in 1905 and had received no intensive battle training.

Yamashita was furious too when Field-Marshal Count Terauchi, commanding the Southern Army, diverted the bulk of the Japanese air force to bombing the Netherlands Indies. The Japanese army was left to attack Singapore almost alone, and the Commonwealth forces were able to retire to the island, whereas with efficient air support the Japanese could have pounded and destroyed the British force before it reached Singapore. Effective use of Japanese air mastery could have played havoc with the convoys bringing in troop reinforcements to Singapore, but until the end of January air raids concentrated on the airfields. The only troopship to be sunk was the *Empress of Asia,* which was bombed in the approaches to the harbour on 5 February. Most of the troops escaped but she took down with her the bulk of the equipment for the 18th British Division.

Japanese newspapers extolled Yamashita's successes and by the time he reached the Johor Strait 'the Tiger of Malaya' was Japan's national hero. But his success roused the jealousy and concern of Prime Minister Tojo and of his commanding officer Terauchi. The latter sent impractical detailed orders for an attack on Singapore, which Yamashita ignored. Yamashita was conscious that he could expect little further co-operation from headquarters and his supply line was drying up.

In Singapore the defenders had no inkling of these problems. In the headquarters at Fort Canning, or 'Confusion Castle' as it was popularly known, there was dissension at all levels. At the war council meetings the Australians were at loggerheads with the British. Gordon Bennett was restive, urging counter attack, and arguing in vain for the appointment of a military adviser to jolt the civilian administration into action.

On 4 February all civilians were evacuated from a belt one mile deep along the north coast, and two days later the demolition of the naval base began. Smoke from its burning oil dumps darkened the sky across the whole island and induced grim foreboding. To quieten the alarm Percival held a press conference next day, declaring, 'Today we stand beleaguered in our island fortress. Our task is to hold this fortress until help can come—as assuredly it will come. This we are determined to do.' His words lacked conviction, and privately he knew that the troop reinforcements still being landed in Singapore were being sacrificed in vain.

Against the advice of his supplies officer Yamashita resolved to attack Singapore before the exhausted Commonwealth troops regained their strength and acquired reinforcements. Since the British had no reconnaissance aircraft and no spies on the mainland, the initiative lay with the Japanese who could choose their point and time of attack.

From their reconnaissance the Japanese were aware that the Johor Strait and the opposite shore were not mined and that the defending troops were spread very thin. Since the Japanese had captured all the British Army's specially prepared maps of Singapore island, they were better equipped with maps of the terrain than the defenders.

Any effective defence depended on preventing the Japanese from establishing a beachhead, which meant that Percival spread his troops along an extended front to guard all the beaches, keeping few troops in reserve and tying himself down in a static defence. Percival stationed his largest force, the British 18th Division, north-east of the Causeway, towards which a Japanese fleet was reported to be approaching and where the Japanese Imperial Guards made feint attacks, occupying Pulau Ubin and firing on Changi. But, as Wavell surmized, Yamashita planned his real onslaught on the north-west, with the object of securing Tengah airfield and the dominant Bukit Timah heights.

An Australian patrol reported the massing of Japanese on the west side of the Johor end of the Causeway on the night of 7/8 February, but the speed and strength of the Japanese onslaught came as a surprise. Hiding in the jungle and rubber until the last moment, the Japanese 5th and 18th Divisions assembled at the waterfront on the evening of 8 February. Using collapsible boats, brought down by rail and sea after the Singgora landings and where necessary linked together to carry field artillery weapons, thousands of Japanese troops landed silently in the darkness on the north-west coast, infiltrating the creeks and inlets until the defending Australian force found itself outflanked and enveloped on all sides. After hours of desperate and confused hand-to-hand fighting, the defenders had to draw back to a neck of land between the Kranji and Jurong rivers, which had defensive possibilities but no prepared position apart from a half-dug anti-tank ditch.

By dawn the 5th and 18th Japanese Divisions were firmly established on the island with part of their artillery. By the end of the day Tengah airfield was in their hands and Yamashita and his staff came across the Strait that night. The Imperial Guards were to force a landing at Kranji but this was almost disastrous, since Nishimura held his troops back and asked for the attack to be called off when the advance party was enveloped in burning oil flowing down the Mandai River. The oil had escaped by accident, but the Japanese feared the defenders might intentionally employ this tactic on a large scale. Yamashita was furious with Nishimura, the attack was resumed and the Japanese gained control of the Singapore end of the Causeway. The defenders' demolition work was only partially effective, since the charge was inadequate to make a big enough breach to allow for low tide, and within four days the Japanese had the Causeway repaired and fully operational.

Once Japanese troops were firmly established on the island, the only hope for the defenders was to hold them along the Jurong-Kranji line, but this position was weakened when one commander interpreted as an immediate order a tentative plan issued by Percival outlining withdrawal to a proposed final battle defensive perimeter.

On 10 February Churchill cabled Wavell insisting, 'There must at this stage be no thought of saving the troops or sparing the population. The battle must be fought to the bitter end at all costs. ... Commanders and senior officers should die with their troops. The honour of the British Empire and of the British Army is at stake. I rely on you to show no mercy to weakness in any form...the whole reputation of our country and our race is involved.'[32] Wavell, who visited Singapore for the last time on that day, urged Percival that there must be no surrender, and recommended a determined counter-attack to hold the Kranji-Jurong line.

The ill-armed but fiercely determined members of Dalforce and other Chinese irregulars fought alongside the Commonwealth troops, many units fighting to the last man, but by the early hours of 11 February the line was broken and the Japanese were in command of Bukit Timah village. Yamashita was delighted to have breached this last defensive position and Japanese aircraft dropped leaflets calling for surrender, but fierce resistance continued. The following day Percival withdrew his troops to a final perimeter round the city stretching from Pasir Panjang to Kallang.

The last British planes flew off to Sumatra on 11 February, by which time Kallang aerodrome was under constant shelling. After that the Japanese could watch everything undisturbed from an observation balloon, and the Penang wireless station poured out messages and propaganda to break morale. Within the town all was confusion and despair. About one million people were now crowded into a three-mile radius from the water-front, exposed to incessant bombing by day and shelling by night. There were no air raid shelters and the dispersal camps on the outskirts of town were in enemy hands. The crowded tenements of Chinatown were death traps in air raids, and it is impossible to say how many civilians were killed in the last days of fighting in Singapore. Some estimate the figure at 500, others as high as 2,000, a day. There were gruesome horrors, such as the destruction by fire of the wooden-hutted Indian base hospital at Tyersall when nearly all the two hundred patients were burned to death. The regular hospitals were crowded and hotels, schools and clubs were taken over as emergency hospitals. Over all hung the pall of black smoke from the burning oil dumps which rained down soot.

The army had not only to fight a last ditch stand in the crowded city but to carry out a scorched earth policy at the same time. The Governor ordered the destruction of rubber stocks and the tin smelting plant on Pulau Brani. To prevent any repetition of the invading army's drunken rampage through Chinese cities, he decreed the smashing of the massive stocks of alcohol which Singapore held as supplier to the whole of South-East Asia: some $1\frac{1}{2}$ million bottles of spirits and 60,000 gallons of samsu. Thomas refused demands by the military to demolish small Chinese workshops on which the livelihood of their owners depended, but he ordered the destruction of the stocks and machinery of British-owned engineering plants, often in the teeth of their owners' opposition. The wireless station was smashed and most of the currency burned, but destruction of the port facilities was hampered because the Harbour Board's key technicians evacuated without notifying the government.

On 13 February, despite fierce and gallant resistance by the 1st battalion of the Malay Regiment, the Japanese broke through the Gap on Pasir Panjang ridge. By afternoon the whole city lay within range of their artillery. No defensive position was left and the heavily populated town lay immediately behind the front line.

All reservoirs were in Japanese hands. They did not turn the water off, knowing the problem they themselves would face in getting it functioning again later, but the pipes in town were so damaged by bombing and shelling that most water was running to waste. By 14 February most areas of town, including hospitals, had no water. Without labour to clear the debris, bury the dead, or mend broken sewers, the town was filled with the stench of filth and death.

Percival appealed to Wavell for discretion to surrender to avoid the inevitable slaughter of the population, but Wavell cabled on 13 February, 'You must continue to inflict maximum damage on enemy for as long as possible by house to house fighting if necessary.' The following day the Governor appealed to Percival to surrender and cabled the Colonial Office to warn how desperate the position was, but Wavell still insisted, 'Your gallant stand is serving a purpose and must be continued to the limit of endurance.'

Not only the Governor but all the military commanders argued the futility of going on, and, without informing Percival, the Australian commander cabled his prime minister declaring he would surrender to avoid loss of life if the enemy entered the city.

Still bound by his orders, Percival ordered resistance to continue, but arrangements were made to evacuate military nurses, vital staff officers and technicians, who were allotted more than half of the three thousand places aboard the little ships which remained in the harbour. The rest were taken up by civilians, mainly European women and children and Chinese, many of whom had been prominent in the anti-Japanese movement and active in the final defence of Singapore. For the first time there was a real scramble to get away from Singapore and many ugly scenes as army deserters struggled to seize places for themselves on the fleeing ships. Clifford Pier and the docks were in turmoil with Japanese planes strafing the evacuees, and the Japanese navy was waiting to intercept those who got away in the 'Bomb Alley' of the Bangka Strait. Of the forty-four ships, all but four were sunk within two days of leaving Singapore and nearly all of the last-minute refugees were captured or killed.

While still urging Percival on, Wavell cabled Churchill on 14 February to tell him the situation was hopeless, and the prime minister gave permission for surrender when no useful purpose could be gained from continuing to fight. On the morning of Sunday, 15 February, Chinese New Year's Day, Percival held a final conference at Fort Canning. Petrol supplies and ammunition were almost exhausted. Makeshift hospitals in schools and clubs were crowded and 10,000 patients were crammed into the one-thousand-bed General Hospital. Parts of the city, including the civilian hospital, had been without water for twenty-four hours, and the danger of epidemic was imminent. Soldiers were deserting in their hundreds and roaming the streets. Thoroughfares were cluttered with overturned cars and trams, and traffic was snarled up bumper to bumper. Any counter attack was out of the question. All agreed on the need to capitulate in order to avert inevitable massacre, and Percival asked the Japanese to discuss peace terms.

In view of the continued fierce resistance, Yamashita was astonished to hear the British wanted to parley and at first suspected a ruse. His own position was critical and he could afford to lose no time. His ammunition was almost exhausted, his supply lines dried up, and he feared that the British would draw him into fierce house-to-house fighting, which would be disastrous for his smaller force. He had decided to bluff by shooting off his dwindling supply of ammunition as if he had limitless stocks, and to launch an all-out attack on the town centre on the night of the fifteenth in order to force defeat on the British before they could exploit his weakness. The bluff succeeded and Percival had no idea of the numerical weakness of the Japanese or their supply difficulties.

Suspicious and wary, Yamashita summoned Percival to come in person to his headquarters at the Ford factory in Bukit Timah. The adversaries began the interview by talking at cross purposes. Percival, taking his surrender as assumed, started discussing terms, while Yamashita kept demanding brusquely whether Percival was offering to surrender or not. Misinterpreting Yamashita's puzzlement, Percival thought the Japanese general was thumping the table to humiliate him. After an hour of confused argument, Yamashita compelled Percival to accept unconditional surrender but acceded to the British commander's request that the Japanese should not enter the city until the following morning. A skeleton force of armed Commonwealth soldiers was to enforce order until the Japanese took over, and all troops were commanded to remain at their posts to ensure an orderly surrender. A few made their escape after the cease-fire, including General Gordon Bennett who succeeded in reaching Australia but was subsequently officially reprimanded.

By mid-afternoon most guns were silent, since both sides had almost used up their ammunition, and at 8.30 p.m. complete silence came to the city. The night of the surrender was one of eerie but foreboding calm and quiet after the horrors of the past week's fighting.

Victory brought a thrill of exhilaration to Japan and her allies. The previous year German military leaders had told Yamashita it would probably take five divisions eighteen months to conquer Singapore.[33] In fact the mission had been accomplished by three divisions in just over two months. For the British the loss of Singapore was the blackest moment of the Second World War and, in the words of Winston Churchill, 'the worst disaster and largest capitulation in British history'.

The scapegoat was the unfortunate Percival; not Brooke-Popham, who had left half-way through the campaign, nor Pownall who was in command for little more than a week, nor yet Wavell, who arrived late on the scene with a hastily improvised and ill-organized command but might have saved the day by appointing a military governor. For Percival Singapore was the end of a promising career which seemed destined to bring him to top command in the British army. After more than three years of hardship and ill-treatment as a prisoner of war in Singapore, Japan and Manchuria, Percival retired without recognition at the end of the war. His reputation remained under a cloud until his death in 1966, but he consistently refused to vindicate himself, seeking only to protect the reputation of the men who had served under him. Even Gordon Bennett, who clashed with Percival more strongly than most men, later admitted that 'the system was more to blame than the individual'.[34]

Percival never realized the close margin between defeat and salvation. At the time Wavell claimed that if Singapore could have held out for one more month, sufficient reinforcements could have been assembled to drive the Japanese back. Yamashita and Tsuji considered that if the British had held on for three more days the Japanese would have been forced to call off their attack. But even if Percival had appreciated the weakness of the Japanese position, the price of further resistance would have been appalling. Amid ruins and carnage, a more ruthless, simple, single-minded fire-eating military commander might have sent Singapore's name down in glory in the annals of British military history. For many Commonwealth troops death would have been kinder than the terrible fate they later suffered in prison camps or on the notorious 'death railway' in Thailand, but for the people of Singapore in February 1942 it was perhaps fortunate that she was not defended by such a commander.

The Malayan campaign was the first encounter between Commonwealth troops and an enemy whose tactics were to defy larger forces of more experienced and better-equipped troops later in the war. In the Japanese Ha-Go offensive on the Arakan front in Burma in February 1944 two years later, it took 180,000 British and Indian troops with overwhelming superiority in aircraft, artillery and tanks to defeat one Japanese division of 8,000 men. The quality and background of the majority of Commonwealth troops fighting in Malaya did not prepare them for a ruthless, savage enemy who fought without regard for his own casualties and who ignored the rules of civilized warfare. As one of their commanders later said, 'It was a case of British academics fighting Jap realists. They are *not* bloody marvels, but they *are* intensely practical and keen, and therefore aggressive and very, very fast.'[35]

While it is true that the defenders made numerous tactical mistakes both on the mainland and in Singapore, the seeds of the ultimate disaster were sown in pre-war days. It grew from official parsimony and bickering, from the administrative fragmentation of the Malay peninsula, from the lack of a generalissimo with powers over all the armed services and, if need be, the civil administration. It came from under-estimating Japanese strength and ingenuity, breeding a complacency which lulled both the local population and the ruling class. It arose from creating a naval base without a navy, and airfields without an adequate air force or ground defence. Ultimately it stemmed from the fact that Britain was never strong enough to defend her eastern empire alone. For the first two decades of the twentieth century she relied on the co-operation of Japan, but threw this over in 1921, without securing a firm alternative American commitment. 'As a substitute for battleships (Britain) built the Naval Base at Singapore',[36] a base created to meet a set of circumstances which never existed. Singapore was not prepared for total war without an effective British ally in the Pacific.

In terms of physical damage to the Allied war effort, the loss of Singapore was immense. It opened the way to the Japanese conquest of the Netherlands East Indies and her acquisition of vast resources of oil, rubber and tin, which would have been invaluable to the Allies. But it did not lead, as the Australians had dreaded, to the invasion of the Australian mainland, because Tokyo refused to support Yamashita's bold plans to conquer Australia. As a naval base Singapore was no more use to Japan than it had been to Britain, and Japanese naval superiority ended at the battle of Midway in June 1942.

When the Japanese took Singapore Tsuji claimed that 'everything that Great Britain had built up here (since 1819) in the Far East had now been beaten to a standstill'.[37] Certainly, as the Japanese took over the city, the economy of Malaya upon which the British régime was founded lay symbolically in ruins before them: the rubber stocks smouldering, the tin-smelting works on Pulau Brani destroyed, the Pulau Bukum oil on fire. Tsuji was wrong in that the British returned to power in Singapore only three and a half years later. Physical disaster did not bring the imperial régime to an end, but the events of the first six weeks of 1942 gave the lie to the basis of colonial rule. It undermined the old assumption of racial superiority and the belief that a colonial power could or should defend its subject people without calling on their co-operation. The ruling class were amazed at the inspired heroism of Dalforce and the Chinese irregulars, the tough fighting spirit of the Malay Regiment and the Asian contingents of the Straits Settlements Volunteer Corps, the spirited devotion of the auxiliary civilian voluntary workers and the ordinary citizen's stoic fortitude in face of danger and death. They were ashamed of their previous doubts about the calibre of Singaporeans and the fact that they had to call on the help of people such as Tan Kah Kee and Lim Bo Seng, who had previously been an embarrassment to them. For a few brief days racial distinctions and aloofness melted away. In the tragic saga of the Malayan campaign most of the actors were foreigners, with the local population until the last scene taking the role of bystanders and victims. But the final battle for Singapore showed of what stuff her people were made.

1. *Sydney Morning Herald,* 14 February 1938, quoted in L. Wigmore, *Australia in the War: the Japanese Thrust* (Canberra, 1957), p. 47.

2. John Gunther, *Inside Asia* (London, 1939), who according to Fujii was 'prize fool of them all'.

3. General Sir Ian Hamilton, *The Times,* London, 24 March 1924, quoted in Wigmore, p. 3.

4. Extract from Malaya Combined Intelligence Summary, No. 8/1940, October 1940, in CO 273/666, 50336.

5. D. Russell-Roberts, *Spotlight on Singapore* (London, 1965), p. 29.

6. *SFP,* 7 January 1941.

7. J.H. Brimmell, *Communism in South East Asia* (London, 1959), p. 148.

8. *Malaya Tribune,* 5 May 1939.

9. S. of S. to Governor, 28 February 1941, CO 273/668, 50695/41.

10. Virginia Thompson, 'Japan Frozen out of British Malaya', *Far Eastern Survey,* X, 20 (20 October 1941), p. 238.

11. C. Brown, *Suez to Singapore* (New York, 1942), p. 280.

12. M. Shinozaki, *My Wartime Experiences in Singapore* (Singapore, 1973), p. 5.

13. Donald Macintyre, *Sea Power in the Pacific* (London, 1972), p. 196.

14. B. Ash, *Someone had Blundered* (London, 1960), p. 151.

15. D. Cooper, *Old Men Forget* (London, 1957), p. 300.

16. Quoted in Wigmore, p. 103.

17. G.A. Weller, *Singapore is Silent* (New York, 1943), p. 65.

18. C. Brown, p. 210.

19. Letter to Editor *ST* by 'Asian', 2 January 1942.

20. A. Bowden to Australian Department of External Affairs, 10 January 1942, quoted in Wigmore, p. 204.

21. *ST,* 29 December 1941.

22. *ST,* 12 January 1942.

23. W.S. Churchill, *The Second World War,* Vol. IV (London, 1951), p. 47.

24. A.G. Allbury, *Bamboo and Bushido* (London, 1955), p. 13.

25. Governor to S. of S. telegram, 3 January 1942, CO 273/668, 50695/41.

26. Governor to S. of S., 4 February 1942, CO 273/669, 50750.

27. S.A. Field, *Singapore Tragedy* (Auckland, 1944), p. 230.

28. J.D. Potter, *A Soldier Must Hang* (London, 1963), p. 84.

29. A.E. Percival, *The War in Malaya* (London, 1949), p. 260.

30. Ian Morrison, *Malayan Postscript* (London, 1942), p. 159.

31. M. Tsuji, *Singapore: the Japanese Version* (Sydney, 1960), p. 60.

32. Churchill, IV, pp. 87–8.

33. Tsuji, p. 215.

34. H. Gordon Bennett, *Why Singapore Fell* (Sydney, 1944), p. 21.

35. Colonel Ian Stewart of the Argylls to Major-General Sir N. Malcolm, New Delhi, 14 November 1942, in CO 273/671, 50790.

36. Sir John Pratt, *War and Politics in China* (London, 1943; reprinted New York, 1971), p. 152.

37. Tsuji, p. 269.

# VI

# Syonan: Light of the South
# 1942–1945

THE agony of battle was over: the ordeal of occupation was to follow. Singaporeans were numbed, hardly crediting what had happened. Up to the last minute they had believed British statements. For more than a century the security of Singapore in British hands had been taken for granted, but suddenly in a few weeks the hollowness of this seeming power had been exposed.

On the morning after the surrender a small body of Japanese *kempei,* or military police, arrived to take control, but the main Japanese army was held back, and the final orderly surrender meant that the city was spared the horrors of indiscriminate slaughter, rape and pillage at the hands of an unrestrained soldiery, which the north-west districts of the island suffered. There was no repetition of the ugly incidents during the last days of fighting, notably when Japanese troops had rampaged through the British military hospital, bayoneting doctors, nurses, and patients.

Despite this, nearly all the Asian population kept indoors on the day after the surrender, and all shops were boarded up. Only the Singapore Cold Storage store remained open, operated by the manager and a handful of staff and doing a roaring trade, mainly among European customers.[1] Otherwise the Japanese found Singapore a 'ghost town',[2] guarded by a small contingent of Indian and British troops, with only listless groups of dejected Commonwealth soldiers to be seen on the streets.

The next morning the European population, men, women and children, were assembled on the padang, inspected and questioned for hours. All British, Australian and allied European prisoners were to be interned at Changi, the military prisoners at Selarang barracks and the civilians, comprising about 2,000 men and 300 women and children, in Changi gaol.

The British and Australian troops set off in the early afternoon on their fourteen-mile journey, marching in orderly ranks and reaching their prison camp about midnight, with stragglers stumbling into the barracks in the early hours of the morning. The Asians, mainly Malays and Indians, who lined the route viewed this spectacle for the most part in bewildered silence, not with enthusiasm and delight as the Japanese expected.

European civilians were marched to Katong, where they were crowded together for a fortnight in empty buildings without food or equipment. Early in March they too set off on the long painful trail to Changi, a few by lorry but most of them trudging on foot.

British officers attached to the Indian and Malay regiments were consigned with their countrymen to Selarang. Indian and Malay officers and men, comprising about 45,000 Indians and 600 Malays, were assembled at Farrer Park on 17 February and urged by the Japanese to disown their loyalty to the British crown and transfer their allegiance to the Japanese emperor.

The eight Malay officers were executed when they refused, but their men were given permission to return home. The first batch of about one hundred were loaded into lorries, ostensibly to be taken to the railway station, but were instead driven away to a mass execution. The rest dispersed, many to join their families who had followed the troops to Singapore during the campaign and were lodged in the Kampong Glam *istana*. A few Malay troops eventually joined the Japanese Volunteer Force, many were sent as forced labourers to Siam, Sumatra or New Guinea, others escaped to join the guerrillas on the mainland, and those who remained in Singapore were kept under close *Kempeitai* surveillance for the rest of the war.[3]

The Indians were greeted as brother Asians and urged to join an Indian National Army to fight the British for the independence of India. Despite the pressures put upon them, most professional soldiers of the Indian Army remained steadfastly loyal to the British, the Gurkhas to a man resisting any inducement to change sides. Many who refused were beaten, tortured and murdered. Others considered such loyalty to former masters who had let them down misplaced. Indian troops had taken the brunt of the fierce fighting in north Malaya, newly-arrived reserves had been thrown untrained and ill-equipped into the Johor battle. About 20,000 now volunteered to join the Indian National Army, some because they saw this as a genuine opportunity to free India from British rule and the majority in the interests of self-preservation. Those who refused were declared to have forfeited their prisoner-of-war status and were imprisoned at Seletar barracks.

Two days after the surrender the Japanese set up their military headquarters at Raffles College and their army vehicles streamed down the Bukit Timah road, all of them flying Japanese flags and their drivers blowing their horns. 'The noise was fierce but cheerful, in fact there was a holiday spirit about the whole affair.'[4]

Yamashita did not intend to stage a triumphal parade but instead held a solemn commemoration service for the dead. He regarded the conquest of Singapore not as a brilliant achievement but 'a bluff that worked',[5] and he saw the island merely as a staging post en route to the Dutch Indies and Australia.

Singapore was renamed Syonan, or Light of the South, and was designated the capital of Japan's southern region. The first task was to repair the physical damage of the fighting, to bury the dead, clear the wreckage, avert the dangers of disease and get municipal services working again. Within twenty-four hours the Japanese cleared the general hospital to accommodate their wounded. Adult patients were sent home or moved to the Cricket Club, the Victoria Hall and the Singapore Club, children were transferred to the mental hospital, and babies were given away to anyone who would care for them.

The Japanese acted swiftly to stop looting by firing into crowds of looters and executing individual offenders on the spot. Indians and Malays were usually released with a warning, but Chinese were summarily decapitated and their heads put on public display as a warning.

Waterworks, gas, electricity workers and municipal employees were ordered to report for duty a few days after the capitulation. Doctors were required to register, and private clinics and dispensaries re-opened on 1 March. Prisoners of war were set to work clearing the debris. The water supply was restored, although it was six weeks before it was fully back to normal, and the air was dull with the smoke of oil dumps, which went on burning for more than a month.

The Japanese were eager to establish their information services quickly. Wireless-station staff were summoned to duty with other essential workers and broadcasting started again in March, with programmes consisting largely of news and propaganda. All receiving sets were sealed to permit reception of medium wave transmission only and it was strictly forbidden to listen in to news from overseas.

A Malay newspaper, in both Jawi and romanized editions, appeared within two days of the surrender, and by the end of the week there were Indian, Chinese and English newspapers. The *Sin Chew Jit Poh* resumed publication as the *Syonan Jit Poh,* and the *Straits Times* became the *Syonan Times.* It continued through to September 1945, but in December 1942, on the anniversary of the outbreak of the Malayan campaign, the newspaper was renamed the *Syonan Shimbun,* issuing both Japanese and English editions. The editor of the English edition was Tatsuki Fujii, former editor of the *Singapore Herald,* who returned in November 1942 as one of a group of Japanese internees released from Indian prison camps in exchange for British internees in other parts of the Far East.

Despite the war in China, Tokyo recognized the need to win the co-operation of the Singapore Chinese, both in rebuilding the economy and using the Nanyang Chinese as a possible tool to bring Chiang Kai-shek to the negotiating table. A secret policy agreement drawn up by the Japanese army general staff as early as March 1941 stressed the need for con-ciliation, once hostile pro-Kuomintang elements had been removed. This policy was couched in vague terms, but the speed of Japanese victory brought their armies to Singapore before any precise plan of execution had been worked out. The manner in which it was implemented by the men on the spot brought tragedy to the Singapore Chinese and left indelible hatred towards the Japanese conquerors.

Yamashita, conscious of his weak position and anxious to avoid any guerrilla attacks on his depleted forces, ordered an immediate rooting out of resistance elements. Major General Saburo Kawamura, commander of the Syonan garrison, was instructed to carry out 'severe punishment of hostile Chinese' in conjunction with Colonel Masyuki Oishi, head of the Syonan *Kempeitai*.

Unlike the German civilian Gestapo, the *Kempeitai* was a military police force administered by the War Ministry. Specially trained in interrogation methods, its task was to crush all resistance to military rule, and it had powers to arrest and extract information from civilians and military alike. At that time there were only about 200 regular *kempei* in Singapore but a 1,000 auxiliaries were recruited from the army, mostly young, rough peasant soldiers, whose passions had been inflamed to fever pitch by the fierce resistance put up by Chinese irregulars in the battle for Singapore island.

Oishi was ordered to act 'in accordance with the letter and spirit of military law', but the instructions were not clear, and the result was a murderous *sook ching,* or purification through purge.

In order to flush out their quarry, orders were given three days after the surrender, probably on Tsuji's authority, for all Chinese males between the ages of eighteen and fifty to report to registration 'camps' for screening. The *kempei* went from house to house driving out Chinese occupants at bayonet point, sometimes seizing women, children and old men too and herding them into five major concentration areas. Here they were examined by the *kempei,* who, with the help of hooded informers, picked out those alleged to be anti-Japanese.

At the registration centres there was neither order, method nor organization. Most of the *kempei* were ignorant auxiliaries, who had no clear idea of what they were doing and spoke only Japanese. In some centres the Japanese were comparatively efficient, sending away women, children and old people, separating those who had been actively involved in anti-Japanese activities and giving the others clearance to go home. Elsewhere tens of thousands were kept for upwards of a week, crowded in the open without food, water or shelter, often kicked and slapped. The *kempei,* many of them rabidly anti-Chinese, condemned at will. In some areas they seized all Chinese school teachers and journalists, and all newcomers from China. Sometimes they arrested all Hainanese, since communism was so prevalent among this community, or men with tattoos, which might indicate membership of a secret society. Elsewhere they picked upon the well-dressed, the intellectuals or those who signed their names in English, and sometimes even the former domestic servants of European households. Those who passed the screening were given a paper with 'Examined' in Chinese, or had square ink marks stamped on their arms or their shirts, which they tried to preserve for months afterwards. The unfortunate were stamped with triangular marks and driven off. Some were taken to prison, but most were roped together and either taken out in boats and dumped overboard off Blakang Mati or herded into the sea off Changi and Siglap and machine gunned to death.

It is impossible to say how many Chinese died in the massacres during the first week of the occupation. The Japanese later admitted to killing 5,000, but many Chinese put the total at more than five times that figure. The massacres were kept secret and the story did not come out until the war was over. Hardly any victims survived and most families hoped their lost relatives had been taken into jail or sent away as labourers.

The major massacres were followed by a mopping-up operation in the eastern rural districts, when hundreds more were executed. By that time the Japanese themselves began to appreciate that these methods were not only barbarous but ineffective. While thousands of ordinary people were slaughtered, many important men escaped the Japanese net. On the orders of Major-General Keishin Manaki, Yamashita's deputy, the mass screening was called off in favour of hunting out key figures.

Some of these had already gone. The remnants of Dalforce had slipped away up-country and taken to the jungle hills to form the Malayan People's Anti-Japanese Army. Tan Kah Kee, prime target of the Japanese, fled to Sumatra eleven days before the capitulation and thence to Java, where he hid throughout the war, despite the high price which the Japanese put on his head. Lee Kong Chian was in the United States and Aw Boon Haw in Hong Kong. Tay Koh Yat, a leading Kuomintang supporter, member of the China Relief Fund committee, and head of Singapore's civil defence, escaped to Java and lived a hermit's existence, but his eldest son was caught and murdered by the Japanese. Lim Bo Seng escaped just before the surrender, but many of his family were seized by the *Kempeitai* and never seen again. Lim Bo Seng himself made his way to India, where he recruited men for the underground movement in Malaya. In 1943 he returned to join the guerrillas in Perak but was arrested by the Japanese and died after torture a few months later.

Others remained. The biggest prize was Lai Teck, secretary-general of the Malayan Communist Party. Lai Teck had escaped arrest throughout the years before the Pacific war, when the British had been most active in suppressing the Malayan Communist Party and may already have been an informer for the British. He now agreed to collaborate secretly with the Japanese.

The Japanese also arrested Tan Lark Sye, vice-chairman of the Chinese chamber of commerce, Yap Pheng Geck, commander of the Chinese company of the Singapore Volunteer Force, Lim Boon Keng, and many other prominent Chinese.

The *sook ching* destroyed Japanese hopes of gaining the co-operation of Singaporeans. The Japanese were never welcomed as liberators in Singapore, as they were initially in some other colonial territories, but they had a splendid opportunity. Their victory inspired awe in a community which had always admired material success, and they had made former British masters look 'shaky and insipid'.[6] While there was no incipient nationalist movement to exploit, the Japanese had the chance to strike a chord of sympathy in a divided and mixed community, united only in subjection to a British régime which had failed them. Many Chinese were so alienated by the Chinese Protectorate that shortly before the fall of Singapore the Chinese chamber of commerce and other Chinese leaders had petitioned the Governor to dismiss the Secretary of Chinese Affairs. The Indians were stirred by the anti-British nationalist movement in India, the Malays resented their economic depression, and the Eurasians had no firm roots in any local community but had been barred from senior posts or social equality by the ruling class.

The Japanese preached an exciting mission of Asian equality in a Greater East Asia New Order comprising Japan, China, Manchuria and South-East Asia. During the campaign Tsuji had sought to impart a sense of mission to his troops. He printed 40,000 copies of a pamphlet 'Read this alone—and the war can be won', for 'front line soldiers, who were on fire with the high ideal of the emancipation of Asia'.[7] 'We embark now upon that great mission which calls upon Japan, as the representative of all the peoples of the Far East, to deal a resolute and final blow to centuries of European aggression in these lands.'

It was declared Japanese policy to bring racial equality to former colonial territories. Five days after the surrender Yamashita promised the people of Syonan, 'We sweep away the arrogant and unrighteous British elements and share pain and rejoicing with all concerned people in a spirit of give and take.' He announced Japan's intention to set up 'the East Asia Co-Prosperity Sphere in which the New Order of justice has to be attained under the Great Spirit Cosmocracy, giving all content to the respective races and individuals according to their talents and faculties'.[8] Condemning the British policy of divide and rule, the Japanese urged that Asians should stand together in a universal brotherhood, or hakko-ichiu, respecting each other's religions, customs and languages.

The Syonan Times declared, 'It is our great duty and pride to place the life of the three million Malayans under the Great East Asia War State and to lead them in obedience to Nippon Military Commands under the aegis of the Empire of Nippon which is the strongest power and leader of East Asia.'[9] The newspaper insisted two months later that 'Nippon not only desires, but insists upon, interracial harmony in all territories within her sphere of influence. . . . The old system of administration in Malaya, with its careful fostered policies of preferential treatment to some and oppressive restrictions to others resulted in political pariahdom as the fate of all.'[10] But by the time these words were written, the Japanese had already squandered their initial assets of admiration, awe and respect. Despite their propaganda, they had shown they were not interested in liberating Asians but in acquiring control of South-East Asian resources for their war needs.

The Japanese urged, 'One of the first imperatives. . . is the breaking down of the habit and custom left behind by the haughty and cunning British. Side by side. . . must proceed the work of reviving Oriental culture based on moral and spiritual principles.' It was easy to sweep away the externals of British power, although the Japanese needed to retain some British doctors, nurses, engineers and other specialist staff as a stopgap measure for a few months, until their own people arrived. The Director of the Botanic Gardens, his assistant, and the Director of Fisheries were retained at the Gardens and the Museum throughout the occupation, a few other internees were employed temporarily in government departments, and for the first twelve months the Bishop of Singapore lived on parole in the town.

The Japanese code of Bushido held it dishonourable for soldiers to surrender, and Japan had never ratified the 1929 Geneva Convention, guaranteeing the rights of prisoners of war to humane treatment. The Japanese did not hesitate to inflict brutal punishments, tortured prisoners to extract information, punished groups for acts committed by individuals and executed men who tried to escape. In theory civilian internees were entitled to better treatment, but in practice there was little difference in living conditions between the military and civilian camps at Changi.

At first prisoners were treated lightly and left to organize themselves, since the Japanese were short of administrators. Initially military prisoners could move fairly freely over the eastern part of the island. These early months were a time of divisions and recriminations, when men relived the disasters of the campaign and blamed their leaders. Bitterness rankled between the British and Australians and between officers and other ranks. Conditions in the prison hospital were dreadful. For many weeks it housed over two thousand patients and more than a quarter of these were buried at Changi by the autumn of 1942.

The soldiers resented Percival's insistence on regular drilling, but within two months some sense of orderliness and discipline had been restored. The Japanese commandeered groups of prisoners as outside work parties and by April 1942 had more than 8,000 at work, building a shrine and war memorial at Bukit Timah, repairing the docks and unloading ships. Such assignments were popular since they meant bigger rations, opportunities to barter or pilfer supplies, particularly in unloading cargoes of food, and working pay, although this only amounted to ten cents a day.

Security was tightened in August 1942. Four hundred senior civilians and military prisoners, including Percival and Shenton Thomas, were removed to Taiwan, and the Japanese put in their own camp administration under Major-General Fukuye. In September 1942 the Japanese assembled all military prisoners, numbering more than 15,000, on Selarang Square and ordered them to sign forms promising not to escape. Stubborn in their refusal, the troops remained for three days without food or shelter, but finally their officers ordered the declarations to be signed, after the Japanese publicly executed four recaptured escapees.

Far from breaking the troops' spirit, the Selarang Square incident rekindled among them a sense of unity and common purpose. Trained to be disciplined, resourceful and self-reliant, the military prisoners shared and developed a diversity of talents. They planted vegetable gardens, kept chickens, and organized camp workshops to produce soap, paper, tooth-powder, brooms and cooking utensils. A library was set up and a camp 'university', which by early 1943 had 120 teachers and more than 2,000 students. They developed a theatre group, issued a camp magazine, and the Australians provided a talented concert party. At first prisoners were permitted to receive copies of the *Syonan Times* and after this was stopped they kept in touch with the outside world through hidden wireless sets, on which they received regular news bulletins from London, New Delhi and the United States.

The Gurkhas too maintained a disciplined camp in true regimental style, but conditions in the Indian camp at Seletar were deplorable. These units had lost all their British officers, many of the Indian officers had been executed or had joined the Indian National Army, and there was constant friction and suspicion between Hindus, Muslims and Sikhs. Discipline was lax even among regular troops, morale was bad, and the incidence of sickness and death very high.

Escape was virtually impossible. Almost unique was the exploit of C.E. McCormac, a former Royal Air Force man, who organized the escape of a seventeen-man working party. With the connivance of a Portuguese Eurasian guard, they fled frcm Pasir Panjang and took a small boat from Kranji. Four survivors were picked up by a Dutch flying-boat in the Straits of Malacca and McCormac eventually reached Australia.[11]

There was no contact between military and civilian prisoners, and little between the men's and women's section in Changi gaol. Civilian male prisoners were sometimes employed on working parties away from the gaol, but, apart from two doctors who worked on a temporary assignment in town, women and children were confined to camp. Life in the women's camp was spartan and bleak, but they ran a school and for eighteen months issued a camp news-sheet.

During the first year conditions in the Changi prison camps were tolerable. Asahi, the Japanese official in charge of enemy aliens, was a considerate man, and the only ill-treatment came from the Sikh and Indian guards. The main hardship was shortage of food. The Japanese reduced rations in all prisoner-of-war and internee camps in October 1942, but food supplies remained fairly constant, if meagre, throughout the twelve months that followed.

In view of her strategic and economic importance, the Japanese intended to retain Syonan as a permanent Japanese colony. In March 1942 they set up a military administration, or *gunseikan-bu,* under Colonel Watanabe, who succeeded Manaki, and a new municipal government, or *tokubetsu-si,* with Shigeo Odate as mayor and a former consul-general,

Kaoru Toyota, as his deputy. In addition to normal municipal functions, the *tokubetsu-si* took over some former government departments and its territorial responsibility included the Carimons and the Riau archipelago.

Odate, who was a first-rate administrator with high-level experience of civil government in occupied China, was given the honorary rank of general. Syonan was Japan's most important centre in the Nanyang, but there were never more than twenty Japanese civilian officials in Syonan at one time. There was constant friction between the civil and military authorities. Sometimes Odate succeeded in overruling Watanabe by virtue of his rank and his personality, but in practice the *tokubetsu-si* was subordinate to the *gunseikan-bu,* which insisted on giving top priority to security and the needs of war.

Because of the shortage of senior men, the *gunseikan-bu* brought in low-ranking Japanese officials and also Taiwanese and Koreans, many of whom were arrogant and cruel. The Taiwanese were particularly useful as interpreters and *kempei* since they spoke the most important Hokkien dialect, while the Koreans, who generally spoke neither Chinese nor English, were employed mainly as prison guards.

During the reign of terror in the first fortnight of the occupation the Chinese were paralysed with fright, and no-one dared to come forward as spokesman. But the more moderate Japanese wanted to reach an understanding, and the initiative appears to have been taken by Shinozaki, newly released from Changi gaol. He found a go-between in Lim Boon Keng, now an old man of seventy-two who had returned from Amoy to retire in Singapore five years earlier. With great reluctance Lim Boon Keng formed an Overseas Chinese Association, with himself as chairman and S.Q. Wong, a prominent Singapore-born Cantonese businessman and banker, as vice-chairman.

Shinozaki persuaded the *Kempeitai* to acknowledge the Association and to release prominent Chinese leaders, such as Tan Lark Sye, to join it. About 250 well-known Chinese congregated at the exclusive Goh Loo Club, where the *gunseikan-bu* issued them with badges as overseas Chinese liaison officers and they formed a peace maintenance committee.

Shinozaki later claimed that he started the Overseas Chinese Association in order to protect the Chinese community,[12] but Watanabe favoured taking a hard line and handed the Association over to Toru Takase, his tough civilian right-hand man.[13] With the help of Wee Twee Kim, a ruthless Taiwanese who had been a storekeeper for a Japanese firm in Singapore before the war, Takase used the Overseas Chinese Association to intimidate the Chinese and extract their wealth.

Tokyo expected local Japanese military authorities to raise their own revenue, and Watanabe decided to do this by a levy on the Malayan Chinese, which would achieve the twin objects of providing administrative expenses and making the Chinese atone for their past hostility. Day after day Takase summoned the Chinese leaders to military headquarters and bullied them with threats. Petrified, they pledged full support for the

Japanese, and eventually were summoned before Watanabe, who ordered them to raise a $50 million 'gift' within a month. A committee was hastily formed under Tan Ean Kiam, managing director of the Oversea Chinese Bank, to organize the collection, and Singapore's liability was fixed at $10 million, the remainder to be raised by Chinese in the Malay states.

The Japanese supplied tax and property records so that no-one could evade payment, and the Chinese in Singapore decided that all individuals should be required to pay 8 per cent on property worth more than $3,000 and companies should pay 5 per cent of their assets. To raise such a sum was a Herculean task, since it represented a quarter of the total Malayan currency in circulation, and at the end of the month only a third of the money had been raised. The Malayan Chinese leaders were summoned to Singapore, threatened with reprisals and the deadline extended for another month. Further failure resulted in another stormy meeting in Singapore, when the date was extended until June, and when by this time barely half of the $50 million had been collected, the Chinese were permitted to raise the balance by loans repayable within a year from the Yokohama Specie Bank, which had taken over the Chartered Bank's premises in Singapore.

Watanabe claimed the 'gift' stemmed inflation by taking surplus money out of circulation and was justified because the revenue was ploughed back into the country. But the demand and the intimidation used to enforce it, coming so soon after the *sook ching*, left a burning hatred among the Singapore Chinese towards the Japanese régime.

Indians, Eurasians and Malays were not sorry to see the Chinese squeezed but were afraid their turn would come next. The Japanese did indeed intend to make the various communities conform to the new state but their attitude to the separate groups differed greatly.

Since they were not interested in fostering any budding Malay nationalism in Singapore, they tended, as the British had done, to leave the Malay community alone.

The Eurasians presented special problems. While they had never been accepted by Britons as equals they had held themselves aloof from the Asian population. English-educated Christians, usually speaking English as their mother tongue, Eurasians gravitated to middle-class white-collar jobs. The Japanese wanted to break down their sense of semi-superiority, claiming 'There are no "superior" people in the New Order.' Those with direct European antecedents were interned. The rest were assembled on the padang early in March and harangued. 'Until now you were spoiled in circumstances of individualism and liberalism. You were used to an easy going life of amusements.' Eurasians were told that 'the time for looking to personal and individual affairs is gone...the New Dawn has come over a new Great Asia', materialism was overthrown and Eurasians should 'gain the spiritualism you have forgotten entirely'.[14] They were commanded to consider themselves as Asians, to forget feelings of racial superiority, and to give up clerical jobs for farming, shopkeeping or other similar employment. A few responded to this challenge, but on the whole the Eurasians remained a distrusted unhappy community, ill at ease with the new régime. Many looked to the French Roman Catholic Bishop Devals as their leader or to the Eurasian Welfare Association, created by Shinozaki and headed by Dr. Paglar.

Japanese policy towards the Jewish community vacillated. All Jews were registered in mid-March, and several wealthy Jews were arrested and released after payment of large sums of money. Eventually all Jewish residents were interned.

Orders were given to treat the Indian population with consideration as allies of the new regime, but most Indian Muslims would have no truck with the Indian National Army and wished to set up an Indian Muslim Association to protect their minority group. The Japanese refused to allow this but at the end of 1943 approved the setting up of an Indian Welfare Association under Dr. Nathan, to provide a link between the municipality and the Indian community. Many Sikhs and 'free Indians' were employed as policemen, patrolmen in the docks, and as guards in the prison camps. Indians who refused to co-operate suffered more from their countrymen in the Indian Independence League and the Indian National Army than from the Japanese.

The municipality worked to restore normal conditions in everyday life. A few days after the capitulation prices were officially pegged, and all refugees were ordered to return up-country to relieve the strain on Singapore's resources. Dr. Kozo Ando, formerly in private practice in Singapore, became chief medical officer for the municipality. Instructions were issued to keep houses clean, to get rid of mosquitoes, to attend for immunization against smallpox and cholera.

Shinozaki became chief education officer with the municipality and tried to reopen schools as quickly as possible. This was difficult because all European and some local teachers were interned, others had been killed, and most school buildings were occupied by the army. Despite this, some English, Malay and Indian schools reopened in April. The Japanese were more reluctant to reopen Chinese schools, but in June 1942 twenty-five Chinese schools also resumed teaching.

The initial preoccupation of the schools was to organize a display to celebrate the Emperor's birthday at the end of April. Thousands of school children marched to the padang carrying flags and singing the Japanese national anthem. Yamashita reviewed the parade and afterwards attended a gathering of about 400 community leaders at the Adelphi Hotel. This was Yamashita's first direct contact with Singaporeans, who regarded him with awe and dread, but the Singapore leaders were relieved when Yamashita told them not to fear the new regime.

Yamashita made a second public appearance two months later to receive the Chinese 'gift'. Sixty leading Chinese attended the ceremony, which was held in the former Singapore chamber of commerce in Fullerton Building. Despite the nerve-racking ordeal they had suffered, the Chinese were impressed with Yamashita, who spoke to them for over an hour about Japanese objectives and ambitions, and concluded that since the Japanese claimed descent from gods and the Europeans from monkeys, in any war between gods and monkeys the gods must win.

This was Yamashita's last official appearance in Singapore. When Terauchi decided to transfer the southern Army's headquarters from Saigon to Syonan, Yamashita's 25th army was moved, and he himself was posted to Manchuria in July 1942. He hoped to visit Tokyo en route to present a report on the Malayan campaign to the Emperor, but the adulation of the Japanese people earned for the 'Tiger of Malaya' Tojo's jealousy and enmity. He was refused permission to visit Tokyo and was ordered to proceed direct to Manchuria, where he remained far from any scene of operations until October 1944, when he was called to resist the American invasion of the Philippines. After a desperate and hopeless campaign Yamashita formally surrendered to the Americans in September 1945, ironically in the presence of Percival, who had recently been released. For both men the fall of Singapore was the beginning of tragedy, but Yamashita's end was the more dramatic. He was the first Japanese general to be tried by the Americans for war crimes and was hanged in February 1946 at an execution described at the time by two U.S. Supreme Court judges as 'judicial lynching', for atrocities in the Philippines over which he had virtually no control.

In the early days Japanese who had advocated a policy of moderation towards the Chinese were regarded as soft and even unpatriotic by the military. In June 1942 Wee Twee Kim accused Shinozaki of treachery in helping the 'enemy' and Mayor Odate sent him back to Japan to avoid arrest. After the payment of the Chinese 'gift' and the departure of the 25th Japanese army, the feud between the military and Japanese civilians died down and the fanatical pressure of the military authorities on the Chinese softened. Watanabe continued to demand firm measures but Takase was sent back to Japan and Wee Twee Kim was dismissed.

In August 1942 Shinozaki returned to Singapore to become chief welfare officer for the municipality, and the Overseas Chinese Association was transferred once more to his charge. For the rest of the occupation the Association acted as a go-between for the Chinese community and the Japanese authorities. But it was rent with dissensions, particularly between the Straits-born and the China-born. The Straits Chinese, who had often been lukewarm in supporting China's cause against Japan before the Pacific war, blamed the China-born for bringing down Japanese reprisals on them. The deep involvement of the immigrant Chinese in pre-war anti-Japanese politics made them perhaps even more anxious to co-operate with the Japanese in order to save their lives. Lim Boon Keng could claim to speak for both communities but he was not an effective leader in the mould of Tan Kah Kee, and many suspected that he had helped the Japanese create the Overseas Chinese Association specifically to milk the Chinese community's wealth.

While the Japanese promised not to discriminate against co-operative Chinese, in practice the Chinese of Singapore and Malaya were treated more harshly than their countrymen in any other part of South-East Asia. In Singapore, Chinese were always the first to be squeezed for money or arrested on suspicion of petty crimes. Many of their young women were seized for Japanese brothels and their young men sent away as labourers. Countless thousands suffered torture and death at the hands of the *Kempeitai*.

For the majority of Chinese it was a question of surviving by adapting to the new régime. The Japanese found the Malayan Chinese puzzling, for they were 'masters at pulling the line of least resistance'.[15] They contributed to Japanese war funds, gave presents, organized dinners and loyal processions, but these were merely aimed to buy peace. Underneath there was bitter hostility. The long years of China's suffering at the hands of the Japanese, the brutality of the first week of the occupation and the extraction of the 'gift' confirmed Chinese hatred for their Japanese masters.

The Japanese policy to sweep away the colonial economic super-structure and incorporate occupied territories into the Greater East Asia Co-Prosperity Sphere caused particular hardship in Singapore which as a regional entrepôt was closely geared to international western economy.

The declared Japanese aim was to convert Syonan into a self-sufficient state, but in practice industry, communications, commerce and finance were harnessed to the war machine. Big Japanese firms such as Mitsui and Mitsubishi were given control of important branches of the Malayan economy: shipping, transport, rubber production, tin and iron mines, palm oil, rice distribution. Subordinate trades and industries were handed over to Japanese or Taiwanese civilian traders, and non-Japanese needed special licences. From the middle of 1942 there was an influx of Japanese businessmen and *rikenyas,* or concession hunters, restaurant, hotel and geisha house proprietors.

The Japanese set up *kumiai,* or guild associations, to control the issue of essential materials which were in short supply. The object of establishing these monopolies was to obtain the army's needs most effectively, but in practice the *kumiai* system produced a government-protected black market, controlled at the top by a handful of Japanese businessmen and operated by local entrepreneurs. Japanese restrictions challenged and sharpened the ingenuity of local Chinese businessmen, and as time went on they came to reassume their former profitable and vital role as middlemen in the economy. The economy became 'a com-bination of Japanese officiousness with Chinese shrewdness, cunning and selfishness'.[16] In many associations the Japanese were front men while

Chinese businessmen were the real power behind them.

In the early months of the occupation the price of luxury goods was low as looters unloaded their booty to evade arrest, and wealthy Chinese sold their possessions to pay their share of the Japanese gift money, but the necessities of life were scarce. Already by April 1942 the shops were nearly empty, householders were storing up supplies and speculators buying up stocks. Everything was 'under the counter' and prices soared. Singapore, with its artificial economy, its dependence on entrepôt trade and imported foodstuffs, was particularly badly hit, and the black market flourished. The cost of living was extremely high, with prices of foodstuffs two to three times those in up-country towns. In June 1943 the *Syonan Shimbun* declared that prices had risen to three times their pre-war level. Strict anti-profiteering regulations issued by the *gunseikan-bu* in August 1943 merely sent prices rocketing further since purchasers now had to pay risk money too.

The influx of Japanese military scrip to replace British currency put the country in the grip of chronic inflation. While the Japanese military offensive continued the currency was sound, but once the fortunes of war turned against Japan, the value of paper money began to slide. Commonly known as 'bananas' or 'coconuts' because they bore designs of plants, the first notes were numbered but subsequent issues were not, and the quality was so poor that notes were easy to forge.

Singapore became glutted with paper money whose face value was meaningless. Everyone knew that Japanese currency would be useless after the war and quickly exchanged it for goods. The price of jewellery, property and other durables rocketed, and at the beginning of 1944 the Japanese tried to stop trafficking in property by imposing crippling taxes on such transactions. These were easy to evade and merely sent prices up further. By March 1945 shophouses which fetched $5,000 to $6,000 before the war were selling for $160,000 to $250,000. Town building-sites fetched fifty or sixty times their pre-war prices, and the housing shortage was so acute that people paid up to $5,000 tea money for a cubicle, or $40,000 to $60,000 for vacant possession of a house. Even bus tickets, cinema tickets and newspapers were sold at black market prices, and by June 1945 a bottle of Hennessy brandy cost $4,000 to $5,000.

This situation encouraged greed and speculation. Racketeers grew rich. Bribery and corruption flourished and those who were squeezed in turn squeezed others. Businessmen could pass on their liabilities, 'like a game in which the Ball of Inflation was quickly passed over to another as soon as it came to them'.[17] Enterprising operators could make fortunes in quick deals, provided they swallowed their scruples, fraternized with Japanese officials, paid bribes and protection money, and contributed to the Japanese war effort. Money was easily made and easily spent because it was not worth saving. Despite shortages, the cafés, amusement parks, gambling establishments and cinemas were crowded, mainly by Japanese, black marketeers and collaborators. Two of the three entertainment 'worlds' were reopened, largely for gambling, and Singapore sported an air of brash gaiety.

Some people refused to have anything to do with the régime, rejecting jobs under the Japanese, selling all their possessions, and living frugally, but the vast majority saw no virtue in letting their families starve and they survived by giving and taking favours. Dealing on the black market was a necessity and so it became respectable. Sharp-witted practice became a virtue, and ruined businessmen who amassed new fortunes were held in general esteem.

Singapore's social world and sense of values turned topsy turvy. It brought to the top a *nouveau riche* class of enterprising businessmen, racketeers and gamblers. It offered profitable opportunities as middlemen to the former lower echelons of society, the hawkers and rickshaw pullers. Owners of restaurants, cinemas and amusement parks flourished, while labourers could demand higher wages or part payment of wages in rice or cloth. Clerks, teachers and white-collar workers, who had formerly enjoyed a favoured position in Singapore, now became a depressed class, finding it very difficult to live on a fixed salary. Old people suffered perhaps most of all since the Japanese refused to honour pensions. Rich men in Singapore had taken pleasure in showing their wealth, but now found it prudent to hide behind a cloak of poverty. Former car-owners took to bicycles. Neckties, shoes and socks were discarded in favour of shorts, open-necked shirts and rubber sandals.

In order to combat inflation and to divert funds to their war effort, the Japanese tried to mop up spare money in state lotteries, gambling and savings campaigns. The first lottery was launched in Singapore in August 1943, while gambling was legalized at the end of 1943 for the first time in more than a century. Both measures were popular but did nothing to stem inflation. Savings drives were started in February 1944, and Singapore was in the middle of its fourth such drive when the war finished, while a government lottery was scheduled to be drawn in early September 1945. Singapore led the way in raising considerable sums of money for savings, amounting to $281,546,000 in 1944–5. The money was paid readily, since it was worth so little, but donors viewed these 'savings' as a gift to purchase peace and quiet, rather than a contribution to the Japanese war effort or a nest egg for their own future.

Food was very short in Singapore, which had always imported most of its supplies. The basic foodstuff, rice, became precious, because imports from Burma dried up and the Japanese hoarded stocks in preparation for further military campaigns. The Japanese encouraged Singaporeans to grow their own food, they organized gardening competitions, offered technical advice, granted loans to smallholders and incorporated vegetable gardening into the school curriculum. The response was so poor that in 1944 Japanese policy changed from encouragement to intimidation. Noncooperation in the self-sufficiency campaign was regarded as sabotage. Government employees were forced to work on vegetable plots. People filled their front gardens with tapioca plants, which put out a lot of greenery without much effort, but by 1945 when the end of the war was in sight even this show of home gardening was abandoned.

The Japanese were more successful in promoting substitute industries, which brought out the constructive inventiveness of Singaporeans. Most products were designed as alternatives for unobtainable imports: twine and ropes were made from pineapple fibre, paper from bamboo, pineapple leaves, and lalang, methylated spirit from tapioca, greases and lubricants from palm oil, motor fuel from rubber oil mixed with petrol. Ammunition was manufactured on a small scale, and in November 1942 the first Singapore-built steamship was launched. Many small soap factories sprang up and for a time Singapore exported soap to Thailand. Few of these substitutes were economic or survived the occupation. The exception was the trishaw, a rickshaw pulled by a bicycle, which was adapted by Chinese mechanics to replace taxis and continued to be a popular and cheap mode of transport until it died out in the early 1970s.

The wartime industrialization campaign was superficial and ephemeral, but it showed the ingenuity of Singaporeans and their innate capacity for future industrialization. The Chinese remained the backbone of Singapore's economy, and the strength of their traditional system of mutual co-operation and regional connexions enabled them to survive and often to prosper during the adversity of the occupation.

The preoccupation of Singaporeans with survival and material security contrasted with the Japanese call for spiritual revival and an end of western colonial materialism. Five days after the surrender Yamashita called on Singaporeans to adopt the Nippon spirit (or *Nippon-Seishin*) and work towards 'moral unification'.

One of Japan's declared aims was to instil Asian consciousness and pride. The press, radio and cinema were devoted to this purpose, and cinemas specialized in cultural and educational documentary films at cheap prices. The Emperor cult was stressed. The Emperor's birthday was declared a public holiday and everyone had to stand facing north-east to Tokyo, observing one minute's silence. Singapore clocks were put forward two hours to bring them into line with Tokyo time, and there was even talk of building a Singapore-Tokyo railway.

The Japanese considered, 'The most profound of all means available to propaganda is education. This can be shaped and altered at will to suit the policy to be propagandized.'[18] Schools were first reopened to get children off the streets and provide teachers with employment. In Shinozaki's words, 'I was just killing time.'[19] By the middle of 1942 the Japanese were in a position to develop a more coherent education policy.[20] They concentrated on vocational and primary education, aiming to provide eight years' schooling as in Japan. They rejected the former British emphasis on academic subjects and laid stress on character building, physical training and vocational instruction, rather than scholastic accomplishment.

The Japanese wished to create a unified education system but in practice had to take over the different language schools inherited from the colonial régime, although all colonial, English, Chinese or religious names were discarded. The Japanese took over the direct running of English, Malay and Chinese schools and set up a few Indian 'national' schools, most of which were staffed by unqualified teachers and were used mainly to disseminate propaganda about the Indian independence movement. Teaching in Malay was permitted in Malay schools since it was the indigenous language, but the Japanese wanted to encourage the study of Nippon-go in other schools, particularly in Chinese-medium institutions. Watanabe wanted to ban the use of English in schools from the beginning, but Odate persuaded him this was impractical, and Japanese was introduced gradually as the medium of instruction.

All teachers were paid on the same scale, whereas in colonial times teachers in English schools enjoyed higher salaries. All primary school fees and book charges were abolished in 1943. The declared aim of education was the 'creation of a feeling of loyalty and the awakening of a national consciousness'. All primary schools adopted a Japanese-style curriculum, beginning each morning by facing towards Japan and singing the Japanese anthem and patriotic Japanese songs. Teachers were brought in from Japan and local teachers were required to learn Japanese. Free Japanese-language evening classes were organized, and Japanese instruction was given over the wireless. Teachers or government servants who learned Japanese received bonuses and those who showed exceptional promise were promoted and sent to Tokyo for further language training. Many teachers and students showed considerable interest in learning the language, and by 1944 most classes in English and Chinese schools were held in Japanese, but the language was too different from the usual Singapore tongues to make it an effective medium of instruction. Much of the school day was taken up with physical drill, gardening and singing. Parents showed reluctance to send their children to school and classes were very small. There were never more than 7,000 children at school and by 1945 the number dwindled to a few hundred.[21]

The accent was on technical and vocational instruction. By March 1943 there were six technical schools in Singapore. The Medical College reopened in Tan Tock Seng Hospital in 1943, readmitting former students, but it moved to Malacca a few months later. Two teacher training schools were opened in 1943. Even in technical institutions the curriculum consisted of indoctrination and rudimentary crash courses designed to meet wartime needs rather than to impart much specialized technological knowledge. In a six-month course at the Naval Construction and Engineering Centre half the time was devoted to learning Japanese. Similarly in the teachers' training colleges and the Leading Officials Training Institute a great deal of time was taken up in studying the Japanese language, 'Nippon spirit', military arts and agriculture.

The Japanese wished to root out the westernized intelligentsia. While they promised religious toleration, in practice religious organizations, particularly the Christian ones, were under constant surveillance. Spies attended services, hymns were scrutinized and sermons were prohibited.

Confident of the superior virtues of their own society, and wishing to develop a small élite under their own control, the Japanese sent carefully selected students to Japan to absorb Japanese ways, but of the four to five hundred students brought from occupied territories to Japan for training during the war, only twelve came from Malaya or Singapore.[22]

Japanese propaganda attacked Anglo-Americanism. 'Asia for the Asiatics! Follow the leadership of Nippon and cast away every trace of Anglo-American influence!'[23] They removed the statue of Raffles, which had been unveiled on the padang in 1887 to celebrate Queen Victoria's golden jubilee and transferred to Empress Place on Centenary Day in February 1919. English signboards were replaced by Japanese. People were encouraged to see Japanese films, but British and American movies remained popular until their showing was prohibited in November 1943. The object was to supersede English. 'We regret that we are forced to use the language of the enemy.... It is a disgrace to use the language of people who exploited and suppressed us,' declared the *Syonan Times* in September 1942. In January 1943 the Japanese threatened to prohibit the use of English in postal correspondence and telephone conversations. In theory Japanese and Malay were the only official languages, but in practice it was impossible to abandon English even in official documents. In other occupied countries the Japanese encouraged the local tongue alongside Japanese to replace European languages, but Singapore had no local *lingua franca,* and Japanese was a difficult alien language.

Singaporeans enjoyed some of the indoctrination, particularly Japanese films and music, but in general were bored with constant repetitive propaganda and a concentrated fare of Japanese victories. All things western were held up as soft and decadent in contrast to Japanese discipline, hardiness and sense of sacrifice. The spectacle of half-starved, half-naked British and Australian prisoners performing manual labour was designed to contribute to this impression. In practice the campaign misfired because the Japanese were equally offensive to the dignity of local Singaporeans.

There were some honourable and respected military and civil Japanese officers, but the shortage of senior officials meant that most of those in authority in Singapore were inexperienced men of inferior calibre. While the new Japanese masters preached a doctrine of Asian equality and of anti-materialistic, anti-western sacrifice for Singaporeans, they themselves showed a predilection for big British and American cars, lording it in former colonial mansions, enjoying tennis, golf and horse racing. The two main department stores, Robinsons and Littles, were exclusively for Japanese customers, and only Japanese could travel in certain lifts in office buildings. Syonan was a soft posting for Japanese, far from the rigours of the battle front. Opportunities to make big fortunes attracted the more unscrupulous Japanese businessmen and adventurers. *Rikenya* became a new word for profiteer in Singaporeans' language, and the most corrupt type of Japanese came to Syonan. Administration was inefficient, rules were evaded, and local businessmen took pride and pleasure in outwitting the Japanese. The result was contempt for the Japanese and for the culture they extolled.

Contempt was mixed with dread, the everyday fear of beatings and face slappings, the constant haunting terror of arrest, prison, torture and death. Civil and criminal courts reopened in May 1942 to try cases by the existing laws if these did not conflict with the military régime, but the old rights of habeas corpus were abolished. Cases were heard in public but were frequently settled by bribery behind the scenes. The judicial system was subordinate to the military, and in April 1942 the Japanese set up a military court in the Supreme Court building to try political offences.

The chief instrument employed to root out anti-Japanese elements was the *Kempeitai,* which had powers of life and death and employed secret agents and informers to denounce those suspected of disloyalty. Citizens found it prudent to get rid of all evidence of connexion with the colonial régime and destroyed their English books, their sons' boy-scout uniforms and western gramophone records. The English-educated, Christians and affluent professional men were particularly vulnerable, often subject to blackmail at the hands of unscrupulous informers.

Many regular pre-war policemen had given up their jobs and new recruits were often cruel and corrupt men. The Special Branch of the police had virtually unlimited powers and were often as arbitrary and oppressive as the *Kempeitai* in their treatment of their own countrymen. Many Chinese sought out a Japanese friend or protector in case of trouble.

The Japanese reverted to a system of collective security reminiscent of the old *kapitan* days. In July 1942 all families were registered and householders were given a 'peace living certificate'. They were responsible for the behaviour of their families, and some householders were appointed as *sidangs* with responsibility for the activities of bigger groups. One-star *sidangs* were accountable for a ward consisting of thirty households and were responsible to district or two-star *sidangs*. Each group of ten wards was placed under an auxiliary police assistant, and in May 1944 these were formed into an association, which arranged for every man between the ages of sixteen and forty-five to enlist for night patrols.

It was not only the brutality but the haphazard and humourless un-certainty of Japanese administration which left the ordinary people of Singapore in a perpetual state of tension and fear. Often people did not know why they were arrested or with what offence they were charged. Different branches of the *Kempeitai* appeared to vie with each other in hunting out suspects, and release from one *Kempeitai* centre did not guarantee freedom from arrest by another. Owning a radio, criticizing the Japanese, even grumbling about high prices were political offences. One word from an informer could mean arrest and some people were denounced to the *Kempeitai* out of sheer personal spite. No-one dared speak up on behalf of the accused. Those arrested were imprisoned without trial in terrible conditions, starved and often tortured, unless their families managed to purchase their release with bribes. The whole period of the occupation was a time of rumour, fear and secrecy, suspicion and informing, when it was unsafe to voice any opinions at all.

The Japanese threw away their opportunities. Their initial aims could have attracted Singaporeans. As one who lived through these years said, 'If Japan had less of *Seishin* and more of common sense, then her history and the history of East Asia would have been different.'[24] Instead of Asian brotherhood, the Japanese brought cruelty and tyranny. In the words of one who suffered under the regime, 'Undoubtedly her achievements were enviable, but Japan forgot to be humane.'[25]

The co-prosperity sphere meant in practice 'co-poverty fear', economic hardship, drabness and exploitation. The gross materialism and corruption of everyday life, which alone ensured survival, undermined the call for sacrifice, spiritual and moral upliftment. The monotonous dullness of Japanese propaganda made a mockery of the idealistic mission to free colonial peoples. While professing to work for Asian unity, the Japanese divided the population more deeply than the British had done, by the varied treatment meted out to the different communities.

The deficiencies of Japanese rule stemmed in part from their need to subordinate everything to the war machine, but it was not merely wartime economic dislocation and military necessity which vitiated the Japanese regime but also racial arrogance. Innate feelings of superiority were increased by the speed of Japan's success in the Malayan campaign, and Japan was confident that South-East Asian countries would admiringly follow her lead.

The Japanese stress of sacrifice, their willingness to die, their devotion to the Emperor, putting the state before the family and individual, inspired some grudging respect in Singapore but did not invite emulation. Japanese racial arrogance and excessive bragging of invincibility stood in stark contrast to the poor behaviour of many officials and military men and the inefficiency and unfairness of their administration.

While the war was going well for the Japanese, conditions in Singapore were not too bad, but by 1943 the tide was turning against them and from that time life became increasingly difficult. Food and supplies dwindled, the currency depreciated rapidly, and the Japanese became more nervous, harsh and erratic in their administration.

Shigeo Odate was promoted to become governor-general of Tokyo city in June 1943 and replaced by a lesser man, Kanichi Naito, who served as mayor of Syonan until the end of the war. The mild Asahi was succeeded in 1943 by a tougher American-educated Japanese, Tominaga, who made life in the Changi camps much harsher.

For military and civilian prisoners alike these were years of overcrowding, disease, hunger and malnutrition, all the more galling when the War Office subsequently proposed to deduct £500 from surviving officers' pay for 'board and lodging' during the occupation.[26] Food and medicines were scarce and internees suffered from dysentery, sores, ulcers, skin diseases, beriberi, and diphtheria. Working parties toiled long hours at heavy manual work, and it was part of Japanese policy to humiliate Europeans by employing them as labourers in public view. Men were subject to beatings and slappings for trivial offences, living always in fear of snap *Kempeitai* inspections for possession of wireless sets or for suspected espionage. Those who were taken away by the *Kempeitai* to the town jails were often imprisoned for months on end, sometimes in solitary confinement, sometimes herded together with a crowd of others, starved, beaten and brutally tortured.

The worst such incident occurred in October 1943, when the Japanese suspected that civilian internees were involved in the sabotage of ships in the harbour. In fact this daring exploit, known as Operation Jaywick, was carried out by six British and Australian soldiers and sailors, who entered Singapore harbour by night in canoes, attached limpet mines to ships in the roads and succeeded in sinking or putting out of action seven ships, including a big oil-tanker. The mission returned safely to Australia, leaving the Japanese convinced that this was the work of British guerrillas from the mainland, acting on information supplied by civilians in town and the inmates of Changi gaol. The internees were not connected with this incident at all.

On 10 October 1943, the notorious 'double tenth', the *Kempeitai* raided the gaol, carried out a thorough search and arrested suspects. This was followed by more searches and arrests, and altogether fifty-seven internees were taken by the *Kempeitai,* including the Bishop of Singapore, H. Fraser, the former Colonial Secretary, Robert Scott, the former Information Officer, and two women, Dr. Cicely Williams, head of the women's camp, and Freddie Bloom, editor of the women's camp newspaper. Many civilians were arrested at the same time, and for the next five months the suspects were kept in *Kempeitai* centres where they were crowded together, with no bedding, lights burning all night, no room to lie down, very little food, and subject to constant interrogation in a vain attempt to establish a link with the sabotage. One suspect was executed, fifteen internees, including Fraser, died under torture, Robert Scott was sentenced to imprisonment in the notorious Outram gaol, and the rest were returned to Changi. It was not until a second Anglo-Australian raiding party, Operation Rimau, was captured off Singapore in December 1944 that the Japanese learned the truth about the earlier raid.[27]

After the 'double tenth' life in Changi gaol became more rigorous, but conditions were still not as bad as in most other prison camps in the region. Those who remained in Changi were more fortunate than their counterparts imprisoned in the Dutch Indies and Malaya, or the thousands who were sent to work in factories in Japan or to build a rail link between Thailand and Burma. They were much better off too than the thousands of Indian prisoners of war sent to work in New Guinea and other parts of the Dutch Indies.

In March 1943 the first batch of 600 military prisoners was dispatched up-country from Selarang. They were told they were moving to rest camps in the mountains but in fact were taken to build the Burma-Siam railway. Throughout 1943 more groups were sent to Thailand, Borneb and Japan and eventually all fit men had left Selarang. At the end of the year the remnants of the working parties began to return from Thailand, with accounts of the dreadful conditions in which more than a third of their number had perished.

Late in 1943 the Japanese decided to build an airfield at Changi using prisoner-of-war labour to clear the ground, fill in swamps and construct runways. In May 1944 civilian internees were moved from Changi prison to a former Royal Air Force camp at Sime Road, and all military prisoners were transferred to the gaol. Others were brought back from Siam and eventually nearly 12,000 prisoners were crowded into the gaol, which had been built to accommodate 600 men. Rations were cut in 1944 and again early in 1945, and inflation was so rampant that the prisoners' meagre wages would buy nothing on the black market. Sick men were expected to work alongside the fit in a feverish attempt to complete the aerodrome. Despite frequent beatings, the exhaustion of heavy work on starvation rations, and a constant tug of war between working hard enough to avoid beatings for malingering and going slow to impede the Japanese war effort, there was some sense of purpose in creating the airfield, which was completed in May 1945 and was strengthened and extended after the war to become a Royal Air Force station.

The Japanese demanded civilian labourers as well as military prisoners for the Burma-Siam railway. It was simple to impress labour since workers had to register with the Labour Department and obtain pass-books in order to take up employment. The unemployed were liable to be rounded up to work for the military or be sent away from Syonan as forced labourers.

In December 1943 the Military Administration formed compulsory labour service corps throughout Malaya. Every group of 150 men had to supply twenty workers between the ages of fifteen and forty-five, and the order was later extended to women. From December 1944 men of military age were forbidden to work as waiters, office peons, salesmen, cooks, tailors, hawkers or in similar occupations, in which women had to take their place. Restaurants, cabarets and other non-essential establishments were closed down. Men were drafted into the military labour corps or defence.

Only about 600 of the civilian labourers for Siam were recruited from Singapore. The first batch of 200 labourers dispatched in May 1943 went voluntarily, attracted by the offer of high wages, and two more groups followed in the next few months. But by August information about the dreadful working conditions in Siam trickled through to Singapore. According to Shinozaki, who as labour and welfare officer was responsible for recruitment, he gained exemption for Syonan from further labour demands and satisfied military objections by sending only one further small group of unemployed vagrants.

In August 1943, in face of the worsening food situation and rising discontent, the Japanese military administration began to tighten security and called for a drastic reduction of Syonan's population. Shinozaki, fearing this might be achieved by another and bigger massacre, set out to promote a voluntary migration to open up agricultural settlements up-country.

The first venture was organized in conjunction with the Overseas Chinese Association. The Japanese promised that the new settlement would be self-governing and that the Syonan municipality would supply food until it was in production. A group of leading Chinese toured Johor and chose a site at Endau. They collected $1 million for the project, sent out men to clear the jungle and recruited voluntary settlers. By September 1944 there were 12,000 settlers in what Lim Boon Keng called 'our Chinese Utopia'. Despite attacks by guerrillas the settlement fared quite well, production was satisfactory, the health record good, but most Singaporeans were city dwellers with no taste for farming or pioneering, and the Endau settlement was abandoned when the war finished.

A similar settlement organized by Singapore Eurasian and Chinese Roman Catholics at Bahau in Negri Sembilan was a disaster from start to finish. The site was unhealthy, the soil poor, and the settlers were mainly middle-class white-collar workers, unsuited to pioneering conditions. Many died at Bahau, including their leader, Bishop Devals, and the others returned to Syonan.

Despite increasing physical hardships, Singaporeans found some compensation in the weakening Japanese position, since it induced Tokyo to allot South-East Asians a larger say in running their own affairs, in order to give them a vested interest in supporting the Japanese regime. Initially the Japanese had intended Malaya to form an integral part of the Japanese empire, as a federation of protected states with a governor-general in Singapore. At first Sumatra was attached to Singapore and Malaya for administrative purposes, and the Japanese stressed the natural ethnic bond between these territories, which the Dutch and British had broken. The administrative link was loose and in 1944 Sumatra was made a separate military area. Japan had no intention of creating an autonomous state of Syonan, but from May 1943, when the Japanese were shifting to the defensive, there was a change of attitude. They made no promises of independence but stopped referring to Malaya as Japanese territory and spoke instead of co-operation in building a 'New Malai'.[28]

Watanabe was succeeded in March 1943 by the more conciliatory Major-General Masuzo Fujimura and Japanese rule gradually began to soften. Advisory Councils were established in the various Malayan states and towns. The Syonan Advisory Council, founded in December

1943, consisted of a Japanese chairman with six Chinese representatives, four Malays, three Indians, one Eurasian and one Arab. The council had no power to initiate policy or discussion, it met only when the mayor thought fit to summon it and in practice it did not advise but merely received instructions, mainly about supporting the war effort. In March 1944 an information and publicity committee was formed under the mayor's chairmanship to report public opinion and explain government policy by means of lectures, pamphlets and broadcasts.[29]

In order to draw more positive Chinese support, in 1944 Colonel Hiroshi Hamada, secretary-general of the Malayan Military Administration, established an *epposho* or reading club for Chinese in Syonan, but it was a failure. The following year, in July 1945, the Japanese set up a *hodosho,* or Help and Guide the People Office, to receive complaints and suggestions from all Syonan communities, but this was also ineffective. The Japanese, on the retreat and seeking means to gain the co-operation of local inhabitants in what was expected to be a long-drawn-out struggle against the allies, talked of giving autonomy to Malaya, but only vague references were made about independence for Syonan.

Tojo called Syonan the 'key point for the construction of Dai Toa'.[30] It was the centre where regional affairs were discussed and political decisions on neighbouring countries were made. Syonan was the place where Tojo met the Burmese leader Ba Maw in July 1943, it was the first headquarters of the Free India government and the centre where preparatory conferences were held in 1945 to debate plans for Indonesian independence. But it had no political prospects or aspirations of its own, nor were there any local administrators or leaders of stature in Singapore or Malaya to demand the power and influence which nationalist leaders acquired in other countries in the later stages of the occupation.

Syonan's one nationalist movement of importance was in support of Indian independence, a political issue which the Japanese began to exploit before they launched their Malayan campaign. From his base in Bangkok Major Iwaichi Fujiwara contacted Pritam Singh, an Indian Independence League organizer, and sent agents to stir up disaffection among the Indian troops in north Malaya. Fujiwara and Pritam Singh accompanied the invading Japanese armies and won the support of Captain Mohan Singh, a regular officer of the British Indian army, who formed a detachment of Indian National Army troops to fight alongside the Japanese. Japanese troops were ordered to deal softly with Indians, not to antagonize them or take reprisals. During the Malayan campaign they tried to induce Indian soldiers to change sides, often sending Indian prisoners back to their units with invitations to surrender. About two hundred Indians took part in the Japanese decoy operation at Pulau Ubin prior to the invasion of Singapore, and they joined in the battle on the island.[31]

At the assembly of Indian troops at Farrer Park which followed the surrender, Fujiwara, Mohan Singh and Pritam Singh addressed the gathering. Mohan Singh became leader of the first Indian National Army, and Pritam Singh organized branches of the Indian Independence League throughout Malaya, with a headquarters in Syonan, and a Singapore lawyer, S.C. Goho, as first president. Fujiwara, Mohan Singh, Goho, Pritam Singh and other Indian Independence League and Indian National Army delegates set off for a meeting in Tokyo in March 1942, but Pritam Singh's plane crashed and he was killed.

In May 1942 Rash Behari Bose, founder and head of the Indian Independence League, arrived in Singapore. Born in 1886, Rash Behari Bose had fled from India to Japan in 1915 after plotting an abortive mutiny. He founded the Indian Independence League in Tokyo in 1921, married a Japanese and became a Japanese citizen in 1923.[32] From Syonan, Rash Behari Bose broadcast to Indians all over the region to join the movement, and in June 1942 the Japanese organized an Indian Independence League conference in Bangkok which voted to end British control in India by force.

The appeal roused considerable response, particularly from Sikhs and Hindus, but the first Indian National Army was a failure. The Japanese were reluctant to create an effective military force, preferring to divide it into small units attached to the Japanese army. Mohan Singh, who was a well-meaning patriot and at first viewed the Japanese as liberators of his country, soon came to realize that they merely intended the force to be an instrument of propaganda.

The Indian community was divided in itself. Many Indian Muslims feared the movement would mean the subjection of their community to the Hindu majority. Even supporters and members of the Indian National Army began to criticize the soft living of Mohan Singh and other leaders, who resided in luxury at Mount Pleasant and moved about Singapore freely, frequently consorting with Japanese in hotels and restaurants. Their easy life was in stark contrast to the spartan existence of their followers, and rumours circulated that Mohan Singh was using the movement to advance his personal ambitions, was diverting public funds to his own use and even that he had engineered Pritam Singh's death.[33]

In December 1942 the Japanese put Mohan Singh under house arrest and the first Indian National Army was disbanded. It was reorganized first under Lieutenant-Colonel Bhonsale, and subsequently under Lieutenant-Colonel Gilani, who had been Mohan Singh's second in command. But the army flagged. Attempts by Rash Behari Bose to keep the Indian independence movement alive met with little enthusiasm, because after all his years in exile he seemed more Japanese than Indian and was regarded as a puppet.

The situation changed dramatically with the arrival in Singapore in July 1943 of a new dynamic leader, Subhas Chandra Bose, who had resigned as president of Congress in India at the beginning of the war in Europe, when the other Congress party leaders refused to make a bid to seize independence through force. When Chandra Bose formed a militant Forward Bloc, the British put him under house arrest in Calcutta, but he escaped to Germany, whence he was smuggled by submarine to Singapore.

Rash Behari Bose, who was old and suffering from tuberculosis, willingly handed over leadership to Subhas Chandra Bose. The vibrant Netaji, or Leader, as he came to be known, stirred the Indian community and brought new life and force into the independence movement. At a mammoth meeting at the Cathay Building in July 1943, the great crowd listened spellbound and roared their approval. Shortly afterwards the Indian National Army paraded on the padang before Premier Tojo, the community leaders of Syonan, and a big audience of about 20,000 spectators. Chandra Bose described Singapore as 'the graveyard of the British empire',[34] and he set out to marshall the efforts of all Indians in the Far East to oust the British from India. He toured the Japanese-occupied countries, raising recruits and money, and at another meeting at Farrer Park in October 1943 he proclaimed the formation of the Azah Hind, or provisional government of Free India, and formally declared war on Britain and the United States.

Not only former members, but also many civilians and prisoners of war who would have nothing to do with Mohan Singh's first army, now rushed to join the new Indian National Army and the Indian Independence League. Indians came from all over the East to enlist in Singapore. Tamil and Malayalam labourers joined in their thousands, girls and boys were organized in a 'Children's army', and about six hundred women joined a parallel women's movement, the Ranee of Jhansi regiment, led by Dr. S. Lakshmi. Affluent families contributed gold and jewellery and rich Indian businessmen donated large sums of money. Muslims were less enthusiastic but most of them contributed, partly out of fear of reprisals and partly because membership of the Indian Independence League conferred some degree of immunity from *Kempeitai* oppression. Unemployed Indians were swept into the army, sometimes press-ganged by the *Kempeitai*.

By the end of 1943 the Indian National Army had two divisions. The first units, ill-equipped, ill-trained but high in spirit, were sent to fight in Burma, and in January 1944 Bose moved his provisional government headquarters to Rangoon. In the months that followed excitement reached fever-pitch in Singapore, the other communities resenting Indian collaboration with the Japanese, but half-envious of their evident enthusiasm and sense of purpose. Throughout February, March and April 1944 news of successes in Burma filled the Singapore newspapers. When Indian National Army units reached the border and raised their flag on Indian soil, new recruits and former fence-sitters rushed to enlist and Indian businessmen contributed willingly to the cause. Indians in Singapore waited to celebrate the expected fall of Imphal, but the success stories and newspaper reports dried up. For weeks there was silence about Burma and eventually stragglers came back to Singapore with news that the Japanese were being pushed back, and that the Indian National Army was breaking up with large-scale desertions.

Subhas Chandra Bose did not lose heart. He returned to Singapore in May 1945, set up his headquarters at Katong and tried to revive support for the cause. But his movement never regained strength. Young men did not wish to risk their lives or businessmen their capital in a doomed venture. When Bose was killed in an air crash in Taiwan in August 1945, the Indian Independence League held a formal service for him in Singapore, but there was no public demonstration and little show of mourning.

Despite a strict prohibition on press reports of Japanese reverses, news of defeats eventually began to filter through the thick Japanese propaganda screen. In November 1944 the American air force carried out its first raid on Singapore harbour, and from that time allied planes were frequently seen, but the allies restricted bombing, not wanting to damage installations which would be useful to them later. They preferred to neutralize Singapore by mining her waters and disrupting rail and sea communications.[35]

The Japanese retreat was welcomed with anticipation tinged with uncertainty and foreboding. Singaporeans feared that the liberation would be grimmer and bloodier than the initial defeat. The Japanese conscripted the local population and concentrated working parties of prisoners of war to construct defences, which they intended to hold to the death. Prisoners feared they would be slaughtered in a last-ditch stand, and rumours went round among the local population that all English-educated Singaporeans and those suspected of sympathy with Britain were on black lists, to be murdered if the British attacked. Singaporeans were convinced that the Japanese intended to fight to the last man and to eliminate any civilians who refused to co-operate.

Everyday living became almost unbearable. Even prisoners brought back from slaving to build the Siam-Burma railway were shocked at the listless hunger and despair of the population. There were long queues for rice. Essential services, such as water, gas, and electricity, were breaking down as machinery wore out and could not be replaced, and hospitals were bare of equipment and drugs. Even the fully employed had to supplement their income to pay soaring black market prices for food and medicines. Many people were dying of malnutrition, and most pathetic of all were Javanese workers, of whom the Japanese brought in about 10,000 as forced labourers, turning them loose on the streets like pariah dogs to die when they were no longer fit for work.

Prisoners of war and civilian internees were at their lowest ebb and many died in the last dreadful months of the occupation, when rations dwindled to starvation point. Early in 1945 the Japanese marshalled nearly 6,000 prisoners into work parties to construct defence works in Singapore and Johor, and from May 1945 intensive military exercises were held on the padang for civilians, including women workers. It was obvious that the Japanese, unlike the British, intended to enrol

Singaporeans as active participants, not merely spectators, in the battle for the recovery of Singapore.

News of the end of the European war in May 1945 and the recapture of Rangoon trickled through to Singapore and was celebrated secretly. By July 1945 allied planes were seen overhead nearly every day and the liberation of Singapore itself was only a question of time.

Japanese rule finished suddenly and quietly in Singapore and she was spared the horrors of a battle for reoccupation. Initial reports about the explosion of atom bombs, the destruction of Japanese cities and the parley for peace were kept secret among senior Japanese military officers, and the abrupt end of the war came as an unexpected shock even to most Japanese officials in Syonan.

Prisoners at Changi gaol heard on their secret wireless sets about Japan's formal surrender on 15 August, but the Japanese made no public announcement until two days later. The prisoners in camp were then informed of the surrender and Shinozaki made a public statement, not mentioning unconditional surrender but merely declaring that the Emperor had decided to end the war. Fearing the reaction of the Japanese soldiers, he warned Singaporeans not to hoist Union Jacks or celebrate openly. The announcement led immediately to a scramble to get rid of Japanese currency, and for a few days prices rocketed, cafés trebled their prices, rickshaw drivers doubled their fares.

On 21 August the Singapore press formally announced the Japanese surrender for the first time. Pro-Japanese organizations disbanded themselves, many policemen and officials quietly slipped away, some rich collaborators fled to Hong Kong, and Taiwanese, who looked and sounded like local Chinese, faded into the general population. For a few days there was sudden deflation as Japanese organizations unloaded their hoarded commodities at give-away prices, and Japanese employers stepped up rations of rice and cloth in a last minute bid for popularity. Japanese signs were pulled down, Rising Sun flags were destroyed, while enterprising tailors started making Allied flags.

The Japanese prepared an internment camp at Jurong, to which most of them retreated with their belongings, leaving only a few officers to hand over to the incoming British administration. Three weeks of anxious waiting followed, since General Douglas MacArthur, Supreme Commander for Allied Powers, ordered that other allied military forces should not land or reoccupy territory until the Japanese had formally surrendered to himself.

Work parties were brought back to Changi and within a few days there were 12,000 prisoners in the gaol. British aircraft dropped leaflets to tell them to remain there, and at the end of the month doctors and stores were dropped by parachute into the camp. The Governor had been taken away, the Colonial Secretary was dead, and, unlike their counterparts in Hong Kong, former officials in Changi, who were numbed and dazed rather than exhilarated, made no attempt to resume control but waited for the return of British troops.

Since guerrilla resistance had been confined to the jungles of Malaya, Singapore was spared the widespread bloodbaths, kangaroo trials, racial bitterness and retribution which the Malay states endured at the hands of resistance fighters in the interregnum between Japan's collapse and the British return. But guerrilla bands held some 'people's trials' in the Geylang district and executed some collaborators, including Wee Twee Kim. Trams and lorries carrying communist flags and filled with Chinese youths sought out collaborators. Some Sikh watchmen and Malay policemen were killed, but most hid away. The former Indian National Army troops lived in terror in their camp at Bidadari and many of them fled. Most Singaporeans waited impatiently for the British to return, afraid to celebrate openly for fear the Japanese soldiers might take retribution. The administration had broken down, the currency was worthless, there was widespread looting.

At last, on 5 September, British warships arrived and Commonwealth troops landed to receive a tumultuous welcome. The three-mile route from the Empire Dock to the Cathay Building was lined with cheering crowds, waving British, American, Russian and Kuomintang flags. A week later, on 12 September, amid the jeers of the assembled crowd, five Japanese generals and two admirals led the delegation which climbed the steps of the municipal building in Singapore to surrender formally to Admiral Lord Louis Mountbatten, Supreme Allied Commander in South-East Asia.

The same Union Jack which was used in 1942 at the time of the British surrender and hidden since then in Changi gaol, was raised over the city. It was a symbol of the old régime. The myth of Japanese invincibility was shattered, British forces were cheered in the streets of Singapore, the old officials were welcomed back.

But it was a different Singapore and a changed South-East Asia to which the Commonwealth troops returned in 1945. As Tsuji put it, the statue of Raffles, which the British restored to Empress Place, had somehow faded in colour, 'The halo of victory must shine on the Union Jack, but today there remains little vestige of its glory of former times.' The régime was welcomed back with genuine relief because it was benign, its weaknesses were sins of omission, its memory was not marred by cruelty or dragooning the population. But the only ultimate justification for a colonial power was its ability to protect and in this the British colonial régime had been tried and found wanting. The old unquestioning trust in British protection had been shattered.

For the moment the return of the British meant the end of a nightmare. Another ten years were to pass before the emergence of leaders of a new generation, who had experienced the shock of the surrender and occupation and the exhilaration of the post-war winds of change, and who were to challenge the British right to rule.

1. K.G. Tregonning, *The Singapore Cold Storage, 1903–1966* (Singapore, 1966).
2. M. Shinozaki, *My Wartime Experiences in Singapore* (Singapore, 1973), p. 14.
3. M.C. ff Sheppard, *The Malay Regiment, 1933–1947* (Kuala Lumpur, 1947).
4. A.J. Sweeting, 'Prisoners of the Japanese' in L. Wigmore, *Australia in the War: the Japanese Thrust* (Canberra, 1957), p. 511.
5. F.A. Reel, *The Case of General Yamashita* (Chicago, 1949), p. 53.
6. Chin Kee Onn, *Malaya Upside Down* (Singapore, 1946), p. 8.
7. M. Tsuji, *Singapore: the Japanese Version* (Sydney, 1960), p. 175.
8. *Good Citizen's Guide* (Singapore, 1943), p. 4.
9. *Syonan Times,* 25 February 1942.
10. Ibid., 25 April 1942.
11. C. McCormac, *You'll Die in Singapore* (London, 1954), autobiographical, Told at second hand in P. Brickhill, *Escape—or Die* (London, 1952).
12. Shinozaki, *Wartime Experiences,* p. 35.
13. Takase, *Principles and Policies Governing Towards the Chinese,* 19 April 1942, English translation in H. Benda, *et al. Japanese Military Administration in Indonesia: Selected Documents* (New Haven, 1965).
14. *Good Citizen's Guide,* 3 March 1942, pp. 17–18.
15. Chin Kee Onn, p. 197.
16. Ibid., p. 89.
17. Ibid., p. 46.
18. Article by T. Fujimori of Propaganda Department Military Administration Singapore in *Syonan Times,* 5 September 1942.
19. Shinozaki, *Wartime Experiences,* p. 52.
20. H.E. Wilson, *Educational Policy and Performance in Singapore, 1942–1945* (Singapore, 1973) gives a brief discussion of wartime education.
21. T.R. Doraisamy (ed.), *150 Years of Education in Singapore* (Singapore, 1969), p. 45.
22. W.H. Elsbree, *Japan's Role in Southeast Asian Nationalist Movements, 1940–1945* (Harvard, 1953), p. 105.
23. Chin Kee Onn, p. 156.
24. Ibid., p. 172.
25. Tan Thoon Lip, *Kempeitai Kindness* (Singapore, 1946), p. 81.
26. D. Russell-Roberts, *Spotlight on Singapore* (London, 1965), p. 229.
27. R. McKie, *The Heroes* (Sydney, 1960); B. Connell, *Return of the Tiger* (London, 1960).
28. F.C. Jones, *Japan's New Order in East Asia: its Rise and Fall, 1937–45* (London, 1954), p. 384.
29. Lee Ah Chai (Ting Hui), 'Singapore under the Japanese, 1942–45', unpublished B.A. academic exercise, University of Malaya (Singapore), 1956, pp. 9–12.
30. Quoted in F.C. Jones, p. 383.
31. J.C. Lebra, *Jungle Alliance* (Singapore, 1971), p. 36; Joginder Singh Jessy, 'The Indian Army of Independence, 1942–1945', unpublished B.A. academic exercise, University of Malaya (Singapore), 1958, pp. 10–11.
32. A.C. Bose, *Indian Revolutionaries Abroad* (Patna, 1971).
33. M.K. Durrani, *The Sixth Column* (London, 1955), p. 74.
34. Quoted in Lebra, p. 118.
35. Supreme Allied Commander's Meetings, 4, 5, 27 February, and 22 April 1945, WO 203/469.

# VII

# The Aftermath of War
# 1945–1955

In the months immediately following the collapse of British power in Malaya, the Colonial Office began drawing up schemes for radical post-war reorganization. The immediate object was to forestall any demands from Washington and Chungking for the permanent dismantling of British colonial rule in South-East Asia, but London officials, and notably Edward Gent, the Assistant Permanent Under-Secretary in the Colonial Office, saw the dramatic break in colonial rule as an opportunity to force through schemes for a remodelled political structure which would ensure administrative efficiency and military security and eventually weld the population together in a sense of Malayan nationhood.

A first proposal grouped the Malay states, Straits Settlements, North Borneo, Sarawak and Brunei into a union, with Singapore as 'the natural centre of trade and communications'.[1] This regional concept was subsequently abandoned as premature, and in 1943 Gent drew up alternative plans to create a Malayan Union, comprising the former four Federated and five Unfederated Malay states, Penang and Malacca, leaving Singapore, with the Cocos Keeling and Christmas Islands as a separate entity. A Governor-General in Singapore would co-ordinate policy in British territories throughout the region.[2]

London did not want to jeopardize the delicate negotiations for Malayan Union by trying to include Singapore. The British were not concerned at that stage with questions of racial balance but considered Singapore should be kept separate as a free port, an imperial defence base, and also because of the Malay states' long-standing fear of Singapore's domination.[3] Whitehall also anticipated that reoccupied Singapore would remain under military rule for a considerable time as the logistics centre for Allied operations in South-East Asia in a long-drawn-out struggle against Japan. The rest of Malaya would probably revert fairly quickly to civil rule.[4]

The only London official opposed to the separation was Sidney Caine, then economic adviser to the Colonial Office and subsequently Vice-Chancellor of the University of Malaya. In a sharp exchange with Gent late in 1943 Caine advised waiting to see what local people wanted before foisting a ready-made plan on them. He urged that Singapore and peninsular Malaya were economically inter-dependent and separating

Singapore would be like cutting London out of Britain. Provided some facilities were retained to protect Singapore's entrepot trade, Caine argued that a union would offer economic and administrative advantages and encourage the growth of a Malayan national consciousness. 'We have everything to gain by blurring and not by sharpening the distinctions between one race and another in the peninsula.' Gent brushed aside this unwelcome advice, insisting that Malayan Union would be easier to achieve without Singapore.[5]

The war cabinet approved the Colonial Office scheme in principle in May 1944, after which detailed planning for post-war civil administration was left to a Malayan planning unit, comprising a handful of former Malayan Civil Service men who were gathered together in London. The British government made its plans in the dark, knowing almost nothing about what was happening in occupied Malaya. Official policy evolved in secrecy and was scarcely influenced by public opinion, although a number of people with pre-war experience in Malaya submitted proposals. They all agreed on the need for radical changes but the majority favoured a federation rather than a unitary state and advocated the inclusion of Singapore.

A large number of refugees from Malaya settled in India during the occupation, including Tan Cheng Lock, his son, Tan Siew Sin, and two pre-war Singapore municipal councillors: John Laycock, a prominent British lawyer, and Tan Chin Tuan, co-managing director of the Oversea Chinese Banking Corporation. More than two-thirds of the Malayan refugees in India joined a Malayan Association of India, which was formed in December 1942. But it was dominated by Europeans, and after some months of bitter wrangling many Malayan Chinese broke away to form their own Overseas Chinese Association in September 1942, with Tan Cheng Lock as president, Tan Chin Tuan as vice-president and Tan Siew Sin as secretary. In November 1943 Tan Cheng Lock sent a long memorandum to the Colonial Office, appealing for a union or federation of the Straits Settlements with the Malay states, and for equal rights and representation for all who made Malaya their home. He emphasized the long connexion of the Straits Chinese with Malaya and pointed to the service of China-born volunteers in the final defence of Singapore as evidence of their potential loyalty as citizens. The Colonial Office approved of the moderate tone of the memorandum but were not swayed by his arguments. They thanked Tan Cheng Lock, referred vaguely to closer liaison in the future, then filed the booklet away and forgot it.[6]

A further memorandum was submitted from India by John Laycock and Tan Chin Tuan, together with Tunku Abu Bakar of the Johor royal house and Oliver Holt, a British Singapore businessman. They objected to any shift of the political centre from Singapore to Kuala Lumpur as 'opposed both to geography and good sense', but the Colonial Office waved this opinion aside with the comment that it 'offered nothing to help to guide our thought in formulating future policy'.[7]

After much controversy, the Association of British Malaya in London produced a proposal for a Malayan federation to include the Straits Settlements, but this too ran counter to the Colonial Office's proposals and was ignored.

London intended to use the supposedly long period of re-occupation and military administration to test 'the temper of the people' and reactions to the proposed new constitutional arrangements. They expected to have plenty of time since they anticipated the Japanese would put up tough resistance in Malaya and would cling to Singapore as long as possible.[8] In June 1945, after the war in Europe had come to an end, the Allies planned to retake Singapore as a first priority in the East, and to use the island to support the needs of ten army divisions, of which only two would be actually maintained in Malaya.[9] The Allies hoped to capture Singapore early in 1946 but doubted whether they would be able to divert all their troops from Europe to be fully operational in the Far East until the summer of 1946, after which they expected many months of hard-fought battle before the war was finally brought to a close.

The order of battle in Operation Tide-race, the plan to re-capture Singapore, was being finalized in Rangoon in mid-August 1945,[10] when Japan suddenly capitulated. This threw all political schemes out of gear and meant that the new constitutional system had to be introduced in Malaya without the extended period of consultation which had been anticipated.

Almost immediately the situation was further complicated when on 25 August 1945, before the British had completed preparations to land re-occupation forces, the Malayan Communist Party's central executive published a manifesto, stressing as its major point, 'To establish a democratic government in Malaya with an electorate drawn from all races of each state and the anti-Japanese army'. To some extent this co-operative 'soft line' policy came as a relief to the British government, who feared the Chinese, communist-dominated guerrilla army as the most influential and dangerous force in Malayan politics. Viewed from another angle, the communist declaration embarrassed London on the grounds that the communists 'have rather stolen our thunder and that we have lost that element of surprise for our progressive policy which would politically have been so valuable'.[11] On paper the communist declaration came so close to the Colonial Office's own plan that London feared their long-deliberated schemes might appear to have been dictated and forced upon them by the Malayan Communist Party.

The British government decided to act immediately and dispatched an emissary, Sir Harold MacMichael, to renegotiate treaties with the sultans, in order to clear the way for Malayan Union. At the same time the secretary of state for the colonies announced the new policy to parliament in October 1945 and set out detailed proposals in a White Paper issued in January 1946. He stressed that Singapore had ties with the mainland but union should not be forced. 'Union must *grow*, if

grow it will, and a premature decision to force into one entity communities with such widely different interests might cause friction and might
cast a shadow over the whole future of the area.'

Former Malayan officials in England protested at the separation. Sir
Shenton Thomas, who had drawn up a detailed proposal for reorganizing
Malaya while he was in internment, considered the scheme for a Malayan
Union and a Colony of Singapore with separate Governors and an
overall Governor-General as 'overloaded and extravagant in conception'.
'The Governor of Singapore will not have enough to do.' But Thomas's
protests carried no weight with the Colonial Office,[12] nor was it swayed
by Sir Cecil Clementi, who argued at a meeting with retired Governors
and senior officials at the Colonial Office in February 1946 that to exclude
Singapore was to 'cut the heart out of Malaya'.[13]

The separation of Singapore would not have seemed so important
had the original scheme been based on a federation to be worked out
leisurely, as most people with experience of Malaya advocated. But the
Colonial Office had set its heart on a Malayan Union and was not prepared
to brook any change in its plans.

The sudden ending of the war brought special difficulties for Singapore
because no detailed plans had been made for her post-war administration.
Once the separation of the island had been agreed by the war cabinet,
the Colonial Office concentrated on the complicated peninsular problems
and virtually ignored Singapore. It anticipated that after a long period
of military administration the island would eventually become 'a sort of
District of Columbia', the headquarters of the British Governor-General
for South-East Asia, with its own local government.[14] The Colonial
Office memorandum on 'Constitutional Reconstruction in the Far East'
drawn up in July 1943 was vague as to whether Singapore should be a
colony proper or treated merely as an enlarged municipality.[15]

The form of Singapore's constitution was still undecided when the
British returned to Malaya in September 1945. As an interim measure
the island became the headquarters of the British Military Administration
under Lord Louis Mountbatten, Supreme Allied Commander, who had
overall political and administrative control in South-East Asia. Singapore
and Malaya remained under British Military Administration until April
1946, but Mountbatten delegated civil government to Sir Ralph Hone,
Chief Civil Affairs Officer for Malaya, with Patrick McKerron as Deputy
Chief Civil Affairs Officer in charge of Singapore.

While serving with the Malayan planning unit during the war McKerron
had drawn up tentative plans for Singapore in which he advocated
changing the island's internal administrative structure as little as possible
in view of her sudden amputation from the rest of Malaya, but once
they arrived in Singapore, both McKerron and Hone changed their
minds and recommended merging central and local authorities into one
Island Council.[16] Such last-minute suggestions irritated the Colonial
Office, who wanted to get Singapore problems out of the way in order

to concentrate on Malayan Union. London decided to play safe or, in their own words, to keep 'well tried and successful organs of government', to retain the hierarchy of executive, legislative and municipal councils and rural board which had served the former Straits Settlements but to expand opportunities for representation.

In November 1945 Hone presided over the first meeting of a Singapore advisory council, comprising seventeen nominated members, including Tan Chin Tuan, Lee Kong Chian and Wu Tian Wang, chairman of the communist Singapore City Committee and former guerrilla leader. The Council's first meeting was amicable and constructive, but it became increasingly critical of the slow pace of reconstruction, the trade restrictions, shortages and hardships.[17]

Singaporeans had welcomed the British forces back as liberators from fear, hunger and poverty, but hopes of a quick recovery soon faded and honeymoon bliss turned sour. As the official British history of the period admits, 'While propagandists contrasted Allied "liberation" with enemy "occupation", the distinction between the two processes was not always so clear to those who were being "liberated"'.[18]

Peace did not mean the end of hunger and want. Food was short, shipping was disorganized and traditional rice-producing countries had no surplus to export. Prices of essential commodities soon soared to ten times the pre-war level, and regulations to control the price of rice, fish and vegetables broke down because they could not be enforced. The *Singapore Annual Report for 1946* spoke of 'the false hopes, the disappointments, the occasional reliefs, and above all, the nightmare expectations of what might happen next month, after scraping the cupboard bare of all supplies'.[19]

The railway and docks had been damaged by Allied bombing. Six major wrecks choked the harbour, 70 per cent of godown accommodation had been destroyed and not a single crane was in working order. More than half the Harbour Board's machinery was destroyed or missing, and all the pre-war tugs and dredgers had vanished.

The town was dirty, neglected and dilapidated, the roads full of potholes, while water, electricity, gas and telephone services had run down. There was chronic overcrowding, poverty and disease. The enormous sums demanded for accommodation during the occupation had forced thousands to become squatters, putting up insanitary shacks without any amenities. The death rate in 1945 was twice the pre-war level, and hospitals were bare of equipment or medicines, often lacking furniture or bedding.

One of the most urgent problems was to restore law and order. During the occupation infringing the law had become a 'patriotic virtue'. The incoming administration found the police force 'nothing more than an ill-clad, badly equipped and poorly disciplined rabble', 'undernourished, dirty, driven to corruption through necessity, and untrained'.[20] The police were so hated and despised as tools of Japanese oppression and cruelty that in the first weeks after the liberation police stations had to be barred and guarded for fear of reprisals.

Permeating the whole of society was the occupation's worst legacy, the corruption of public and private integrity: flourishing gambling dens and brothels, both legalized by the Japanese, the resurgence of opium smoking, universal profiteering and bribery. Less spectacular but perhaps most insidious of all was the selfish cynicism and contempt for the old virtues of honesty, hard work and thrift in favour of quick profits and easy spending. Profiteers and former collaborators prospered, whereas many loyal government employees were subject to humiliating investigations before being reinstated in their former posts. The restored British administration often leaned on men who had been useful to the colonial régime in the past and equally adaptable to the Japanese: the professional survivors, who had grown rich and influential during the occupation.

Senior British Military Administration officials were honest men of high calibre, but minor officials were often not so scrupulous, and the opportunities for black market enterprise which had attracted the worst sort of Japanese during the occupation now brought in the most corrupt of Europeans. 'We Chinese never realized that there were Europeans like them', a senior Malayan Civil Service official was told.[21] The British Military Administration requisitioned private property arbitrarily and grossly mismanaged the distribution of rice. Its financial inefficiency and scandalous corruption were criticized openly in the advisory council and the 'BMA' was commonly referred to as the Black Market Administration.[22] In seven months it destroyed the goodwill which existed at the time of the liberation and brought British prestige in Singapore to a lower point even than in February 1942.[23]

Despite disappointments, inefficiencies and corruption, the British Military Administration made some positive achievements, and at least the fear and brutality of the occupation had gone. Top priority was given to restoring public utilities, water, electricity and gas supplies. The Royal Navy transferred the port to civilian control in eight weeks, courts reopened, collaborators and undesirables were weeded out of the police force and a new police recruiting campaign was launched.

The administration came to grips quickly with the problems of education, and within three weeks reopened fourteen Malay and fourteen English schools. Despite lack of equipment and neglected buildings, teachers set to with enthusiasm and vigour on the task of rehabilitation, trying not only to satisfy the great hunger for education but also distributing food and other supplies and coping with many problems of social distress. The Chinese also rushed to reopen their schools, and by the end of 1945, 66 Chinese, 37 English, and 21 Malay schools were in operation. In addition to the normal intake, a generation of over-age children who had received no schooling during the occupation had to be absorbed, and by March 1946 62,000 children were in school. It took a little longer to revive higher education, but the Medical College took back former students in June 1946, and, together with Raffles College, admitted the first new intake in October that year.

The main necessity, on which all else depended, was to revive the Malayan economy. To this end the military administration selected seven leading industrial, transport and mining companies, six based in Singapore and the seventh in Selangor, giving them priority in importing supplies and getting staff released from military service.[24] But the intention was to restore free private enterprise as quickly as possible and not to interfere with Singapore's free port status.

By the end of the military regime the port was almost back to pre-war capacity and the supply of water and electricity exceeded pre-war consumption. The police force was functioning fairly efficiently. Except in the case of rice, price controls and rationing were beginning to work as shortages became less desperate.

A war crimes commission was established to investigate atrocities. *Kempei, Kempeitai* informers, prison guards, and some local community leaders, such as Paglar and Goho, were arrested, and in October 1945 a special court was established to try such cases.

Japanese accused of committing atrocities were put in Changi gaol to await trial, but the rest of the Japanese community, almost 7,000 strong, was left in its Jurong camp. Japanese military prisoners were brought in later from the surrounding countries and about 12,000 were employed as labourers for the next two years.

Indian National Army men and Indian Independence League supporters were screened, most were exonerated, but many former regular soldiers were discharged from the British army and the officers sent to stand trial in Delhi. Indian troops pulled down the monument which the Indian National Army had put up on the Esplanade, and the Japanese shrine and war memorial were also blown up.

Public demand for punishment of collaborators was loud but most accusations took the form of complaints against informers and blackmailers. The court often found it difficult to weigh evidence and distinguish spite from genuine grievances, so that many culprits escaped, bringing the courts and the administration into disrepute. In their concern to heal wounds, the British administration in practice came to condone collaboration where no physical brutality was proved. Lai Teck, the most important of all the collaborators, gave himself up to the British, with whom he co-operated in secret for the next two years, while remaining secretary-general of the Malayan Communist Party.

The most celebrated collaboration case was the trial of Dr. Paglar, former president of the Eurasian Welfare Association, which opened in Singapore in January 1946. The British regarded collaboration by Eurasians as special treachery and the case roused considerable passions. Shinozaki, who had been released and employed by the British field security service as a translator and interpreter, spoke in defence of Paglar, who was eventually freed but not acquitted.

The first war crimes case, which opened in Singapore in January 1946, dealt with allegations of cruel treatment of Indian prisoners of war consigned as forced labour to the East Indies. This was followed by the 'Double Tenth Trial', in which twenty-one members of the Singapore *Kempeitai*, including its then chief, Lieutenant Colonel Sumida Haruzo, were accused of the torture and murder of internees and civilians in the reign of terror which began at Changi gaol on 10 October 1943. The gruesome horrors were related in the testimony of men such as the Bishop of Singapore and the accused were convicted.

The outcome of the Chinese massacres trial was very different. The trial, which was the last of its kind, opened in the Victoria Memorial Hall in March 1947, and the accused included General Kawamura and Colonel Oishi. Rich Chinese, such as Tay Koh Yat, whose eldest son had been murdered in the massacre, worked hard to collect testimony which proved the enormity of the crime. But evidence of individual responsibility was inconclusive. Of the chief people allegedly responsible, Yamashita had been executed, Tsuji had disappeared, and others had been killed during the war. Few victims survived to act as witnesses and the perpetrators of the crimes were small fry, who could not be identified or who had perished in the war. Kawamura and Oishi were condemned to death and five others to life imprisonment, but the Chinese community was incensed at the leniency of the verdict. A Singapore Chinese Massacre Appeal Committee petitioned the Governor to review the sentences, but in vain. The British considered there was insufficient evidence to warrant heavier sentences, but to the Chinese it seemed that the British were only interested in securing justice for crimes committed against a handful of their own people and cared little for the much greater brutality inflicted on countless thousands of Chinese.

At the time of the liberation the communists were the great heroes of the day in Singapore. By the end of the war the communist-dominated Malayan People's Anti-Japanese Army numbered about 4,500 including many non-communist patriotic Chinese. The Malayan Communist Party had gained prestige both among the masses and many middle-class Chinese by being identified as anti-Japanese patriots, but the leaders realized the party was not strong enough to resist the return of the British or to set up a united Malayan republic. Adopting a soft-line technique, the party agreed temporarily to disband its military arm and to work towards its goal by political subversion.

The Malayan People's Anti-Japanese Army was formally disbanded in January 1946 at a moving final parade on the padang in Singapore, when Mountbatten presented medals to the resistance leaders, including the guerrilla commander, Chin Peng. Arms and ammunition were surrendered, but the Malayan Communist Party secretly retained stocks of weapons and formed an ex-servicemen's association to keep the army together.

Singapore's post-war political climate was ideal for cultivating communist influence. Mountbatten, a man of liberal views, was eager to encourage the free expression of political opinions, and as a reward for wartime co-operation the British felt obliged for the first time to recognize the legality of the Malayan Communist Party. Wu Tian Wang's appointment to the advisory council enabled him to make political capital by taking a public stand against the corruption of the administration.

The small communist Singapore City Committee operated through several front organizations, and in the immediate post-war months the Malayan Communist Party could command about 70,000 supporters in Singapore. Its most important organization was the General Labour Union, through which it sought to consolidate a mass following among Singapore's workers. Here the communists had a virgin field to plough. The Japanese had stamped out labour unrest, there were no existing trade unions, while the liberal labour legislation passed just before the war permitted people who were not connected with the trade to share in the management of unions and placed few restrictions on the use of union funds.

Immediately after the surrender, the General Labour Union set up its headquarters in Singapore with branches in other Malayan towns and promised to campaign for better working conditions, shorter hours, and the creation of an All-Malayan Working Class United Front. The glamour and prestige which the Malayan Communist Party had acquired during the war, combined with genuine grievances of workers arising from the immediate post-war dislocation, unemployment, inflation and shortages, enabled the General Labour Union to build up its membership quickly.

Labour unrest began in October 1945 with a successful strike by 7,000 dockers to obtain higher wages. It was soon followed by strikes among Singapore Traction Company employees and other groups of workers, including hospital staff, firemen and even cabaret girls.

Mountbatten, not wanting to use force against organized labour or to revive the pre-war weapon of banishment, pleaded for disputes to be settled by amicable negotiation without intimidation. But the increasingly aggressive tactics of the General Labour Union led to a tougher official line and the use of Japanese prisoners of war to replace strikers, which in turn generated further labour trouble.

The source of discontent was genuine enough. There was widespread unemployment, food was scarce and the cost of living was rising steeply. In December 1945 a reduction of the rice ration to three katis a week provoked a mass demonstration of 6,000 workers who assembled on the padang to demand bigger rations and higher wages, after which the authorities banned meetings and processions except under licence.

By the end of 1945 the Singapore General Labour Union covered more than sixty trade unions and when the British Military Administration jailed Soon Khwong, its secretary-general, on charges of intimidation and extortion, the union staged a two-day general strike in January 1946. 173,000 workers stopped work and transport came to a halt. The authorities then released Soon Khwong, a step which convinced the communists that the British Military Administration was weak and would take no action against them.

In February 1946 all the unions incorporated in the General Labour Unions of Singapore and Malaya formed a Pan-Malayan Federation of Trade Unions, with two constituent parts, one on the mainland and the other registered as the Singapore Federation of Trade Unions. Both were dominated by the Malayan Communist Party and affiliated to the World Federation of Trade Unions.

The Pan-Malayan Federation of Trade Unions, which claimed a membership of 450,000 was formally inaugurated on 15 February 1946, the anniversary of the British defeat in Singapore, when the Malayan Communist Party applied to hold a procession to lament this 'day of mourning'. The British Military Administration refused a permit and on the eve of the planned procession arrested twenty-seven leading communists, ten of whom were subsequently banished without trial.

After this setback the communists gave up direct action in favour of quietly extending their hold over the trade union movement and supporting other radical groups in seeking constitutional change.

The period of military administration came to an end in April 1946, when the Malayan Union was enforced on the mainland and Singapore reverted to civil administration as a crown colony, under the governorship of Sir Franklin Gimson.

The British Labour government agreed with some reluctance to accept the wartime cabinet's decision to dissolve the Straits Settlements.[25] And Singapore in fact preserved many links with the Malayan Union: currency, higher education, immigration, income tax, civil aviation, posts and telegraphs were to be administered on a pan-Malayan basis. As the British government declared, 'It is no part of the policy of His Majesty's government to preclude or prejudice in any way the fusion of Singapore and the Malayan Union in a wider union at a later date should it be considered that such a course was desirable.'[26]

Britain's post-war constitutional proposals had taken Malaya by surprise. The war had weakened colonial authority without creating a positive nationalist movement to replace it, and the country lacked political organizations to respond to the proposed change. Most Singaporeans showed little interest but vocal minorities objected to the separation of Singapore from various viewpoints. The Malayan Communist Party saw it as a threat to its projected united Malayan republic, the Kesatuan Melayu Singapura did not want to raise barriers between peninsular and Singapore Malays, and the Chinese chamber of commerce objected to cutting off Singapore as 'the centre of Malayan economy, politics and culture'.[27]

The Malayan Union proposal provoked the formation of Singapore's first indigenous political party, the Malayan Democratic Union, which was created in December 1945 and supported a Malayan Union provided Singapore were included. It was a multi-racial party, formed by two radical Cambridge-educated lawyers, Lim Kean Chye and John Eber, and communists Wu Tian Wang, Gerald de Cruz and Lim Hong Bee, under the chairmanship of a respected British-Guiana-born lawyer, Philip Hoalim, who had practised law in Singapore since 1932.[28]

Most of the party's leaders were English-educated, middle-class, university-trained professional men, who were not themselves communists but believed that all opponents of imperialism should unite to agitate for independence. The party's manifesto, issued in December 1945, was a moderate document, proposing to work towards self government by extending representation in the legislative council and liberalizing citizenship requirements, with the eventual aim of making Singapore part of a self-governing Malaya within the British Commonwealth.

The Malayan Democratic Union also called for social and educational reform. The party advocated official multi-lingualism, the creation of integrated schools where different language streams would study under one roof, and the opening of a local university. It demanded social reforms, a more extensive housing programme, encouragement of democratic trade unions, and it was the first local organization to welcome the introduction of income tax in order to finance a more radical social policy.

Meanwhile in peninsular Malaya the Malayan Union scheme alarmed politically active Malays into forming the United Malays National Organization (UMNO) in Kuala Lumpur in March 1946 on the eve of the inauguration of the new form of government. UMNO claimed that the transfer of sovereignty over the Malay states was invalid since the sultans had been forced to sign away their rights, and that the proposed citizenship laws offering equal political status to immigrant communities were unfair to the Malays. This spirited opposition and the widespread and vociferous support which UMNO aroused among the Malays came as a shock to the British who, after consultation with UMNO leaders and the Malay sultans, drew up revised proposals based on a federation of the peninsular states, stricter citizenship requirements, more safeguards for Malays and their rulers, and postponed elective representation to an unspecified date.[29] The only feature of Malayan Union which survived was the separation of Singapore. The Malay leaders insisted on this, since if Singapore were incorporated in the Malayan federation the Chinese would outnumber the Malays.

The upsurge of Malay nationalism sparked off a counter movement in Singapore and the peninsula among those who objected to the proposed more restrictive constitution as a retrograde step. The communists, denouncing the new constitutional proposals as 'the cloven hoof of British imperialism', called a mass rally of 20,000 people at Farrer Park in September 1946 to demand self-government for Malaya and equality for all who made it their home. In October 1946 the Malayan Democratic Union asked the government to call a committee representing all parties and communities to discuss new constitutional proposals, but the British wanted no truck with the communists or the Malayan Democratic Union.

The disparate opposition groups decided to form a united front to campaign against the new federation scheme. In December 1946 they created a Pan-Malayan Council of Joint Action, which was re-named the All-Malaya Council of Joint Action in August 1947, with the veteran Straits Chinese leader, Tan Cheng Lock, as chairman. The body comprised the Malayan Democratic Union, the Straits Chinese British Association, the Pan-Malayan Federation of Trade Unions, and various communal, commercial, women's, and youth organizations. While the Malayan Communist Party was not officially a member, it was the dominant force behind the scenes and represented by a number of front organizations, notably the Malayan People's Anti-Japanese Ex-Service Comrades' Association.

The All-Malaya Council of Joint Action allied with the Pusat Tengga Ra'ayat (People's United Front or PUTERA) formed by the left-wing Malay Nationalist Party, which opposed the conservative, aristocratic-dominated UMNO and saw Malaya's future as a union with Indonesia. For a time the alliance also enjoyed the support of the Chinese chambers of commerce in Singapore and Malaya.

The British refused to recognize the Pan-Malayan Council of Joint Action as representative of domiciled non-Malay opinion, and in May 1947 published a draft Federation Agreement, which had been approved by UMNO and the Malay sultans. John Eber, as secretary-general of the now re-named All-Malaya Council of Joint Action, then drew up a counter scheme in the form of *The People's Constitutional Proposals for Malaya*.[30] This demanded the inclusion of Singapore in a federated Malaya, with an executive council responsible to a legislative assembly elected by all adults domiciled in Malaya, but with certain safeguards to ensure the predominance of Malays in the assembly during a transitional fifteen-year phase.

The All-Malaya Council of Joint Action organized mass rallies and in October 1947 obtained the support of Chinese chambers of commerce throughout Singapore and Malaya for a nation-wide *hartal*, or economic boycott. This marked the high-water mark of opposition unity and was supported with enthusiasm by the immigrant communities. But it aroused passionate Malay hostility and kindled little response among the English educated. The British bowed to the Malay leaders' view that communal differences were too deep to create an immediate self-governing state with racial equality, and accepted the UMNO proposal for the gradual assimilation of immigrants into a Malay state which would work towards independence under British guidance. On this basis the Malayan Union gave way to a Federation of Malaya in February 1948 and Singapore remained a separate crown colony.

The polyglot All-Malaya Council of Joint Action-PUTERA alliance disintegrated rapidly. The Chinese chambers of commerce opposed the separation of Singapore and restrictive citizenship clauses but had no liking for the radical *People's Constitutional Proposals,* nor did they relish any communist connexion. They refused to respond to Tan Cheng Lock's call for a second *hartal* in January 1948 and turned their back on the movement. In March 1948 the Malayan Communist Party withdrew its support, so that the All-Malaya Council of Joint Action, deprived of financial backing and mass support, fell apart.

Singapore was left to follow her separate course of political development, although events in the Federation were soon to have a powerful impact upon the colony.

For the present most Singaporeans were preoccupied with the hardships of everyday living. Food shortages persisted and in May 1947 the weekly rice ration fell to 1½ katis a head equivalent to the lowest level of the occupation. Singaporeans had to revert to eating tapioca and there were queues for bread, tinned milk and other foodstuffs. Malnutrition and tuberculosis were rife, and wages did not keep pace with rising prices. Some employers issued workers with free or cheap rice supplies and the government set up people's restaurants in 1947 to provide meals at controlled prices, but these measures went only a small way in alleviating the general misery.

Secret societies flourished and violence reached such a pitch that the pre-war Societies Ordinance, which was held in abeyance in the immediate post-war period, was reinstated in April 1947.

The Malayan Communist Party set out to exploit the widespread misery for its own political ends in a bid to capture the labour movement. In 1946 and 1947 the General Labour Union organized strikes in the Harbour Board, public transport, fire and postal services, hospitals and many private firms, both European and Chinese. Some stoppages involved thousands of workers, dragging on for weeks at a time. Most of them succeeded in gaining higher wage awards, which gave the Malayan Communist Party great kudos and attracted more workers to its unions.

Those who were reluctant were forced to join. The Singapore Federation of Trade Unions formed a Workers' Protection Corps, consisting largely of secret society gangsters and former Malayan People's Anti-Japanese Army members, who broke up or intimidated existing non-communist unions. By the beginning of 1947 the Singapore Federation of Trade Unions claimed control of three-quarters of the entire organized labour force and aimed to dominate the port, the municipality, public works and transport.

The combination of determined leadership, successful strikes and intimidation gave the communists a stranglehold over labour which was difficult to break, but by the latter months of 1947 the Singapore Federation of Trade Unions began to weaken in the face of changing circumstances and government action. From March 1947 the colonial authorities began to register unions under the 1940 Trade Union Ordinance, which gave the government closer supervision over finance and membership and forbade the use of funds for political purposes.

In an effort to build up a legitimate democratic trade union movement the British government had sent John Brazier, a former organizer for the National Union of Railwaymen, to Singapore in December 1945 as Industrial Relations Adviser to the British Military Administration and subsequently Pan-Malayan Trade Union Adviser. 'Battling Jack' Brazier was an energetic and determined man, disliking both communism and imperialism, and anxious to create non-political unions. His position was extremely difficult. Employers resented him, the colonial government gave him only lukewarm support, and he found workers reluctant to become involved, caught between fear of communist intimidation on the one hand and repression by security forces on the other.

Despite this, by 1947 a number of independent unions emerged, and at the same time workers' conditions began to improve at last as a world-wide demand for rubber and tin hastened Singapore's recovery. Despite quotas, currency restrictions and strikes, by 1947 the volume of her trade was considerably heavier than before the war, and in 1948 rubber production exceeded the wartime 1940 peak. Trade expansion, the more effective enforcement of rationing and price controls, and abundant harvests in 1948 brought an end to the worst shortages and hardships. By 1949 trade and productivity had been restored, social services were at least equal to pre-war levels, while infant mortality and general death rates were the lowest on record.[31]

The combination of firm government action and the steadily improving economic position undermined the effectiveness of communist agitation, which up to that point had played with considerable success on genuine grievances among workers. By the end of 1947 many Singapore workers were disillusioned by the Malayan Communist Party's use of trade unions to promote political ends instead of fighting for better conditions. A mission sent out from Britain early in 1948 to investigate the state of trade unions revealed how the communists used strikes for purely political purposes. They 'call strikes but pay no strike pay...frame demands but carry out no negotiations...while pushing forward union leaders whom they interfere with and often intimidate'.[32] The communist leaders alienated many workers when they embarked on a programme of defiance which had little to do with wages or conditions of labour. Workers became less willing to take strike action or to contribute to union funds, and strikes staged by the Malayan Communist Party late in 1947 petered out ineffectively.

After the separation of Singapore in 1946, the colonial authorities aimed to work gradually towards internal self-government and to build up a feeling of common loyalty towards the island as a permanent home. Singapore's inhabitants were still cosmopolitan and mixed, comprising approximately 78 per cent Chinese, 12 per cent Malay and Indonesian, 7 per cent Indian, and 3 per cent European, Eurasian and other small minorities.[33] But the character and outlook of the population had changed greatly from pre-war days as a result of the immigration restrictions introduced in the 1930s, followed by the dislocation of war.

The population was less transitory and more balanced, with a large proportion of women, children and old people. Male adults comprised half the population in 1931 but only one-third in 1947.

The Chinese in particular were more settled. At the 1931 census only 36 per cent of Singapore Chinese were Straits-born, but by 1947 the proportion rose to 60 per cent and by the mid-1950s to 70 per cent. According to a 1947 social survey more than half of the China-born immigrants had neither revisited China nor sent remittances to families there, so that the link with the motherland was more tenuous than was generally supposed.[34]

The Indians kept stronger personal ties with their land of origin. It continued to be common practice for Indian men to come to work in Singapore on their own, and the proportion of women was smaller than among any of the other communities. The majority of Indians sent money to families in India and travelled frequently between India and Singapore.

Between 1947 and 1957 Singapore's Indian population increased rapidly. Two-thirds were migrants from the Federation of Malaya, who were attracted by higher salaries and better opportunities of employment in Singapore or who wished to escape the dangers and hardships of the communist emergency. There was also an influx of northern Indians, particularly Sikhs and Sindhis, who emigrated to Singapore in 1947 and 1948 during the unrest which followed independence and partition in India. In addition many Malayalis came from Kerala in the immediate post-war years. Some were employed as building workers, but most were clerks and shopkeepers, often finding employment in or round the mushrooming British military installations.

While most Indians, Pakistanis, and Ceylonese still looked with pride to their homeland and many continued to return there to marry, to educate their children, or to retire, increasing numbers settled down permanently in Singapore. From the late 1950s when immigration restrictions were tightened, the stream of Indian immigrants dwindled to a trickle of professional and wealthy businessmen and their families.[35]

For the first two years, from 1946 to 1948, the Governor of Singapore, ruled with the help of an advisory council consisting entirely of officials and nominated non-officials. Gimson started by appointing six non-officials, later increasing the number to eleven, when for the first time non-officials outnumbered officials and Asians outnumbered Europeans. The advisory council remained a consultative body, but the only occasion on which Gimson exercised his right to force measures through was on the question of income tax. Attempts to impose income tax in 1860, 1910, and 1921 had been strenuously resisted, and the tax had hitherto only been levied in Singapore in time of war. The Malayan Democratic Union was the only group to support the Income Tax Ordinance, which the Governor enacted by decree in November 1947 in the face of opposition from the non-official advisory councillors, the chambers of commerce and the Singapore Association, successor to the Straits Settlements (Singapore) Association.

The 1947 census, which revealed an unexpectedly large proportion of local-born Singaporeans, strengthened arguments for developing political responsibility and self-government. The colonial authorities, in co-operation with the advisory council, planned to transfer power to Singaporeans in stages by developing the existing executive and legislative bodies and widening representation.

As a first step a new constitution, to be implemented after elections scheduled to be held in March 1948, created an executive council with an official majority and a legislative council with nine officials and thirteen non-officials, of whom four would be nominated by the Governor, three chosen by the chambers of commerce and the remaining six elected by adult British subjects who had been resident in Singapore for one year prior to the election.

The Colonial Office had visualized a legislative council in which representatives would be elected on a racial basis, but the Malayan Democratic Union opposed this vigorously and the advisory council insisted unanimously that legislative councillors should represent geographical constituencies, not racial communities. The special commercial representation through the chambers of commerce was retained, but some members of the advisory council criticized the practice as 'repugnant to all ideas of democracy'.[36]

The Governor retained powers over reserved subjects and could veto the legislative council's proceedings. He still remained subject only to the ultimate control of the secretary of state for the colonies in London. But the Singapore constitution was more liberal than the constitutions of the Malayan Union and the subsequent Federation of Malaya, which made no provision for elected legislative councillors.

The constitutional reforms did not satisfy the Malayan Democratic Union, which by that time was dominated by militant radicals and had become a communist-front organization. The party decided to boycott the elections and staged mass rallies at Farrer Park to protest against the new constitution.

This left the new political opportunities to the class of European and English-educated commercial and professional men who had traditionally been associated with the colonial régime. In August 1947 three lawyers, C.C. Tan, John Laycock, and N.A. Mallal, formed the Singapore Progressive Party to fight the forthcoming elections. Laycock and the Pakistan-born Mallal had served as municipal councillors in the 1930s, but C.C. Tan, the Progressive Party's first chairman, Singapore-born and London-trained, first appeared in public life as a non-official member of the advisory council in 1946. Mild, tolerant and rational, Tan typified the Progressive Party, which was essentially a moderate party, advocating no radical political, social or economic change. The Progressives were willing to co-operate with the British to promote steady constitutional reform by gradually extending the numbers of elected councillors and eventually creating a cabinet of ministers responsible to a legislative assembly. They did not set a definite target date for self-government and, unlike the Malayan Communist Party and the Malayan Democratic Union, aimed to achieve self-government in Singapore before merging with the Federation of Malaya as a fully independent country. The party attracted English-educated professional men from the upper social strata of colonial society, many of them members of the Singapore Association or the Straits Chinese British Association. Of the latter the most prominent were Tan Chin Tuan and Thio Chan Bee, a Sumatra-born, Singapore-educated headmaster and member of the advisory council.

The Progressives were the only party to fight the 1948 election and won half of the six elected seats, the remaining three falling to independents. All the successful candidates were lawyers, three of them Indian, one Chinese, one European, and one Malay.

The prominence of the Indian minority in Singapore politics was one of the unique features of the immediate post-war years. Indians enjoyed a favoured position since active participation in politics was confined to British subjects, but they also showed more enthusiasm than other communities in taking advantage of their opportunities. Only 23,000 voters registered out of a potential electorate of more than 200,000. Of these more than 10,000 were Indians and eight of the fifteen candidates were Indian.

The enthusiasm of Indians was partly a measure of their concern about their place as a minority in a future self-governing Singapore, but it also reflected a natural predilection for national and industrial politics and an upsurge of confidence at the success of the nationalist movement in India. The achievement of independence in India in 1947 gave status and a sense of pride to the Indian community and a pre-eminence in Singapore politics which they never achieved before or since. Successful Indian contestants did not, however, stand for communal interests, and the 1948 election revealed a refreshing freedom from racial friction.

In October 1948 Gimson commented with satisfaction, 'Communalism as known in other countries has never carried any weight in Singapore, and I am confident that it never will, as no truly democratic system can ever be founded otherwise.' No major Singapore party has been a communal party, and Malayan communal parties such as UMNO, the Malayan Chinese Association or the Malayan Indian Congress failed to attract a big following in Singapore.

The British also planned to expand the municipal commission's authority and make it more democratic as a training for self-government. The pre-war administration, in which all members of the municipal commission and rural board were officials or the Governor's nominees, was restored in 1946 as an interim measure, but a committee was appointed under John Laycock to recommend a more liberal scheme. The Laycock proposals that two-thirds of the municipal commissioners should be elected by British subjects or British-protected persons possessing certain property and residential qualifications were accepted. At the first municipal election, held in 1949 to choose eighteen out of a twenty-seven member municipal commission, the Progressive Party triumphed, winning thirteen seats. But the public showed as little interest in municipal as in legislative council politics, and less than 10 per cent registered of a potential electorate of 100,000.

By the time the new legislative council assembled in 1948 Singapore seemed poised for steady if unspectacular constitutional and social reform.

The Malayan Communist Party had failed in its bid to influence the constitutional developments in Malaya and Singapore and was rent by internal discord and scandal. In March 1947 the party was left reeling from the shock of Lai Teck's defection, when he disappeared amid rumours that he was a double agent and had absconded with the party's funds.

The new communist leader, Chin Peng, favoured militant action to make up for the party's failure to exploit labour unrest and the constitutional debate, which ended in February 1948 with the establishment of the Federation of Malaya. The following month the party decided on a new policy of mass struggle against British imperialism. The Malayan Communist Party may also have received instructions to adopt a militant stand at a communist international meeting held in Calcutta in February 1948, which two of its members attended. Lawrence Sharkey, the Australian communist leader, spent a fortnight in Singapore on his return from Calcutta to Australia, and may possibly have given the orders at that time for a revolt in Malaya.

The first trial of strength came in February 1948 after the Singapore Harbour Board decasualized labour and began to employ dockers directly instead of working through contractors. This benefited workers but threatened the hold which the Malayan Communist Party exerted over contract labour. The communist-controlled Singapore Harbour Board Labour Union staged a strike, but this collapsed within forty-eight hours and convinced many workers that the communists were not working for their interests. The strike led to the arrest of union leaders and the discovery of documents relating to the illegal communist Singapore Workers' Protection Corps, which the authorities broke up. The Singapore Federation of Trade Unions then attempted unsuccessfully to launch a general strike. It also planned a May Day rally, hoping to marshal 100,000 participants, but the government banned the procession, the leaders·called it off, and May Day 1948 proved to be the first crime-free day Singapore had enjoyed for years.

It was obvious that the Malayan Communist Party had lost its hold over the labour movement and that urban revolution in Singapore had no chance of success. The party defeated its own purposes partly because of its precipitate and blatant bid for power in Singapore in 1945–6 which put the government on its guard and precluded more insidious infiltration, and partly because the years of immediate post-war economic hardship in Malaya coincided with a time when Russia was pre-occupied with her own internal reconstruction. By 1948, when Russia revived her interest in promoting international communism and exploiting political and economic difficulties for western European countries in their colonies, the Malayan Communist Party's golden chance in Singapore had passed.

In May 1948 the majority of leading communists left Singapore for the Federation, the former Malayan People's Anti-Japanese Army was revived, and acts of violence in May and June led to the declaration of a state of emergency in the Federation. The Singapore Federation of Trade Unions disbanded itself on the eve of the outbreak of the rising up-country, and when police raided its offices they found the premises deserted and all its papers gone.

The twelve-year armed struggle was confined to the mainland, but a state of emergency was declared in Singapore a week after the outbreak of the revolt, and emergency regulations put restrictions on meetings, associations and strikes and permitted the detention of individuals without trial. All radical political groups were suspect, since they had been associated with the Malayan Communist Party in the arguments about labour legislation and the constitutional future of Malaya and Singapore. The Malayan Communist Party was proscribed, many Malay Nationalist Party leaders were arrested, and the Malayan Democratic Union, fearing the government would break it up, voluntarily dissolved itself in June 1948.

At its height the Malayan Democratic Union numbered only a few hundred members and was never taken seriously by the British, but many of the constructive ideas of its early days were adopted by later Singapore politicians.

The first side-effect of the Malayan emergency in Singapore was to cripple left-wing political movements and leave the stage to conservative politicians, who were willing to co-operate amicably with the colonial authorities in working for constitutional reform, modest social change and the retention of the colonial economy.

The Progressive Party's only rival was the Singapore Labour Party, formed in September 1948 a few months after the elections by M.A. Majid, president of the Singapore Seamen's Union, with two trade unionists, Indian-born M.P.D. Nair, and Ceylon-born Peter Williams. Nair and Williams were leaders of the Army Civil Services union and the early leadership was dominated by English-educated Indians. They also recruited an English schoolmaster, Francis Thomas, who had worked in Singapore as a teacher for fourteen years, and in 1949 won over Lim Yew Hock, a member of the Progressive Party, who became president of the Singapore Labour Party. A third-generation Straits Chinese, born in Singapore in 1914, Lim Yew Hock was a former clerk, who became full-time general secretary of the Singapore Clerical and Administrative Workers' Union, was subsequently a founder member of the Singapore Trade Union Congress, and had been nominated by the Governor in 1948 to represent the interests of labour in the legislative council.

Modelled on Britain's Labour Party, the Singapore Labour Party

sought to break communist influence in the labour movement by further-
ing the practical interests of workers, bettering their conditions and
redistributing wealth. It aimed to achieve self-government for Singapore
by 1954, followed by full independence through merger with the Federation, to produce a 'socialist society in Malaya' in which the rubber and
tin industries would be nationalized. Like all other Singapore parties,
the Singapore Labour Party was multi-racial in its leadership and membership, but drawn from a lower income group than the Progressives.
Most of its leaders were English-educated, many of them immigrant
Indians. A few had university training, but none was socially prominent,
and most were trade unionists and clerks. Discipline was slack, the
party had little financial backing and was weakened by personal jealousies
and rifts.

The moderate Lim Yew Hock and the Fabian Francis Thomas were
soon at loggerheads with Peter Williams's radical wing. Quarrels over
nomination of candidates to municipal elections in 1951 and squabbles
over personal ambitions split the party into factions. By 1952 Williams
gained control and expelled Lim Yew Hock, but the party disintegrated
in confusion and survived only in name, leaving the Progressives a clear
field in legislative council and municipal politics.

Both the colonial authorities and the Progressives recognized the need
for a new approach to social welfare and education if Singapore was to
be converted into a settled, self-governing society.

Before the war social welfare was left in the hands of voluntary organizations, sometimes helped by government grants, but in June 1946
the government established a social welfare department. Initially it
took over responsibility for dealing with exceptional post-war hardships
through people's restaurants, children's feeding centres and a citizens'
advice bureau, set up to help refugees and displaced persons.

As conditions returned to normal the department's work expanded
to provide more permanent social services. In 1947 it carried out a survey
of living conditions, which revealed an appalling state of misery and
chronic overcrowding. Singapore's population had risen from 560,000
in 1931 to 941,000 in 1947. Most were crowded in the inner city area,
where the majority of households lived in one room or cubicle, and a
quarter of the unskilled worker families had even less.[37]

A housing committee reported in 1948, 'The disease from which
Singapore is suffering is Gigantism. A chaotic and unwieldy megapolis
has been created...by haphazard and unplanned growth.'[38] Barely
one-third of the urban population was housed satisfactorily, and the
population was expanding so fast that the housing built by the Singapore
Improvement Trust could only accommodate the equivalent of one-third
of the annual population increase. The Trust could not begin to eliminate
slums or to clear the thousands of miserable squatter huts.

In view of the shocking revelations in the social survey, in 1948 the
government increased loans to the Singapore Improvement Trust,

launched an interim plan to house 36,000 people and arranged for a detailed survey to frame a master plan for creating satellite towns. The Progressives suggested establishing a Housing Trust, which was the forerunner of the Housing and Development Board.

The post-war colonial government also accepted greater responsibility for providing education and recognized that pre-war education policy was outdated. It had not only to make up for schooling which had been interrupted by the occupation but also to expand facilities to meet the increasing demands and different requirements of a more settled society with growing numbers of children. At the same time a new approach to education was needed as a training for self-government and to inculcate a sense of common citizenship.

The general Commonwealth policy at that time was to concentrate upon primary education in the mother tongue. In Singapore too a growing body of intelligent opinion in the immediate pre-war years felt that facility in the English language was bought at the expense of cutting Singaporeans off from their cultural roots.[39] When the Director of Education followed up this line of thinking and proposed to give official support to expanding vernacular primary education, confining English primary schools to native English speakers, the non-officials in the advisory council objected on the grounds that English was the only language in which all races could share a common ground. C.C. Tan condemned the suggestion that English-medium primary education be confined to the English-speaking as 'a sinister move' and racially divisive, and advocated that *all* children should be taught in English at the primary level.[40]

In deference to these views, the government modified its proposals and in 1947 launched a ten-year programme which aimed to provide six years of primary education in any of the four main languages, in accordance with parents' choice. The government continued to finance Malay schools and to subsidize Tamil and Chinese schools which met its requirements, but the demands for English education were so great that in practice the bulk of funds were devoted to expanding English-medium schooling. This was eagerly sought after by ambitious parents, since it offered the best prospects for secondary and tertiary education and for profitable employment, and by 1957 attendance in English-medium schools was four times the pre-war 1941 figure. The trend pleaseu the colonial government, which regarded the English schools as 'hitherto the nursery for the more Malayan minded of our youth' and was content to plough more and more money into English-medium education to the neglect of Chinese and other vernacular schools.

While the emphasis at that stage was on expanding primary education, the localization of the civil service and the modernization of society created a need for a well-educated élite. In 1949 the King Edward College of Medicine merged with Raffles College to form an independent English-medium University of Malaya,[41] to serve Singapore, the Federation of Malaya and the British Borneo territories. This was followed the next year by the opening of a Singapore teachers' training college.

Modest advances were made in improving social services. In 1949 a Young Persons Ordinance consolidated and extended laws protecting young people, enforcing the pre-war legislation against the *mui tsai* system, setting up a juvenile court, a probation service and approved schools. In the same year a ten-year medical plan was launched to expand health services and hospital facilities, and a five-year social welfare plan was adopted. Social benefits were paid to the old, unfit, blind, crippled and to widows with dependent children, and in 1954 the Progressives put through a central provident fund bill, which was implemented by the next government in 1955.

The expansion of education and other social services was financed partly through the proceeds from the new income tax and partly from revenue arising from the economic boom brought to Singapore by the Korean war. The year 1951 was a record trading year, when the price of rubber rose to almost two dollars a pound and tin to five times its pre-war level.

Constitutional reform proceeded slowly. In 1951 the colonial authorities increased the number of elected seats in the legislative assembly to nine and allowed the non-official legislative councillors to elect two of their number to serve on the executive council. Gimson described this as 'a new political experiment'. For the first time non-officials would equal officials on the executive council, but the Governor retained his casting vote and his reserve powers over currency, banking, trade duties, treaties, defence, and racial or religious privilege.

At the 1951 elections the Progressive Party won six of the nine elected seats and continued to dominate the legislative council for the next four years, with Tan Chin Tuan as deputy president of the council. At first the Progressives were content with the leisurely pace of constitutional advance, but developments in the Federation of Malaya quickened their interest in attaining more effective self-government in Singapore. In 1951 Tunku Abdul Rahman, the new president of UMNO, took up the cry of 'Merdeka!' or 'Freedom!' for the Federation, and a Member system was introduced in Kuala Lumpur, whereby Members would have ministerial responsibility for certain government functions.

In 1953 the Progressives set a ten-year target date for achieving self-government, to be followed by full independence through merger with the Federation, and in the meantime they advocated introducing a predominantly elected legislative council, with a Member system comparable to that in the Federation.

The colonial authorities welcomed these suggestions, and indeed the new Governor, Sir John Nicoll, prodded the Progressive Party into drawing up definite plans for responsible government. The colonial authorities regarded the Progressives as a reliable group, in whose hands the transition to stable self-government could be made in an orderly, peaceful fashion, without upsetting the economy. The British feared that public apathy was the main obstacle to the development of democratic government in Singapore and felt 'the present constitution has fallen considerably short of Chinese aspirations'.[42] They were convinced that enthusiasm could be stimulated only by more radical and challenging opportunities in central and local government.

Accordingly, in 1953 Sir George Rendel was appointed to head a commission to review the constitution of the colony, including the relationship between the central and municipal government. The Rendel Commission included the attorney-general and the president of the city council, together with Chinese, Malay and Indian representatives nominated by the non-official members of the legislative council, and a European non-official nominated by the Governor. It set out to devise a 'complete political and constitutional structure designed to enable Singapore to develop as a self-contained and autonomous unit in any larger organization with which it may ultimately become associated'.[43]

While it was not in its terms of reference to consider closer association with the Federation, the Rendel commission felt the two territories were so linked in geography, economy, politics and defence that 'it makes it difficult to visualize any permanent solution of either problem which does not take account of the other'. The commission wished to ensure that its recommendations would not impede the ultimate closer association of Singapore with the Federation of Malaya as a basis for gaining full independence.

In the meantime the commission followed the main features of the scheme for extending responsible elected government devised by the Progressive Party. Its object was to encourage political awareness and responsibility among the electorate by putting effective control over domestic policy into the hands of a predominantly elected government, a 'genuinely responsible body with real power and authority', which would provide a base for further constitutional development.

The commission recommended keeping local government separate in the hands of a new island-wide, wholly elected 'City and Island Council'. For the central government it proposed to create a single chamber legislative assembly of 32 members, consisting of 25 elected councillors, 3 ex-officio ministers, and 4 nominated non-officials. The chambers of commerce were to lose their special voting privileges. Voters would be registered automatically and according to geographical constituencies, not racial communities.

The commission suggested that the executive council be replaced by a council of nine ministers, three appointed by the Governor, and the remaining six recommended by the leader of the strongest party in the legislative assembly, who would enjoy many of the functions of a prime minister. The council of ministers, acting like a cabinet with collective responsibility, would have authority over all matters except external affairs, internal security and defence. Elected assemblymen would gain control over commerce, industry, labour, immigration, social welfare, education, housing, communications, public works and health, leaving the three crucial ministries in the hands of the financial secretary, the attorney-general and the chief secretary, successor to the former colonial secretary. The commission recommended retaining English as the sole official language.

The British government accepted the Rendel proposals concerning central government and arranged to hold elections to implement the new constitution in 1955. The final decision on reorganizing the local authority was left to the incoming government.

The armed communist revolt in Malaya ultimately failed, but it distorted the development of nationalism in both the Federation and Singapore by destroying the former radical parties and pan-Malayan political movements. Singapore followed a course separate and distinct from mainland Malaya and was left to work out her own constitutional problems.

The enforcement of emergency regulations, the banning of political meetings except during election times, and the proscribing of left-wing parties gave Singapore a few years of superficial peace, when the colonial authorities worked quietly towards a more liberal and representative administration and the minority of Singaporeans in the political limelight concentrated upon trying to secure some form of ministerial powers and more elected seats in the legislature.

The colonial authorities were misled by the placid moderation of the legislative council. In clamping down on subversion the emergency regulations in effect suppressed nearly all political activity outside of the legislative council. The colonial authorities looked to this body to keep them informed about public opinion, but in this the legislative council was a hindrance rather than a help since its members were out of touch with the mass of the population. In particular the Chinese non-officials were exclusively English-educated upper-class Straits Chinese and closer in outlook to the ruling class than to the majority of their own countrymen.

The political institutions of the first post-war decade were remote from the real issues and developments of the day. The British saw the path to self-government starting with a municipal council and a legislative council, which would gradually become more elective and Asian-dominated, steadily taking over more responsibility for Singapore's affairs. Far from being a liberal training ground for democracy and a stepping-stone to independence, legislative councils could be a barrier to progress. The directors of the reactionary East India Company had perhaps come nearer the truth in distrusting elected legislative councils, on the grounds that elected members would be the English-educated wealthy minority, who would promote their selfish commercial interests to the detriment of the mass of the population. In Singapore the provisions for voting rights and insistence on English as the sole official language meant that the legislative and municipal councils were the preserve of Europeans and of English-educated, western-oriented well-to-do professional and commercial men, whose interests and thinking were in line with the ruling community. In the first post-war decade the sole occasion on which the non-official legislators clashed with the government was over the imposition of income tax.

The legislative council spent its time debating issues which seemed remote and irrelevant to the bulk of the population. It did not stimulate mass interest in politics, and it failed to keep the government in touch with the trends of the time. Indeed the support of non-officials for government policy blinded the authorities to the social discontent simmering just under the surface.

The four nominated non-official legislative councillors, sometimes known as 'The Queen's Party', were regarded as colonial puppets, and the three representatives of the chambers of commerce were criticized by labour leaders as the voice of commercial capitalism.

The elected members were no more representative. The Progressives, who held most of the elected seats, remained a stable fairly homogeneous group, continuing under the same leadership. At its peak the party had a membership of approximately four thousand and was supported by substantial donations from wealthy individual backers. But the Progressives had little contact with the working class, nor did they seek mass support. Full membership was open only to British and British-protected subjects and three-quarters of the members came from the middle and upper-middle class. Conservative in their economic policy, the Progressives wanted to uphold Singapore's traditional economy and give equal opportunities to local and foreign-financed industrial enterprises. They wished to keep political control in the hands of the English-speaking and to support a leisurely programme of constitutional reform and slow Malayanization of the civil service. The Chinese masses regarded them as collaborators, supporting the colonial government's unpopular policies on education, language, immigration, citizenship, and national service.

To the Chinese-educated and a minority of English-educated radicals the activities of the legislative council were unreal and irrelevant, and the genuine political issues of the time took place outside of the council chamber.

The communist victory in China in 1949 hardened the colonial power's attitude towards the involvement of Chinese Singaporeans in China's politics and reopened rifts between the Kuomintang and communist supporters among the Chinese-educated in Singapore. Both parties by that time were proscribed in Singapore, since the Malayan Communist Party was outlawed when the Malayan emergency broke out and the Kuomintang failed to register in 1949. But the conflict of loyalties persisted in the background. Tay Koh Yat, director of the anti-communist newspaper the *Chung Hsing Jit Pao*, led the Kuomintang faction, but Tan Kah Kee, still the most influential of the Nanyang Chinese, saw the Chinese Communist Party as the saviours of China and came out publicly in support of their cause.

Most Singapore Chinese, whatever their political feelings, were stirred by the Chinese Communist Pasty's triumph in their motherland. This did not necessarily imply sympathy with the Malayan Communist Party or its plans for establishing a Malayan republic, but the British, hard-pressed by the mainly Chinese communist guerrilla army in the Federation, feared that Peking would stir up the Malayan Chinese against the colonial authorities.

At first it appeared that the new regime in China intended to take over the Kuomintang policy of harnessing the loyalties of the Nanyang Chinese. In 1949 Peking created an Overseas Chinese Affairs Commission and asked Nanyang Chinese organizations, schools and newspapers to establish links with the commission. Former overseas Chinese were elected to represent the interests of the Nanyang Chinese on the National People's Council. Peking began broadcasts to the overseas Chinese in 1949 and started the China News Service for their benefit three years later. It declared an interest in supporting Chinese education overseas, encouraged Nanyang Chinese to maintain contact with and send remittances to their relatives in China, invited them to send their children for education in China and appealed for qualified doctors, engineers and teachers to go back to help rebuild the motherland.

The Singapore authorities regarded this policy as a threat to their attempts to build up a sense of common civic loyalty in Singapore and a menace to the physical security of Singapore and Malaya. They clamped down on contacts between Peking and the Singapore Chinese. When Tan Kah Kee visited China in 1950 to supervise the rehabilitation of the educational institutions which were his special interest and which had fallen into disarray during the years of civil war, the British authorities refused to re-admit him, and he was never able to set foot in Singapore again. The Chinese Communist Party gave Tan Kah Kee a party post, but this was a token of esteem for an ageing patriot rather than a position of power. He continued to live in Fukien province, travelling to Peking for occasional meetings, and died in his home village in 1961.

The traditional leaders of the Chinese-educated resented the colonial government's harshness towards Chinese patriotism. The Chinese chamber of commerce, which had been the most influential spokesman for the Chinese community before the war, was still considered in 1950 to be the 'premier society of the Chinese in Singapore',[44] with 2,000 individual members and more than sixty associations representing a further 10,000.

The chamber's confidence increased with the emergence of China as a big power, and many of its leaders, such as Lee Kong Chian and Tan Lark Sye, made new fortunes during the Korean war boom. Yet they felt excluded from the local political scene and nervous about their future in a self-governing Singapore or an independent Malaya. They resented paying taxes to support measures which detracted from what they conceived to be the interests of the China-born, particularly an

English-medium education system which hit at the roots of their own language and culture.

The regulation confining participation in politics to Straits-born or naturalized British subjects who were literate in English excluded the mass of immigrant and vernacular-educated Singaporeans, who constituted about half the adult population in the immediate post-war years. In 1946 the Chinese chamber of commerce began agitating for multi-lingualism in the legislative and municipal councils and for Chinese to be admitted as an official language. The chamber was incensed at an Immigration Bill passed in 1950 which was designed primarily to restrict the immigration of Chinese who might have communist sympathies, and from 1951 it campaigned for a special local citizenship to give political rights to long-term residents who were not British subjects. But the colonial authorities refused to waive naturalization requirements and in this they had the support of the Progressive Party and the Straits Chinese British Association.

To the traditional Chinese the most alarming aspect of colonial policy was its threat to Chinese education. The Singapore Chinese were concerned about a new education policy launched in the Federation in 1952, which concentrated on English and Malay schooling to the exclusion of Chinese. They also feared that the authorities were bent on suppressing Chinese education in Singapore, since in devoting the bulk of finances to the English-medium schools it appeared the colonial government was content to see Chinese education atrophy and die.

Chinese schools showed no desire to integrate with any national unified system and continued to be run by independent management committees, but despite the large grants given by the Chinese Nationalist government to rehabilitate Singapore's Chinese schools in the immediate post-war years, they could not match the facilities in the government-aided English schools. Chinese schools were overcrowded, their teachers were often untrained and earning about one-third the salary of their counterparts in English-medium schools.

The declining standards in Chinese schools and greater opportunities offered by English education drove increasing numbers of children into English-medium schools, and in 1954, for the first time, the new intake into English schools was greater than into the Chinese.

Most Chinese-educated pupils finished school at the primary stage to take unskilled or semi-skilled jobs. There were only nine Chinese middle schools in Singapore and no opportunities for Chinese-medium tertiary education. Large numbers of young Chinese flocked to mainland China for further education, often leaving tearful and protesting parents behind on the quayside. Peking at that time welcomed overseas Chinese students, giving them privileges and subsidies, waiving minimum educational qualifications, and opening special schools to provide intensive language instruction and political indoctrination. By 1954 the steady stream of young Singapore Chinese going off to seek their new Mecca swelled to a flood, but the colonial immigration laws precluded them from returning to the colony from China.[45]

In 1953 Tan Lark Sye declared that English education resulted in 'increasing taxes, laying traps, turning out fools and wasting public funds.'[46] His proposal to open a Chinese-medium Nanyang University in Singapore as a centre for the whole region met with enthusiastic response from rich and poor Chinese alike. Millionaires contributed handsome donations, the Hokkien *huay kuan* presented a magnificent site at Jurong, while taxi and trishaw drivers gave up one day's earnings, amounting to $20,000, for the university, which was eventually opened in 1956.

The reaction from the Chinese leaders impelled the government into belatedly paying more attention to the problem of Chinese schools. Under the terms of a White Paper published in December 1953 grants were offered to Chinese schools provided they were efficiently managed and gave bi-lingual instruction in Chinese and English. But by that time the education question had become part of wider political issues, and the leadership of the wealthy Chinese was challenged by new radical elements among the Chinese-educated.

It was impossible for left-wing politics to flourish overtly in Singapore during the early years of the Malayan emergency and the Malayan Communist Party concentrated on the mainland struggle. The Singapore City Committee continued to operate secretly and in 1949 organized an Anti-British League and a Singapore Students' Anti-British League with cells in Chinese middle schools. But the Special Branch of the police force was vigilant in hunting out suspected subversives. Under a new School Registration Ordinance, which gave them increased powers to search and close suspected schools, they closed two leading middle schools for a few weeks in 1950, dismissed some teachers and expelled a large number of students. The police succeeded in rounding up most of the Singapore City Committee in 1950, and the following year arrested thirty-four English-speaking radicals, including John Eber, C.V. Devan Nair of the Singapore Teachers' Union, and James Puthucheary of the University of Malaya Socialist Club. Altogether about twelve hundred Singaporeans were arrested under the emergency regulations in the period from 1948 to 1953, and the Anti-British League was virtually broken up.

The Communist Party failed to exploit the one opportunity which presented itself for fomenting trouble, the Hertogh riots of December 1950. These began when the Singapore government decided to return to her mother in Holland a Dutch Eurasian girl, Maria Hertogh, who had lost contact with her interned parents during the Japanese occupation, been brought up by a Muslim family, and married a Muslim. Stirred up by leaders of the Malay Nationalist Party and by the Muslim press, Malays, Indonesians and Indian Muslims in Singapore protested violently against the government's action. The commissioner of police allowed the situation to get out of hand, Europeans and Eurasians were attacked indiscriminately, and eighteen people were killed and 173 injured in two days of rioting. The Chinese secret societies were quick to take advantage of the trouble, but the Communist Party was caught by surprise. By the time it intervened to call on all races in Singapore to unite against British rule, law and order had been restored.[47]

The outbreak of the Malayan emergency dealt a blow not only to Chinese patriots and communists but also to legitimate radical politics and trade union activities. The atmosphere of fear and uncertainty inhibited freedom of speech, stifled debate and deterred students, intellectuals and trade unionists from taking an active part in public life. But by 1953 the atmosphere of intense political repression began to lift. As the Federation government gained the upper hand against the communist insurgents, tension slackened in Singapore too and detainees were released.

The Malayan Communist Party took advantage of this period of milder repression to infiltrate open organizations, notably Chinese schools and labour unions, playing upon the genuine grievances of students and workers.

The frustration of intelligent and ambitious Chinese school students combined with intense pride in communist achievements in China to feed pro-Chinese and anti-colonial feeling. Chinese middle school graduates were not qualified to gain access to the English-medium University of Malaya or to English-speaking universities overseas. Nor were there any openings for them in government and quasi-government organizations. A number of senior schoolboys were young men in their early twenties, since secondary schools were closed during the occupation and many over-aged pupils were admitted in the immediate post-war years. These youths and their teachers had good reason to be bitter against the colonial government. They admired the new Peking régime and eagerly absorbed books and communist propaganda from China.

Most outstanding among these young men were two Chinese High School graduates and former Singapore Students' Anti-British League cell leaders, Lim Chin Siong, born in Singapore in 1933, and Malayan-born Fong Swee Suan who was two years his senior. They had been involved in organizing class boycotts which resulted in the police raiding the Chinese High School. Fong Swee Suan left school after narrowly escaping arrest and Lim Chin Siong was expelled in 1952. They took low-paid jobs with bus companies, Fong Swee Suan as a bus conductor and Lim Chin Siong as a clerk, and devoted most of their energies to helping build up communist influence.

In 1953 the communists began to co-ordinate their activities in Chinese schools and seized upon the government's decision to enrol 2,500 youths for part-time national service as a suitable issue to foment discontent. They organized mass student protest demonstrations in May 1954, which were broken up by the police and many students were arrested. This stirred up further demonstrations to demand their release, and nearly all students refused to register for national service.

To counter this, in September 1954 the government passed a School Registration Amendment Ordinance, extending the government's powers to close schools on grounds of subversion. They coupled this the following month with a new financial offer of a $12 million grant which would raise aid for Chinese schools to the level offered to English schools.

This offer had strings attached. While leaving the management committees to conduct everyday affairs in the schools, the government proposed to appoint a nine-man board, consisting of three officials and six Chinese representatives, to allocate grants and supervise discipline, curricula and textbooks, with the Governor having the final say. The Chinese chamber of commerce protested that the board should be appointed and run entirely by Chinese, and the new offer failed to satisfy the growing revolutionary feelings among the student population. Chinese school committees, which were often dominated by rich businessmen of Kuomintang sympathies, found it increasingly difficult to enforce discipline among the unruly, over-aged students, and communist cells in the school intimidated principals and teachers. Students protested against the government having any say in the content and method of teaching. Negotiations broke down, three-quarters of the Chinese schools including the leading middle schools refused aid, and communist student leaders set up a Singapore Chinese Middle School Students' Union, which the government refused to register.

By mid-1954 communist leaders began to bring students into supporting labour disputes. The labour movement was in disarray and ripe for communist infiltration. Official policy aimed only to suppress communist-dominated unions but in practice its vigilance over trade union activities after the outbreak of the Malayan emergency stunted the growth of legitimate unions, since workers were afraid to become involved and invite police persecution.

Legislation was amended in 1948 to require trade union leaders to have three years' employment in the industry they represented and to restrict federations of unions to allied occupations, which excluded professional political agitators from leadership and automatically dissolved the Pan-Malayan Federation of Trade Unions. In the months which followed the outbreak of the emergency, trade union membership slumped and most unions disappeared.

The colonial government wished to build up a democratic trade union movement as part of the battle against communism and from 1949 encouraged the formation of a Singapore Trade Union Congress. After much dissension this was eventually set up in 1951 and within a year claimed a membership of 23,000 workers. These were mainly English-speaking, white-collar clerical workers since the congress failed to attract the mass of Chinese-speaking manual workers, and most of the leaders were Indians. The congress's organization was inefficient, its finances shaky, and it found difficulty in collecting dues, since it offered little benefit to its members. It soon splintered into factions and by 1953 the body was almost dormant.

The government's failure to stimulate democratic trade unionism, and the short-sightedness of Singapore employers in exploiting the labour movement's disarray to keep wages low despite rising profits during the Korean war boom, played into communist hands. The Singapore Trade Union Congress was discredited, its leadership rent by the same personal dissensions which split the Singapore Labour Party with which it was closely associated. It had done nothing to better the lot of its worker members. In 1954 the unemployment rate was higher than it had been at the time of the 1947 social survey and most working-class families still lived in appalling conditions.[48]

The mass of Chinese blamed their troubles on the colonial regime and resented the privileged position of the English-educated. This was ideal ground for communism and the new generation of militant young student leaders set out to harness the labour movement to the anti-imperialist cause. In May 1954 Lim Chin Siong became secretary-general of a recently formed Singapore Factory and Shop Workers' Union. Despite his youth and slight boyish appearance, Lim was a dedicated radical and a charismatic orator who could charm and sway mass audiences. Membership of the Singapore Factory and Shop Workers' Union expanded and by 1955 the organization included thirty industrial unions and was efficiently administered by a hierarchy of committees.

The Singapore Factory and Shop Workers' Union employed similar tactics to those used by the General Labour Union in the immediate post-war years, building up support by successful strikes bringing concrete benefits for the strikers. A number of small-scale stoppages in 1954 gained the first improvements for workers for many years and the first big strike was organized in the Paya Lebar bus company in February 1955. From that point the Singapore Factory and Shop Workers' Union launched a series of strikes, which extracted higher wages and better conditions and attracted thousands of recruits. Membership soared from 375 in April 1954 to nearly 30,000 by the end of 1955. The majority of members were Chinese but the union's twelve-man executive committee included both Chinese- and English-educated militants: Fong Swee Suan, secretary of the Singapore Bus Workers' Union; C.V. Devan Nair, now adviser to the Singapore Traction Company Employees' Union; and three founder members of the University of Malaya Socialist Club also came to prominence in the labour movement: James Puthucheary, Jamit Singh, secretary of the Harbour Board Staff Association, and Sandra Woodhull, secretary of the Naval Base Labour Union.

For the first time Chinese-educated and English-educated radicals linked together student and labour politics into a militant anti-colonial movement, which ran counter to the designs for steady constitutional reform planned by the British and accepted by the Progressives. Radical Singaporeans had no wish to see an independent Singapore with a colonial-type economy and ruled in the interests of the traditional English-educated élite.

Parallel with this development came the emergence of a new breed of Singaporean politicians, brought together as students in British universities. The overnight collapse of a seemingly unshakeable colonial regime in 1942 and the need for ingenuity to survive the hard years which followed provided the nursery which bred a crop of remarkable political leaders among the English-educated middle class, who had formerly accepted without question the colonial society and their semi-privileged position within it.

In 1949 six young Malayans studying in London formed a Malayan Forum discussion group to bring politically-minded Malayan students together. These informal discussions built up support for the Malayan independence movement, and a group of Singapore students resolved to work for Singapore's independence as part of a united Malaya within the British Commonwealth, to create racial equality and redistribute wealth more fairly.

The most outstanding member of this group was Lee Kuan Yew, a fourth-generation Singaporean. Lee's great-grandfather exemplified the successful mid-nineteenth century penniless immigrant who made sufficient money to return to China and buy an official rank. The family prospered and Lee Kuan Yew was born in 1923 into a comfortable middle-class Straits Chinese background. Educated at Raffles Institution, he was a Raffles College freshman when Singapore fell to the Japanese. After the war Lee Kuan Yew read law at Cambridge, where he acquired academic distinction.

Through the Malayan Forum he established contact with other young Malayans, notably two Raffles College graduates, Goh Keng Swee, an economist, and Toh Chin Chye, a physiologist. Goh Keng Swee, born in Malacca in 1918, a civil servant and former member of the Singapore Volunteers Corps, was the founder and first chairman of the Malayan Forum. Toh Chin Chye became the Forum's second chairman.

Lee Kuan Yew returned to Singapore in August 1950, where he quickly made a reputation as a quick-thinking and effective courtroom lawyer. Lee was well connected with the affluent Straits Chinese upper class, being Tan Chin Tuan's nephew by marriage and son-in-law of a senior official of the Oversea Chinese Bank, heart of the Lee Kong Chian commercial empire. Initially Lee Kuan Yew took the traditional path to political influence, becoming secretary of the Straits Chinese British Association and campaigning for the Progressives in the 1951 election. But he was impatient with the slow pace of the Straits Chinese politicians and realized that the future did not belong to the 'Queen's Chinese' but to those who could command wider support. Together with Goh Keng Swee, once more a Singapore civil servant, and Toh Chin Chye, who had become a lecturer at the University of Malaya, Lee developed his political plans and extended his contacts with other politically-minded individuals and groups.

He became legal adviser to various trade unions, first of all among English-speaking government employees. Through this work he met

Sinnathamby Rajaratnam, a journalist, who was born in Ceylon in 1915 but had lived in Malaya from infancy. Educated at Raffles Institution and London University, Rajaratnam was associate editor of the *Singapore Standard* and president of the Singapore Union of Journalists.

Union work also brought Lee Kuan Yew in touch with senior local officials who were bitter against racial discrimination in the public service. In 1946 the British government adopted the principle of localization in the colonial service.[49] From 1948 local officials were admitted to upper administrative grades, and a public services commission was set up to handle local recruitment in 1950 when the first students graduated from the local university. Asian officials were recruited in growing numbers but quickly became dissatisfied at the disparity between themselves and foreigners in conditions of service and promotion prospects. In practice the public services commission dealt only with lower posts and London continued to control the civil service, without any date being set for Malayanization. Expatriate officials saw the civil service as a body of administrators aloof from politics and visualized Malayanization as a gradual process, by which local officials would rise through the service and take over as expatriates retired. Local officers took a contrary view, considering political reforms were meaningless unless Singaporeans gained control of the bureaucracy at the same time.

Discontent came to a head in 1952 over a government decision to pay special expatriation allowances to European officials, and in protest a Council of Joint Action was formed by Lee Kuan Yew, Goh Keng Swee and Kenneth Byrne, a Malayan-born, Oxford-educated Eurasian official, who had served as a magistrate during the occupation. The council had representatives from twenty-one government unions, including the Local Senior Officers' Association which Byrne had formed two years previously. It organized a successful mass-demonstration which forced the authorities to pay more allowances to low-paid local employees, and it converted the question of Malayanization into a major political issue.

Most important of all was Lee Kuan Yew's connexion with C.V. Devan Nair of the Singapore Teachers' Union, through whom he met left-wing extremist Chinese student leaders and University of Malaya undergraduates. Lee acted as supporting counsel to the radical English Queen's Counsel, D.N. Pritt, in defending Chinese students arrested during the anti-national-service riots of May 1954 and University of Malaya Socialist Club undergraduates charged with publishing an allegedly subversive editorial in their paper *Fajar (Dawn)*.[50] These two trials caused a public furore, brought Lee Kuan Yew into the limelight and opened his eyes to the power of militant left-wing forces in Singapore.

The publication of the Rendel report in February 1954 and the prospect of elections to establish a measure of self-government the following year stimulated a flurry of discussions and negotiations to form new parties and alliances.

10. David Marshall, Chief Minister of Singapore, 1955–1956
(By permission of the *Straits Times*)

11. Lee Kuan Yew, Prime Minister of Singapore
(By permission of the Prime Minister's Office, Singapore)

The Singapore Labour Party existed in name only. In July 1954 Lim Yew Hock and Francis Thomas drew former socialists together to form a Labour Front, under the leadership of David Marshall, a prominent lawyer. Marshall, then forty-seven years old, was a member of the small but notable Jewish community, although he did not belong to one of its richer families. He qualified as a lawyer in England in the mid-1930s, fought with the Volunteers during the Japanese invasion and was subsequently sent as a prisoner of war to work in the coal mines of Hokkaido. By the early 1950s he had built up a reputation as an outstanding criminal defence lawyer. A man of warm human sympathies, a powerful speaker and persuasive court-room advocate, Marshall was a passionate defender of the underdog. His admiration for the British legal system and concern with the dignity and freedom of the individual made him in many ways European in outlook and perhaps for that reason the more bitter at what he considered to be the degradation and humiliation of colonial rule. An outspoken critic of British colonialism before the war, he was invited to join the Malayan Democratic Union but was repelled by the communist-style intemperate abuse of the party's language. He joined the Progressives but resigned because the party was content to move so gradually towards independence, and in 1954 he accepted the invitation to head the new Labour Front.

The Labour Front leaders approached Lee Kuan Yew but negotiations were fruitless, since Lee saw more advantage in alliance with the extreme militant radicals. The illegal Malayan Communist Party welcomed the possibility of using the English-educated left-wing as a front political party to exploit the new constitution in preparation for eventual armed struggle. Lee Kuan Yew's group, now fully alive to the force and discontent of the Chinese-educated masses, realized that an alliance with such men, dangerous though it might be, offered the only path to political success. The future belonged to politicians who could command the allegiance of the Chinese-educated.

The People's Action Party with Lee Kuan Yew as secretary-general, Toh Chin Chye as chairman, and a committee comprising trade unionists and Chinese- and English-educated radicals, was inaugurated in October 1954 in the Victoria Memorial Hall. The gathering of more than 1,500 people was the largest meeting held in Singapore since the emergency regulations were introduced in 1948. The presence of Tunku Abdul Rahman, head of UMNO, and Sir Tan Cheng Lock, now leader of the Malayan Chinese Association, underlined the new party's intention to get away from narrowly parochial Singapore affairs to a wider Malayan horizon. The party pledged itself to agitate in the coming elections for immediate independence for Singapore in union with the Federation, for the repeal of the emergency regulations, a common Malayan citizenship, complete Malayanization of the civil service, free compulsory education, the encouragement of local industry, the amendment of trade union legislation and for a workers' charter.

The wealthy China-born business community was slower to appreciate the new political opportunities which the Rendel constitution offered to the Chinese-educated, but shortly before the 1955 election an influential section of the Chinese chamber of commerce formed a Democratic Party. Despite its name, the new party was conservative in its economic outlook and frankly communal, pledged to foster Chinese education and culture, to make Chinese an official language and to obtain liberal citizenship terms for the China-born. It had little organization but strong financial backing, notably from Tan Lark Sye, former president of the Chinese chamber of commerce and head of the Hokkien *huay kuan*.

The battle lines were drawn for the electoral contest which was to open a new era in Singapore's development.

1. C.O. Memorandum, 28 July 1942, CO 825/35, 55104/42.

2. Colonial Office, 'Future Constitutional Policy for British Colonial Territories in Southeast Asia', C.M.B. (44) 3 of 14 January 1944, CO 825/43 B, 55104/15/44.

3. C.O. Memorandum: 'Plans for constitutional reconstruction in the Far East', 20 March 1943, CO 825/35 I, 55104/1.

4. C.O. minute, 18 November 1943, CO 825/35 I, 55104/1.

5. Minutes between Caine and Gent, 30 November and 1 December 1943, CO 825/35 I, 55105/1.

6. Tan Cheng Lock, *Memorandum on the Future of British Malaya* (Bombay, November 1943), and C.O. minute, 11 July 1945, 55104/1/3A, CO 825/42A.

7. John Laycock, Tan Chin Tuan, Tunku Abu Bakar, and Oliver Holt, *Memorandum on Proposals for Political Changes in Malaya* (Bombay, May 1944) and C.O. minute, 29 July 1944, 55104/1/3D, CO 825/42A.

8. Supreme Allied Command (SAC), South-East Asia, Director of Intelligence paper on 'Japanese Overall Strategy and its effect on Japanese Strategy in S.E. Asia', 18 May 1945, WO 203/286.

9. Report on 'Maintenance of operations after the capture of Singapore', Adv. H.Q. ALFSEA 151/AQP, 11 June 1945, WO 203/888; War Office Plan, 26 June 1945, WO 203/1105.

10. H.Q. ALFSEA to Chief of Gen. Staff, 13 August 1945, WO 203/941.

11. Supreme Allied Command South-East Asia to F.O., 3 September 1945, 50823/46, CO 273/675.

12. Shenton Thomas, Memorandum, Formosa, 29 February 1944, 50984/45, CO 273/677; Thomas to Gent, 20 October 1945, and C.O. minutes 50823/17, CO 273/675.

13. Clementi, Comments at meeting at the Colonial Office, February 1946, and Colonial Office, 'Notes for guidance of Secretary of State at meeting, February 1946'. 50823/35, CO 273/676.

14. C.O. minutes (Gent and Gater), March 1943, CO 825/35 I, 55104/1.

15. 'Constitutional Reconstruction in the Far East', 21 July 1943, and revised Colonial Office memorandum, 30 July 1943, CO 825/35 I, 55104/1.

16. McKerron and others, 'Memorandum on Constitution for Singapore', 1 May 1945; McKerron to Gent, 30 November 1945; Hone to Gent, 5 December 1945, 50823/17, CO 273/675.

17. Sir Ralph Hone, 'Papers relating to the Military Administration of the Malayan Peninsula, 5 September 1945–1 April 1946', Rhodes House, MSS Brit.Emp. S 407/3; British Military Administration, *Singapore Advisory Council Proceedings*, 14 November and 12 December 1945 and January 1946.

18. F.S.V. Donnison, *British Military Administration in the Far East, 1943–46* (London, 1956).
19. Colonial Office, *British Dependencies in the Far East, 1945–1949*, Cmd. 7709 (London, May 1949), p. 33.
20. Colonial Office, *British Dependencies*, p. 161.
21. A. Gilmour, *My Role in the Rehabilitation of Singapore: 1946–1953* (Singapore, 1973), p. 6.
22. C. Gamba, *The Origins of Trade Unionism in Malaya* (Singapore, 1962), p. 45.
23. T. Silcock and Ungku Aziz, 'Nationalism in Malaya', in W.L. Holland (ed.), *Asian Nationalism and the West* (New York, 1953; reprinted New York, 1973), p. 300.
24. United Engineers, Hume Pipe Company, Singapore Cold Storage, Wearne/Borneo Motors, Fraser & Neave Breweries, Singapore Traction Company, Malayan Collieries.
25. Arthur Creech-Jones Papers, Rhodes House, MSS Brit.Emp. S 332, Box 26, File 11
26. *Malayan Union and Singapore: statement of policy on future Constitution*, Cmd. 6724 (London, January 1946).
27. *New Democracy*, 24 January 1946 (also *Chung Hwa* and *Sin Chew*, 24 January 1946), *Malayan press comment on the White Paper on Malayan Union*, Special supplement to *Malayan Press Digest*, 1/MPD. 15/16.2.
28. P. Hoalim, *The Malayan Democratic Union: Singapore's First Democratic Political Party* (Singapore, 1973).
29. Malayan Union, *Constitutional Proposals for Malaya: Summary of a Report of the Working Committee appointed by a Conference of the Governor of Malayan Union, the Rulers and the Representatives of the United Malays National Organization* (Kuala Lumpur, 1946).
30. PUTERA and All-Malaya Council of Joint Action, *The People's Constitutional Proposals for Malaya* (Kuala Lumpur, November 1947).
31. Colonial Office, *British Dependencies*, pp. 30, 41. The infant mortality rate was 80.79 in 1948, compared with 191.30 in 1931 and 285 in 1944.
32. S.S. Awberry and F.W. Dalley, *Labour and Trades Union Organization in the Federation of Malaya and Singapore* (Kuala Lumpur, 1948), p. 27.
33. M.V. del Tufo, *A Report on the 1947 Census of Population* (London, 1949).
34. Department of Social Welfare, *A Social Survey of Singapore* (Singapore, 1947), pp. 114, 119–21.
35. Kernial Singh Sandhu, *Indians in Malaya* (Cambridge, 1969), p. 151.
36. Tan Chin Tuan, quoted in *ST*, 4 July 1947.
37. Department of Social Welfare, *A Social Survey of Singapore* (Singapore, 1947), p. 75.
38. Quoted in Colonial Office, *British Dependencies*, p. 35.
39. This thesis was forcibly argued in D.D. Chelliah, *A History of the Educational Policy of the Straits Settlements* (Kuala Lumpur, 1947; 2nd edition, Singapore, 1960). Based upon a Ph.D. thesis submitted to the University of London in 1940, this work was published by the Malayan Union government and carried weight in post-war thinking on education policy.
40. Quoted in D.S. Samuel, 'A Comparative Study of the Powers of the Malayan and Singapore Legislatures, 1945–59', unpublished M.A. dissertation, University of Singapore, 1967, p. 22.
41. The University opened a division in Kuala Lumpur in 1958, and in 1961 split into two separate institutions: the University of Malaya (in Kuala Lumpur) and the University of Singapore.
42. F.C. Carnell, 'Constitutional Reform and Elections in Malaya', *Pacific Affairs*, XXVII, 3 (1954), p. 219.
43. *Report of the Constitutional Commission* (Singapore, 1954). The Rendel Report.
44. Homer Cheng, 'The Network of Singapore Societies', *Journal of the South Seas Society*, VI, 2 (1950), p. 12.
45. V. Thompson and R. Adloff, *Minority Problems in Southeast Asia* (Stanford, 1955), p. 33.

46. Quoted in Yeo Kim Wah, *Political Development in Singapore, 1945–1955* (Singapore, 1973), p. 161.
47. *Report of the Singapore Riots Inquiry Commission* (Singapore, 1951).
48. Goh Keng Swee, *Urban Income and Housing* (Singapore, 1954).
49. Colonial Office, *Organization of the Colonial Service*, Cmd. 197 of 1946 (London, 1946).
50. D.N. Pritt, *Autobiography, Vol. III. The Defence Accuses* (London, 1966).

# VIII

# The Road to Merdeka
# 1955–1965

THE Rendel constitution was designed to stimulate an appetite for self-government among seemingly reluctant Singaporeans. The colonial authorities had spent ten years prodding life into a movement towards political maturity with little apparent sign of success, but the 1955 election marked a lusty, vociferous political awakening. It heralded years of vigorous constitutional struggle when new nationalist leaders emerged and issues which really concerned the mass of Singaporeans were brought into the political arena.

The election held in April 1955 to implement the Rendel constitution was the first lively political contest in Singapore's history, and the temporary easing of emergency restrictions bred election fever. This spirited competition did not come from the biggest and ostensibly strongest contestants, the Progressive and Democratic parties, who fielded large teams of candidates and aimed to win outright control of the assembly. Regarding each other as the only serious competitors, they appealed to the traditional middle-class electorate, made little attempt to woo the masses, ignored the left-wing parties and clashed in no less than eighteen constituencies.

It was the new parties of the left which stirred the mass of the population, despite the fact that neither the People's Action Party nor the Labour Front aspired to win office. The People's Action Party considered that 'to form a government under the Rendel constitution was to work with our hands tied behind our backs',[1] nor was it yet strong enough to make a successful bid for power. The extreme left-wing favoured boycotting the election and concentrating on direct action, but the moderates prevailed and the party decided to field a token force. They campaigned intensively, attracting mass rallies, including large numbers of Chinese voters who had shown no interest in previous elections.

The Labour Front stood for immediate independence within a merged Singapore/Malaya and promised to Malayanize the public administration within four years, extend Singapore citizenship to include the 220,000 China-born inhabitants, abolish the emergency regulations and introduce multi-lingualism in the legislature. The party fielded seventeen candidates and aimed to produce a strong opposition party in the new legislative assembly. In a stirring and emotional election manifesto, 'I Believe',

Marshall denounced colonialism as exploitation and promised 'dynamic socialism' to counter 'the creeping paralysis of communism'. Flamboyant in speech, Marshall brought the histrionics of his court-room technique to sway large audiences, making ever more extravagant election promises, warning of 'the near-erupting volcano of impatient youth thirsting for independence'.[2]

The election results were a shock to the victors, the losers and the British alike. David Marshall's Labour Front emerged the strongest party with ten seats, and the PAP won three of the four seats it contested. But the Progressives won only four and the Democratic Party, two. Apart from Lim Yew Hock, no former legislative councillor won through to the new Assembly. Some who had previously been nominated or chosen by the chambers of commerce preferred not to face the hurly burly of an election. Others were discredited because of their association with the old regime and close co-operation with the colonial authorities. C.C. Tan, John Laycock, and Nasir Mallal all lost their seats.

The right-wing parties failed partly because they split the moderate conservative vote between them but mainly because they had not appreciated the changed character of the electorate. Automatic registration of voters increased the electorate from 76,000 to more than 300,000, of whom the majority were working-class Chinese. The left-wing parties appealed for the new voters' support, whereas the Progressives offered only a continuation of the unpopular, pro-colonial conservative policies of the past. The Democratic Party championed Chinese culture, language, education and citizenship but its strident chauvinism attracted little enthusiasm among middle-class Straits Chinese, while its capitalist economic policy was indistinguishable from that of its Progressive rivals and drove the mass of Chinese towards the more radical Labour Front and the PAP.

The 1955 election was the funeral of conservative politics and ended the days when the Chinese chamber of commerce could exert direct political power. The following year the Progressives merged with the Democratic Party to form a Liberal Socialist Party, but this inappropriately named organization attracted no popular support and was decisively trounced in the next election. The future belonged to politicians of the left who aimed to seize self-government as quickly as possible and to build up mass support against colonial rule.

Marshall's Labour Front formed a government with the support of the three Alliance[3] members, the ex-officio members and two nominated non-officials, who together formed a motley group of 18 in an Assembly of 32. The position was precarious but the opposition was also divided, comprising six Liberal Socialists, three PAP members, including Lee Kuan Yew and Lim Chin Siong, three Independents and two nominated non-officials.

A left-wing minority government, facing a part-conservative, part extreme left-wing opposition, was a situation which no-one had envisaged.

The British expected the ruling Progressive Party would command the support of the first assembly and the familiar figures of the old legislative council would fill the new assembly's front ranks. It assumed that a strong Progressive Party, stimulated by a small radical opposition, would guide Singapore in a peaceful and gradual transition to political internal self-government, leaving existing economic and defence interests undisturbed. This did not happen.

The Rendel constitution created a cabinet which was responsible to the assembly but did not define the powers or place of the chief minister, and David Marshall found himself suddenly thrust into power, or rather into titular power without substance. He was new to politics, parliament and authority, and was temperamentally unsuited to be a minority government leader, requiring special qualities of restraint and diplomacy. Unable to remain in opposition, in which role he could probably have been highly effective, yet not strong enough to carry out his ambitious election promises, Marshall was forced to compete with the PAP opposition for the extremist left-wing position. From the beginning Lee Kuan Yew denounced the Rendel constitution, 'We say this Constitution is colonialism in disguise.' Marshall also felt it was a mere sop to nationalist aspirations and he was put into the difficult position of having to operate a constitution which he despised. At the same time the PAP opposition goaded Marshall on to fulfil election promises, to repeal the emergency regulations and demand immediate self-government, so that from the first Marshall was driven into demanding more power for his government.

To make this complicated situation work required political subtlety on the part of the Governor and the new chief minister and a mutual sympathy which neither possessed. The British were quick to acknowledge strong nationalist leaders, as in the Federation of Malaya where elections also produced unexpected results in 1955. The Alliance was returned to power in Kuala Lumpur with such an overwhelming mandate that London agreed to speed the process towards independence and the Federation soon overtook Singapore's initially more liberal constitutional status to become a fully independent state in 1957.

The British response to the new political situation in Singapore was very different. The minority government lacked firm foundations and the Governor, Sir John Nicoll, made it clear that Marshall's victory did not give him a clear mandate. The Rendel constitution laid down that the Governor must consult his chief minister but did not specify that he must act on his advice. The somewhat stiff and unimaginative Nicoll attempted to treat the chief minister as a figurehead, for a time even refusing to allot him a room, until Marshall threatened to set up his desk under a tree in front of the secretariat. Nicoll had anticipated that the leader of the house would be Minister of Commerce and Industry, but Marshall, who was not a man to be browbeaten, insisted on making the office of chief minister a full-time appointment and created a separate Ministry of Commerce and Industry.

Marshall's victory also created unexpected difficulties for the PAP moderates, because they had to keep to the left in order to be more radical than the government, and this gave a fillip to the extremist element in the party. From the start the PAP was anti-imperialist and socialist but divided into two wings, the non-communists under Lee Kuan Yew and the pro-communists under Lim Chin Siong. The alliance of communist and non-communist was a particularly hazardous game in Singapore in the mid-1950s. While Lee Kuan Yew was the party's most vocal member in the eyes of the English-educated community, during the early years Lim Chin Siong and the militant wing were the real force in the PAP, commanding the support of organized labour and the mass of Chinese.

The days of leisurely, gentlemanly political debate were over, and the verbal duels of the two leading political rivals, Marshall and Lee Kuan Yew, both powerful speakers and strong personalities, electrified the legislative chamber and brought crowds to its previously empty public benches. The two men shared some features in common. They belonged to the English-educated middle-class but were members of minority groups, the Jews and Hakkas, noted for their toughness, enterprise and resilience. They were newcomers to parliament but enjoyed the turmoil of the hustings, the cut and thrust of parliamentary debate. Both were English-trained Middle Temple lawyers, who sought to work through British constitutional methods to create a non-communist Singapore as part of a wider independent Malaya.

Here the resemblance finished. They differed fundamentally in their principles, style and methods. While Marshall loved the limelight of political life, he was not adept at treading the corridors of power. Impetuous, impatient and quick tempered, he wore his heart on his sleeve and met problems head on, disdaining compromise as deceit. Lee was both a man of vision and a careful schemer, with no trace of sentimentality, cold and calculating in his analysis, his whole life centred round politics. To Marshall the rights and liberties of individuals, human justice, dignity, equality and protection for the underprivileged took first priority. Lee Kuan Yew put society before the individual and was impatient with those whom he took to be weaklings or fools. Marshall made no secret of his antipathy towards the Malayan Communist Party and wanted no dealings with the extreme left-wing in Singapore, relying for popular support on the non-communist Singapore Trade Union Congress. He tried to bridge the gap between his middle-class English-educated background and that of the ordinary population by 'Meet the People' sessions, in which he held open house in person to discuss individuals' problems. Lee Kuan Yew, on the other hand, considered that the only means of acquiring mass support among the Chinese-educated majority was to work in alliance with left-wing leaders among the trade union movement and Chinese middle schools. As he said in 1955, 'Any man in Singapore who wants to carry the Chinese-speaking people with him cannot afford to be anti-Communist.'

Marshall felt deeply about the political and social ills of the time and was eager to come to grips with the vital problems which had been largely swept under the carpet during the post-war years: vernacular education, language, citizenship and Malayanization. The extremists were quick to take advantage of the new government's weakness to exploit these issues, while the moderate elements of the PAP were equally anxious to see these problems dealt with speedily in order to take the fire and power out of the left wing of their own party.

The outcome was a stormy and acrimonious battle, which in fact produced solid and lasting benefits for Singapore, but at the time Singapore appeared to be descending into chaos. Lim Chin Siong and extremist leaders decided to ignore constitutional methods and launch the student and labour movements into a joint direct militant campaign of obstruction and violence. On the eve of the election nearly 10,000 Chinese middle-school students staged a strike and boycotted classes, demanding the registration of the Singapore Chinese Middle School Students' Union. Organized by a small minority, Chinese school students campaigned en masse for the PAP during the election and continued afterwards to support riots and labour strikes and to demand registration of their union.

In May 1955 students and workers converted a strike at the Hock Lee bus company into a violent demonstration which led to a night of terror and death. Ignoring the Governor's advice, Marshall refused to call in troops to restore order, and the strike resulted in triumph for the Singapore Bus Workers' Union and its Singapore Factory and Shop Workers' Union allies.

The Labour Front government arrested some students and threatened to close schools involved in the trouble unless they expelled student ringleaders and restored discipline. Two thousand students then barricaded themselves in the Chung Cheng High School, demanding the release of their leaders and repeal of restrictive school legislation, while the Singapore Factory and Shop Workers' Union threatened to call a general strike in their support if Marshall closed the schools.

The chief minister refused to take stern measures, because he genuinely sympathized with the Chinese students' cause and attributed blame to colonial education policy. 'Our son is as one who is ill. This is not the time for the whip and the knife,' he insisted. Marshall reopened the schools and appointed an all-party committee to examine the Chinese education problem. This committee ultimately produced a long-term compromise policy, but at the time Marshall's move was interpreted as weakness, and jubilant students held a big victory parade at the Chung Cheng High School.

Marshall also agreed to register the Singapore Chinese Middle School Students' Union, provided it kept out of politics. The Malayan Communist Party ordered the students to accept this offer but had no intention of honouring the conditions. At the union's inaugural meeting in October 1955 it attacked the Public Security Ordinance and supported strike action by the Singapore Traction Company. The Singapore Chinese

Middle School Students' Union was efficiently organized by an executive committee, with branch committees in each middle school, subcommittees and cells at form level, and a membership of nearly 10,000. The union became the dominant power in the Chinese schools, physically attacking teachers who did not conform to its revolutionary views, and school managements found themselves powerless to enforce discipline.

During May and June 1955 labour trouble mounted, fomented by Lim Chin Siong and the militants. Membership of the Singapore Factory and Shop Workers' Union expanded dramatically, and in June the extremist labour leaders tried to escalate a Harbour Board dispute into a general strike. The Labour Front government forestalled this by arresting five leaders, including Fong Swee Suan, but the incident revealed the intentions and the power of the Malayan Communist Party to manipulate trade unions for political ends, and Marshall accused the PAP members in the legislative assembly of 'an open effort to substitute mob government for government by the people's elected representatives'. Of nearly 300 strikes in 1955 only a third involved claims for better wages and conditions, while the rest were sympathy strikes or demands for the release of imprisoned trade union officials.

The new government had taken off to a troubled start, and the weakness of Marshall's minority position forced him to be all the more bellicose in his dealings with the colonial authorities. The British deplored what they considered to be Marshall's excessively soft handling of riots, while the chief minister's lack of political guile and his sympathy with dissident workers and students made his relationship with Government House more difficult. This was particularly so with regard to the emergency regulations, which offended Marshall's respect for individual liberty and which he was pledged to repeal, yet needed to retain. In order to enable Marshall to fulfil his election promise, Nicoll suggested that the chief minister should repeal the emergency regulations and then the Governor would reimpose them, a step which would give Marshall kudos, throw all the blame on the colonial authorities and yet preserve the colony's peace and order. Marshall dismissed this compromise as a piece of political chicanery.

In order not to be outdone by the extremist opposition, Marshall sought more power and in July 1955 demanded the appointment of four assistant ministers. When the new Governor, Sir Robert Black, refused, Marshall threatened to resign unless Singapore were given immediate self-government, claiming that the issue was 'whether the Governor governs or we govern'. In view of his turbulent few months in office, the demand seemed preposterous. But the British feared Marshall's departure would open the way to a more radical and irresponsible government. The Colonial Office ruled that the Governor should henceforth act on the chief minister's advice and agreed to hold constitutional talks after the assembly had been in existence for one year, instead of allowing it to run its full term.

Despite his difficulties and inexperience Marshall had accomplished a great deal. He had forced the British to respect his interpretation of the chief minister's role, he had succeeded in appointing further ministers and had brought the British to the conference table. He had also taken steps to deal with fundamental grievances by appointing the all-party committee to investigate Chinese education and a Malayanization committee under the chairmanship of a distinguished doctor, B.R. Sreenivasan. His government passed a Labour Ordinance in December 1955 to restrict hours of labour and drew up proposals for a single Singapore citizenship. While the Colonial Office and the Governor found Marshall a cross to bear, he aroused their grudging respect.

The Colonial Office approached the constitutional talks in London in April 1956 with caution. 'We do not intend that Singapore should become an outpost of Communist China, and, in fact, a colony of Peking,' the secretary of state warned, and he rejected Marshall's contradictory view that 'merdeka will rally the majority of the people against Communism'. Marshall demanded full internal self-government by April 1957, leaving foreign policy and external defence in Britain's hands but allowing Singapore a veto on defence and rights of consultation on foreign affairs.

The British government was prepared to grant a great deal: a fully-elected assembly, the removal of ex-officio members, special Singapore citizenship, local control of trade and commerce. But it insisted on a defence council on which Britain and Singapore should have equal representation, with a casting vote in the hands of a British High Commissioner. The Colonial Office promised to use this power only in an emergency but refused to agree to Marshall's demand to abolish the casting vote, and the talks broke down on this point.

The Singapore delegation was divided about whether to accept London's offer, but Marshall had made a pre-commitment leaving no room for bargaining. He refused to compromise and returned to Singapore empty handed to face bitter press criticism and hostile debate in the legislative assembly.[4] He had staked his pledge on getting internal self-government and resigned in June 1956. This was a personal decision, not forced upon him by his colleagues, and caused no rift in the Labour Front. His place was taken by Lim Yew Hock, the deputy chief minister and Minister for Labour, who retained Marshall's entire cabinet and continued to rely on the co-operation of the Labour Front and Alliance parties.

Lim Yew Hock's position was far from strong. The Labour Front had been hastily put together to fight the 1955 election, at which time it was merely a collection of some 300 to 400 individuals. After coming to power it began to build up its organization and by the end of 1955, on paper at least, had some 5,500 members. But the troubles and dissensions of the first year in office put immense strains on its fragile structure. Two Labour Front assemblymen became opposition Independents, so that by September 1956 Lim Yew Hock could command the support of only eleven of the twenty-five elected members. He depended on the fact that the opposition remained divided.

This weak government soon faced a new crisis in the Chinese middle schools. The committee on Chinese education issued its report in February 1956, condemning the divisive colonial educational policy and recommending equal treatment for all schools and all four leading languages and cultures.[5] The committee concluded that the best hope for creating a harmonious multi-racial Singapore lay in breaking down exclusiveness in educational streams and encouraging young people of different racial groups to mix. To this end the committee urged bi-lingual primary education, with a common syllabus, common textbooks, equal grants, equal pay for teachers and equal opportunities for school leavers from all language streams to enter government service. They also recommended banning students from active politics, and the government's decision to implement the report[6] brought it into head-on conflict with communist aspirations and with politically-minded Chinese students and teachers.

As part of a general campaign to counter subversion, in September 1956 the Lim Yew Hock government dissolved seven communist-front organizations, including the Singapore Chinese Middle Schools Students' Union, closed two Chinese schools and expelled 142 middle school students, some of them 'professional students' in their mid-twenties. Five thousand students, organized by Lim Chin Siong and extremist leaders, then staged a protest sit-in at six Chinese schools. When neither teachers nor parents could dislodge the students, the police drove them out with tear gas, whereupon they formed processions which resulted in rioting in many parts of the city. Fifteen people were killed, more than one hundred were injured and for two days Singapore was under curfew, while police and troops were rushed from the Federation to help quell the disturbances. Documents found in a police raid on the headquarters of the Singapore Factory and Shop Workers' Union proved the implication of labour leaders in the student demonstrations. As a result the union was dissolved and extremists, including Lim Chin Siong and James Puthucheary, were arrested.

This determined action strengthened Lim Yew Hock's position when he led a second all-party delegation to London in March 1957 to renew discussions about self-government. The Colonial Office responded more sympathetically to the quiet conciliatory style of this self-effacing, unassuming, pliable man of smiles than it had to Marshall's explosive rhetoric. The 1957 negotiations were also easier because the Federation of Malaya was about to become independent. The Colonial Office proposed to create a seven-member internal security council on which Britain and Singapore would have equal representation, while the Federation would appoint the seventh representative. This satisfied Singapore's pride and her aspirations towards merger. At the same time it put the casting vote in the hands of the Federation, which shared Britain's concern to curb subversion in Singapore. Otherwise the Singapore delegation accepted similar constitutional terms to those which

Marshall had refused the previous year.[8]

When the offer came to be debated in the legislative assembly, Marshall criticized the delegation and in particular Lee Kuan Yew for accepting what he dubbed the 'fraud constitution' which they had rejected under his leadership. Following this challenge both Marshall and Lee Kuan Yew resigned from the assembly. Lee immediately fought and won a by-election in defence of this issue, but Marshall retired temporarily from the political arena.

A majority in the assembly agreed to accept the British offer and a third all-party mission was to go to London in 1958 to settle final terms for the new constitution.

The prospect of a self-governing Singapore in which Britain and the conservative Federation held control over internal security provoked the communists into new forms of militancy.

Communist student activity shifted from the middle schools to the new Nanyang University, which was formally opened in March 1956 amid great enthusiasm from all the Chinese community, conservative and radical, wealthy and poor. Thousands crowded to the opening ceremony, causing an unprecedented traffic jam, which lasted until the early hours of the morning, along the country lane to the then remote Jurong.

Very quickly the new university became a hotbed of trouble, since student extremists who had belonged to the banned Singapore Chinese Middle School Students' Union set up the Nanyang University Students' Union and organized acts of protest and violence reminiscent of the former middle school troubles.

At the same time the Malayan Communist Party set out to revive its strength in the trade unions, to infiltrate the Trade Union Congress and to gain complete control of the PAP. Despite the arrest of trade-union agitators and the dissolution of the powerful Singapore Factory and Shop Workers' Union in October 1956, by mid-1957 the communists had built up a new central union. They tried to dominate Labour Day celebrations in May 1957, and after that organized mass rallies under the guise of picnics and extended their influence in the PAP through the party's cultural and education committee. The left-wing leaders than set out to oust the moderates from the party's central executive committee.[9]

At the first party conference in 1955 the extremists had not stood for election to the party's central executive committee, of which Toh Chin Chye was chairman and Lee Kuan Yew secretary-general. At the second conference in 1956 the left-wing gained only four of the twelve seats, although Lim Chin Siong won the highest individual number of votes. The third annual conference in August 1957 witnessed an all-out battle for control of the party between the moderates and the extremists, who objected to the terms of self-government accepted by Lee Kuan Yew as a member of the all-party mission to London, to the proposed internal security council and to the principle of independence through merger with the Federation. The extremists succeeded in winning half of the seats, the future of the moderates appeared precarious, and Toh and Lee stood down from the leadership.

In face of the widespread communist threat, the Lim Yew Hock government stepped in to arrest thirty-five active communists, including five members of the newly elected PAP central executive committee and eleven PAP branch officials, together with trade union leaders, students and journalists. Lim Yew Hock's object was to purge extremist influence· from the student and labour movements, including the Singapore Trade Union Congress which was the basis of his own party's power. But the arrests also crippled extremist power in the PAP and gave the moderates the opportunity to regain mastery of their party without incurring un-popularity by taking action themselves against their rivals. This dramatic change of fortune was so propitious for Lee Kuan Yew and his associates that many, including his extremist colleagues, felt that Lee had been privy to the intentions of Lim Yew Hock and the colonial authorities.

In order to consolidate their hold over the party, the moderates ex-tended the executive committee's term of office to two years and created a cadre system by which the PAP was divided into four categories of members: probationary, ordinary, probationary cadre and full cadre, of whom only the last group could vote for the central executive committee. Cadres had to be literate Singapore citizens, over twenty-one years of age, thus automatically excluding most students and many China-born working-class members, who were the most enthusiastic supporters of the communist wing. Cadre membership had to be approved by the central executive committee, which thus perpetuated the supremacy of the English-educated moderate leaders, although most PAP members continued to be Chinese-educated.

The moderates continued outwardly to support their left-wing col-leagues and to agitate for the release of their imprisoned associates, thus ensuring popularity with the masses. At the same time, despite the outspoken anti-colonialism of the English-educated PAP leaders and their acrimonious opposition to the Labour Front government, Lee Kuan Yew was able to play a strong role in the legislative assembly. As a member of the all-party committee appointed by Marshall to deal with the problem of education and of the teams which went to London to seek self-government, he took a constructive part in the developments of the 1955–9 period without being identified with the ruling régime.

The British government was pleased in general with the activities of the Lim Yew Hock government in countering subversion, and the in-dependence granted to the Federation of Malaya in August 1957 was a further stabilizing factor. The Singapore legislative assembly sent its greetings, 'We of Singapore look forward to that day when our strength will be added to your strength and our separation will be ended.'

Further progress was made on the crucial issues of Malayanization, citizenship and education. In December 1956, after some heated debate, the legislative assembly accepted the Malayanization committee's majority report, which advocated complete localization of administrative posts in two years and the rest of the service in four. The following year the public service commission was given full executive powers and Malayanization proceeded rapidly.

The citizenship controversy was settled by a Citizenship Ordinance in 1957, which offered Singapore citizenship to all born in Singapore or the Federation and to British citizens of two years' residence, and offered naturalization to all those resident for ten years in the colony who were prepared to swear loyalty to Singapore. This enfranchised the majority of the 220,000 alien-born Chinese.

In December 1957 an Education Ordinance based upon the all-party committee's recommendations gave parity to the four main language streams. It continues to be the foundation for Singapore's educational policy to the present day. Already by that time educational reforms undertaken since 1955, when the department of Education was converted into a ministry, were beginning to take effect. By the end of 1957 the ministry had opened ninety-six new primary schools and eleven new secondary schools. It started technical and commercial schools, initiated an energetic programme of adult education, established training courses for Malay and Tamil teachers and opened a polytechnic in 1958.[10]

When the third all-party constitutional mission went to London in April 1958 the situation looked brighter and the terms of the new constitution were quickly agreed. The British parliament passed a State of Singapore Act in August 1958, which converted the colony into a state with control over all domestic affairs, including finance.[11] Internal security would be in the hands of the internal security council, comprising representatives from Singapore, Britain and the Federation.[12] A fifty-one member legislative assembly, elected on the basis of adult suffrage by all Singapore citizens, could conduct its debates in English, Malay, Mandarin or Tamil. The prime minister would select his cabinet, and after a short interim period a local *Yang di-pertuan negara*, or chief of state, would be chosen. While the British government retained control of foreign affairs and external defence, it could only suspend the constitution and assume full powers of government through its Commissioner in the event of a dire emergency. The only controversial point was the British insistence that known subversives should be excluded from the first elections, which were scheduled to be held in May 1959 to bring the new constitution into force.

Meanwhile in Singapore the centre of interest shifted from the legislative assembly to the hitherto quiet, stately, rather dull City Hall. In the post-war years the scope of local government increased appreciably and Singapore acquired city status in 1951. During the following four years three commissions were set up to make recommendations for reorganizing local government. The first was a one-man commission in the person of Dr. L.C. Hill, a local-government expert from Britain, appointed in 1951. Hill recommended increasing the powers of the city council by making it all-elected on the basis of universal adult suffrage and transferring to it government and quasi-government functions such as public health, communications and housing. He proposed having an elected mayor instead of a seconded civil servant as president of the council. He also suggested expanding the responsibilities of rural district councils and aimed to involve the whole adult population in local government as a training for political freedom.[13]

The Rendel committee was also asked to consider local government within the framework of its constitutional proposals and recommended streamlining local government functions into one island-wide City and Island Council.

Marshall rejected the Rendel proposals for local administration, fearing that the proposed island-wide local authority would rival the legislative assembly. In 1955 he appointed another committee under T.P. McNeice, the municipal president, to plan separate city and district councils along the lines of the Hill report.[14]

As a result new local-government legislation came into force in July 1957. The Singapore Improvement Trust and Singapore Harbour Board retained their independent status, and the city council's powers remained largely the same, while the rural district councils continued to be 'no more than glorified rural district advisory committees'.[15] But the composition of the city council and its electorate changed radically. The council became an entirely elected body of thirty-two members, one of whom would be chosen as mayor. Candidates literate in any of the four main languages were eligible to stand and all four languages were to be permitted in council debates. All adults were automatically registered as voters, subject to certain residence qualifications, and in this way the vote was extended to about half a million new voters who were not British subjects.

The city council elections held in December 1957 roused interest and fire for the first time. The Liberal Socialists, who had dominated the old council, retained only seven seats. Victory went to new men, in particular the PAP, who promised in their election campaign to fight corruption and reorganize the council to serve the people. Despite the setback suffered by the arrest of its most radical leaders a few months earlier, the PAP won thirteen of the fourteen seats it contested, to become the largest party in the new council.

Ong Eng Guan, a Johor-born, Australian-trained accountant, founder member and treasurer of the PAP, was elected mayor. Ong was a favourite with the Chinese masses, a bitter anti-colonialist but not a communist, an unorthodox and unpredictable individualist. No specific powers were laid down for the mayor, but Ong Eng Guan disdained to be a 'ceremonial figurehead attending cocktail parties' and converted the council into what he rightly described as 'the most controversial Municipal

Council in the world'.[16] He appointed and dismissed staff at will, forced resignations, issued instructions without reference to the council, and harangued the council for hours on end concerning the alleged wrongs of colonialism. Stormy, abusive meetings raged all day and long into the night. 'A Chinese carnival for baiting the British and cuddling the hawkers',[17] they played to crowded public galleries, packed with labourers who had never set foot in the council chamber before. At length the other parties rallied together to stop the mayor's activities, objecting to his attempt to create a special mayor's fund, which they alleged was being used for political purposes, accusing him of dismissing staff on political grounds and using his powers, particularly in the granting of hawkers' licences, to gain political influence.

In March 1959 the government took over part of the city council's functions, the next month Ong Eng Guan and the other PAP councillors resigned, and the Lim Yew Hock government appointed a commission of enquiry to investigate alleged irregularities in the working of the council.

The moderate PAP leaders prepared to make a bid for power in the elections scheduled to implement the new constitution in 1959. They drew up a comprehensive political, economic and social programme, and in February 1959 launched a pre-election campaign of weekly mass rallies to publicize their party's policy. At the first meeting they charged the Labour Front with receiving political funds from the United States government, which the Education Minister, Chew Swee Kee, was alleged to have converted to his own use. Lee Kuan Yew called for the immediate resignation of the entire Lim Yew Hock government 'in view of public disgust and loss of public confidence in the government as a result of recent disclosures'. Francis Thomas, Minister for Communications and Works, who disapproved of Lim Yew Hock's methods and his willingness if need be to use underworld support to smash the PAP, resigned from the government and supported Lee Kuan Yew's demand for a commission of enquiry.

The Labour Front had fallen apart. Lim Yew Hock organized a new Singapore People's Alliance Party to fight the coming elections, but this was merely a new name for the old Labour Front leadership with a few Liberal Socialist allies.

The disclosures, rumours and allegations, which came to light at the hearings of the commission of enquiry held in the weeks immediately prior to the May 1959 election, lent an unsavoury air which discredited the existing régime. By contrast PAP candidates, dressed in white as a symbol of incorruptibility, offered the electorate a constructive programme of economic and social reform. Claiming to be 'a party founded on principle, not opportunism',[18] the PAP leaders promised 'honest and efficient government', which would tackle the problems of education, labour, trade unions, social security, housing, rural development, health and the status of women. They pledged to work towards uniting Singapore with the Federation. Their primary aim was to 'infuse into our multi-racial society the spirit of belonging to a nation', and the next priority was to transform Singapore from a trading to a productive industrial society, 'to obtain for the general masses of the people a happy, full and secure livelihood'.[19]

The PAP contested all fifty-one constituencies and swept the polls to secure forty-three seats. Of the remaining eight seats, four went to the Singapore People's Alliance, three to UMNO-MCA Alliance candidates and one to an Independent. For the first time Singapore had a fully-elected government and one with a strong working majority.[20]

After 1959 the former leaders ceased to play a dominant role in Singapore politics. Lim Yew Hock returned to the new assembly but with diminished prestige, and David Marshall, who used trade union support to form a new Workers' Party, was defeated at the polls.

The old leadership had failed to realize that the balance of political power lay with the Chinese-educated masses. Unable to create a strong disciplined political organization to harness support at grass-roots level, it petered out in 1959 in dissensions, accusations and ignominy, which clouded the substantial achievements of the past four years. In the words of Francis Thomas, the Marshall government 'gave a tremendous psychological boost to the people'.[21] The two Labour Front governments won full internal self-government within the lifetime of the Rendel assembly, they created a special Singapore citizenship, drew up a programme for swift Malayanization of the public services and established the principle of official multi-lingualism. They inaugurated an education policy which averted a dangerous crisis and gave equality to the four main streams of Singapore's culture. They kept the path to merger open by maintaining a harmonious relationship with Kuala Lumpur.

The Labour Front governments also acted as a safety valve in tackling basic issues which threatened the future of Singapore, because by 1955 the colonial government was dangerously out of touch with the mass of Singaporeans. An official described the Singapore special branch in 1956 as 'unquestionably the world's greatest authorities on Communism in Asia',[22] but the efficiency of colonial repression tended to blind the authorities and to delude them into interpreting real grievances as subversion.

For all its faults, and despite the irresponsibility of Ong Eng Guan's tenure of office at City Hall, the Labour Front handed over the machinery of government intact and unimpaired, providing the foundation for the later success of the more disciplined, hard-hearded, calculating and practical People's Action Party.

THE PAP GOVERNMENT

The PAP's clear victory at the polls struck chill in the hearts of most conservatives, businessmen, and property owners, especially expatriates, who regarded the election as the prelude to irresponsible and vindictive government and ultimately to communism. Up to that time the party's activities had on the surface been almost entirely disruptive, and Lee Kuan Yew's group had given open encouragement to the extravagant demands of the extremist wing. The storms in the legislative assembly, the pandemonium at City Hall, the anti-capitalist tirades, the strikes and demonstrations which had troubled Singapore in the past four years had already undermined the confidence of businessmen. The intensity of the PAP's election campaign, the party's record of extremism and its inciting workers against employers frightened the professional and commercial community. European clubs prepared to be closed down, the price of property slumped, there was a flight of capital, many foreign firms moved their headquarters to Kuala Lumpur, and a general air of gloom and foreboding in business circles augured badly for the future economic health of Singapore, which was still largely dependent upon expatriate investment.

The immediate aftermath of the election seemed to confirm these predictions. Lee Kuan Yew refused to take office until PAP detainees were released and gave several of them posts in his government. The new régime launched an attack upon western culture and pressed heavily upon the hitherto privileged English-educated middle class. Six thousand civil servants suffered a cut in allowances and were drafted into carrying out 'voluntary' manual work on Sundays. Western films and magazines which were held to have a corrupting influence or to belittle Asian culture were banned. Special terms for British subjects to obtain Singapore citizenship were withdrawn. Even Raffles almost fell victim to the wave of anti-westernism, but after much debate the new leaders decided to let his statue remain for the time being.

The situation was in fact less unsettling than it appeared. Some of Singapore's most critical problems, such as education, language, and citizenship, were already well on the way to solution. Widespread fears of retribution against capitalism and colonialism were unfounded. Despite their fiery election speeches and appeals to mass emotionalism, the party's English-speaking leaders were not extremist, and the exuberance of the election obscured what they really stood for. After the 1958 constitutional talks in London, Lee Kuan Yew had satisfied the Colonial Office that if he formed a government its policies would be moderate and the disruptive elements in the PAP contained.

In the 1955 and 1959 assembly elections and in the municipal election of 1957 the PAP moderates ranted against colonialism and promised socialism, but they preached social welfare not ideological Marxist-Leninism. In 1959, while emphasizing self-reliance, they acknowledged that foreign capital was essential for building up the economy. They aimed to effect radical changes in Singapore society, but, as Lee Kuan Yew promised in a broadcast speech at the time of assuming office, this was to be 'a social revolution by peaceful means'.

Lee Kuan Yew's need to retain the support of the Chinese-educated masses and to keep to the left of the Labour Front government had driven him to cultivate an extremist public image, which was at variance with his long-term political thinking. Few in Singapore at that time were aware of the views which he had urged as a student in favour of a mildly socialist non-communist state, with independence to be achieved through constitutional means within the framework of the British Commonwealth. Nor was it generally appreciated how the moderates within the PAP had skilfully used the opportunities of the past few years to win control of the party's central machinery.

Lee Kuan Yew manipulated his grasp of English constitutional practice with great skill to give strength to his leadership and exploited this advantage over his left-wing allies. Realizing the suicidal mistake made by the Malayan Democratic Union in boycotting the 1948 elections, he had prevailed over Lim Chin Siong, Devan Nair and other left-wing advocates of direct action, in insisting the PAP should get a foothold in the 1955 assembly.

It was the PAP moderates who came to power in June 1959, and before their extremist colleagues were released from prison Lee organized the re-election of the existing central executive committee for a further two year period. Lim Chin Siong and three other ex-detainees were appointed political secretaries in the new government but were put in ministries where they could exert little power, nor did they obtain cadre membership of the party.

The new cabinet presented an imposing display of talent. The inner corps comprised Lee Kuan Yew, Toh Chin Chye, Goh Keng Swee and S. Rajaratnam, whose ability to act as a team despite personal differences proved a major source of strength to the moderate faction of the PAP. Toh Chin Chye was a dedicated party chairman, Goh Keng Swee was a practical economist and pragmatic thinker, and Rajaratnam was an able journalist. All three were willing to leave the limelight to Lee Kuan Yew, the most impressive public personality among the English-speaking group in the PAP, a compelling orator, fluent, direct, fundamental and analytical, who possessed the power to impress not only the English-educated of his own people but also foreign men of affairs and intellectuals.

The last British Governor, Sir William Goode, who acted as *Yang dipertuan negara* for the first six months, worked in close co-operation with the new government, helping by his sympathetic personality and unobtrusive tact to achieve a smooth transfer of power. In December 1959 he was succeeded by Yusof bin Ishak, former chairman of the public services commission. Born in Perak in 1910, the son of a government official, Yusof completed his schooling at Raffles Institution. An above-average student and keen sportsman, he became a journalist and founded the new *Utusan Melayu* in 1938. After a wartime in semi-retirement he revived the *Utusan* and attracted to the newspaper young, thinking Malays, some of whom rose to prominence in the later independence movements in Malaya and Singapore. A simple-living, hard working, disciplined, rather shy man, Yusof exemplified the radical, modern-minded Muslim. He stood for multi-racialism and secular modernization and worked to lift the condition of the Malays through their own efforts and through education.

When the office of Governor was abolished, the leading British authority was a Commissioner for the United Kingdom, who combined the office with that of Commissioner-General for the United Kingdom in South-East Asia. The British Commissioner remained in the background but had considerable powers, being entitled to see the agenda of cabinet meetings, together with all cabinet papers. He was also chairman of the internal security council, with the ultimate right in time of emergency to suspend the constitution and assume charge of the government, although these powers were never invoked.

In a statement of policy read by the *Yang di-pertuan negara* at the opening of the first session of the new legislative assembly, the government declared its stand, 'to end colonialism and establish an independent, democratic, non-Communist, socialist Malaya'. But from the start the PAP stood for incompatible objects. The moderates wanted to expand and diversify the economy and to achieve independence for Singapore through merger with the Federation of Malaya. The economic programme put forward by Goh Keng Swee as Minister of Finance ran counter to communism and was based upon achieving a common market with the Federation and encouraging industrialization in conjunction with private and, if need be, foreign capital. The pledge to achieve independence through merger with the anti-communist Federation also alarmed the extreme wing of the PAP. The problem of keeping extremists in check without losing the mass support behind them was more difficult to deal with in office than in opposition, and the new government was soon threatened with disaster when its leaders sought to establish economic stability and ease the way for union with Malaya.

The PAP pledged to achieve merger with the Federation of Malaya within its term of office. The *Yang di-pertuan negara's* policy statement declared, 'The future of Singapore lies ultimately in re-uniting with the Federation of Malaya as a state in an independent country.'

The British government also looked forward to an ultimate reunion of the two territories. The Governor of Singapore in opening the second session of the legislative assembly in August 1956 had said, 'The government will continue to foster and strengthen those links so that ultimately the narrow gap will be bridged bringing about the fusion of the two territories in a single united nation.'

The 'narrow gap', small in physical terms across the Johor Straits, was psychologically broad and was widening. Since their separation in 1946, different constitutional development and divergent education policies drove Singapore and the Federation further apart. Initially Tunku Abdul Rahman was prepared to consider incorporating Singapore into a confederation as a single state unit, but this was unacceptable to Singapore leaders, and discussions between Marshall and Tunku Abdul Rahman in December 1955 produced no agreement. By the time the

Federation achieved her independence in 1957 and Singapore was rent by political strife, the Malayan prime minister was no longer prepared to envisage merger on any terms.

While the official PAP policy aimed to dispel the impression of Singapore 'setting the pace in the social revolution of the whole of the South-East Asian archipelago',[23] their victory in 1959 intensified resistance in Kuala Lumpur to any ideas of union. To the essentially right-wing conservative Alliance the PAP was an ultra left-wing party. But the new Singapore government rejected any suggestions that it should seek a separate independence. A Malayan nation was, in the words of Rajaratnam, 'a historical necessity'.[24] 'Nobody in his senses believes that Singapore alone, in isolation, can be independent,' an official publication stated in 1960.[25] 'Without this economic base (the Federation), Singapore would not survive,' declared Lee Kuan Yew. 'Whatever we do,' commented Goh Keng Swee, 'major changes in our economy are only possible if Singapore and the Federation are integrated as one economy. The political reason for merger has a strong economic basis.'

The new government realized 'we must also resolve the...fears which make the Malay majority in the Federation not want the Chinese majority in Singapore'.[26] In 1954, when the party was born, the PAP created a Malay Affairs Bureau, under the direction of a journalist, Othman bin Wok, who became an assemblyman in 1963 and a cabinet minister two years later. Initially the PAP hoped to reach an understanding with the Singapore UMNO comparable to the alliance between the UMNO and the MCA in the Federation. It proposed a link in the city council in 1957 but was rebuffed by the Singapore UMNO on instructions from Kuala Lumpur. As a result a number of radical Singapore Malays resigned from UMNO to join the PAP, which devoted increasing attention to Malay problems.

In 1956 the PAP moderates advocated a unified education system to draw the Federation and Singapore together. The 1958 constitution acknowledged the Malays as the indigenous people, and the new government appointed a Malay as the first local *Yang di-pertuan negara,* recognized Malay as the national language and adopted a policy of bettering the condition and prospects of Singapore Malays through education and social development. A Malay education advisory committee was set up in 1959, the first Malay secondary school was opened the following year, and free secondary and university education was offered to suitably-qualified Singapore Malay citizens, together with liberal bursaries and allowances. More schools and community centres were established in Malay areas, and in 1960 a new Malay settlement was set up at Sembawang, with its own board of management, school, community centre and mosque.

Despite this policy of conciliation, talks held with Federation leaders in 1960 to discuss the possibilities of a pan-Malayan common market bore no fruit, and the PAP government found it impossible to woo the Federation and satisfy its own extremists at the same time. While the PAP moderates regarded the internal security council as the first constitutional link with Malaya, to the left wing it was a symbol of colonialism and oppression. The left wing criticized the government for accepting Malay as the national language and making Chinese schools conform to the policy laid down by the Labour Front regime.

The PAP leaders sought merger as a matter of urgency not only to achieve political independence but also to guarantee Singapore's economic survival. During the 1950s the preoccupation of the British and nearly all Singapore politicians with political issues obscured the fact that Singapore's most critical problem was her economy. In 1959 she was still a largely non-industrial society, dependent upon international entrepôt commerce, servicing the Malayan commodity trade, and income from British military bases. But her population was growing rapidly. Already there was considerable unemployment among the unskilled and semi-skilled, and the traditional colonial economy was not geared to meet increasing demands for employment and rising expectations in social services. In the mid-1950s more than half the population was under the age of twenty-one and Singapore had one of the highest rates of population growth in the world. At the same time expenditure on public health and other social services increased dramatically in the post-war years, and the education budget multiplied nineteen-fold in the decade from 1947 to 1957.

Goh Keng Swee, who became Finance Minister in 1959, aimed to throw off the degradation of poverty by rapid economic growth. The key to this was large-scale industrialization, which would mop up unemployment and finance social measures, of which the most crying need was to rehouse the population decently.

The immediate problem was to achieve financial stability and confidence. Before the election Goh Keng Swee had called for industrialization as the main economic priority, but his careful programme had gone almost unnoticed during the frenzied polemics of the election, and the subsequent PAP victory scared away foreign and local capital needed for Goh's programme.

Nor were the long-term prospects for industrialization bright. The International Bank for Reconstruction and Development feared that Singapore's economic expansion would not continue on a scale sufficient to keep pace with her growing population, the pressure on social services and demands for employment.[27] Singapore needed to curb her population growth, discipline her labour force and achieve an expanded domestic common market with the Federation.

Little was done to remedy this situation during the Labour Front's tenure of office. A master plan drawn up in 1958 mapped out future land use for the whole of Singapore island, and a start was made in building the first satellite town at Queenstown. But the government was largely preoccupied with problems of self-government, education, citizenship, and Malayanization while, as Lee Kuan Yew later admitted, the PAP opposition had used the trade unions as 'a banner behind which we challenged the whole system' and threatened to bring the economy to the point of collapse. The pan-Malayan common market seemed a remote dream. Meanwhile Singapore's birth-rate continued to soar. A voluntary Family Planning Association was started in 1949 but children continued to be regarded as a social and economic asset even among the poorest of Singaporeans.

It needed strong government to introduce a planned economy, to take ruthless action to curb population growth and discipline workers, but despite its landslide victory the PAP was not a united, monolithic party. Its election victory brought immediate internal strains between the moderates, who wanted to woo the Federation and capitalists in order to boost the economy, and the extremists who wanted to establish a socialist independent state and destroy capitalism and colonialism. The result was that political storm-clouds gathered in the first two years of the new government and industrialization was at a standstill in an atmosphere of uncertainty and labour unrest.

The PAP moderates wanted to change the trade unions into partners of the establishment, but for many trade unionists this transformation was difficult and unwelcome. Lee Kuan Yew had declared in 1959 that 'a PAP government is a government on the workers' side',[28] and promised to see that workers received a fair share of increased wealth in the form of better wages and good working conditions. But he warned against damaging the economy by a tussle between labour and capital. The objective was to secure 'industrial peace with justice', to achieve collective bargaining without strikes. An Industrial Relations Ordinance was enacted in 1960 providing for conciliation, arbitration and settlement of disputes by collective bargaining, and the following month an industrial arbitration court was set up whose decisions were binding in law. Trade unionists resisted government attempts to unify and reorganize the labour movement by new legislation providing for a National Trades Union Congress, which would co-operate closely with the government and have sole authority for calling strikes. The government then withdrew its trade unions bill and instead used the weapon of withholding and withdrawing registration from trade unions. This led to internal dissensions within the party, which were reflected in public bickering and militated against the political stability needed to lay the foundations for a sound economy.

The first open quarrel came not with the left-wing extremists but with the maverick Ong Eng Guan. Ong's standing in the party and his popularity with the masses had not been damaged as a result of the commission of enquiry into the proceedings of the city council, which was adjourned when heated allegations and arguments among witnesses and counsel threatened to prejudice the 1959 election. It was never reconvened, and controversy ended in July 1959 when the PAP absorbed the city council into the central government. For good or ill the days of municipal democracy were over, and the merging of local and central authority which Governor Ord had first proposed ninety years earlier was pushed through by the PAP government within a few weeks of taking office in order to streamline the machinery of government.

Most city council functions were transferred to a Ministry of National Development, which also directed economic planning and supervised the Harbour Board and a Housing Board, created in 1960 to take over and expand the functions of the Singapore Improvement Trust. Despite Ong Eng Guan's unsettling and unorthodox record as mayor, he was given this key ministry and was one of the three Singapore members on the influential internal security council. The appointment soon led to a clash of personalities and principles. Ong resented the rising star of Lee Kuan Yew as a threat to his own ambitions, while the party executive feared that Ong's appeal to Chinese chauvinism jeopardized their policy of courting Malaya and building up the economy. Moreover Ong used the same disruptive techniques to run his ministry which he had brought to his office of mayor, with the result that the ministry was ineffective, industrialization was at a standstill, and construction of housing fell below the level of previous years.

Within a few months Ong's powers were clipped: local government and the Harbour Board were removed from his portfolio. Ong then decided to challenge the party executive. In June 1960 he produced sixteen resolutions, charging the leaders with creating an undemocratic party structure and failing to advance with sufficient speed towards independence and socialism. But he found little support within the party and was opposed by both the moderates and the pro-communists. The party executive charged him with raising the resolutions to cover up his own ambitions and maladministration. He was dismissed from his ministry and expelled from the party, the first victim of the authoritarian discipline which he himself had helped to create.

Ong Eng Guan resigned from the legislative assembly, and a sordid and vindictive squabble ensued in which the executive sought to discredit Ong on personal moral grounds. This tarnished Ong's public image but did not diminish his charismatic appeal among the mass of supporters in his constituency at Hong Lim, where he fought the by-election to fill his former seat in April 1961. Using his personal popularity to exploit Chinese chauvinism and anti-colonialism, Ong demanded immediate and unconditional independence from Britain. He won a landslide victory, despite communist support for the government's candidate, and in June 1961 he formed a rival United People's Party.

This by-election was crucial. It threatened to topple the government, but the very danger of the ruling group in the PAP led to its salvation. Hitherto Tunku Abdul Rahman had aimed to keep the Federation clear from the turbulent politics of Singapore. Now, in view of the possible overthrow of the Singapore government and the rise of more extreme left-wing leaders, the Malayan leader feared that Singapore might achieve independence in 1963 as a communist state, potentially a 'second

Cuba'[29] and a danger to Malaya's security. Despite the immense difficulties of establishing a successful merger, the Malayan prime minister came to the reluctant conclusion that the dangers of a hostile, independent, communist-controlled Singapore were even more frightening.

In a luncheon speech to the Foreign Correspondents' Association in Singapore in May 1961, Abdul Rahman tentatively suggested that 'sooner or later' Malaya, Singapore, and the Borneo territories should work for closer 'political and economic co-operation'. This informal and unexpected suggestion received a delighted official welcome from the Singapore government but caused consternation among the PAP's left wing and precipitated an open confrontation between the moderates and extremists. The left wing dreaded the prospect of Singapore coming under the control of the anti-communist government in Kuala Lumpur and instead wanted independence for a separate Singapore, in which they were confident they would have the upper hand.

Conflict between the PAP party executive and its left wing was bound to come, and the ruling group was relieved to fight the inevitable battle on the issue of merger, on which it was difficult for the opposition to whip up popular emotions. Despite this the ensuing struggle almost resulted in annihilation of the PAP.

The test came as a result of a by-election in the Anson constituency in July 1961, when Lim Chin Siong, together with other left-wing PAP assemblymen, party officials and trade union leaders, withheld support from the government's candidate and backed his opponent, David Marshall, chairman of the Workers' Party. Marshall, who won by a small majority, stood for immediate independence, the abolition of the internal security council and the evacuation by Britain of her military bases in Singapore. Lim Chin Siong's group supported these demands and in addition protested against the proposed merger with Malaya and called for 'internal democracy in the PAP' and the release of all political detainees.

Meanwhile James Puthucheary, with Lim Chin Siong, Sandra Woodhull, and Fong Swee Suan, sought an urgent interview with Lord Selkirk, the British Commissioner-General for South-East Asia, at his residence at Eden Hall. In view of their suspicion that Lee Kuan Yew had long been collaborating with the British, they wished to assure themselves that Britain would not suspend the constitution if the prime minister were voted out of office and they themselves came to power. Not knowing why they wished to see him, and in accordance with his open-door policy, Lord Selkirk received the four dissident PAP members and stressed that the constitution was a free one, which they should respect.

The British intended to keep to the constitutional arrangements and timetable which had been laid down, but the 'Eden Hall tea party', coming at such a dangerous moment for Lee Kuan Yew, drove him to fury. He labelled it as a sinister British plot, in which they were conspiring to encourage the communists to political licence in order to force Lee either to smash the left wing for them or to resign and allow the British to step in and suspend the constitution.[30]

Whether or not Lee Kuan Yew believed the accusation he was making, which the opposition derided as 'a fairy tale of British lions and communist bears', he used it to stir up popular support and demanded a vote of confidence from the legislative assembly, although he could no longer be sure of commanding a majority.

During the debate in the legislature which raged all night, the extremists denounced the proposed merger as an imperialist plot. When the final division came, twenty-seven assemblymen voted for the government and twenty-four, including thirteen of the PAP's left wing, either abstained or voted against the motion of confidence.

The PAP rebel assemblymen, who included five parliamentary secretaries, then proceeded to form an opposition party, the Barisan Sosialis or Socialist Front, with Lim Chin Siong as its secretary-general. But they continued to sit in the assembly as representatives of their constituencies.

The PAP executive's strong parliamentary majority of 1959 had almost dwindled away, but its position in the party outside of the assembly was even more precarious. While the moderates had been in control of the central executive committee since 1957, the communists continued to consolidate their strength at the second level of leadership and at the base of the party structure. When the split came in July 1961 most key figures in the party's branches defected to the Barisan, and at the lower level the PAP's organization was almost crippled. Thirty-five branch committees resigned, and nineteen of the twenty-three paid organizing secretaries defected. Large numbers of cadres quitted, and only 20 per cent of the party's former members paid their subscriptions in 1962.[31] Many branches were almost destroyed. Eleven had less than twenty-five members each and one had only ten. The PAP lost most of its active party workers and a great mass of supporters, many of whom were not pro-communist but thought the party was doomed and scrambled to leave the apparently sinking ship.

The Barisan Sosialis started with a great deal of strength at grass-roots level and controlled most of the secondary political associations formerly attached to the PAP. It also had strength outside of the party organization among Nanyang University students and graduates and among trade unionists. At the time of the split the Barisan controlled two-thirds of organized labour, and forty-three unions publicly pledged their support for the new party.

This dangerous time proved to be the turning point in the fortunes of Lee Kuan Yew and the PAP. Impelled by the domestic crisis, the Singapore government continued its negotiations for merger with a vigour born of near-desperation. Tunku Abdul Rahman feared that a simple merger of Singapore and Malaya would give dominance to Singapore and to the Chinese, who would be the largest single community in a united Singapore/Malaya, comprising 43 per cent of the total population compared with 41 per cent Malays. He decided therefore to promote a looser partnership, based on a federation of Malaya, Singapore, and the British Borneo territories.

The principle of merger was approved at a regional conference of the Commonwealth Parliamentary Association held in Singapore in July 1961 with representatives from Malaya, Singapore, North Borneo, Brunei, and Sarawak, and formal agreement in principle was announced after the prime ministers of Singapore and Malaya conferred the following month. By November 1961 it was agreed that Singapore should be a special state with greater autonomy than the other units in the proposed federation, but Singapore citizens would not automatically become Malaysian citizens, since the terms for obtaining citizenship were more stringent for immigrant communities in Malaya. Singapore would have a smaller representation in the federal government than her population would otherwise warrant, but would be able to retain her own executive state government. Britain agreed to these merger terms, provided she retained control of the Singapore military bases.

The Barisan Sosialis opposed the government's approach to merger, criticizing in particular the restrictive citizenship stipulations. The communists would have liked to see Singapore part of a united republican Malaya but not of a conservative federation including the Borneo territories, which was designed by Tunku Abdul Rahman to prevent a communist takeover in Singapore, not to facilitate it.

Lee Kuan Yew set out in a series of broadcasts to enlist popular support for the proposed merger, portraying the Barisan as a communist organization, intent upon sabotaging the whole issue. The government decided to submit the question to a general referendum, presenting three alternative forms of merger, but not offering the choice of voting against the union.

The different elements in Singapore, Kuala Lumpur and the Borneo territories who opposed the merger began to make common cause. Some Barisan Sosialis members attended a meeting of the Indonesian Communist Party in December 1961 at which a resolution was taken against the Malaysia proposal, and in January 1962 a conference was held in Kuala Lumpur, at which the (Malayan) Socialist Front, Barisan Sosialis, Sarawak United People's Party, and Brunei Parti Ra'kyat combined to oppose the project. Subsequently the Barisan Sosialis, supported by David Marshall's Workers' Party and Ong Eng Guan's United People's Party, sent a mission of nineteen assemblymen to appeal to the United Nations committee on colonialism against the form of the proposed merger, but in July 1962 Lee Kuan Yew went to New York and successfully defended the issue.[32] He then proceeded to London to join the British and Malayans in working out final details.

The campaign leading up to the Singapore referendum held in September 1962 was as heated as an election, since the government's survival depended on the issue. Seventy-one per cent of the electorate voted in favour of the government's proposals, but 25 per cent showed their disapproval by returning blank or spoiled votes. The PAP's troubles were far from over, because by that time it had lost its parliamentary majority with the defection of an assemblywoman to the Barisan in July 1962. This meant that the government had to rely upon Lim Yew Hock and the Alliance representatives, who supported the PAP on the central issue of merger but on nothing else. The government's position was so precarious that a vacancy in the assembly arising from the death of a government minister was left unfilled, since the seat would almost certainly have fallen to the Barisan.

The position eased after February 1963, when the internal security council ordered the detention under Operation Cold Store of more than a hundred political, trade union, and student leaders, who had shown support for a rebellion in Brunei. The detainees included Lim Chin Siong and half of the Barisan's central executive committee, and the arrests provoked riots of protest, which in turn led to further arrests, mainly of second-echelon Barisan leaders. Once again the PAP party executive's rivals had been removed at a dangerous time in circumstances in which the Singapore government could lay the responsibility at the doors of others, this time the British and Malayans. The arrests were a severe blow to the Barisan. Tension in Singapore over the impending merger lessened, and Lee Kuan Yew gained considerable personal success in negotiating the final terms of the union which were very favourable to Singapore.

Under the Malaysia agreement, which was concluded in July 1963, Singapore, Sarawak and North Borneo (Sabah) were federated with the existing states of Malaya to form Malaysia.[33] Singapore left control over foreign affairs, defence and internal security to the central government but kept considerable powers over finance, labour and education. She was allotted fifteen seats in the new 127 member federal legislature but was to retain her own executive government and assembly, with her own *Yang di-pertuan negara* and separate public services commission. The Singapore government was to be responsible for executive administration and day-to-day policies in Singapore, and was obliged to pay to the central government only 40 per cent of her income from taxes, which amounted to 27 per cent of her total revenue.

The Federation of Malaysia was scheduled to come into being on 31 August 1963,[34] but Tunku Abdul Rahman deferred implementing the agreement until mid-September because of objections to the creation of the new state on the part of President Sukarno of Indonesia, who viewed the amalgamation of the former British territories in South-East Asia as a threat to the area and a denial of ethnic and cultural unity. Sukarno dreamed of uniting the Malay world and saw the formation of Malaysia as a menace to this pan-Indonesian concept. In June 1963 the foreign ministers of Malaya, Indonesia and the Philippines held an abortive conference at which the Philippines urged the formation of 'Maphilindo' to include all their countries and Sukarno condemned the Malaysia concept as a 'neo-colonialistic plot'. To satisfy his complaints, Tunku Abdul Rahman arranged for a United Nations survey, which confirmed that the people of the Borneo territories favoured the merger, but Sukarno refused to acknowledge Malaysia and organized an armed confrontation against the new state, which lasted for nearly three years.

Lee Kuan Yew declared Singapore's freedom unilaterally on 31 August 1963, the date originally set for the coming into being of the new federation, so that the island enjoyed an anomalous fifteen days of full independence before becoming part of Malaysia.

During that transitional period the PAP government called a snap election. Once union with Malaya was achieved, the basis for co-operation with the Alliance assemblymen disappeared. Hitherto the government had relied on their support to ward off left-wing attacks, but now it needed a fresh mandate to renew its power.

Three major parties contested the September 1963 election: the PAP, the Barisan Sosialis and a new Singapore Alliance, which consisted of the remnants of Lim Yew Hock's Singapore People's Alliance, together with the Singapore branches of the UMNO, Malayan Chinese Association and Malayan Indian Congress.

The result of the contest hung in doubt. While the PAP had lost much of the mass support it commanded in 1959, it had made a vigorous attempt to revive its organization and recruit new members, particularly among the Malay and Indian communities. The PAP's position was much stronger than it had been in its darkest hours two years before. Many of its leading opponents were in jail, but there were also more positive reasons for the party's improved fortunes. It had achieved its main political goal in successfully negotiating merger with the Federation and winning independence from colonial rule within the time limit promised in 1959. As the ruling party it held the initiative. For a long time the government had intended to hold an election immediately Malaysia came into being and planned its strategy accordingly. From the early months of 1963 Lee Kuan Yew took advantage of his position as prime minister to carry out extensive personal tours in all constituencies, particularly in the rural areas where the left wing had built up strong support in the mid-1950s.

The government controlled broadcasting and also television, which began a pilot service early in 1963. It developed local community centres as channels of communication under the direction of a People's Association, formed as an independent statutory body in 1960 under the prime minister's chairmanship. The 1952 Hill report on local government had recognized that the 'community centres should be the nursery of citizenship', whereas 'central government is anonymous, it is impersonal, to most people it is nothing more than an idea'.[35] In 1959 there were still only twenty-four community centres, but during the next four years the PAP built more than a hundred new ones, providing a social meeting place, recreation facilities, literacy classes, wireless and later television. Community centres were to become one of the most important instruments of government and consolidation of PAP power.

PAP rule had brought material benefits to large numbers of people. It had begun to build a broad base for industrialization and a better livelihood and had advanced some way in redistributing national income through extended social services, housing, education and health facilities. It had improved the status of women and brought relative peace to industrial relations. ·

After Ong Eng Guan's supersession, the government had turned its back on doctrinaire socialism and embarked on a vigorous pragmatic programme of economic expansion and social reform. In 1961 a four-year economic development plan was launched, based on a United Nations industrial survey mission headed by Dr. Albert Winsemius. The plan laid stress on economic development and industrial growth, with the government participating directly and providing background services.[36]

In 1961 an Economic Development Board was set up and work began on building an industrial estate at Jurong. Nearly 4,000 acres of swamp and wasteland were allotted for this project, which was developed with the help of World Bank experts.[37] Foreign and local investors were wooed with incentives in the form of tax holidays for pioneer industries and low rates of taxation for export-oriented manufactures, together with temporary protective tariffs against imports. In the early stage the main aim was to provide employment and the emphasis was on import substitution to develop the domestic market and on labour intensive industries, such as textiles.

By 1963 the government claimed to have the 'most advanced and enlightened labour legislation' in South-East Asia. The path to industrial peace was not easy. When the Barisan Sosialis splintered from the PAP in July 1961, the trade union movement also split into factions. Since pro-communists now dominated the secretariat of the Singapore Trade Union Congress, the government de-registered this body and encouraged the formation of the National Trades Union Congress in its place. The left wing formed a rival Singapore Association of Trade Unions, but many of its leaders were arrested in Operation Cold Store in February 1963.

The battle to expand the economy and overcome unemployment was accompanied by an attack on social problems. Under the direction of Lim Kim San, a successful businessman and member of a wealthy Singapore family, the Housing and Development Board set up in 1960 built almost as many houses and shops in its first three years as the more limited Singapore Improvement Trust had constructed in its thirty-two years. Initially the Board dealt with housing, slum clearance and resettlement but in 1962 it set up an urban renewal department and widened its scope to include urban development and redevelopment.

A public utilities board was established in 1963 to take over the water, electricity and gas functions of the former city council. Health facilities were improved. A mass X-ray campaign was launched in 1960 to combat tuberculosis, which was then the main killing disease. School health services were expanded, more maternal and child welfare clinics set up, better sanitation and immunization provided, particularly in outlying villages.

Vigorous attempts were made to enforce law and order. Full use was made of the emergency regulations to arrest secret-society men and keep others under supervision. Kidnapping gangs were broken up, and by 1963 the number of secret-society incidents dropped to less than half the monthly average of 1959.

The PAP fulfilled its promises to enhance the status of women by passing a Women's Charter in 1962, which prohibited polygamy, except among Muslims, and made divorce illegal other than by court order.[38]

The PAP accepted the principle of bi-lingualism and parity of the four language streams embodied in the education policy laid down in 1956 and promoted this policy vigorously. Expenditure on education rose from $600,000 in 1960 to $10,000,000 in 1963, and the school population increased over the same period from 290,000 to 430,000. The PAP pledged itself to provide universal free primary education as the first priority in education, and soon after taking office they embarked on a crash school-building programme and stepped up the recruiting and training of teachers. The number of students at the teachers' training college doubled from 2,500 in 1959 to 5,000 in 1965. In 1960 the first integrated schools were opened, where pupils could study in different language media but mingle socially under the same roof, and eighty-four such schools were built in the next seven years.

By September 1963 the four-year development plan was ahead of schedule,[39] the housing programme was up to the target set, and considerable strides had been made in education. Despite this, the PAP was afraid that the Singapore Alliance would split the moderate vote and that the Barisan might win outright control of the assembly. While the Barisan had suffered from the arrest of so many of its key officials, active party workers, and trade union and student supporters, it still had considerable mass appeal among workers and influential backing from Tan Lark Sye, chairman of the Nanyang university council, and other Chinese educational and community leaders.

The end of British colonialism had not settled the problem of the Chinese-educated, who felt that the fruits of self-government had fallen to the English-educated while they themselves continued to be excluded from influence and discriminated against.[40] Under the official education policy, Chinese schools received similar grants-in-aid to English schools, Chinese teachers enjoyed the same salaries and conditions, and Chinese school graduates were admitted to government service. Despite these material benefits, Chinese schools resented being drawn into the state system. Chinese schoolchildren boycotted examinations in December 1961 in protest against attempts to unify curricula and examinations.

The situation at Nanyang University threatened to erupt into violence when the Prescott commission, appointed in 1959 to report on the university, criticized its academic standards and advised against recognition of its degrees. This would have revived in more severe form the explosive position of 1955, in throwing frustrated graduates with unacceptable qualifications on the labour market. As a compromise Nanyang University graduates were admitted to the public service on an individual probationary basis, and the government proposed to raise the university's standards and open it to students of all races. But the university and its sponsors objected to the proposed erosion of its exclusively Chinese character. In view of falling enrolment in Chinese schools, in August 1963 the Chinese chamber of commerce called for more money to be spent on Chinese education, more Chinese schools, expanded facilities for higher education in the Chinese medium, together with more outlets for employment. This ran counter to the PAP's policy of creating a unified educational system, which many Chinese community leaders regarded as sabotaging Chinese education and culture.

Chauvinists wanted to preserve Chinese education intact without any compromise and the communists continued to use the issue to foment political dissent. Nanyang University students and guild of graduates supported the Barisan's election campaign, to which Tan Lark Sye contributed substantial funds.

The PAP fought the 1963 election on the issue of its past record as evidence of its effective economic and social policies and used every legal means to defeat its opponents. The government called the election in the minimum permissible time, excluded imprisoned Barisan leaders from standing by requiring candidates to present their papers in person, restricted meetings, froze funds of hostile trade unions and withdrew the registration of seven Barisan-dominated trade unions.[41]

To the surprise of Barisan and PAP supporters alike, the ruling party gained a clear victory in the election, winning thirty-seven of the fifty-one seats. The Barisan won thirteen, and the remaining seat fell to Ong Eng Guan, sole victor of the United People's Party. The biggest surprise of the election was the total defeat of the Alliance. It also saw the disappearance from the assembly of familiar leading figures, notably Lim Yew Hock, who did not contest the election, and David Marshall, who was heavily defeated at the polls. When the new assembly met in September 1963, Lee Kuan Yew was the sole survivor of the 1955 legislative assembly.

The PAP's victory was unique in that it was the first Singapore election to swing away from the left. The ruling party's success resulted partly from clever manipulation and pushing constitutional practice to the limit of the letter of the law. It owed much to the British-type system of one-member constituencies without proportional representation, designed to produce strong effective government in a two-party system, by which the PAP with less than 47 per cent of the vote won nearly 73 per cent of the seats. But the main reason for the party's victory was that it offered the best hope of orderly government to the business and professional community and had provided social and economic benefits to the middle and a large part of the working class. Many former right wing and moderate opponents now backed the PAP as the best guarantee for stability, law and order. The left wing stood in disarray, still commanding the sympathies of a large part of the population, but disunited and many of its leaders imprisoned or expelled.

The electoral victory gave the ruling party a clear mandate and it used this new power and confidence, backed by central government support, to put further checks on both Chinese chauvinism and communism. One of its first actions was to revoke Tan Lark Sye's citizenship, and it also prepared to destroy the base of the Barisan Sosialis. After the Barisan's defeat at the polls, the party reverted to the direct action tactics which its leaders traditionally preferred. The Malaysian government ordered the arrest of communist Nanyang university student leaders late in September 1963 following clashes with the police, boycotting of classes and protest marches. After calling abortive strikes in October 1963, the Barisan-dominated Singapore Association of Trade Unions was de-registered and its leaders, including three Barisan assemblymen, were arrested. The government also dissolved Barisan-dominated rural associations and hawkers' organizations, withdrew the registration of more Barisan-controlled trade unions and encouraged employers to dismiss Barisan trade union cadres.

The result was that within a few weeks of the formal coming into being of Malaysia the political situation in Singapore was quieter and more controlled than at any time since 1955.

On his return to power in September 1963 and against the new background of confidence, Lee Kuan Yew looked forward to turning Singapore into the 'New York of Malaysia, the industrial base of an affluent and just society'. He announced his government's first task would be to establish harmony with the central Malaysian government. The relationship was far from happy. The months before the final Malaysia agreement was drawn up had been a time of acrimonious haggling over finance, taxation, and trade, and for a time it appeared that negotiations had reached an impasse because Singapore was trying to drive too hard a bargain.

The terms hammered out in July 1963 were financially favourable to Singapore and included provision for a common market, which Singapore sought more eagerly than Kuala Lumpur. Both Malaya and Singapore were industrializing and ultimately wanted the expanded domestic market which economic union would bring. But their immediate economic interests conflicted. Singapore was unwilling to abandon her free port status, while the Federation did not want to open her tariff walls to the competition of Singapore industry with its initial benefit of tax-free raw materials. Singapore succeeded in getting a provision written into the Malaysia agreement for a progressive common market to be introduced over the next twelve years, causing the least possible upset to her entrepôt trade.[42]

Singapore had secured financial advantages at the expense of losing a great deal of goodwill in Kuala Lumpur, and the wounds inflicted on the relationship failed to heal. Despite the clash of economic and financial interests, it appeared in September 1963 that the two territories' immediate political interests coincided, because both governments wanted to hold in check the extreme left wing in Singapore. Paradoxically, it was political conflict which embittered the relations of the two partners and within two years brought the brief unhappy marriage to stormy divorce.

Lee Kuan Yew's unilateral declaration of independence and staging an immediate election irritated the central government, and Tunku Abdul Rahman visited Singapore personally to express pained shock at the rejection of the UMNO-Alliance candidates in Malay areas during the Singapore election. The Tunku declared there were 'a few traitors' in the Singapore Malay community but the attraction of Singapore Malays to the PAP was in fact widespread, since the party seemed more effective in advancing Malay interests than the Singapore UMNO. The PAP government had taken steps to promote the Malay language and education and had achieved a union with Malaya from which the Singapore Malays expected great benefits. After the breakaway of the Chinese left wing in 1961, Malay membership of the PAP expanded.

Lee Kuan Yew did not wholly welcome this shift of loyalties on the part of the Singapore Malays, since he wished the PAP to work in alliance with UMNO in the central government. The PAP leaders regarded the formation of Malaysia as the launching point for the creation of a socialist society and saw the conservative Malayan Chinese Association as a major obstacle in achieving this goal. In May 1963 Tan Siew Sin, Federal Finance Minister and president of the Malayan Chinese Association, declared that his party had 'a duty to perform in Singapore. It is Singapore's only hope for future stability and progress.'[43] The PAP resisted this proposed intrusion into Singapore politics and aimed eventually to supplant the Malayan Chinese Association as the second partner in the Malaysian Alliance. On the eve of the Singapore election in September 1963, when PAP candidates were opposing UMNO men, Lee Kuan Yew declared, 'It is my belief that the Tunku and Tun Abdul Razak will work with us— not today or next month, but in years to come. We calculate in terms of decades, not in terms of elections.'[44]

At that time the prime minister of Singapore declared the PAP would not contest the federal elections in 1964, and for some months the Singapore government wooed federal UMNO leaders, but the Singapore UMNO, backed by Kuala Lumpur, set out to reorganize its strength in opposition to the PAP.

The PAP then changed its tactics. Feeling that the exclusion from a share of power in Kuala Lumpur failed to reflect its new strength, and at the same time alarmed at the force of opposition to the new federation within Malaysia and in neighbouring countries, the PAP decided to bring forward its plans for taking an active role in Malaysian politics. In March 1964, on the eve of the federal elections, Toh Chin Chye, deputy prime minister of Singapore, announced the PAP would field a token team to show that the party was 'a force to be reckoned with in five years' and thus a worthy partner for UMNO. The PAP's immediate fear was that the radical Chinese urban population in Malaya might turn away from the Malayan Chinese Association, now renamed the Malaysian Chinese Association, and be driven into the arms of the communist-influenced Socialist Front. The Socialist Front, which had opposed the formation of Malaysia from the start, now joined forces with radical Malays, who looked to ultimate union with Indonesia. This anti-Malaysia front was reminiscent of the curious alliance of left-wing extremists and Malay-Indonesian nationalists who had opposed Malayan Union nearly twenty years earlier, and to the PAP it appeared to threaten the whole basis of the new federation.

The PAP based their election stand on support for Malaysia. They did not put themselves forward as a communal party, nor challenge the privileged position of the Malays, and they recognized Malay as the national language. They declared they were not fighting the central government nor UMNO but only the Malaysian Chinese Association. Lee Kuan Yew claimed, 'A vote for the MCA is a vote for continued inactivity, complacence and decadence...there must be a jolt in the leadership of the government.'

The party's election campaign was disastrous. The central government interpreted it as a breach of faith, and at his opening election rally Tunku Abdul Rahman declared his solidarity with the Malaysian Chinese Association, repudiating the proffered alliance with the PAP. 'We don't want them,' he declared.[45] Despite their non-communal stand, PAP candidates drew the main force of Malay attack, because they appeared as the spectre of potential Singapore Chinese dominance, long feared by the Malays.

The campaign was hastily undertaken, without adequate preparations, with no election organization or local branches on the mainland. Of the PAP's eleven parliamentary and fifteen state candidates, only one was successful, and that by a slender majority in a constituency formerly held by a Chinese independent, not in a Malaysian Chinese Association stronghold. The successful candidate, C.V. Devan Nair, former leftist union leader and detainee, had remained loyal to the PAP in the 1961 split. His lone voice was ineffective in the Malaysian parliament and his absorption with Malaysian politics in the next few years was a major factor in the slow growth of the National Trades Union Congress in Singapore.

The ill-judged intervention into federal politics arose partly from impatience, which was characteristic of the PAP leadership. In reviewing its first year in office in 1960, a PAP publication had admitted to 'minor mistakes of haste, born out of impatience to put the world right...errors not of the rashness of the policy to be implemented but of the intemperate haste in not preparing and carrying the people.'[46] The urge to set the world aright was firmly imbedded in PAP philosophy, and the same precipitate haste marked its activities in Malaysia in 1964 and 1965. The Singapore rulers believed that racialism could best be eliminated by vigorous attack upon economic and social inequalities and injustice affecting all races. The Alliance leaders, on the other hand, were convinced that racial distrust ran deep and could only be soothed away by cautious and gradual learning to live together. 'Young men...want to rush things,' complained the Tunku, 'Why rush?...why not take time to make a strong nation.'[47]

The Singapore government's election bid was not merely an error of tactics. The socialist leaders of Singapore were out of tune with the inherent conservatism and communalism of federal politics, and in the 1964 elections they entered an unfamiliar arena. The electoral tussle revealed the innate incompatibility and lack of understanding between the two territories, which threatened the incorporation of Singapore into Malaysia from the beginning. To bring together the essentially urban, commercial and industrial society of Singapore with the rural, racially-divided society of the Federation of Malaya was a most difficult undertaking, given even the most favourable of circumstances. The basic economic needs of the two communities were so fundamentally different that any effective government in the two places must clash on priorities and direction. Constitutional development and nationalism had followed diverse paths. Malaya's independence had been gained by a westernized multi-racial élite, but after 1957 the quest for nationhood led, as it did in other South-East Asian nations, to the development of cultural nationalism, in this case Malay nationalism. As in other parts of South-East Asia, local nationalists saw the prosperous Chinese middle class, which controlled a large part of the region's trade, as a threat to its own economic nationalism. But anti-Chinese feeling held a unique place in Malay nationalism. Malayan Chinese tended to be identified with communism, since the movement in Malaya was almost exclusively a Chinese concern. Distrust of the large Chinese community's loyalty was intense. Despite Peking's attempts from the mid-1950s to spell out a new doctrine, repudiating the Kuomintang *jus sanguinis* principle and urging overseas Chinese either to take up local citizenship or steer clear of local politics, fears and suspicions of the loyalty of the Chinese community ran as strong as ever.

Alarmed by the upsurge of Malay cultural nationalism, the PAP sought to divert politics from communalism towards socio-economic questions. This inevitably appeared to be anti-Malay and so aroused the very communal passions which the PAP aimed to allay.

Singapore's premature rush into federal politics was fatal to the unity of Malaysia. Tunku Abdul Rahman and Tun Abdul Razak, Malaysia's deputy prime minister, considered Lee Kuan Yew had broken a pledge to stay clear of federal politics and not mobilize the peninsular Chinese. This drove the UMNO/MCA partners closer together, created suspicions about the personal ambitions of Singapore leaders, particularly of Lee Kuan Yew, and set the relationship between Singapore and the central government on a downhill track, along which it continued to slide with increasing momentum.

Singaporeans began to resent the strains and irritations which merger in Malaysia involved.[48] Indonesian confrontation brought physical violence and damaged trade. Indonesian saboteurs exploded a number of bombs in Singapore between September 1963 and May 1965, and gunboats seized many Singapore fishing-craft. By 1964 Singapore felt the pinch at the cutting off of her vital Indonesian trade, and the central government demanded a larger proportion of her revenue to help meet expanded defence expenditure.

Industrialization progressed but at a disappointingly slow pace in the mid-1960s. It was difficult to attract new industries to the Jurong industrial estate, which acquired the nickname 'Goh's Folly'.[49] Despite taxation incentives, capitalists were wary of investing in a politically unstable spot, with fairly high wages and a tiny domestic market. Singapore's traditional Chinese firms and British agency houses, which dominated the economic scene, were not geared to spearhead industralization. Foreign capital was reluctant to be wooed. The main attraction was to textile manufacturers from Hong Kong and Taiwan, who found in Singapore a means of by-passing quota restrictions on imports of textiles into Britain, but their activities merely soured Singapore's relations with Britain and did little to provide substantial employment, let alone lay a healthy foundation for an industrial Singapore.

Singapore industrialists, who hoped merger would solve many of these problems, soon complained that they were unfairly treated in the granting of pioneer status certificates, which were subject to Kuala Lumpur's approval, and in the sharing out of textile export quotas. There was a growing feeling that membership of Malaysia had been purchased too expensively.

The most disappointed group of all were the Singapore Malays who had hoped union with Malaya would bring them the same preferential quotas in employment opportunities, promotions and licences which applied in the Federation. At the time of merger the Singapore government undertook to encourage Malay as the national language and to safeguard Malay 'political, educational, religious, economic and cultural interests'. But apart from offering financial benefits in education to give Malay children the chance to better themselves, the Singaporeans did not intend to adopt the Malayan system of privileges. In addition many Malays, particularly in the Geylang area, saw urban renewal schemes, which proposed to move them from their *kampongs* into modern high-rise flats, as a threat to their established way of life.

The Singapore UMNO, which reorganized itself after the 1963 debacle, found a ready response among the Malay community and in June 1964 asked for legislation to give economic advantages to Malays. Lee Kuan Yew invited representatives of Malay organizations to meet him and state their grievances, but in the meantime the Singapore UMNO called a convention with representatives from 150 bodies. At this meeting held early in July ultra-UMNO leaders from Kuala Lumpur, notably the secretary-general, Dato Syed Jaffar Albar, played upon the fears and grievances of the Singapore Malays to stir up feelings against the government. The convention decided to demand special rights for Malays and formed a Singapore Malay National Action committee. The Malay press meanwhile waged a constant campaign against the PAP, the *Utusan Melayu* accusing Lee Kuan Yew of trying to turn Singapore into another Israel and suppressing Muslims.

Representatives from a hundred Malay political, religious, educational, cultural and literary organizations met the prime minister a few days later, but Lee Kuan Yew refused to give special concessions to the Malay minority, except in the field of education. The *Yang di-pertuan negara,* Yusof bin Ishak, appealed for forbearance, but tension reached breaking point, and fighting broke out between Malay and Chinese youths during a Muslim procession in the Geylang district in celebration of Prophet Muhammad's birthday. The whole island was put under curfew and the trouble continued for a week. Twenty-two people were killed, hundreds injured, and the atmosphere was heavy with bitterness and fear. Early in September communal violence broke out again, this time partly induced by Indonesian provocation and coinciding with Indonesian parachute landings on the mainland. Again law and order were restored within a week, but tension remained.

The violence was confined to a small minority, and most people were glad to keep to their houses and steer clear of trouble, but the riots came as a deep shock. In 1949 the colonial government had dismissed problems of race in Singapore with the remark, 'There are no social problems of race or cultural relations of any magnitude. All races live and work harmoniously together.'[50] Singapore had prided herself on her racial tolerance and communal peace, which now seemed threatened for the first time in her history. A commission of enquiry was appointed to investigate the riots but its findings were never published.

Lee Kuan Yew and Tunku Abdul Rahman were both distressed at the outbreak of communal violence, and in September 1964 they made an agreement to avoid sensitive issues for two years, but it was an uneasy truce. The following month a Malaysian minister, Khir Johari, declared that the Singapore Alliance aimed to win the next election in Singapore, and Toh Chin Chye retorted that the PAP should be reorganized to 'get at Malaya'.[51] Early in 1965 Lee Kuan Yew made public speeches in several Malayan towns in which he accused extremist Alliance leaders of trying to force Singapore's political parties into communal lines.

After their setback in the 1964 federal election, the PAP had declared it would continue its policy of 'multi-racialism and Malaysian nationalism, offering the democratic socialist way to a more equal and just society— appealing to Malay and non-Malay have-nots to raise educational and living standards'. Impelled by the merging in April 1965 of the four separate Alliance parties in the states of Malaya, Singapore, Sabah, and

Sarawak to form a Malaysian National Alliance Party, the PAP set out to draw together the radical parties of the various Malaysian territories to form a united opposition.

In May 1965 delegations from the PAP and four opposition parties from the states of Malaya and Sarawak met in Singapore to form a Malaysian Solidarity Convention. Its slogan was 'a democratic, Malaysian Malaysia', and it appealed for an end to communal politics and for political affiliation on the basis of 'common political ideologies and common social and economic aspirations'. It insisted the main problem was 'how best to meet quickly and effectively the economic, social and cultural aspirations of the under-privileged majority of all races without destroying economic stability'.[52]

While the Malaysian Solidarity Convention claimed to be a non-communal party, organized on ideological and socio-economic lines, in practice it appealed mainly to non-Malays, particularly to the Chinese, and the equality it sought implied the ultimate withdrawal of Malay privileges. Consequently instead of reducing communal tensions, the Malaysian Solidarity Convention widened racial rifts.

By the middle of 1965 Lee Kuan Yew was the focal point of hatred among the right wing of UMNO, who feared the Singapore government planned a Chinese takeover of Malaysia. However much Lee Kuan Yew might regard himself as a non-communal exponent of secular modernization, to conservative Malays he personified what Malays feared in the Chinese: harsh, grasping and aggressive ambition, a threat to their religion and their culture. UMNO extremists saw the Malaysian Solidarity Convention as a naked attempt by Lee Kuan Yew to link Singapore, Sarawak, and Sabah against Kuala Lumpur and seize power for himself. They were alarmed at Lee's growing international stature, his continual attacks upon the central government and his open contempt for many features of Malay life.

Lee himself did nothing to soften this impression. In May 1965 he declared, 'If we must make trouble, let us have it now instead of waiting for another five or ten years.'[53] Lee's abrasive personality came out clearly in his frequent appearances on television, which quickly supplanted radio as the most compelling channel of political communication in homes and community centres. UMNO leaders demanded the suppression of PAP speeches, and in May 1965 the Malaysian Minister of Information and Broadcasting threatened to take over radio and television services in Singapore if they discredited the central government. Meanwhile Kuala Lumpur protested when the Singapore Ministry of Culture distributed its *Malaysian Mirror* to schools in Malaya, but Lee Kuan Yew declared this was necessary since 'every day dreadful poison is being poured out in (the Malay press) about the PAP being communalistic and anti-Malay'.

Parliamentary sessions in Kuala Lumpur in May and June 1965 were filled with abuse, even the moderate leaders of the Alliance being drawn into bitter dispute. Tan Siew Sin declared it was impossible for Kuala

Lumpur and Singapore to co-operate while Lee Kuan Yew remained prime minister, and UMNO extremists demanded the arrest of Lee and other Singapore ministers. Tunku Abdul Rahman insisted there were no constit itional grounds for arresting them, but he was becoming increasingly incensed by the speeches made by the PAP leaders, sensitive to the impact Singapore leaders were making abroad, and to criticism of the central Malaysian government in the foreign press.

At the beginning of June, saddened and anxious, Tunku Abdul Rahman left to attend a British Commonwealth prime ministers' conference in London. Later that month, at Lee Kuan Yew's request, the Singapore prime minister met Tun Abdul Razak to try to resolve their differences. No compromise could be reached, and the talks merely brought fresh outbursts from Malay extremists and the Malay press. The weeks which followed were filled with false rumours of arrests and assassinations. In July the central government ordered the closure of the Bank of China in Singapore, which was of crucial importance to the island, since it financed many small businessmen and also the large food trade from China.

The crisis became more acute with the prolonged absence of Tunku Abdul Rahman, who fell ill in London. The special branch reported the build-up of pressures and the possibilities of racial riots, and Razak flew to visit Tunku Abdul Rahman in his London hospital. The Malaysian prime minister feared the situation was slipping from his control, that no compromise was possible with the PAP leaders and that he was losing his grasp over the extremists in his own party. Tunku Abdul Rahman and Abdul Razak decided they must either depose the Singapore government or eject Singapore from Malaysia. To remove the PAP government by force was not practicable, and in any event such a move would have been resisted by the British and Australians, who still held a crucial place in defence and security. The expulsion of Singapore seemed the only solution.

The Tunku determined to do this on his return to Kuala Lumpur early in August but knew that if his intentions leaked out, Malaysia's Commonwealth partners would put pressure on him not to evict Singapore, particularly in the middle of Indonesian confrontation. Therefore the Malaysian leaders determined to act quickly and secretly. Lee Kuan Yew was summoned to Kuala Lumpur and tried in vain to argue against the decision, still hoping for a compromise which would provide for a looser association in Malaysia. Learning of the Tunku's decision a few hours before the formal announcement was due, the British and Australian diplomatic representatives urged him to change his mind, but the Tunku was adamant.

Singapore's independence was proclaimed on 9 August 1965, and she assumed full sovereignty over her territory.[54] She was immediately recognized as an independent republic within the Commonwealth by Britain, Australia, New Zealand, and the United States, and in September 1965 she was admitted to the United Nations.

1. People's Action Party, *The Tasks Ahead* (Singapore, 1959), p. 6.

2. *ST,* 29 March 1955.

3. The Malay Union Alliance, a parliamentary coalition of UMNO and Malayan Chinese Association.

4. Singapore Legislative Assembly, *Report of the All Party Mission to London, April/May 1956,* Cmd. 31 of 1956 (Singapore, 1956).

5. Singapore Legislative Assembly, *Report of the All Party Committee of the Singapore Legislative Assembly on Chinese Education,* Cmd. 9 of 1956 (Singapore, 1956).

6. Singapore Legislative Assembly, *White Paper on Education Policy,* Cmd. 15 of 1956 (Singapore, 1956).

7 .Singapore Legislative Assembly, *Singapore Chinese Middle Schools Students Union,* Sessional Papers, Cmd. 53 of 1956 (Singapore, 1956).

8. Singapore Legislative Assembly, *Singapore Constitutional Conference, March/April 1957* (Singapore, 1957).

9. Singapore Legislative Assembly, *The Communist Threat in Singapore,* Sessional Cmd. Paper No. 33 of 1957 (Singapore, 1957).

10. Ministry of Education, *First Triennial Survey of Education, 1955–57* (Singapore, 1959).

11. Great Britain, *State of Singapore Act 1958,* Chapter 59, 6 & 7 Eliz. II (London, 1958); *Singapore (Constitution) Order in Council,* laid before parliament 27 November 1958, *Gazette Supplement* No. 81 of 27 November 1958 (Singapore, 1958). See also Creech-Jones Papers, MSS. Brit.Emp. S 332, Box 26, File 11 (Rhodes House, Oxford).

12. Great Britain, *Exchange of Letters on Internal Security Council of Singapore,* Cmd. 620 of 1958 (London, 1958).

13. Singapore Legislative Council, *Report on the Reform of Local Government* by L.C. Hill, November 1951 (Singapore, 1952).

14. Singapore Legislative Assembly, *Report of the Committee on Local Government* (the McNeice Report), (Singapore, 1956).

15. Lim Choon Meng (Liberal Socialist) in *Singapore Legislative Assembly Proceedings* (Singapore, 1956–7), Vol. 2, Col. 2452.

16. Singapore, *Minutes of City Council Proceedings,* 30 July 1958.

17. W.A. Hanna, *Sequel to Colonialism* (New York, 1965), p. 31.

18. Toh Chin Chye in People's Action Party, *The Tasks Ahead,* February 1959, p. 2.

19. Ibid., April 1959, pp. 8, 9; Goh Keng Swee in *The Tasks Ahead,* March 1959, p. 19.

20. For detailed commentary on the election see Ong Chit Chung, 'The 1959 Singapore General Election', *JSEAS,* VI, 1 (1975), pp. 61–86.

21. F. Thomas, *Memoirs of a Migrant* (Singapore, 1972), p. 99.

22. J.B. Perry Robinson, *Transformation in Malaya* (London, 1956), p. 66.

23. *Petir,* III (no. 1), p. 1, 17 July 1959.

24. S. Rajaratnam, April 1959, *Tasks Ahead,* p. 12.

25. Singapore Ministry of Culture, *The Socialist Solution: an Analysis of Current Political Forces in Singapore* (Singapore, 1960).

26. People's Action Party, *Sixth Anniversary Celebration Souvenir* (Singapore, 1960).

27. International Bank for Reconstruction and Development, *The Economic Development of Malaya* (Singapore, 1955), p. 28.

28. Lee Kuan Yew, March 1959, *Tasks Ahead,* p. 24.

29. *Straits Budget,* 21 November 1962.

30. Lord Selkirk in letter to author, 12 December 1973. The reason for Lee's anger given by Dennis Bloodworth in the London *Observer* 22 July 1961 and repeated in V. Purcell, *The Revolution in South East Asia* (London, 1962), p. 11, namely an allegation that the British Commissioner-General had conferred with the extremists on his return from London before he saw Lee himself, was incorrect. Lord Selkirk had in fact been in contact with the prime minister a few days earlier.

31. Pang Cheng Lian, *The People's Action Party* (Singapore, 1971), p. 15.

32. *Comments by the Singapore government on the Memorandum by Nineteen Singapore Opposition Assemblymen to the United Nations Committee on Colonialism* (Singapore, 1962).

33. Singapore Legislative Assembly, *Malaysia Agreement concluded between the U.K., Federation of Malaya, North Borneo, Sarawak and Singapore*, Cmd. paper 24 of 1963 presented to Legislative Assembly, 30 July 1963 (Singapore, 1963); *Malaysia Agreement: Exchange of Letters between Prime Minister and Ministers of Singapore, Deputy Prime Minister and Ministers Federation and British Colonial Office*, Misc. 5 of 1963, presented to Singapore Legislative Assembly by Prime Minister, 26 July 1963.

34. *Malaysia Act No. 26 of 1963* (Kuala Lumpur, 1963); *Sabah, Sarawak and Singapore (State Constitutions) Order in Council*, 29 August, 1963, *State of Singapore Government Gazette, Subsidiary Legislation Supplement*, 16 September 1963, No. 1493 Malaysia.

35. Colony of Singapore, *Report on the Reform of Local Government*, (Singapore, 1952).

36. Ministry of Finance, *State of Singapore Development Plan, 1961–1964* (Singapore, 1961).

37. Economic Development Board, *The Jurong Story* (Singapore, 1967).

38. Singapore Legislative Assembly, *Report of the Select Committee on the Women's Charter Bill* (the Oehlers report), L.A. 16 of 1960 (Singapore, 1960).

39. Ministry of Finance, *State of Singapore First Development Plan, 1961–64. Review of Progress for the Three Years Ending 31 December 1963* (Singapore, 1964).

40. Discussed in Wang Gungwu, 'Traditional Leadership in a New Nation: The Chinese in Malaya and Singapore', in G. Wijeyewardene (ed), *Symposium on Leadership and Authority* (Singapore, 1968), pp. 209–26, and in S.T. Alisjahbana (ed.), *The Cultural Problems of Malaysia in the Context of Southeast Asia* (Kuala Lumpur, 1966).

41. F.L. Starner, 'The Singapore 1963 Elections', in K.J. Ratnam and R.S. Milne, *The Malayan Parliamentary Election of 1964* (Singapore, 1967).

42. International Bank for Reconstruction and Development, *Report on the Economic Aspects of Malaysia* (Rueff Report), (Kuala Lumpur, July 1963) supported the proposed common market.

43. *ST*, 23 May 1963.

44. *ST*, 10 September 1963. Tun Abdul Razak was then deputy prime minister of Malaysia.

45. *Sunday Times*, 15 March 1964.

46. Singapore Ministry of Culture, *The Socialist Solution* (Singapore, 1960).

47. *ST*, 8 March 1965.

48. See M. Leifer, 'Singapore in Malaysia: the politics of Federation', *JSEAH*, VI, 2 (1965), pp. 54–70, and P. Boyce, 'Policy without Authority: Singapore's External Affairs Power', *JSEAH*, VI, 2 (1965), pp. 87–103, for contemporary comment.

49. See W.A. Hanna, 'Go-ahead at Goh's Folly', *American Universities Field Staff Inc., Southeast Asia Series*, Vol. XII, no. 3 (New York, 1964) for these early difficult years.

50. Colony of Singapore, *Information on Singapore for 1949 transmitted to the United Nations* (Singapore, 1949).

51. *Straits Budget*, 1 November 1964.

52. Singapore Ministry of Culture, *Separation: Singapore's Separation from the Federation of Malaysia, 9 August 1965* (Singapore, 1965).

53. *ST*, 22 May 1965.

54. *Independence of Singapore Agreement* in *Singapore Government Gazette Extraordinary*, VIII, no. 66, 9 August 1965.

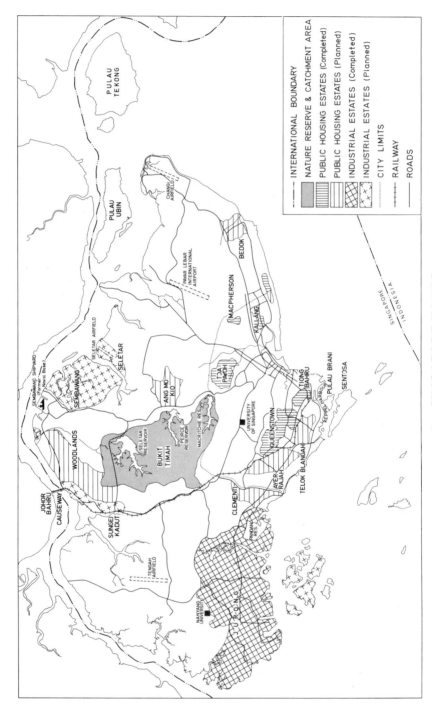

2. SINGAPORE IN 1975

INTERNATIONAL BOUNDARY

NATURE RESERVE & CATCHMENT AREA

PUBLIC HOUSING ESTATES (Completed)

PUBLIC HOUSING ESTATES (Planned)

INDUSTRIAL ESTATES (Completed)

INDUSTRIAL ESTATES (Planned)

CITY LIMITS

RAILWAY

ROADS

# IX

# Independence: The First Decade
# 1965–1975

SINGAPORE'S expulsion from Malaysia destroyed the basis on which responsible Singapore politicians had considered the state viable. She was unique among colonial countries in having independence thrust upon her unilaterally, her prime minister publicly lamenting in tears this 'moment of agony'. The PAP leadership had consistently repudiated any suggestion that Singapore should seek a separate independence. Only three years earlier an official memorandum to the United Nations committee on colonialism had declared, 'Singapore ... is dependent on the Federation of Malaysia for its water supply, its trade and its survival. It is not viable by itself.'[1] Now Singapore was alone, and the impossible had to be achieved. She must survive.

For Lee Kuan Yew, Singapore's expulsion from Malaysia was a bitter personal defeat and destroyed his foremost political achievement. On separation day he was distraught and in despair, convinced that Singapore was doomed. Less than two months earlier he had declared, 'The question of secession is out. Any change must be a step forward and not backward.'[2] He had fought to achieve a working relationship with Kuala Lumpur in the last months, but on his terms, and the passionate energy with which he waged the battle contributed much to the final break.

For his senior colleagues, all of whom came from the Federation, the separation meant personal anguish of a different order. Lee himself was a Singaporean, but Toh Chin Chye was born in Taiping, Goh Keng Swee in Malacca, Rajaratnam's family lived in Seremban, and the majority of the Singapore cabinet were Malayan-born.

Most Singaporeans were shaken but did not share the top leadership's deep dismay. Many were relieved that Singapore was to be spared further bouts of the communal stress which caused the bitter racial riots of 1964 and rose to a crescendo of hysteria in the middle of 1965. Some businessmen welcomed liberation from Kuala Lumpur's economic policy with unconcealed glee. Even within the PAP hierarchy some central executive committee members were convinced that separation was inevitable and in some ways desirable.[3]

At first the Singapore government spoke of Malaya as 'one people now divided into two arenas', 'one people in two countries', and aimed to make Singapore a model of tolerance which would eventually lead to the rebuilding of the Malaysian federation.[4] Malay remained Singapore's national language, the new national anthem was sung in Malay and her Muslim *Yang di-pertuan negara,* Yusof bin Ishak, became the republic's first president. Few Malaysian leaders took so sanguine a view of reunification, but in his speech to the federal parliament announcing the separation in August 1965 Tunku Abdul Rahman declared, 'In diversity I am convinced we can find unity, or in ordinary everyday parlance absence will make the hearts grow fonder.'

Initially this hope was not fulfilled. The separation agreement provided for co-operation in economic questions, defence and foreign policy, but the early months of separation put new strains on the relationship between Malaysia and Singapore.[5] The two governments set out to produce competitive, instead of co-operative, economies. Quotas, duties, and retaliatory tariffs caused great distress, particularly among manufacturers who had set up industries based upon a united Singapore/ Malaysia domestic market.

The pan-Malayan immigration policy ended soon after separation, and immigration controls at both ends of the Causeway brought considerable hardship to people who had moved freely between the mainland and Singapore to live and work.

Kuala Lumpur was incensed when immediately after separation Lee Kuan Yew expressed interest in resuming friendly trading relations with Indonesia, despite the state of political confrontation. When Indonesia and Singapore revived a limited barter trade in January 1966, Malaysia threatened in retaliation to divert all her rubber and palm oil exports to Port Swettenham, the present Port Klang.

The following month quarrels flared up over Malaysia's right to station troops in Singapore, and to Tunku Abdul Rahman's annoyance Singapore withdrew unilaterally from the joint defence council and combined operations committee.

The political and personal abuse which had tarnished relationships during the union persisted, although in a lower key. Lee Kuan Yew offended Malaysia by speaking of her as 'a mediaeval feudal society',[6] while UMNO singled out PAP Malay leaders for special attack as disloyal to their race, 'like peas who have lost their pod'.[7]

From the middle of 1966, with rising confidence that independent Singapore could survive, talk of reunification with Malaysia began to fade away. Singapore's leaders set out to cultivate a sense of separate nationhood with such success that within a few years most Singaporeans accepted their independent status as inevitable. Strange myths sprang up concerning Singapore's brief involvement in Malaysia. Some regarded the merger as a PAP tactic to get rid of the left-wing opposition and seize total independence for Singapore. Others saw it as an anti-Chinese plot devised by Britain and Kuala Lumpur, a 'curiously quixotic, drawing-room plan'.[8]

At the time of Singapore's expulsion from Malaysia the PAP government was in a strong position at home. The merger, however painful at the time, had saved Singapore's ruling régime and averted the apparently inevitable political chaos which the island faced in 1961. Kuala Lumpur's arrest of key Barisan figures brought a crisis of leadership in the opposition party, and the Barisan's 'Crush Malaysia' slogan had little appeal to the mass of Singapore Chinese.

The PAP's strength was demonstrated in July 1965, when Ong Eng Guan resigned from the assembly and the PAP carried the seat by a large majority in a straight by-election fight with the Barisan. Indeed this victory in the Hong Lim constituency, where the PAP's defeat four years before had driven Tunku Abdul Rahman into proposing the merger, showed that Kuala Lumpur need no longer fear a communist take-over in Singapore and made the Malaysian cabinet less reluctant to force the break.

Most Singaporeans did not hold the PAP leadership to blame for the eviction from Malaysia. There was no cabinet split nor any move to change the leadership, and many new recruits joined the party in the later months of 1965. The PAP cabinet was a strong and effective team, in command of their party. Control of the central executive had been kept tightly in the hands of the trusted few since the communist bid to take over the party in 1957, and ·in reconstructing the party after the 1961 split the central executive extended its hold at the grass-roots level and over outside supporting organizations, such as cultural groups and trade unions. The need for cohesion in the struggles of the 1950s and early 1960s forged a remarkable solidarity of PAP leadership in later years, preserving a united outward front despite personal differences.

The Barisan Sosialis sapped its strength further by repudiating Singapore's independence as spurious, an unpopular stand which split the party's rank and file. It claimed the new republic was a neo-colonial state, tied to Britain by a defence treaty, her economy dominated by foreign capitalists and her freedom trammelled by emergency regulations. The five remaining Barisan assemblymen who had escaped arrest in the past few years boycotted the new parliament when it met in December 1965 and formally resigned their seats in October 1966.

Again the Barisan attempted to use student discontent as a political weapon and organized boycotts at Nanyang University in October and November 1965, which led to the expulsion of eighty-five students. Government moves to exclude political agitators from the universities by insisting on the grant of suitability certificates as a requirement of admission led to fresh outbursts of violence in Nanyang University, to restiveness in the Ngee Ann College and the normally quiet University of Singapore. A Students' National Action Front was formed in November 1966, but the government intervened to stifle this, expelling 112 students from Nanyang University and eighty-one from Ngee Ann College, and banishing those who were not citizens. At the same time they imprisoned Barisan Sosialis members involved in the student troubles.

The Barisan was in no position to take effective militant action. Arrests and de-registration of unions had destroyed its control over organized labour. Nor could the party command external support. Links with the communist Malayan National Liberation League in Djakarta were shattered in September 1965 with the annihilation of the Indonesian Communist Party. At the same time the Moscow-Peking split weakened Russian influence and communist China maintained a low profile in South-East Asia.

While the Chinese government valued remittances and investments from the Nanyang, it soon came to doubt the usefulness of the overseas Chinese as instruments for international revolution. From 1954 Peking had officially encouraged overseas Chinese to identify with their host countries and assured David Marshall when he visited China the following year that Singapore Chinese, including the China-born, could take up the new Singapore citizenship.

The Maoist régime could not control the actions of overseas Chinese students, who often carried militant action much further than Peking intended. China found herself blamed for the violent student demonstrations in Singapore in 1956, and the actions of her would-be followers among the overseas Chinese were an impediment to friendly foreign relations.

Students from overseas proved an embarrassing strain on the Chinese educational system, and by the late 1950s they were unwelcome unless of above average calibre. Singapore students who had previously flocked to China lost interest, disillusioned by their predecessors' difficulties and finding the new Singapore education policy and Nanyang University offered them more opportunities at home.

Despite these changes in Peking's attitude, the Singapore government continued to fear that communist China was dictating policy to the Nanyang Chinese. Briefly during the 1967 Chinese cultural revolution it appeared that Peking would stir up overseas Chinese, but in practice the quiet disengagement continued. The policy consistently followed since the late 1890s by Chinese royalists, reformists, revolutionaries and the Kuomintang was unobtrusively laid to rest.

By the time Singapore's first parliament met in December 1965 the PAP leaders had recovered from the shock of separation and laid down an ambitious policy to tackle the new city-state's problems of survival. No radical changes were needed in Singapore's machinery of government. Her constitution as a Malaysian state was retained but amended and her legislative assembly became a parliament.[9]

PAP policy aimed to create national cohesion, based on a multi-racial, multi-lingual secular society. Addressing parliament in December 1965 Lee Kuan Yew stressed, 'We have a vested interest in multi-racialism and a secular state, for the antithesis of multi-racialism and the antithesis of secularism hold perils of enormous magnitude.'

To create a feeling of nationhood posed special problems. Singapore had no indigenous pre-colonial traditions, the colonial period had left no strong cultural legacy among the mixed, transient immigrant society, and post-war emphasis on achieving merger with the Federation precluded building up any exclusively Singaporean identity. Every divisive force was present in Singapore, in language, colour, religion and culture, but the island state was small and compact. Each community centre had its wireless and television set, and under the Ministry of Culture the government-operated Radio Television Singapura was harnessed to the task of nation building.

Singapore profited from the experiences of other newly-formed nations, such as Israel, which found that initial attempts at total assimilation threatened to produce a muddled, rootless culture. Instead of trying to merge and suppress ethnic differences, official policy stressed the richness of cultural diversity but sought to superimpose on this a specifically Singaporean identity and sense of values. As the Foreign Minister, S. Rajaratnam, explained to the United Nations general assembly in 1965, 'If we of the present generation can steadfastly stick to this policy for the next thirty years, then we would have succeeded in creating a Singaporean of a unique kind. He would be a man rooted in the cultures of four great civilizations but not belonging exclusively to any of them.'

This was accompanied by a policy to inculcate discipline and dedication, to toughen moral fibre by spartan puritanism, to build a 'rugged society' and wipe out corruption, both in high politics and in everyday administration. On the whole the anti-corruption campaign was effective, although strong and trusted family and clan loyalties still encouraged nepotism, and the keen official eye to detect corruption sometimes threatened to make civil servants over-cautious.

Differences in race, colour, religion, and language were of minimal importance in public life, but the impact of the multi-racial policy was more difficult to assess at the social level. Inter-racial marriage was still uncommon. Such marriages doubled from two hundred registered in 1964 to four hundred in 1969 but were a negligible proportion of the total. Despite this, tolerance, goodwill and inter-racial acceptance gained ground. The policy of mixing different racial groups in public housing, resettlement schemes and integrated schools produced some friendships and understanding and appeared to rouse little friction.

While in principle equality was given to all the major languages, religions and cultures, all Singaporeans were required to conform to the general political, economic and social ethos of modern Singapore. In a state where nearly 80 per cent of the population were of Chinese ethnic origin, this meant in practice a strongly traditional Chinese flavour: an insistence on discipline, hard work, competition, self reliance, respect for worldly success and desire for material gain. Some communities were more adaptable than others in conforming to these ideals.

Of the Malays, who formed the largest minority, many found difficulty in fitting into the national mould. After independence the rapid expansion of the economy, intensive measures to weld the nation together and major schemes for urban renewal and rehousing swept them into the mainstream of Singapore social life. Thousands of *kampung* dwellers were compelled to move to high-rise apartment blocks in resettlement estates or new towns alongside non-Malay neighbours. Large numbers of Malays had to change their occupations. Malay fishermen and farmers found their livelihood drying up and had to take up employment in town.

These years were perhaps more unsettling for Malays than for any other community, because many were forced to adopt a radically changed life-style, while former concessions were gradually withdrawn. While Malay continued officially to be the national language, in practice it was used less and less, and English became the main common tongue. Special educational bursaries for Malays were awarded more sparingly and were restricted to students of proved merit.

Some Malays adapted readily to the new situation, taking up jobs in factories and offices, welcoming the modern facilities of apartment blocks, and sending their children to English-medium schools. But for the broad mass adjustment was painful. Many Malays held PAP Malay politicians responsible for their community's troubles but they had no alternative leaders. President Yusof died in 1970, and in any event the nature of his office and increasing ill health prevented his acting as more than a symbol. After Singapore's expulsion from Malaysia, the Singapore UMNO was cut off from the Malaysian UMNO and went into decline. No political organization remained to channel Malay dissatisfaction, foreboding and resentment, which was expressed in the 1972 election in a sizeable protest vote. This surprised and alarmed the government, but it appeared that the Malay community would find itself obliged to accept conformity and assimilation in the PAP ideal of modern Singapore.[10]

The 160,000 Indians, Pakistanis, and Ceylonese, who constituted the second largest minority, were mixed in religion, in social, linguistic and economic background. In general they remained the least assimilated community, maintaining the strongest ties with their home countries and cultures, but they had a political punch out of proportion to their size and were heavily represented in the upper ranks of the civil service.[11]

Eurasians, who numbered a little over 20,000 in the early 1970s tended to be middle-class official, professional, and commercial people, whose fluency in English and experience in administration and commerce gave them an initial advantage, although many were too steeped in western ways to conform happily to the new society.

The importance of distinctive minority groups declined. The Jews dwindled to about 600 in the early 1970s, since many found themselves more at home in western countries than in modern Singapore and emigrated to Britain or Australia. The Armenian community, so flourishing in the mid-nineteenth century, shrank to about thirty in the 1970s. The Arabs, who had owned vast tracts of land in Singapore in the 1930s, sold much of their property after World War II and reverted to trading activities. Many emigrated to surrounding Muslim countries.

In general the lot of Singapore's women improved, irrespective of ethnic background. Protected by the Women's Charter and released from the traditional burden of raising large families, women were encouraged to play a full and active part in contributing to progress. For the well-educated minority, the pursuit of a career to use their skills became a patriotic duty, encouraged officially by tax incentives. Exempt from the obligations of their male counterparts to undertake national military service and freed to a large extent from the pressures and strains put on young male Singaporeans in a highly competitive meritocracy, women enjoyed an enviable position compared with their sisters in most other countries. But this was not reflected in any increased political influence. Despite, or perhaps because of, the revolution in the status of Singapore's women in the decade following the passing of the Women's Charter, women retreated from the political scene. The last woman member of parliament, a veteran battler for women's rights, resigned in 1970, leaving the political arena an exclusively masculine concern.

As in 1959, the spotlight in 1965 was again on the political crisis but the most vital immediate problems were economic. Prospects of a common market with Malaysia were shattered, and Singapore might eventually lose her former role as the financial, banking and shipping centre for the Malay peninsula. Malaysia wanted to reduce her traditional dependence on Singapore, to by-pass her port and raise tariff walls against her industries, in order to protect her own economic programmes.

Rapid industrialization geared to export markets was essential to meet the challenge of the new position. Despite vigorous government policies over the past few years, Singapore was still heavily dependent in 1965 on entrepôt trade. Her industrialization programme had concentrated upon labour-intensive industries to mop up unemployment and on import substitution to cater for the proposed Malaysian common market.

Successive finance ministers continued Goh Keng Swee's policy of developing Singapore as a mixed economy, a combination of private enterprise with state encouragement and participation. In November 1965 Goh handed over the Finance Ministry to Lim Kim San, who had an impressive record as chairman of the Housing and Development Board from 1959 to 1963 and as Minister for National Development from 1963 to 1965. Goh Keng Swee acted as Finance Minister again from 1967 to 1970 when he was succeeded by Hon Sui Sen, a former civil servant, who had become permanent secretary of the Economic Development division of the Ministry of Finance in 1959, first chairman of the Economic Development Board in 1961, and first president of the Development Bank of Singapore in 1968.

Further incentives were offered to local and foreign capital, Singapore's economic attractions were widely publicized and potential investors were wooed more ardently. An Economic Incentives Act of 1967 consolidated existing laws and provided new financial inducements to encourage export industries and the application of science and technology to industry. The aim was not only to diversify the economy but also the pattern of trade and investment, in order to escape from dependence on individual nations. Hitherto more than 70 per cent of foreign investment in Singapore had been British, and Singapore now set out to attract other investors and build up new trading relationships.[12]

The early years of independence were a time of international prosperity when Singapore's economy grew quickly. Indonesian trade revived with the end of confrontation in June 1966, and growing American involvement in the Vietnam war boosted Singapore's role as a supplies centre. Even the Seven Days' war in the Middle East in 1967, leading to the closure of the Suez Canal on which modern Singapore's fortunes had largely been built, caused her little setback. The increased proportion of trade with Japan and the United States reduced her dependence on the canal, and improvements in steamer design cut the time required for the Cape of Good Hope route.

This atmosphere of prosperity and growing confidence was clouded in January 1968 when Britain decided to withdraw from her Singapore bases within three years. This posed a serious threat not only to Singapore's physical security but also to her economy.

At the time of separation Malayan defence was guaranteed under treaty by Britain, who indicated in February 1966 that her bases would be retained as long as Singapore and Malaysia were happy to accept them. Four months later the British prime minister, Harold Wilson, stated that any proposal to withdraw British forces from east of Suez would be 'the surest recipe for a nuclear holocaust'. But in the twelve months which followed this statement mounting economic troubles convinced the British government that it could no longer afford to guarantee protection for Malaysia and Singapore.

It is surprising that this inevitable policy change was delayed so long. The fall of Singapore and the granting of independence to India had brought British paramountcy east of Suez to an end and required a re-appraisal of the British role.[13] But this was not done for another two decades, during which time a much-weakened Britain continued to commit herself to defending the area, pouring in expenditure on defence installations in Singapore on an unprecedented scale. Twenty years of such spending in the East and elsewhere, the Malayan emergency, and the drain imposed by the three-year confrontation against Indonesia involving 50,000 British troops, shook Britain's economy. At the end of 1966 she announced her intention to give up the extravagant role which she could no longer afford to play and produced a White Paper on defence, which proposed to run down the Singapore bases by the mid-1970s.

Britain assured Singapore that the withdrawal of forces would be gradual, and when mounting financial problems brought about a devaluation of sterling in November 1967 Denis Healey, the British Defence Minister, promised that this would not speed up the pull-out. Wilson gave similar assurances in Australia a month later, but as a result of financial readjustments which followed the devaluation, in January 1968 the British government suddenly decided to accelerate the timetable and to evacuate the Singapore bases by the spring of 1971.[14] Whereas the 1966 White Paper had been a balanced scheme, the decision of January 1968 was dictated purely by Britain's domestic political considerations with no military consultation, and it created grave and unexpected problems for Singapore.[15]

Hitherto the Ministry of the Interior and Defence, set up in November 1965 under Goh Keng Swee, had concentrated on building up Singapore's army under the umbrella of the Anglo-Malaysian defence agreement. At the time of independence Singapore's armed forces consisted of two regular infantry battalions, the first created in 1956 and the second in 1962, one partially mobilized volunteer infantry battalion, a volunteer artillery regiment, an armoured car squadron, some engineers and signals.

Soon after independence plans were laid down for a small regular army supported by a large force of national servicemen, and the two regular infantry regiments were amalgamated with the Volunteers to form the first Singapore infantry brigade. A Singapore Armed Forces Training Institute was opened at Jurong in 1966 and Israeli advisers were appointed to train the army. They were selected largely because Israel had developed methods to overcome immensely superior enemies in war and had used military service to help create an Israeli identity in their own small country. In 1967 legislation was passed requiring that all male Singapore citizens undergo a period of national military service at the age of eighteen, after which they were put on the reserve. This extensive use of national service was designed to create and maintain a large defence force at minimum cost and also to engender a sense of national unity through universal service. In 1968 this small army was not yet an effective deterrent force, and Singapore had left naval and air defence entirely to Britain. Her sea-going navy, comprising one patrol boat, was not adequate even to defend merchant shipping against casual piracy, and she had no aircraft.

The British withdrawal also threatened Singapore's economy. Britain's spending in Singapore, totalling $450 million a year, accounted for 25 per cent of Singapore's gross national product and had been a vital factor contributing to economic growth in the mid-1960s. The bases employed 25,000 local people, of whom 21,000 were Singapore citizens, and thousands more derived their livelihood indirectly from the British service community. Despite Singapore's efforts to industrialize and to diversify her economy, there seemed little chance of absorbing the large-scale unemployment threatened by the British withdrawal, with its consequent threat to political stability.

In the first surge of angry panic Singapore leaders contemplated retaliation in the form of withdrawal from the sterling area and action against British shipping, insurance and banking interests, but realized this would damage Singapore more than Britain. Lee Kuan Yew flew to London, where he argued his case forcibly and effectively, not only in private talks with British government leaders but also before the British public on television.[16] British economic interests, such as the Confederation of British Industry, added their voice, and as a result the British cabinet agreed to postpone the final withdrawal until November 1971, to pay substantial compensation terms, to hand over valuable assets, to help retrain redundant employees and create an air defence system.

Always adept in turning adversities into opportunities, the PAP leaders used the prospect of the accelerated British withdrawal to renew the feeling of crisis and challenge and to draw Singaporeans closer together. The result was even greater vitality in the effort to build up Singapore's economy and to muster her defence in the two years which remained before the British departure.

In order to tackle the new tasks, the ruling party went to the polls in April 1968 to seek a new mandate. The result was a foregone conclusion. The opposition parties were disorganized and had little appeal. Most Singaporeans, impressed by their leaders' firm and prompt reaction to the crisis, regarded the present leadership as most capable of leading them out of the current dangers. There was no need for the political manoeuvrings which had ensured victory in the 1963 election. The Barisan Sosialis boycotted the election, the Alliance fielded no candidates, and the Workers' Party put up only two. PAP candidates won every parliamentary seat and were returned unopposed in 51 of the 58 constituencies.

With this new power the government seized the chance to enforce strict labour discipline in order to encourage domestic and foreign capital investment. At the opening of the first meeting of the independent parliament in December 1965, the government had declared, 'The excesses of irresponsible trade unions. . .are luxuries which we can no longer afford.'[17] 'Change is the essence of life,' Lee Kuan Yew urged the National Trades Union Congress in April 1967, at the same time appealing to the Singapore Employers' Federation to work together to build up the prosperity of the state, of employers and workers alike. It was difficult to change attitudes which had been built up over a generation, but the sudden prospect of wide-scale unemployment and the need to divert resources to defence expenditure induced workers to accept unpalatable changes, which they had not been prepared to consider in the easy years when Singapore sheltered under the umbrella of Britain's military protection and the bases brought money and employment to so many of her people.

An Employment Act and an Industrial Relations (Amendment) Act passed in August 1968 aimed to restrict trade union disputes, prevent strikes and increase productivity. The new labour laws gave employers clearer powers in promoting, transferring and dismissing workers, but gave workers the right of appeal to the Ministry of Labour. The laws permitted longer working hours, reduced holidays, restricted overtime and bonus payments, and curtailed fringe benefits enjoyed by some white-collar workers. But for the mass of workers they gave compensating benefits in providing for the first time for sick leave and retrenchment payments. Legislation was also passed at the same time to increase employers' contributions to the central provident fund.[18]

The initial reaction of the National Trades Union Congress was one of shock, fearing that employers would use the legislation to exploit workers, but in view of the crisis the trade unions accepted the necessity for tough new laws.

The labour legislation succeeded in almost eliminating strikes. The year 1969 was the first strike-free year since the PAP came to office, and the second industrial arbitration court was closed in January 1970 for lack of business.

Confident that its labour problems were solved, the Singapore government intensified its wooing of foreign and local investment. In July 1968 the Economic Development Board was reorganized and development financing operations were transferred to a Development Bank of Singapore, which provided long-term financing to manufacturing industries and took a sizeable but minority equity in new industries in partnership with private capital. Six months later the government supervised the setting up of an International Trading Company (Intraco), jointly owned by the government, the Development Bank and private capital, with the initial task of dealing with countries whose international trade was under government control.

Singapore grew rapidly as a financial centre and capital market. In 1968 she was made the headquarters of the Asian Dollar Market, and in 1969 she became a gold market and quickly outstripped Hong Kong and Beirut. By 1970 she had thirty-six commercial banks, twenty-six foreign and ten Singaporean.

The government set out to make Singapore Asia's biggest shipping, ship-repairing and shipbuilding centre after Japan. In 1966 Singapore set up her own register of local ships, and two years later offered tax-free registration of foreign ships on terms more liberal than Panama or Liberia, thus creating the first Asian 'flag of convenience'. In 1968 she launched her own national shipping line, the Neptune Orient Line, and in 1972 created a National Shippers' Council, which aimed to break the monopoly held by the Far Eastern Freight Conference. The conference, which was dominated by the old European, mainly British, shipping lines, dated back to 1897, when the major shipping lines made an agreement with leading exporting firms to use only ships belonging to the conference.[19] The conference shipping companies still monopolized shipping and dictated freight rates in the early 1970s, but the new National Shippers' Council set out to end Singapore's dependence on foreign shipping.

Singapore's shipbuilding and repairing business almost doubled from $64 million in 1966 to $120 million in 1968. Jurong Shipyard, financed by private capital, started operating in 1964, Keppel Shipyard was separated from the Port of Singapore Authority in August 1968 to form a commercial enterprise wholly owned by the Singapore government, and four months later Sembawang Shipyard was founded, taking over the former British naval dockyard.

In 1969 Singapore outstripped London to become the busiest port in the Commonwealth, with the completion of her container complex in 1972 she became the container trans-shipment centre for South-East Asia, and by 1975 she claimed to be the third port in the world after Rotterdam and New York.

In the new atmosphere of industrial peace and political quiet, foreign investors whom the government had been courting for many years now began to pour into Singapore. In 1968 manufacturing activity suddenly speeded up in Jurong after the town was reorganized into the Jurong Town Corporation, which also managed eleven other industrial estates. Jurong's function changed from an industrial estate mopping up unemployment into the base for a viable independent industrial, export-oriented economy. Applicants rushed to set up new manufacturing industries and by the end of 1970 Jurong had 264 factories in production, employing 32,000 workers, and another 106 factories under construction.

Singapore's dependence on Britain declined with the influx of capital from other countries, mainly from the United States, but also from western Europe, Japan, Hong Kong, Taiwan, Malaysia and Australia. In 1972 the United States accounted for 46 per cent of the new foreign capital invested, and in 1973 she became, after Malaysia, Singapore's second trading partner.

By 1972 one quarter of Singapore's manufacturing companies were foreign or joint-venture firms, accounting for nearly 70 per cent of the value of the republic's industrial production and 83 per cent of her direct exports, and employing more than half of her labour force. Singapore provided an attractive base for the growth of multi-national organizations, mainly of American origin, which were welcomed as an effective means of expanding the economy, since they also provided technical expertise, management and export outlets.

The quest for oil in neighbouring Indonesia brought an influx of capital, equipment and expertise to Singapore, which provided the natural centre for supporting servicing operations. In the early 1970s thirty major oil exploration companies were located in Singapore, together with more than a dozen exploration consulting concerns, diving companies, construction and specialist engineers.[20] By 1970 petroleum was Singapore's leading export industry, accounting for nearly 40 per cent of her total manufactured products, and she was the oil storage and distribution centre for the whole region. In 1973 Singapore claimed to be the third largest oil-refining centre in the world after Houston and Rotterdam.

A world-wide boom in shipbuilding and repairing, the demands of the Vietnam war, the recovery of the Indonesian economy, and the increasing search for off-shore oil in South-East Asia enabled Singapore to make notable economic gains. A World Bank team reported: 'In 1968

Singapore entered a new phase of accelerated growth with boom conditions in private investment, a decline in unemployment, buoyancy of government revenues, the emergence of an over-all surplus of savings over investments, and a significant build-up of external reserves.'

By the end of the 1960s Singapore could look back on a decade in which she had managed to diversify and expand her economy. Her gross domestic product expanded by a compound annual rate of over 9 per cent in the 1960s, her annual rate of increase in industrial production was more than 20 per cent, and the number of factories more than trebled. Employment quadrupled and the spectre of mass unemployment as a result of the British evacuation was laid to rest. By 1970 Singapore had achieved a state of near-full employment, with labour shortages in certain categories. In 1971, despite the retrenchment of 17,000 civilian employees by the British services, Singapore needed to relax her immigration laws to give work permits to non-citizens, and by 1972 immigrant workers constituted 12 per cent of the labour force.

Singapore's open economy was dangerously vulnerable to international fluctuations over which she had no control, but at the same time competition with her larger neighbours kept her alert, adaptable and ready to upgrade her services, in extending and modernizing port and airport facilities, ship-repairing services and manufacturing facilities for the offshore oil industry.

Boom conditions and the enthusiasm of foreign capital soon put Singapore in a better position to safeguard her own interests and to demand a bigger share in the profits. She had completed the first stage of industrial development, which stressed providing employment for an over-abundant labour force and attracting capital and entrepreneur skills. She could now offer political stability and a disciplined labour force, rather than cheap labour and tax holidays, as the main attractions to foreign developers, and could seek highly skilled employment which would better her people's standard of living and ensure permanent prosperity. Singapore became more discriminating in the choice of investment and tried to break away from her 'sweat shop' image by encouraging more sophisticated industries which would develop the technical skills of her labour force.

Foreign investors were prepared to offset somewhat higher wage prospects against disciplined and skilled labour, but the favourable climate could only be maintained if Singapore could avoid being caught in the inflationary spirals and soaring production costs which had induced manufacturers from the major industrial countries to come. By 1972 she had to redirect industries because of lack of labour. Such a shortage of skilled workers would normally have sparked off a general wage rise, but the government wished to guarantee Singapore's continued competitiveness. In December 1971 a national wages council was set up, comprising government, trade union and employers' representatives, to formulate guidelines on wages policy and ensure that higher wages and improved benefits should reflect greater skills and increased productivity.

For the first eight years after independence Singapore achieved a spectacular expansion in her economy, but at the end of 1973 she felt the first effects of international monetary system disorders and a world-wide oil crisis when Arab producers restricted oil exports and raised prices dramatically.[21] With her heavy dependence on the import of crude oil from the Middle East, this was the biggest threat to Singapore since independence. Coupled with this, Singapore suffered when the traditional balance of trade was reversed in favour of primary producers, sending import prices of raw materials, food and energy sources soaring in manufacturing countries. For Singapore this spelt particular danger, since she was an urban, commercial and industrial economy, with a small agriculture, which could supply only a fraction of her people's needs. In 1974 her growth slowed down as a result of the world-wide recession,[22] and the following year expansion almost came to a halt.

To help counter this the republic sought to build up friendly relations with oil-producing states and encouraged Arab participation in the economy. Rajaratnam visited the Middle East early in 1974 and succeeded in ensuring that no retaliatory action was taken against Singapore because of her past friendship with Israel. As a result her refinery capacity was barely affected by the crisis. An Arab trade delegation visited Singapore in November 1974 and two months later Singapore signed an agreement for a petrochemical complex as a joint venture between Japanese, Singaporean and Arab capital.

To maintain and raise the standard of living, economic expansion needed to be accompanied by a check on Singapore's population growth, which reached a peak of 4.4 per cent per annum in 1957. The voluntary Singapore Family Planning Association succeeded in stemming this spectacular rate of increase in the late 1950s,[23] but stronger measures were needed to achieve an ideal zero growth-rate, and in 1966 the government created a Singapore Family Planning and Population Board, which launched a five-year programme. Official direction, maximum publicity and generous funds, coinciding with new developments in medical knowledge and improved techniques, enabled the board to achieve dramatic results among a receptive population. Conquering traditional Asian respect for large families, family planning gained acceptance among the middle class of all racial and religious groups. As a further inducement, abortion laws were liberalized, priorities in government housing formerly given to large families were withdrawn, and hospital fees for third and subsequent confinements were raised. The board's success was so marked that in 1969 its chairman was appointed director of the World Bank's population projects department.

The first family-planning programme reduced Singapore's population growth to the level of the world's advanced industrial nations, but the problem was not yet solved. In 1971 the birth rate began to rise again, partly because of the large proportion of young women born during the population bulge of the immediate post-war years, and partly because family planning had made less headway among the lower paid and uneducated. To ensure that improved economic benefits would not be eaten away in pressures on social services, health and education, family-planning programmes were intensified, penalties on large families were extended by withdrawing priorities for school entry in the case of fourth and subsequent children, and in 1975 preference in school admissions was given to the children of parents who had undergone sterilization.

By 1975 population growth had fallen to 1.3 per cent but the target of zero growth based upon a two-child family would take a further fifty years to achieve, by which time the population would have doubled to four million.[24] The most densely populated country in the world with 3,787 persons per square kilometre, Singapore needed substantial economic growth if she were to avoid being forced to take draconian punitive measures to curb her population increase.

In 1968 the attention of most Singaporeans focused on the threatened economic hardships arising from the accelerated British withdrawal, but the government's immediate concern was military security. Hitherto Singapore had devoted only a small part of her resources to defence. She had the nucleus of an army but negligible naval and air forces. An air force command was created in April 1968 and a maritime command in December 1968.

Fortunately there was no immediate threat of war and the economy was thriving, so that the process of diverting energy and resources to defence was comparatively easy. The demands of the situation provided a chance to unite the new nation in patriotic effort. Citizens were called upon to contribute to a defence fund, and the challenge gave new opportunities for stronger cohesion and national service.

Singapore had come a long way in preparing herself against the withdrawal of the British bases when in June 1970 a general election in Britain brought to power the Conservative party, which had opposed the Labour government's decision to accelerate the pull-out. The change of government in London did not in fact bring a reversal of policy, since both parties accepted that the Singapore base was an outdated military concept and Britain could never again afford to be caught in an open-ended commitment such as the confrontation with Indonesia.

Despite this, the Conservatives did not want to shed all responsibility for the region, and after some months of discussions, agreement was reached in April 1971 to replace the Anglo-Malaysian defence pact by a five power Commonwealth defence agreement, signed by Singapore, Malaysia, Britain, Australia and New Zealand. This pact replaced definite commitment to military aid by a deliberately nebulous provision for consultation and discussion should a crisis arise.

Modest contingents of Australian, New Zealand and British troops (ANZUK) were stationed in Singapore, supported by air and naval contingents. The small force was intended to be a show of confidence and to provide further technical back-up to the defence capability of

Singapore and Malaysia.

The effectiveness of the five power Commonwealth defence agreement was never put to the test, and at best Singapore leaders regarded it as providing a breathing space to build up Singapore's own defences. Australia pulled out her ground troops in 1975 and the last British troops left early the next year. Singapore viewed their departure with mixed feelings, confident that her defences were now sufficient for her local needs,[25] but regretting that the departure coincided with the communist victory in Vietnam.

Meanwhile the withdrawal of the British forces meant that large tracts of prime land, together with valuable buildings, schools, hospitals, sports complexes and other amenities were handed over to the Singapore government, since at its height the British military occupied more than one tenth of the total area of Singapore island, including some of its most favoured locations. The government inherited valuable technical installations, particularly the magnificently-equipped naval dockyard which became the foundation for a new shipbuilding industry.

Great changes were made in education, which was recognized as the most important long-term means to inculcate national values. In 1959 the PAP had insisted that 'education must serve a purpose' and be tailored to suit society.[26] After 1965 the education system was adapted to mould a nation.[27]

Between 1959 and 1967 the Ministry of Education built schools at the average rate of one each month, and by the time of independence universal free primary education had been achieved. The educational five-year plan for the period 1966 to 1970 concentrated on expanding secondary and tertiary education. Greater importance was given to scientific and technical studies and to physical education. From 1966 the use of a second language became compulsory in secondary schools, following the recommendations of a commission set up two years before to report on the new education system.[28]

During its first nine years in power the PAP government spent nearly a third of the budget on education, but Britain's decision to hasten withdrawal of her forces compelled the Singapore government to reappraise its education policy. After 1968 finance for education had to give priority to defence, which by 1971 absorbed a quarter of the budget. At the same time education needed to be geared more closely to industrialization and to improving the quality of Singapore's labour force, which constituted her only natural resource.

In 1968 it was decided to continue the general policy laid down in 1956 but to bring all schools closer into the national system, to promote multi-lingualism more vigorously and to divert more pupils into technical and vocational schooling. At the university level emphasis veered from producing arts graduates in favour of training the engineers, scientists and business managers whom Singapore required for the development of her economy.

High-calibre students from both English- and Chinese-medium schools were creamed off for intensive pre-university training, and in 1969 the first national junior college was set up for this purpose. The policy of highly selective, intensive secondary education was intended to produce not an élite class but a meritocracy, to give equal opportunities for all and reward ability, but to develop the talents of individuals for the good of society.

Greater emphasis was put on second-language training. Insistence on bi-lingualism meant that more children studied their mother tongue in schools, but increasingly the vernacular became a child's second language. Despite the provision of better facilities for Malay, Chinese and Tamil education, career opportunities in government service, commerce and industry favoured the English-speaking, strengthening the traditional concern of ambitious parents to send their children to English-medium schools. By 1968 more than 300,000 pupils attended English schools compared with only 135,000 in Chinese schools. At that time 13,000 children studied Tamil as a second language in English-medium schools, but the enrolment of new pupils in Tamil primary schools was falling off rapidly. Attendance at Malay primary schools fell from 5,000 pupils in 1966 to 2,000 three years later, despite the fact that there were by then ten Malay secondary schools.

This spontaneous drift towards English schooling was not the result of deliberate official policy. The government resisted pressure to make English-medium education universal, notably from Malay spokesmen who felt that vernacular education held back their community as it had done in colonial times. While Malays formed 15 per cent of the total population, only 2 per cent of the professional and administrative class were Malays. Malay was not a language of opportunity in either commerce or the public service, and in 1970 the Singapore Malay Teachers' Union formally appealed for a national system of education based on English as the main language of instruction. Such a measure posed political problems: resentment from Indonesia and Malaysia, and, perhaps more important, hostility from those Singapore Chinese who wanted to maintain traditional Chinese education.

Chinese education, which had flourished in times of discrimination under colonial rule, withered when it was incorporated on equal terms into a national system. Government leaders made no secret of their conviction that the Chinese-educated tended to be more politically active, more resilient in misfortune and more willing to make personal sacrifices for the common good. The prime minister and other prominent English-educated leaders chose to send their children to Chinese schools, claiming that Chinese education provided better character training. But forward-looking parents lower down the social scale, who could not offer the same facilities for learning English at home, preferred to opt for English schooling.

Chinese education was no longer a dead end, as it had been in the 1950s. All Chinese now studied their mother tongue either as a first or second language, but also had the opportunity to learn English, and Chinese education provided an outlet to Nanyang University. Despite this, the opportunities for the Chinese-educated university graduate did not equal those for his English-educated counterpart. Nanyang graduates found greater difficulty in securing employment in commerce and industry, and even within government service they were rarely put in line for senior appointments. In 1970 they constituted nearly 40 per cent of the executive civil service, few of them gaining admittance to the upper administrative grade.

The steady decline in Chinese-school enrolment caused growing concern among those who regarded Chinese education, in the words of Lim Boon Keng long ago, as a system 'to ennoble man's mind and purify his character'. It also worried Chinese-language newspaper publishers who saw their potential readership dwindling away, and by the early 1970s there was renewed murmuring from the Chinese press and the Chinese chamber of commerce.

In an attempt to take heat out of the situation, the government offered to register six-year-olds at the half year in Chinese primary schools, which gave a head start to children who would normally have had to wait until the following January for admission. But this gesture could not solve the deep-seated problem of Chinese education and its place in modern Singapore.

At the other end of the scale affluent westernized parents continued to send children to boarding schools and universities in Britain, Australia or the United States. To curb this practice, private foreign schools in Singapore were closed to most Singapore citizens, and from 1971 heavy financial penalties were imposed on parents sending boys overseas, mainly to prevent the evasion of national service obligations. Increasing pressure and exhortation were used to induce parents to educate their children in Singapore, in order to increase national cohesion, to instil the national ethos and to ensure that they were trained in the skills and professions the government deemed necessary for Singapore. This was only partially effective. Some rich families continued to send their sons abroad, and there was no restriction on daughters.

British colonial and Chinese traditions both set great store on formal examinations, and the ideal of meritocracy appealed to the materialistic, competitive, success-worshipping society of independent Singapore. The system opened attractive opportunities and rewards for able young people whatever their social and linguistic background, while for the mass of Singaporeans the concern to tailor vocational education to the actual demands of the economy dispelled the spectre of unemployment.

The object was to develop every child's economically useful capabilities to the full. The system offered tempting opportunities but put great strains on talented youngsters and pushed the weak and less intelligent to the wall. Poor youths who won through to personal success were admired, but 'equality' of educational opportunity usually meant better chances for the children of ambitious professional and middle-class parents.

By the mid-1970s it was obvious that bi-lingual education was too arduous for many young Singaporeans and threatened to turn Singapore into what Lee Kuan Yew described as a 'calypso society', a hybrid with no language or distinctive culture of its own. Politicians and education leaders, even at the university level, stressed that English was merely the language which Singaporeans needed to cope with modern technology and commerce. Study of their mother tongue would provide their basic values, without which they would be 'completely deculturized and lost.'[29] But English was the language of government, in 1971 it became the official language of the armed forces, and it was rapidly becoming the language of the schools and homes. Singapore had to face the problem whether indigenous cultural roots would dry up in a national education system based mainly on an alien language.

In order to speed up the physical development of the island, after independence many legal limitations laid down by the original master-plan were withdrawn and the government assumed greater powers of land acquisition.

A series of United Nations missions, which visited Singapore between 1962 and 1965, culminated in an ambitious State and City project in 1967, under which new towns would provide employment, housing, health and recreational amenities to cater for an estimated population of three million in the 1990s, stabilizing at about four million in the twenty-first century. The government embarked on urban renewal, large-scale drainage schemes to alleviate flooding and giant projects covering the reclamation of the coast at Pasir Panjang and along the entire coast from the Singapore river to Changi.

This programme dispersed the population from the central areas where it had remained heavily concentrated since the settlement was first founded. Queenstown was completed by the mid-1960s and a second larger town at Toa Payoh was finished by 1973. In the early 1970s work began on new towns at Bedok and Telok Blangah, after which the emphasis would shift to the northern part of the island and the creation of the largest and most ambitious of the new towns at Woodlands, which was designed to equal Queenstown and Toa Payoh combined.

In the city area ambitious schemes of urban renewal transformed decaying districts into modern, high-rise flats, hotels and offices. Slums, squatter shanties and dilapidated *kampungs* on the outskirts of town gave way to new townships of self-contained flats with electricity, piped water and sewerage, in modern housing estates with their own shopping centres, schools, markets, clinics and recreational facilities.

Public utilities expanded to cater for the growing population, the needs of industry and the new housing estates. Extensions to the Seletar reservoir were finished in 1969 to help cope with the demand for water, which doubled between 1966 and 1971. By the early 1970s nearly 95 per cent of the population had a piped water supply, and work was in hand to link the whole island to the main sewerage system by 1980.

Amid the flurry of reconstruction, with the rise of new towns in hitherto undeveloped areas and the growth of hotels and shopping complexes in the Orchard Road district, the old heart of Singapore city remained the financial and administrative centre. But its appearance changed rapidly, as old shophouses and decaying office blocks were replaced by modern steel and concrete skyscrapers, and Shenton Way, an undeveloped parking lot a few years ago, became the Wall Street of Singapore.

Chinatown and the Malay *kampung* areas disappeared rapidly as their occupants moved to resettlement estates. Rambling colonial-style mansions in their spacious compounds gave way to blocks of luxury flats, in face of the ruthless pressure of redevelopment and the soaring price of land. The former Chinese, Malay and colonial European architecture, which had given Singapore its distinctive character, was replaced by an anonymous modern style in both public and private buildings.

By 1975, 42 per cent of the population lived in government-built housing, and the Housing Board began constructing higher-quality housing for sale to middle-class Singaporeans who found difficulty in meeting rising costs of land and property. By the end of the decade it was anticipated that nearly 70 per cent of Singaporeans would occupy public housing. But the object was to encourage home ownership in order to give Singaporeans a vested interest in preserving stability and to release capital for further house building. From 1964 Housing and Development Board flats were sold on favourable terms to Singapore citizens with low incomes.

A small self-contained island with a strictly enforced immigration policy, Singapore was protected from the influx of rural migrants and the lumpen-proletariat problems which faced most cities in the developing world. As the housing situation eased some measures were taken against squatters, and many of the unsightly, insanitary shanty settlements were swept away. In 1968 an Environmental Health Act was passed to curb pollution and promote beauty and cleanliness in physical surroundings by imposing harsh fines on offenders. Singaporeans had been responsive even in colonial times to measures designed to better their health and material well-being, and an independent government had no inhibitions about disciplining its citizens for their own good.

Improvements in the general environment and in public housing raised health standards. By the early 1970s an infant mortality rate of 21 per thousand and an average life expectancy of over 64 years compared favourably with most developed countries. Smallpox, cholera, diphtheria and polio virtually disappeared as a result of vigorous vaccination and immunization programmes, whilst tuberculosis lost its traditional place as the main killer to the 'diseases of civilization', cancer and heart disease.

Official encouragement was given to advancing physical fitness. The British had imparted some of their enthusiasm for sports but only to middle-class Singaporeans, notably the Eurasians and Indians, and favourite British sports, such as golf, cricket and tennis, were decried by many Singaporeans as colonialist rich men's hobbies. After independence the attitude changed. Physical fitness was a national ideal, and expensive sports became fashionable among those who could afford them. Physical education was vigorously promoted in the schools as a means to improve the health of the rising generation and to build up a robust national defence force. From 1966 a *Pesta Sukan*, or festival of sport, was organized annually to accompany National Day celebrations, and a mammoth international sports complex, opened at the old Kallang airport in 1973, enabled Singapore to play host that year to the South-East Asia Peninsular Games.

The post-independence years appeared to be the most constructive and exciting in Singapore's history and inspired admiration in many western countries, who saw the tiny republic overcoming apparently insuperable obstacles while more developed societies floundered in indecisiveness. As a result the island state and its leadership acquired an international reputation out of proportion to the country's size or importance. The period held something akin to the excitement of the early days of Singapore, when the settlement lived on its wits, seeking a way out of its artificial and precarious position.

The outside world came increasingly to identify Singapore with Lee Kuan Yew, who emerged as a prominent international figure, dominating by reason of his impressive personality, his experience and predilection for television debate, his clear, compelling oratory and plain speaking. Making use of his long-time friendship with the leaders of the then ruling British Labour Party and his status in the international socialist movement, Lee made a great impact in 1966 at the congress of the Socialist International in Stockholm, at the 1967 Scarborough Labour Party conference,[30] and in his public appearances in Britain the next year, when he protested against the new defence decisions.

The announcement of the accelerated British withdrawal early in 1968 acted as a renewed stimulant to Singapore, enhancing her sense of solidarity, instilling discipline and energy to tackle the problems of her threatened survival. She celebrated her 150th anniversary in 1969 in an atmosphere of buoyant optimism and festivity. In the four years since independence was thrust upon her Singapore could claim many solid achievements, which had seemed remote and unattainable at the time of separation. Much had been done to create a sense of multi-racial nationhood, particularly among the younger generation, and Singapore was spared the severe racial conflicts which struck Kuala Lumpur and other parts of peninsular Malaysia in May 1969

The World Bank and International Monetary Fund report in 1970, said that the young republic exuded 'a general atmosphere of ebullience and optimism'...and...'It is this proper sense of urgency which makes Singapore such an exciting place to live in and which, tempered as it is with humanity and concern for the well-being of the individual citizen, lies at the heart of Singapore's outstandingly successful development and achievements.'

In a week of brilliant weather in January 1971 Singapore, one of the youngest and smallest of independent Commonwealth countries, played host to a conference of Commonwealth heads of government. Lee Kuan Yew as chairman displayed unusual tact and this, coupled with the republic's general euphoria of confidence and prosperity, did much to smooth the passions and arguments of an otherwise unproductive conference. Singapore symbolized the pride of independence within the Commonwealth, a beautiful, thriving city-state which had risen in little over a century and a half to be one of the world's great ports and a fast-developing modern independent nation. A disciplined society showed an absence of undue political, labour or student unrest which was unusual anywhere in the world in 1971 and in marked contrast to Singapore's own turbulence of only ten years before.

When the once dreaded day of the final troop withdrawals arrived in November 1971, the *New Nation* carried the headline, 'The British pull-out causes scarcely a ripple'.[31] Singapore was fast moving from the ranks of the developing nations into an affluent society.

But Singapore's remarkable rise had been purchased at a price. Success itself was in a sense self-defeating, quickly driving out memories of hardships and dangers. Singaporeans began to question restrictions and discipline which irked in easier times, while foreign observers, often with little appreciation of past events, criticized the authoritarianism of the regime and sometimes belittled its achievements. The leadership, accustomed to the euphoria of applause, reacted with excessive sensitivity to domestic and external criticism. They tended to read political subversion and sinister plots into the lessening plaudits of the outside world, which became growingly indifferent to the republic as a small nation in a troubled region.

Political quiet, economic prosperity and the incipient sense of nationalism had been achieved by compromising some of the early PAP's principles: democracy, socialism and close amity with her neighbours.

The early dangers and later successes gave the PAP increasing strength and encouraged authoritarianism. Its leaders' dexterity in exploiting good fortune and turning setbacks into opportunities, which had won them the early battles, gave them almost a stranglehold of power in more stable times.

The PAP leadership itself had recognized this danger in its early years. At the end of its first year of office in 1960 an official publication commented that a government must restrict the rights of individuals, but 'if it does so to a point where it becomes in fact a totalitarian society, the purpose of the restriction has been negated'. In December 1965, shortly after the separation from Malaysia, Lee Kuan Yew declared in parliament that Singapore had inherited a tendency for too great a concentration of power in the hands of the executive and needed 'to liberalize the constitution and make the weight of executive authority less inhibitive to the legislature and to the judiciary'. No such changes were made.

A constitutional commission, headed by the Chief Justice and comprising lawyers of the different racial and religious communities, which was appointed in 1966 to recommend safeguards against racially discriminating legislation, reported unanimously that communalism was a negligible danger but that some means was needed to protect the rights of individuals where circumstances had combined to give the ruling party a monopoly of power. British constitutional practice vested strong powers in the Singapore parliament, which were further increased by the absence of a second chamber, the elimination of separate local authorities in 1959 and the voluntary abdication of the only opposition party, the Barisan Sosialis, in 1965. The commission recommended certain safeguards to avert the potential tyranny of a parliament monopolized by one party, which could overturn the constitution itself by a simple majority. They proposed the creation of a council of state, comprising eminent citizens with no political affiliations, which would be an advisory body, meeting in public to debate laws after their first reading in parliament and to draw attention to proposed legislation which threatened minorities. The commission suggested the creation of an independent Ombudsman to deal with faults and abuses in administration. It recommended too that fundamental constitutional provisions should be altered only by a two-thirds parliamentary majority, confirmed by a two-thirds majority of all the electors in a referendum.[32]

The government accepted some of the commission's proposals, but rejected the suggestion for a referendum and opted for the safeguard of a two-thirds parliamentary majority. They agreed in principle to appoint an advisory council of state but preferred that it should meet in private and should include some permanent members, who might be leading politicians. While approving the principle of an Ombudsman, they postponed appointing such an officer.

The new constitutional proposals raised fundamental issues basic to the future of liberty in Singapore but provoked little public or press comment.[33] In 1967 parliament accepted the report with the government's modifications, despite some backbencher criticism,[34] and a presidential council came into being in 1970[35] with the Chief Justice as chairman. Its members, some appointed for life and the rest for three years, included serving cabinet ministers, notably Lee Kuan Yew, Goh Keng Swee and S. Rajaratnam, and former political leaders, such as C.C. Tan, Francis Thomas, and David Marshall.

The council's powers were further restricted by excluding from its purview any bills certified by the prime minister as affecting defence, security or good order in Singapore, and Marshall resigned after seven months, objecting to the limited nature of the council's functions, the secrecy of its proceedings, and the inclusion of active politicians, cabinet ministers and permanent secretaries in its membership.

In 1973, on the presidential council's own recommendation, it was reduced to a smaller Presidential Council for Minority Rights, whose functions were confined to drawing attention after the final reading to measures which discriminated against particular communities. The council's objections could be overruled by a two-thirds parliamentary majority and it no longer had power to consider any proposed legislation which was 'inconsistent with the fundamental liberties of the subject'.

Political skill, material success and the continued use of emergency regulations combined make the PAP almost synonymous with the state. Singapore was not a one-party state, but after 1965 the party held every seat in parliament. The republic continued to hold elections based on universal adult citizen suffrage at regular intervals, conducting its parliamentary business openly and meticulously according to the British parliamentary model from which it derived. Backbenchers were encouraged to take upon themselves the role of a 'loyal opposition' in debating official policy, but such parliamentary debates were mere academic discussions. Backbenchers could not hope to alter official policy except in minor detail, and parliament became as staid and tedious as the pre-1955 colonial legislative council.

Singaporeans showed little concern over growing PAP power in the immediate post-independence years. They were quick to respond to new policies and practical programmes and to discard customs which inhibited economic growth. But they left initiative to the politicians and were content to follow energetic and dedicated leadership. The impetus for construction and development planning came from the cabinet and senior civil servants, not the professions, the universities, the press or other institutions. Lee Kuan Yew claimed with some justification that independent Singapore was built on the ability, drive and dedication of about 150 individuals. The bulk of the population accepted PAP leadership since it was effective, but the quiet homage paid to success contained the seeds of danger, because the government's intense activity tended to deaden the sense of involvement on the part of the community as a whole. Singaporeans fell into the habit of following directions, while the ruling group, conscious of the efforts they had put into building the state, became obsessed with efficiency and impatient of criticism.

Western liberals looked somewhat askance at Singapore-style democracy, but in the words of Rajaratnam, 'The people are more interested in what is good government than in having an opposition.' Singapore was following a trend common to most countries of South-East Asia by the early 1970s in preferring 'guided democracy' to misguided democracy.

The leadership could claim to have produced a political stability and economic prosperity which seemed unattainable in the restless days of the mid-1950s. The cabinet was an able and vigorous team. They avoided ostentation in their way of living, and the prime minister, although often domineering in manner, tried to dispel the image of dictatorship. Neither he nor his colleagues sought to glorify their reputation by the erection of statues and monuments or the naming of buildings and roads and they retained old colonial titles and relics.[36]

With a monopoly of patronage and power, the party could co-opt or neutralize potential dissenters. By 1965 the PAP had already established channels of control and communication within the party and outside, which were further developed in the years which followed. Government leaders toured constituencies frequently, making speeches and attending social gatherings, and members of parliament held regular meet-the-people sessions on the lines started by David Marshall in 1955. Since 1959, when none of the English-educated ruling group could speak the Chinese mandarin dialect, the leaders, and particularly Lee Kuan Yew, had mastered it sufficiently to establish direct contact with the mass base on which the strength of their party lay. Lacking a parliamentary opposition, the government tried to keep its fingers on the pulse of popular opinion through PAP branch committees, the People's Association and citizens' consultative committees.

After the debacle of 1961 the party leaders took care not to let power accumulate again in the hands of branch committees, formerly elected by local members, which had given active communists control. Instead the central executive committee appointed the branch committees, with the local member of parliament as chairman, and the leadership kept contact through regular lectures organized for branch committees and cadres.

The People's Association, with the prime minister as chairman of its management board, administered 180 community centres, nearly 400 kindergartens and other amenities. The community centres had government-trained organizers and provided social and recreational facilities, particularly for young people. All People's Association kindergarten teachers had to be PAP members, so that a popular service was combined with indoctrination.[37]

Citizens' consultative committees were set up in each electoral district early in 1965, and within each constituency *kampungs* and streets had their own committees. In theory the citizens' consultative committees were independent of party organization, and the government co-opted prominent individual residents who commanded local respect, but inevitably these government-nominated committees became organs of the PAP, a means of supporting the party and attracting new blood to its ranks. Citizens' consultative committees and community centres served as listening-posts and provided the opportunity for the party leadership to explain official policy, but most of the communication was downwards. They were sounding boards for public opinion, not vehicles for criticism or opposition.

In one sense the absence of formal parliamentary opposition freed government ministers from the inhibiting need to tailor their public utterances to political tactics. This suited the analytical intellectual tastes of the party's leaders, who explained government policy and sometimes admitted mistakes with a candour rarely seen in countries with greater freedom of press and speech. But this expounding of public policy did not imply any bending to public opinion.

The government virtually controlled the mass media. All broadcasting and television was in the hands of a government department and soon after independence the government declared its intention to use these means 'to continue to inculcate national attitudes and political understanding'.[38]

The emergency regulations, dating back to 1948, inhibited press criticism of official policy by requiring newspapers to renew their licences annually. Censorship was not nakedly imposed but consisted of subtle pressures from government and self-restraint by newspaper editors. This situation did not encourage a lively free press, and public confrontation between the press and government was rare.

At the beginning of 1971 there were four English newspapers: the *Straits Times*, the oldest, largest and wealthiest, and the only newspaper with a circulation in excess of 100,000; and three newcomers, the *Eastern Sun*, the *Singapore Herald*, and the *New Nation*. Of four Chinese daily newspapers, the *Nanyang Siang Pau* and the *Sin Chew Jit Poh*, each with a circulation of about 60,000, continued to be the most influential. In addition there were three Indian vernacular newspapers and one romanized Malay daily, the *Berita Harian*, which was published by the *Straits Times*. The Jawi *Utusan Melayu* was banned in 1970 on the grounds that the newspaper incited racial passions.

The Singapore government, growingly sensitive to pressures from outside, suspected that foreign interests were acquiring a foothold in the Singapore press, planning to gain control, which might ultimately be used for political purposes. In 1970 the *Sin Chew Jit Poh* began criticizing the alleged neglect of Chinese education, and bitter press opposition culminated in May 1971 in the arrest of the four leading editorial staff of the *Nanyang Siang Pau* on the grounds that they were stirring up chauvinism among the Singapore Chinese.

This action was followed immediately by accusations that communist money from Hong Kong was behind the *Eastern Sun*. The senior staff immediately resigned and the newspaper closed. Within a few days an attack was launched on the *Singapore Herald*, on information supplied from abroad that foreign money was being put in to control the newspaper through East Malaysia, Hong Kong and possibly America. The *Herald*, which had shown some spirited but moderate criticism of government policies during its ten months' existence, protested and tried to fight back but had to give up the struggle when the government put pressure on the Chase Manhattan Bank to foreclose the *Herald's* account.

After this the Singapore press remained quiet and tamed, and in 1974 its freedom was further curtailed by a regulation that newspaper directors must be personally approved by the prime minister.

The voices of labour leaders and students, who had traditionally led opposition in Singapore politics, were stilled. The trade union movement had gone into decline since the stormy days of the early 1960s, and after the arrest of militant leaders and the disintegration of the communist-controlled Singapore Association of Trade Unions in 1964, the organized labour movement ceased to be an important political force. The labour legislation of 1968, which was so largely responsible for Singapore's swift economic growth, sapped the purpose of trade unions to agitate for better conditions and accelerated the withering of the movement. Membership of the National Trades Union Congress dropped rapidly.

The veteran trade union leader, C.V. Devan Nair, returned to Singapore in 1969 as adviser to the trade unions. Deploring the 'appalling inertia which inhibits the treading of new ground and the blazing of new trails of endeavour', he set out to find a fresh role for the trade union movement in partnership with the government and to build up its financial resources. 'A modern Singapore with an old-fashioned trade union movement is an intolerable contradiction,' he insisted. Advising against either militancy or passive docility, Devan Nair pressed for 'active acceptance' of government measures. With official encouragement, the National Trades Union Congress entered the world of co-operatives, insurance, and business, and set out to raise its finances and to train a new generation of trade union leaders. But there was no fire in the new-style unionism.[39]

With the economy booming and an abundance of attractive jobs for graduates, the universities became politically quiet and almost docile. Trouble died down at Nanyang University by 1967 and restiveness among Ngee Ann College students was smoothed out by 1968. English-educated University of Singapore student leaders, while in general support of Singapore's version of pragmatic, democratic socialism, sought the chance to dissent on some aspects. The government, fearing a repetition in Singapore of the revolt of youth in more developed countries, discouraged such debate, and the student body did not contest the issue strongly, since it realized that dissident views might jeopardize careers in a small society where the bulk of patronage lay with the government. A moderate University Democratic Socialist Club, started in 1964, challenged the more radical pro-Barisan University of Singapore Socialist Club, which went into decline and was struck off the register of societies in 1971.

While external political opposition was almost extinct, the PAP itself showed no signs of breaking up into opposing groups. The leadership sought to groom their own successors, mainly from the English-educated professional class, intelligent men but untried, since the majority of them had never had to face electoral heckling or make personal sacrifices to achieve success.

Parliamentary candidates were selected by the central executive committee on account of their intellectual calibre and conformity to party discipline. The rank and file of the party continued to be largely primary-school educated but the leadership lay in the hands of the educated middle class, and all three new senior ministers of state chosen in 1975 were university-educated technocrats in their thirties, men in the cabinet's own image.

To foster a loyal opposition would mean relaxing its hold to an extent unnatural in Singapore's ruling group, who dreaded to see the results of twenty years of effort spoilt by a younger and softer generation, unhardened in the school of bitter experience. Far from showing any wish to abdicate power into the hands of younger men, the ruling leadership revealed a hardening of control, growing insensitiveness, increasing rejection and impatience with criticism, and insistence on conformity, particularly from the young.

As the safety valves for institutionalized criticism closed, some Singaporeans became more concerned about the nature of the régime. The PAP's sweeping victory in the 1968 election was an expression of popular confidence and trust. At the same time it marked a potentially dangerous voluntary abdication of power by the electorate into the hands of one political group, threatening the isolation of government and encouraging an arrogance of power. The following year saw the beginnings of dissent in the form of public protests, opposition from the Bar Council, and in particular from David Marshall, when the government abolished trial by jury for capital offences in favour of trial by a panel of two judges.

The action taken against the Chinese and English press in 1971 came as a shock, and the unexpected enthusiasm and vigour of support for the *Singapore Herald's* fight revealed an undercurrent of liberal opposition to the régime and sympathy with those features which the government found alarming and perhaps sinister: the *Herald's* implied criticism of over-disciplined regimentation in Singapore society.[40]

The international press gave these incidents maximum publicity and Lee Kuan Yew came under attack when he spoke at the International Press Institute meeting in Helsinki shortly afterwards. There was universal condemnation of the Singapore government's action in the foreign press and Amnesty International tried to intervene, but Lee Kuan Yew appeared indifferent to this adverse publicity.

By the time Singaporeans went to the polls in the general election of 1972 there were murmurings of discontent among the Malay minority, English-educated intellectuals, Chinese-educated conservatives, and workers. The swift pace of modernization inevitably brought stress. Urban renewal uprooted families, disrupted jobs and imposed unfamiliar ways of life. But the ruling party's strength and the stability and prosperity which it brought made it difficult for the old opposition parties to survive or for effective new ones to emerge. Opposition parties offered only negative or outmoded platforms with no credible alternative to the ruling regime.

Of fifteen legally registered political parties, all of them claiming to represent 'democratic socialism', five opposition parties contested the 1972 election.[41] Only the Barisan had any following, but it was weakened by the imprisonment of many of its leaders and by long years in the political wilderness, cut off from power and patronage. Throughout their career the left-wing extremists had committed tactical errors in preferring direct action to constitutional battle, leaving the moderate element of the PAP to profit from the maximum exploitation and manipulation of the constitutional system. The Barisan repeated earlier mistakes in boycotting parliament in 1965, refusing to take part in the 1968 election and 1970 by-elections.[42] Most of its rank and file were opposed to contesting the 1972 election. The party was divided, and its leader, Dr. Lee Siew Choh, did not command the support accorded to the fiery early leaders, who by this time had withdrawn from Singapore's politics. James Puthucheary, Sandra Woodhull and Fong Swee Suan had moved to Kuala Lumpur after their release from prison. Lim Chin Siong was freed in 1969 but was immediately deported to England. He was still only thirty-six years old but was a broken and disillusioned man, repudiated as a traitor by the Barisan.

Once again the ruling party won all the seats, but only eight seats were uncontested and nearly a third of the votes went against the PAP. Lee Kuan Yew had predicted such a verdict but the government stepped in swiftly to deal with the protest vote. They alleged foreign backing and interference, insisted on parties opening their accounts to inspection and became tougher in suppressing opposition. This culminated in the crippling of the Barisan Sosialis as a result of a heavy fine imposed on it in a libel action.

Democracy was the first casualty to the independent government's success and socialism the second. In order to convert herself into an industrial society, Singapore had to shed her radical image, to woo nervous foreign capital and provide incentives to hesitant local capitalists. This meant not only ensuring political stability but drastically modifying socialist principles, both in state planning and in the ownership of economic wealth. In 1960 the PAP leadership had said, 'We have clearly stated that we stand for an independent, democratic, non-Communist, socialist *Malaya*. We have never stated that we stand for an independent, democratic, non-Communist, socialist *Singapore*...because we realize that a socialist Singapore is an economic impossibility.'[43] After independence socialist theory was dropped to suit changed circumstances. Long-term central planning was abandoned in favour of a more pragmatic approach, an economic planning unit formed in 1964 was abolished, and three draft second-development plans for the public sector were discarded before publication because of rapidly changing conditions.

The Singapore government did not intend to nationalize the means of production. As Lee Kuan Yew stated in 1969, 'In an under-developed situation where you have no managerial or technological class, the State ownership of all basic industries simply does not make sense.' The Singapore government believed that capital and skills could best be built up by private entrepreneurs, rather than civil servants, but it was prepared to go beyond merely providing the infrastructure for development. It took extensive ownership in commercial enterprises through shareholding and representation on boards of directors, and by 1974 had direct or indirect participation in 124 firms.[44] The government took part ownership in certain vital industries such as iron and steel, shipbuilding and shipping, and supplied 'seed capital' where private investors were hesitant. The Development Bank helped finance projects, such as hotels, real estate, oil refining, publishing, sugar refining, and insurance, with the twin aims of bringing profit to the state and hastening the process of replacing foreign by local expertise. But the authorities did not intend to use public money to bolster ailing or uneconomic activities.

These policies produced a mixed private-public economy based on supervised private enterprise. Singapore's brand of 'socialist democracy' was difficult to reconcile with the western concept of this term. The state did not aim to own the means of production nor to establish a welfare state, but the government initiated planning, supervised economic development and taxed the profits for the benefit of the state. Goh Keng Swee declared, 'The government has to be the planner and the mobilizer of the economic effort', but 'the free enterprise system, correctly nurtured and adroitly handled, can serve as a powerful and versatile instrument of economic growth.'[45] The government aimed to distribute the fruits of prosperity more widely by using fairly high personal and company taxation to finance benefits in education, housing and public health. The necessity to attract outside capital, to offer a secure haven to the industrialist and yet furnish a good living for the mass of the people, produced a pragmatic socialism akin to paternal capitalism.

Foreign capital, expertise and technology were vital to achieve rapid economic growth, and a small island, where it was difficult to build up an export trade with a limited domestic market, needed special efforts to attract foreign investors and to keep ahead of local neighbours in technology. Singapore's success in achieving this difficult feat laid her open to the charge that she was continuing to be an economic and political dependency in a neo-colonialist world.[46]

Rapid economic expansion accentuated disparities of wealth which the PAP had pledged in its early socialist days to abolish. By 1973 Singapore's *per capita* income was second only to Japan in Asia, but a disproportionate share fell to a small multi-millionaire group and to the professional and business classes. Managerial skills were at a premium in Singapore's developing society, so that honours and well-paid appointments were the prerogative of the highly-educated minority. Profits from the booming economy went into the pockets of business tycoons, while workers bore the main brunt of economic sacrifice. The line between haves and have-nots was almost as clearly marked as it had been in colonial times. Between 1959 and the early 1970s the wages of workers earning less than $500 a month increased by only about 5 per cent, whereas executive-grade salaries doubled or trebled.

The very advantages which Singapore enjoyed in her contacts with developed economies, her sound educational system, high standard of English and opportunities for overseas training for her people, meant that qualified personnel might be lured abroad by higher material incentives unless terms at home were attractive. Singapore could not close her society while she developed, in the same way as countries such as China or Russia. To remain competitive she needed to enlarge the economic cake before attempting to divide it up fairly. The result, as Lee Kuan Yew said in 1970, was 'We are developing painfully, unequally, often unjustly.'

The new state philosophy of meritocracy and self-reliance, and the concentration of state resources on providing decent housing, good education and jobs, left little compassion for the handicapped, the weak and the less gifted. Central provident fund obligations were extended, both for employers and employees, to make provision for retirement and old age, but schemes for social insurance, old-age pensions and unemployment benefits, which had been mooted in the immediate post-war years, were set aside in the interests of promoting the economy. Shunning a welfare state, official policy concentrated on measures to enable people to pull themselves out of poverty and to secure economic progress.

The amount paid out in public assistance to individuals in distress declined after 1965. Public health and hospital services, which had formerly been provided free to the needy, were now subject to small charges, except in maternity and child-welfare clinics and in the treatment of socially dangerous diseases such as tuberculosis. Care of the handicapped, the infirm and the aged was left almost entirely to the family or to the many voluntary charitable agencies. By the early 1970s more than ninety such bodies belonged to the Singapore Council of Social Service, which received a government subsidy but relied mainly on private contributions.

The young republic's success in forging a sense of nationality and building up her military security threatened her long-term interests, which lay in preserving international peace and regional harmony. She was too small to defend herself effectively against anything more than a localized attack except in alliance with other powers, nor could she afford to devote a large proportion of her revenue to defence for any length of time without jeopardizing the commercial prosperity which was her life blood. As a small nation dependent upon peace and goodwill to preserve her international commerce, Singapore needed to follow a policy of neutralism and to find a role and status in South-East Asia which were acceptable to her neighbours. She had to blur the image of a Chinese city-state, centre of an overseas Chinese regional trade network, and to seek a profitable part of an expanding South-East Asian prosperity, rather than compete for the lion's share of a static regional economy.

Singapore needed to counteract her military and economic vulnerability by adopting a policy of non-alignment, aiming to win recognition and to establish friendly relations and trading links with all countries, regardless of ideology. Soon after independence Toh Chin Chye, the deputy prime minister, and Rajaratnam, the Foreign Minister, embarked on extensive travels, particularly in Africa and eastern Europe, signing trade agreements, explaining the facts of separation, and seeking to ward off possible criticism by the anti-colonial bloc in the United Nations about the retention of British military bases.

These efforts were largely successful, but Singapore's relationship with other South-East Asian powers was not so happy. Her concern to build up a sense of nationhood and to fight for her survival gave her an abrasive and selfish character which often irritated her neighbours, particularly Malaysia and Indonesia. Kuala Lumpur resented the emergence of Singapore and her leaders into international prominence and also viewed with alarm her Israeli military experts, with their emphasis on aggressive, pre-emptive strike tactics, and Singapore's implied affinity with Israel as a small nation in a potentially hostile area of 'jungle Arabs'.

Singapore's urgent nationalism had stressed her individuality, her separateness from her immediate neighbours. The need for survival engendered a self-centred outlook, while success bred arrogance. Her leaders cultivated a style of plain speech which was effective in Singapore and often admired in developed countries but grated and jarred when it was used to criticize and denigrate her neighbours. On an official visit to Thailand in 1973 Lee Kuan Yew's hosts welcomed him to the house but remonstrated gently that they did not want to be told it was dirty. A mini-Middle Kingdom, cocksure and proud of her own rapid achievements, Singapore was impatient with other nations' difficulties, prone to offer unsought advice and unable to appreciate that methods which worked well in her own small community could not be transplanted to other countries with more complex, if perhaps less stark, problems.

Throughout her history the profits made by Singapore in providing the servicing infrastructure for the development of neighbouring areas, which were more liberally endowed with natural resources, had been a source of resentment. In modern times this acquired a new bitterness with racial undertones, since, despite her multi-racial policy, Singapore was essentially a Chinese city. While Malaysia and Indonesia tried to diversify the internal control of their own economies, the Chinese in both countries continued to play a dominant commercial role. Singapore remained the channel for a major part of the Chinese-controlled commerce of South-East Asia, so that her prosperity was a source of political embarrassment and isolation in the region. The political leadership in Indonesia and Malaysia looked upon Singapore as an economic parasite.

Both Indonesia and Malaysia strove to free themselves from economic dependence on Singapore. Indonesia set out to attract major oil-servicing activities and build up her own rubber-milling industry. Malaysia broke the formal economic links which had survived the political separation of Singapore and Malaysia. Malaysia Singapore Airlines was dissolved in 1972, after which the two countries operated separate national airlines. In 1973 the Malaysian government decided to separate the joint currency and to split the Malaysia-Singapore stock exchange. The end of common currency control and stock market trading was followed a few weeks later by the setting up of an independent rubber market in Kuala Lumpur, which threatened Singapore's pre-eminence as rubber broker.

Singapore's interests clashed with those of Malaysia and Indonesia over the Straits of Malacca, which Singapore was anxious to keep as an international waterway but Malaysia and Indonesia wished to treat as part of their territorial waters.

During confrontation Singapore had said many harsh things about Indonesia, at one point likening her ambitions to those of Japan in the 1930s and accusing her of 'grooming itself for the role of protector in South-East Asia'.[47] Singapore's insistence in October 1968 on executing Indonesian saboteurs responsible for bomb killings during confrontation, despite President Suharto's personal pleas for clemency, sparked off anti-Singapore violence in Djakarta, during which the Singapore ambassador had to flee for his life.

This friction hurt Singapore's real interests. Malaysia was Singapore's major trading partner, and while trade figures with Indonesia were a jealously guarded secret, probably one-fifth of Indonesia's trade passed through Singapore.

Britain's military run-down forced Singapore and Malaysia to draw closer together, and the international 'cold war' thaw dictated a fundamental reappraisal of South-East Asian relations. The admission of the People's Republic of China to the United Nations in 1971, its subsequent normalization of international relations, the lessening antipathy between China and the United States from 1972, the *rapprochement* between Washington and Moscow, America's withdrawal from Vietnam at the end of 1972 and the fall of Indo-China to communist rule in 1975 all combined to change the premises upon which international relations had rested since the end of World War II.

Singapore feared that in the new international climate small vulnerable powers might be trampled underfoot. During the 1950s and 1960s while the 'third world' of the Afro-Asian anti-colonial group was a force to be reckoned with in the United Nations and presented something akin to a united front, the big powers paid court and looked for its support in the east/west 'cold war'. In the early 1970s, as the big powers reverted to policies based on traditional national interests, the fragile Afro-Asian group disintegrated and small nations lost their bargaining power. The prospect of general international peace did not mean the end of localized wars and in some ways made them more likely.[48] When President Nyerere of Tanzania, at the Commonwealth heads of government conference in Ottawa in 1973, quoted an African proverb that it was the grass which was hurt when elephants fight, Lee Kuan Yew countered grimly that 'when elephants flirt the grass also suffers. And when they make love, it is disastrous'.

For the countries of South-East Asia the best chance of preservation lay in setting their own neighbourhood in order, cultivating prosperity and contentment within their countries, building up regional co-operation and persuading friendly big powers to guarantee their integrity. While seeking friendship and active support from powerful countries, Singapore wanted to forge closer links and repair damaged relationships with her neighbours. In a world of changed priorities, where South-East Asian cohesion was an important factor, Singapore recognized Indonesia as the natural leader of the region. Political unity with Malaysia had failed, but the defence of the two countries was inseparable and a close working relationship was necessary to counter the artificial and vulnerable nature of Singapore's existence.

The path to regional co-operation was not easy. Singapore was a founder member of the Association of South-East Asian Nations (ASEAN), formed with Indonesia, Malaysia, Thailand and the Philippines in 1967, but in the early 1970s ASEAN remained a collection of disunited states, competitive rather than complementary in their economies and threatened by internal tensions.

As a first step the Malaysian and Singapore leaders began to patch up their differences. In 1970 Goh Keng Swee inaugurated tax concessions to encourage Singaporeans to invest in the Malaysian and Indonesian economies. In 1972 Lee Kuan Yew paid his first visit to Kuala Lumpur since separation, and in cordial talks with the prime minister, Tun Abdul Razak, promised co-operation and increased support for Singapore investment in Malaysia. The following year Tun Abdul Razak reciprocated the visit in a spirit of warmth and harmony.

In 1973 Lee Kuan Yew visited Indonesia for the first time in thirteen years. It was an unexpected success. After a solemn ceremony at the graves of the saboteurs whom Singapore had executed five years before, Lee Kuan Yew and Suharto held friendly talks, and the two leaders issued a joint communique, speaking in terms of 'increasing cordialitv'. These were not empty platitudes, for both realized the need for firm friendship and regional solidarity to safeguard themselves as small fry in a dangerous sea. President Suharto reciprocated the visit in 1974, when the Singapore and Indonesian leaders again met on friendly terms.

The need to find a formula to protect the Straits of Malacca brought Indonesia, Malaysia and Singapore together in frequent conference in 1972. The three nations recognized their inter-dependence in checking communist subversion following the arrest in March 1972 of a Malayan Communist Party agent, smuggled out of Indonesia with plans to step up guerrilla activity in Malaysia, using Singapore as an infiltration base. Both Indonesian and Malaysian leaders realized that, whatever their antipathy towards the PAP, the present régime constituted the surest safeguard against a communist Singapore. Singapore shed her Israeli military advisers, whose presence had alarmed Indonesia as much as Malaysia, and played down her image as the Israel of South-East Asia, 'a far-fetched analogy', as Goh Keng Swee called this in December 1972.[49]

While ASEAN members were agreed on the need for closer co-operation in principle, they differed in their view of the region's international role. In 1972 ASEAN supported a proposal put forward by Tun Abdul Razak that South-East Asia should be a 'zone of peace, freedom and neutrality', seeking the support of all the small powers in the area, backed by the guarantee of non-interference from the big powers. But while Singapore saw the Association of South-East Asian Nations as a useful political force, she put little trust in the dream of neutralization and had more faith in winning guarantees of protection from big powers.

The unexpectedly swift collapse of Indo-China to the communists in the spring of 1975 put the ASEAN nations in a quandary. It revived fears that communism would spread to the rest of South-East Asia and give a fresh lease of life to guerrilla movements, which China might support as a counterweight to Russian influence in Indo-China.

The dangers of the new situation drew the ASEAN countries closer together, and at a summit meeting held in Bali in February 1976 their leaders showed a spirit of harmony and agreement to co-operate. But practical policies were left flexible and undecided. The fall of Indo-China to communist rule destroyed South-East Asian confidence in the United States as its protector and led each country to re-assess its relationship with China, the Soviet Union and Indo-China. In 1974 Malaysia had been the first South-East Asian country to establish diplomatic relations with China. Now the Philippines and Thailand also began talks with Peking and hurriedly began to loosen their ties with the United States. Singapore still looked to trade with the United States, Japan and western Europe to help maintain prosperity as the most effective bulwark against communism, but she sent goodwill and trade missions to Peking in 1975, and Lee Kuan Yew paid a state visit to China the following year. Anxious to play down Singapore's image as a Chinese city, the prime minister re-iterated in January 1976 that his country would be the last ASEAN country to establish formal diplomatic ties with Peking. At the same time he wished to cultivate friendship with China as the most benign super-power and a check against any southward Vietnamese expansion.

On the tenth anniversary of independence in August 1975 Singapore celebrated National Day in a sober mood. After nearly a decade of spectacular economic expansion, in 1975 she registered near zero growth. She had weathered the international economic turbulence of 1973–75 without wage cuts, high unemployment or great social strain, but the immediate prospects of renewed economic growth were poor, and in the long term the end of the cheap fuel age meant that Singapore might never again enjoy the boom of her early years of independence. With a third of her total manufacturing investment in refinery capacity, she was more hard hit than any other country in the region by the rising cost of crude oil and consequent increases in transportation costs.

The government had encouraged the type of dynamic economy which was becoming increasingly vulnerable in the modern world. It needed to remain highly competitive vis-à-vis Singapore's neighbours, predicating constant expansion and greater sophistication in industrial production and finance. Against this no new political leadership was emerging with the flair to cope with the changing situation or to take the economy on to a higher plane. In the mid-1970s the old leaders still showed some of their customary resilience and adaptability in reacting to the world recession and regional political changes. But they found it more difficult to galvanize the new generation of Singaporeans into urgent response to the crises, nor did the situation draw out younger men with a new approach to a radically changed world.

In continuing to silence dissent when such suppression was often no longer relevant the government removed opportunities for new ideas and thought to emerge. Strong leadership produced an outwardly stable disciplined society at the expense of sapping initiative and independent thought. The result, as Goh Keng Swee complained as early as 1970, was, 'We have in Singapore intellectual conformity in place of intellectual inquisitiveness and the sum total is a depressing climate of intellectual sterility.'

Singapore had left Malaysia in 1965 with vague suggestions that she might eventually return, but as the years passed this became less realistic. She had achieved independence not by her own design but as a result of outside pressures. Even then she remained under the shield of British military protection, her economy still largely geared to Britain. She continued tied to colonial apron strings longer than any other country in South-East Asia. In the 1970s these strings were severed, and Singapore had to establish her status as a South-East Asian country, specifically in her membership of ASEAN.

With the strengthening of the Suharto regime in Indonesia and of Tun Abdul Razak's administration in Malaysia, Singapore's brief pre-eminence faded and she needed to adapt to being one unit in ASEAN, the smallest in size and in population of the member countries and the odd man out ethnically and culturally.

Her attitude of mind changed to meet the new circumstances. The Arab oil-embargo of 1973 underlined Singapore's economic vulnerability and compelled her to drop the arrogant economic stance which she had adopted since independence. She came to terms with the oil-producing Arab states and, more important, began assuming a more modest role with her immediate neighbours.

At many times in her past Singapore was faced with the prospect of danger and sometimes of extinction. Yet each time the prophets of doom were confounded. According to astrologers, the combination of stars under which modern Singapore was established spelt her lasting good fortune. But throughout her history she was saved by the intelligent and vigorous exploitation of good luck. Her ethnic composition and the lack of indigenous raw materials, which her neighbours have in abundance, create a constant need for delicate balancing and quick wittedness. Singapore's independent existence defies all accepted modern concepts of politics and economics. It is a place which can never relax in its continuing struggle for survival.

1. State of Singapore, *Comments of the Singapore government on the Memorandum by Nineteen Singapore Opposition Assemblymen to the United Nations Committee on Colonialism* (Singapore, 1962).

2. *ST*, 25 May 1965.

3. T.J. Bellows, *The People's Action Party of Singapore* (New Haven, 1971), pp. 56–7.

4. Lee Kuan Yew, *Singapore Parliamentary Debates*, Vol. 24, 14 December 1965.

5. Detailed in Lau Teik Soon, 'Malaysia-Singapore Relations: Crisis of Adjustment, 1965–68', *JSEAH*, X, 1 (1969), pp. 155–76; Background in R.S. Milne, 'Singapore's Exit from Malaysia: the Consequences of Ambiguity', *Asian Survey*, VI, 3 (1966), pp. 175–84.

6. *ST*, 20 October 1965.

7. *Utusan Melayu*, 20 March 1967.

8. Garth Alexander, *Silent Invasion: the Chinese in Southeast Asia* (London, 1973), p. 214. Reprinted as *The Invisible China* (New York, 1974).

9. Singapore Constitution 1966. Reprinted with amendments. *Republic of Singapore Government Gazette Reprints Supplement (Acts)* No. 14, March 1966.

10. See Ismail bin Kassim, *Problems of Elite Cohesion: a Perspective from a Minority Community* (Singapore, 1974); W.A. Hanna, 'The Malays' Singapore', *American Universities Field Staff Reports, Southeast Asia Series*, Vol. XIV, Nos. 2–6 (New York, January–February, 1966); Sharom Ahmat and James Wong (eds.), *Malay Participation in the National Development of Singapore* (Singapore, 1971).

11. Anirudha Gupta (ed.), *Indians Abroad: Asia and Africa* (New Delhi, 1971) discusses problems of role, citizenship, language etc. in Singapore and Malaysia.

12. H. Hughes and You Poh Seng (eds.), *Foreign Investment and Industrialization in Singapore* (Canberra and Wisconsin, 1969) gives a useful analysis of foreign investment. See also P.J. Drake, *Financial Development in Malaya and Singapore* (Canberra, 1969); Economic Development Board, *The Jurong Story* (Singapore, 1967).

13. P. Darby, *British Defence Policy East of Suez, 1947–1968* (London, 1973). An able discussion on decolonization and defence policy.

14. Harold Wilson, *The Labour Government, 1964–1970: a Personal Record* (London, 1971), p. 483.

15. D. McDougall, 'The Wilson Government and the British Defence Commitment in Malaysia/Singapore', *JSEAS*, IV, 2 (1972), pp. 229–40 discusses British defence policy between 1964 and 1970.

16. See Alex Josey, *Lee Kuan Yew in London* (Singapore, 1968).

17. *Yang di-pertuan Negara's* opening speech, 8 December 1965, *Singapore Parliamentary Debates*, Vol. 24.

18. Text of industrial legislation and political speeches in Alex Josey, *Labour Laws in a Changing Singapore* (Singapore, 1968); see also W.E. Chalmers, *Crucial Issues in Industrial Relations in Singapore* (Singapore, 1967) for background study.

19. Chiang Hai Ding, 'The Early Shipping Conference System of Singapore, 1897–1911', *JSEAH*, X, 1 (1969), pp. 50–68.

20. *Financial Times*, London, 1 October 1973.

21. Ministry of Finance, 'Economic Survey of Singapore', 1 March 1975, and Hon Sui Sen, Budget Statement, March 1975, reported in *The Mirror*, 18 March 1974, Vol. 10, no. 11.

22. Hon Sui Sen, Budget statement, March 1975, reported in *The Mirror*, 17 March 1975, Vol. 11, no. 11.

23. Goh Keng Swee in speech to annual meeting International Monetary Fund and World Bank, Washington, October 1969.

24. *Singapore Bulletin*, July 1975, p. 9.

25. Goh Keng Swee, Minister of Defence, 12 July 1974, *The Mirror*, 22 July 1974, Vol. 10, No. 29.

26. Yong Nyuk Lin, April 1959, People's Action Party, *The Tasks Ahead* (Singapore, 1959), p. 2.

27. Lee Kuan Yew, *New Bearings in Our Education System* (Singapore, 1966).

28. Singapore Legislative Assembly, *Commission of Inquiry into Education (final report)*, (Lim Tay Boh report), Cmd. 8 of 1964 (Singapore 1964).

29. *The Asian*, 19 November 1972, quoting Lee Kuan Yew.

30. Lee Kuan Yew, *Social Revolution in Singapore* (Singapore, 1967) gives text of this speech.

31. *New Nation*, 2 November 1971.

32. *Report of the Constitutional Commission* (Singapore, August 1966).

33. *ST*, 18 March 1967. Editorial comment.

34. *Singapore Parliamentary Debates*, 14, 15, 16, 17 March 1967, Vol. 25, Nos. 17, 18, 19, 20.

35. Constitution (Amendment) Act No. 19 of 1969.

36. Lee Kuan Yew on London television, 4 January 1972, reported in *New Nation*, 5 January 1972.

37. See Seah Chee Meow, *Community Centres in Singapore: their Political Involvement* (Singapore, 1974).

38. *Yang di-pertuan*'s speech, 8 December 1965. *Singapore Parliamentary Debates*, Vol. 24.

39. Singapore National Trades Union Congress, *Why Labour Must Go Modern* (Singapore, 1970); Singapore National Trades Union Congress, *Towards Tomorrow* (Singapore, 1973).

40. Lee Kuan Yaw at Rural East District Citizens' Consultative Committee, reported in *New Nation*, 7 September 1971.

41. Alex Josey, *The Singapore General Elections 1972* (Singapore, 1972) gives a detailed, pro-PAP account.

42. For details of this by-election see Alex Josey, *Democracy in Singapore* (Singapore, 1970).

43. Lee Kuan Yew, *The Battle for Merger* (Singapore, 1961), p. 166.

44. Tan Chwee Huat, *New Directions*, Vol. I, No. 2 (April 1974).

45. *The Asian*, 20 August 1972.

46. The thesis of Iain Buchanan's controversial *Singapore in Southeast Asia* (London, 1972).

47. S. Rajaratnam, *Malaysia and the Changing Patterns of World Politics* (Singapore, January 1964).

48. S. Rajaratnam, *The Asian*, 20 August 1972.

49. *The Asian*, 10 December 1972.

# Bibliography

## OFFICIAL RECORDS

OFFICIAL records of Singapore in the period from 1819 to 1867 when she was administered from India are to be found in the National Archives in Singapore, the India Office Library and Public Record Office in London, the Archives of West Bengal in Calcutta, and the National Archives of India in New Delhi.

The National Archives in Singapore house Straits Settlements Records in the series A to Z and AA to FF inclusive. The India Office Library in London holds Directors' Despatches, Board's Collections, Proceedings and Correspondence of the East India Company up to 1858 and Correspondence of the India Office from 1858 to 1867. Proceedings and Consultations of the East India Company and the India Office period are to be found in Calcutta and New Delhi. The Public Record Office in London houses Colonial Office, Foreign Office and War Office records relating to Singapore prior to 1867. The nature of these records are detailed in C.M. Turnbull, *The Straits Settlements, 1826–67* (London and Kuala Lumpur, 1972), pp. 392–4.

Official records relating to Singapore after 1867 are to be found in the National Archives in Singapore and the Public Record Office in London. The National Archives in Singapore hold dispatches between the Governor and the Colonial Office in the series:

| | |
|---|---|
| COD | Colonial Office Despatches to Governor from 1867 |
| COD/C | Colonial Office Despatches (Confidential) to Governor from 1867 |
| GD | Governor's Despatches to Colonial Office from 1867 |
| GD/C | Governor's Despatches (Confidential) to Colonial Office. |

These holdings are incomplete since much material was destroyed during World War II.

The Public Record Office in London has more complete holdings in the series:

| | |
|---|---|
| CO 144 | Labuan original correspondence (which contains material relating to the Straits Settlements prior to 1867) |
| CO 273 | Straits Settlements, original correspondence, 1838–1946 |
| CO 274 | Straits Settlements, Acts, 1867–1940 |
| CO 275 | Straits Settlements, Sessional papers, 1855–1939 |
| CO 276 | Straits Settlements, government gazettes, 1867–81 |
| CO 277 | Straits Settlements, Miscellanea, 1867–1939 |
| CO 537 | Supplementary correspondence, Straits Settlements, Federated Malay States and Singapore, 1873–1926 |

| | |
|---|---|
| CO 825 | Colonial Office, Eastern Department, original correspondence, 1927–46 |
| CO 865 | Colonial Office, Far Eastern Reconstruction, 1942–4 |
| WO 32 | War Office, General series. |
| WO 172 | Containing the Mountbatten Diaries |
| WO 203 | Military Headquarters Papers Far East (World War II) |
| CAB | Cabinet papers |

Colonial Office records pertaining to post-World War II in the series CO 953 Singapore, original correspondence 1946 onwards (a continuation of CO 273), are closed to public inspection until 1980.

## PARLIAMENTARY RECORDS

SINGAPORE
Straits Settlements Executive Council Proceedings, 1867–1941
Straits Settlements Legislative Council Proceedings, 1867–1941
Singapore, British Military Administration Advisory Council
   Proceedings, November 1945–March 1946
Singapore Advisory Council, Public Sessions, 1946–8
Singapore Legislative Council Proceedings, 1948–55
Singapore Legislative Assembly Proceedings, 1955–65
Singapore Parliamentary Debates, from 1965

BRITAIN
Hansard's Parliamentary Debates
British Parliament Accounts and Papers
British Sessional Papers

INDIA
Proceedings of the Legislative Council of India (1st ser.) 1854–61
Proceedings of the Legislative Council of India (2nd ser.) 1862–7

## PRIVATE PAPERS

The Royal Commonwealth Society Library, London, houses the British Association of Malaysia Historical Collection: 15 boxes of documents, personal reminiscences, manuscripts, typescripts and press cuttings relating to Singapore and Malaysia. This collection comprises mainly twentieth century materials but includes some earlier papers, notably the Straits Settlements Association minute books, 1887–1920, and letter books, 1876–1916.

Rhodes House Library, Oxford, has miscellaneous personal papers and diaries, relating to Singapore in the MSS British Empire and MSS Indian Ocean series. Most material relates to the twentieth century but some items date back to the 1840s.

The Public Record Office, India Office Library and British Museum in London, and the National Archives, Kuala Lumpur, house various collections of private papers relating to Singapore.

The India Office Library holds the minute books of the Association of British Malaya (subsequently the British Association of Malaysia), which was founded in 1920 and wound up in 1973.

## NEWSPAPERS

The main English-language press sources are:
*Malaya Tribune,* Singapore, 1914–51.
*Singapore Chronicle,* Singapore, 1824–37.
*Singapore Free Press,* Singapore. 1st ser. 1835–69
    2nd ser. 1884–1962 (incorporated into *Malay Mail* 1962).
*Singapore Herald* (1) (Japanese-owned), Singapore, 1939–41.
*Singapore Herald* (2), Singapore, 1970–1.
*Singapore Standard,* Singapore, 1950–9.
*Straits Times,* Singapore, 1845–1942, 1945 onwards.
*Syonan Times,* (later the *Syonan Shimbun*), Singapore, 1942–5.
    *The Asian,* Hong Kong, 1971–3 also carried articles on Singapore.

For details of the Malay vernacular press, see W.R. Roff, *Bibliography of Malay and Arabic Periodicals in the Straits Settlements and Peninsular Malay States, 1876–1941* (London, 1972). The major contemporary Malay-language newspapers are the *Utusan Melayu,* Singapore, 1939–57; Kuala Lumpur, 1957 onwards, and the *Berita Harian* (romanized), Kuala Lumpur, 1957 onwards.

The emergence of the Chinese press is treated in Chen Mong Hock, *The Early Chinese Newspapers of Singapore, 1881–1912* (Singapore, 1967). The leading Chinese-language newspapers are:
*Nanyang Siang Pau,* Singapore, 1923 +
*Sin Chew Jit Poh,* Singapore, 1929 +
Details of newspapers are given in P. Lim Pui Huen, *Newspapers published in the Malaysian area: with a union list of local holdings,* Institute of Southeast Asian Studies, Occasional paper No. 2 (Singapore, 1970).

## PERIODICALS

The most useful periodicals relating to Singapore's history are:
*Journal of the Straits Branch, Royal Asiatic Society* (Singapore, 1878–1922), 86 vols.
*Journal of the Malayan* (subsequently *Malaysian*) *Branch, Royal Asiatic Society* (Singapore and Kuala Lumpur, 1923 onwards), successor to the *Journal of the Straits Branch.*
*Journal of the Indian Archipelago and Eastern Asia* (Singapore, 1847–59), 12 vols.
*Memoirs of the Raffles Museum,* 1955 onwards.
*Journal of the South Seas Society* (Singapore, 1940 onwards).
*Journal of Southeast Asian History* (Singapore, 1960–9), 10 vols.

*Journal of Southeast Asian Studies* (Singapore, 1970 onwards) successor to the *Journal of Southeast Asian History*.
*Straits Chinese Magazine* (Singapore, 1897–1907).

The following discussion of sources is not a comprehensive bibliography, and further references on points of detail appear in the Chapter Notes.

## GENERAL

Singapore's history is treated as part of the Malay peninsula by N.J. Ryan, *A History of Malaysia and Singapore*, 5th revised edition (Kuala Lumpur, 1976), which provides a useful introduction for the general reader.

Various authors covered particular aspects of Singapore's development in W.E. Makepeace, R. St. J. Braddell and G.S. Brooke (eds.), *One Hundred Years of Singapore*, 2 vols. (London, 1921). The first history of Singapore as a separate entity was H.F. Pearson's short *Singapore: a Popular History, 1819–1960* (Singapore, 1961). Donald and Joanna Moore, *The First 150 Years of Singapore* (Singapore, 1969), viewed her history largely through the medium of contemporary accounts. The *Journal of Southeast Asian History*, X (1), 1969, and *Journal of the Malaysian Branch, Royal Asiatic Society*, XLII (1), 1965, were special issues commemorating the 150th anniversary of the founding of modern Singapore.

K.G. Tregonning (ed.), *Papers on Malayan History* (Singapore, 1962) contains articles on a number of Singaporean topics.

Much useful information is contained in official census reports, pre-World War II *Straits Settlements Annual Reports, Singapore Annual Reports* 1947–63, and *Singapore Yearbooks* from 1964.

Saw Swee-Hock, *Population in Transition* (Philadelphia, 1970) treats Singapore's population growth historically up to the mid-1960s. Further sources are indicated in Saw Swee-Hock, *The Demography of Malaysia, Singapore and Brunei: a Bibliography* (Hong Kong, 1970), and Saw Swee-Hock and Cheng Siok-Hwa, *A Bibliography of the Demography of Singapore* (Singapore, 1975).

Song Ong Siang, *One Hundred Years' History of the Chinese in Singapore* (London, 1923; reprinted Singapore, 1967) deals with the Singapore Chinese community in an anecdotal form. Other works put the Singapore Chinese in the broader setting of Malaya, such as V. Purcell, *The Chinese in Malaya* (London, 1948; reprinted Kuala Lumpur, 1967), and V. Purcell, *The Chinese in Modern Malaya* (Singapore, 1956; 2nd revised edition, Singapore, 1960), or of South-East Asia, such as V. Purcell, *The Chinese in South-East Asia* (Oxford, 1951); C.P. Fitzgerald, *The Southern Expansion of the Chinese People* (London, 1972); Naosaku Uchida, *The Overseas Chinese* (Stanford, 1959); Wang Gungwu's brief but useful survey, *A Short History of the Nanyang Chinese* (Singapore, 1959); and an unusual Marxist interpretation, N.A. Simoniya, *Overseas*

*Chinese in Southeast Asia: a Russian Study* (Ithaca, 1961).

Chinese migration and labour are discussed in individual periods, but W.L. Blythe, 'Historical Sketch of Chinese Labour in Malaya', *JMBRAS,* XX, 1 (1947), pp. 64–114, (reprinted Singapore, 1953) gives a general outline.

C. Gamba, 'Chinese Associations in Singapore', *JMBRAS,* XXXIX, 2 (1966), pp. 123–68 gives details of various contemporary associations and their historical antecedents.

The most comprehensive history of Chinese secret societies in Malaya is W.L. Blythe, *The Impact of the Chinese Secret Societies in Malaya* (London, 1969), which expands and challenges M.L. Wynne's pioneer study, *Triad and Tabut* (Singapore, 1941), L. Comber, *Chinese Secret Societies in Malaya* (New York and Singapore, 1959), and L. Comber, *The Traditional Mysteries of Chinese Secret Societies in Malaya* (Singapore, 1951). Mak Lau Fong, 'The Forgotten and Rejected Community: a Sociological Study of Chinese Secret Societies in Singapore and West Malaysia', (Sociology Department, University of Singapore, 1973) provides a new insight, using field interviews rather than colonial records.

Studies of the Indian community concentrate on peninsular Malaya. The most comprehensive account of the history of the Singapore Indian community is contained in Kernial Singh Sandhu, *Indians in Malaya* (Cambridge 1969). S. Arasaratnam, *Indians in Malaysia and Singapore* (Bombay and Kuala Lumpur, 1970) is a useful shorter work. G. Netto, *Indians in Malaya* (Singapore, 1961) is a short pioneer account. U. Mahajani, *The Role of Indian Minorities in Burma and Malaya* (Bombay, 1960) is concerned with the peninsula and has little to say about Singapore Indians.

Minority groups are considered in S. Durai Raja Singam, *A Hundred Years of Ceylonese in Malaya and Singapore, 1867–1967* (Kuala Lumpur, 1968); M. Teixeira, *The Portuguese Missions in Malaya and Singapore 1511–1958,* 3 vols. (Lisbon, 1963), of which Volume III, *Singapore,* has interesting material about Portuguese and some prominent Eurasian families; and J. Vredenbregt, 'Bawean Migration: some preliminary notes', *Bijdragen Tot de Taal-, Land-, en Volkenkunde,* CXX (1964), pp. 109–37, which looks at the Boyanese community.

The development of education before World War II is discussed in D.D. Chelliah's influential *A History of the Educational Policy of the Straits Settlements* (Kuala Lumpur, 1947; reprinted Singapore, 1960), and post-war development in S. Gopinathan, *Towards a National System of Education in Singapore, 1945–1973* (Singapore, 1974). T.W. Doraisamy (ed.), *150 Years of Education in Singapore* (Singapore, 1969) gives an overall treatment. E. Wijeysingha, *A History of Raffles Institution, 1823–1963* (Singapore, 1964) tells the story of Singapore's oldest English-medium school.

There is no comprehensive economic history of Singapore, which has hitherto been treated as part of South-East Asia or Malaya as in G.C. Allen and A.G. Donnithorne, *Western Enterprise in Indonesia and Malaya*

(New York, 1957, reprinted New York, 1968), and Lim Chong Yah, *The Economic Development of Modern Malaya* (Kuala Lumpur, 1967), which covers the period 1874–1963. Li Dun-jen, *British Malaya: an Economic Analysis* (New York, 1955) is a small factual book covering the period 1895–1938 and mostly about the peninsula. C.D. Cowan (ed.), *The Economic Development of South-East Asia* (London, 1964) is a collection of papers weighted heavily on Malaya and Singapore.

Economic studies relating to specific periods are noted in the following sections, but some works cover a wider span of time. These include histories of Singapore companies, such as: K.G. Tregonning, *Home Port Singapore* (London, 1967), a substantial history of the Straits Steamship Company from 1890 to 1965; S. Cunyngham-Brown, *The Traders* (London, 1970), concerning Guthries, Singapore's longest surviving firm.

K.G. Tregonning, *The Singapore Cold Storage Company, 1903–1966* (Singapore, 1966) and *Straits Tin: a Brief Account of the First Seventy Five Years of the Straits Trading Company Ltd., 1887–1962* (Singapore, 1962); and E. Jennings's handsomely illustrated *Mansfields: Transport and Distribution in Southeast Asia* (Singapore, 1973) and *Wheels of Progress: Seventy Five Years of Cycle and Carriage* (Singapore, 1975) are shorter works but contain much interesting material.

J.W.N. Kyshe, *Cases Heard and Determined in H.M. Supreme Court of the Straits Settlements, 1808–84*, 3 vols. (Singapore, 1885) gives a valuable introduction to the early history of legal development in Singapore. R. St. J. Braddell, *The Law of the Straits Settlements*, 2 vols. (Singapore, 1916; 2nd edition, Singapore, 1931) has a chapter on the reception of English law into the Straits. Ahmad Ibrahim bin Mohammed, *Towards a History of Law in Malaysia and Singapore* (Singapore, 1970), in an interesting lecture looks behind British law to customary law and its survival. Constitutional questions are discussed in C.M. Turnbull, 'Constitutional Development of Singapore, 1819–1968', in *Modern Singapore*, ed. by Ooi Jin Bee and Chiang Hai Ding (Singapore, 1969).

## THE FOUNDATION OF THE SETTLEMENT, 1819–1826

### EARLY SINGAPORE/TEMASEK

The major part of *JMBRAS*, XLII, I (1969), the Singapore 150th Anniversary Commemorative Issue, is devoted to reprints of articles appearing in past issues of the *JMBRAS* and *JSBRAS* concerning pre-colonial Singapore and the early years of the modern settlement.

The earliest indigenous history of Temasek/Singapura is the *Sejarah Melayu (Malay Annals)*, probably written in the early seventeenth century, the most outstanding and colourful of Malay histories. The best English version is C.C. Brown (trans.), 'Sejarah Melayu or "Malay Annals"': a translation of Raffles MS 17', *JMBRAS*, XXV, parts 2 and 3 (1953); reprinted as *Sejarah Melayu: 'Malay Annals'* (Kuala Lumpur, 1970).

O.W. Wolters, *The Fall of Srivijaya in Malay History* (Ithaca, 1970) is a controversial but stimulating interpretation of Temasek's history in the fourteenth century.

There is useful discussion on fourteenth-century Temasek in P. Wheatley, *The Golden Khersonese* (Singapore, 1961), an impressive historical geography of early Malaya, and P. Wheatley, *Impressions of the Malay Peninsula in Ancient Times* (Singapore, 1964).

Haji Buyong Adil, *Sejarah Singapura: Rujukan Khas Mengenai Peristiwa-peristiwa Sebelum Tahun 1824* (Kuala Lumpur, 1972) tells the story from the Malay viewpoint.

THE FOUNDING OF MODERN SINGAPORE

Malay historical sources relating to the background of Malay politics are discussed in J.C. Bottoms, 'Some Malay Historical Sources' in Soedjatmoko (ed.), *An Introduction to Indonesian Historiography* (Ithaca, 1965), being a revised version of J.C. Bottoms, 'Malay Historical Works', *JSSS*, XV, 2 (1959), pp. 69–98, reprinted in K.G. Tregonning (ed.), *Malayan Historical Sources* (Singapore, 1962).

The best Malay source is the *Tuhfat al-Nafis* (or *Precious Gift*), written by Raja Ali Al-Haji bin Raja Ahmad of Riau in 1865, covering the history of Riau and south Malaya from the seventeenth to the mid-nineteenth centuries. There is no English translation but a romanized version was published as *Tuhfat al-Nafis: Sejarah Melayu dan Bugis* (Singapore, 1965). The Jawi text with an English summary appears in R.O. Winstedt (trans. and ed.), 'A Malay History of Riau and Johore', *JMBRAS*, X, 2 (1932), pp. 1–299 (text) and 300–20 (summary). C.H. Wake, 'Raffles and the Rajas', *JMBRAS*, XLVIII, 1 (1975), pp. 47–73 uses this source to place the foundation of modern Singapore in the setting of Malay politics.

Sophia, Lady Raffles, *Memoir of the Life and Public Services of Sir Thomas Stamford Raffles* (London, 1830) gives a vivid personal portrayal of her husband and incorporates many of his letters. See also J.R. Logan (ed.), 'Notes Illustrative of the Life and Services of Sir Thomas Stamford Raffles', *JIA*, IX (1855), pp. 306–24.

The definitive biography of Raffles remains to be written. Of existing biographies the best and most meticulously researched is C.E. Wurtzburg, *Raffles of the Eastern Isles* (London, 1954). Older studies by D.C. de K. Boulger, *The Life of Sir Stamford Raffles* (London, 1897, reprinted London, 1973); H.E. Egerton, *Sir Stamford Raffles: England in the Far East* (London, 1900), and R. Coupland, *Raffles, 1781–1826* (London, 1926), 3rd edition as *Raffles of Singapore* (London, 1946), tended to be uncritically admiring. E. Hahn, *Raffles of Singapore* (London, 1946, reprinted Kuala Lumpur, 1968) is a racy but readable account and more perceptive than M. Collis, *Raffles* (London, 1966). Syed Hussein Alatas, *Thomas Stamford Raffles, 1781–1826: Schemer or Reformer* (Sydney, 1971) gives an individual, over-critical interpretation.

The diplomatic background to the founding of modern Singapore is covered in detail in H. Marks, 'The First Contest for Singapore: 1819–

1824', *Verhandelingen van het Koninklijk Instituut voor Taal-, Land-, en Volkenkunde,* XXVII (The Hague, 1959), and N. Tarling, *Anglo-Dutch Rivalry in the Malay World, 1780–1824* (Cambridge and Queensland, 1962). For additional matter relating to John Palmer, the Calcutta merchant, see N. Tarling, 'The Prince of Merchants and the Lion City', *JMBRAS,* XXXVI, 1 (1964), pp. 20–40; reprinted in Ǹ. Tarling, *Imperial Britain in South East Asia* (Kuala Lumpur, 1975).

There are two excellent collections of documents relating to early Singapore: T. Braddell, 'Notices of Singapore', *JIA,* VII (1853), pp. 325–57; *JIA,* VIII (1854), pp. 97–111, 329–48, 403–19; *JIA,* IX (1855), pp. 53–65, 442–82; and C.D. Cowan, 'Early Penang and the Rise of Singapore', *JMBRAS,* XXIII, 2 (1950), 210 pp.

J. Crawfurd, *Journal of an Embassy from the Governor-General to the Courts of Siam and Cochin China* (London, 1828, reprinted Kuala Lumpur, 1967), describes a visit to Singapore in 1822 and some aspects of Crawfurd's period as Resident from 1823–6. A vivid description is given by Munshi Abdullah bin Abdul Kadir, *The Hikayat Abdullah* (Singapore, 1849), of which the best English translation is the annotated edition by A.H. Hill, *JMBRAS,* XXVIII, 3 (1955), reprinted as *The Hikayat Abdullah* (Kuala Lumpur, 1970). Munshi Abdullah, who was born in Malacca of Malay/ Arab/Tamil descent, came to Singapore about 1820 and remained there for most of his life until he died in 1854. He had many connexions with the European community, and his colourful autobiography provides the only detailed Asian eye-witness account of Singapore's first thirty years. He was not in Singapore when the settlement was first founded, however, and his remarks about its establishment are not accurate.

C.B. Buckley, *An Anecdotal History of Old Times in Singapore, 1819– 1867* (Singapore, 1902, reprinted Kuala Lumpur, 1965), uses mainly contemporary newspapers to describe the early years.

A small book, H.F. Pearson, *This Other India* (Singapore, 1957) deals lightly with early Singapore, and K.G. Tregonning, *The British in Malaya: the First Forty Years, 1786–1826* (Tucson, Arizona, 1965) has a final chapter on the origins of modern Singapore.

## SINGAPORE, 1826–1867

The period is covered by L.A. Mills, 'British Malaya, 1824–67', *JMBRAS,* III, 2 (1925), revised as *JMBRAS,* XXXIII, 3 (1960), reprinted as *British Malaya, 1824–67* (Kuala Lumpur, 1966), and by C.M. Turnbull, *The Straits Settlements, 1826–67* (London and Kuala Lumpur, 1972), both of which have comprehensive bibliographies.

The *Journal of the Indian Archipelago and Eastern Asia,* edited by J.R. Logan, 12 vols. (Singapore, 1847–59) has many valuable articles on contemporary affairs in Singapore.

There are a number of valuable eye-witness accounts, notably A.H. Hill (ed. and trans.), 'The Hikayat Abdullah', *JMBRAS,* XXVIII, 3 (1955), reprinted as *The Hikayat Abdullah* (Kuala Lumpur, 1970).

G.W. Earl, *The Eastern Seas* (London, 1837, reprinted Kuala Lumpur, 1971) gives the best English view of Singapore in the 1830s, while P.J. Begbie, *The Malayan Peninsula* (Madras, 1834, reprinted Kuala Lumpur, 1967) and T.J. Newbold, *Political and Statistical Account of the British Settlements in the Straits of Malacca,* 2 vols. (London, 1839, reprinted Kuala Lumpur, 1971) each have a chapter on Singapore. Unfortunately a second volume of J.H. Moor (ed.), *Notices of the Indian Archipelago and the Adjacent Countries,* Vol. I (Singapore, 1837, reprinted London, 1968), which was to contain material on Singapore in the 1830s, was never published.

The best contemporary description of Singapore in the last years of Indian rule is J. Cameron, *Our Tropical Possessions in Malayan India* (London, 1865, reprinted Kuala Lumpur, 1965). Further factual information about this period is given in T. Braddell, *Singapore and the Straits Settlements Described* (Penang, 1858) and *Statistics of the British Possessions in the Straits of Malacca* (Penang, 1861).

J.T. Thomson, *Some Glimpses into Life in the Far East* (London, 1864) and *Sequel to Some Glimpses into Life in the Far East* (London, 1865) are unduly scathing about the Straits administration and Governor Butterworth in particular. O. Cavenagh, *Reminiscences of an Indian Official* (London, 1884) includes a detailed but uninspired account of his governorship. W.H. Read, *Play and Politics: Reminiscences of Malaya by an Old Resident* (London, 1901) is a disappointing book, the ramblings of an old man who played a prominent part in public affairs in mid-nineteenth-century Singapore.

J.F.A. McNair, *Prisoners their Own Warders* (London, 1899) is a valuable first-hand account of the convict system under the Indian régime.

J.D. Vaughan, *The Manners and Customs of the Chinese of the Straits Settlements* (Singapore, 1879, reprinted Kuala Lumpur, 1971) is a sympathetic contemporary account. Seah Eu Chin, 'The Chinese in Singapore: General Sketch of the Numbers, Tribes and Avocations of the Chinese in Singapore', *JIA,* II (1848), pp. 283–9 was contributed by a leading Chinese. Other useful studies by well-informed contemporaries are T. Braddell, 'Notes on the Chinese in the Straits', *JIA,* IX (1855), pp. 109–24; W.A. Pickering, 'The Chinese in the Straits of Malacca', *Frazer's Magazine,* October 1876; and W.A. Pickering, 'Chinese Secret Societies and their Origin', *JSBRAS,* I (1878), pp. 63–84 and II (1878), pp. 1–18.

J. Crawfurd, *A Descriptive Dictionary of the Indian Islands and Adjacent Countries* (London, 1856, reprinted Kuala Lumpur, 1971), pp. 395–402, has a long entry on Singapore.

C.B. Buckley, *An Anecdotal History of Old Times in Singapore, 1819–1867* (Singapore, 1902, reprinted Kuala Lumpur, 1965) is based mainly on excerpts from the *Singapore Free Press* from the late 1830s onwards.

Turning to more modern work, M. Freedman throws valuable light on Chinese society at that time in 'Immigrants and Associations: Chinese in 19th Century Singapore', *Comparative Studies in Society and History,* III,

(The Hague, 1960–1), pp. 25–48; 'Chinese Kinship and Marriage in Early Singapore', *JSEAH*, III, 2 (1962). See also Wong Choon San, *A Gallery of Chinese Kapitans* (Singapore, 1964), pp. 27–37; Lea E. Williams, 'Chinese Leadership in Early British Singapore', *Asian Studies*, II, 2 (1964), pp. 170–9; and Yong Ching Fatt, 'Chinese Leadership in Nineteenth Century Singapore', *Journal of the Island Society (Hsin-shê Hsüeh-pao)*, I (1967), pp. 1–18, which studies the background of fifteen important community leaders.

N. Tarling, 'British Policy in the Malay Peninsula and Archipelago, 1824–71', *JMBRAS*, XXX, 3 (1957), reprinted as *British Policy in the Malay Peninsula and Archipelago, 1824–71* (Kuala Lumpur, 1970) deals in meticulous detail with the relations between Singapore and the neighbouring regions. This theme is developed further in relation to piracy in N. Tarling, *Piracy and Politics in the Malay World: a Study of British Imperialism in the Nineteenth Century* (Melbourne, 1963).

Wong Lin Ken, 'The Trade of Singapore, 1819–69', *JMBRAS*, XXX, 4 (1960), 315 pp., is a thorough study of Singapore's trade prior to the opening of the Suez Canal.

## HIGH NOON OF EMPIRE, 1867–1914

Many aspects of this period are dealt with in W.E. Makepeace, R. St. J. Braddell and G.S. Brooke (eds.), *One Hundred Years of Singapore*, 2 vols., (London, 1921).

The leading English-language newspapers, the *Straits Times* and the *Singapore Free Press*, flourished during much of this period, and the first vernacular newspapers begin to throw light on some of the activities of the Muslim and Chinese communities. But there were no outstanding contemporary books.

J.D. Ross, *Sixty Years: Life and Adventure in the Far East*, 2 vols. (London, 1911, reprinted London, 1968) is a colourful story about himself and his relatives in Singapore, Borneo and the region in the second half of the century. But the most evocative picture of Singapore in the 1880s, although the port is not specifically named, appears in the stories of Joseph Conrad, and in particular 'The End of the Tether' in *Youth: a Narrative, and Two Other Stories* (Edinburgh, 1902) and *The Shadow Line* (New York and London, 1917). These are discussed in N. Sherry, *Conrad's Eastern World* (Cambridge, 1966), especially in a chapter on Singapore, pp. 173–94.

Conrad had more opportunity to study Singapore's port life than upper-class casual visitors who left brief impressions, such as Isabella Bird, *The Golden Chersonese and the Way Thither* (New York, 1883, reprinted Kuala Lumpur, 1967) or F. Caddy, *To Siam and Malaya in the Duke of Sutherland's Yacht 'Sans Peur'* (London, 1889). J.A. Bethune Cook, *Sunny Singapore* (London, 1907) has useful information about mission activities. E.A. Brown, *Indiscreet Memories* (London, 1935), a detailed diary of European social life at the beginning of the twentieth century, contains much trivia but has some revealing glimpses. R.O. Winstedt, *Start from Alif: Count from One* (Kuala Lumpur, 1969) describes his brief first impressions of Singapore when he arrived as a Malayan Civil Service cadet in 1902. Otto Ziegele, 'Singapore Diary, 1886–1890', unpublished MSS Ind. Ocn. S 95 (Rhodes House, Oxford) portrays the social life of young European commercial assistants.

Large-scale 'pride of empire' books published at the turn of the century tended to give potted histories and factual descriptions of Singapore but reflected the confident atmosphere of the time, such as N.B. Dennys, *A Descriptive Dictionary of British Malaya* (London, 1894), which was designed as a follow-up to Crawfurd's *Dictionary*; A. Wright and H.A. Cartwright, *Twentieth Century Impressions of British Malaya* (London, 1908), a monumental tome which devoted a section to Singapore's background, pp. 20–48; or A. Wright and T.H. Reid, *The Malay Peninsula: a Record of Progress in the Middle East* (London, 1912), a complacent work with a chapter on contemporary Singapore, pp. 217–36.

There is a wealth of literature on Singapore's relations with the Malay states and the spread of British rule, starting with the partly autobiographical work by Frank Swettenham, *British Malaya* (London, 1948, reprinted London, 1955).

Of modern histories based on original research into contemporary sources, Khoo Kay Kim, *The Western Malay States, 1850–1873* (Kuala Lumpur, 1972) shows the involvement of the Straits Settlements with the Malay states before the British formally intervened. The intervention is the subject of C.D. Cowan, *Nineteenth Century Malaya: the Origins of British Control* (London, 1961), and C.N. Parkinson, *British Intervention in Malaya, 1867–77* (Singapore, 1960). W.D. McIntyre, *The Imperial Frontier in the Tropics, 1865–75* (London and New York, 1967) and J.S. Galbraith, 'The "Turbulent Frontier" as a Factor in British Expansion', *Comparative Studies in Society and History*, II, 2 (1960), pp. 150–68, put the Malay states frontier problem in its imperial setting. E. Sadka, *The Protected Malay States, 1874–1895* (Kuala Lumpur, 1968) and E. Thio, *British Policy in the Malay Peninsula, 1880–1910, Volume I: the Southern and Central States* (Singapore, 1969) are excellent studies of the extension and consolidation of British rule.

E.M. Merewether, *Report on the Census of the Straits Settlements taken on the 5th April 1891* (Singapore, 1892) and J.R. Innes, *Report on the Census of the Straits Settlements taken on 1st March 1901* (London, 1901) contain vital information concerning Singapore's population.

Song Ong Siang, *One Hundred Years History of the Chinese in Singapore* (London, 1923, reprinted Singapore, 1967) is the major source of information on the Singapore Chinese in this period. The *Straits Chinese Magazine* (Singapore 1897–1907) has many pertinent articles, notably, G.T. Hare, 'The Straits Born Chinese', *Straits Chinese Magazine*, I, 1 (March, 1897), and Lim Boon Keng, 'The Role of the Straits Born Chinese in the Development of China', *Straits Chinese Magazine*, VII, 3 (September, 1903).

Wu Lien-Teh, *Plague Fighter: the Autobiography of a Modern Chinese Physician* (Cambridge, 1959) portrays Straits Chinese life at the turn of the century, although it relates primarily to Penang.

Turning to modern works, E. Thio, 'The Singapore Chinese Protectorate: Events and Conditions leading to its Establishment 1823–1877', *JSSS*, XVI, 1 & 2 (1960), pp. 40–80, is a careful study of the origins of the Chinese Protectorate. R.N. Jackson, *Pickering: Protector of Chinese* (Kuala Lumpur, 1965) is a short but interesting biography written by a former administrator in the Chinese secretariat in Malaya. R.N. Jackson, *Immigrant Labour and the Development of Malaya, 1786–1920* deals mostly with the Malay states but sets the work of the Protectorate in its Malayan context.

Png Poh Seng, 'The Straits Chinese in Singapore: a Case of Local Identity and Socio-Cultural Accommodation', *JSEAH*, X, 1 (1969), pp. 95–114 investigates problems facing Singapore Chinese society at this time.

W.R. Roff, *The Origins of Malay Nationalism* (New Haven and Kuala Lumpur, 1967) is a fine study of the Malayo-Muslim community at this period. Particularly relevant is the chapter published as 'The Malayo-Muslim World of Singapore in the late 19th Century', *Journal of Asian Studies*, XXIV (1964), pp. 75–89.

There are a number of good economic studies, notably Francis E. Hyde, *Far Eastern Trade, 1860–1914* (London, 1973); G. Bogaars, 'The Tanjong Pagar Dock Company, 1864–1905', *Memoirs of the Raffles Museum,* III (1956), pp. 117–266, a well-researched account of port development; Chiang Hai Ding, 'Sino-British Mercantile Relations in Singapore's Entrepôt Trade, 1870–1915', in J. Ch'en Chi-Jang and N. Tarling (eds.), *Studies in the Social History of China and South-East Asia* (Cambridge, 1970), pp. 247–66; G. Bogaars, 'The Effect of the Opening of the Suez Canal on the Trade and Development of Singapore', *JMBRAS*, XXVIII, 1 (1955), pp. 99–143.

## SINGAPORE, 1914–1941

The English-language press, joined in 1914 by the *Malaya Tribune*, and the Chinese newspapers, notably the *Nanyang Siang Pau* and the *Sin Chew Jit Poh*, both founded in the 1920s, are an invaluable source of material for this period.

The system of government attracted on-the-spot investigation in the late 1930s by a number of able North American scholars who produced some admirable studies of British colonial administration on the eve of World War II. R. Emerson, *Malaysia: a Study in Direct and Indirect Rule* (New York, 1937, reprinted Kuala Lumpur, 1964) is the most acute analysis and commentary on government and society in the Straits Settlements in the 1930s, though often critical and controversial in its day. L.A. Mills, *British Rule in Eastern Asia* (London, 1942), written before the Japanese war, is a balanced and sober assessment based on a 1936–7 visit and documentary study. Virginia Thompson, *Postmortem on Malaya* (New York, 1943) is a scholarly, well-researched and substantial analysis but highly critical of the colonial system in the light of the 1941–2 debacle. See also R. Emerson, L.A. Mills and V. Thompson, *Government and Nationalism in Southeast Asia* (New York, 1942).

The flavour of life in Singapore in the 1930s is conveyed in a number of interesting contemporary autobiographical accounts by Europeans, notably R. St. J. Braddell, *Lights of Singapore* (London, 1934) by a third-generation British Singaporean lawyer; R.C.H. McKie, *This Was Singapore* (London, 1950), the colourful account of a young journalist's life in the late 1930s; R.H.B. Lockhart, *Return to Malaya* (London, 1936), which compares the Singapore of the mid-1930s with the pre-World War I era. Two police officers published worthwhile reminiscences: R.H. de S. Onraet, *Singapore: a Police Background* (London, 1947), written by an Inspector-General of Police of the inter-war years; and A. Dixon, *Singapore Patrol* (London, 1935), describing a junior policeman's work in the mid-1920s. Victor Purcell, *The Memoirs of a Malayan Official* (London, 1965) are the experiences of a Malayan Civil Service official who served from 1921 to 1946, becoming Adviser on Chinese Affairs to the British Military Administration in 1945–6. In the inter-war years Purcell worked with the Chinese Protectorate, mainly in the Straits Settlements and part of the time in Singapore. A. Gilmour, *An Eastern Cadet's Anecdotage* (Singapore, 1974) gives some glimpses into a junior official's life, although his reminiscences relate mainly to up-country Malaya.

There are no comparable contemporary descriptions by Asian writers, with the exception of Janet Lim, *Sold for Silver* (London and New York, 1958), the fascinating autobiography of a *mui tsai* of the 1930s, who subsequently became a hospital matron.

The earlier years are not so well served by contemporary accounts. C. Wright, *Cameos of the Old Federated Malay States and Straits Settlements (1912–1924)* (Ilfracombe, 1972), letters written home by an ex-rubber planter who took an office job in Singapore, portrays something of life, particularly entertainment, among young Europeans. L. Guillemard, *Trivial Fond Records* (London, 1937) gives a disappointing description of his governorship from 1919 to 1927. H.M. Bleackley, *A Tour in Southern Asia (Indo-china, Malaya, Java, Sumatra and Ceylon, 1925–26)* (London, 1928) is a superficial tourist's impression.

C.A. Vlieland, *Census of British Malaya, 1931* (London, 1932) gives a detailed analysis of Singapore's population.

Victor Sim, *Biographies of Prominent Chinese in Singapore* (Singapore, 1950) gives short uncritical biographies in English and Chinese of many leading figures, including Tan Kah Kee, Lim Boon Keng, Lee Kong Chian, Tan Lark Sye and Aw Boon Haw. Singapore Chinese Chamber of Commerce, *Fifty Years of Enterprise* (Singapore, 1964), also has interesting material about Chinese leaders. There is as yet no English translation of Tan Kah Kee's autobiography, *Ch'en Chia-keng. Nan-ch'iao hui-i lu*, 2 vols. (Singapore, 1946).

A number of studies of the overseas Chinese and their home background throw valuable light on the Singapore Chinese as the major Nanyang community, notably Chen Ta, *Emigrant Communities in South China: a Study of Overseas Migration and its Influence on Standards of Living and Social Change* (Shanghai, 1939, and New York, 1940), based upon field work carried out in China in the mid-1930s. See also H.F. MacNair, *The Chinese Abroad, their Position and Protection: a Study of International Law and Relations* (Shanghai, 1925, reprinted Taipeh, 1971). Chen Ta, *Chinese Migrations, with special reference to Labour Conditions* (Washington, 1923, reprinted New York, 1967), has only a small section on Malaya.

J. Chesneaux, *The Chinese Labor Movement, 1919–1927* (French original edition, 1962; trans. by H.M. Wright, Stanford, 1968) is invaluable as a background study. There are several useful works on the inter-war labour movement in Singapore, which affected mainly the Chinese: C. Gamba, *The Origins of Trade Unionism in Malaya: a Study of Colonial Labour Unrest* (Singapore, 1962) is a substantial well-researched work. J.N. Parmer, 'Attempts at Labor Organization by Chinese Workers in Certain Industries in the 1930s' in K.G. Tregonning (ed.), *Papers on Malayan History* (Singapore, 1962), pp. 239–55, gives an interesting insight into the labour movement in Singapore among seamen, pineapple industry and building workers. This is amplified in Tai Yuen, 'Labour Unrest in Malaya, 1934–1941', unpublished M. Phil. thesis, University of Hong Kong, 1973. Virginia Thompson, *Labour Problems in Southeast Asia* (New Haven, 1947) is a survey of the inter-war labour position, but her chapter on Malaya, pp. 62–116, deals mainly with the peninsula. Bruno Lasker, *Human Bondage in Southeast Asia* (North Carolina, 1950) is concerned briefly with the Singapore *mui tsai* question.

On the political activities of the Singapore Chinese, Y. Akashi, *The Nanyang Chinese Anti-Japanese National Salvation Movement, 1937–41* (Kansas, 1970) is a valuable pioneer study, based on Japanese, English and Chinese sources. Pang Wing Seng, 'The Double Seventh Incident, 1937: Singapore Chinese Response to the Outbreak of the Sino-Japanese War', *JSEAS*, IV, 2 (1973), pp. 269–99, offers an insight into leadership and institutions among the Singapore Chinese.

Kuomintang activities are discussed in Png Poh Seng, 'The KMT in Malaya', *JSEAH*, II, 2 (1961), pp. 1–32, reprinted in K.G. Tregonning (ed.), *Papers on Malayan History* (Singapore, 1962).

J.D. Brimmell's excellent study, *Communism in South East Asia* (London, 1959) sets the movement in Singapore in the context of the region, while C.B. McLane, *Soviet Strategies in Southeast Asia: an Explanation of Eastern Policy under Lenin and Stalin* (Princeton, 1966) sets Singapore in the communist international background. J.D. Brimmell, *A Short History of the Malayan Communist Party* (Singapore, 1956) is very brief. Harry Miller, *Menace in Malaya* (London, 1954) has a good readable account of the early communist movement in Singapore.

The private papers of Tan Cheng Lock, the most politically active

Straits Chinese leader, are housed in the National Archives, Malaysia. Tan Cheng Lock, *Malayan Problems: from a Chinese Point of View*, ed. by C.Q. Lee (Singapore, 1947) comprises speeches and pamphlets composed by Tan Cheng Lock before, during, and immediately after World War II. The Arthur Creech-Jones Papers, MSS Brit. Emp. S332, Box 26, File 11, (Rhodes House, Oxford) relate to Singapore in the 1930s, including Tan Cheng Lock's activities and questions of legislative council reform.

D.D. Chelliah's seminal, *A History of the Educational Policy of the Straits Settlements* (Kuala Lumpur, 1947; 2nd edition, Singapore 1960), completed before the Japanese war, is the most comprehensive treatment of the subject. Victor Purcell, *Problems of Chinese Education* (London, 1936) is a substantial and useful book by an official directly involved. J.S. Nagle, *Educational Needs of the Straits Settlements and Federated Malay States* (Baltimore, 1928) contains much detailed information about the system, and R.O. Winstedt, *Education in Malaya* (Singapore, 1924), a booklet written when the author was Director of Education, is a useful summary.

No definitive study has been published about the sepoy mutiny of 1915. Rhodes House, Oxford, and the Royal Commonwealth Society Library, London, house some personal reminiscences, R.W. Mosbergen, 'The Sepoy Rebellion: a History of the Singapore Mutiny, 1915', B.A. academic exercise, University of Malaya (Singapore, 1954) is a readable narrative; Lauterbach's role is described in a dated but once popular book, Lowell Thomas, *Lauterbach of the China Sea* (London, 1930). A.C. Bose, *Indian Revolutionaries Abroad* (Patna, 1971) has a little about the mutiny and the attempts to build up anti-British feeling in Japan in World War I.

## WAR IN THE EAST, 1941–1942

### Pre-war Defence Policy

W.R. Louis, *British Strategy in the Far East, 1919–1939* (Oxford, 1971), puts the Singapore base in the context of general British strategic policy in the Far East.

The naval-base question is considered in C.N. Parkinson, 'The Pre-1942 Singapore Naval Base', *United States Naval Institute Proceedings*, Vol. 82, no. 9 (1956), pp. 939–54; C.N. Parkinson, *Britain in the Far East: the Singapore Naval Base* (Singapore, 1955); W.D. McIntyre, 'The Strategic Significance of Singapore, 1917–42; the Naval Base and the Commonwealth', *JSEAH*, X, 1 (1969), pp. 69–94; and W.D. McIntyre, 'New Zealand and the Singapore Base between the Wars', *JSEAS*, II, 1 (1971), pp. 2–21.

N. Shorrick, *Lion in the Sky: the Story of Seletar and the Royal Air Force in Singapore* (Kuala Lumpur, 1968) is a fairly detailed study. H.A. Probert, *History of Changi* (Singapore, 1965) is a small book but contains some interesting information.

I.H. Nish, *Alliance in Decline: a Study of Anglo-Japanese Relations, 1908–23* (London, 1972) is a sound scholarly treatment of the early diplomatic background.

### THE MILITARY CAMPAIGN

There are voluminous first-hand and secondary accounts in English, but few written by Japanese or Singaporeans.

Of accounts by leading participants, the most essential reading are Lt.-Gen. A.E. Percival, *The War in Malaya* (London, 1949) and *Operations of Malaya Command, from 8th December 1941 to 15th February 1942* (HMSO, London, 1948); and Lt.-Gen. H. Gordon Bennett, *Why Singapore Fell* (Sydney, 1944). See also Sir W.S. Churchill, *The Second World War, Vol. IV: the Hinge of Fate* (London, 1951). John Connell (ed. and completed by Brigadier Michael Roberts), *Wavell, Supreme Commander, 1941–1943* (London, 1969), contains many documents; Sir Henry Pownall, *Chief of Staff: the Diaries of Lieutenant-General Sir Henry Pownall, Vol. II, 1940–44*, ed. Brian Bond (London, 1974) refers to Pownall's brief command in Singapore; Brigadier I. Simson, *Singapore: Too Little, Too Late* (Singapore, 1970) is a bitter account by the Chief Engineer, Malaya Command; Duff Cooper (Viscount Norwich), *Old Men Forget* (London, 1957) contains one useful chapter on Singapore in 1941–2 when Cooper was Resident Cabinet Minister.

Colonel Masanobu Tsuji, *Singapore: the Japanese Version* (Sydney, 1960; first published in Japanese in 1952) is a fascinating first-hand narrative from the Japanese standpoint.

A number of servicemen described their experiences, notably: K. Attiwill, *The Singapore Story* (London, 1959), a vivid account of the last days before the city's fall by a former soldier and prisoner of war who was dissatisfied with the official histories; A.G. Donahue, *Last Flight from Singapore* (London, 1944), the experiences of an American fighter pilot with the R.A.F. in the last days before the fall of Singapore; D.C. Eyre, *The Soul and the Sea* (London, 1959), in collaboration with Douglas Bowler, a R.A.F. wireless operator, telling the story of the small ships which fled at the fall of Singapore; and D.H. James, *The Rise and Fall of the Japanese Empire* (London, 1951), which sets his personal story as a soldier in the Malayan campaign and prisoner of war in the context of the rise and fall of Japan.

There were a number of accounts by journalists, notably: Ian Morrison, *Malayan Postscript* (London, 1942) a short but compelling book by the London *Times* correspondent; Cecil Brown, *Suez to Singapore* (New York, 1942), a blistering indictment of the colonial régime by an American journalist who was on the *Prince of Wales* when she was sunk, in the form of a detailed diary kept until mid-January 1942 when he was expelled; G.A. Weller, *Singapore is Silent* (New York, 1943) by the last American war correspondent to leave Singapore, on the day the Causeway was blown up; O'Dowd Gallagher, *Retreat in the East* (London, 1942), the bitter impressions of a South African correspondent of the London *Daily Express* who was on the *Repulse* when she sank; E.M. Glover, *In 70 Days* (London, 1946; rev. ed. London, 1949) by the general manager of the

*Malaya Tribune* who had worked in Malaya as a journalist since 1927. Of less interest is D. Crisp, *Why We Lost Singapore* (Bombay, 1945), a small book comprising articles written for newspapers in 1942 and 1943.

The story is told from the opposite side in (Johnny) Tatsuki Fujii, *Singapore Assignment* (Tokyo, 1943) by an American-educated Japanese journalist who worked with the *Singapore Herald* from 1939 to 1941, and edited the *Syonan Shimbun* during the occupation.

Other civilians left eye-witness impressions of everyday living during the last weeks before Singapore's fall, notably: G. Playfair, *Singapore Goes Off the Air* (London, 1944), the diary of a newly-recruited Malayan Broadcasting Corporation employee, who arrived in Singapore the day the Pacific war broke out and escaped three days before the capitulation; O.W. Gilmour, *Singapore to Freedom* (London, 1943), the impressions of the deputy municipal engineer, who had lived in Singapore since 1926; S.E. Field, *Singapore Tragedy* (Auckland, 1944), by a New Zealand government employee who fled from Kuala Lumpur and stayed in Singapore from mid-January to early February 1942; Carline Reid, *Malayan Climax: Experiences of an Australian Girl in Malaya, 1940–42* (Hobart, n.d.), who escaped from Kuala Lumpur in mid-January 1942 and worked in local defence in Singapore until her evacuation four days before the surrender; D.G. Kin (Plotkin), *Rage in Singapore: the Cauldron of Asia Boils Over* (New York, 1942), the curious reminiscences of a Russian-born American about life in Singapore and Malaya on the eve of the surrender.

The few descriptions by Singaporean eye-witnesses are included in the following section, but Lim Thean-Soo, *Southward Lies the Fortress: the Siege of Singapore* (Singapore, 1971) gives a somewhat muddled historical account in novel form.

Of the innumerable secondary accounts of the military campaign, the best is Major-General S. Woodburn Kirby, *Singapore: the Chain of Disaster* (London, 1971). The official histories are thorough, essential reading and based on original documents but suffer from the inevitable limitations of official accounts: S. Woodburn Kirby (ed.), *The War Against Japan, Vol. I, The Loss of Singapore* (London, 1957), the British version; L. Wigmore, *Australia in the War: the Japanese Thrust* (Canberra, 1957); B. Prasad (ed.), *Official History of the Indian Armed Forces in the Second World War, 1939–45: Campaigns in South-East Asia, 1941–42*, by K.D. Bhargava and K.N.V. Sastri (Combined Inter-Services Historical Section, India and Pakistan, 1960).

Basil Collier, *The War in the Far East* (London and New York, 1969) is a readable one-volume account of the whole war. Arthur Swinson, *Defeat in Malaya: the Fall of Singapore* (New York, 1970) is a balanced, straightforward narrative. Frank Owen, *The Fall of Singapore* (London, 1960) and James Leasor, *Singapore: the Battle that Changed the World* (New York, 1968) are more biased journalistic accounts.

Noel Barber, *Sinister Twilight: the Fall and Rise Again of Singapore* (London, 1968), and K. Caffrey, *Out in the Midday Sun: Singapore,*

*1941–45* (New York, 1973), which set the general story against personal reminiscences of European residents in Singapore, make compelling reading.

Captain Russell Grenfell, *Mainfleet to Singapore* (London, 1951) is a good account of the naval war, starting from the rise of Japan in the early twentieth century to the Battle of Midway in May 1942. G.M. Bennett, *The Loss of the Prince of Wales and Repulse* (London, 1973), a small book, describes this sea battle in close-up. Bernard Ash, *Someone Had Blundered: the Story of the Repulse and the Prince of Wales* (London, 1960) is more dramatic and concerned with the 'human interest' of this incident. H.M. Tomlinson, *Malay Waters: the Story of Little Ships Coasting out of Singapore and Penang in Peace and War* (London, 1950) recounts the activities of small ships during the Japanese campaign.

Compton Mackenzie, *Eastern Epic*, Vol. I (London, 1951) tells the story of the Indian troops' involvement in the campaign. M.C. ff Sheppard, *The Malay Regiment, 1933–1947* (Kuala Lumpur, 1947) is short but has some interesting material. There is no specific account of the Volunteers' role in the campaign to update T.M. Winsley, *A History of the Singapore Volunteer Corps* (Singapore, 1937).

L.D. Gammans, *Singapore Sequel* (London, 1944), is a propaganda pamphlet to combat wartime allegations of British failure in Malaya.

Turning to biographical material, Frank Legg, *The Gordon Bennett Story* (Sydney, 1965) has five chapters on the Malayan campaign and the aftermath. Sir John Smyth, *Percival and the Tragedy of Singapore* (London, 1971) aims to clear Percival's name but is a disappointing book.

There is no definitive biography of Yamashita. The most interesting study appears in Arthur Swinson, *Four Samurai* (London, 1968). J.D. Potter, *A Soldier Must Hang: the Biography of an Oriental General* (London, 1963) is a favourable, simplistic view, an interesting early attempt at reassessing Yamashita. Two studies by F.A. Reel, *The Case of General Yamashita* (Chicago, 1949) and A.S. Kenworthy, *The Tiger of Malaya* (New York, 1953), by authors who were connected with Yamashita's trial, relate mainly to his later years but provide interesting insight to his character.

## THE JAPANESE OCCUPATION, 1942–1945

Many vivid first-hand accounts were written about the occupation by Singaporeans, notably Chew Hock Leong, *When Singapore was Syonan* (Singapore, 1945), the earliest, brief and hurriedly-written narrative; Tan Yeok Seong, 'History of the Formation of the Oversea Chinese Association and the Extortion by Japanese Military Administration of $50,000,000 from the Chinese in Malaya', *JSSS*, III, 1 (1946), pp. 1–12; Tan Thoon Lip, *Kempeitai 'Kindness'* (Singapore, 1946), a poignant account, written by an English-educated lawyer, grandson of Tan Tock Seng; Janet Lim, *Sold for Silver* (London, 1958); Chen Su Lan, *Remember Pompong and Oxley Rise* (Singapore, 1969), the personal experiences of a prominent doctor; N.J. Low and H.M. Cheng, *This Singapore (Our City of Dreadful Nights)* (Singapore, 1947), describing the experiences of a teacher and a civil servant. N.J. Low, *When Singapore was Syonan-to* (Singapore, 1973) is largely a duplication of this work, with additional chapters about other people's experiences. Chin Kee Onn, *Malaya Upside Down* (Singapore, 1946) is mostly about Perak but is relevant to Singapore.

Many European prisoners of war and civilian internees described their experiences in great detail. Perhaps the best are R. Braddon, *The Naked Island* (London, 1952) by an Australian soldier who was in Changi Camp in 1942 and during the last year of the war, and D. Russell-Roberts, *Spotlight on Singapore* (London, 1965) written by one of the comparatively few mi'itary prisoners who spent the whole occupation period in Singapore. Ẋ. Hastain, *White Coolie* (London, 1947) is an understated, disciplined narrative by a British sergeant-major. W.S. Kent Hughes, *Slaves of the Samurai* (Melbourne, 1946) is an account in verse by an Australian colonel, imprisoned in Changi but removed later in 1942 with other senior officers to Taiwan. The most detailed, unvarnished and unabridged portrayal of Changi, and of work camps in Singapore and Thailand is K.J. Ball, 'Diaries as a Prisoner of War in Singapore, 1942', 4 vols., unpublished MSS Ind. Ocn. r 3 (Rhodes House, Oxford), although Ball in fact only spent from January to November 1942 in Singapore. L. Greener, *No Time to Look Back* (London, 1951) is a novel of camp life written by an ex-prisoner of war.

Of civilian accounts, Constance Sleep, 'Letter to Son from Changi Internment Camp', unpublished MSS Ind. Ocn. s 130, (Rhodes House, Oxford), is a running letter describing life in the women's camp from 1942 to the end of the war in considerable detail. A.B. Jeffrey, *White Coolies* (Sydney, 1954) is the story of an Australian army nurse, who fled from Singapore and was subsequently interned by the Japanese in Sumatra.

There are also a number of second-hand accounts: D. Norman, *Road from Singapore* (London, 1970), the story of John Dodd, an R.A.F. corporal, captured in Java but interned at Selarang for the rest of the war; E. Lambert, *MacDougal's Farm* (London, 1965), about a crippled Australian prisoner kept in Selarang all the war; A. Dally, *Cicely, the Story of a Doctor* (London, 1968), biography of a paediatrician who came to Singapore in 1937, was imprisoned in the women's camp in Changi, employed for some months by the Japanese in Singapore town and later arrested by the *kempeitai*; L. Bell, *Destined Meeting* (London, 1959), about the civilian internment camps. The first two chapters of R. McKay, *John Leonard Wilson, Confessor for the Faith* (London, 1973) describe wartime Singapore where Wilson was then Bishop.

Lee Ah Chai (Ting Hui), 'Singapore under the Japanese, 1942–45', unpublished B.A. academic exercise, University of Malaya (Singapore, 1956), gives a useful outline of Japanese administration. Syonan, *The Good Citizen's Guide. Handbook of Declarations, Orders, Rules and Regulations etc. issued by Gunseikan-bu (Military Administration Department), Syonan Tokubetu-si (municipality) and Johore Administration between February*

*2602 (1942) and March 2603 (1943)* (Singapore, 1943) is a good source for the early months of the occupation.

Two valuable studies by Japanese writers set Japanese policy in the wider Malayan context, namely Y. Akashi, 'Japanese Policy towards the Malayan Chinese, 1941–45', *JSEAS*, I, 2 (1970), pp. 61–89, which has a lot of detail about Singapore; and Yoichi Itagaki, 'Some Aspects of the Japanese Policy for Malaya under the Occupation, with special reference to Nationalism', in K.G. Tregonning (ed.), *Papers on Malayan History* (Singapore, 1962), pp. 256–73, written by a Japanese who was serving in Singapore during the war.

Mamoru Shinozaki, *My Wartime Experiences in Singapore* (Singapore, 1973) and *Syonan—My Story* (Singapore, 1975) are fascinating reminiscences by a Japanese who played an important role in Singapore before, during and after the war.

Other works deal with Japanese policy in South-East Asia as a whole, notably J. Lebra (ed.), *Japan's Greater East Asia Co-Prosperity Sphere in World War II: Selected Readings and Documents* (Kuala Lumpur, 1974), a valuable collection and commentary, taken mainly from Japanese sources; W.H. Elsbree, *Japan's Role in Southeast Asian Nationalist Movements, 1940–1945* (Cambridge, Mass., 1953); F.C. Jones, *Japan's New Order in East Asia: its Rise and Fall, 1937–45* (London, 1954).

Two books deal with the 'double tenth' trial held in Singapore in March–April 1946 concerning the Changi gaol investigations: C. Sleeman and S.C. Silkin (eds.), *Trial of Sumida Haruzo and Twenty Others: the Double Tenth Trial* (London, 1951), being the full proceedings, edited by the prosecution counsel and court president; and B.A. Mallal (ed.), *The Double Tenth Trial* (Singapore, 1947). Lord Russell of Liverpool, *The Knights of Bushido* (London, 1958) discusses the Chinese massacres.

There are a number of studies of the Indian National Army. J.C. Lebra, *Jungle Alliance: Japan and the Indian National Army* (Singapore, 1971), is a readable but scholarly account which puts the movement in the wider context of Japan and India. Joginder Singh Jessy, 'The Indian Army of Independence, 1942–1945', unpublished B.A. academic exercise, University of Malaya (Singapore), 1958, is a lively account of the army's activities in Malaya. Shah Nawaz Khan, *My Memories of I.N.A. and its Netaji* (New Delhi, 1946) was written by an ex-I.N.A. officer and great admirer of Bose. K.K. Ghosh, *The Indian National Army: Second Front of the Indian Independence Movement* (Meerut, 1969) was the first detached historical account by an Indian. C. Kondapi, *Indians Overseas, 1828–1949* (New Delhi, 1951) has a section on the Azad Hind movement and Japanese occupation. H. Toye, *The Springing Tiger* (London, 1959) tells the story of Subhas Chandra Bose. Mahmood Khan Durrani, *The Sixth Column* (London, 1955) is a fascinating first-hand story by an Indian Muslim who infiltrated the Indian National Army. Gurchan Singh, *Singa, the Lion of Malaya* (London, 1949), told by a Sikh ex-police inspector, is only partly about Singapore but gives unusual insight into life among the Indian community during the occupation.

B. Prasad (ed.), *Official History of the Indian Armed Forces in the Second World War, 1939–45, Vol. II, The Reconquest of Burma* (India and Pakistan, 1959) deals with the Indian National Army. S. Woodburn Kirby, (ed.), *The War Against Japan, Vol. V, The Surrender of Japan* (London, 1969), the official British war history, is useful for the general background of the later war years.

## THE AFTERMATH OF WAR, 1945–1955

The standard work on the British Military Administration is F.S.V. Donnison, *British Military Administration in the Far East, 1943–46* (London, 1956), written with access to official documents. V. Purcell, 'Malayan Politics' in S. Rose (ed.), *Politics in Southern Asia* (London, 1963), pp. 218–34, is a brief narrative up to 1962 by an official of the Malayan planning unit and British Military Administration.

Major General Sir Ralph Hone, Chief Civil Affairs Officer Malaya, 'Papers relating to the Military Administration of the Malayan Peninsula, 5 September 1945–1 April 1946', MSS Brit. Emp. S 407/3 (Rhodes House, Oxford) includes Singapore Advisory Council papers, letters about early civil administration and Malayan Union.

The official view of the immediate post-war years is given in *British South East Asia Recovers* (Singapore, 1949), reprinted by the *Straits Times* from Colonial Office, *British Dependencies in the Far East, 1945–49*, Cmd. 7709 (London, 1949), supplemented by Great Britain, *Information on Singapore for 1949 Transmitted to the United Nations* (London, 1949).

O.W. Gilmour, *With Freedom to Singapore* (London, 1950) is an interesting personal commentary on newly liberated Singapore. The final chapter of E.M. Glover, *In 70 Days* (first published London, 1946; rev. ed., 1949) has brief post-war impressions.

A number of politicians and officials have published interesting personal recollections, notably: Philip Hoalim, *The Malayan Democratic Union* (Singapore, 1973) by the party's chairman; Andrew Gilmour, *My Role in the Rehabilitation of Singapore: 1946–1953* (Singapore, 1973) by a senior Malayan Civil Service official; David Marshall, 'Singapore's Struggle for Nationhood, 1945–59', *JSEAS*, I, 2 (1970), pp. 99–104, from a talk given by the first chief minister in 1969, reprinted as *Singapore's Struggle for Nationhood, 1945–1959* (Singapore, 1971); Francis Thomas, *Memoirs of a Migrant* (Singapore, 1972), a refreshingly candid short autobiography.

Desmond Neill, *The Elegant Flower* (London, 1956) by a Chinese-speaking Malayan Civil Service official gives the flavour of Chinatown at this time. Tan Kok Seng, *Son of Singapore* (Singapore, 1972) is the remarkable autobiography of a Chinese-educated labourer who grew up in the 1950s.

R. Jumabhoy, *Multi-racial Singapore* (Singapore, 1970) is the rather disjointed, anecdotal story of an Indian-born businessman, who came to Singapore in 1915 and served as a municipal and legislative councillor.

Other autobiographical works are less illuminating, such as Patrick

Anderson, *Snake Wine* (London, 1955), the entertaining but slight reminiscences of a university lecturer; F.D. Ommaney, *Eastern Windows* (London, 1960), by a Fisheries Research official who came to Singapore in 1952; Oliver Crawford, *The Door Marked Malaya* (London, 1958), by a British army subaltern who served in Singapore and Malaya from 1954 to 1955.

Two valuable official reports throw light on social conditions at this time, namely Department of Social Welfare, *A Social Survey of Singapore* (Singapore, 1947) and Goh Keng Swee, *Urban Incomes and Housing* (Singapore, 1956), a report on the 1953/4 social survey. C. Gamba, 'Some Social Problems in Singapore', *Australian Quarterly*, XXVI, 2 (1954) gives a grim picture of poverty.

Most studies of politics in this period concentrate on peninsular Malaya, notably A.J. Stockwell, 'The Development of the Malayan Union Experiment, 1942–1948', unpublished Ph.D. thesis, University of London, 1973, an excellent treatment based on recently opened documents; J. de V. Allen, *The Malayan Union* (New Haven, 1967), mainly concerning the negotiations; T.H. Silcock and Ungku Aziz, 'Nationalism in Malaya' in W.L. Holland (ed.), *Asian Nationalism and the West* (New York, 1953, reprinted New York, 1973), a stimulating study of incipient nationalism; K.J. Ratnam, *Communalism and the Political Process in Malaya* (Singapore, 1965); and R. Emerson, *Representative Government in Southeast Asia* (Cambridge, Mass., 1955). Mohamed Noordin Sopiee, *From Malayan Union to Singapore Separation: Political Unification in the Malaysia Region, 1945–65* (Kuala Lumpur, 1974) treats Singapore's position in more detail, and the origins of the post-war separation are considered in C.M. Turnbull, 'British Planning for Postwar Malaya', *JSEAS*, V, 2 (1974), pp. 239–54. S. Rose, *Socialism in Southeast Asia* (London, 1959) devotes a large amount of attention to Singapore's politics between 1945 and 1957 in a chapter on Malaya.

The most thorough treatment of Singapore politics in this decade is Yeo Kim Wah, *Political Development in Singapore, 1945–1955* (Singapore, 1973), a substantial and scholarly work based on original materials. Sections appeared as 'A Study of Three Early Political Parties in Singapore, 1945–1955', *JSEAH*, X, 1 (1969), pp. 115–41, and 'A Study of Two Early Elections in Singapore', *JMBRAS*, XLV, 1 (1972), pp. 57–80. See too D.S. Samuel, 'A Comparative Study of the Powers of the Malayan and Singapore Legislatures, 1945–59', unpublished M.A. dissertation, University of Singapore, 1967. G.L. Peet, *Political Questions of Malaya* (Cambridge, 1949) is a brief commentary by the then editor of the *Straits Times*.

S.W. Jones, *Public Administration in Malaya* (London and New York, 1953) is a useful description of the political and administrative framework of Malaya and Singapore by a pre-war Colonial Secretary. W.C. Taylor, *Local Government in Malaya* (Alor Star, 1949) refers only briefly to Singapore and is mainly a detailed analysis of the Penang municipality.

S. Gopinathan, *Towards a National System of Education in Singapore,*

*1945–1973* (Singapore, 1974) is a brief but useful study. Education policy is detailed in Singapore Advisory Council, *Education Policy in the Colony of Singapore. Ten Years' Programme adopted in the Advisory Council on 7th August 1947* (Singapore, 1948).

M.V. del Tufo, *A Report on the 1947 Census of Population* (London, 1949) shows the changed structure of population in the post-war years.

A number of excellent field studies were carried out by anthropologists and sociologists in Singapore in the 1950s. Concerning the Singapore Chinese community see particularly: M. Freedman, *Chinese Family and Marriage in Singapore* (London, 1957); Barrington Kaye, *Upper Nankin Street Singapore* (Singapore, 1960); M. Freedman and M. Topley, 'Religious and Social Realignment among the Chinese in Singapore', *JAS*, XXI, 1 (1961), pp. 3–23; M. Topley, 'The Emergence and Social Function of Chinese Religious Associations in Singapore', *Comparative Studies in Society and History*, III (1960–61), pp. 289–314; A.J.A. Elliott, *Chinese Spirit and Medium Cults in Singapore* (London, 1955).

For the Malay community see Judith Djamour, *Malay Kinship and Marriage in Singapore* (London, 1959) based on field work carried out in 1949–50.

Numerous studies have been made of the communist emergency in Malaya. Of greatest relevance to Singapore are: M.R. Stenson, *Industrial Conflict in Malaya: Prelude to the Communist Revolt of 1948* (London, 1970), an important study of the labour background; M.R. Stenson, *Repression and Revolt: the Origins of the 1948 Communist Insurrection in Malaya and Singapore* (Ohio, 1969), a small but interesting paper; R. Clutterbuck, *Riot and Revolution in Singapore and Malaya, 1945–1963* (London, 1973), by a senior British army officer serving in Malaya during part of this time; G.Z. Hanrahan, *The Communist Struggle in Malaya* (New York, 1954; rev. ed., Kuala Lumpur, 1971); V. Thompson and R. Adloff, *The Left Wing in Southeast Asia* (New York, 1950) which has a chapter on Malaya, the growth of the Malayan communist movement and Singapore politics.

The best and most detailed scholarly study of the labour movement in post-war years is C. Gamba, *The Origins of Trade Unionism in Malaya: a Study in Colonial Labour Unrest* (Singapore, 1962), which takes the story up to the formation of the Singapore Trade Union Congress in 1951. Alex Josey, *Trade Unionism in Malaya* (Singapore, 1954; rev. ed. Singapore, 1958) is a shorter account by a left-wing journalist. Virginia Thompson, *Labour Problems in Southeast Asia* (New Haven, 1947) deals with immediate post-war strikes. S.S. Awberry and F.W. Dalley, *Labour and Trades Union Organisation in the Federation of Malaya and Singapore* (Kuala Lumpur, 1948) is the report of an investigation carried out in 1947–8 at the invitation of the Malayan and Singapore governments. C. Gamba, *Labour Law in Malaya* (Singapore, 1955) gives a brief synopsis of labour law.

International Bank for Reconstruction and Development, *The Economic Development of Malaya* (Singapore, 1955), the report of a mission to Malaya and Singapore January–May 1954, is a weighty and valuable commentary not only on the economy but on education, social welfare and health.

## SINGAPORE, 1955–1965

Very few studies have been made of the period of the Labour Front governments. A number of legislative assembly papers provide valuable discussions of major issues, notably *The Report of the All Party Committee of the Singapore Legislative Assembly on Chinese Education*, Cmd. No. 9 (Singapore, 1956); *White Paper on Education Policy*, Cmd. 15 of 1956 (Singapore, 1956); *The Communist Threat in Singapore*, sessional paper, Cmd. 33 of 1957 (Singapore, 1957).

Few personal reminiscences of this period have been published, apart from Francis Thomas, *Memoirs of a Migrant* (Singapore, 1972); David Marshall, *Singapore's Struggle for Nationhood, 1945–1959* (Singapore, 1971); and D.J. Enright, *Memoirs of a Mendicant Professor* (London, 1969) by a university professor who came into conflict with the PAP authorities.

Singapore is included with Malaya in N. Ginsburg and C.F. Roberts, *Malaya* (Seattle, 1958, rev. ed. 1960), which provides a useful factual background; L.A. Mills, *Malaya: a Political and Economic Appraisal* (Minneapolis, 1958); and J.N. Parmer, 'Malaysia' in G. McT. Kahin (ed.), *Governments and Politics of Southeast Asia* (Ithaca, 1959, 2nd edition Ithaca, 1964), pp. 281–365.

There are two well-researched and informative studies of the People's Action Party: T.J. Bellows, *The People's Action Party of Singapore* (New Haven, 1971) and Pang Cheng Lian, *Singapore's People's Action Party* (Singapore, 1971), which amplifies Pang Cheng Lian, 'The People's Action Party, 1954–1963', *JSEAH*, X, 1 (1969), pp. 142–54. The party leadership is very vocal. Annual reports and anniversary souvenirs were issued from 1955. *Petir*, the PAP's official organ, began publication in 1956. The *Tasks Ahead* (Singapore, 1959) gives a comprehensive exposition of the party's policy prior to the 1959 election. From 1959 the Ministry of Culture issued numerous booklets detailing the ruling party's policy, notably: *Towards a More Just Society* (Singapore, 1959), on assuming office; *Towards Socialism* (Singapore, 1960–1), a seven-volume analysis of policy, including Vol. I, Lee Kuan Yew, *The Socialist Solution* (1960), a commentary on current political forces in Singapore, and Vol. V, Lee Kuan Yew, *The Battle for Merger* (1961); *Democratic Socialism in Action, June 1959–April 1963* (Singapore, 1963), summing up the party's first ministry; *Social Transformation in Singapore* (Singapore, 1964); *Separation: Singapore's Separation from the Federation* (Singapore, 1965).

The present political leaders have not written any memoirs but many of their speeches have been published. Chong Peng-Khaun (ed.), *Problems in Political Development in Singapore* (California, 1968) is a reprint of articles, Ministry of Culture publications and Lee Kuan Yew's speeches. See also Lee Kuan Yew, *Towards a Malaysian Malaysia* (Singapore, 1965);

*Malaysia—Age of Revolution* (Singapore, 1965); *Malaysia Comes of Age* (Singapore, 1965). Goh Keng Swee, *Some Problems of Industrialization* (Singapore, 1963) was based on a series of radio talks. Goh Keng Swee, *Economics of Modernisation and Other Essays* (Singapore, 1972) is an important collection of speeches made between 1959 and 1971, giving a good picture of Goh's changing views and pragmatic approach. S. Rajaratnam, *Malayan Culture in the Making* (Singapore, 1960); *Challenge of Confrontation* (Singapore, 1964); and *Malaysia and the World* (Singapore, 1964), reflect his views as Minister of Culture and subsequently Foreign Minister.

There is no definitive biography of Lee Kuan Yew but he is portrayed from opposed angles in Alex Josey, *Lee Kuan Yew* (Singapore, 1968; rev. ed. 1971) and *Lee Kuan Yew: the Struggle for Singapore* (Sydney, 1974), a very sympathetic treatment by a friend and adviser, based in large part on Lee Kuan Yew's speeches; and T.J.S. George, *Lee Kuan Yew's Singapore* (London, 1973), a hypercritical study by an Indian journalist. A. Roland, *Profiles from the New Asia* (London, 1970) includes a chapter on Lim Kin San and his Singapore background.

Michael Leifer, 'Politics in Singapore: the First Term of the People's Action Party, 1959–63', *Journal of Commonwealth Political Studies*, II (1963–4), pp. 102–19, is a useful commentary. A number of perceptive studies have been made of Singapore's incorporation into and expulsion from Malaysia, notably: W.A. Hanna, *Sequel to Colonialism* (New York, 1965) about the formative years from 1957 to 1960; W.A. Hanna, *The Formation of Malaysia* (New York, 1964); Milton E. Osborne, *Singapore and Malaysia* (Ithaca, 1964); and Nancy Fletcher, *The Separation of Singapore from Malaysia* (Ithaca, 1969, reprinted 1971). Friction and growing tensions in the Malaysia relationship are shown in Michael Leifer, 'Singapore in Malaysia: the Politics of Federation', *JSEAH*, VI, 2 (1965), pp. 54–70; Peter Boyce, 'Policy without Authority: Singapore's External Affairs Power', *JSEAH*, VI, 2 (1965), pp. 87–103; R.S. Milne, 'Singapore's Exit from Malaysia: the Consequences of Ambiguity', *Asian Survey*, VI, 3 (1966), pp. 175–84. R.C.H. McKie, *Malaysia in Focus* (Sydney, 1963) is a readable personal impression of events and prominent personalities on the eve of the formation of Malaysia.

The left-wing Barisan Sosialis opposition party published a fortnightly *Plebeian* (1962–3), which continued at irregular intervals as the *Plebeian Express* (1963/4–8) and *Plebeian* (1968–70). J.M. Van der Kroef, *Communism in Malaysia and Singapore* (The Hague, 1967) is the only full-length study of the subject and an important work, although some of the author's conclusions are challenged in Stephen Fitzgerald, *China and the Overseas Chinese: a Study of Peking's Changing Policy, 1949–70* (Cambridge, 1972), a stimulating interpretation, based largely on Chinese official sources. R.S. Elegant, *The Dragon's Seed: Peking and the Overseas Chinese* (New York, 1959) is a readable account of the impact of China and Chinese communism on Singapore Chinese in the mid-1950s. Jay Taylor, *China and South-east Asia: Peking's Relations with Revolutionary Move-*

*ments* (New York, 1974) has some interesting sections on Singapore; A. Doak Barnett, 'Reports on the Chinese in Singapore and Malaya', *American Universities Field Staff Report* (New York, 1955), comprising 'Self rule and Unrest: Overseas Chinese in Singapore'; 'Notes on Three Growing Forces among Singapore Chinese: Political Parties, Students and Workers'; and 'A Chronology of Three Months of Unrest in Singapore', is a useful first-hand report. R. Clutterbuck, *Riot and Revolution in Singapore and Malaya, 1945–1963* (London, 1973) is also relevant to this period, as is A.C. Brackman, *Southeast Asia's Second Front: the Power Struggle in the Malay Archipelago* (London, 1966). F.L. Starner, 'Communism in Malaysia: a Multifront Struggle', in R.A. Scalapino (ed.), *The Communist Revolution in Asia* (New Jersey, 1965) includes Singapore but not in great detail.

Malaysian Government, *Communism in the Nanyang University* (Kuala Lumpur, June 1964), and J.M. Van der Kroef, 'Nanyang University and the Dilemmas of Overseas Chinese Education', *China Quarterly*, No. 20, October–December 1964, pp. 96–127, deal with student political activities.

S.C. Chua, *State of Singapore: Report on the Census of Population in 1957* (Singapore, 1964) analyses population statistics. Ismail Kassim, *Problems of Elite Cohesion: a Perspective from a Minority Community* (Singapore, 1974) is a well-researched study of the Malay community by a political scientist. The legal position of the Malay minority is considered by the then State Advocate-General of Singapore, Ahmad Ibrahim, in 'The Legal Position of Muslims in Singapore', *Intisari*, I, 1 (1962), pp. 40–50, and *The Status of Muslim Women in Family Law in Malaysia, Singapore and Brunei* (Singapore, 1965). See also an interesting study by Judith Djamour, *The Muslim Matrimonial Court in Singapore* (London, 1966) based on field work carried out in 1963.

C.H. Crabb, *Malaya's Eurasians: an Opinion* (Singapore, 1960) is a slight work but throws light on contemporary attitudes.

Turning to the economy, D.J. Blake, 'Patterns of Singapore's Trade, 1961–66', *Malayan Economic Review*, XIII, 1 (1968) presents a detailed analysis. P.J. Drake (ed.), *Money and Banking in Malaya and Singapore* (Singapore, 1966), is an interesting collection of articles with commentary. J. Puthucheary, *Ownership and Control in the Malayan Economy* (Singapore, 1960) is interesting for the economic views of a left-wing politician.

## FIRST DECADE OF INDEPENDENCE, 1965–1975

Basic sources for official information can be found in the *Singapore Yearbook*, first published in 1964 and replacing the former *Annual Reports*; in annual publications of the People's Action Party; in *The Mirror, a Weekly Almanac of Current Affairs*, published by the Ministry of Culture since 1965. Also useful is the *Mirror of Opinion—Weekly Highlights of Malay, Chinese and Tamil Press*, translations from the vernacular press issued by the Ministry of Culture from 1965 onwards.

J. Victor Morais (ed.), *Who's Who in Malaysia and Singapore* (Kuala

Lumpur, 1956 onwards) has biographical details of prominent Singaporeans.

Ooi Jin Bee and Chiang Hai Ding (eds.), *Modern Singapore* (Singapore, 1969) is a collection of essays on many facets of contemporary Singapore.

Sally Backhouse, *Singapore* (London, 1972) is a sensible, factual book for the general reader, looking to the past but concentrating on modern Singapore. Dick Wilson, *East Meets West: Singapore* (Singapore, 1971) is a brisk, topical informative book, written to publicize Singapore to the outside world. Dick Wilson, *The Future Role of Singapore* (London, 1972) is thought-provoking. R.C.H. McKie, *Singapore* (Singapore, 1972), a small book written on revisiting Singapore, almost comes into the category of a guide book but gives some impression of the changed frenzied hurry of the present day compared with his earlier books.

Chan Heng Chee, *Singapore: the Politics of Survival, 1965–1967* (Singapore, 1971) is a stimulating and scholarly study of the immediate post-independence years. Robert Shaplen, *Time Out of Hand: Revolution and Reaction in South East Asia* (New York and London, 1969) contains an intelligent commentary by a journalist on Singapore's experience in Malaysia and during the early years of separation.

Chan Heng Chee, *The Dynamics of One Party Dominance: the PAP at the Grass Roots* (Singapore, 1976) and P.A. Busch, *Legitimacy and Ethnicity: a Case Study of Singapore* (New Haven, 1974) are based on field studies in parliamentary constituencies and schools respectively. Wu Tehyao (ed.), *Political and Social Change in Singapore* (Singapore, 1975) is a useful collection of papers dealing mainly with contemporary social issues and international relationships. Chan Heng Chee, 'Nation Building in Southeast Asia: the Singapore Case' in B. Grossmann (ed.), *Southeast Asia in the Modern World* (Wiesbaden, 1972), pp. 165–79, is also published as *Nation Building in Southeast Asia: the Singapore Case* (Singapore, 1971).

W.A. Hanna has published a number of useful commentaries in *American Universities Field Staff Reports, Southeast Asia Series*, particularly 'Success and Sobriety in Singapore, Vol. 16, nos. 2–5 (New York, 1968).

The greatest concentration of writing has been in the economic sphere: R. Ma and You Poh Seng, *The Economy of Malaysia and Singapore* (Singapore, 1966); You Poh Seng and Lim Chong Yah (eds.), *The Singapore Economy* (Singapore, 1971), a useful work dealing with economic development in the 1960s; P.J. Drake, *Financial Development in Malaya and Singapore* (Canberra, 1969), dealing with the system up to 1967; H. Hughes and You Poh Seng (eds.), *Foreign Investment and Industrialization in Singapore* (Canberra, 1969); Goh Chok-tong, *Industrial Growth in Singapore, 1959–68,* Economic Development Division, Ministry of Finance (Singapore, 1968), an informative paper with useful statistics; Wong Kum Poh and M. Tan (eds.), *Singapore in the International Economy* (Singapore, 1972), a small but useful collection of symposium papers in a specialized field; P.P. Courtenay, *A Geography of Trade and Development in Malaya* (London, 1972); Lee Soo Ann, *Papers on Economic Planning and Development in Singapore* (Singapore, 1971) for the general reader.

Goh Keng Swee's economic philosophy is shown in his collection of speeches, *The Economics of Modernisation and Other Essays* (Singapore, 1972), and in 'Economic Development and Modernization in South-East Asia' in H.D. Evers (ed.), *Modernization in South East Asia* (Singapore, 1973).

Iain Buchanan, *Singapore in Southeast Asia* (London, 1972), a highly critical and controversial but important book, concentrates on economic and social aspects.

R. Gamer, *The Politics of Urban Development in Singapore* (Ithaca, 1972) is an interesting field study by a sociologist on planning and its political repercussions. See also Riaz Hassan, 'A Note on the Development Process in Singapore', *JSEAS*, VI, 1 (1975), pp. 87–94.

Pang Eng Fong and Thelma Kay, *Change and Continuity in Singapore's Industrial Relations System* (Singapore, 1974) provides a useful brief discussion of the position of organized labour since the 1968 legislation.

Some of the reports of SEADAG (Southeast Asia Development Advisory Group) of the Asia Society, New York, relate to Singapore, particularly Roy Fonseca, 'Planning Experience in Singapore', (New York, April 1974).

Interesting comparisons between economic development in Singapore and Hong Kong are made in M. Herrmann, *Hong Kong Versus Singapore* (Stuttgart, 1970); and T. Geiger, *Tales of Two City States: Development Progress of Hong Kong and Singapore* (Washington, 1973).

S.H.K. Yeh (ed.), *Public Housing in Singapore* (Singapore, 1975) shows the social impact of housing policy in the post-1959 period.

R. Nyce, *The Kingdom and the Country: a Study of Church and Society in Singapore* (Singapore, 1970, 2nd edition, 1972) gives an interesting sociological insight into the social revolution of the 1960s.

Government of Singapore, *Census Report for 1970* (Singapore, 1973) is an invaluable source of information on population. Chang Chen-Tung, *Fertility Transition in Singapore* (Singapore, 1974) is a well-researched examination of the National Family Planning Programme's role. Tan Lee Wah, 'Changes in the Distribution of the Population of Singapore, 1957–1970', *Journal of Tropical Geography*, XL (1975), pp. 53–62, has some informative maps.

A.W. Lind, *Nanyang Perspectives: Chinese Students in Multiracial Singapore* (Hawaii, 1974) is a scholarly detailed study, based on fieldwork carried out in 1969.

On foreign policy, P. Boyce, *Malaysia and Singapore in International Diplomacy: Documents and Commentaries* (Sydney, 1968) is useful. Chan Heng Chee, 'Singapore's Foreign Policy, 1965–68', *JSEAH*, X, 1 (1969), pp. 177–91, deals with the early years. There are some pertinent points in F.H.H. King, 'The Foreign Policy of Singapore' in R.P. Barston (ed.), *The Other Powers: Studies in Foreign Policies of Small States* (London, 1973), pp. 252–86. Lau Teik Soon (ed.), *New Directions in the*

*International Relations of Southeast Asia: the Great Powers and Southeast Asia* (Singapore, 1973) has some stimulating discussion. D.C. Hawkins, *The Defence of Malaysia and Singapore: from AMDA to ANZUK* (London, 1972) is a short but useful commentary about British defence arrangements for Malaysia and Singapore.

Seah Chee Meow (ed.), *Trends in Singapore* (Singapore, 1975), the proceedings of a seminar held in 1974, presents discussion by Singaporean specialists on current political, economic and social trends.

# Index

ABDULLAH, EX-SULTAN OF PERAK, 100
Abdul Rahim Kajai, 148
Abdul Rahman, Tunku, becomes head of UMNO, 241; and formation of PAP, 253; Prime Minister of the Federation of Malaya, 273–4, 277–8, 279–80, 299; Prime Minister of Malaysia, 281, 287, 288, 289, 291, 293, 298
Abdul Razak, Tun, 287, 289, 293, 295, 330, 332
Abdul Samad, Dr., 148
Abdullah b Abdul Kadir, Munshi, 27
Abdu'r Rahman, Temenggong of Johor, 1, 5, 30; and founding of Singapore, 6, 8–11; and early Singapore, 12, 14, 17, 18, 23; moves to Telok Blangah, 21–2, 30; and Singapore Institution, 26; signs Treaty of Friendship and Alliance of 1824, 29; and Crawfurd, 30; and piracy, 6, 41; death of, 51
Abdu'r Rahman, Sultan of Riau-Lingga, 9, 10
Abu Bakar, Temenggong, Maharajah and Sultan of Johor, 52, 83, 100, 118
Abu Bakar, Tunku, 221
Acheh, 7–8
Adamson & Gilfillan, 93
Adelphi Hotel, 200
Aden, 86
Admiralty, 124, 165; jurisdiction, 41
Afghanistan, 123
Africa, 327
African Institution, 26
Agriculture, 43–5
Alaska, 91
Albert Dock, 95
Alexander the Great, 2, 3
Alexandra Barracks, 129
Ali, Bendahara of Pahang, 51
Ali, Sultan of Johor, 51, 52, 100
Aliens Ordinance of 1933, 137
Al-Imam, 122
Al-Junied family, 100, 101
Al-Junied Syed Mohammed bin Harun, 15

Al-Junied, Syed Omar bin Ali, 15
Alkaff family, 148
Alkaff, Syed Shaik, 101
All-Malaya Council of Joint Action, 231–2
All-Malayan National Liberation Movement, 152
Alliance Party, in the Federation of Malaya, 259, 274, 287, 289–90, 291, 292; in Singapore, 263, 270, 281, 282, 285, 287, 306
Alsagoff family, 101, 147
Alsagoff, Syed Ahmed, 47
Alsagoff, Syed Mohammed bin Omar, 148
American Board of Commissioners of Foreign Missions, 61
American Civil War, 43
American Methodist Mission, 119, 146
Americans (see also United States of America), 132, 169; as arms dealers, 6; and trade in early Singapore, 39–40, 138; first consul, 44; canning industry, 91; banking, 92; and boycott of trade, 133; and Pearl Harbor, 166, 172; evacuated from Malaya, 174; and World War II, 175, 176, 201; bomb Singapore, 216; and Vietnam war, 304
Amoy, 13, 17, 54, 85, 113, 152, 198
Amoy University, 113, 150
Anderson, John (of Guthries), 93, 97
Anderson, Sir John (Governor of the Straits Settlements), 97, 117–18
Ando, Dr. Kozo, 200
Anglicans, 61, 104
Anglo-American Convention of 1815, 39
Anglo-Chinese Boys' School, 119, 145
Anglo-Dutch Treaty of 1824 (see London, Treaty of)
Anglo-French Entente, 125
Anglo-Japanese Alliance, 130, 162
Anglo-Malaysian Defence Agreement, 305, 311
Anglo-Siamese (Bowring) Treaty, 39,

43
Anson by-election, 278
Anti-British League, 247
Anti-Comintern Pact, 163
ANZUK, 311–12
Arabs, and Temasek/Singapura, 2; in early Singapore, 14, 15, 22, 25, 29; in Straits Settlements Residency, 38, 40, 47, 50; in Straits Settlements Colony, 97, 99, 100–1, 115, 122; and newspapers, 147; in inter-war years, 148; in Japanese Occupation, 213; in Republic of Singapore, 302; oil producers, 310; oil embargo, 332
Arakan, 187
Argyll & Sutherland Highlanders, 175, 178
Armenian Church, 46, 47
Armenians, 14, 15, 29, 38, 40, 63, 302
Army Civil Services Union, 238
Arong Bilawa, 15
Asahi, 197, 209
ASEAN (Association of Southeast Asian Nations), 330–1, 332
Asiatic Petroleum Company, 92
Association of British Malaya, 158, 222
Australia, 40, 86, 141, 186, 197, 237, 302, 314; immigrants from, 65; tin from, 91; food imports from, 116; and Malayan defences, 162, 163, 164, 165; in World War II, 170, 173, 174, 175–7, 182, 183, 185, 188, 191; troops in Japanese Occupation, 190, 196, 207, 210; and Singapore's separation from Malaysia, 293; and defence of Malaysia/Singapore, 304; investment in Singapore, 308; troops for ANZUK, 311–12
Aw Boon Haw, 131, 133, 134, 147, 153, 194
Axis powers, 166, 168
Azad Hind (Government of Free India), 215

BA MAW, 213
Baba Chinese, 14, 55, 94, 102–8, 110, 117, 122, 123, 138, 153, 154–5, 158
Baghdad, 38
Bahau, 212
Balestier, Joseph, 44, 48
Bali, 39; ASEAN summit at, 331
Bangka, 91; Strait, 185
Bangkok, 14, 39, 43, 170, 213, 214
Bank of China, 293
Bannerman, James, 8, 10, 11, 18

Barisan Sosialis (Socialist Front), formed, 279; and Malaysia negotiations, 280, 281; in 1963 elections, 282, 284, 285, 286; and trade unions, 283; in Republic of Singapore, 299–300, 306, 319, 323, 324–5
Batavia (see also Djakarta), 14, 39, 40, 110, 168
Bawean, 44, 99
Bedok, 315
Behn Meyer & Company, 92, 128
Ben Line, 93
Bencoolen, 6, 7, 13, 14, 16, 17, 18, 19, 20, 22; Singapore separated from, 27; and convicts, 46
Bengal, 67, 68
Bengal Engineers, 60
Bengalis, 37
Bennett, Major-General Gordon, 173, 176, 182, 186
Bentham, Jeremy, 32, 57
Berita Harian, 322
Bermuda, 79
Bernard, Francis, 18, 31
Best, Captain, 60
Beurel, Father, 62
Bhonsale, Lt. Colonel, 214
Bidadari camp, 218
Biduanda Orang Kallang, 5, 37
Billiton, 91
Bintang, 3
Bintang Timor, 105, 122
Bishop of Singapore, 196, 210, 227
Black, Sir Robert, 262
Blakang Mati (see also Sentosa) 123, 194
Bloodworth, Dennis, 294n
Bloom, Freddie, 210
Blue Funnel Line (see Ocean Steamship Company)
Blundell, Edmund, 35, 60, 69–72
Board of Control, 11, 50
Boat Quay, 21, 46, 48
Boer War, 104
Bonham, George, early career, 20; as Governor, 35, 36, 41, 67; and Temenggong Ibrahim, 51; retires, 69
Borneo, 4, 39, 100, 211, 240, 278, 280, 282
Borneo Company, 48, 92–93, 95
Bose, Rash Behari, 214–15
Bose, Subhas Chandra, 214–16
Botanic Garden, at Government Hill, 22, 46; at Tanglin, 91, 196
Boustead and Company, 40, 81, 92

Boustead, Edward, 47
Boyanese, 25, 44, 90, 97–8
Braddell, Thomas, xiii
Bras Basah River, 1, 14
Brazier, John, 232–3
Brazil, 91
Britain, 68, 188, 212, 221, 290, 302, 314; and Malay states, xiii; enters European Economic Community, xiv; and South-East Asia during French wars, 6–7; and Raffles, 7; and Treaty of London, 29–30; and steamship services, 40; and proposed naval headquarters, 60; contacts with Singapore in mid-19th century, 66; and transfer movement, 72, 74; and defence of Straits Settlements, 86, 123–5; and naval power, 91; and World War I, 132; and trade quotas, 139; and labour legislation in Straits Settlements, 144; and Wilson mission, 156; pre-war policy in Far East, 162–5, 188; and World War II, 166, 167, 168, 169, 171, 175–7, 180–1, 182, 188; troops in Japanese Occupation, 190, 196–7, 207; and post-war trade unions, 233; & 1956 constitutional talks, 263; and Singapore's internal security, 265, 267; & Lim Yew Hock government, 266; and state of Singapore 1959, 273; and Eden Hall, 278–9; and Malaysia negotiations, 280; and Singapore's separation from Malaysia, 293, 298; withdraws military bases, 304–6, 309, 311, 312, 318; and military protection, 306; and ANZUK, 311; Lee Kuan Yew visits, 317
British Guiana, 137, 230
British Conservative Party, 163, 311
British Labour Party, attitude to naval base, 163; and dissolution of Straits Settlements, 229; and Singapore Labour Party, 238; and Lee Kuan Yew, 317
British Malayan Broadcasting Corporation, 140
British Malaysia Association, wound up, xiv
British Military Administration, 223–6, 233
Brooke, Rajah James, 71
Brooke-Popham, Sir Robert, 166, 169, 171, 173, 174
Brunei, and piracy, 41; becomes

British protectorate, 90; post-war reconstruction, 220; and Malaysia negotiations, 280; rebellion in, 281
Brunei Parti Ra'kyat, 280
Bugis, 6; in Riau-Lingga empire, 9; and trade, 13, 15, 38, 39, 40, 43; in early Singapore, 14, 15, 22, 29; and slave trade, 24–5; in Straits Settlements Residency, 37, 38, 47, 50, 58; and piracy, 41; and labour, 43; and education, 61, 62; in Straits Settlements Colony, 97–8, 100
Bukit Chermin, 48, 52
Bukit Larangan (Forbidden Hill), 1, 22
Bukit Timah, 31, 48, 140, 196; and tigers, 45; and Japanese invasion, 183, 184, 186, 191
Bulan Island, 5
Burma, 31, 176, 187, 215; Burma Road, 153, 154; Burma-Siam railway, 210, 211–12, 216
Butterworth, William John, 35, 36, 51, 52, 54, 67–9
Byrne, Kenneth, 252

CAINE, SIDNEY, 220–1
Cairnhill, 48
Calcutta, 1, 8, 12, 18, 20, 22, 23, 26, 29, 30, 31, 39, 43, 48, 54, 57, 71, 98, 215; and founding of Singapore, 11; Singapore made a dependency of, 27; and currency, 41; and piracy, 41, 50; and port dues, 50; and defence, 60; and education, 62; and steamship communications, 66; and justices of the peace, 67; legislative council (1854) in, 69; and convicts, 73; and taxes, 73, 74; and 1948 international communist meeting, 237
Cambodia, trade with, 13; communist victory in, xiv
Cameron Highlands, 140
Cameron, John, 121
Canada, 165
Canning, Lord, 36
Canton, 14, 16, 38, 85, 105, 152, 165
Cantonese, 36–7, 55, 102, 103, 111, 112, 153, 198
Cape of Good Hope, 7, 16, 304
Carimon Islands, 8, 20, 198
Carlyle, Thomas, cited, 78
Carnie, Charles, 48
Castlereagh, Lord, 11
Cathay Building, 215, 218

Cathedral of the Good Shepherd, 47, 142
Cavenagh, Orfeur, 35, 43, 45, 52, 58, 72–5, 79
Cavenagh Bridge, 113
Celates, 5
Celebes, 39, 43, 99
Celestial Reasoning Society, 108
Ceylon, 89, 116, 137, 179, 238, 252
Ceylonese, 97, 140, 234, 302
Chang Chen-hsun (Thio Tiauw Siat), 109–10
Changi, 73, 198, 226, 315; defences, 163–4, 179–80; and Japanese invasion, 183; in Japanese Occupation, 190, 191, 196, 197, 209, 210, 211, 217, 218, 227
Chartered Bank of India, Australia and China, 40, 92, 199
Chase Manhattan Bank, 322
Cheang Hong Lim, 102, 106, 113
Cheang Wan Seng school, 106
Chen Tsu-nan, 111, 112
Chew Swee Kee, 269
Chi Nan school, 134
Chiamassie, 1
Chiang Kai-shek, 151, 153, 154, 168, 192
Chin Joo and Company, 94
Chin Peng, 227, 237
China, 40, 114, 117, 121, 160, 198, 251, 326; trade with, 4, 9, 13, 17, 35, 38, 39, 43, 113; treaty ports opened, 39, 43; 1857 war in, 71; remittances to, 88, 94, 234; relaxes emigration laws, 105, 108, 109; 1911 revolution, 107, 112, 128; and Nanyang consulates, 108–11; and Hundred Days' Reform, 110; Tan Kah Kee visits, 154, 245; Japanese war, 163, 166–7, 168, 170, 171, 173, 192; and Greater East Asia New Order, 195; communist victory in, 244; communist régime's attitude to Overseas Chinese, 246–7, 248, 300; Cultural Revolution, 300; People's Republic admitted to United Nations, 329; and communism in South-East Asia, 331; diplomatic contact with Malaysia, 331; Lee Kuan Yew visits, 331
China News Service, 245
China Relief Fund, 194
China Sea, 4, 42
Chinese, and Temasek/Singapura, 1–2, 4; in early Singapore, 5, 10, 12,

13, 14, 17, 18, 19, 22, 29; and gambier production, 5, 13, 44–5; in Nanyang trade, 14, 94; in Straits Settlements residency, 36, 38, 40, 44, 47, 53–6, 57, 58, 61, 63–4, 70, 71, 78, 82–3; and tin mining in Malay states, 82–4; in Straits Settlements Colony, 82–3, 84, 86–90, 94, 97, 102–13, 115, 131; in inter-war years, 132–8, 139, 150–5, 167–8; in battle for Singapore, 177–8, 184, 185, 188, 193; in Japanese Occupation, 192–4, 198–9, 200–3, 205, 212, 213; and massacres trial, 227; in Singapore Colony, 233–4, 240, 244–7; and communist China, 245–6; and 1955 election, 258; and 1959 election, 270
Chinese Advisory Board, 89, 103, 106, 124
Chinese Chambers of Commerce, 231–2 (see also Singapore Chinese Chamber of Commerce)
Chinese Communist Party, 152, 166, 244, 245
Chinese consul (general), 106, 107, 108–11, 117; and anti-Japanese campaign, 133, 151, 152
Chinese Coolie Immigration Bill, 83
Chinese education, 61, 62, 105–6, 108, 119, 121, 134, 136, 137, 140, 145, 146, 147, 150, 225, 246–7, 248–9, 261–2, 264, 275, 284–5, 313–14
Chinese High School, 136
Chinese Immigrants Ordinance (1877), 87
Chinese Marriage Committee, 143
Chinese National Liberation Vanguard Corps, 152
Chinese Protectorate, 25, 86–90, 99, 135, 143, 144, 151, 177, 195
Chiu Eng Si (Chinese Free School), 106
Cholera, 63, 117
Christians, 142; and secret societies, 54; missions and education, 61–2, 107, 118, 119, 146; and Straits Chinese, 104; in Japanese Occupation, 206–7, 208
Christmas Island, 80, 220
Chua Chong Long, 14, 55, 56
Chulan, Raja, 2
Chulalongkorn, King, 90
Chung Cheng High School, 261
Chung Hsing Jit Pao, 244
Chung Hua Girls' School, 107

Chung Kuo Council (*see* Mobilization, Council for General)
Chungking, 153, 154, 165, 178, 220
Churchill, Winston, 165, 167, 168, 170, 176, 184, 185–6, 187
Cinnamon planting, 44
Citizenship Ordinance (1957), 267
City, Singapore acquired status of, 267; Council, 268–9; merged into central government, 277
City Hall, 132, 270, 271
Civil Marriage Ordinance, 143
Clarence, Duke of, 104
Claridge, Sir John, 34, 35
Clarke, Sir Andrew, 85
Claymore, 59
Clementi, Sir Cecil, 136–7, 139–40, 155–7, 223
Clementi-Smith, Sir Cecil, 89–90, 103, 119, 124
Clifford Pier, 185
Cloves, 44
Cochin China, 13, 27, 38
Cockpit Hotel (*see* Hotel de l'Europe)
Coconut Grove, 141
Coconut planting, 44, 48
Cocos-Keeling Islands, 80, 128, 220
Coffee planting, 44, 91, 93
Coleman Bridge, 113
Coleman, George Drumgold, 46–7
Collyer, Captain, 60, 72
Collyer Quay, 73, 114, 115
Colonial Office, Straits Settlements transferred to, 43, 72, 74–5; and Ord, 79–82; and British intervention in Malay states, 83–4; and Straits Settlements legislative council, 85; and Straits Civil Service, 85; and opium, 117; and defence, 123–4; and imperial preference, 139; and *mui tsai*, 143; and Guillemard's reforms, 157; and Wilson report, 157; and Japanese invasion, 185; and post-war reorganization, 220–4; and 1948 legislative council, 235; and Marshall government, 262–3; and 1956 constitutional talks, 263; and 1957 constitutional talks, 264–5; and 1958 constitutional talks, 271
Commercial Square (*see also* Raffles Place), 21, 22, 29, 46, 73, 113, 114
Comintern, 135, 136, 144, 151, 165
Commonwealth Defence Agreement (1971), 311–12
Commonwealth Parliamentary Association, 280
Communism, in 1920s, 134–6; and Kuomintang, 144; and anti-Japanese movement, 151–2; in World War II, 165–7, 177–8; after liberation, 222; under British Military Administration 224, 227–9; and Malayan Union, 229–32; and trade unions, 232–3; and Malayan Democratic Union, 235; in Singapore Colony, 237–8, 247–9, 250, 261–2, 263, 264, 265–6; victory in China, 244–5; and Singapore special branch, 270; and Malay nationalism, 289; in Indonesia, 300; Moscow/Peking split, 300; victory in Indo-China, 331
Confederation of British Industry, 306
Connaught, Duke of, 104
Constitutional Commission (1966), 319
Contagious Diseases Ordinance (1870), 87–8
Convent of the Holy Infant Jesus, 46, 62, 63
Convicts, 113; in early Singapore, 24; and tiger hunting, 45; transferred from Bencoolen, 46; as labour, 46, 56–7, 73; opposition to transportation of, 70, 71, 79; transportation stopped, 73
Cooper, Duff, 169, 171, 173, 175
Copra trade, 91
Cotton planting, 44
Council of Joint Action (1952), 252
Couperus, Abraham, 21
Crawfurd, John, early career, 27; Resident of Singapore, 27–31, 35; and trade, 28, 40, 50; relations with Sultan and Temenggong, 30, 51; later career, 31; on European community, 38; and transfer movement, 68, 72; and Straits Settlements Association, 82
Creech-Jones, Arthur, 159
Cricket Club, 66, 192
Crimean War, 60
Criminal Procedure Bill (1873), 84
Crimping Ordinance (1877), 87
Currency, and East India Company, 41, 70, 71, 79; stabilized in 1906, 92; exchange rates, 114–15; in Japanese Occupation, 203, 209, 217, 218; separation from Malaysia, xiv
Curtin, John, 176–7

DALFORCE, 177, 181, 184, 188, 194
Dalhousie, Lord, 68, 69
Dalley, Lt. Col. John, 177
D'Almeida and Sons, 43
D'Almeida, Joaquim, 48, 70
D'Almeida, Dr. Jozé, 29, 70
Dangerous Societies Suppression Ordinance, 82
Darbishire, C.W., 158
Davidson, G.F., 43
De Cruz, Gerald, 230
Defence, in Straits Settlements Residency, 59–61, 72; in Straits Settlements Colony, 86, 123–5; in World War I, 128–30; inter-war years, 162–4; in World War II, 168, 169–89; and Japanese Occupation, 216; joint defence council with Malaysia, 298; in Republic of Singapore, 304–6, 311–12
Democratic Party, 254, 257–8
Devals, Bishop, 200, 212
Development Bank of Singapore, 303, 307, 326
Diana, 42
Diehn, 128, 130
Dindings, 80
Djakarta, 300, 329 (see also Batavia)
Dobbie, Major General William, 164, 170
'Double Tenth' incident, 210; trial, 227
Ducroux, Joseph (see Lefranc, Serge)
Dunkirk, 166
Dunlop, Major S., 88, 89
Dunman, Thomas, 48, 58–9, 73
Dusserah, 57
Dutch, 167, 169, 212; and Pulau Brani, 5; East India Company occupies colonies, 6; and Raffles, 7–8, 11; and founding of Singapore, 8, 9, 10–11, 29–30; commercial policy, 10, 39; and Riau-Lingga empire, 9, 15; Anglo-Dutch negotiations, 11–12, 18, 29–30; in Sumatra, 42; and oil, 92; shipping lines, 93; Eurasians, 98; and Java communist rising, 135; and negotiations with Japan, 168; in World War II, 175
Dutch East Indies, 6, 58, 110; trade with, 38, 39, 42–3, 78, 90; currency, 41; and Straits convict system, 57; and Chinese immigration, 82, 97; and secret societies, 89; tin from, 91; and Mecca pilgrim trade, 99;

and Chinese fund raising, 108; and rubber restriction, 138; freezes Japanese assets, 168; and Japanese invasion, 182, 188, 191; Japanese Occupation, 210
Dyaks, 41

EAST ASIA CO-PROSPERITY SPHERE, 195
East Beach, 16, 21
East India Company, 18, 40, 49, 51; and founding of Singapore, xiii, 9–10, 11; and Raffles, 1, 6–7; and Singapore Institution, 26; signs Treaty of Friendship and Alliance, 1824, 29; forms Straits Settlements Presidency, 34; loses China trade monopoly, 35; and China trade, 39; and currency, 41; education policy, 61; charter renewed, 69; petition for abolition, 71–2; and transfer movement, 68–9, 71–2; and legislative councils, 84, 243
Eastern Sun, 322
Eber, John, 229, 231, 247
Economic Development Board, 283, 303, 307
Eden Hall, 278–9
Edinburgh, 105
Education, & Raffles, 26, 61; and Crawfurd, 28; in Straits Settlements Residency, 61–3; and Baba Chinese, 104–5; in Straits Settlements Colony, 118–21; interwar years, 134, 136, 140, 144–7, 149, 150, 154; in Japanese Occupation, 200, 205–7; under British Military Administration, 225; in Singapore Colony, 240–1, 246–7; in Federation of Malaya, 246; Committee on Chinese education (1955), 261, 264; Education Ordinance (1957), 267; and Labour Front government, 270; under PAP government, 284–5, 300, 312–15 (see also Chinese education, Malay education and Tamil education)
Egypt, 122
Elgin Bridge, 73
Elgin, Lord, 56
Embok Suloh, Haji, 100, 149
Emden, 128, 129
Emergency, declared in Federation of Malaya, 238, 243, 248; regulations in Singapore, 238, 247, 257; impact on Singapore, 243; and Marshall,

262; and Britain, 304
Empire Dock, 95, 218
Employment Act (1968), 306–7
*Empress of Asia*, 182
Empress Dowager of China, 110
Endau, 212
Environmental Health Act, 316
Esplanade, 46, 47, 113, 116, 226
Eurasian Association, 157
Eurasian Welfare Association, 200, 226
Eurasians, in early Singapore, 14; in Straits Settlements Residency, 58, 59, 63; in Straits Settlements Colony, 97–8, 119; newspapers, 122, 147; inter-war years, 154; in Japanese Occupation, 195, 197, 199–200, 212, 213, 226; in Singapore Colony, 233; in Hertogh riots, 247–8; in Republic of Singapore, 302, 316
European Economic Community, xi
Europeans, in early Singapore, 14, 15, 17, 20, 22, 24, 28, 29; in Straits Settlements Residency, 38, 40, 41, 42, 46, 49–50, 51–2, 58, 59, 61, 62, 63, 64–5, 65–6, 67–72; in Straits Settlements Colony, 79, 92, 94, 97–8, 115–16, 140–2; in World War II, 167, 168; in Japanese Occupation, 190–1, 196–7, 209–11, 216–17; in British Military Administration, 225; in Singapore Colony, 233, 243; and Hertogh riots, 247–8; and 1959 election, 270–1
Evangelicals, 32

*Fajar*, 252
Far Eastern Freight Conference, 307
Farquhar, Colonel William, 8, 9, 10, 11–17, 19–21, 25, 28, 31, 35, 48, 49
Farrer Park, 141, 191, 213, 215, 230, 235
Federated Malay States, formed, 91, 96; relations with Singapore, 96–7, 156; education, 146; and Malayan Union, 220
Federation of Malaya (*see* Malaya, Federation of)
Fisher, Admiral Sir John, 125
Flint, Captain William, 20, 28–9
Fong Swee Suan, 248, 250, 262, 278, 325
Forbidden Hill (*see* Bukit Larangan)
Ford factory, 186
Formosa, 42 (*see also* Taiwan)

Fort Canning, 1, 60–1, 73, 81; in World War II, 182, 186
France, 109, 124, 129, 162, 166, 168
Franco-Russian Alliance, 124
Fraser, H. (Colonial Secretary), 210
Fraser, John, 93
Fraser and Neave Ltd., 93, 255n
French, 61, 90, 92, 93, 136, 141
*Friend of India*, cited, 43
Fu Ta Ching, 134
Fujii, Tatsuki, 165, 189n, 192
Fujimura, Major General Masuzo, 212
Fujiwara, Major Iwaichi, 170, 213–14
Fukien province, 36, 53, 131, 133, 245
Fukuye, Major General, 196
Fullerton Building, 132, 201
Fullerton, Robert, 34–5, 36, 49, 50

Gambier, 58, 100, 101; in Singapore, 5, 13, 16, 44–5; spreads to Johor, 45; and Seah Eu Chin, 55
Gambling, 24, 25, 29, 49, 58, 67, 88–9, 204, 225
Gan Eng Seng, 102, 106, 117
Gan Eng Seng Free School, 106
Gas Company, 115
General Labour Union (*see* Singapore General Labour Union, Malayan General Labour Union, and South Seas General Labour Union)
Gent, Edward, 220–1
Germany, 166; fears of competition, 124, 125, 129, 162; makes Anti-Comintern Pact, 163; makes Russo-German Pact, 165; makes Japanese pact, 166; invades Russia, 167; Yamashita visits, 171; on fall of Singapore, 186; Gestapo in, 193
Germans, and trade, 40, 94; residents in World War I, 128–30; brewery, 140
Geylang, 101, 218, 290; Geylang Serai, 149
Ghee Hok Society, 82
Gibraltar, 74, 86, 163, 164, 176
Gilani, Lt. Col., 214
Gillon, Captain, 28
Gimson, Sir Franklin, 229, 234, 236
Glover, E.M., 165
Goa, 61
Goh Keng Swee, 251, 252, 272, 274, 275, 297, 303, 319, 326, 330, 332
Goh Loo Club, 198
Goho, S.C., 214, 226
Golden Khersonese, 1

Goode, Sir William, 272
Goodwood House, 45
Goodwood Park Hotel, 116
Gordon Highlanders, 178
Government Hill, 22, 46
Government House, 114, 115, 262;
    first Government House, 22, 29, 46,
    60; second Government House
    (present Istana), 73, 81, 104, 116,
    158
Greater East Asia New Order, 195,
    202
Guillemard, Sir Laurence, 155, 157–8
Gujaratis, 37, 98, 129
Gurkhas, 191, 197
Guthrie, Alexander, 16, 17, 93
Guthrie and Company, 16, 40, 93, 94,
    95, 97, 102, 131
Guthrie, James, 48, 93
Gutta percha, 51

HAGUE, THE, 11, 12
Hainan, 152, 165
Hainanese, 87, 102, 134, 135, 144, 193
Hakkas, 15, 36–7, 102, 109, 110, 131,
    153, 260
Hamada, Colonel Hiroshi, 213
Hamilton, Captain Alexander, 20
Haruzo, Lt. Col. Sumida, 227
Hastings, Lord, 7, 11, 18
Healey, Denis, 304
Heath, Major General Lewis, 173
Helsinki, 324
Hertogh, Maria, riots over, 247–8
Hewetson, Thomas, 48, 59
Hill, Dr. L.C., 268, 282
Hindus, 57, 197, 214
Hindu Advisory Board, 157
Ho Chi-minh, 136
Hoalim, Philip, 230
Hock Lee Bus Company strike, 261
Hokkaido, 253
Hokkien Huay-kuay, 103, 123, 247,
    254
Hokkiens, 15, 36–7, 47, 54, 62, 102,
    106, 112, 133, 138, 151
Holland, 166, 247
Holt, Alfred, 93
Holt, Philip, 93
Holt, Oliver, 221
Hon Sui Sen, 303
Hone, Sir Ralph, 223–4
Hong Kong, 36, 95, 116, 129, 137,
    194, 217, 290, 322; founded, 39, 43;
    as naval headquarters, 60; and
    troops, 74, 86; and secret societies,
89; and *mui tsai*, 143; and naval
    base, 163; Japanese invade, 172;
    investment in Singapore, 308
Hongkong and Shanghai Banking
    Corporation, 92, 123
Hong Lim by-elections, in 1961, 277;
    in 1965, 299
Hoo Ah Kay (*see* Whampoa)
Horsburgh Lighthouse, 69
Hotel de l'Europe, 47, 140
Hospitals, 63, 116–17, 120, 131; in
    Japanese invasion, 184, 185, 186,
    190; in Japanese Occupation, 192,
    196, 216; post World War II, 224,
    241
Housing and Development Board,
    240, 277, 283, 303, 316
Houston, 308
Hsu Ch'ing, 111
Huang Nai-seng, 110
Huang Tsun-hsien, 109
Hui-hsien Cultural Club, 108
Hullett, R.W., 119
Hume Pipe Company, 255n
Hundred Days' Reform Movement,
    105, 110
Hussein, Sultan of Johor, 50–1; and
    founding of Singapore, 9–11; signs
    June 1819 agreement, 12; moves to
    Kampong Glam, 14, 22; and trade,
    17; and early Singapore administra-
    tion, 17, 18, 23; and Singapore
    Institution, 26; signs Treaty of
    Friendship and Alliance, 29; and
    Crawfurd, 30; dies, 51

IBRAHIM, TEMENGGONG OF JOHOR, 42,
    47, 51–2, 62–3
Ibrahim, Sultan of Johor, 100, 130
Immigration Restriction Ordinance,
    137; Immigration Ordinance (1950),
    246
Imperial Airways, 141
Imperial Guards (Japanese), 171, 182,
    183
Imphal, 215
India, 98, 116, 160, 194, 214; and
    trade, 13, 38, 44; and steamship
    services, 40; Japanese internees
    sent to, 173, 192; gains independ-
    ence, 236, 304
India Office, 72, 78
*Indiana*, 16
Indian Independence League, 200,
    213–16, 226
Indian Mutiny, 71, 73

Indian National Army, 191, 197, 200, 213–16, 218, 226
Indian Welfare Association, 200
Indians, 43, 138; in early Singapore, 14, 15, 22, 29; in Straits Settlements Residency, 37–8, 47, 52–3, 56–7, 70; in Straits Settlements Colony, 90, 97–9, 115; 5th Light Infantry regiment, 128–30; in World War I, 130; Muslims, 148; in inter-war years, 154; troops in World War II, 166, 170–1, 173, 175, 177, 184; in Japanese Occupation, 190, 191, 195, 197, 199, 200, 210, 213–16; war crimes trial, 226–7; in Singapore Colony, 233, 234; in post-war politics, 236, 238; and PAP, 282; in Republic of Singapore, 302, 316
Income tax, 74, 117, 241; in World War I, 132; Guillemard's proposals for, 158; in World War II, 165; and 1947 Ordinance, 234, 244
Indigo planting, 44
Indo-China, 331; and French, 90, 124; Japanese occupy north, 166; Japanese bases in South, 168; Paris peace agreements (1973), xiv; Communist victory in, xiv, 331
Indonesia, 281, 288; communism in, 134, 280, 300; confrontation with, 290, 291, 293, 298, 304, 329; trade with, 304; and Singapore Republic, 328–9; and ASEAN, 330; Lee Kuan Yew visits, 330; and Suharto régime, 332
Indonesian Communist Party, 280, 300
Indonesians, 101; immigrants to Straits Settlements Residency, 50; immigrants to Straits Settlements Colony, 99–100, 122; and Singapore Colony, 233; and Hertogh riots, 247
Industrial Courts Bill, 140
Industrial Relations (Amendment) Act (1968), 306–7
Industrial Relations Ordinance (1960), 276
International Bank for Reconstruction and Development, 275
International Press Institute, 324
International Trading Company (Intraco), 307
Ipoh, 141
Iskander, 3–4
Israel, 291, 301, 330; military advisers from, 305, 328
Italy, shipping lines, 93; and World War II, 166; Yamashita visits, 171

JAFFAR ALBAR, DATO SYED, 291
Jagat Singh, 129
Jamit Singh, 250
Japan, 111, 128, 307, 326, 329; and Straits convict system, 57; defeats Chinese navy, 109; naval competition from, 124; Anglo-Japanese alliance, 125; in 1915 Singapore mutiny, 130; and imperial preference tariffs, 139; Chinese anti-Japanese movement, 133, 134, 150; prostitutes, 143; invades Manchuria, 150, 163; Sino-Japanese War, 163–15, 192; Japan and South-East Asia, 162–218 (Chapters V and VI), 253; invades Malaya, 144; first air raid on Singapore, 162; Occupation of Singapore, 121, 190–218 (Chapter VI), 224–5, 228; Japanese Volunteer Force, 191; capitulation, 217–18, 222; Japanese under British Military Administration, 226–7, 228; trade with Republic of Singapore, 304, 331; investment in Singapore, 308, 310
Jardine and Company, 48, 95
Java, 27, 44, 194; and Temasek/Singapura, 1, 2, 3, 4; and East India Company, 6; and Raffles, 6–7; trade with, 14; rivalry of Javanese ports, 95; immigrants from, 99; communist revolt in (1927), 135; in World War II, 175
Javanese, in early Singapore, 22, 25; in Straits Settlements Residency, 44, 47; in Straits Settlements Colony, 97–8; in Japanese Occupation, 216
Jawi-peranakan, 38, 57, 99, 100, 101, 148
*Jawi-peranakan*, 101, 121–2
Jellicoe, Lord, 162
Jervois, Sir William Drummond, 86
Jews, in Straits Settlements Residency, 38, 40, 47, 63; in Straits Settlements Colony, 97–8, 115; in Japanese Occupation, 200; David Marshall, 253, 260; in Republic of Singapore, 302
Johnston, Alexander Laurie, 16
Johnston, A.L. and Company, 16, 52,

68, 92

Johor, 7, 8, 9, 37, 52, 63, 88, 97, 132, 221, 268; gambier and pepper production in, 45; 1855 treaty, 52; and telephone service, 92; and railway, 96; accepts British Adviser, 96; and 1915 mutiny, 130; and defence, 164, 173; in Japanese invasion, 175, 176, 180; and Occupation, 216

Johor Bahru, 52, 96, 147, 169, 179

Johor Causeway, 31, 178, 183, 298

Johor empire, 5, 20, 21, 30

Johor Lama, 4

Johor Strait, 31, 37, 48, 163, 171, 179, 183

*Journal of the Indian Archipelago*, xiii

Judicial system, 24, 27–8, 34–5, 36, 50, 70, 81, 208

Jurong, 305; river, 183; Japanese internment camp, 217, 226; industrial estate, 283, 290; Town Corporation, 308

Jurong Shipyard, 307

Jury, 34, 70, 71, 74, 84, 88, 324

KADIR, TENGKU, 148

Kallang, 141, 184; river, 5; Extension River Scheme, 115; airfield, 149, 179

Kampong Bencoolen, 14, 99

Kampong Bugis, 15, 30

Kampong Glam, 14, 15, 18, 22, 39, 46, 47, 51, 52, 99, 100, 122, 148, 191

Kampong Jawa, 50

Kampong Malacca, 99

Kampong Melayu, 149

Kampong Sumbawa, 50

Kandang Kerbau Maternity Hospital, 131

K'ang T'ai, 1

K'ang Yu-wei, 110, 111

Kao Ling-pai, 151, 154

Kassim Mansoor, 129

Katong, 44, 48, 98, 191, 216

Kawamura, Major General Saburo, 193, 227

Keasberry, Benjamin Peach, 62, 101, 118; his school, 62–3

Kedah, 96

Kelantan, 96

*Kempeitai*, 190, 191, 193, 194, 198, 202, 208–9, 210, 215, 226–7

Ken, Tsurumi, 169

Keppel Harbour, 5, 32n, 37, 48, 163, 180

Keppel, Admiral Sir Henry, 60

Keppel Shipyard, 307–8

Keppel Strait, 4–5

Kerr, William Wemys, 48, 52

Kesatuan Melayu Singapura (Singapore Malay Union), 148–9, 159, 229

Khir Johari, 291

Khoo Seok Wan, 107, 110, 111

Kiichi, Gunji, 151

Killiney, 48

Kim Seng and Company, 94

King Edward VII Medical School, 120, 131; College of Medicine, 145, 206, 225, 240 (*see also* Medical School)

King George VI Dock, 163

Kipling, Rudyard, cited, 94

Korea, 171; War in, 241, 245, 250; Koreans, 198

Kota Bharu, 164, 172

Kra Isthmus, 124

Kranji, 96, 183, 197

Kreta Ayer incident, 135

Ku Seng Wui Kun Association, 103

Kuala Lumpur, 141, 155, 230, 259; capital of Federated Malay States, 96; Japanese occupy, 175; and post-war reorganization, 221; capital of Federation of Malaya, 241, 271, 274, 278, 280, 286; capital of Federation of Malaysia, 287, 290, 291, 292–3, 297, 298, 317, 328, 330

Kuala Temasek, 2

Kuang-hsu, Emperor, 109

Kuantan, 83, 164

Kuching, 70

*Kumiai* system, 202–3

Kuomintang, 111, 113, 133, 134–8, 150–4, 156, 194, 245, 249, 289, 300; and trade unions, 144; in World War II, 168, 177; in Japanese Occupation, 192; and communist victory in China, 244

Kwangtung, 36, 53

Kwong Yik Bank, 92

LABOUR COMMISSION (1890), 87

Labour Front, 253, 257–70, 271, 275

Labouring Classes Anti-Enemy-Backing-Up Society, 152

Labuan, 80

Lai Teck, 151, 166, 194, 226, 237

Lake, Captain Edward, 60

Lakshmi, Dr. S., 215

Larut, 100

*Lat Pau*, 106, 108, 123

Lauterbach, Oberleutnant Julius,

129–30
Laycock, John, 221, 235, 236, 258; Laycock Committee, 236
League of Nations, 163
Lee Cheng Yam, 94
Lee Kong Chian, 131, 134, 150, 152, 194, 224, 245, 251
Lee Kuan Yew, early career, 251–2, 253; in 1955 Assembly, 258–60, 265; and PAP extremists, 265–6; first term as prime minister (1959–63), 271–85; as prime minister of Singapore in Malaysia, 286–93; as prime minister of Republic of Singapore, 297–331
Lee Rubber Company, 131
Lee Siew Choh, 325
Legislative Council, of Calcutta, 69; attitude of East India Company to, 84; demand for in Straits Settlements, 71; Straits Settlements Legislative Council formed, 79–80; resignation of non-officials (1873), 84; non-officials reinstated, 85; Chinese representative on, 102–3; and defences, 123–4, 180; and Chinese immigration, 138; and imperial preference, 139; Malay representative on, 148–9; and Straits Chinese, 154; Guillemard's reforms, 157–8; and Tan Cheng Lock, 159; in 1930s, 160; reformed 1948 council, 235–7; 1951 reform, 241 (*See further* under Singapore Legislative Assembly)
Lefranc, Serge (Joseph Ducroux), 136, 151
*Lembaga, Malaya*, 147
*Lembaga Melayu*, 122, 147
Leprosy, 63
Liberal Socialist Party, 258, 268, 269
Liberia, 307
Lim Bo Seng, 178, 188, 194
Lim Boon Keng, Dr., 103–7, 110, 113; as Queen's scholar, 103; and Volunteers Corps, 104; and education, 105, 314; on commission of enquiry into poverty, 116; and Kuomintang, 133; and press, 147; in Japanese Occupation, 194, 198, 201–2, 212
Lim Chin Siong, 248, 250, 258, 261–2, 264, 265, 272, 278–9, 281, 325
Lim Kean Chye, 229
Lim Kim San, 283, 303
Lim Nee Soon, 111, 112, 133

Lim Yew Hock, 238–9, 253, 258, 263–4, 266, 269–70, 281, 282, 285
Lingga, 5, 6
Little, Dr. Robert, 64–5
Little's Department Store, 207
Lo Tsung-yao, 110
Local Senior Officers' Association, 252
Logan, Abraham, 70, 74
London, 11, 18, 31, 50, 71, 72, 81–2, 84, 91, 93, 105, 123, 128, 158, 159, 163, 165, 170, 173, 197, 221, 235, 252, 293, 308; and Malayan Union plans, 220; and 1957 constitutional talks, 264–5, 266; and 1958 constitutional talks, 265, 267; and Malaysia merger negotiations, 280; withdraws bases, 305
*London and China Telegraph*, cited, 79
London Hotel, 46, 47
London Missionary Society, 61, 62
London, Treaty of (Anglo-Dutch Treaty of 1824), 29–30

MACAO, 29, 61
MacArthur, General Douglas, 217
Macassar, 38, 43
MacDonald, Ramsey, 163
Maclaine, Fraser and Company, 92
MacMichael, Sir Harold, 222
MacRitchie, James, 114–15
Madras Army, 67
Madras Engineers, 60
Mahdi, Rajah (of Selangor), 100
Mahmud, Raja (of Selangor), 100
Ma'it, 1
Majapahit, 1, 3, 4
Malacca, 39, 51, 69, 110, 138, 158, 159, 206, 251, 297; sultanate of, 3, 4; in French wars, 6–7; and Dutch administration, 10; and early Singapore, 12, 14; immigrants from, 14, 18, 37; ceded to Britain in 1824, 29; and charter of justice, 36; and sago manufacture, 44; part of Straits Settlements Colony, 80, 96, 100; Chinese business connections with, 94; and Malayan Union, 220
Malacca Straits, 4, 7, 9, 11, 20, 41, 42, 43, 90, 123, 197, 330
Malaria, 63, 116, 117, 131
*Malay Annals*, 2–3, 4
Malay education, 61, 62, 100, 118–19, 121, 145–6, 200, 206, 225, 240, 267, 274, 302, 313
Malay Nationalist Party, 231, 238,

247
Malay Regiment, 181, 185, 188
Malay Seamen's Association, 143
Malay States, early trade with, 38, 39, 78, 91; extension of British protection to, xiii, 42, 78, 83; and Indian immigration, 98; and education, 146; and naval base, 163; and constitutional proposals in 1930s, 155–6; and Chinese 'gift', 199; in Japanese occupation, 218; and Malayan Union, 220–1 (see also Federated Malay States, Unfederated Malay States)
Malay States Guides, 129
Malaya, Federation of, 235, 238, 240, 289; formed, 231–2, 237; independence movement in, 241; and Rendel Commission, 242; Communist Emergency in, 238, 243, 245, 248; education policy, 246; gains independence, 259, 266, 274; relations with Singapore colony, 264, 265, 266; and Singapore Internal Security Council, 267; merger with Singapore, 269, 273–6, 277–8, 279–81; and Operation Cold Store, 281; and Malayan common market, 286
Malaya Tribune, 122, 147, 165, 168, 169–70
Malayan Association of India, 221
Malayan Chinese Association, 236, 253, 270, 282, 287; subsequently Malaysian Chinese Association, 288, 289
Malayan Civil Service, 96, 154, 155, 174–5, 221, 225
Malayan Collieries, 255n
Malayan Communist Party, founded, 136; and early trade unions, 144; in 1930s, 151–2, 153; in World War II, 165, 167, 177–8; in Japanese Occupation, 194; after liberation, 222; under British Military Administration, 226, 227–9; and Malayan Union, 229, 231–2; and post-war trade unions, 232–3; and Singapore Colony, 236, 237–8, 244–5; and Malayan Emergency, 238; banned, 238, 244; in 1950s, 247–8; in Chinese schools, 248–9; and PAP, 253, 260, 265; and David Marshall, 260; under Labour Front government, 262, 265–6; in Republic of Singapore, 330
Malayan Breweries, 140

Malayan Democratic Union, 229–31, 234–6, 238, 253, 272
Malayan Forum, 251
Malayan General Labour Union, 144, 165
Malayan Indian Congress, 236, 282
Malayan National Liberation League, 300
Malayan People's Anti-Japanese Army, 194, 227, 238
Malayan People's Anti-Japanese Ex-Service Comrades' Association, 231
Malayan Planning Unit, 221
Malayan Union, 220–3, 224, 229–31, 235, 288
Malays, in Temasek/Singapura, 2–4; in early Singapore, 5–6, 8–10, 12–13, 18, 23, 24, 25–6, 29; in Straits Settlements Residency, 37, 40, 43, 47, 50–1, 56, 58, 90; in Straits Settlements Colony, 97, 99–101; and vernacular press, 101, 121–2, 147–8; in Japanese Occupation, 190, 191, 192, 199, 213, 218; Singapore Malays and Malayan Union, 229; Malay nationalism, 230–1; in Singapore Colony, 233; and Hertogh riots, 247–8; in state of Singapore, 272–3; and PAP, 274, 282, 287, 288, 290–1; in Republic of Singapore, 301–2
Malaysia, Federation formed, x, 281; Agreement, 281, 286; and state of Singapore, 286–93, 297, 301; 1964 federal election in, 287–9; expulsion of Singapore from, xiii, 293, 297, 318; relations with Republic of Singapore, xiv, 297–8, 303, 308, 328–9, 330, 332; and defence, 304; and ANZUK, 312; 1969 riots in, 317; and ASEAN, 330; diplomatic contact with China, 331
Malaysian Chinese Association (see Malayan Chinese Association)
Malaysian Mirror, 292
Malaysian National Alliance Party, 292
Malaysian Solidarity Convention, 292
Malayur, 2
Mallal, Nasir A., 235, 258
Malta, 86
Manaki, Major General Keishin, 194, 197
Manchuria, 150, 163, 171, 195, 201
Manchus, 42, 53, 54, 107, 109, 110, 123, 133, 134, 136

Mandai river, 183
Manila, 14
Mansfield and Company, 93, 94
Mansfield, Walter, 93
Mao Tse-tung, 154
Marco Polo, 1
Marsden, William, 1, 8, 10
Marshall, David, early career, 253; as Chief Minister, 258–63, 264, 265, 273, 321; in opposition, 265, 324; and local government, 268; and Workers' Party, 270, 278, 280; and 1963 election, 285; visits Peking (1955), 300; and Presidential Council, 319
Martin, Dr., 48
'Matador' Plan, 172
Matheson, John, 16
Maxwell, Sir Benson, 81
May Day, 1940 rally, 165; 1948 planned rally, 237; 1957 celebration, 265
McAlister and Company, 93
McCormac, C.E., 197
McKerron, Patrick, 223
McLean Commission, 145, 146
McLean, Sir William, 145
McNeice, T.P., 268
Mecca, 44, 99, 101
Medical School, 107, 154 (see also King Edward VII College of Medicine); school for apothecaries (1889), 119
Mediterranean Sea, 125, 165
Menangkabau, 18, 100, 122
Mercantile Bank of India, 40, 92
Methodists, 104, 118, 119, 145
Methodist Girls' School, 119
Meyer, Manasseh, 98
Middleton Isolation Hospital, 131
Midway, Battle of, 188
Milburn, William, 21
Mindanao, 41
Ming emperor of China, and Temasek/Singapura, 2
Mitsubishi, 202
Mitsui, 202
Mobilization, Council for General, 177–8
Mohammed Eunos bin Abdullah, 122, 148–9
Mohammed Said bin Dada Mohyid-din, 121
Mohan Singh, Captain, 213–14
Moluccas, 7
Montgomery, Field Marshal Bernard, 180

Morgan, John, 28
Moscow, 300, 329
Moses, Aristarchus, 15
Mount Elizabeth, 48, 59
Mountbatten, Lord Louis, 218, 223, 227–8
Muar River, 175
Muhammedan Advisory Board, 157
Mui tsai, 143, 241
Municipal Building (later City Hall), 132
Municipal Committee, first committee (1848), 67; reform in 1850s, 70; and Cavenagh, 74; Chinese representative appointed, 102; Municipal Ordinance (1887), 114–15; Municipal Ordinance (1913), 118, 131–2; first Malay councillor, 148; Guillemard's reforms, 157; and communism, 166; in Japanese Occupation, 200; and post-war reform, 236–7; achieves city status, 267
Muslim Association of Singapore, 101, 148
Muslim Institute, 148

Nagarakretagama, 2
Nahuijs, Colonel, 30
Nair, C.V. Devan, 247, 250, 252, 288, 323
Nair, M.P.D., 238
Naito, Kanichi, 209
Nanking, 107, 134, 153
Nanyang Chinese National Salvation Movement, 151–4, 166, 168
Nanyang Chinese Relief General Association, 152–4
Nanyang Communist Party, 135
Nanyang Hua Chiao Middle School, 134
Nanyang Siang Pau, 133, 147, 152, 153, 322
Nanyang University, 247, 265, 279, 284–5, 299, 300, 314, 323
Nathan, Dr., 200
National Shippers' Council, 307
National Trades Union Congress, 276, 283, 288, 306, 307, 323
Naturalization Law of 1852, 37
Naval Base, 150, 163–4, 171, 172, 179, 180, 308
Naval Base Labour Union, 250
Naval Limitation Treaty (1922) (see Washington Agreement)

Neave, David, 93
Negri Sembilan, 83, 90, 212
Neptune Orient Line, 307
Netherlands (see under Dutch, Holland)
New Delhi, 197, 226
New Guinea, 191, 210
New Harbour (later Keppel Harbour), 47, 48, 52, 94, 115; defence of, 60, 123
New Harbour Dock Company, 95
New Nation, 318, 322
New World Cabaret, 178
New Year's Day sports, 37, 66
New York, 280, 286, 308
New Zealand, 140, 162, 163, 164, 165, 293; and ANZUK, 311–12
Newcastle, 124
Ng Ah Choy, 110
Ngee Ann College, 299, 323
Ngee Ann Kongsi, 103
Nicoll, Sir John, 241, 259, 262
Nishimura, Takuma, 171, 182, 183
Norddeutscher Lloyd Company, 93
North Borneo, 90, 220, 280, 281
Nutmeg planting, 44, 47, 48
Nyerere, President of Tanzania, 329

OCEAN STEAMSHIP COMPANY (BLUE FUNNEL LINE), 93
Odate, Shigeo, 197, 198, 201, 206, 209
Oishi, Colonel Masyuki, 193, 227
Ong Eng Guan, 283; as Mayor, 268–9, 270; in PAP government, 276–7; and United People's Party, 280, 285; resigns from Assembly, 299
Onn bin Ja'afar, Dato, 149
Operation Cold Store, 281, 283
Operation Jaywick, 210
Operation Rimau, 210
Operation Tide-race, 222
Opium, Commission on (1907), 93, 117; smoking, 24, 29, 64–5, 142; anti-smoking campaign, 107–8, 117; and Japanese Occupation, 225
Opium wars, First Opium War, 39, 61; Second Opium War, 43
Orang Gallang, 5, 6
Orang Gelam, 5, 37
Orang Kallang (see Biduanda Orang Kallang)
Orang laut, 5, 8, 10, 37, 41, 47
Orang Seletar, 5, 37
Orchard Road, 45, 47, 316
Ord, Sir Harry St. George, 79–85, 87, 158, 277

Oriental Bank, 40
Oriental Telephone and Electric Company, 92
Othman bin Wok, 274
Ottawa, 329
Outram prison, 130, 210
Oversea Chinese Bank, 199, 221, 251
Overseas Affairs Bureau, 133
Overseas Chinese Affairs Commission (1949), 245
Overseas Chinese Association (Bombay), 221
Overseas Chinese Association (Syonan), 198, 201–2, 212
Oxley, Dr. Thomas, 48

PAGLAR, DR., 200, 226
Pacific Ocean, 162, 188
Pahang, 9, 83, 90
Pakistanis, 234, 302
Palembang, 2, 3, 4
Pan-Malayan Council of Joint Action, 231
Pan-Malayan Federation of Trade Unions, 229, 231
Pan-Pacific Trade Union Secretariat, 144
Panama, 307
Pangkor Engagement, 85
Parameswara, 3–4
Paris Peace Agreement on Indo-China, xiv
Parliament (see under Singapore Parliament, United Kingdom Parliament)
Parliament Building, 46
Parsis, 37, 38, 40, 52, 63
Pasir Panjang, 117, 141, 149, 184, 185, 197, 315
Patani, 164, 172
Patent Slip and Dock Company, 95
Paterson and Simons, 52, 93, 95
Paterson, William, 52
Pavlova, Anna, 141
Paya Lebar Bus Company strike, 250
Pearl, James, 16
Pearl Harbor, 166, 167, 172
Pearl's Hill, 64
Pearl's Hill Reservoir, 115
Peirce Reservoir, 115
Peking, 108, 109, 110, 111, 117, 150, 245, 246, 248, 263, 289, 300
Penang, 6, 8, 14, 16, 39, 69, 83, 110, 111, 112, 121, 141, 148, 156, 184, 188; attitude to founding of Singapore, 10; and Raffles, 18; revenue

of, 29; as capital of Straits Settlements presidency, 34, 36; and Indian immigration, 43, 98; 1857 riots in, 71; and transfer petition, 72; part of Straits Settlements Colony, 80, 96; wants separation from Straits Settlements, 80; secret society riots in (1867), 82; in Japanese invasion, 173–4, 180, 184; and Malayan Union, 220

Penang Chamber of Commerce, 158

Peninsular and Oriental Steam Navigation Company (P & O), 48, 66, 93, 95

Pepper planting, 44–5, 55, 58, 100, 101

Perak, 80, 83, 84, 85, 90, 100, 102, 129, 194, 272

People's Association, 282, 321

People's Action Party, formed, 253; and Labour Front government, 257–62; and communists, 265–6; and City Council (1957–9), 268–9; and 1959 elections, 269–70; first term of office (1959–63), 270–85; and 1963 election, 282, 285–6; and state of Singapore (1963–5), 286–93; in Republic of Singapore, 297–332 (Chapter IX); and Malaysia since 1965, 297–8; and 1968 election, 306; and 1972 election, 324–5

*People's Constitutional Proposals for Malaya*, 231

Percival, Lt. General Arthur, 164, 168, 169, 170, 173, 178, 180–1, 183–7, 196, 201

Perlis, 96

Persekutuan Islam Singapura (*see* Muslim Association of Singapore)

Philippines, 90, 172, 176, 201, 281, 330, 331

Phillips, Admiral Sir Tom, 170, 172

Philomathic Society, 106

Pickering, William, 86–90

Pillai, Naraina, 15, 22

Piracy, in Temasek, 2; in Riau archipelago, 5–6; and Straits Settlements Residency, 41–2, 50, 51–2, 70, 79

Pires, Tomé, 4

Po Leung Kuk, 88

Police force, 17–18, 58–9, 67, 70, 73, 88, 90, 135, 142, 144, 166, 208, 224–5

Ponggol, 91

Port of Singapore Authority, 307

Port Swettenham (later Port Klang), 98, 298

Portuguese, and 16th century histories, 2, 3, 4; and Malacca, 4; and Johor, 4; and Singapura, 4; in early Singapore, 29; in Straits Settlements Residency, 40; and Singapore Institution, 61; Eurasians, 98, 197

Pownall, General Sir Henry, 174, 175

Presbyterians, 104, 105, 111

Prescott Commission, 284–5

President of Singapore, 81, 298, 302

Presidential Council (later Presidential Council for Minority Rights), 319–20

Press, in Straits Settlements Residency, 70, 71; Malay press, 101, 121–2, 147–8, 192; Chinese press, 123, 137, 147, 152; in World War II, 165; in Japanese Occupation, 192; and PAP government, 322, 324

*Prince of Wales*, 170, 171

Pritam Singh, 213–14

Pritt, D.N., 252

Protected Malay States, 82, 85, 87, 89, 90, 92, 96, 109

Protestants, missions and education, 61–2

Ptolemy, 1

P'u Luo Chung, 1

Public Services Commission, 252, 281

Public Utilities Board, 283

Pulai Reservoir, 132

Pulai River, 37

Pulau Brani, 5, 91

Pulau Bukum, 92, 188

Pulau Ubin, 31, 183, 213

Pulau Ujong, 1

Punjabis, 37

Purvis, John, 16

PUTERA (Pusat Tenaga Ra'ayat, or People's United Front), 231

Puthucheary, James, 247, 250, 264, 278, 325

QANTAS, 141

Quarry Workers' Union, 178

Queen's Scholarships, 103, 106, 119, 120

Queenstown, 275, 315

RAEBURN, 48

Raffles, Sir Thomas Stamford, 99, 125, 158; early career, 6–7; founds Singapore, xiii, 1, 7–10, 16, 31, 51; revisits Singapore (1819), 12; and

Naraina Pillai, 15; and Arabs, 15; last visit to Singapore (1822–3), 18–27, 30; administration of Singapore, 16–17, 31–2, 35; and Bencoolen, 18, 20; quarrels with Farquhar, 19–21; trade policy of, 23–4, 50; and education, 26, 61, 83; and slavery, 24–5, 32; leaves Singapore, 26, 27; and Crawfurd, 27; death of, 31; and Americans, 39; siting Singapore town, 48; and gambling, 49; statue of, 207, 218, 271

Raffles College, 144–5, 154, 191, 225, 240, 251

Raffles Girls' School, 62, 63

Raffles Hotel, 116, 140, 178

Raffles Institution (formerly Singapore Institution), 26, 28, 46, 61–2, 63, 73, 93, 105, 106, 118, 119, 120, 121–2, 145, 251, 252, 272

Raffles Place (*see also under* Commercial Square), 21, 162

Raffles, Sophia, Lady, 19

Rajaratnam, Sinnathamby, 252, 272, 274, 297, 301, 310, 319, 320, 327

Rangoon, 98, 129, 131, 215, 217, 222

Read, William Henry, 52, 68, 72, 74, 82, 84, 92

Reform Islam movement, 121

Reid, Arnold, 121

Rendel, Sir George, 242; constitution, 242–3, 252, 254, 257, 259, 270; and local government, 268

*Repulse*, 170, 171

Riau, 8, 9, 10, 11, 14; and trade, 13, 15, 40; immigrants from, 37, 58, 99

Riau-Lingga archipelago, 5, 7, 9, 30, 37, 41, 198

Riau-Lingga empire, 8

Ridley, Henry, 91

Rice milling, 94, 102

River Valley, 48

Robinson, Sir Hercules, 74

Robinsons store, 207

Rochore, 22, 115

Roman Catholics, 47, 142; and schools, 61, 62; and missionaries, 104; and Japanese Occupation, 200, 212

Rotterdam, 308

Rubber, 91, 138, 139; grown in Botanic Garden, 91; and Guthries, 93, 94; rubber trade, 96; Javanese labour for, 99; processing, 102; price of, 131; in World War II, 165;

separation from Malaysian market, xiv

Rubber Association, 91

Russia, 326; fears of strength, 60, 123, 124; and 1915 mutiny, 130; Russo-German Pact (1939), 165; Japanese fears of, 167; in World War II, 170, 171, 176; and international communist movement, 237–8; in modern South-East Asia, 331

Russo-Japanese War, 125

SABAH, 281, 291, 292

Sabara, 1

Sago manufacture, 44

Saigon, 94, 95, 181, 201

St. Andrew's Church (later Cathedral), 47, 57, 73, 142

St. Andrew's School, 119

St. Anthony's School, 119

St. Clair, W.G., 121, 147

St. James, 48, 132

St. John's Island, 8, 12

St. Joseph's Institution, 62, 63, 98

St. Margaret's School, 61, 63

San-Min-Chu-I youth Corps, 153, 167

Sang Utama, 2

Sarawak, 90, 220, 280, 281, 291–292

Sarawak United People's Party, 280

Scandinavian, Shipping lines, 93

Scarborough, 317

Scott, Robert, 210

Scott, Thomas, 93

Seabridge, 165, 174

Seah Eu Chin, 55, 82, 90, 102

Seah Liang Seah, 102, 103, 105

Seaview Hotel, 140

Secret Societies, 53–4, 58, 80, 82, 83, 88–90, 134–5, 232, 248, 284

See Ewe Lay, 123

See Tiong Wah, 123

Selangor, 83, 84, 85, 90, 226

Selarang barracks, 163, 190, 191, 196–7, 211

Seletar 73, 141; River, 3; reservoir, 132, 315; airfield, 162, 163, 179; barracks, 191, 197

Selkirk, Lord, 278

Sembawang, 141, 274; airfield, 163, 179; Shipyard, 308

Sentosa, 4, 123

Sepoy Lines, 29

Sepoy Mutiny (1915), 128–30, 162, 174

Serangoon, 48, 101

Seremban, 297

Seychelles, 100
Shanghai, 94, 114, 134, 136
Shantung, 150
Sharkey, Lawrence, 237
Shell Company, 92
Shellabear, Dr. W.G., 118
Shi Chu Ching, 110
Shinozaki, Mamoru, 166, 198, 200, 201, 205, 211–12, 217, 226
Siak, 44
Siam (see also Thailand), 27, 57, 61, 91, 96, 191; and trade, 13, 38, 39, 40, 90, 94, 113; education, 61, 62
Sikhs, 37, 90, 98, 99, 129, 197, 200, 214, 218, 234
Simons, Henry, 52
Simson, Brigadier Ivan, 168, 169, 175
Sin Chew Jit Poh, 133, 147, 153, 192, 322
Sindhis, 98, 234
Singai Nesan, 122
Singapore Advisory Council, 224, 225, 228, 234–5
Singapore Agricultural and Horticultural Society, 44
Singapore Alliance Party, 282, 284, 285, 287, 291, 306
Singapore Anti-Opium Society, 117
Singapore Annual Report for 1946, 224
Singapore Armed Forces Training Institute, 305
Singapore Association, 234, 236
Singapore Association of Trade Unions, 283, 286, 323
Singapore Bus Workers' Union, 250, 261
Singapore Chamber of Commerce, 55, 72, 74, 91, 139, 157, 158, 159, 201, 234, 235
Singapore Chinese Chamber of Commerce (see also Singapore Chinese Commercial Association), 102, 111, 113, 157, 159, 194; and anti-opium campaign, 107–8; and anti-Japanese movement, 133, 152; and immigration, 138; in Sino-Japanese war, 151, 195; and Malayan Union, 229; and income tax, 234; and legislative council, 235; and education, 245–7, 249, 285, 314; and Democratic Party, 254
Singapore Chinese Commercial Association (later Singapore Chinese Chamber of Commerce), 110, 111, 118, 123
Singapore Chinese General Associa-

tion for the Relief of Refugees in China, 151
Singapore Chinese Middle Schools Students' Union, 249, 261–2, 264, 265
Singapore Chinese Middle Schools Teachers' Federation, 136
Singapore Chronicle, 31, 70
Singapore City Committee (communist), 224, 228, 247
Singapore Clerical and Administrative Workers' Union, 238
Singapore Cold Storage Company, 116, 140, 190, 255n
Singapore Council for Social Service, 327
Singapore Electric Tramways Company, 115, 132
Singapore Employers' Federation, 306
Singapore Eurasian Advocate, 122
Singapore Factory and Shop Workers' Union, 250, 261–2, 264, 265
Singapore Family Planning Association, 276, 310
Singapore Family Planning and Population Board, 310–11
Singapore Flying Club, 140
Singapore Federation of Trade Unions, 229, 232, 237, 238
Singapore Free Press, 36, 42, 51, 56, 70, 119, 121, 122, 147, 165, 167
Singapore General Labour Union (see also Malayan General Labour Union, South Seas General Labour Union), 152, 228, 229, 232, 250
Singapore Harbour Board, 95–6, 159, 165, 185, 224, 232, 237, 262, 268, 277
Singapore Herald (1939–41), 165, 169
Singapore Herald (1970–71), 322, 324
Singapore Improvement Trust, 132, 239, 268, 277, 283
Singapore Labour Party, 238–9, 250, 253
Singapore Legislative Assembly, Rendel proposals for, 242–3; Rendel Assembly, 258–60, 266–7, 270; State of Singapore Legislative Assembly, 267, 273, 279, 281, 282, 285–6, 299
Singapore Malay Union (see Kesatuan Melayu Singapura)
Singapore hippo, 169
Singapore Parliament, 299, 300, 303, 306, 318, 319, 323, 325

Singapore People's Alliance Party, 269–70, 282
Singapore Progressive Party, 235–7, 238, 239, 241–2, 244, 246, 250–1, 253, 257–8, 259
Singapore River, 1, 3, 5, 8, 21, 37, 46, 48, 60, 315
Singapore Seamen's Union, 238
*Singapore Standard*, 252
Singapore Strait, 4, 5, 29
Singapore Students' Anti-British League, 248
Singapore Students' Federation, 136
Singapore Swimming Club, 66, 116, 140
Singapore Teachers' Union, 247, 251
Singapore Traction Company, 132, 228, 255n
Singapore Traction Company Employees' Union, 250, 261
Singapore Trade Union Congress, 238, 249–50, 260, 265, 266, 283
Singapore Turf Club, 140
Singapore Union of Journalists, 252
Singapore Volunteer Corps, 129, 130, 167, 168, 169, 177, 181, 188, 194, 251, 253, 305
Singapore Volunteer Rifle Corps, 59, 104, 106; wound up, 129
Singapura, 1–4, 5, 8
Singgora, 164, 172, 183
Singosari, 4
Siva temple, 47
Skinner, A.M., 118
Slim River, 175
Smallpox, 63
Smith, Adam, 32
Smith, Captain Ross, 141
Socialist Front (Malayan), 280, 288
Socialist International, 317
Somerset, Duchess of, 12, 19
Song Ong Siang, 103, 104, 105, 106, 110, 122
Soon Khwong, 228
South Africa, 91, 140
South Seas General Labour Union, 134, 144
Southern Army Command (Japanese), 181, 182, 201
Sreenivasan, Dr. B.R., 263
Sri Mariamman temple, 47
Sri Tri Buana, 2–3, 4
Srivijaya, 2, 3
Stamp Act, 73, 74
State of Singapore Act (1958), 267
Steamships, 40, 66, 90, 93, 99, 105

Stevenson rubber restriction scheme, 131, 138
Still, Alexander William, 121, 147
Stockholm, 317
Straits Chinese British Association, 103–4, 105, 106, 112, 113, 144, 154, 157, 158–9, 231, 236, 246, 251
*Straits Chinese Magazine*, 106
Straits Chinese Recreation Club, 104, 106
Straits Civil Service, 85
*Straits Echo*, 147
Straits Legal Service, 155
Straits Medical Service, 155
Straits Settlements, 122, 160, 224; as Presidency, xiii, 34; reduced to Residency, 34; separation from Bengal, 68; converted to crown colony, xiii, 43, 72, 74–5, 80, 124, 164; and Malayan Union proposals, 220–1; dissolved, 229
Straits Settlements Association, 31, 81–2, 123, 157–8, 159
Straits Settlements Civil Service, 155, 159
Straits Steamship Company, 94
*Straits Times*, 63, 65, 70, 79, 81, 85, 92, 121, 140, 147, 158; in World War II, 165, 174–5, 192; in Republic of Singapore, 322
Straits Trading Company, 91, 93
Subramaniam temple, 47
Suez, 86; overland route, 65; railway opened, 66; canal, xiii, 78, 86, 90, 91, 95, 130, 304
Sugar planting, 44, 48, 91
Suharto, President, 329, 330, 332
Sulu, 41
Sukarno, President, 281–2
Sumatra, 100, 122, 139, 194, 236; and Temasek/Singapura, 4; and piracy, 6; and Raffles, 7, 18; and Riau-Lingga empire, 9; trade with, 13, 39; settlers from, 14, 37, 97, 99; and slave trade, 24; and Dutch expansion, 42; and gutta percha trade, 51; and World War II, 179, 184, 191; and Japanese Occupation, 212
Sun Yat-sen, Dr., 110–12, 132, 133, 135, 150
Sunda Straits, 7, 90
Sungei Ujong, 83, 100
Supreme Court, 47, 84, 142, 208; Supreme Court Bill, 81
Suzuki, Lt. General Sosaku, 171

Swatow, 85, 152
Swettenham, Sir Frank, 110
*Sydney Morning Herald*, 163
Syonan, 190–219
Syonan Advisory Council, 212–13
*Syonan Jit Poh*, 192
*Syonan Shimbun*, 192, 203
*Syonan Times*, 192, 195, 197, 207

TAIPING, 129, 297
Taiwan, 170, 196, 216, 290, 308;
  Taiwanese, 198, 202, 217
Takase, Toru, 198, 201
Tamil Association, 146
Tamil education, 61, 62, 119, 121,
  137, 140, 145, 146, 200, 240, 267,
  313
Tamils, 52, 98, 122, 215
Tan Beng Swee, 94, 102–3, 108
Tan Boon Liat, 117
Tan C.C., 235, 240, 258, 319
Tan Che Sang, 14, 22, 55
Tan Cheng Lock, 138, 145, 156, 158–
  9, 221, 231, 253
Tan Chin Tuan, 221, 224, 236, 241,
  251
Tan Choon Bock, 94, 102
Tan Ean Kiam, 153, 199
Tan Jiak Kim, 94, 102, 103, 104, 105,
  107, 118, 120
Tan Kah Kee, 113, 131, 133–4, 145,
  147, 150–4, 177–8, 188, 194, 202,
  244, 245
Tan Kah Kee and Company, 113
Tan Keong Saik, 94, 102
Tan Kim Ching, 94, 95, 102
Tan Kim Seng, 55, 56, 94, 102, 106,
  116
Tan Lark Sye, 131, 194, 198, 245,
  247, 254, 284, 285, 286
Tan-ma-hsi pirates, 2
Tan Malaka, 135
Tan Seng Poh, 102, 113
Tan Siew Sin, 221, 287, 292
Tan Tock Seng, 15, 55, 102; founds
  pauper hospital, 64, 206
Tanglin, 48, 59, 100
Tanglin Club, 66, 128
Tanjong Katong, 12
Tanjong Malang, 12
Tanjong Pagar, 22, 25, 132
Tanjong Pagar Dock Company, 40,
  95, 96
Tay Koh Yat, 131, 194, 227, 244
Telegraph, with Batavia, 40; with
  Europe, 92; with Protected Malay

States, 92
Telok Ayer, 25, 47, 94, 95
Telok Blangah, 22, 30, 47, 51, 52, 99,
  100, 118, 149; New Town, 315
Temasek, 2–4, 45
Tenasserim, 69
Tengah Airfield, 162, 163, 179, 183
Teo Eng Hock, 111, 112
Teochews, 36–7, 55, 88, 102, 103
Terauchi, Field Marshal Count, 182,
  201
Teutonia Club, 66, 116, 128, 141
Thailand (*see also* Siam), 187, 205;
  and Temasek/Singapura, 3–4; Jap-
  anese invade, 172; in Japanese
  Occupation, 210, 211; relations
  with Singapore Republic, 328; and
  ASEAN, 330; and Peking, 331
Thian Hok Keong temple, 47
Thio Chan Bee, 236
Thomas, Francis, 238–9, 253, 269,
  270, 319
Thomas, Sir Shenton, 139–40, 155,
  157, 168, 173, 174, 175, 177, 180,
  184–5, 196, 223
Thong Chai Medical Institution, 117
Tiao Tso-chi'en, 151
*T'ien Nan Shin Pao*, 110
Tigers, 45, 65
Timor, 39
Tin; in Malay states, 82, 83–4, 87;
  smelting, 91; trade in, 96, 138–9;
  influx of European capital, 94;
  price of, 131; in World War II, 165
Tiong Wah Girls' School, 136
Toa Payoh, 315
Toh Chin Chye, 251, 265–6, 272,
  287–8, 291, 297, 327
Tojo, General Hideki, 171, 182, 193,
  201, 213, 215
Tokyo, 109, 128, 166, 168, 181, 188,
  201, 205, 206, 214
Tominaga, 209
*T'oo Nan Daily News*, 111, 112
Toyota, Kaoru, 198
Trade Unions, 152; pre-World War
  II, 143–4; trade union legislation
  (1940–1), 144, 232; under British
  Military Administration, 228–9; in
  Singapore colony, 232–3, 237–8,
  249–50, 276; Lee Kuan Yew ad-
  viser to, 251–2; and PAP govern-
  ment, 276, 322–3; and Barisan
  Sosialis, 283, 286; and 1968 legisla-
  tion, 306–7
Trafalgar Coconut Plantation, 91

Trafalgar Home for Lepers, 131
Travers, Captain Thomas, 19
Treasury (British), 72, 155
Trengganu, 96
Trincomalee, 86
Tso Ping-lung, 108
Tsuji, Colonel Masanobu, 170, 171, 181, 188, 195, 218, 227
Tung-ming Hui, 111–12, 132
Turkey, 129
Tyersall, 100, 184

UNFEDERATED MALAY STATES, 156, 157, 220
Union Times (Nanyang Chung Hwei Pao), 111, 112, 123,
United Kingdom Parliament, and judicial system (1830), 35; and transfer petition, 72; and defences, 124; and Tan Cheng Lock, 159; and Malayan Union, 222–3; and 1958 State of Singapore Act, 267
United Malays National Organization, 149, 230–1, 236, 241, 253, 287–8, 289, 291, 292, 298; in Singapore, 270, 274, 282, 287, 290–1, 302
United Nations, 301, 327, 329; Committee on Colonialism, 280, 297; Industrial Survey Mission to Singapore, 283; Singapore admitted member of, 293; Missions on development, 315
United People's Party, 277, 285
United States of America, 140, 162, 163, 165, 166, 167, 168, 171, 194, 197, 269, 293, 304, 308, 314, 322, 329, 331
United States Exclusion Act, 133
University Democratic Socialist Club, 323
University of Malaya (in Singapore), 220, 240, 248, 251, 252, 255n
University of Malaya Socialist Club, 247, 250, 252, 323
University of Singapore, 120, 299, 323
Utilitarians, 32
Utusan Melayu (1907–22), 122
Utusan Melayu (1938 +), 147–8, 149, 272, 291, 322

VAN DER CAPELLEN, 11
Vichy France, 168
Victoria Dock, 95
Victoria Memorial Hall, 115, 192, 227, 253

Victoria, Queen, 104, 115, 116, 207
Victoria School, 145
Victoria Theatre, 115
Vietnam, 304, 308, 312, 329, 331

WALLICH, DR., 22, 26, 27
Wang Ching-wei, 153
Wang Ta-yüan, 2, 4
War Cabinet, 221, 223
War Crimes Commission, 226
War Office, 74, 86, 123, 164, 167, 180, 181, 209
Warta Melayu, 147
Washington, 109, 128, 167, 220, 329
Washington Agreement (1922), 162–3
Watanabe, Colonel, 197, 198–9, 201, 206
Wavell, Field Marshal Sir Archibald, 176, 178, 181, 183–5
Wearne/Borneo Motors, 255n
Wee Twee Kim, 198, 201, 218
Weld, Sir Frederick, 124
Whampoa (Hoo Ah Kay), 48, 55, 56, 67, 82, 84, 90, 105; appointed to legislative council, 80; as Chinese consul, 108
Whitehall, 167, 172, 220
Wilberforce, William, 26, 32
Williams, Dr. Cicely, 210
Williams, Peter, 238–9
Wilson, Harold, 304
Wilson, Sir Samuel, 156–7, 159
Winsemius, Dr. Albert, 283
Winstedt, Sir Richard, xiv, 145–6
Wolf H.M.S., 42
Women's Charter, 284, 302–3
Wong Kim Geok (see Lai Teck)
Wong S.Q., 198
Woodbridge Mental Hospital, 131
Woodhull, Sandra, 250, 278, 325
Woodlands New Town, 315
Woods, Robin, 70, 74
Woolley Committee, 118
Workers' Party, 270, 278, 280, 306
Workers' Protection Corps, 232, 237
World Bank, 283, 308–9, 310, 317–18
World Federation of Trade Unions, 229
World War I, 97, 101, 102, 104, 113, 125, 128–30, 131, 132, 148, 149, 155, 157, 162, 167
World War II, 99, 104, 117, 118, 133, 139, 143, 146, 147, 150, 154, 155, 159, 162, 165–218 (Chapters V and VI), 302, 329
Wu Lien-teh, Dr., 110

Wu Tian Wang, 224, 228, 230
Wu T'ieh-ch'eng, 153, 154

YAMASHITA, LT. GENERAL TOMOYUKI,
171, 172, 179, 181–4, 186–7, 188,
191, 193, 194, 195, 200–1, 205, 227
*Yang di-pertuan negara*, 267, 272, 273,
274, 281, 291, 298
Yap Pheng Geck, 194

Yasin, Sayid, 25
Yin Suat Chuan, Dr. 117
Yiu Lieh (Yiu Lit), 111, 112
Yokohama Specie Bank, 199
York, Duke and Duchess of, 104
Young, Sir Arthur, 155
Yuan Shi-K'ai, President of China,
133
Yusof bin Ishak, 272, 291, 298, 302